SILENT STARS

SILENT STARS

JEANINE BASINGER

ALFRED A. KNOPF ❧ NEW YORK 1999

This Is a Borzoi Book
Published by Alfred A. Knopf

Copyright © 1999 by Jeanine Basinger

All rights reserved under International and Pan-American Copyright Conventions.
Published in the United States by Alfred A. Knopf,
a division of Random House, Inc., New York, and simultaneously
in Canada by Random House of Canada Limited, Toronto.
Distributed by Random House, Inc., New York.

www.randomhouse.com

Knopf, Borzoi Books, and the colophon are registered trademarks of Random House, Inc.

Library of Congress Cataloging-in-Publication Data
Basinger, Jeanine.
Silent Stars / by Jeanine Basinger. — 1st ed.
p.   cm.
Includes bibliographical references and index.
ISBN 0-679-43840-8 (cloth)
1. Motion picture actors and actresses—United States—Biography.
2. Silent films—United States—History and criticism.   I. Title.
PN1998.2.B373   1999
791.43'028'092273—dc21
[B]   98-48060   CIP

Manufactured in the United States of America

First Edition

FRONTISPIECE: The ultimate in silent star exotica—
Rudolph Valentino and Nita Naldi in *Blood and Sand*

This book is lovingly and respectfully dedicated to all the stars of silent film that I have either written about only briefly or did not have room to mention: first and foremost Blanche Sweet, along with Wallace Reid, Raymond Griffith, Betty Bronson, Harry Carey, Eleanor Boardman, Charley Chase, Mary Miles Minter, Pearl White, Florence Vidor, Hoot Gibson, Thomas Meighan, Dolores Del Rio, Vilma Banky, Broncho Billy Anderson, Ben Turpin, Milton Sills, Laurel and Hardy, Jackie Coogan, Dorothy and Lillian Gish, William Haines, Mae Marsh, the comedy greats (Chaplin, Keaton, Lloyd, and Langdon), Esther Ralston, Richard Dix, Corrinne Grifith, Charles Ray, Sessue Hayakawa, Emil Jannings, and on and on . . .

Contents

Acknowledgments

I AM GRATEFUL to the many friends and colleagues who supported the research for this book, especially in helping me locate prints and videotapes of the movies. My particular thanks go to Elaina Archer of the Mary Pickford Foundation for her generosity, her enthusiasm, and her insight into both Mary Pickford and Clara Bow. I also want to thank Dennis Doros of Milestone Film and Video; Mary Lea Bandy, Steven Higgins, and Charles Silver of the Museum of Modern Art; Paolo Cherchi-Usai, Ed Stratmann, Caroline Yeager, and especially Carol Radovich and her bunch of volunteers, all of George Eastman House in Rochester, New York; David Francis and Madeline F. Matz of the Library of Congress; Maxine Fleckner Ducey of the Wisconsin Center for Film and Theatre Research; the Mandelbaums of Photofest; Linda Mehr of the Margaret Herrick Library at the Academy of Motion Picture Arts and Sciences; John Horn of the San Simeon District of California's Department of Parks and Recreation; and Bruce Goldstein of the Film Forum. People who must be thanked for providing me with insights, research aid, copies of their own materials, and encouragement include Audrey Kupferberg and Rob Edelman, Bob Smith and Michael Geragetelis, Nancy Katz Colman, Jeffrey Lane, Jeremy Arnold, Liz Garcia, Bill Wolkoff, Morgan Fahey, Annette Tapert, Nancy Klawans Dunn, Frank Thompson, Brenda Keating, Jessica Rosner, Robbins Barstow, Cari Beauchamp, Lisa Dombrowski, Ken Wlaschin, and Rusty Casselton, who was particularly generous with his time in helping me with Colleen Moore. Leonard, Alice, and Jessie Maltin always deserve thanks on any movie project I undertake, as does the wonderful Co-curator of the Wesleyan Cinema Archives, Leith Johnson. I also want to pay tribute to the many silent film experts whose work I admire and whose insights I depended on: Kevin Brownlow, Richard Koszarski, Anthony Slide, David Shephard, and the late DeWitt Bodeen, who was so kind to me many years ago. They are to be thanked for the insights I received from them, but in no way blamed for any mistakes in judgment or lapses in taste.

No book I write could be done without the support of Wesleyan University and all my colleagues there—Richard Slotkin, Leo Lensing, Akös Östor,

Joe and Kit Reed, Bill Francisco, Jean Shaw, and Brenda Keating—or without Adele Wise, who transcribes my text onto the computer and who works long and difficult hours. As always, I must thank my husband, John, and our daughter, Savannah Jahrling, both of whom provided so much discussion and encouragement. Without John, this book would never have been finished, because he did so much to support it.

I must also thank the people at Knopf who worked so hard in behalf of *Silent Stars:* Ken Schneider, Karen Mugler, Iris Weinstein, Tracy Cabanis, Andy Hughes, Carol Carson, and Susan Innes.

My final thanks are reserved for my editor, Bob Gottlieb, who has helped me so much with all the projects we have undertaken together, but who this time around did more than anyone could reasonably expect. For his insight and patience—and for accompanying me on journeys to screen movies in faraway places—he can never be thanked enough. It is a true friend who'll share the burden of rapidly translating silent film titles that are half in French and half in Spanish as they swiftly roll by. (Between us we could just about cover them.)

SILENT STARS

INTRODUCTION

THE PURPOSE OF THIS BOOK is to celebrate a group of silent film stars who are somehow forgotten, misunderstood, or underappreciated. They are all important stars, not minor figures—actors and actresses who made a major impact in their own time. I wanted to watch their movies and consider what was significant about them then and what they seem like now. My primary interest lay in sharing the experience of viewing their work, since their movies are mostly not readily available to audiences today. Although I wanted to present an overview of each star's life and career, I didn't plan to write detailed biographies. And in no way would I be writing a history of silent cinema.

The stars I selected are not a representative group, and someone else might have made a somewhat different list. (When I told a friend I was embarking on this book, he immediately said, "You absolutely have to do Harry Carey." Well, I didn't do Harry Carey, even though I think he's first-rate. No doubt my friend will be disappointed.) My choices were not whimsical, but they *were* personal. I began by considering everyone, including names I had barely heard of, and names I knew, but had limited experience with. For instance, anyone with a nodding acquaintance of silent film has seen Constance Talmadge as the Mountain Girl in D. W. Griffith's *Intolerance*, but who knows her as the title character in *The Duchess of Buffalo* or *Venus of Venice*? And there were so many stars then! Soon I had lists of the well-known, the lesser-known, the unknown, and the known-then-but-not-now—many names, many faces. As it turned out, the greatest stars were by far the most interesting, and many of them were very different from what I had expected. I had assumed that the really big names would not fit into the categories of "forgotten, misunderstood, or underappreciated," but to my surprise, many of them *did* qualify. Even though they still have loyal fans, or excellent books written about them, or revivals and tributes mounted, or have written their autobiographies, there was very little detail available about their actual films, particularly the more obscure ones. The more movies I watched, the more I kept coming back to the actors I liked best, those who piqued my curiosity or made me laugh or captured my heart. In the end, I followed my moviegoer's instincts, and chose the ones I wanted to know more about. Thus, my final choices were influenced by pleasure, by surprise and delight, and by a new awareness of how these stars defined their times. I was, of course, indirectly influenced by the availability of titles to watch, since I wanted to see as many movies starring the same person as possible. Marguerite Clark sounded intriguing and looked very pretty in still photographs and, for a while, reviews called her "a rival to Pickford." But since apparently the only one of her films to survive is 1916's *Snow White,* she had to go.

My first two choices were Mary Pickford and Douglas Fairbanks. Obviously, they are not forgotten, but most people have an oversimplified idea of them, so that despite their continuing fame, they really are underappreciated. In addition they represent the birth of superstar celebrity; their success, their talent, and their marriage to each other made them the first King and Queen of Hollywood, and they have never been superseded. Next I chose Valentino. He, too, isn't forgotten, but he is badly misunderstood, locked into an effeminate image that is only one aspect of his persona and that ignores his considerable charm and humor. A similar misunderstanding plagues Gloria Swanson, who has become Norma Desmond, her comedy skills and decidedly undemented grasp of reality totally unknown, and Pola Negri, a superb actress who is remembered now—if remembered at all—as something of a nut who walked around with two Russian wolfhounds and flung herself on Valentino's grave. Colleen Moore was once the definitive 1920s flapper, the essential emblem of her decade, but she has never been given her rightful place in film history. The underappreciated Marion Davies and Clara Bow suffer from misunderstandings: for Davies, that she had no talent and that her career was manufactured by her wealthy lover, and for Bow, that hers consisted mainly of sex scandals. John Gilbert is a slave to his legend, that of the prototypical silent actor ruined by the coming of sound, while Lon Chaney is still admired, but his marvelous roster of unique characters has been reduced to two major roles, the phantom of the opera and the hunchback of Notre Dame. William S. Hart and Tom Mix are "cowboys," which inevitably means underappreciated, and Mabel Normand and the Keystone Kops, surreal comedy artists, are lumped together as part of Mack Sennett's slapstick. As to the Talmadge sisters, Norma and Constance, once envied and worshiped by their fans—well, they are just forgotten. And finally there's Rin-Tin-Tin. He's become a minor-league Lassie instead of the mortgage-lifting canine star he really was.

Eliminating names was sometimes easy, sometimes difficult. Earle Williams and Elliott Dexter were popular leading men in the years 1910–19. Both were handsome. Both were good actors. Both appeared in major films opposite important female stars. But what reason was there to include them? I couldn't find one. It wasn't hard to give up Carol Dempster, a Griffith favorite,

Blanche Sweet and Wallace Reid

or Charles Ray, a celebrated "country boy," but it was hard not to grieve over a beauty like Dolores Del Rio, or Theda Bara, the original movie vamp, or Pearl White, the intrepid serial queen, or the darkly handsome Richard Barthelmess, or the deliciously hilarious comic Raymond Griffith. It was especially difficult to give up such important names as Wallace Reid and Blanche Sweet.

Wallace Reid was a particularly good-looking man who died unexpectedly of drug addiction at a young age and at the top of his fame. He was the supreme example of the "all-American" or "Arrow Collar ad" type. On-screen, he exuded self-confidence and cheerful good health, and his charm and acting ability were such that he carried his movies, most of which were slight vehicles designed to showcase his stardom. He was one of the most successful of the popular leading men of the teens and early twenties, who were expected to be strong physically, exceptionally handsome, youthful, and excellent actors in the theatrical tradition. Reid fit the bill, but he was almost *too* perfect, with no particular quirks or individual characteristics. Unlike

Fairbanks and Valentino, he is generic—*only* a type. There was no pressing need to write about him.

Blanche Sweet was a major figure, a top star in the first two decades of film history, being especially important in the early days of 1910 to 1914. She was a fine actress, emoting from deep inside herself, predating modern acting techniques by speaking directly to her audience through the camera. She was unique, quite unlike the girlish little heroines of her day, and Adela Rogers St. Johns said she had "a personality so stimulating, so intriguing, so full of interesting vibration . . . [that] she'd certainly never, never bore you." Sweet's role in such landmark movies as *The Lonedale Operator, Judith of Bethulia,* and the 1923 version of *Anna Christie* ensure her place in film history. But even though she was an important pioneering actress, her career was marred by inexplicable absences from the screen. Film historian Anthony Slide concluded that "she did not handle her professional life successfully," although she was "capable of fine and subtle emotional performances." And because she *was* so talented, she was less the movie star and more the actress, and didn't develop one distinct persona to analyze. (Her work was remarkably varied over the years.)

It was difficult deciding not to include Sweet and Reid and some of the others—Betty Bronson, Mae Marsh, Thomas Meighan, Ben Turpin, Mae Murray, Dorothy Gish. It wasn't difficult eliminating such giants as Charlie Chaplin, Buster Keaton, Harold Lloyd, Laurel and Hardy, Lillian Gish, Greta Garbo, and even Louise Brooks, a minor figure in her own time. They have defied the odds against silent film stars and are all still "alive" today. Furthermore, their films have been extensively analyzed. Although I love every one of them, they didn't seem to be in need of reexamination.

As I sifted through the names and watched the movies, I became increasingly aware of the incredible influence silent stars had on their audiences. This was especially true of the people I finally did choose, the Valentinos and Pickfords and Swansons. The fame they achieved was dizzying, a level of adulation that simply had not existed before movies were invented. And it all happened so fast! (And ended so swiftly. From the time the fan magazines first began promoting movie stars in 1911 to the end of the silent era in 1927 was only sixteen years.) Of course there had been stars before the movies were born—in theatre, opera, ballet, burlesque, sports, and vaudeville—but there had never been a stardom like theirs. Their fans felt they knew them, understood them, owned them. Their audience believed in them. These stars appeared in close-up on gigantic screens, and their movies were distributed *to* their audiences, into every small town; they came often, and stayed long; and they could be watched over and over again, performing the same role in exactly the same way, never flubbing a line, never changing, never failing. They offered intimacy, a secret and intense relationship that was one-on-one in the comfort of a cozy darkness. Because title cards could easily be translated into other languages, their stardom was international, knowing no boundaries of politics or culture. And it wasn't snobbish, because anyone could afford a ticket.

Silent stars bonded with their audiences. Between them and the men and women in the seats was a strong connection forged in a quiet world of dreams and imagination. Sometimes they played ordinary people like their fans and sometimes they played fantasy figures who were rich and royal; but always they connected. And as the fan magazines promoted them, the myth was born that they were special, yes, but also just like the audience. The implication was clear: You, too, could be a star. With no education, no experience, not much brains and a minimum of talent, you yourself might leave the gas station, the ten-cent store, the barber shop, or the manicure table and become a tremendous success. Like your heroes, you could become class—or pseudoclass—because if you acquired money and status by just being yourself on-screen, in America that meant you were royalty. (As Elizabeth Taylor summed it up decades later, "There's no deodorant like success.")

None of that notion of democracy was true. Stars were unique, not ordinary, and they worked hard for their success and even harder to maintain it. But for the first time, everyone seemed to have easy access to stardom: you could see it on the screen, and dream of its possibility in your own life. Silent film stars were doubly powerful, both as objects of desire and as role models.

The first star (although it's dangerous to use the word "first" in film history) is reputed to have been the softly beautiful Florence Lawrence, who emerged around 1908. When Lawrence first appeared in movies for Biograph, she wasn't identified by name, and when audiences started asking exhibitors, "Who *is* that girl?," Biograph was unwilling to answer—their policy was not to allow players to become known, since billing identity might give actors bargaining power in salary negotiations. The public was not deterred, however; they merely called Lawrence the "Biograph girl," bestowing on her a popularity that catapulted her into stardom and soon enough into oblivion. (Lawrence represents movie stardom in all its horror. In 1938, she committed suicide by eating ant paste.) When Lawrence left Biograph in 1909, Mary Pickford was just making her film debut. The fickle public fell even more in love with *her*, and soon she became the "Biograph girl," and then "America's Sweetheart, Mary Pickford," the person who deserves the official title of "first real star" in motion picture history.

In the beginning, the public found its own favorites and singled them out as they had Lawrence and Pickford. Once businessmen discovered that popular players with recognized names helped to sell tickets, they changed their policy about allowing billing for actors. Soon, with the help of fan magazines, they began actively promoting—and creating—movie stars.*

These magazines understood their purpose, and didn't shrink from it. Their excesses of prose and attitude are often both hilarious and inexplicable. Consider, for instance, an article on an alleged invention of Gloria Swanson's, the "Stop-Go Hat." Underneath a photograph of Swanson wearing her creation is a caption that identifies it as "a very useful, in fact, indispensable article for motoring." A fur structure atop the hat conceals a periscope that enables a driver to see where "he" is going and where "he's" been: "For night driving, the periscope is equipped with a red and green light making the driver practically [his] own traffic cop."

Writers automatically employed flowery descriptions, as in a full-page layout from *Motion Picture* of October 1918, in which famous actresses are described in poetic terms. Lillian Gish is "a potted lily in a lonesome window" . . . Norma Talmadge is "scarlet poppies in a white field, sable and ermine, a studio tea in Greenwich Village" . . . her sister Constance, on the other hand, is "April showers, a college campus, a ride in the rain, a kiss in the dark" . . . and Mary Pickford is "every little girl's dream, white kid gloves and white tulle, a playground and children's laughter." This gushing tone is not the whole story, however; the magazines could be acerbic. A piece appears in the very next issue of the same magazine which "explains" to movie fans what the advertising they see for films *really* means: "A thrilling spectacle is 50 horsemen riding around in and out of the picture; a masterpiece is a picture that cost more than expected; and a crowning achievement of the screen is something in which the author is starred."

Most of these magazines promoted stars through superbly photographed, full-page portraits suitable for cutting out and framing. They held popularity contests and endless discussions of who was the handsomest, who the prettiest—and there were many candidates, because these early stars were the most beautiful people of their time. The faces of silent film stars, particularly the actresses, are not the faces one sees on-screen today, nor are they the faces of women like Garbo, Dietrich, and Crawford (who all started in silents, but who were not typical of the era). The silent stars look rounder. Their faces aren't shadowed or hawkish, with razor-sharp cheekbones, but romantic and soft, with apparently no bones at all. (Detractors sometimes call this look a "pudding face.")

To say that "they had faces" is true, but that's only the beginning. They had radiance, and projected a kind of magnificent emotionalism that today's

---

*The earliest fan magazines, founded in 1911, were *Motion Picture Story* (after 1914 known as *Motion Picture*) and *Photoplay. Motion Picture Classic* (1915) and *Shadowland* (1919) followed.

more ironic times can't sustain, much less inspire. In their world of silence, these actors and actresses use their complete bodies in performance, treating the self as a single expressive unit. Every big star in those years has enormous physical control, whether it's Colleen Moore trying to keep her balance on a whirling fashion dais, Gloria Swanson flouncing past a lineup of mocking soldiers, or Rudolph Valentino holding his partner tight for a sudden moment of hesitation in the tango. They were not afraid of their bodies. Clara Bow constantly hugged herself. Douglas Fairbanks leapt off a building in a suit and sensible shoes (or slid down a ship's sail in a pirate's costume). Lon Chaney twisted himself into legless creatures and crippled hunchbacks. They boldly used their arms to express emotion—raising them dramatically and reaching out their hands, things no actor today would do under any circumstances. Each star had a distinctive body and put it to use in developing a character which in turn developed into a persona that the audience fell in love with and wanted to be in the presence of as often as possible.

Sometimes, watching these gorgeous people, I had the sense that I was kneeling down and peeping through a knothole, spying on another world, a perfect world full of beautiful little people. They are all so small! The women are often barely five feet tall, and the men are short, compact, and well proportioned. (Where do these teeny people come from, and where are such people today?) The women hop about on feet that look as if they might have been bound at birth. They're like today's gymnasts, without real breasts or hips or shoulders, but with large heads and enormous masses of hair. The men have small hands and feet and make perfect matches for the little women they are wooing. When a genuinely substantial woman—a Greta Garbo—or a really tall man—a Gary Cooper—enters the frame of silent film, it's startling.

Most of the silent stars play representational types: the all-American, the Latin Lover, the stalwart hero, the country rube for the men; the vamp, the city siren, the unhappy wife, the small-town sweetheart for the women. The male stars made their heroes energetic, optimistic, and quintessentially American on the one hand, or, as in the case of Valentino, exotic, sensual, and inherently foreign. The various types of women add up to reflect the emergence of the modern woman. There is something touching about the covert desire for liberation their characters collectively represent. Often, the stars are grown women pretending to be little girls, denying their female bodies and thus rejecting their roles as wives and mothers in some hidden, visually nuanced way. These girls are called "hoydens" or "tomboys," and the desire to escape the traditional female self is obvious. In the teens, women like Pickford and Mabel Normand, two very different stars, both play tomboys who do physical comedy and who trick the world into giving them what they want. They control other people and their environment with their cleverness, and they spend more than half of every movie uninvolved in a romantic tangle or a sexual situation. Although the later flapper type would be sexualized by Clara Bow, the original flapper was, as Colleen Moore once described herself, "sexy, sexless"—both liberated and old-fashioned. There's a single image that provides a crystalizing glimpse of the 1920s modern girl in transition. As *Broken Chains* (1922) opens, Claire Windsor (playing second lead to Colleen Moore and wearing a huge hat with feathers) is driving her roadster at top speed and busily planning her "radiophone" dance for the coming evening's entertainment. She's "new"—driving a powerful machine at high speed—and "old"— she's got feathers on her head and her "work" is merely social.

Different types of male stars all have the same goal: success. They're going to make it somehow, against all odds. The only variance has to do with how the success is defined. It can be getting rich, winning the game, marrying the beautiful girl, stopping the villains, inventing the cure for a mysterious disease, finding the treasure, or perhaps just figuring himself out, finding a value system that will work best for his character and its world. For the men, it's an open world, with unlimited opportunity for good or evil, romance or seduction, but always with the challenge to succeed.

The fictionalized world these stars inhabit is never silent in the viewer's mind, even today when there's often no musical accompaniment. Sound is never missed, because silent films are about emotion and action—two things that don't require it. The absence of sound becomes irrelevant as viewers read titles aloud inside their heads and "hear" everything that is happening. In fact, the representation of sound is often embedded in both titles and story action. Shouts are presented in BIG LETTERS on a title card and simulated by such things as Norma Talmadge shaking a coal scuttle in *Kiki* (1926), while Ronald Colman is trying to talk on the telephone. (He covers his ears.)

Title cards provide an ongoing conversation with the viewer. When well done, they're folded into the story, never interrupting it needlessly, never breaking the mood, and never providing unnecessary information. (A bad film will often have too many titles, most of which supply only dialogue.) In a good film, titles are used for historical background, exposition, commentary, mood and atmosphere, irony, moralizing, dialogue, and touches of wit. The brilliant pacing of many silent films is helped by title cards that cover narrative developments which, if visualized, would slow down the action.

When you enter the world that silent stars inhabit and bring to life, you enter a strange and private place, a world of reinvention and sudden redemption. It's not outdated—there are too many modern concepts and too much that's surprising and fresh—but it's not our world, either. It's an Ur-world, full of strong emotion, and you seem to be constantly sharing lives in secret ways, looking on at secret moments, watching scenes of deeply felt and hyper-expressive revelation. More than any other type of film, silent film is voyeuristic. If porn had a *pure* counterpart, it would be silent film. The secret watching, the silent sharing—the sense that we're intruding in emotional space that has no easy words to explain itself, no noise to distract us from our feelings. It's a world of beautiful lovers, friendly old parents (much better than your own), and exciting monsters to stir you up and get you going. Safe monsters, however, along with safe floods, safe love affairs, safe dangers, safe sex—anything and everything in its purest possible form, one that gives you all you want but robs you of nothing. It's a world of adventure and romance, and it takes you to exotic times and places: Revolutionary Russia, Napoleonic France, jungles, the days of knights and ladies, imaginary kingdoms, and of course, the wonderful world of wealth. You enter a magnificent mansion where there are fresh grapes in silver bowls, lace tablecloths, crystal glasses, velvet draperies, all kinds of *things*. The high-class woman of the house dresses in a fur-trimmed cape with no buttons or sleeves, the ultimate in the irresponsible garb of the very wealthy, something she can toss lightly over her dress and hold together with her own delicate yet superbly manicured hands. She isn't going to need those hands for anything practical such as driving a car or carrying a purse; she has people to do that for her. And she isn't going to have to worry about bad weather, either—she's going to be untouched by the elements, riding in cabs, carriages, limousines, the conveyances of wealth and position. Again and again in these movies, exquisite women in silk shoes clutch their wraps around them and move effortlessly through time, living in a world where the snow is never cold, their feet never get wet, and pneumonia strikes only when needed for plot development.

In contrast to the mansion with the grapes, there's a bucolic landscape that is unrecognizable today—a world of quiet dignity. Scenes could easily be shot on real locations since there was no need to worry about chirping birds, honking motorcars, or airplanes overhead ruining the take. This world offers real information, an honest glimpse into dreams of the past. A heroine stands in the farmyard while a gentle wind ruffles the apple trees and blossoms drop around her feet. The rural world of the teens and twenties is a sunny fantasy, something beautiful, innocent, and lost. "Six spring broilers" at the Busy Pie Café would cost you $5, and a piece of homemade pie, a nickel. (Wine, however, would be $49.) Characters are freely using "arnica" (which has not been seen in American homes in at least four decades) and clothes are made of "linsey-woolsey." A biscuit is a "clinker," a bad dancer a "corn shredder," a half-smoked cigarette a "dincher." Sometimes you haven't a clue to what's going on. When a villain gets out of prison and discovers his shoes squeak, he goes immediately to the waterfront and dips his feet. This means something—but what?

It's a world where railroad tracks run alongside every back road, and railroad handcars are free and available for stealing to use in a freewheeling chase. These chases can be serious, with a heroine needing rescue; or comic, with an eloping groom frantically chasing the speeding train that carries his would-be bride; or western, where the outlaws are creeping up on the train they're going to rob. The handcar is an all-purpose story element recognized by everyone, and none of us today has so much as seen one, much less commandeered one to solve a problem.

It's a world full of strange rituals and a great deal of attitude, and the films that illustrate it best are probably the wacky silent film comedies. Anything that can possibly go wrong absolutely does, and there's always a gun somewhere: in a pocket, a purse, or a drawer. When "Help! Help! Police!" rings out (on a title card), those reliable troopers always arrive promptly. They arrive, but they don't help much. People fall down, jump, scream, run, and bump into things, but just when all settles down, fresh disasters strike, from new and unexpected sources. All the women are indignant and the men don't know what to do about it. They just try to be stoic, and withstand assault. Everyone is concerned with money. There are rich people, and there are poor people, and there's a big gap between the two. However, lines can be crossed, because the poor victimize the rich with real dedication and true imagination and resource. This doesn't mean that silent film comedy—or silent film in general—suggests that there is no evil in the world, no poverty, no catastrophe. But it suggests that individuals can triumph and bad things can be overcome with enough enthusiasm, hard work, optimism, and decency. To look at these films today is to learn about the optimism of Americans. It's not just that people are so ingenious at solving problems, but that there are so many problems to be solved. While characters lie asleep in their beds at night, burglars are breaking in downstairs. If they stand under a drainpipe, it will break and they will be drenched. If they take to the floor in a rented tuxedo to tango, trouser seams will give way. All the machinery they try to operate will backfire, break down, or run away with them. Opportunity knocks, but on their heads as well as their doors. On the other hand, they have a chance to move forward and accomplish something, even while waging a constant battle against disaster. Their glass is both half empty and half full. They teeter between profit and loss, winning and losing, loving and hating. It's a wild and unpredictable place full of crooks and con artists, suckers and rubes. Anything can happen. It does. They survive. And that's America.

Watching silent films from the teens and twenties, one observes a society undergoing rupture. At first, the films reflect an attempt to hold on to innocence. The women are childlike, the men impossibly heroic. Many of the stories concern children, and sex is always a cautionary tale. D. W. Griffith's is the dominant sensibility, with its roots in agrarian society and the melodramatic theatrical tradition. By the end of 1919, after World War I has given the nineteenth century the coup de grâce, the twentieth century cracks open. The tempo changes from the waltz to the Charleston, and the energy, pace, and rhythm of silent films begin to produce unexpected riffs, shifts in tone, and wildly improvisational scenes. The silent film becomes visual jazz. Women cut their hair, shorten their skirts, and become aggressive. Men start swanning around in impeccable evening clothes or exotic Arabian garb. Both women and men are looking for sexual satisfaction or, rather, sexual stimulation. The rural world of sun-dappled forests, flowing rivers, and lazy farms with clucking chickens fades away to be replaced by art deco apartments, limos, and roadhouses selling "hooch." Stars become more casual, and the acting style shifts from one of declamation, broad gesture, and overt emotion to a loose naturalism that will lead directly to the sound era. The fantasies of the audience change from grand dreams of a generic quality—settling the frontier, owning their own land, escaping oppression—to specific dreams fueled by the movies themselves: wealth, social position, passion, clothes, furniture, glamour, exotica, and, of course, sex.

The twenties became a movie-dominated decade, and the silent stars its beautiful, representative citizens. F. Scott Fitzgerald wrote, "It was an age of miracles, it was an age of art, it was an age of excess, it was an age of satire." It's the perfect introduction to silent film and the world of stars who did not speak.

MARY PICKFORD

PERHAPS CECIL B. DEMILLE said it best: "There have been hundreds of stars. There have been scores of fine actresses in motion pictures. There has been only one Mary Pickford." He wrote those words in 1955, but they ring even truer today, when it's clear that not only has there been only one, there's never going to be another. Pickford was the biggest of the big, a top box office draw, an international superstar, and a strong woman who took charge of her own career in a tough business run by competitive men. The early film historian Benjamin Hampton assessed her career in 1931 by saying, "Mary Pickford is the only member of her sex who ever became the focal point of an entire industry," but he got it wrong. She was the only member of either sex to do so—and still is. And yet today, although people know her name, and though silent film historians keep trying to set the record straight, they have no real grasp of who she was, how important and beloved she was, or how she pioneered stardom and the concept of the career woman. Isn't it ironic that the biggest female star in history ends up being the most misunderstood?

People think of Mary Pickford as a bargain-basement Shirley Temple—that she was an older actress who masqueraded as a child, dimpling around, cheering everyone up while her characters lived a Dickensian existence with nothing but a bowl of gruel and a brave smile between them and disaster. While it's true that many of Mary's characters were relentlessly optimistic, she was no dimwit blonde who created problems; she was a clever minx who solved them. Furthermore, she usually played a young girl, not a child, and often appeared as the lovely woman she was in real life. She was an actress, not an infant phenomenon. She was sometimes sentimental as befit her times, but there's a difference between sweet and cloying, and Mary Pickford was never cloying. Her film character connected directly to her audiences because she was funny and nothing got her down. Whatever grim turn of the plot presented itself, she exhibited no self-pity and kept on trucking. Her determination to set things right often resulted in hilarious movie chaos, but she offered hope and escape, two things Americans have always been happy to embrace. Her cheeky females make a go of it on their own, standing in gamely for anyone in the audience who was poor, who had ever faced real trouble, and whose pants might fall down at a crucial moment.

Mary was one of the big three of the silent era, along with her husband, Douglas Fairbanks, and their friend, Charlie Chaplin. Fairbanks is generally accepted as the energetic male *Zeitgeist* of the silent era, Chaplin is called its social conscience, but Pickford rarely gets credit for being its female soul. She can match them joke for joke, caper for caper, heart for heart. Her characters exhibit inner fire, and her arguments have no gender bias. Over the years more than one large male gets kicked in the butt by Mary Pickford; she's a fairly astonishing role model for women, a modern woman before such a concept was fully understood.

Her acting style is of its own time, of course. She first learned how to perform onstage, and she never lost the basics she mastered there: how to hold the audience's eye, how to move her supple body to convey specific meanings, how to lift an arm or cock her head to shift attention to herself, how to hold that attention without losing pace. These were the tools of her trade, and she brought them with her to movies, sharpening them and miniaturizing them, adjusting them for a subtle camera that could come up close to her expressive face. Like other stars of the new medium, she quickly understood that actors in motion pictures could win an audience by more or less allowing their physical presence—their essence—to fill out the role. She became more natural. "I lived my characters," she said. "That's the only way you can be. You have to live your parts." Thus, she was perfect for movies—an actress who loved the camera and feared nothing from it, being able to ignore its presence and "live" in front of it. She was one of the first to combine the old and new performance styles, linking her new knowledge of movies to the theatrical tradition her audience knew and understood.

In some ways, Pickford is a female Charlie Chaplin. She has the same remarkable physical control over her own tiny body. Like him, she can enter the frame, focus the eye, and perform a series of actions that are both comic and inherently honest. Chaplin's bizarre and careful carving of his boiled shoe for lunch in *The Gold Rush* is hilarious in content and unrealistic in action, but it's grounded in the ability to cook, cut, and eat. Pickford was similarly adept. When she straps wet brushes onto her feet in *Through the Back Door* to "skate" across dirty kitchen floors so as to wash them more efficiently, she too links comedy and reality, skating and scrubbing, with a dancer's awareness of the first and a poor girl's familiarity with the second. She "skates" in perfect character, that of a tomboyish little girl anxious to get the job done so that she can run outside to play. Slipping, sliding, twisting and turning, falling down on her behind, she never loses the awkwardness of the girl, her determination,

Pickford on "skates" in *Through the Back Door*

her inventiveness. In her little socks and Mary Janes, slippery brushes sliding her forward, she performs a perfect ballet of both physical control and detailed characterization.

Pickford is delightfully natural and spontaneous, but she's also a beauty, a far greater one than can be inferred from still photographs. Her sparkle worked well in comedy, and her radiance illuminated melodrama. Lamenting that for inexplicable reasons she has come to be more associated with the latter (and to "represent silent film tragedy"), historian Kevin Brownlow said, "Nothing could be more ludicrously inaccurate. Mary Pickford was essentially a comedienne, although that description cannot do justice to her rich talents as a dramatic actress."

Her best films showcase both abilities. Although she has been criticized for having a narrow range, her movies reveal the opposite: she has the broadest range of any silent film actress. She can play a spunky tomboy, a grand lady, a royal princess, a deformed cripple, a freckled farm girl, a tragic heroine, an old woman, a young girl, and a little child that is really a little child and not a grown-up's falsification of a little child. Lillian Gish, unquestionably a great actress, had a narrower range in the roles she undertook. What Gish had was depth, real depth, and what Pickford had was the ability to do many different things across a broad surface.*

Pickford's fans adored her beyond the usual level of popularity. They themselves picked her out of the pack and made her "America's Sweetheart." It wasn't a title invented to sell her, like the "sweater girl," the "oomph girl," or the "It" girl. It was first a fact, and then an advertising slogan, lovingly bestowed, and it came from honest and direct feelings: moviegoers called her their sweetheart because that's who she was. And she accepted the responsibility of their adoration, saying, "I am a servant of the public. I've never forgotten that." She took everything about her career seriously. She wanted her films to make money, but she also wanted them to be good. She paid close attention to every aspect of production, always hiring the best talents and constantly monitoring their work. ("I frightened them," she said.) If she hadn't been a star, she might have become the best producer in Hollywood. Pickford gave the business everything she had, both behind the scenes and in front of the camera. "Mary Pickford deserved to be named America's Sweetheart," said Adolph Zukor, president of Paramount Pictures, praising her commitment to her fans, to her career, and to the business itself. (Zukor was in a position to know. He admitted, "I started out giving her $500 per week, but I finally paid her $10,000.")

The sum of Mary Pickford is impressive. She could act. She had comedy skills. She had beauty and personality. She had charisma (lots of charisma), and she definitely had brains—she was a tough negotiator who managed her own career brilliantly, and she supported her entire family from childhood to old age. She was no Rebecca of Sunnybrook Farm, and certainly no Pollyanna.[†] The great film historian and collector William K. Everson said she and her films had it all, "a happy mixture of quantity, quality, variety and spontaneity." To understand her, and to restore to her the status she deserves, one has to consider three things: her career, her marriage, and her celebrity.

---

*It's inappropriate to suggest they were in competition, in that they were friends who started out together as children, and they were never rivals. Pickford was a top star, wildly popular, and Gish never achieved that level of celebrity, nor would she probably have wanted to. Gish had the good fortune to have a genius to guide her (D. W. Griffith), and she escaped the labels that stardom, with its attendant restrictions of persona, inevitably forces on actors.

†One has only to read her tart-tongued comments on Chaplin to realize that. Near the end of her life, her stepson, Douglas Fairbanks, Jr., suggested to her that Chaplin had mellowed in his feelings toward her. "I don't care," she replied. "He's still a son of a bitch."

THE CAREER

Mary Pickford firmly stated: "My career was planned. There was never anything accidental about it. It was planned, it was painful, it was purposeful." She went for full control in a way that few actresses ever pursued and even fewer ever achieved. "Mary had her hand in everything, writing scripts, arguing with directors, making suggestions to other players . . . and her ideas were helpful," said Adolph Zukor. "I am convinced that Mary could have risen to the top in United States Steel if she had decided to be a Carnegie instead of a movie star." Her cameraman, Charles Rosher, added, "She knew everything there was to know about motion pictures." In the beginning, of course, she knew nothing, but her determination, hard work, and intelligence took her where she wanted to go, and where she wanted to go was the very top.

Like most of her contemporaries, she came from nowhere and nothing. Born in Canada as plain Gladys Smith in 1892 (not 1893 as is sometimes suggested), she faced poverty and hard times throughout her youth. Her father, a poor provider, died when she was about six years old, leaving her mother, Charlotte, a penniless widow with three small children to raise—Gladys and her sister, Lottie, and brother, Jack, both of whom would also have substantial movie careers. Charlotte did the best she could by taking in sewing, but on September 19, 1898, things took an upturn: it was the day Gladys, age six, made her stage debut at the Princess Theatre in Toronto with the Cummings Stock Company. Within three years, she became a well-known theatre personality in Toronto, and was invited to go on tour in a play entitled *The Little Red Schoolhouse.*

Pickford's story has been written—first in her autobiography, *Sunshine and Shadow,* and later in biographies by Scott Eyman and Eileen Whitfield. The story of her early years, in which she and all her family became regular troupers and she literally grew up onstage, has been told. Her motivation for getting into movies is linked to a decision she made in 1906, when she was fourteen. She had been on tour for six years, and felt she had mastered the craft of acting. And, as she always would, she knew what she wanted: to stop touring and live in one place, and to have real success, the kind that only the Broadway stage could bring an actress in those years.

Pickford's legend begins with the story of how she decided she must be hired by David Belasco, the famous New York impresario. In this tale, she is cast as the determined female who always insists on what she wants and always gets it. It's a simple plot: a little girl, just barely in her teens, demands an audience with a formidable theatre maestro. He's too busy, but she persists. He hasn't time for her, but she won't give up. He hasn't heard of her, but she overrules him. And finally she enters his office, a small, delicate creature with a head of beautiful golden curls. She's a child, really, but she looks him straight in the eye. She never blinks. She never wavers. She faces him with courage and strength, telling him, "I am an actress, but I want to become a good one." Naturally she wins him over and is immediately cast in the important role of Betty Warren in William de Mille's latest play, *The Warrens of Virginia,* for twenty-five dollars a week. Belasco has only one problem with Gladys: her name. It's too plain for a star. Gladys suggests one of her other family names, Pickford, and says she always liked the name "Marie." They agree on "Mary Pickford," and that evening, the newly christened Mary sends her mother a telegram: GLADYS SMITH NOW MARY PICKFORD ENGAGED BY DAVID BELASCO TO APPEAR ON BROADWAY THIS FALL. This scene is by all accounts reasonably true and is also a perfect Mary Pickford movie scenario—little girl, big man, she wins.

Pickford's career with Belasco went well, but in the spring of 1909 she and her family were thinking about the summer season that lay ahead: since theatres weren't air-conditioned in those days, there would be little work for stage actors. Her mother suggested she consider motion pictures, the new medium that provided summer work and paid a hefty five dollars a day. Mary allegedly was unhappy at the suggestion. Was she not a Belasco actress, and would it not diminish her status to work in the upstart medium of the movies? But the lure of the money and the prospect of being able to keep her family together through the summer motivated her. She took a trolley car to the Biograph studio, and again, as legend has it, she found an opportunity to play a grand scene involving "the little girl and the very big man." This time the big man was D. W. Griffith, and she sniffed at the five dollars per day because she was "a Belasco actress" and demanded "at least ten." Furthermore, she added, "I must have twenty-five dollars a week guaranteed." She was hired, and on April 20, 1909, Mary Pickford, with her makeup applied personally by Griffith, made her movie debut in *Her First Biscuits,* "a comedy subject." (According to Scott Eyman, who consulted Biograph records, she appeared in the background, as the film starred Dorothy Bernard. Pickford later said Griffith's makeup job made her look like Pancho Villa.)

These stories about Mary's early encounters with Belasco and Griffith are charming and grounded in fact, and they are deeply revealing. First, they emphasize the hard fact that she was already a tough-minded professional as a teenager, having started supporting her family while still a child. Second, they show her sharp negotiating skills. She went alone to meet two powerful men and to work out a deal for herself; no agent accompanied her to ask for ten dollars a day or a guaranteed weekly salary. Last, they reveal how Mary Pickford's life is the stuff that legends are made of, or, perhaps that legends are made up to accommodate. They are part of the larger-than-life story that ultimately became the movie of her life.

After going to work for Griffith at Biograph in 1909, Mary rapidly became an audience favorite. Like Florence Lawrence before her she became identified as the "Biograph girl," but also as "the little girl with the golden curls." When for convenience her characters were named "Mary," audiences started singling her out as "that little Mary." It's no legendary story that moviegoers fell in love with her and made her a star. That is fact, the foundation of her popularity.

Once she started in movies, Mary shrewdly sized up the new medium, grasping its financial possibilities as unlimited. According to the Eyman biography, Belasco searched for her when fall came, but she was too ashamed to tell him she was in the movies, and avoided him. Later, William de Mille wrote to Belasco that he had bumped into her and "the poor kid is actually thinking of taking up motion pictures seriously. She says she can make a fairly good living at it . . . I pleaded with her not to waste her professional life . . . but she's a rather stubborn little thing for such a youngster and she says she knows what she's doing . . . So I suppose we'll have to say goodbye to little Mary Pickford. She'll never be heard from again, and I feel terribly sorry for her." (So much for the wisdom of William de Mille.)

Typical films from 1910, her second year, include *All on Account of the Milk* and *An Arcadian Maid.* In *All on Account of the Milk,* she is the central female character, a girl who pretends to be shocked when she's kissed, revealing later when she's alone how delighted she really is. Her ability to include the audience in this secret relationship ("It's just the two of us—don't tell") is remarkable. She portrays demure shock, a little surprise, and the secret pleasure with great clarity and specificity but also with considerable subtlety. She brings an audience to her. Her performance in *An Arcadian Maid,* a tragedy about a naive girl conned into becoming a thief, is totally different from that in *All on Account of the Milk.* It would be easy to believe that the two movies featured two different actresses.

During Mary's formative years, she switched effortlessly from comedies to dramas, from westerns to romances, from the role of child to that of grown woman, from pixieish tomboy to elegant lady. What they had available for her to play, she played. She made forty-two titles in 1909 and another thirty-two in 1910,* with titles like *The Lonely Villa* and *The Violin Maker of Cremona* (both directed by Griffith), *The Peach Basket Hat, The Country Doctor, His Wife's Visitor, The Little Teacher,* and *To Save Her Soul.* The examples available

---

*Pickford's long filmography is printed complete in both the Scott Eyman and Eileen Whitfield biographies.

for my viewing were flickering, hazy copies that caused eyestrain and narrative frustration. Often a complex story is performed in broadly pantomimed action, with great gaps in exposition so that it's difficult to be certain what is happening, since there are no titles other than the name of the movie itself. But even under such conditions, it's easy to see why Mary Pickford became a star. Besides her obvious assets of beauty, youth, and self-confidence, she stands out through her ability to delineate what her actions are and what emotions they represent. She eclipses others because she can make clear what is going on in the story and what her character is thinking and feeling. She is distinctive right from the very beginning of her career.

Five of her 1909 movies display this ability in its embryonic form: *The Way of Man, The Broken Locket, The Awakening, Getting Even,* and *The Renunciation.* Although she's not much more than a child, she plays a grown woman with a grown woman's problems, as they are stories of romance, marriage, and problems with men. (The last two are comedies.) In these first months before the camera, she is an uncommonly pretty young girl, with the typical big head and small body of the silent film star. She has a mass of blonde curls, but, seen mostly in long shots, she looks like a traditional "little woman" from the previous century: wasp waist, huge hat, blob of hair, long skirt, ample bosom harnessed for the fashionable hourglass look. At this time, she weighs about 115 pounds, and she's only five feet one inch tall (later, she would slim down to 95 pounds), so she's somewhat stocky, a Queen Victoria figure packed with solid flesh. She's not at all like the girlish Pickford she would later become.

By 1911, Mary was developing rapidly, learning her way around the business. She had a sharp nose for anything that might earn her an extra dollar, and when she realized people got paid for writing movie stories, she wrote one called *The Goose Girl* and sold it for twenty-five dollars. When she noticed that her stage makeup didn't look right on the screen, she began trying new blends and checking how she looked with her cameraman, finally purchasing top-quality materials and demanding reimbursement, with a percent for her innovations. When she realized that brother Jack and sister Lottie could bring in cash by playing in movies, she found them steady work. And when she discovered that her popularity was great enough to make her desirable to other movie companies, she started negotiating for more money wherever she could find it. In 1911, she made *When a Man Loves, White Roses, The Italian Barber, Three Sisters,* and *A Decree of Destiny* for Biograph, and then decamped to join the Independent Motion Picture Company (IMP), because the founder (Carl Laemmle) offered her $175 per week.* She wasn't motivated by money alone.

---

*In only three years, Mary traveled from Biograph to IMP and from IMP to Majestic and from Majestic back to Biograph, always increasing her salary.

Her new husband, Owen Moore, a successful leading man, had signed with IMP, and she wanted to join him. IMP was under the direction of Thomas Ince, and various legal concerns prompted him to open his new studio in Havana, Cuba. Mary traveled there to make approximately thirty-four films.

For IMP in Cuba, in 1911, Mary made such movies as *The Dream, The Mirror, Sweet Memories, Artful Kate,* and *In Old Madrid.* Her work is strong, and she plays mature roles. In *The Dream,* she's the good wife of a drunken husband who dreams she smokes, drinks, and runs around town (he wakes up a reformed man); in *The Mirror* she's wooed by two men and consults a fortune-teller as to which to choose. In *Sweet Memories,* a sentimental portrait matched to a series of title cards that contain a poem ("We played at artists on the green . . . He painted my portrait at sweet fourteen"), she has a small role, but in *Artful Kate* and *In Old Madrid* she's the leading lady. She and Moore wrote the story for the former, and in the latter she tests her sweetheart's love by pretending to be a Spanish senorita who woos him (an early example of her ability to be two different people on screen).

By the end of 1912, she was a name, a major motion picture star. According to Belasco, "Mary Pickford was famous, and had become known as 'The Queen of the Movies.' " Nevertheless, he was able to lure her back to the stage for a production of *A Good Little Devil,* which opened on Broadway in January of 1913. She received excellent reviews, and for a time seemed happy, having always claimed she wanted to return to the legitimate theatre. But when Adolph Zukor filmed *A Good Little Devil* for his Famous Players in Famous Plays series, Mary started negotiating her return to the screen. By mid-1913, she was back where she belonged and where she would stay—in the movies—and back where she had started out, at Biograph.

The return to Biograph meant, of course, a return to D. W. Griffith and a working relationship that was never comfortable for either of them. Mary was not as pliant as Gish, and she fought Griffith on many fronts, claiming he only gave her roles that other actresses in the company turned down. Years later, she was still complaining. She told Kevin Brownlow: "I respected him, yes. I even had an affection for him, but when he told me to do things I didn't believe in, I wouldn't do them. I would *not* run around like a goose with its head cut off, crying 'Oooooh . . . the little birds! Oooooh . . . look! A little bunny!' " As Eileen Whitfield points out, however, Griffith actually "increased her expressive range to a degree she would never achieve again" by casting her in *Friends* (1912) as "a prostitute . . . [and] in *Fate's Interception* (1912) . . . as a wronged woman who asks an admirer to kill her lover . . . and *Female of the Species* (1912), a film so atmospheric it is almost surreal."

Pickford and Griffith engaged in shouting matches. She is said to have bitten him, and he allegedly once shoved her down. (Whitfield says that Mary declaimed from the floor, "You call yourself a Southern gentleman! You're not only a disgrace to the South, but to the North as well! Never speak to me again, sir!" It's another great Pickford scene from real life.) It's interesting to speculate what would have become of Mary's career had she followed Griffith's guidance. Clearly, he was shaping her, as he did all his actresses, into his own concept of "female." It reflects Mary's determined nature off-screen—as well as the one she assumed on-screen—that she broke away from his domination and forged her own persona and career.

One of the most successful of the Pickford/Griffith collaborations of this period is the 1913 release *The New York Hat* (made in late 1912), from a story by Anita Loos. Lionel Barrymore plays the male lead opposite Mary in a story that modern women find appealing. As a mother lies dying, she gives a letter to her young minister (Barrymore) which says she has lived with her daughter's stepfather for years, and although that was good enough for her, she knows he won't give her daughter certain "things." She leaves the minister money "for things she want and don't need [*sic*]." Pickford plays the daughter, Mollie, who later dreams of a New York hat she has seen in a store window. But it costs ten dollars! Following the dead mother's instructions, the minister buys it, giving it to her as a gift, but telling her to keep this a secret. Since townswomen shopping in the store saw him make the purchase, they naturally assume the worst when she wears it to church. Enraged, her father destroys the hat, and she is shunned and called a Jezebel. The minister is warned he will have to right the wrong he's done her, but he shows everyone her mother's letter and all ends well when he suddenly proposes to Mary of his own accord. Eyman makes the point that this film shows how Pickford had "already mastered the art of projecting emotions through the lens directly to the audience—the true art of screen acting." He is specifically referring to a scene in which her character dreams of the hat she would like to own. She wakes up and feels for it on top of her head, as if it were there. When it isn't, her face falls into what Eyman calls a "perfectly judged it-was-only-a-dream disappointment."

In late 1913, Pickford signed a contract with Famous Players Film Company. It was then that she went into high gear as a star, finding enormous popularity in such 1914 releases as *The Eagle's Mate, Such a Little Queen, Behind the Scenes, Cinderella,* and her first version of *Tess of the Storm Country.* In 1915 she made nine features: *Mistress Nell, Fanchon the Cricket, The Dawn of a Tomorrow, Little Pal, Rags, Esmerelda, A Girl of Yesterday, The Foundling,* and *Madame Butterfly. Mistress Nell, Rags,* and *Madame Butterfly* are good examples of Mary, the star, at this time.

In *Mistress Nell* Mary is introduced sitting sidesaddle on a large white horse, and her title card defines her character: "Mistress Nell of Drury Lane

The New York Hat, her final film with D. W. Griffith

Theatre, of whom 'twas said 'England would be worse than a Puritan funeral without her.' " Playing opposite her husband, Owen Moore, Mary is utterly natural, and completely at home in the frame. Her comic timing and precise gestures seem uncontrived—she seems to be about behavior rather than performance, yet she makes the most out of every moment. For instance, when Nell arrives at the Blue Boar for a rendezvous with the king, she draws out her entrance, taking as much time as possible. As she approaches the doorway, she lifts a dainty foot to lean forward and peek in one of the windows. Then, she ties a veil over her face as a disguise. Next she trips ever so slightly as she steps up onto the threshold, and when she knocks on the door, she makes sure to let the audience understand this hurts her knuckles. Finally, she kicks the door with her foot as a final knock (to save the knuckles, of course). It's early 1915, and Mary Pickford films are already all about Mary Pickford, yet it's never annoying; she knows exactly what she can get away with. Later, she passes that supreme test for any movie actor—an eating scene—by sitting in the center of the frame, easily dominating two other stars, and managing to devour a chicken as if she hasn't eaten in days. The range of her skill is evident in two sequences: when she masquerades as an Irish lad, walking with a pseudo-male swagger, and when she enacts the role of Nell enacting the role of an Arabian princess. She's natural and modern as

Two 1915 releases: *The Dawn of a Tomorrow*, intense drama,
and *Rags*, charming comedy

Nell, but broadly posturing in Nell's seventeenth-century performance-within-the-performance.

Rags represents the popular Pickford formula of the day to such a degree that *Variety* said, "One thing about Miss Pickford . . . she and her bag of tricks are so well established in the minds of film followers no matter what she does in a picture they are sure to term it 'cute.' " Pickford starts out as a young woman of about twenty who marries a bank cashier found short in his accounts. Allowed to leave town, the young couple end up in poverty in a mining camp, where the husband becomes an alcoholic. The poor twenty-year-old Mary dies in childbirth, making way for a second Mary, who becomes the sixteen-year-old Rags, the tomboy terror of the camp. (Mary playing her own mother caused *Variety* to sneer, "Mighty few of us can be a mother to ourselves, even in a film.") Rags is the Mary Pickford the public had fallen in love with: she stomps around town terrorizing everyone—until, of course, she falls in love with costar Marshall ("Mickey") Neilan. It's one thing to see Mary attack a group of small boys who are tormenting a dog—she's ferocious—but quite another to see her go after a saloon full of grown men who are being cruel to her father. She lets 'em have it but good, rushing them, socking them, bashing them with the furniture, until they're finally cowering back against the wall. Then she stalks out, with an "I hope I don't have to do this again" scowl on her face. The audience loved this aspect of Mary Pickford, and it's the one that has more or less been lost over the years. As the critic Andrew Sarris observed, "Good may have prevailed in Mary Pickford's movies, but the set of her tough little jaw told you that it damn well better."

Pickford's version of Madame Butterfly, with Marshall Neilan

The *Rags* "formula" referred to by *Variety* gave viewers two Marys for the price of one. First, she's the lovely mother, soft hair piled atop her head, a bouquet of roses in her arms, then the Calamity Mary, who is in turn herself replaced by someone like her mother, the romantic leading lady she becomes after she's sent to boarding school and returns to win Neilan's heart. Her fans liked her all these ways, yet she still made films in which she undertook a single dramatic identity, such as her Cho Cho San (*sic*) in *Madame Butterfly*. Although there are a few moments of light charm, the screenplay stays within the tragedy of the story. Mary walks, bows low, lowers her head, and sits in a style that was considered appropriate for a Japanese woman, and she never forgets or loses the posture. Usually boisterous in her movies—leaping around, girlishly jumping up and down—here she is the opposite, and her performance is highly effective.

In June of 1916 Famous Players merged with the Jesse L. Lasky Feature Play Company to form Famous Players/Lasky, with the product to be distributed by Paramount Pictures. In July the company set up Artcraft Pictures to release the films of Mary Pickford—and she became the first actress to have her own production unit: the Pickford Film Corporation, which would be housed within Adolph Zukor's Famous Players organization. She could choose her own directors and supporting cast, and she had approval over advertising, a voice regarding final cut, and the right to question any role she didn't like. Zukor was not so much her boss as he was her colleague. Throughout 1916 she continued her string of successes with *The Foundling* (a second version, shot in late 1915), *Poor Little Peppina, The Eternal Grind, Hulda from Holland,* and *Less Than the Dust.* In 1917 she began an astonishing run of films, almost all of which would be enormous hits, although her first release, *Pride of the Clan,* was one of her few movies that didn't do well at the box office (possibly because it was self-consciously beautiful). The story, directed by Maurice Tourneur, is set in a fishing village off the coast of Scotland, and the production is greatly enhanced by superbly designed sets by Ben Carré. Tourneur is one of the great visual artists of the silent cinema, and he uses silhouettes and compositions to create a strong sense of atmosphere. The image looks stark, spare, and dramatic. The houses that the simple folk inhabit are dark and dim, with low ceilings (clearly visible in the shots), giving a cramped and tight feeling to the interiors. The movie often uses a single source of light for dramatic effect. Mary gives a fine performance, but the movie, with a dour Scottish ambience that lacked comedy, didn't appeal widely to her audiences, even though her character is within the range of what they liked to see her do and doesn't depart significantly from her persona.

Her next, *The Poor Little Rich Girl*—enhanced by fanciful dreamlike sequences—was just the sort of thing her fans loved. Although many people think of Mary as always playing a child, this was the first movie in which she actually did so. Based on a successful play, *Poor Little Rich Girl* had first-rate artists working in all areas of production: Frances Marion wrote the scenario, Tourneur directed, and Ben Carré again did the scenery. It became a landmark film for Pickford, because of the enormous influence it had over the rest of her career. She touchingly plays a lonely little girl whose wealthy parents seldom have time for her, until she accidentally poisons herself by taking too much of a sleeping drug. While she is in recovery, she hallucinates an imaginative dream world, populated with bears, lonely children, and the Angel of Death. She recovers, of course, and her parents are suitably chastened, ready to pay her more attention in the future. *Poor Little Rich Girl* was an enormous success, providing an excellent outlet for Pickford's skills, both in portraying a lonely and pretty little girl, and in showing her to be quite a handful. She sticks a plate of gooey cake under the seat of a nasty playmate, romps with an organ grinder, tosses her ornate gowns out the window in a fit of pique, and dresses up in male clothing, announcing, "I'm Gwendolyn, and I'm a boy."

Also released in 1917 was the excellent *A Romance of the Redwoods.* It was to be the first of two films Mary Pickford would make with director Cecil B. DeMille, but they were not a happy match. Both were strong-willed and

Cecil B. DeMille directing Pickford in *A Romance of the Redwoods*

opinionated about their work. Although the end product was satisfactory and did well at the box office, these two determined individuals—some have called them tyrants—were respectful of each other but not comfortable together. (Mary Pickford was not content to be DeMille's "little fella," a kind of on-the-set pet—which is what Gloria Swanson would later become.)

Shot outdoors on real locations, *Romance* is the story of a resourceful young woman in California Gold Rush days, who loses everything, but manages to cope and ultimately endure. Mary plays a character who is always prepared and always plans ahead. Where others are passive, she is active. Her character is, in fact, that of a provider, the role she was forced to play in her own life. *Variety* said, "Herewith enters Mary Pickford, actress. No longer does the queen of the unspoken drama rely on curls and pouts for effect, for in *A Romance of the Redwoods,* she actually acts and does it in such manner as to land her points with surprising effectiveness."

The Little American (1917) was her second DeMille. Pickford was cast as a young American girl with two suitors, a Frenchman and a German, during World War I. At this stage of her career she's very confident. In a scene in which a German general commands her to remove his boots, she skillfully conveys her character's unfamiliarity with the dirt she finds on her fingers, as well as her repugnance for what she smells, and her distaste and inner outrage at having been asked to perform the service. Her response is partly political, partly female, partly sexual, and partly practical. It's a delicate piece of acting.

The typical Pickford
"little girl," *Rebecca
of Sunnybrook Farm*

Variety fell all over itself regarding her next film, *Rebecca of Sunnybrook Farm:* "Superlatives, so indiscriminately used with reference to pictures in many instances, seem inadequate in properly approximating the transcendent merit of . . . *Rebecca of Sunnybrook Farm* . . . with Mary Pickford. It is a master work that is going to stand supreme . . . for several years to come." Frances Marion adapted the famous book by Kate Douglas Wiggin which tells the story of Rebecca, who is sent away from her large family to live with her aunts. Today, when an excerpt is chosen as a typical Mary Pickford scene, it's often one from this film. Mary, living with the two stingy aunts, is shown getting set to steal herself a piece of pie when she suddenly notices one of her aunts' embroidered samplers: "Thou Shalt Not Steal." Looking slightly guilty but assuming a pious expression, she starts to leave the room until she spots another needlepoint: "God Helps Those Who Help Themselves." Immediately she starts gobbling! It's unfortunate that this movie should be chosen as "typical" Mary Pickford, because actually it presents one of her more heavy-handed performances. More than one film historian has suggested that *Rebecca* is the main source of today's misunderstanding of Pickford's image because it was remade by Shirley Temple in 1938 (in a version that had almost nothing to do with the original book), and stills from it show Mary in her Temple-like golden curls. It's certainly true that Mary never lets up for a minute in *Rebecca*—winking, stomping, prancing, too cute for words. Fans loved her to caper around in this manner, but she does more than enough of it in this film, and her actions lack the spontaneity she displays in her best roles, except for one marvelous sequence in which she first arrives in town and sits alone waiting to meet her aunts. As girls from the town walk by, Pickford's facial expressions shift from open friendliness to suspicion—as she realizes they aren't friendly—and on to outright concern as they scorn her, and finally to a menacing posture as she gets set to defend herself. The issue regarding the age of her character is neatly dealt with by a conversation in which one of her friends (Marjorie Daw) points out that "it will be four years before we're ladies." Pickford, playing age twelve, covers by adding, "Well, we're the *beginning* of ladies." In the meantime, as a lively female, she gets to pound her rival "into jelly," have a series of small-town adventures with her gang, and create a huge drama by running away on a windy and rainy night. She's out the window and down the drainpipe, executing a nice stunt. In the end, she's a grown-up woman graduating from school with honors, and preparing to marry her sweetheart. *Rebecca* was another huge hit for Pickford.

The year 1917 had been one of remarkable success for her, and her final release kept up the pace. It was her very popular version of *The Little Princess*, based on the beloved novel by Frances Hodgson Burnett. Pickford plays Sara Crewe, a girl about ten or eleven years old. (Pickford's role made her fans happy, as she was beautifully dressed in little short skirts, big bows, and long golden curls.) The good reviews said such things as "a more fitting story for Mary Pickford could not have been thought of," and "Miss Pickford at her best," and "her most fitting role." Such comments reflected what was becoming the most popular response of the day—the audience liked Mary Pickford when she pretended to be a little girl.

In *Stella Maris* (1918), one of her best films, Pickford plays both the title character, a wealthy young woman who is crippled and thus overprotected, and Unity Blake, a deformed servant girl—two *totally* different people. Although the wronged husband in the plot points out that there's a strange resemblance between Stella and Unity if only Unity were cleaned up a bit, no one seems to agree. And why should they? Thanks to Pickford's ability to control her body, walk with a crooked gait, and find a new set of gestures, they really don't look that much alike. As Stella, Pickford is sunny, all smiles, and she displays her famous head of curly ringlets to advantage. In this role we can see how pretty Mary Pickford really is. She has a lovely natural smile and a perfect complexion. As Unity, however, she looks dull-skinned, sallow, deformed, and downright ugly. (Mary obviously didn't care how she looked if it was important to her performance.) The most difficult thing for any actor or actress to disguise is his physical self—voice, gesture, walk, even body shape (Lon Chaney is the exception who proves the rule). But Pickford could do it, too, as she demonstrates in *Stella Maris*.

The two Marys in *Stella Maris*

Pickford's next release was *Amarilly of Clothesline Alley,* a charming comedy/drama in which she plays "a debutante" of a New York slum. It's a story of class, with the typical American movie attitude: poor people are really rich and rich people are really poor—poor people have an inborn elegance and rich people have the souls of louts. (The upper-class Mrs. David Phillips is described in a title as believing in the "14th Amendment": "Thou shalt not forget thy pose.") Pickford plays a comic hoyden from a poor Irish family whose heart is generous and whose energy never flags. She washes windows, does laundry, sells cigarettes, and chews gum with equal determination, and she's got up in a ridiculous wardrobe to indicate her poor taste and lack of fashion education. When she's taken "as a social experiment" to the Phillips mansion, she's outfitted tastefully and transformed into a beauty. (As always, clothes make the woman.) In the end, Amarilly/Mary returns home, because "you can't mix ice cream and pickles."

Amarilly is full of knockabout charm and a kind of pseudosocialist look at the slums. Pickford is particularly effective in a scene in which, to humiliate her, Mrs. Phillips invites her washerwoman mom and uncouth siblings to the mansion for tea. At first, Pickford is delighted, thrilled to have her loved ones with her again. As the event disintegrates (Mom dances a wild Irish jig with the butler and discusses the price of soap), she slowly begins to understand that Mrs. Phillips and her fancy friends are looking down on her family. Her pain at this understanding, her loyalty to her roots, and her peppy refusal to let the betrayal get her down are all beautifully conveyed in a complex mixture of intelligence, tenderness, and fire.

Mary was on top, number one in popularity, and her success enabled her to advance the careers of her siblings, Jack and Lottie. In early May of 1918, all three of the Pickfords were on-screen in first-rate material. Jack appeared in *Mile-a-Minute Kendall,* and Lottie played a supporting role as the villain. Mary herself opened in *M'liss,* based on a Bret Harte story. (The *New York Times* carried a big headline, PICKFORDS ALL HERE: MARY, JACK, LOTTIE, Famous Screen Family in New Plays at Broadway Houses.) Reviews for *M'liss* were excellent, because Mary was very good at playing naughty little girls like the heroine. Her M'liss is supposed to "swear like a trooper" as she raises plenty of hell, running around town doing as she pleases until love calms her down. (She meets the man of her dreams by beaning him with her slingshot—and also does battle with a big bear and a huge snake.) *M'liss* was a solid production, once again surrounding her with first-rate talent. Frances Marion wrote the screenplay, Marshall Neilan directed, and her love interest was the very handsome Thomas Meighan, a big star in his own right.

Pickford finished 1918 with two movies that aren't well known today: *How Could You, Jean?* and *Johanna Enlists. Variety* commented about *How Could You, Jean?* that "the story is weak enough, but the direction is altogether uninspired by even a touch of brilliancy or originality." (The director was "William D. Taylor,"* of whom *Variety* cruelly said, "It will probably be some time before he secures another opportunity to direct a Mary Pickford feature.") Frances Marion again wrote the scenario, and it was a familiar one: Pickford plays a young woman who loses all her money and has to go to work as a cook, only to find wealth again by marrying it. In *Johanna Enlists,* she plays a Pennsylvania Dutch backwoods girl whose world comes to life when a regiment of soldiers encamps on her father's farm. This film presents the Mary Pickford formula clearly. In the beginning, she's a freckled mountain urchin, her face described as "a rice puddin' stuck full of flies." She sleeps in a laundry basket, wears a clothespin on her nose while she feeds the pigs, and falls backward off the porch—a slapstick comedy-relief character. After the soldiers arrive, she perks up and starts studying photos in fashion magazines and using her freckle cream. She takes a milk bath, gets a new hairdo (her own famous blonde curls), a new dress—and a toothbrush. As the film progresses,

---

*This is the infamous William Desmond Taylor, who was mysteriously murdered in 1922. He would direct Mary in two more films—*Captain Kidd, Jr.* and *Johanna Enlists.* Mary described him as "a very charming man who directed me in three very bad pictures."

Mary becomes prettier and prettier, ending up in a ruffled, fancy white organdy dress and hat. This transformation—from bumpkin to beauty—is done with humor, including her very funny imitation of Isadora Duncan, a send-up of modern dance technique that inspires her parents to dump water on her.

Johanna Enlists, a wartime effort, had patriotic intentions. A final title card reads, "Now over there are all the soldiers who took part in this picture. They are the 143rd Field Artillery—of which regiment, Mary Pickford is God-mother and Honorary Colonel. 'God Bless them all, and send them safely back to us.' " The final image is a stunning look at "Colonel Mary Pickford" and Colonel Ralph F. Faneuf, the "gallant commander of the famous 143rd." Mary, looking very trim and spiffy in her uniform, executes a snappy salute to her audience.

Looking back over her 1918 releases, one realizes two things about the Pickford career: she had developed a screen character of her own; and she was already attempting to expand the boundaries of that character. Established on-screen as a young American girl with plenty of moxie, off-screen she was a married woman of twenty-six. Her fans loved her as a spunky kid, and she was smart enough to hold on to that image. She began, however, playing in films that afforded her a chance to be something else at the same time: a grown-up version of "America's Sweetheart." Throughout 1918, she appeared successfully in movies that gave the public "two Marys": *Stella Maris, Amarilly of Clothesline Alley, M'liss,* and *Johanna Enlists.* In each she played her traditional character and a better-looking, better-dressed version of herself.

This is the major issue of the Mary Pickford career. The generally accepted opinion is that she became locked into her image as a feisty young girl because her fans wouldn't have it any other way. As early as 1918, critics begin to refer to her movies as formulas (as if those of Fairbanks, Swanson, and others were not) and to suggest that she was going to have to grow up to survive. Pickford took their comments seriously (she was somewhat thin-skinned about criticism). As she aged, she complained to friends and coworkers about having to play her familiar screen character and about wanting to try more mature roles. Yet watching her movies suggests that it might be time to rethink some of this. She began her career by playing girls (she was one) as well as mature women. As she advanced, she undertook roles that put her remarkable acting skills to work, often allowing her to play two versions of one character. After she defined her traditional persona, she generally found release from its youngster format in some way: by growing up, by having a dream or fantasy, or by playing a second, older character. Perhaps she wasn't held hostage to her "sweetheart" persona as much as we think. Perhaps it became a convenient excuse to be used by an aging actress who was tired of wearing hair bows. Instead of seeing her career as a tragedy in which a woman has to play younger than she is, perhaps it should be seen as a triumph in which an actress developed a persona, found a way to vary it, and kept it going far longer than most of her counterparts. Yes, she outgrew herself, but so did Fairbanks and Chaplin.

In December of 1918, after more than two years of constant success, Pickford got proof that she was at the very top: a Motion Picture Hall of Fame contest in which all of America's movie fans were invited to vote for their favorite stars was won by her with 159,199 votes, considerably out in front of the number two entry, Marguerite Clark, who had 138,852. (Marguerite Clark, a forgotten name today, was, along with Mary Miles Minter, one of Pickford's closest rivals during these years.) The top twelve, after Pickford and Clark, were Douglas Fairbanks, number three, with 132,228, Harold Lockwood, William S. Hart, Wallace Reid, Pearl White, Anita Stewart, Theda Bara, Francis X. Bushman, Earle Williams, and William Farnum. Norma Talmadge had 88,040 votes, Charlie Chaplin 86,192. (Lillian Gish, who ranks sixty-fifth, had 37,340 votes, and Mabel Normand 19,605.)

Pickford's first film of 1919, *Captain Kidd, Jr.,* was her last release by Artcraft, and her last produced by the Pickford Film Corporation. It was treated more or less as a film with nothing to offer except its star. During this period, Mary's romance with Douglas Fairbanks was in full flower, and she was probably as distracted from her work as she had ever been—or ever would be. But in late 1918, she had begun to feel that her career was stalling. Movies like *How Could You, Jean?* (which she said should have been called "How could you, Mary?") were disappointments to her, and in general, she felt that Artcraft hadn't always handled her or her movies in the best way possible. After their long and fruitful association, Zukor and Mary had reached an impasse. She wanted total control over her work, and he, a good businessman, felt that he should retain input about how his money was spent. Finally, on November 9, 1918, Mary signed a contract with First National and broke off with Zukor. (Their parting has been reported as being of dramatic simplicity. She telephoned him to say, "Mr. Zukor, I've done it." He replied, "God bless you, sweetheart." She started to cry, and hung up.)

Mary's First National contract began on December 1, 1918, and all her movies were to be jointly copyrighted. After a five- to six-year period of distribution, the ownership of the movies and the copyrights were to revert to her, a shrewd business move that put her in control not only of the money they could earn later on but also of her historical destiny. During the same period, she dissolved the Pickford Film Corporation and set up the Mary Pickford Company, which was co-owned fifty-fifty by Mary and her mother. Mary would copyright all her productions personally, and she now had full creative control over all aspects of her films—and, in addition to a big salary, a guarantee of 50 percent of the profits. In 1919, she made some of the most successful films of her career: *Daddy Long Legs, The Hoodlum,* and *The Heart o' the Hills.* Each of these movies successfully employs what was by now Pickford's established pattern of young girl/grown woman performance. *Daddy Long Legs* begins with her in an orphanage, a child-mother to the other poor kids. After she's been taken under the wing of a mysterious guardian who doesn't reveal his name (her "daddy long legs"), she grows up to be the beautiful young woman he decides to marry.

Daddy Long Legs was so successful that it was used in promoting her next film, *The Hoodlum.* Since it had come from her own studio, that, too, was touted. The ads for the movie proclaimed: "Hey! look out for THE HOODLUM when she comes to your theatre. She is MARY PICKFORD in her Second Picture from her own Studios. Miss Pickford is now personally responsible for every detail of her new pictures. That this one will prove a worthy successor to her first personal production, *Daddy Long Legs,* she confidently hopes. A First National Attraction."

The Hoodlum begins with a significant demonstration of Mary's raw star power. Prior to the beginning of the movie, she appears on-screen, dressed for her traditional "little Mary" role, with a big hair bow, long curls, and a short, lacy white dress with little shoes and short socks. She is seen writing on a blackboard that is supported by an old-fashioned artist's easel: "Be an American. Help Uncle Sam pay for the war. The fighting's over but the paying ain't." Obviously prompted from off-screen, she listens carefully and adds the word "not" after "ain't." Prompted again, she erases "ain't" and puts in "is," dimpling beautifully and making sweet faces at both the audience and the off-screen presence. Then she erases it all and writes BUY WAR SAVINGS STAMP. Prompted again, she adds the "s," smiles, and curtsies like a little princess. Here was proof of the Mary Pickford success as well as the Mary Pickford curse. Her power and popularity were so great that she was chosen to be the star who could best sell the audience the savings stamps concept, because everyone knew that no one would be impatient with a sales pitch from "America's Sweetheart." Ironically, however, it was assumed that people might not be as responsive to the real Mary Pickford, a mature woman, making a direct and simple pitch to the audience as herself. They liked her both ways, but they preferred the young girl with the long golden curls. Yet, paradoxically, Pickford's face is made up like a grown woman's, with lipstick and mascara. She is not appearing as a child, but as Mary Pickford, movie star, in one of her most popular roles, the girl child.

The Hoodlum is vintage Mary Pickford. She plays the spoiled granddaughter of an old tycoon whose business methods are sometimes less than honorable. The early scenes of the film allow Mary to let it rip: she stamps her foot, screams, throws things, and storms into her grandfather's business meeting in pajamas and slippers, demanding his attention. *The Hoodlum* reverses the usual formula, in which Mary travels from slums to a mansion, by having her travel from a mansion to the slums. Her father, who is writing a book about poor people, returns home from Europe and the two of them go to live in the poverty-ridden section of the city to aid his research. Her irritated grandfather comes to the slums himself, disguised as "Peter Cooper," to see what will happen to her. What happens, of course, is that she turns into Amarilly of Clothesline Alley, making a superb adjustment and busily solving most of the problems of the neighborhood. Having arrived in the slums like a star, in silks and high heels and an expensive town car, she's soon bouncing around in a silly hat with a feather on it and various striped dresses designed to scream "poverty." Mary learns to shoot craps, to share everything, and to help the poor. In one wonderful sequence, she takes to the alley to do a wicked dance with a little slum boy. (Her grandpa watches, horrified, while she tangos around, shaking her little body and high-stepping through the trash.) While it can't exactly be said that Mary gets down, at least she shows herself willing to boogie. She even dresses up like a street boy and burgles her grandpa's house to help the young man she's fallen in love with. Movies like *Amarilly* and *Hoodlum* make it hard to understand why modern audiences have such a mistaken idea about Mary Pickford. Apart from the obvious problem—her films haven't been easy to find—how did the false notion of her as saccharine heroine come to define her work? Mary had such toughness in her, and such a willingness to deglamorize herself. When James Cagney received the American Film Institute Life Achievement Award, he referred to his success as being partly due to "the unmistakable touch of the gutter" he carried with him out of the slums. Pickford, another great Irish actor, carried with her "the unmistakable touch of the really tough female breadwinner." This quality is fully on display in *The Hoodlum*.

The *New York Times* review of *The Heart o' the Hills* indicates that critics were catching on to Mary's strategy regarding her persona: "Apparently Mary Pickford is facing the realization that she cannot go on forever as the sweet, cute, and kittenish little darling of the screen, for her latest . . . shows her in more serious moods and with more mature manners than her previous productions." Pickford played an untamed Kentucky mountain girl in a story taken from a novel by John Fox, Jr., a popular fiction writer of the day. The clever way in which she and her collaborators addressed the problem of her age— and of her fans' unwillingness to let go of their "little Mary"—is effectively demonstrated. For more than half the movie, Mary is the fans' darling, particularly when she beats the stuffing out of several boys on the school grounds, scaring them half to death. She's at her best in an extended scene at a mountain hoedown, dancing up a storm, socking a citified partner who tries to put his arm around her waist (the young John Gilbert), and threatening to poke the eyes out of a beautifully turned-out rival. (This upper-crust female promptly faints dead away, leaving Mary to haul her off the dance floor, while an old-timer warns, "We'll have no upscuddle here!") In the final third of the film Mary becomes a grown-up, suddenly wealthy, having been conveniently adopted by "Colonel Pendleton." She's fashionably dressed in an elegantly cut riding habit, and she is a radiant, glowing young woman, her real off-screen self. In the end, reunited with her childhood mountain beau, the tomboy is seen to be still enclosed within the very elegant bosom of the mature young woman. Dressed in a beautiful organdy dress with a bow, she becomes again the playful young girl as she and her true love jump up and down in a stream and Mary falls on her bottom in the water. At this point, she gives her audience both her womanly self and her familiar youthful screen character.

Early in 1919, First National, which was releasing Mary's movies, was rumored to be planning a merger with the powerful Famous Players/Lasky corporation, and the shrewd businesswoman in Mary Pickford understood at once that the control she had gained over her films could be lost. Acting swiftly, Mary, Douglas Fairbanks, D. W. Griffith, William S. Hart, and Charles Chaplin created their own organization to counter this potential loss of creative power, forming a company that would be known as the United Artists Association. (Hart soon left the group.) Their plan was to increase their profits, stop other organizations from using them for block booking purposes, and gain complete control once and for all over their careers. It was an unprecedented move on the part of major artists. "Freedom," Mary said years later. "It's a heady wine, and having tasted it, you find it impossible to go back to working for someone else."

Mary released only two movies through United Artists in 1920: *Pollyanna* and *Suds*. Reviewing the first, the *New York Times* once again raised the issue of when Mary was going to grow up on-screen. In a very telling piece, the *Times* opened up with, "People have been asking recently, 'Why doesn't Mary Pickford grow up?' The question is answered at the Rivoli this week. It is evident that Miss Pickford doesn't grow up because she can make more people laugh and cry, can win her way into more hearts, and even protesting heads, as a rampant, resilient little girl than as anything else. She can no more grow up than Peter Pan. When she stops being a child on the screen, she'll probably just stop." Chilling words, although the *Times* added a cheerful note: "But that time is a long way off."

Pollyanna, the popular Eleanor Porter story, is about a little girl who is determined to "be glad" no matter what happens to knock her for a loop. This concept is enough to drive a modern audience crazy. (Even in 1920, the *Times* pointed out that meeting such a person in real life was "provocation to a justifiable homicide.") It's difficult for viewers today to understand a property like *Pollyanna* and how it was received in its own day, often assuming that no one found it overly sentimental or cloying at the time. However, *Variety* pointed

Pollyanna

out cheerfully that the charming world of *Pollyanna,* a nice place to live in, was "a fat lie, but it helps to believe it." It was voluntary escapism even then. There's something magnificent about the ridiculous concept of "be glad," and also something terribly American in its incurable optimism. When Pollyanna's beloved father dies and she is swept away from her familiar life to live with a wealthy maiden aunt, she finds a stern, unrelenting relative. For this, Pollyanna finds a way to "be glad," and she soon has the aunt—and the entire town—twisted around her little finger. It's perversely satisfying. And Pickford understands the story's irony as well as its subtext, which is about a girl so tough that nothing can get her down. She arrives in New England during a downpour, and is blown around the streets, so that when she first appears before her austere aunt, soaking wet and muddy, she looks like a bedraggled rat, her clothes dripping and her shoes ruining the carpets. When her aunt lets her have it—not exactly a warm welcome for the bereaved orphan—she puts magazines under her shoes to keep the mud off the floors and carpets, but finds it difficult to lift her feet, which are now stuck to the paper. She begins to walk around, lifting her knees high with each step, taking on a crazy goose-stepping gait, but behaving as if this is perfectly natural and no one will notice. (She's solved a problem, after all.) For several minutes, everything

Pickford does is hilarious, yet very matter-of-fact. For antics like these, she received rave reviews.

Suds, her other 1920 release, was a modest hit. In it, Mary Pickford played a role that had been acted on the stage by Maude Adams (in a play called *'Op o' Me Thumb*). She's a hardworking washer-girl in a cheap French laundry in London, and some fans complained because her character never becomes wealthy—where was the rainbow and the pot of gold? Seen today, her performance is suspiciously Chaplinesque. Her downtrodden laundress is played more for pity than usual despite comedy sequences involving a horse brought up to her rented room and a fast-paced ride down the street in a wagon, which ends up with her newly washed laundry in the dirt. The carpers were right: for once, Mary got nowhere and found no wealthy lover, no rich daddy, and no moral to explain why, either.

Mary Pickford at her worst—and least accessible for modern audiences—can be seen in *Love Light,* her first release of 1921. There's way too much of her in the movie—she appears in a series of incidents that stop the plot dead as she caters to her audience. Without a fresh conception in either script or direction, these incidents become nothing more than shtick, and in performing them, Mary both loses our interest and destroys the pace. For instance, a bunch of chickens get drunk (don't ask) and reel around the yard, so "little Mary" can coyly chase them, to put them in her stew. This tiresome event goes on and on, yet it in no way reflects the tone of the rest of the film, which turns into a tragedy. Later, Mary, grown up and married, gives birth and goes temporarily mad, and as if that weren't enough, her husband turns out to be a German spy. Nothing seems to matter except providing moments for Mary to be the little tomboy (beating up her brother) or to show her dramatic skills (stealing a neighbor's baby after her own child dies). In *Love Light* we get a definite sense that Mary Pickford may be shoving what audiences wanted from her down their throats.

On the other hand, the idea of casting Mary Pickford in *Little Lord Fauntleroy* (1921) was so perfect, with Mary playing both the little boy and his beautiful mother, Dearest, that the *Times* had only to say: "Is there anything more to be said?" The movie is extraordinarily well made, with photography by Charles Rosher, honest settings, lovely costumes, solid direction, and a strong supporting cast. To play a young boy, Pickford—who was not only not a boy but was twenty-nine years old—uses her full bag of tricks. One of the most professional aspects of the movie is its superb exploitation of double exposure so that she can play the little lord and his mother together. There's a marvelous moment in which Pickford reaches out—to herself—that is perfectly matched. (She's portraying people of two different heights; she stood on six-inch lifts as the mother.) And she manages not only to be taller than herself but totally different from herself. As Dearest, she's calm, regal, and

Pickford as little Lord Fauntleroy and as his beloved mother, Dearest

sweetly loving. As the child, she's antsy, energetic, and full of curiosity. She presents a properly boyish character, fighting, punching, climbing, jumping, wrestling, and executing a neat handstand. (One sly reviewer pointed out that she must have used her husband, Doug Fairbanks, as a model for these scenes.) At the gala opening of the movie at the Apollo Theatre in New York, Mary and Doug made a personal appearance. The crowds were so huge that the police had to cut their way through the throngs. Mary's fame and popularity were at their zenith. (A 1921 issue of *Motion Picture* gushed, "Five years ago, Mary Pickford was the Queen of the movies. Today she is the Empress.")

In her final release of 1921, *Through the Back Door,* Pickford plays a child given to French peasants so that her mother can marry a wealthy man who's not interested in having a child around, "sacrificing the joy of being a mother for the joy of being a wife." She's very much the public's favorite Mary, riding a reluctant mule, splashing in a stream, and strapping brushes on her shoes to perform her famous "skating"-around-the-room sequence. It was the usual rags-to-riches, tomboy-to-becurled-heiress routine. *Variety* summed it up neatly as "a market product—that's all—full of sweetness and light, a money maker and probably designed as such."

In 1914 Pickford had made *Tess of the Storm Country* with great success, and it was a logical decision for United Artists to remake it in 1922. Although it had only been eight years since the original, Mary's stardom had grown

Pickford made *Tess of the Storm Country* in 1914 and again in 1922,
when she appeared with Jean Hersholt.

hugely. The money now available to spend on her productions was generous,
and film techniques had greatly improved, so there was a solid business reason for re-creating the story. The remake of *Tess* turned out to be one of Pickford's best films, as all of her talent was put to use. In *Tess*, her character is
shown going about her daily work in great detail. To watch Mary cooking,
preparing the wood for a fire, or cleaning house is to see totally credible action,
which, in turn, makes her character totally credible. In addition, her Tess is
very confrontational. She is living on her own in a highly independent manner,
daring to ignore what others might think of her. She stomps into the frame completely free of the usual 1920s female trappings. She wears big boots—men's
boots—and a long, floppy coat, still the tough little tomboy. Pickford, of
course, was a tiny person, inherently feminine, so when she becomes energetic
or athletic (here she jumps into a roaring river to save a pregnant woman from
drowning), she never becomes masculine. She defeminizes the female form in
Tess, playing a woman cut loose from convention and societal expectations, but
in the end she finds love and accepts motherhood in a believable manner.

    In *Tess* can be seen the essential paradox of the Pickford image. She is
young and old, she is male and female, she is childish and mature. Her filmed
image embodies virtue—her characters are often saying indirectly to a
viewer, "I am wonderfully the sum of all virtues." At the same time, however,

she's a bad-tempered little devil. As Molly Haskell wrote of her, "Even at her most arch-angelic, Pickford was no American Cinderella or Snow White whose only claim to consequence was a tiny foot or pretty face. She was a rebel, who, in the somewhat sentimental spirit of the prize pup as underdog, championed the poor against the rich, the scruffy orphans against the prissy rich kids. She was a little girl with gumption and self-reliance who could get herself out of trouble as easily as into it." Pickford managed to be likable and unthreatening yet also a character who was all about will, something audiences clearly responded to in her. (Off-screen, she was well known to possess an indomitable will.)

Rosita, Pickford's only 1923 movie, was directed by Ernst Lubitsch, and it has one of the worst reputations in silent film history. Pickford was instrumental in bringing the great German director of such delights as *Oyster Princess* and *Madame Du Barry* to America, and their planned collaboration was eagerly awaited by everyone. Yet the movie, long unavailable in the United States, accumulated a bad reputation over the years, mostly perpetuated by the star herself, who was never comfortable with the end result. *Rosita*, however, is an excellent movie, and Pickford is excellent in it. In a public showing at New York's Film Forum in August of 1997, a full house responded with laughter and applause to its sexy and sophisticated story. Its reputation is completely undeserved.* Almost everything said about *Rosita* is wrong: it earned excellent reviews, it made money, Pickford is wonderful, and Lubitsch has a firm hand on the direction. *Variety* said that Pickford "with her hair done up, pretty as a picture and displaying action ability few thought her capable of . . . tops the splendid work of *Stella Maris,* the greatest picture she ever made until the current feature." The movie itself was called "one of the biggest pictures of the year." Lubitsch, making his American directorial debut, also earned raves: "[He is] responsible for turning out a production replete with infinite detail, delightful atmospheric touches, consummate characterizations . . ." The *New York Times* said, "Nothing more delightfully charming . . . has been seen on the screen for some time," adding such adjectives as "exquisite," "swiftly flowing," "impressive," "witty," and "pleasingly pictured." Its conclusion was: "One of the most charming productions in which Miss Pickford has appeared." As to money, *Rosita* grossed over $940,000 in America, Canada, and South America, and its European release brought in even more.

---

*Over the years, I've heard a great deal about *Rosita:* It's a flop, it lost money, Pickford is an embarrassment, Lubitsch was off his feed . . . but something I hadn't heard was that it essentially tells exactly the same story as *The Spanish Dancer,* the Lubitsch German film starring Pola Negri. In fact, it's almost a direct remake, except that *Rosita* is a far more expensive production, and the leading character is tailored more specifically to Pickford's charm than to Negri's passion.

What happened so that between 1923 and now these accolades and all that money were reduced to flop status? Basically, what happened was Mary Pickford. She was disappointed by *Rosita* and began defining it as a failure very early on. ("It's the worst picture I ever did; it's the worst picture I ever *saw.*") She was proud she had brought Lubitsch to America, and their personal relationship wasn't terrible, but she described him as "a director of doors," adding, "he didn't understand me." Knowing what we know about Lubitsch's career—and knowing what we know about Pickford's—it's easy to understand that they were not a marriage made in movie heaven. Lubitsch was sly, sophisticated, and sexy. Pickford was fresh, direct, and, while not sexless, more or less disengaged from the concept. Lubitsch was European, and Pickford was prototypically American. Both wanted control of their movies. Yet *Rosita* is a testament to what professionals they both were, and how very talented; despite their incompatibility, they made a wonderful movie that shows them both to advantage. Neither suffers at the other's hands.

Rosita has costly settings, including an outdoor Seville, beautiful gardens, castle rooms with vaulted ceilings, ornate furniture, and magnificent mirrors and doors. The pace is superb, and Lubitsch's direction of the typical "cast of thousands" delineates a world of real people and colorful action. Holbrook Blinn as the lecherous old king is absolutely wonderful, and the costumes, hairdos, and jewelry are all beautiful. Pickford is excellent as the street singer who dances, flirts, and entertains the masses. Her eyes sparkle, her smile is enchanting, and she's her traditional tough little self—throwing a would-be tax collector out into the streets after knocking him a good one—and yelling at the king, "I hate you!" She plays an excellent comedy scene in which Rosita, a hungry street girl, is first brought to the palace, where she spots a large bowl of sweets. Eyeballing the dish carefully, she begins to stalk it. As the camera holds steady on the bowl sitting in the middle of a large table, she walks back and forth past it, in and out of frame. After a few moments of "casing the joint," she grabs up a bonbon and pops it into her mouth, smoothly sailing by again for another one. This scene is a perfect example of how Lubitsch and Pickford wed their styles harmoniously. The camera setup—static—and the clever action that allows the star to go in and out of frame while the audience gets the joke from watching an inanimate bowl—is pure Lubitsch. But the sly comedy of a little girl getting ready to steal from the big rich folks, and the resulting cleverly timed comedy action, is pure Mary Pickford.

Rosita's reputation—and the fact that it was lost to viewers for so many years—illustrates one of the more depressing aspects of Pickford's career. She had worked hard for her image, and she wanted it kept intact. Fearing that her films would be laughed at by later generations, she decreed that her work be destroyed after her death. As early as the May 1931 issue of *Photo-*

Four famous figures clown around on the set of *Rosita:* Charlie Chaplin, director Ernst
Lubitsch, Douglas Fairbanks, and Pickford.

Dorothy Vernon of Haddon Hall

play, Pickford was thinking about eradicating any chance for history to judge her unfavorably. In an article entitled "As Mary Faces Forty," Pickford states flatly, "I am adding a codicil to my will. It says that when I go, my films go with me. They are to be destroyed. I am buying all my old films for this purpose. I would rather be a beautiful illusion in the minds of people than a horrible example on celluloid. I pleased my own generation. That is all that matters."

In *Dorothy Vernon of Haddon Hall* (1924), Mary played in a costume film in which she was the spunky heir to Haddon Hall, betrothed as a child to the heir of the Rutlands, whose estate lies alongside. A slight touch of Fairbanks has crept into her work, as she races to the rescue of her lover in an extended sequence in which she rides her horse over hill and dale, along a castle wall, executing a brilliant jump. There's a complicated plot involving Mary, Queen of Scots, and it did give Mary Pickford a grown-up role to play. However, it was not a critical or financial success, and is often cited by historians as an example of how, when she attempted to play a grown-up role, her audiences rejected her. Of all Mary Pickford's films, *Dorothy Vernon of Haddon Hall* seems the best argument for that case. Seeing it today, there is no reason to object to the film *except* that Pickford plays a grown-up woman quite straightforwardly and is not the "little Mary" that audiences loved best.

Dorothy Vernon is a well-designed film, with expensive costumes in which Pickford looks lovely, but it's also a lively, playful movie with comedy, charming love scenes, and exciting action. (Many film historians, including Kevin Brownlow and Elaina Archer, believe that Pickford's astonishing action sequences were probably performed by Douglas Fairbanks in a wig and cloak.) She was always honest with herself about the failure, saying, "So many costume pictures just then . . . and most of them were better than mine." In her memoirs she told the truth about how she felt afterward: "I was quite ready to surrender to public demand and become a child again."

So back to childhood she went for her next two movies—*Little Annie Rooney* (1925) and *Sparrows* (1926). In the former, she's showcased in the kind of film that had made her a star a decade earlier. She plays a twelve-year-old (at age thirty-three) who is boss of a bunch of street kids, a sort of early Our Gang. *Variety* summed up the film's appeal: " 'Our Mary' is back again in *Little Annie Rooney* . . . She's dirty-hands, dirty-face . . . and the fans are going to love her to death."

Sparrows is an excellent example of why Mary Pickford was a success, although a *Variety* review at the time called it "one of the few duds put out by Mary Pickford." Seen today, it is far more likable than *Little Annie Rooney*. *Sparrows* is a dark story concerning a group of pathetic children who are trapped like slaves on a baby farm deep in an alligator-infested swamp. Rather than making the film seem old-fashioned, this Dickensian situation lifts it up into a classic mold, giving it a fairy-tale quality, so that its melodrama and sentiment can be taken as unreal in a stylized manner that is really very modern. Its horrific tale—basically about child abuse—is presented almost jauntily, with considerable panache. There's a constant vein of humor to it, which undercuts a modern audience's potential rejection of the plot, and it has a tense and thrilling escape through the swamp that culminates in an insane boat chase that is practically madcap in its execution. (This chase is partly marred by the use of inadequate miniatures.)

Mary is perfect as the surrogate mother to the other swamp orphans. Here is the great movie star, Miss Pickford, who never gave birth (although she did adopt two children late in life), picking up babies and feeding them, rocking them, changing them, singing to them, as if she were an old hand at the job. (As she aged, Mary was often cast as the "little mother" to a brood of younger children. This gave her an excuse to have children without sex, and her movies to tackle mature plot responsibilities without threatening her image.) Her gestures with the children, and her rhythms in ministering to them, are all perfect. Mary's film persona is well illustrated by *Sparrows,* as she holds off the old villain with a pitchfork and rescues a tormentor (having decided to feel sorry for him) by pulling him out of quicksand with a horse and rope.

Sparrows

My Best Girl in 1927 would be Mary Pickford's final silent film. She was the greatest of the great, but she was near the end of her run. *My Best Girl* paired her with the man who was to become her third and final husband, the handsome Charles "Buddy" Rogers. She enters the movie for all the world as if it were 1917 instead of 1927 and she was still the little kitchen slavey of her early films. Although she plays a grown-up working as a stock clerk in one of those 1920s wonderlands, the department store, she is first seen as nothing but a pair of feet in worn shoes and dark stockings. This time the shoes have high heels, but she's still the same resourceful "little Mary" as she hurries down the store aisle overburdened with pots and pans. She drops one, picks it up, drops another, picks it up, until finally she puts her foot in one of the pans to slide it along. Of course, her foot gets stuck! Just about when she gets where she's going, her underpants fall down, and she steps out of them, rushing over to the counter to figure out what to do. In the meantime, another woman comes along, steps inside them by accident, looks down, and assumes they're hers. It's an appropriate comic introduction for a child actor, but Mary is now play-ing a flapper (or perhaps a semi-flapper). Her hair is shorter, although not

Pickford and the man who would become her husband, Buddy Rogers,
in *My Best Girl*

fashionably bobbed, and she wears makeup (not too much), but she's still the
poor girl whose family depends upon her.

My Best Girl is full of charm, however. Rogers plays a stock clerk who's
the boss's son in disguise. When he and Mary fall in love, Rogers takes her to
his mansion for dinner, telling her that the slogan of the boss is "We are all
one happy family" and they're sure to be welcome. She plays a wonderful
scene. Winking to let his butler in on things, Rogers escorts Mary to the dinner table where they pretend to be "Mr. and Mrs." She's on home territory,
carefully wiping her silverware before she uses it, grabbing items off the butler's tray for Rogers before they can be served properly, and confidently signaling him to use his soup spoon instead of his cocktail fork when they bring
in the "lobster sundae." After she mistakes the consommé for tea and dumps
milk and sugar into it, she tells him privately, "They may have great waiters
here, but the food is terrible." When his parents come home unexpectedly,
she hides under the table and has to be coaxed out. Everything she does is
standard Mary, the kinds of things her fans still loved her to do, and she is at
her best doing them . . . but it *is* 1927. She has a final grand scene in which
she pretends to Rogers that she was fooling him all along, so that he can be
free to marry a suitable girl. She struts around, smearing lipstick on her face,
choking over a cigarette she tries to puff, and dancing a hot Charleston, a nice

girl pretending to be naughty. Pickford still knows how to strike exactly the right note of half-funny, half-touching waiflike behavior. Breaking down, she cries, climbs into his lap, and says, "I'm not really a bad girl, Joe . . . I love you, Joe, but I can't marry you." But, of course, she does. Both on-screen and in real life.

Pickford made her sound debut in *Coquette,* released in early April of 1929. She would win the 1928–29 Best Actress Oscar for her performance in it, which pretty much sums up critical opinion as to whether she could talk or not. *Variety* said, "She talks and she looks different with the new bob." Otherwise, the implication was, she's our Mary and that's that. The *Variety* review concludes by quoting a woman in the audience overheard saying, "Well, after spending an entire night with a man in a cabin, Mary Pickford is still America's sweetheart." In an unprecedented tribute contained inside a review, *Variety* continued: "A notice on Mary Pickford in her first talker would not be complete without a personal comment. Miss Pickford's screen career stands without parallel, in any way, in every way. For longevity, for stardom, for cleanliness and for the promotion of the American film industry. What Jolson did for the talkers, Miss Pickford did for the pioneer silents."

In *Coquette,* which had been a popular stage success with Helen Hayes in the role of Norma Besant, Mary Pickford appeared before her adoring public completely transformed. It wasn't just that she had a voice. This time she really *was* a flapper . . . and a distinctly flirtatious one at that. Her first spoken words were an off-screen reply to her brother, "Mind your own business, Marty, I'm just trying to get my skirt to hang a little straight." When she appears shortly after, she comes flurrying downstairs as if she were Clara Bow. Her very blonde hair is now cropped short, a true 1920s bob of tight curls around her head. She has on a low-cut, spaghetti-strap evening gown that's all gauze and fluff, topped off with a diamond clip at her stomach and a long chain of diamond beads. Her skirt is short and her little satin heels are high. She's a new person, and definitely a woman with a sex life. (Perhaps her Oscar was awarded partly because she had challenged her image, playing a grown-up anti-Pickford role. Whatever might be said about *Coquette*—it has the quality of a high school play—Mary Pickford can't be said not to have deserved her Oscar. She had earned it by a lifetime in the business, and by her unprecedented popularity, and hers would not be the last acting Oscar awarded for the wrong reasons.)

The story is about her falling in love with a man her father does not approve of, and she and this love (Johnny Mack Brown, the hunk of his day) have lots of steamy embraces. Pickford's voice goes a little high from time to time, and slightly false as she "acts" the devil out of the dialogue, which is frequently over the top. However, she speaks in a less exaggerated southern accent than the rest of the cast, and she delivers her dialogue more naturally

The "new" Pickford in her sound debut and Oscar-winning role in *Coquette*

than they do. (They're all busily enunciating everything very clearly, in case we're not listening.) Sometimes she makes the error of showing emotion and delineating response physically when she should be placing that response in the dialogue that's carrying it. On the whole, though, she makes a respectable debut in sound.

After *Coquette*, Pickford assembled her old creative team of Marshall Neilan and Frances Marion for a movie to be called *Forever Yours*, but things went badly. Neilan was drinking heavily, and they quarreled. Pickford said the footage was "stupid" and she scrapped it, taking a huge loss and claiming to have burned the unreleased film. (Actually, she was too practical for that. The remaining footage is now at the Library of Congress.) She made only three more movies: *The Taming of the Shrew* (1929), in which she costarred with Fairbanks and the famous credit line "additional dialogue by Sam Taylor" appeared, and *Kiki* (1931) and *Secrets* (1933), both of which were remakes of silent films that had starred Norma Talmadge. *Secrets*, beautifully directed by Frank Borzage, was *Forever Yours* completely reshot from top to bottom. *Kiki* and *Secrets* are not disasters, and the latter holds up well. However, Pickford seems no longer unique, and somewhat distanced from the new, tougher era of the 1930s.

When she completed *Secrets*, Mary Pickford was forty-one years old. Shrewd and clear-minded about her work as she had always been, she stepped aside. It was over. Despite reports that she continued to consider projects—and missed working—she terminated her career. Years later, she gave a coolly detached, honest appraisal: "I left the screen because I didn't want what happened to Charlie Chaplin to happen to me. When he discarded the little tramp, the little tramp turned around and killed him. The little girl made me. I wasn't waiting for the little girl to kill me."

THE MARRIAGE

By 1915 Mary Pickford was the girl who had everything. She was "America's Sweetheart," hugely wealthy, respected in her profession, her emotional life linked to her work and to her family, to whom she always remained devoted. (A reporter once observed, "Her greatest interest in life is her mother," and that may well have been true.) But Mary was flesh and blood and she found time to be interested enough in a young man to marry him behind her mother's back. Charlotte Pickford was Mary's partner in her career, and the two were very close in every respect, yet when Mary fell in love with the handsome Owen Moore, she defied her mother in a way she never had before, and really never did again. Moore and Mary were both at Biograph during her formative years as a star, and they fell in love. (Moore and his brothers, Matt and Tom, had significant careers as leading men of the stalwart variety.) In her autobiography, she described her love as "five feet eleven inches tall, extremely handsome, with a ruddy Irish complexion, perfect teeth, dark blue eyes, and a very musical voice . . . He was the Beau Brummel of Biograph, always dressed with immaculate elegance." In other words, he was irresistible to an impressionable young girl, who managed to overlook stories about his heavy drinking and also her mother's firm advice: "He's too old for you."

On January 7, 1911, when she was just eighteen, Mary married Owen Moore, who had turned twenty-four in December of 1910. "If ever there was a sadder wedding," she wrote, "I have yet to hear of it." She described how she worried because "I'm disobeying Mother . . . I don't want to leave my family." However, she *did* marry him, but to put her deep attachment to her family—and her guilt—in perspective, she went home to Mom right after the ceremony, climbing into bed on her wedding night to fall asleep beside her sister, Lottie. (With a start like this, it was hardly likely the marriage was going to be a success.) Mary finally told her mother, whose explanation was "He must have bewitched her."

This early marriage is usually referred to as a disaster, and no doubt that is a fair assessment. However, testimony to what inspired it and perhaps kept it going for a while exists: Owen Moore and Mary Pickford together in *Cinderella* (1914) and *Mistress Nell* (1915). In *Cinderella*, they meet playfully in the forest and seem to be genuinely smitten with one another; they have an easy physical familiarity, and a quick response to each other. In *Nell*, there is a golden moment in which she leans back against her husband in a very unchildlike manner. Obviously feeling the comfort of his familiar body, she lifts her arms to bring his head close to hers, her face lighting up in a radiant, sensual smile. Their playful love scenes and visible mutual attraction are evidence of theirs having been, at least for a time, a very hot romance.

Owen Moore, however, was never fully accepted into the tight-knit Pickford circle, and over the next few years his drinking increased, her disillusionment kept pace, and the final straw was her stardom, for which she earned much more money than he did, leaving him feeling emasculated and embittered. When Mary finally divorced him in 1919, their marriage had been dead for years, but her motivation was the man who really filled her life, her male counterpart in stardom, Douglas Fairbanks.

When the two great stars, Douglas Fairbanks and Mary Pickford, fell in love and began courting, it was unprecedented. They were the top male and female stars of their time. The public loved them both individually, and to have them get together was beyond a fan's wildest dreams of star heaven. From the beginning, their devoted public dubbed them "Doug and Mary," "Mary and Doug"—just two down-to-earth, lovable people the fans felt they knew on a first-name basis. Their stardom was a gift from an adoring public who saw in them something honest and believable. In the public's mind, who else would either of them ever possibly want to marry? They deserved each other and belonged with each other.

They are said to have first met in 1914 at the home of Elsie Janis, a popular Broadway musical comedy star. Doug was still wed to his first wife, Beth, and Mary to Moore. He was a stage success, but not yet a film star, and she was already successful. Of this fateful meeting, she later wrote, "I've always felt that my meeting with Douglas Fairbanks was predestined. I had no social life after working hours. And my only friends were those associated with me in the making of my films. Owen and I, needless to say, were anything but compatible . . ." The couple did not meet again for approximately a year, and by that time, Fairbanks's first movie, *The Lamb*, was on-screen. They both attended a party at the Algonquin Hotel, and while they danced and Fairbanks praised Mary's work, something began to happen between them. "I had been living in half-shadows," Mary wrote in her autobiography, "and now this light was cast on me, this sunlight of Douglas's approval." Frances Marion, the screenwriter who knew them both well, said about Doug, "He'd listen to Mary. He treated her like an intelligent person. Any woman goes for that."

For most of the three years Douglas Fairbanks and Mary Pickford carried on a passionate affair, the public knew little about it. These years of contrivance and denial served to increase their ardor, and finally they felt they simply had to marry, although neither of them was confident that it would be a good thing for their careers. In particular, Mary felt that divorcing and then marrying a man who would also have to divorce, as well as leave his young son (Douglas, Jr.), could easily destroy her image as "America's Sweetheart, a pure and honest little creature." But they went ahead. On Sunday, March 28, 1920, Douglas Elton Fairbanks and Gladys Mary Smith Moore, ages thirty-six and "twenty-six" (Mary had reduced her age) were wed at Fairbanks's home. Present were her family, Doug's brother and his wife, Charles Chaplin, actress Marjorie Daw, Doug's press agent, and the playwright Edward Knoblock. It was a simple ceremony with close friends and family, but then all celebrity hell broke loose. When the world's most famous girl, radiantly beautiful, abundantly talented, and truly beloved, married the world's most virile and handsome man, equally beautiful, talented, and beloved, it was a blockbuster situation. And the wonderful part was that they deeply loved each other, and it showed. In her autobiography, Mary includes a photograph that she has captioned "The dress I wore when I was married to Douglas." She is meltingly beautiful and looks almost dumbstruck with love. Her head is backed by a satin pillow with a ruffle around the edge, and she is holding a fragile bouquet just underneath her bosom. Her dress is delicate, with the tiniest of bows below her throat. Her hair curls sweetly around her face, and although she's not smiling, she looks utterly happy. The fact that she was already a divorcée, a tough business negotiator, and a seasoned actress is nowhere indicated. She could be any small-town girl, innocent and virginal, awaiting her wedding ceremony.

The fan magazines of the day naturally went all out covering the romance and marriage of Doug and Mary. In "The Pickford-Fairbanks Wooing," from the August 1920 issue of *Motion Picture*, Billy Bates reassures fans that "there is a great love story behind the famous wedding." And he gives details: "When Mary Pickford stood before the minister, she stood there as any woman might stand, radiant with love for the man at her side, a bit tearful perhaps for the tender memories left behind, but with smiling hope for the future. Except for the sensation-hungry world waiting just outside the door, she might have been the plumber's bride looking forward to the honeymoon trip to Niagara Falls." Some plumber's bride. And not only had both Fairbanks and Pickford been married before, but there is no evidence that Billy Bates had attended the ceremony. Under a magnificent photograph of Fairbanks, this issue carries the caption: "There never was a more envied bridegroom than 'Doug' and, incidentally, it is doubtful if there is another who could have married 'America's Sweetheart' and remained anything else in the

Pickford and Fairbanks, mobbed by fans in London

world other than 'Mary's husband.' " (This caption, at least, makes a cogent
point.) The magazine also presents a lavish photo layout: MEET MR. AND MRS.
DOUGLAS FAIRBANKS. The bride and groom, extremely fashionably dressed and
inexplicably carrying hats inside their own house, are seen posing with dogs,
then cats, then in the grape arbor, and out-of-doors on a huge lawn.

After Mary completed work on *Suds*, Mr. and Mrs. Fairbanks left for a
four-week honeymoon in Europe. As Mary wrote, "Neither of us had any suspicions of what lay ahead for us either in Europe or in America . . . So dense
were the crowds that we didn't dare set foot out of our suite at the Ritz-Carlton
Hotel [in New York] . . . [In England] Douglas and I were swept up by mobs of
fans till I could neither eat nor sleep, let alone drink in the historic sights. Our
first stop was the Ritz in London. Outside our window we saw them, thousands
and thousands of them, waiting day and night in the streets below, for a
glimpse of us. I felt so inadequate and powerless to show my gratitude that it
actually made me ill." At an outdoor benefit in Kensington Gardens, Mary and
Doug arrived seated in the back of an open Rolls-Royce, and as the crowds
surged forward, Mary was grabbed and pulled out of the car. Doug managed to
rescue her by clutching her by the ankles, but when they were finally able to
step out, the crowds again closed in around them "like quicksand," and she
had to be carried on Doug's shoulders to keep from being crushed. On the

Continent, the mobs did not diminish. "I spent my honeymoon on a balcony waving to crowds," Mary said.

After Mr. and Mrs. Fairbanks took up residence in Hollywood, they became the social leaders of the movie world. Like the royalty they were, King Doug and Queen Mary resided in the fabled palace of Pickfair, a twenty-two-room Tudor mansion that was a wedding present from the groom to the bride. Set on eighteen acres with a stunning view, the house had beautifully designed leaded windows, parquet floors, rich wood paneling, and high, frescoed ceilings. There was a lakelike pool (in which Mary and Doug were photographed rowing a canoe), tennis courts, a library (which Mary called "the book room"), a formal dining room, but only four bedrooms. (Luxurious though it was, it was more of a home than a mansion.) But there was plenty of staff: a head butler, two assistant butlers, two chauffeurs (for two stars), a cook, a gardener, a kitchen maid, a scullery maid, a laundress, Mary's personal maid, a watchman, a handyman, and anyone else they needed. And in case the fans thought they were living too well, they economized by having one of the chauffeurs double as a projectionist.

Everything Doug and Mary did at Pickfair was not only legendary but hard-core important in the business. In a town in which the A-list/B-list concept was only just forming, to be invited there was to have arrived, a striking departure from the earlier, more democratic days of filmmaking. Joan Crawford once described to me what it was like to dine at Pickfair. Always a bit intimidated by (and resentful of) the grand Mary, who had arrived in a way Joan never felt she *could* arrive no matter what level of success she achieved, she detailed how what you wore had to be right, what you said had to be right, where you sat defined your status, and God forbid if you didn't know how to use a finger bowl properly. For all of that, she said, the evenings at Pickfair were wonderful—and entertaining. There were always glamorous and famous people, good conversation, and superb food. She felt that parties at San Simeon were much more down-to-earth than those at Pickfair, despite the awesome surroundings of the Hearst castle. "Remember," she told me, "Marion Davies was always just one of the gals, and Hearst put the catsup bottle on the table, but Mary was a Queen and everyone knew it."

The Pickford/Fairbanks marriage—and the happy days at Pickfair—tragically came apart in the 1930s, after both Doug and Mary had passed their prime as stars. No one knows for certain what went wrong between them, but no one believes they ever really stopped loving each other. Their lives had changed when sound came in, and their stardom—while it didn't exactly end for them—wasn't at the same level, nor did they have the same passion for it. How can any superstar marriage survive? Did Doug and Mary just get tired of playing "Doug and Mary"? Or did the public tire of them playing "Doug and Mary" and render the roles passé? All anyone knows, despite many opinions on the subject, is that on December 8, 1933, Mary Pickford filed for divorce, and although they came close to reconciling, she ended up marrying Buddy Rogers after Fairbanks wed Lady Sylvia Ashley, a woman Douglas junior wrote frankly about in his autobiography, saying he had come "to actively dislike her."

It is said that when years later, Mary's niece, Gwynne (Lottie's daughter), called her in the wee hours intending to tell her of Doug's death, Mary Pickford was psychic, saying immediately, "Don't tell me, my darling is gone." Later, Robert Fairbanks, fulfilling a private promise to his brother, called to give Mary a coded message from their first days of courting that was meaningful only to them. It was 1939, and Mary Pickford would live, no doubt feeling alone in many ways, forty more years.

THE CELEBRITY

The Doug and Mary romance was only part of the phenomenon of Mary Pickford's enormous stardom: if she had never married Douglas Fairbanks she would still be an object of tremendous interest. The way fans picked her out of the crowd and dubbed her "America's Sweetheart"—and the way critics revered her—is the first real marking place in the history of fandom, stardom, and mass hysteria in twentieth-century America. About this fan adulation Mary made a simple, pared-down statement: "I've been loved." It was a perfect understatement from a woman whose box office popularity has never been equaled by any other woman. Her stardom lasted twenty years, and she was named "number one" by *Photoplay* for fifteen of them. Over the years, those who've understood this seem to have stretched themselves to the limit to get it across. When she received an honorary Oscar in 1976, her film clips were introduced with "For more than three generations of movie goers, *this* was the face of the most popular woman in the world." Social historian Edward Wagenknecht made a sweeping evaluation: "I do not believe anybody can understand America in the years during and after the First World War who does not understand the vogue of Mary Pickford." The movie magazines and critics and allegedly hard-bitten journalists of her own time fell over themselves with superlatives such as "She is the glory of the American stage," "She's so simple, so competent, so enthusiastic, so natural," "Any land might be proud of her," "She's a veritable Shakespeare's pen in animated human form," and "She's unique."

Mary Pickford is a quintessential specimen for the study of fan worship, but it isn't generally grasped just how popular she really was. Although the fan magazines of the era carry articles on everyone, those on Pickford are unlike those about anyone else (and there are more of them). Ads and articles and fan letters demonstrate the crazy, worshipful adoration that Pickford inspired. People wanted a piece of her in whatever form they could get it, and her popularity pointed the way for fan passion to be translated into money *outside* the box office. For instance, Mary Pickford is all over the July 1918 issue of *Motion Picture* magazine, but one of the most interesting items is an ad for Pompeiian Beauty Powder, which features a large portrait of her, treating her as if she were the greatest beauty of her time. There is also on display "The Mary Pickford Art Panel," which is available for a mere dime and, of course, proof-of-purchase from a jar of Pompeiian Beauty Powder and Day Cream. The ad says, "The world's most beloved little woman has honored the makers of Pompeiian by posing exclusively for the 1918 Pompeiian Art Panel." It is 28 inches by 7¼ inches, and it comes "in beautiful colors." All you have to do is clip the coupon, add your dime, and your proof, and you, too, can own this panel, which shows Mary in a white ruffled dress, her curls hanging forward over her shoulders, holding a large spray of lilacs and daisies and tulips, with roses mixed in.

The same issue features a worshipful "Eulogy to Little Mary" by Arthur S. Brooks:

Mary Pickford

Say, Mary. I fell
Like a German "Ace" with
A bullet thru his gas-tank
For you . . .
Just a little appreciation
of the Immeasurable services
You are doing the people
You are helping to polish
The pewter of their lives.
Well, so long, Mary.
Thanks!

In December 1919, *Motion Picture* advertises "The Mary Pickford Manicure File," made from "the very wood of the house in Canada where Pickford was born and spent her girlhood." This holy grail is "A Lucky Piece" and it will be "the envy of all your friends, a magnetic charm, a treasured keepsake, an inspiration, a close association with filmdom's most winsome, beautiful, lovable, dainty star, MARY PICKFORD." And it costs a mere fifty cents. (Right under this ad runs this notice: "TO OUR READERS: Motion Picture Magazine guarantees the reliability and integrity of its advertisers. However, should there be any misrepresentation whatever, notify us promptly, and either the advertiser or ourselves will refund your money.")

This adoration of Mary Pickford reflects the more innocent era of the earliest fan magazines. In those days, the magazines followed the public's interest in the stars; whom the public liked the fan mags wrote about—in giddy terms. Later, the magazines, fueled by the studio flacks, would promote and actively sell stars to the public, but in the early years the coverage is a confirmation of how the public actually felt. Articles about Mary Pickford— and there's at least one in every magazine—show how passionately she was loved. In the May 1918 *Motion Picture*, there's an article entitled "Do We Love Mary Pickford? (from a Fan's Own Viewpoint)" by Clara Louise Leslie. She writes:

> Mary Pickford is a fairy! She is not of this world. She just hap-pened down here to help rub a little of the soot off of everybody's viewpoint and whisper to us of a place where perchance butter and eggs are within reason, where folks never have toothaches, and where they tell legends about divorce courts . . . There is yet to be found a woman who is jealous of Mary Pickford . . . We love her curls, we love her sunshine, we love her self-forgetful little ways; and most of all we love Mary Pickford because she loves us . . . Mary Pickford, sweetheart, is the sweetheart of America . . . Now and then one hears of some one who does not like Mary Pickford, but that person is like a highbrow and is generally a full-fledged fan's idea of the type of individual who would steal, plague the cat, and gossip about the dead.

Ironically, this gushing and foolish piece touches in its own way on the real strengths of Mary Pickford. Her films took viewers out of their daily lives into a more innocent and likable world; they appealed to the average working man and woman; and she was believed to be genuinely nice. In March 1920, *Motion Picture* ran an article called "We Meet Mary" (by Gladys Hall) which explained Mary's popularity. "Mary might have been you or me, you know, for all the air of import there was about her. She was sweet; she was wholly unaf-fected; she was interested and winning and sincere." Before going to meet Pickford for the first time, says the writer, she was plagued by many questions. "What was she going to be like? What would she wear? Would she wear her hair in the famous curls? Would she be 'upstage'?" and then, she writes dra-matically: "She came. She didn't in any sense take a stand or strike an atti-tude. She is . . . a good business woman . . . but she is, nonetheless, just a girl, able to meet other girls on their own footing, able to talk . . . with . . . a winsome sort of friendliness, wearing her honors, but wearing them lightly." Pickford seemed to her fans to be a real person; in that sense she truly was "America's Sweetheart."

Not unlike the "Do We Love Mary Pickford?" article that actually defined her persona, "We Meet Mary" both treats her as royalty and claims she's just one of the girls. Contemporaries of Mary's in the business gave ample testimony over the years to her legend—her royalty, as well as her kindness and generosity. In *The Real Tinsel,* Bernard Rosenberg and Harry Silverstein printed a series of interviews with pioneer silent film people which speak of Mary Pickford in positive terms. Wini Shaw talks about Mary's kindness. In her first days in Hollywood, Shaw went to the Brown Derby by herself and ordered liver and bacon, but when it came she couldn't eat it because she had been crying from sheer loneliness. The captain came over and asked her name, and soon she was given a note reading, "Dear Miss Shaw: You look so lonesome sitting over there. I wonder if we may join you?" It was signed "Mary Pickford." Shaw added in her interview, "Here I am a punk kid, and she's the queen. So far as I'm concerned, she always will be. I'll never forget that act of kindness until my dying day." Conrad Nagel spoke of her generosity. "Mary was one of the few great stars of that era who had a social conscience." Maxine Elliott Hicks, who played the other little girl with Mary in *The Poor Little Rich Girl,* said, "Mary Pickford was wonderful to me. Momma and I would go over on the streetcar or whatever we could get in the morning. In the evening, Mary would ask me if I was going straight home, and I would say yes. She'd say, 'I'm having my chauffeur take you home, and I'm going with Mother.' She sent us home more than one time in a limousine." Madge Bellamy tells how Mary helped her fix her hair, taught her about lighting, and let her wear one of her dresses for a part. "I was always in love with Mary," she says.

These anecdotes, told years after Mary's golden days, when there was no gain to be had from them, illustrate part of what made Mary great. She never forgot her own lonely days, and she never forgot that some people had less than she did. In that sense, she was democratic, and the fans were responding to something they felt was part of her that really *was* part of her.

The fan mag articles on Pickford are very different from those on such luminaries as Gloria Swanson and Norma Talmadge. Instead of stressing fashion tips and glamour, the writing on Pickford treated her more seriously, and allowed her to express herself as if she were both wise and down-to-earth. In the April 1918 *Motion Picture,* in a large photo layout entitled STUDIO ACTORS KNIT WITH MARY PICKFORD, she's seen knitting for the doughboys between scenes of her new movie, and teaching everyone else how to knit, too. The movie is *Amarilly of Clothesline Alley,* and not only is the entire supporting cast reduced to the level of schoolchildren here, but her director, Marshall Neilan, sits patiently holding her yarn. Mary reigns supreme, and the magazine calls attention to how she spends her off-screen time: no idle shopping and gossipy chitchat for the sweetheart; *she* knits for chilly soldiers.

In *Motion Picture* of June 1919, Mary was interviewed in an article entitled "On Location With Mary Pickford." She was shooting the graduation scene for *Daddy Long Legs* at the Busch mansion gardens in Pasadena. Mary was full of "gay humor," reported her interviewer, who had ridden out to the location with the star in Mary's green Pierce Arrow. "I believe that a sense of humor is the greatest gift we can have," said Mary, although later she admitted that "My thoughts are full of business these days." Mary reflects "within herself" all humanity, said her interviewer, describing Mary's life as one of denial, struggle, and disappointment. "Mary Pickford believes that it is neither wealth nor success that brings happiness and contentment. It is service, doing our share and not being drones." Presumably, they all rode home together in the green Pierce Arrow after exchanging these philosophies.

Like the other big stars of the day, Mary Pickford was subjected to "character nose reading" in the February 1923 issue of *Photoplay* and even Mary's nose was treated with respect! It was interpreted to mean that she was "evenly balanced, emotional, responsive, but not hypersensitive, practical, with a capacity for thought and emotion." She had "strength, thrift, reserve, financial ability," but exhibited in her dealings "caution, affection, and sympathy." The upshot of all this science was a simple statement: "Her mind controls her heart." (Though sometimes her control would slip. In the 1920 April–May issue of *Motion Picture*, Mary let loose. Sitting in the most expensive suite at the Ritz, she passionately cries out, "I hated being poor.")

IT WOULD BE NICE to end the story of Mary Pickford on the lawn of Pickfair at the height of her fame, but things seldom fade out that way, particularly in the lives of movie stars. It would also be very wrong to sentimentalize the life of a woman who never had a real childhood or even a girlhood of her own. There is every indication that she herself wasn't sentimental in her private life. ("I've worked and fought my way through since I was twelve," she said.) She was married young and badly to an alcoholic actor, and was rumored to have lost her ability to have children through an early abortion. She lived through her brother's messy life, which included marriage to the drug-addicted Olive Thomas and his early death in 1932 at the age of thirty-six. She was heartbroken when her closest confidante, her mother, died of a horrible cancer in 1928 (age fifty-five), and she lost her only sister, Lottie (like her brother, Jack, no saint), who died in 1936 at the age of forty-one. Finally, she faced the end of her career and great fame, and the bitter loss of the great love of her life, Doug Fairbanks. On a more positive note, she married her handsome costar from *My Best Girl,* the charming Buddy Rogers, on June 26, 1937. He was twelve years her junior, but they made an attractive couple, and seemed very right for each other. Their marriage lasted for forty-two years, until her death, and Rogers remained devoted, ever handsome and attentive.

Pickford spent the final years of her life out of the spotlight, and these years are sad to read about. She is rumored to have drifted into alcoholism, and she became reclusive, sometimes spending the day in bed at Pickfair. (Well, heaven knows she'd earned a rest.) For a while, she produced movies, kept United Artists going, and busied herself with charities—in particular, the Motion Picture Relief Fund and Home. Then she just seemed to fade away, last seen in March of 1976 propped up in a chair receiving an honorary Oscar, looking somewhat bewildered by it all, but making a game go of her performance. On May 29, 1979, she died, with Buddy Rogers at her bedside.

Why did the public lose interest in her? Obviously, the coming of sound, her age, and changing public taste all played a part. And she contributed to her disappearance by decreeing that her films should not be shown. Thanks to Buddy Rogers and Lillian Gish—and many others devoted to preservation—she was finally persuaded to let her movies survive beyond her death and be shown to a new generation.

Kevin Brownlow summed up Pickford brilliantly: "The ideal American girl is still the Mary Pickford character: extremely attractive, warm-hearted, generous, funny—but independent and fiery-tempered when the occasion demands . . . She had legions of imitators, but no rivals." Mary expressed her own feelings about what her movies meant to her by saying, "There is something sacred to me about that camera . . . I think Oscar Wilde wrote a poem about a robin who loved a white rose. He loved it so much that he pierced his breast, and let his heart's blood turn the white rose red . . . Maybe this sounds *very* sentimental, but for anybody who has loved a career as much as I've loved mine, there can be no short cuts."

Mary Pickford took no shortcuts in life. She deserves to sit in her rightful chair, the throne of the Queen of Film History. And she deserves respect for what she really was: America's first sweetheart—but also one hell of a woman.

Sincerely

Mary Pickford ©

HARTSOOK
PHOTO
S.F. · L.A.

Pickford as her fans
liked to see her
(LEFT) and (ABOVE)
as she herself liked
to be seen (1929)

MABEL AND THE KOPS

AMERICANS ARE THE PEOPLE WHO, when the French decided that Jerry Lewis was a genius, never stopped to ask why but immediately branded France a nation of idiots. (That may well be, but not because they like Jerry Lewis.) It's safe to say that almost all of American comedy except Chaplin and Keaton is under-valued due to our depressing national tendency to award our prizes and honors to anything perceived as "serious." Lip service is paid to our great tradition of "slapstick," but no one actually knows much about who did it and what it really was. Although a Mack Sennett chase has become a symbol of silent film comedy, the true brilliance of the work is not generally appreciated and not enough credit is given to two glories of the old Sennett gang, the beautiful and intrepid comedi-enne Mabel Normand, and those truly amazing Keystone Kops . . . Mabel and the Kops.

The Kops! Ah, the Kops. On the road and out of control. See how they run, or, more to the point, see how they drive, steering firmly but dangerously over curbstones, around trolley cars, through plate glass windows, and on top of a row of terrified ditchdiggers who drop their shovels and duck. Ignoring not only all traffic laws but the laws of gravity and sanity as well, the Kops are out there doing what we all secretly long to do: not giving a good god-damn as they relentlessly pursue their goal. Oh, those Kops. How rewarding it is to watch them. How little they care about their fellowman, and—oh, boy—what a good time they're having at very, very high speeds.

And Mabel. The whoop-de-doo girl, a tiny creature who could ride a horse, drive a car, fall on her butt, clamber over a rooftop, and still look like a million bucks when she was through. Mabel was the babe who got tied to the railroad tracks while the villain twirled his mustache—but only in jest. She was a figure of delicious liberation who made a joke out of the idea of a damsel in distress. When Mabel showed up, it was everyone else who was potentially in distress, because nothing stopped her, nothing slowed her down.

No discussion of Mabel and the Kops can begin without first considering the King of Comedy, the man whose work first presented us with the three noblest inventions of movie comedy—the pie, the banana peel, and the car:

Mack Sennett, who once proclaimed his philosophy of comedy as "slap 'em down good." Under Sennett's guidance, Mabel and the Kops achieved phenomenal popularity, as did many more of Sennett's comedy stars, including at one time or another Charlie Chaplin, Fatty Arbuckle, Chester Conklin, Mack Swain, Marie Prevost, Marie Dressler, and Gloria Swanson.

Sennett is certainly acknowledged to be the great pioneer of silent film comedy, but not always recognized is the startling quality of his fantastical movies, the bizarre and surrealistic nature of his world. The critics of his own time had a keen appreciation of his comedy that is much broader than the one generally held today. In a 1928 issue of *Photoplay*, the novelist Theodore Dreiser, who was also a film critic and fan, called Sennett "a master" and "Rabelaisian." His movies are a world unto themselves—a world that's always falling apart, collapsing out from under its hapless characters. No one has described it better than Dreiser, who, after praising "the pie throwers, soup spillers, bomb tossers," went on to pay tribute to

> bridges, fences, floors, sidewalks that give way under the most unbelievable and impossible circumstances. The shirt-collars, too tight during attempts to button them, which take flight like birds. The houses which spin before the wind, only to pause with a form of comic terror on the edge of a precipice, there to teeter and torture all of us. The trains or streetcars or automobiles that collide with one another and by sheer impact transfer whole groups of passengers to new routes and new directions. Are not these nonsensicalities illustrations of that age old formula that underlines humor—the inordinate inflation of fantasy to heights where reason can only laughingly accept the mingling of the normal with the abnormal?

Mack Sennett is one of the great artists of the early cinema, although art was never his goal. His high-speed comedies of people chasing each other exist in a kind of free-floating universe of action detached from anything natural. They contain characters with wonderful names like Marmaduke Bracegirdle and Mr. Whoosiz, and they have plots in which anything imaginable—and much that isn't—can happen. They have endearing intertitles that comment on "a mother-in-law who never lost an argument"; or, about a character presumed deceased who suddenly starts breathing—"not so darn dead!" The world of Sennett is one in which machinery fails you or runs away with you, and characters are loose in a wild and unpredictable landscape populated with crooks and con artists. Everyone is busy getting hold of money in any way possible, yet policemen are everywhere, standing on every corner, under every tree. There is a clear line drawn between the rich and the poor, but jumping across that line can be accomplished through daring, danger, and driving very fast.

This doesn't mean there are no rules. It's axiomatic that if anyone is wearing polka-dot underwear, his pants are sooner or later going to fall down and reveal all. And if a cook is hired, she won't know how to fire up the stove, and a chauffeur is probably a burglar in disguise. Furthermore, if one man chased by a bear is funny, two men chased by two bears is funnier. Twelve men chased by two bears, three goats, four policemen, two hyenas, and a giraffe is *hysterical*. The Sennett comedies are always physical. Since they were made at a time when Americans performed real labor (as opposed to today's more cerebral daily work), this makes sense; the characters are all attempting to *do* things: cook, drive, build, repair, feed the animals. At the same time, these practical souls are being undermined by others, less practical, who hope to gain by doing nothing at all, so they scheme, plot, plan, foil, and seduce. The stories seem to develop spontaneously because, in fact, they were spontaneous, often improvised on the spot. The bottom line about all these movies is that they were—and are—universally understood.

Mack Sennett's accomplishment was that he defined the American version of slapstick by making physical comedy cinematic. To the old forms of burlesque and carnival, he added the tricks only movies can provide, using editing, fast cranking, camera angles, and dissolves to create a fresh new approach to the genre. For instance, for the Kops Sennett developed a wonderful set of routines, including one in which a patrol wagon, like the Marx Brothers' stateroom that would postdate it, unloaded an unbelievably endless supply of Kops, or the one in which a hapless Kop was dragged down the street behind a speeding auto. In the former, each Kop just disappeared out of camera range, at which point the camera was stopped so that he could return to the wagon and disembark again. In the latter, the cameraman operated at a speed that appeared to be much faster when it was shown on the screen, and the actor actually was riding a small platform mounted on wheels. Sennett also discovered that by editing out every third or fourth frame, a sequence seemed to move even faster when screened.

There may have been chases in films before Sennett, and, in fact, most people think the idea originally came from French cinema, Méliès or Pathé, but it is Sennett who lifted the chase into an art form and made it an American event. Obviously, the grand chase over a landscape as a finale to the theatrical process couldn't have happened before the invention of film. And film without the encumbrance of sound meant that the chase could really cover ground, over hill and dale, in ways that staggered the imagination. If people think the chase as practiced by Sennett is not an art form, they have only to look at the highly capable chases in *It's a Mad, Mad, Mad, Mad World* and *The Pink*

Panther to realize how very much better Sennett's were. It's the precision timing, the careful orchestration of action, and the ever-escalating chaos that is remarkable. No one today seems able to do it at the same pace, with the same energy, and with the same wild abandon. Perhaps we're all too conscious of the actual dangers involved for the actors, animals, automobiles, and various other objects involved. Today we can imagine the ASPCA standing by to make sure the horses clopping ahead of the fire wagon aren't being mistreated, or the actress's hairdresser demanding that the pace be adapted to her hairdo, or the actor himself insisting on either his double doing the work or that he be paid extra and protected in the close-ups. Back then, they just hopped in and drove. They were getting paid, and what the hell?

There are chases of all kinds in the Sennett films, involving men and women and animals and vehicles on the land, in the air, and on the water, with an assortment of impediments along the way: flying bricks and stones, detours that appear out of nowhere, mud holes deep enough to sink the *Titanic,* innocent street-crossers, chicken coops full of cluckers, houses, windowpanes, and, of course, the railroad tracks. If an automobile full of characters was barreling down the highway and had to cross a railroad track, the railroad ties, through some mysterious force known only to movie magic, would stall the car—and always just at the moment an express train was bearing down. But Sennett knew how to establish the joke—car on railroad track—use it well, and next time, vary it. The train switches to another track, or the people jump out of the car, or the train actually hits the car, or whatever. Sennett always came up with a new twist, a new madness. He understood the audience, knowing how to surprise them, repeat something for renewed laughter, and then switch to a newer, more sophisticated variation on the laugh. Sennett worked with his audience—and against them—with true genius.

And then there was the pie. Mack Sennett and the pie, an American love story. At some point in the history of the Sennett company, the first pie was thrown into the first face. Mabel Normand was reputed to have been the initial pie thrower and credit was given to her for inventing the idea. Certainly, *A Noise from the Deep* (1913) has Mabel tossing a pie into the round and startled face of Roscoe "Fatty" Arbuckle. There is something deeply poetic about the fact that the first movie pie was probably thrown by a woman, Mabel Normand, into the face of a surprised male actor. It's a great feminist statement— the revolt of the pie maker. (The pie was a constant Sennett joke. In *Tillie's Punctured Romance,* her rich uncle is described as "a pie manufacturer.")

The Sennett pie was not a pie as we mortals know it. It was a concoction of paste that would hold together as it flew through the air, and there was an art to tossing it. It couldn't be crudely heaved; it had to be pushed forward with balance, form, and a smooth follow-through. Expert opinion had it that six to eight feet was the ideal distance, and Fatty Arbuckle was hailed as an

Mack Sennett as an actor in
Stolen Magic

ambidextrous pie thrower who amazed everyone because he could launch from as far back as ten feet. The banana peel—the other key comic food-stuff—was manipulated to advantage by everyone connected to silent film comedy, not just by Sennett and his troupe, though he played his part by escalating the pratfalls generated by the slippery item.

Where did Sennett come from, that he understood comedy so perfectly and could adapt it to the new medium with such panache? Mack Sennett entered movies early, and as an actor. He was born Michael Sinnott in Canada, probably in 1880, to an Irish Catholic family who were not wealthy. He had a marvelous bass singing voice, and after working as a laborer, he resolved to go to New York City (in about 1902) and try to get into the Metropolitan Opera. Instead, he got a job at a burlesque theatre and soon gave up his singing ambitions and began playing comedy on the burlesque circuit. Most biographical entries on Sennett suggest that he entered films in 1909, but there are scholars who think that by that date he had already acted in approximately twenty-two movies for D. W. Griffith. There are records that indicate that he made twenty-three movies in 1908 (only seven of which are comedies). In 1909, he appeared in approximately fifty-eight dramas and thirty-five comedies, almost two a week. In 1910, there were twenty-five dramas and twenty-four comedies, and finally, in 1911, he began to direct. By

August of that year, Mack Sennett was solidly established as a successful maker of comedies. What is important about these early years is that he was under hire to Biograph. Sennett once said, "I learned all I ever learned by standing around and watching people who knew how," and one of the people he was watching definitely knew how—Biograph's D. W. Griffith, who befriended him in his first years in the movie business.

Throughout 1911 and 1912, Sennett cranked out movies, among them two films that are considered possible forerunners to the concept of the Kops, *When the Firebells Rang* (the hapless professionals are firemen, not police) and *The Would-Be Shriner,* in which a parade of Shriners is constantly interrupted by policemen. In 1912, Sennett joined two film producers, Adam Kessel and Charles Bauman (owners of the New York Motion Picture Company), to form the Keystone Film Company, which gave him the freedom to do whatever he wanted to in production. Under contract was not only Sennett but Mabel Normand, among others. An ad was run in the trades: "KEYSTONE FILMS. A Quartet of popular fun makers. Mack Sennett, Mabel Normand, Fred Mace, Ford Sterling, supported by an all-star company in split-reel comedies. A Keystone every Monday." From that point on, Sennett was a major creator of comedies, some of which starred Charlie Chaplin, who came to Keystone in late 1913 and remained for a year; he had been brought in as a potential replacement for a disaffected Ford Sterling. Although he made thirty-five comedies for Keystone, Chaplin was reputedly unhappy there, even though his Little Tramp character was perfected during this time. (Some historians feel that Chaplin never gave Sennett and Mabel enough credit for the Tramp's development.) By the fall of 1914, Chaplin was becoming a real star and was advertised as one of Sennett's trio of popular comics, along with Arbuckle and Mabel: an issue of *Photoplay* presented a comic "menu" that offered "Chaplin Supreme, Stuffed Arbuckle, and Normand, Scrambled." Chaplin left Sennett largely because he had a star's mentality and did not like taking orders from others. Furthermore, his personal style of comedy was grounded in a burlesque of real life, and Sennett's was surrealistic.

Sennett went on making films for Keystone until 1917, when he took control of the company, changed its name to the Mack Sennett Comedies Corp., and began releasing his movies through Paramount. The actual "Keystone Comedies" were made between 1912 and 1917. Typical is *Love, Speed, and Thrills* (1915), a title that says it all, and it more than lives up to its name. Mack Swain and Chester Conklin play characters they portrayed in a number of Sennett's works, Ambrose (Swain) and Walrus (Conklin). The film builds toward a magnificent chase, in which a man on a horse, three cops on foot, and a woman riding in the sidecar of a motorcycle driven by the villain (Walrus) tear across the countryside. Later in the action, the cops commandeer a rowboat, just in time to collect the villain as he falls off a huge bridge. The girl, also falling, has been lassoed and saved by the man on the horse (Ambrose, her husband). As the chase plays out, the horse gallops alongside the sidecar, and the heroine is swept up onto it, but when the horse and two riders collapse and turn over, the motorcycle speeds by, tipping the woman back into the sidecar. Everybody falls down. Everybody switches from foot to car and from car back to foot, and it's fast, funny, inventive, and amazing. This is the essence of Mack Sennett's silent comedy.

These movies are not always politically correct. *Toplitsky and Company* (1913) contains a blatant stereotype of a Jewish store owner within a farce that concerns the leading character's attraction to his partner's wife. The resulting mixup, in and out of bedrooms, is not viciously anti-Semitic, but it's uncomfortable viewing today. The villainous store owner jumps out of the wife's bedroom window and goes on the run, taking refuge by running into a bathhouse to hide. (Why a bathhouse?) During the escape, he runs past a large black bear tied up on a chain outside a suburban house. Hence, the surreal: why is a bear on a chain outside an ordinary home? Later the bear gets loose ("Trouble," says the succinct title card) and, naturally, wanders into the bathhouse, chasing everyone out and down the street. The combination of black bear, husband, store owner, wife, and bathhouse . . . well, it's crazy, isn't it?

Another early Sennett comedy, *One Night Stand* (1915), is set on a stage in a little theatre. On the walls are written warnings such as ASBESTUS (*sic*), NO SMOKING, DO NOT TOUCH LINES, and DO NOT SEND YOUR LAUNDRY OUT TILL WE SEE YOUR ACT. Throughout the action, the characters are constantly smoking, touching things, and, we presume, sending their laundry out. Certainly they ignore the big one: WATCH YOUR STEP. Chaos reigns. All the stage flats fall down, and offstage characters poke sharp objects through them, sticking those trying to perform on stage, a kind of crude early *Noises Off* concept. The stagehands finally attack the actors, and everyone runs around, both offstage and on, bopping everyone else. Seen today, it's a great visual metaphor: film comedy destroys Victorian theatre.

In the 1915 *Love, Loot, and Crash* (a perfect title), a banker and his daughter have no cook and cannot cope on their own. They run an ad in the paper, and two crooks read it, deciding that one of them will dress up as a woman and get the job so they can loot the place later. ("Put on your frills, and grab the job.") Meanwhile, the girl loves a boy her father doesn't approve of, and keeps jumping out the window to meet him, but Dad always stops her. Eventually the fake cook, the father and the girl, and the friendly neighborhood cop who drops in for coffee are all inside the house together. Outside are the boyfriend, arriving to elope with the girl, and the other crook, arriving to help burgle the joint. All three actions ingeniously entwine. The boyfriend drives up on a motorcycle, and the fake cook (still in drag) jumps out the window to escape the cop and gets on the motorcycle. He thinks it's his cohort, and the boy thinks it's the girl. Off they go! A stolen car arrives, driven by the cohort, and the girl jumps in, thinking it's the boy. The cop has been trapped in the kitchen by the cook, but now he breaks out and takes off after them. He and his fellow cops commandeer a vehicle to chase the stolen car, and all three groups race off at top speed, with various disasters along the way, down to the seaside. Everyone falls in the water except the girlfriend, who watches from the boardwalk, and the movie ends.

A Muddy Romance (1913) is a madcap romp featuring the "water police," who leap into a rowboat to stop a marriage ceremony that is taking place in another boat in the middle of a lake. They row wildly forward, firing their guns and falling into the water, until some distant force shuts off the water source, draining the lake and dumping all the participants into thick, viscous mud, in which they wallow helplessly.

The typical Sennett comedy is full of inventive action, and props and sets are equally inventive, such as a real swimming pool built on the set and, for *Astray from the Steerage* (1921), a chair that twirls (for which Sennett came up with an optical effect that showed the point of view of the character who was spinning). Titles are also an inventive part of Sennett's comedy—"All your fault—as usual" and "Enjoying her jealousy in a woman's way." And some are slightly off-color, such as a tasteful introduction of today's comedy favorite, the fart joke: "The cheese makes itself known," with all the characters delicately holding their noses, not daring to look at each other. Mostly, however, the characters run around, fall down, and accuse each other in a series of bizarre events. In *The Surf Girl,* an ostrich swallows the heroine's locket. Like the bear outside someone's home in *Toplitsky and Company,* this ostrich is conveniently available.

Sennett not only incorporates unlikely animals and ordinary cars into his stories, he also makes use of any other conveyance he can put his hands on: boats, trains, wagons, bicycles, anything that moves. As new inventions appear, movies always incorporate them into the plot. Today we have computers. Heavily muscled heroes and heroines who've worked out in the gym all day to perfect those bodies sit down at a computer terminal, loom heavily over the machine, and brilliantly type in questions that will not only resolve the plot but will explain EVERYTHING. (And the actors never have trouble figuring out access codes.) In the days of the Sennett comedy, things were reversed. Little people, looking overwhelmed and confused, struggled with cook stoves that belched sooty smoke all over them. They burned the eggs. Their clothes were ruined. They couldn't cope. Today, the questions are big but easily solved. Then, the questions were small but required heroic individual effort to figure out. We've progressed from brave little humans tackling small troubles and prevailing to big humans tackling imaginary woes (aliens and dinosaurs) and blowing them to kingdom come, the final resolution.

These early comedies set up a situation, vary it, milk it, take it to its moment of highest chaos, and then leave it unresolved. For instance, *Toplitsky and Company* ends when all the characters are fighting each other in the bedroom and the bed collapses. In *Love, Loot, and Crash*, the movie is over once everyone falls into the water. Critics often complain that American comedies set up hilarious premises but are unable to resolve the action in an equally funny way. It's interesting to note, watching Sennett, that a sensible narrative resolution was never part of the American comic tradition. With Sennett, the explosion of utter chaos *was* the resolution, and there was no better way to achieve it than through the rapid chase. What the big number with 200 blonde tap dancers, 100 roller skaters, and 50 American flags is to the musical, what the final shoot-out in dusty streets is to the western, the chase is to the Sennett comedy. Down the road, over the bridge, under the viaduct, across the landscape, off the pier, and into the water is the final resolving action. Logic plays no part in the setup and thus has no role in the payoff.

Between 1913 and 1915, Sennett made comedies in which both Mabel Normand and the Keystone Kops emerged as audience favorites, and of the two, the Kops—at least in name—are the better known today. Kalton C. Lahue and Terry Brewer, in their book, *Kops and Custards: The Legend of Keystone Films,* state flatly, "The Keystone Kops were Sennett's major contribution to Americana and to the American language." They explain that the Kops were not born on-screen as a unit but rather emerged after a gradual evolution of an idea that Sennett nurtured for years. The book dates the first "recorded existence of a Kop picture from Keystone as the December 23, 1912, release of *Hoffmeyer's Legacy,*" and adds, "From this point on, one or more policemen were in nearly every comedy." Throughout 1913, new comics who signed on with Keystone were given a trial period in a Kop uniform, so that, Lahue and Brewer explain, it was "quite easy for Sennett to determine whether the man actually had what it took to be a true Keystone comedian . . . if he had the stamina to stand up under the sometimes brutal punishment and still come across as being funny."

The Bangville Police (1913) is a perfect introduction to the Kops. The guys are a bunch of rubes in straw hats, clunky shoes and boots, and nonmatching outfits. They ride to farm girl Mabel Normand's rescue, she mistakenly believing that thieves are lurking about her homestead. As they rush forward, the Kops fall down in the dusty street, tripping over each other and their own feet, before they clamber aboard their lone automotive pursuit vehicle (ridiculously marked with the number 13, although the first twelve vehicles are nowhere to be seen). The chief summons this motley group by firing his pistol into the ceiling. Some come on foot, carrying shovels as their weapons, and others run straight to the scene of the "crime." The fast-paced comedy mixes parallel story lines in which Mabel mistakes her own family for

The Keystone Kops
on the job:
running . . .

. . . crashing . . .

. . . and living up to their reputation for crime-fighting

the bad guys, and the family mistakes her for those typical silent film villains, "Burglars!", when she hides from *them*. The Kops arrive and add to the confusion, but everything is, as usual, wrapped up within minutes.

With the Kops, there was always frenzied activity. In 1958, when Sennett was in his late seventies, he gave an interview to *Newsweek* magazine in which he defined comedy: "The key is comic motion, which is sometimes like lightning. You see it, but you don't hear the thunder until seconds later . . . A wise guy once asked me, 'What exactly did you have to know to be a good Keystone cop?' I said, 'You had to understand comic motion.' "

Most experts agree that the high point of Kopdom was the 1914 two-reeler *In the Clutches of the Gang*. The Kops are called in on a kidnapping case, and their bumbling Chief Teheezel (the admirable Ford Sterling) urges his inept crew forward with the usual incompetence. Paying no attention to their leader, and more or less bungling everything they try, the gang end up arresting the mayor in one of their larger miscarriages of would-be justice.

The Kops were always a collective unit, famous for being the Kops, sort of like Our Gang and the Dead End Kids. Audiences knew some of their indi-

The Kops . . . a cake . . .

vidual names but probably not all. They were like one actor, a unit of movie meaning and pleasure, not distinct from one another. The original seven Keystone Kops were Charles Avery, Bobby Dunn, George Jesks (who became a screenwriter), Edgar Kennedy (famous for his slow burn, which he carried over into sound), Hank Mann (with the walrus mustache and the droopy look), Mack Riley, and Slim Summerville (the skinny, homely guy who not only went on to sound as an actor and director, but who gained immortality when a studio head described Bette Davis as having "as much sex appeal as Slim Summerville.") As time passed, other comics came and went in the Kops aggregation: Fatty Arbuckle, Chester Conklin, Charlie Chase, James Finlayson, Henry Lehrman, Eddie Sutherland, Eddy Cline. The great chief of the Kops, the bearded man who presided over the chaos, was Ford Sterling.

The Kops are a brilliant concept. To take a gaggle of inept policemen and display them over and over again in a series of riotously funny physical punishments plays equally well to the peanut gallery and the expensive box seats. People hate cops. Even people who have never had anything to do with cops hate them. Of course, we count on them to keep order and to protect us when we need protecting, and we love them on television shows in which they have nerves of steel and hearts of gold, but in the abstract, as a nation, collectively we hate them. They are too much like high school principals. We're very happy to see their pants fall down, and they look good to us with pie on their faces. The Keystone Kops turn up—and they get punished for it, as they crash

. . . and the
inevitable

into each other, fall down, and suffer indignity after indignity. Here is pure
movie satisfaction.

The Kops are very skillfully presented. The comic originality and timing
in one of their chase scenes requires imagination to think up, talent to execute, understanding of the medium, and, of course, raw courage to perform.
The Kops are madmen presented as incompetents, and they're madmen rushing around in modern machines. What's more, the machines they were operating in their routines were newly invented and not yet experienced by the
average moviegoer. (In the early days of automobiles, it was reported that
there were only two cars registered in all of Kansas City, and they ran into
each other. There is both poetry and philosophy in this fact, but most of all,
there is humor. Sennett got the humor.)

The Kops go fast because they can. They whiz along, as when they're
dragged on their bellies, single file on a rope, behind a speeding automobile
that takes a fast corner and inadvertently wraps them around a telephone
pole, breaking the rope and setting them loose. Along comes another car, however, and it accidentally reattaches them, jerking them off the pole and back
out onto the highway, again on their bellies at top speed. The miracle is not
that we laugh but that they weren't killed.

Watching a Keystone Kops chase today is almost like watching a dream
sequence, in that many prints have no musical accompaniment and one sits in
deep silence as people fly through space, suffer falls, collisions, and bumps

apparently without harm. These movies have a manic quality, a terrific pacing in which, as the speed escalates, they almost seem to fall away into a kind of serene flow of safe movement, a warp speed of comedy. Nothing bad is going to happen here, but everything that can go wrong is going to go wrong. You'll fall down—but get up. You'll be knocked off the pier—but not drown. You'll be chased by bad guys—but get away. Perfect timing safely presents characters in a weird and abstract world, a Caligariesque place. A dreamlike state at high speed. It's the American dream, all right: just keep moving and every-thing will turn out fine. As the great Satchel Paige famously observed, "Don't look back. Something might be gaining on you," and with the Kops, it always is. (One of the Kops once allegedly remarked, "I was even kicked by a giraffe.")

ALTHOUGH THE KEYSTONE KOPS didn't achieve top fame individually, Mabel Normand became Sennett's biggest and best attraction. There is still nobody quite like her, because she was everything at once. Another of the tiny women of silent film, Mabel could nevertheless project herself into tall if she had to, even suggesting a willowy, elegant mannequin if the part called for it. She could also become a little boy, a pretty young girl, and a daredevil stunt-woman. What she had was plenty of talent, with the good looks the visual medium required and comedy timing that was nothing short of perfection.

Watching Mabel Normand is a challenge. In one movie, she looks like Buster Keaton (or maybe Stan Laurel), and in the next she's Gloria Swanson. She wasn't one of the little boy–girls of the silent era, because she had the body of a sex symbol: bosomy, curvaceous, and well formed. Yet because she was so small, she could disguise herself as a boy in baggy pants, a flannel shirt, and a loose cap, and because of her athletic ability, get away with it. But she could also, as a comic once said, "clean up real good," swanning out with a fur muff, a diamond necklace, and a hat with an ostrich feather on top. Her glamorous shape, which made her a beauty and a desirable woman, was undercut by her big head (which looked even bigger with the enormous poundage of hair that women wore in those years) and a big pair of clown's feet. She was by nature a contradiction perfect for comedy: a sexy, full-bodied woman with the head and feet of a clown. In other words, Mabel Normand is a true comic, but a beautiful one, who looked elegant one minute and hoydenish the next. She isn't in the tradition of the actress who becomes a comedienne because she's basically homely and can never play romantic leads. She wasn't driven to comedy because her nose was too big, her teeth too bucked, or her voice too gravelly (anyway, audiences couldn't hear her speak). As the beauti-ful comedienne who wears gorgeous clothes but also does pratfalls, Normand is the forerunner of a comedy tradition that American women excel at: the female comedy hero, like Lucille Ball, Betty Hutton, and even Carole Lombard, who took plenty of slapstick hits in her time. In America, we ask our women to sacrifice glamour if the situation calls for it, because we prize the "good Joe" quality in women. A heroine needs to be able to roll with the punches, take it on the chin, and dish it out as necessary. Mabel Normand could and did do all this in spades, and she more or less defined the tradition.

Unlike many of the early stars of the silent era, Mabel Normand wasn't trained in the theatre. She was never taught how to project, or declaim, or gesture. She entered the movies in a natural state—and she retained that naturalism. She just wheeled in, full of high spirits, afraid of nothing and no one, and with no sense of herself as a great actress worried about her dignity. The people she fell in with most closely shared her love of life, practical jokes, and high living, and most of them were making comedies. Mabel was like one of those characters who are standing innocently on the street corner when the Keystone Kops roar by at what looks like a hundred miles an hour. The car sideswipes her and inexplicably she falls inside, drawn into the chase, hanging on to her hat but game for the ride. As it turned out, Mabel was more game than anyone else. Her ride was a wild one, but, alas, it was also a short one.

All the silent film stars fell prey to the fanciful biographical invention that the fan magazines loved to create for the adoring public. Just as Tom Mix was supposed to have been born in a log cabin in Texas, and Valentino was the son of a nobleman, Mabel had her own tall tales. The chief difference was that she tended to invent them herself. According to her biographer, Betty Harper Fussell, Mabel liked to say that she "had set off for Manhattan from Boston after inheriting a legacy from a seafaring uncle enriched by the Oriental trade" or that her mother had sent her out when she was "only thirteen, to bear her share of earning for the needy household." What really happened was that Mabel sent herself out in about 1908 to seek her own fortune, knowing she could rely on herself better than on anyone else she knew. She had been born in Boston in 1892 (her crypt claims 1895), an uncommonly pretty little girl with a strong will. She went to New York City and became a successful advertising model, stepping up to the more prestigious label of "artist's model," posing for the covers of such magazines as the *Saturday Evening Post.* Nevertheless, money was always tight, so when she heard about the good pay for appearing in movies at Biograph, she took the trolley downtown to Fourteenth Street, climbed the stairs, and met a man who turned out to be D. W. Griffith's assistant. She was soon hired, but only as an extra girl. However, she also met someone who was going to be very important to her future—Mack Sennett, who had been working for Griffith for about two years, and who was at least twelve, perhaps fourteen, years older than she was.

When the Biograph company made its first move to California, in 1909, Mabel Normand was not invited to come along. It's easy to see that she wasn't D. W. Griffith's type, hardly being a Victorian maiden and having no experience of serious acting. Griffith suggested that she try finding work at the Vitagraph Studios in Brooklyn, and her first movies are listed by Fussell as 1910 Vitagraphs: *The Indiscretions of Betty, Over the Garden Wall, Willful Peggy,* and *Betty Becomes a Maid.* When Sennett returned to New York with Biograph, in 1911, he talked Griffith into hiring her, making the point that Griffith could use her in his dramas and he himself could put her to work in his comedies. The first movie Mack and Mabel made together was *The Diving Girl,* in August of 1911, and it showcased everything Mabel had to show. Wearing a bathing costume with black stockings and slippers and a kerchief on her head, Mabel strikes a blow for the all-American female of the twentieth century. She plays a tomboy who likes to dive, and Sennett let her pose at the end of a diving board like a little goddess. The story concerns the effect she has on everyone, until her uncle persuades her to go inside. Mabel is fresh and perky. Instead of peeking into a nickelodeon to see some hootchy-kootchy dancer of an advanced age wiggle her rear, Americans got to see a pretty young girl strut her stuff. And Mabel could strut. It was the beginning, not only for Mabel the star but for Mack and Mabel, the comedy team, and somewhere along the line, Mack and Mabel, the lovers.

One of Keystone's handouts for fans: Mabel Normand, the "Keystone Girl"

Sennett once said that the essence of comedy was "contrast and catastrophe involving the unseating of dignity." By that definition, Mabel Normand was a perfect leading lady for Sennett because she carried within her an inherent dignity and beauty that she wasn't afraid to toss to the four winds, thus providing her own contrast. Mabel could run very fast, jump very high, and fall down very hard. Mabel could dive from a high rock, and hang out of an airplane with a smile on her face. Mabel could steer a car with pie on her face, and drive fearlessly at high speed. Mabel could do it all, and she did. (Unfortunately, as it turned out, she did a little too much of everything off-screen, too.)

Griffith also used Mabel, most particularly in the 1912 *Mender of Nets,* which costarred her with Mary Pickford. It was the first film Mabel made in California, having just arrived there. (By the time she returned to New York again, it would be New Year's Eve in 1915, and she would step off the Twentieth Century Limited train a tremendous star, rich and famous and adored, and known everywhere as "Keystone Mabel" or "The Sugar on the Keystone

Mabel in action

Grapefruit.") Mabel and Mary make a perfect contrast—Mabel's dark hair and Mary's blond, Mabel's sexy body and Mary's little-girl form. Mabel steals Mary's beau but dies after giving birth. Mary proves her worth by caring for Mabel's child. The movie was dubbed "a seaside romance," and Mabel was cast as "The Weakness: His Old Infatuation."

When Griffith again returned east with Biograph, Sennett, Kessel, and Bauman stayed behind and started Keystone, and Mack and Mabel were off on their wild comedy ride. Their first two movies were *The Water Nymph* and *Cohen Collects a Debt,* in 1912. Betty Fussell eloquently describes the formula they were going to follow by saying that "from the beginning, sex, crime, and money were the source of the Keystone comedy and the context of their lives. Mabel provided the sex, the male clowns provided the crime, and the combo brought in the money." The formula worked. The troupe ground out the two-reelers: *Mabel's Lovers, A Midnight Elopement, Saving Mabel's Dad, The Mistaken Masher, A Red Hot Romance,* and many more, fifty-three pictures within the first Keystone year (1912–13). However, according to Fussell, only seven of them exist today. One is the aforementioned *Bangville Police* and another is *Barney Oldfield's Race For A Life* (1913). Barney Oldfield, a famous race car driver of the era, plays himself in a delightful example of the Mack and Mabel style. Mabel plays "Mable, Sweet and Lovely," and Mack plays "a bashful suitor." Cleverly using familiar ploys from the popular melodramas of the day, the movie provides a comic variation of the damsel-in-distress story, with Mabel ending up tied to the railroad tracks while the villain twirls his mustache, and Mack and Oldfield racing to the rescue in Oldfield's famous car. One of the great treats of the movie is a scene in which Mack woos Mabel, shyly handing her a flower. They are both young, slim, healthy, full of beans— and clearly in love with each other. It's a golden moment frozen in time.

Mack and Mabel were on a roll, making other 1913 hits such as *Mabel's Awful Mistake, Mabel's Dramatic Career, The Gusher, The Speed Queen, Mabel's Heroes,* and *For the Love of Mabel.* In the first of these appears one of those images automatically associated with silent film: Mabel and a buzz saw! A handsome man persuades her to elope with him, even though he already has a wife and a bunch of kids. Her boyfriend follows the elopers, and watches outside while poor Mabel is tied to the table with the buzz saw coming at her. This scene had already become a cliché, having been fully explored in the serials starring the intrepid heroines of *The Perils of Pauline* and *The Exploits of Elaine.* Sennett and Mabel and the gang send up the idea, spoofing those heroines and turning the villain into an exaggerated cartoon. The genius of this plan was that the send-up is funny, yet still tense and scary. The audience got more bang for its buck. (Sennett never forgot that comedy was partly rooted in tension, and that frightening situations followed by the release of a laugh always pleased a crowd.)

In *Mabel's Dramatic Career,* Mabel plays a hired girl who becomes a movie queen. Her coplayers are Mack Sennett, Ford Sterling, and Fatty Arbuckle. The film is particularly interesting because in it, Sennett, as her former boyfriend, goes to see a Keystone Comedy that Mabel is starring in. (The title of the movie-within-the-movie is *Mabel and the Villain.*) The Sennett character, who loves her, starts waving at the screen and shouting, eventually shooting at it because Mabel is in danger before the Kops arrive to save her. (In the movie-within-the-movie they are called the "Keystone Kids.") After the movie is over, Sennett walks out and sees the actor who played the villain—actually a mild-mannered family man—and takes out after him. This Pirandellian concept is very modern. A similar idea would be used in 1916's *A Movie Star,* which shows great sophistication in its send-up of the popular westerns of the era. Mack Swain plays a movie star who poses outside a theatre, standing by his own photo, until his female fans finally notice him. This movie has a film-within-a-film called *Big Hearted Jack,* and Swain loves watching it with the audience. The females continue to mob him—until his wife and kids show up. It's interesting that as early as 1916 there was a complete awareness of what the movie star's problem was going to be: the contrast between image and reality!

In *The Gusher,* Mabel copes with an out-of-control oil well and various attempts to poach on her discoveries. In *The Speed Queen,* she's arrested for speeding, and in *For the Love of Mabel,* she has to be rescued from a dynamite bomb. In all these movies, Mabel worked like a Trojan, never shying away from the thick of the wildest action. She was a true daredevil, evolving from the pretty youngster originally billed as "the Venus diving girl" into a slapstick comedy queen who executed stunts that would have stopped any other movie star in her tracks. There was no trick to Mabel Normand. She went out on her own and did it all, without gimmicks, without camera cheats, and without, presumably, any real fear.

In 1914 Sennett undertook a highly ambitious project: *Tillie's Punctured Romance,* advertised as "The 'Impossible' Attained—A SIX REEL COMEDY!" Sennett's idea was to make a comedy that had status. Griffith had begun shooting a full-length feature, *Birth of a Nation,* on July 4 (to be released in early February 1915). If Griffith could make a film like *Birth of a Nation,* why couldn't he, the King of Comedy, lift comedy movies to the same heights? *Tillie's Punctured Romance* was one of the greatest hits of the Sennett troupe, with Chaplin, Normand, the Kops, and Marie Dressler all appearing together. Often referred to as "the first feature-length comedy," it *is* a full six reels. Sennett's backers thought he had gone mad, but the film was an immediate winner.

Chaplin plays a bounder whose accomplice in fleecing naive women is his girlfriend, Mabel. Their target is the hapless farm girl, Tillie, played magnificently by Dressler, a major stage star who had made a big success on

Mabel and her pop-
ular partner Fatty
Arbuckle, in *Mabel,
Fatty and the Law*

Broadway in a comedy called *Tillie's Nightmare.* Sennett had the story
adapted for the screen, and to fill out the expanded running time, he comes up
with trick after trick. Despite the competition of Chaplin and Normand,
Dressler makes the film her own. Her large size is played with, as she goes
about bumping into things (shattering them). When she playfully tries to flirt
with Chaplin by slinging a sexy hip out toward him, she knocks him flat. She
goes with Chaplin to the city dressed in an outfit that belongs in the Smithson-
ian: a print monstrosity covered with ruffles and a long string of beads, topped
off by the world's most improbable hat with a duck—or is it a goose, or perhaps a swan or a chicken?—smack dab on top of it. Mabel plays Dressler's
opposite: cool, elegant, and dressed in great taste—well, great comedy taste,
anyway. She's very glamorous. Mabel has a wonderful scene in which she and
Chaplin go to a movie entitled *The Thief's Fate,* and she sees the girlfriend of
the thief get arrested. This starts her thinking, and after much action, including a ballroom dance between Dressler and Chaplin that is a direct satire on
Vernon and Irene Castle, and a great chase in which Dressler falls off a pier,
the movie ends with an ironic look at Chaplin. "Curse the beauty that holds
women slaves to such men," jokes a title, and suddenly, Normand and
Dressler, two great queens of silent film comedy, embrace, throw Chaplin out,
and declare, "He ain't no good to either of us."

The years 1914–16 brought more of the same Sennett fare for Mabel,
including *Mabel's Nerve,* where she rides a bucking bronco, and *Mabel at the*

Mabel in the big hit
*Tillie's Punctured
Romance*

Wheel, in which Chaplin tries to sabotage a road race but Mabel saves the day by taking the wheel herself and driving madly to victory. In movies like this, Mabel was a kind of pratfall Pearl White, combining her athletic ability, her nerve, and her beauty to make her the comic relief, the romantic lead, and the stuntwoman all in one person.

Mack Sennett not only made Mabel Normand a star but was instrumental in combining her with a great comic foil, the underrated genius Roscoe "Fatty" Arbuckle, a Jackie Gleason/Oliver Hardy prototype. Arbuckle started working with Sennett in 1913 for five dollars a day, and Mabel—a shrewd judge of talent—saw his potential. Watching him work, she noticed how many different things he could do, and in particular realized that he was amazingly light on his feet. She talked Sennett into starring her with Fatty, and within a short time the two comedians were Keystone's most popular team.

Fatty was five feet ten inches to Mabel's barely five feet, and 266 pounds to her less than 100. Together in the frame, they were a great visual joke: a big, fat guy and a tiny woman. Just the way they looked standing side by side could get a laugh, and their contrasting size and shape were exploited for all kinds of comic variations. Arbuckle was also an excellent acrobat, so he could match Mabel's athletic ability. Their work together was a glorious blend of compatible comic styles. Fatty could fume and Mabel could flounce.

The best title of all the Mabel and Fatty movies is the 1913 *Passions, He Had Three* (they were milk, raw eggs, and girls). Fatty is a doctor and Mabel is his elegant wife. In the brief running time, Fatty tries to tie his bow tie and Mabel has to help (a brilliant piece of physical comedy). Mabel's old school boyfriend comes to dinner and Fatty gets jealous. They sit down to eat lobsters, which gives them nightmares that turn into dream sequences, and in the meantime that old favorite, a burglar (posing as a cripple), interrupts the meal and later tries to rob the house. It ends with everyone running up and down stairs and around the elegant house, showing off the furniture and providing hilarious pratfalls and entrances and exits.

Mabel continued to appear without Fatty during these years. Among these solo efforts was one of her most popular movies, *Mabel's Blunder* (1914), in which both her boss and his son have designs on her. Again, an elaborate scenario plays out within a short running time: Mabel pretends to be her brother, her brother pretends to be her, her boyfriend kisses another girl but it's really his sister, which Mabel doesn't know, etc. Mabel, stylishly dressed, shows herself to be a master of comic pantomime. There's a particularly superb moment in which, dressed as her brother in long coat and with a cap pulled down over her eyes, she swiftly pilots a big open-air car down the streets of Los Angeles, a simple act that shows exactly who and what she was: a modern girl of speed and daring, unafraid of the new machines.

The title cards of these comedies rely very little on detail. Instead, they speak simple facts: "A MISUNDERSTANDING," or "TROUBLE ARRIVES." The stories *are* complex, however, and one must pay attention. A lot of detail is never explained or presented, and the audience is asked to make assumptions and draw conclusions—or just go with the flow, waiting for the big chase scene. An actress like Mabel is essentially pantomiming a great deal of her character's story, and this is not exactly the same as acting. What is remarkable about her is that she was able to grow, moving beyond such simple demonstrations in which the object is never subtle emotion but always the broad event for comic purposes.

Even while her career was thriving, Mabel was frequently ill with respiratory problems. She complained of sinus trouble, bad headaches, and a chronic cough, and was reported to be frequently hemorrhaging, a sign of tuberculosis. However, she made no effort to rest as a result of these problems. Rest was not a part of Mabel's lifestyle. She partied all night, worked nonstop, and medicated herself with a concoction she referred to jauntily as her "goop," a cough syrup available over the counter but which was laced with opium.

In December of 1914, Sennett announced that "Mabel Normand, leading woman of the Keystone Company since its inception, is in the future to direct every picture she acts in." Mabel directed only movies in which she starred, but her accomplishment as one of the first female directors, and one of the few to do comedy, is singular. She and Mack Sennett had formed a true creative partnership—or so it appeared. By the end of 1915, their combined efforts were solidly established. They were not only a moviemaking team; they were also an item. However, a marriage planned for July 4, 1915, derailed at the last minute, allegedly because she walked in on him in bed with the beautiful Mae Busch shortly before the ceremony was to take place. They were soon quarreling both on and off the set.

Motion Picture World of July 1915 listed Mabel as one of the winners of a popularity contest to determine "The Great Cast." Pickford won "leading woman," Chaplin won "male comedian," and Mabel, "female comedian." Yet, Chaplin was given a raise at Essenay and would begin earning $10,000 per week. Pickford was raised to $700,000 per year, and she was earning a percent of profits, a six-figure bonus each year, and a generous weekly expense account. Mabel was paid $500 per week—and there was no increase in sight. But she had become a big star, and she wanted more: more money, more control of her films, more respect, and more opportunities to play romantic leading ladies in feature-length films. Disgruntled, she accompanied Fatty to New York at the end of 1915 to make a group of short films with eastern settings. When she returned to Hollywood in May of 1916, she demanded her own production company. Sennett reluctantly agreed, and established the Mabel Normand Feature Film Company.

With this newly acquired status, she reported to work at her own little studio that Sennett built for her, located just over the hill from his, and settled down in her own dressing room with a Japanese chef, an Oriental rug, and a canary. And she began work on a feature film that was designed to allow her to make the kind of transformation within the plot that Mary Pickford handled so successfully in her tailor-made movies: from tomboy little girl to romantic leading woman. The film was to be called *Mickey*, and from the minute that production began in 1916, it was a war of wills—and a fight for control— between Mack and Mabel. Filming was completed in the spring of 1917, and after shooting ended, Mabel left Sennett to sign with Samuel Goldwyn. "I decided I'd had enough of the Keystone Company," she said.

Mickey, which was not released until August 1918, was an enormous hit. Mabel's reviews were excellent: "Mickey and Mabel Normand are one and the same . . . She could not have appeared in a title role in which she was better suited . . . She is a wonderful little actress," said *Variety*. Mabel is dressed, as so many silent film stars often were, in patched trousers, a flannel undershirt, and a coat way too big for her, which served to emphasize her tiny frame. She plays the perfect tomboy, always getting into trouble, who is sent east to live with rich relatives. Naturally, these are horrible people who turn her into a servant—a bad idea, since she wrecks everything she touches until, of course, she snags the handsome young man who appreciates her honest qualities and loves her, only her.

Even before the release of *Mickey*, everything Mabel did was news, and

Mabel as the comic hoyden in *Mickey* . . .

since she did so much, the fan magazines ate her up. She became famous for her beautiful clothes and her wild lifestyle, which included not only playing bizarre practical jokes on coworkers but also out-of-control drinking and partying. Mostly, the magazines paid tribute to her comedy skills. In June 1918, *Motion Picture* dubbed her "Thalia . . . the muse of comedy" in an article called "The Muses of Movie Land." (Pickford was Calliope, the Muse of Eloquence.) But though the fan magazines cleaned up her act, they hinted at the erratic behavior in thinly veiled articles like one called "Mabel in a Hurry," in the November 1918 *Motion Picture*. The interviewer tells us of his "thrilling day with Mabel Normand," referring to her, however, as a "young lady of tempestuous moods and moments." To illustrate, he cheerfully writes of how he waited for her on the set from 9:30 to 11:30 a.m. (To make sure the point gets across, he adds that the studio guide told him that Normand "never keeps an appointment. If she has an appointment for 4, it usually occurs to her to begin dressing for it at 4:30.")

Mabel, however, finally turns up. "In décolleté, partially hidden by a dressing robe," she dashes in. "Rushed! Late! Back in a minute!" After her rehearsal, she does return to talk to the writer, telling him about her latest location shoot, about her new maid acquired from a millionaire's home, about how her two greatest weaknesses are black lace stockings and dime savings banks, and how she cares only for purple flowers. She snaps at him when he wants to talk of other things, and he allows himself to write, "She has a

... and as the
would-be star in
The Extra Girl

chameleon personality." At some point in the discussion, Mabel really takes off, telling him she once lived for thirty days on ice cream, that she thinks Charlie Chaplin is the screen's greatest actor, and that she always signs her letters "Me" and calls people "Old Peach" if she likes them. (She does not call the reporter "Old Peach.") She would rather do drama than comedy, but drama with an occasional smile. She always carries a tiny ivory elephant for good luck. As they conclude their conversation at 1:30 p.m., the interviewer really nails her, saying that in nearly four hours, they probably talked "fully eight minutes in all," and adds that someone once told him Mabel Normand reminded him of a "dancing mouse, whirling madly all the time, but without purpose." It's hard to tell today whether Mabel was giving a performance or revealing her normal self. At one point, she tries for pathos, real or feigned, by saying that while she must seem ever so gay most of the time, she really isn't. "I get terribly blue and sad. Life is such a rush." But her final shot at the reporter probably gives the real picture. "Good-bye!" she suddenly sings out, dismissing him summarily. Turning to her maid, she then bellows out, "Gimme my grapefruit and a gas mask."

Mabel went increasingly out of control in her interviews. She was once reported to have said, in answer to a standard fan magazine query about what her hobbies were: "Say anything you like, but don't say I like to work. That sounds too much like Mary Pickford, that prissy bitch."

After Mabel left Sennett for Goldwyn, the interviews became even more erratic. She told reporters such things as "I love to punch babies and twist their legs" or, in describing her ideal man, "A brutal Irishman who chews tobacco," or "I love dark, windy days when trees break and houses blow down." There is anger in her words, and she began to be late to the set and behave erratically with people, going out to lunch and ordering nine martinis and a baked Alaska. She spent money recklessly, and during her Goldwyn years she perhaps went beyond her "goop" and fell under the spell of drugs, never fully to recover her health again.

In the wake of her huge success with *Mickey*, Mabel was at the top of her stardom, and Goldwyn promoted her heavily. She made a series of popular films for him, many of which have titles that sound like ideal Mabel movies: *The Pest, Peck's Bad Girl, A Perfect 36, Sis Hopkins, Jinx,* and *Slim Princess,* among others. The only one available for viewing today is the 1921 *What Happened to Rosa?* Directed by Victor Schertzinger, it presents Mabel as a little department store clerk, "Mayme Ladd," a dreamer whose "dull, drudging life has never been brightened by a single gleam of romance." Mabel is perfectly cast as the little comic loser, her big eyes rolling and her hair hanging in her face. Her expressive body and excellent timing are put to good use in her comedy scenes, and her true beauty is drawn on when she turns into Rosa. Mabel's character consults a psychic who gives her a "prelim spirit shampoo," tells her she is inhabited by the spirit of "Rosa Alvaro, a beautiful Spanish maiden," sticks a rose in her teeth, and says calmly, "That will be five dollars."

Mabel looks tired, but she's still up to the down-and-out clowning. She plays out an extended comic sequence in which she wrestles with putting silk stockings on the legs of a store mannequin, and after having to swim to shore off a pleasure boat, she makes a comic tour de force out of pulling a fish from her blouse. It is obvious in this film what a compelling personality Mabel Normand really was, especially when she portrays the beautiful Rosa. Such a romantic beauty is well within her range, not just because she is good-looking but because she has considerable dramatic ability. (Many thought that she could have been the greatest dramatic actress of her time had she so chosen.) When the action calls for her to dress up as a boyish street urchin, her physical comedy reaches a high point, and she can still do it with great energy. *Rosa,* however, was not a big success, and everyone realized that Mabel Normand was ill. Her life had taken on an even faster pace, the acceleration appearing somewhat the way the old Sennett chases were conducted: start slow, move out, then take off at high speed and never let up until the chaos explodes and there's no future.

Mabel had made no real progress. Now she was grinding out movies for Goldwyn the same way she had once ground them out for Sennett. In the beginning, Goldwyn had promoted her the way she wanted to be promoted, wearing lovely clothes and romantically photographed; he treated her with what she thought of as class. He had promised her he would present her in "artistic" movies, and her first film was a serious drama, with some comedy, *Joan of Plattsburg,* in which she played an orphan who imagines she's Joan of Arc reincarnated. Filming went badly, and Goldwyn shelved it, shoving Mabel into a full comedy, *Dodging a Million.* When *Joan* was later released (in May 1918), the miscast Mabel was criticized by *Variety* as not having the required "spirituality." After that, Goldwyn fell back on the popularity of her character from *Mickey.* The rest of the sixteen features she made for him over the next three years were slapstick romantic comedies. Disenchanted, Mabel began to give Goldwyn and his staff the same kind of hard time she had once given Sennett. "Oh, what a little devil she was," said Abraham Lehr, Goldwyn's manager.

In 1920, the Goldwyn Pictures Corporation collapsed, and Mabel completed her filming for him by the end of that year.* Shortly after, Sennett announced that Mabel Normand would return to his company. These years of Mabel's life are hazy. Her biographer, Fussell, whose research was thorough, admits, "I was confused about Mabel's chronology" because "until [the fall of 1919] Mabel was turning out a feature every two or three months. Then there were long stretches between films." Fussell feels that, during this time period, Mabel went to what fan magazines and friends called "a small New England village" to rebuild her "wrecked nervous system."

In 1921 she made *Molly O',* and in 1922 *Suzanna,* both with Sennett. Both were Mickeyish stories. The former is a Cinderella plot in which a sweet girl marries a rich hero, and the latter is a costume film set in Spanish California, also in the Cinderella mode. She received excellent reviews for the first, with *Variety* reporting, "Mabel Normand does manage to get to the audience . . . The picture will get patronage." The *New York Times* also predicted the masses would like it, but gave Mabel credit by saying the film's success was "due chiefly to the pantomime of Mabel Normand." For *Suzanna, Variety* said Mabel's performance was "a worthy feature" of the story, also pointing out that she had been toned down, and was playing a more refined heroine than usual, but not without losing all of her tomboy mannerisms. It seemed that Mack and Mabel were trying to compromise—give her a little romance and a little slapstick, mixed together.

Mabel continued her by now established pattern of work hard, play hard. Explaining herself as "shanty Irish," she reeled along through life and got away with it because she was generous and lovable. Blanche Sweet said, "We all granted her the license of an enchanted princess . . . When she spoke, toads came out of her mouth, but nobody minded."

* Her final Goldwyn films were released later, in 1921 (*What Happened to Rosa?*) and 1922 (*Head Over Heels*).

The public, however, was about to start minding. While Mabel was becoming more and more famous for her fancy clothes, big spending, out-of-control interviews, and wild life, the public's romantic vision of Hollywood and its stars started to come apart. The first big scandal occurred in September of 1921, just before the release of *Molly O'*, and it involved Mabel's old costar, Fatty Arbuckle, who was accused of a particularly obscene rape which resulted in a starlet's death. Although Fatty was ultimately acquitted after three successive trials, his career as a charming fat comic was virtually ended. Then in 1922, while she was filming *Suzanna,* the handsome director William Desmond Taylor was shot to death, and rumors said he was wearing a silver locket containing Mabel's picture. Mabel, the last person to see him alive, had her name drawn into the mess, as she had been involved with him. Perhaps to rest and perhaps to escape the scandals, which had taken a harsh toll on her, Mabel left Hollywood and fled to Europe in 1922 on an extended "grand tour." When she returned, things seemed to be getting back to normal until—ten days following the successful release of *Suzanna*—another scandal occurred. On January 14, 1923, the handsome Wallace Reid, known as an all-American, clean-cut actor, suddenly died and was revealed to have been a drug addict. Although Mabel had no direct connection to Reid, the known presence of drugs in Hollywood made Mabel and her environment subject to even closer scrutiny and newer, deeper criticisms. But the worst was yet to come.

First, however, came *The Extra Girl* (1923), one of Mabel's best movies, although not a huge success at the time. With a story written for her by Sennett, Mabel plays a small-town girl who tries to get into the movies, but fails. She's given a job as prop girl, and in one excellent sequence she places a lion's head on a dog—the usual way the cheapo outfit she works for creates a lion—only to have a real lion show up, a case of mistaken identity similar to the leopard charade in *Bringing Up Baby.* Mabel ambles around the studio dragging the lion behind her, pushing it, cajoling it, and bossing it around with total confidence. She's both hilarious and touching, and the action plays out in a way that affords her the chance to show her stuff at the highest level.

Finally, just after the release of *The Extra Girl,* on New Year's Day, 1924, another big scandal hit Mabel. Her chauffeur, Joe Kelly, shot the playboy Courtland Dines, and "Kelly" turned out not to be his real name; he was an ex-con named Horace Greer. Although Dines didn't die, Greer had shot him with Mabel's own gun while Mabel and Edna Purviance were in his bedroom changing their clothes for dinner. Various reports of drunkenness were included in the different versions of the story people put forth regarding this event. A definitive statement was made by the state attorney general of Ohio, as he announced the state's banning of Mabel's movies: "This film star has been entirely too closely connected with disgraceful shooting affairs."

A spunky Mabel in *Mickey,* and showing some effects of her high living in *Molly O'*

The story of the life of Mabel Normand becomes increasingly visible on her face as the years go by. She begins to look thin. Circles appear under her eyes, and she has the nervous, slightly askew look that might be associated with mental illness, a physical malady—or alcoholism and drug use. Comparing a series of photographs of her shows clearly what was happening to her, and how rapidly it was happening. In 1916, as she prepares to shoot *Mickey,* she poses in her costume for the film. Relaxed and smiling, she leans against a cabin wall by a window. Her hair is thick and long and full, her eyes dark and mischievous. She wears a man's shirt, vest, and pants, with a pair of old shoes on her big feet. Her hand is on her hip. She looks saucy and ready for anything. A photo taken in February of 1920 on location for *Pinto* shows her in a similar outfit: pants, plaid shirt, and boots. She's reading a newspaper and looks haggard, dark circles under her eyes and an obvious tension around her mouth. A third photo, taken in the late twenties, reveals her as a sad-eyed woman without a smile, dressed in expensive silks and satins, studded with jewels, a fur coat loosely draped about her shoulders. There is a bored look to her, but also a haunted, gaunt quality. Still quite young, she's already looking burned out.

After the Dines scandal, Mabel's career began to fall apart. She began to drift even more, spending money recklessly, drinking even more heavily, and finally leaving Hollywood for an unsuccessful attempt at a stage career in New York. Although her fans turned out loyally, her reviews were not good. She returned to Hollywood in 1926 at the invitation of Hal Roach, who gave her a three-year contract for eight short comedies and eight features. Sadly, she completed only five of the shorts before her contract was terminated: *The Nickel-Hopper, Raggedy Rose, Anything Once, Should Men Walk Home?*, and *One Hour Married. Nickel-Hopper* and *Raggedy Rose* (both in 1926) are typical examples.

In *Nickel-Hopper*, she effectively plays a little slum girl who works all day scrubbing floors and baby-sitting, and all night as a dance instructor who gets "2½ cents a dance." She's on top of her comedy action as she's twirled around the floor at top speed by a series of dangerous partners (or, as the bandleader puts it when the dance begins, "Choose your opponent"). A young Boris Karloff is one of her would-be suitors, but the showstopper is an elderly man with a long beard who dances up a storm. "You've been eating too much reindeer meat, Santa Claus," she tells him. An effective comedy chase and a madcap marriage wrap up the plot.

In *Raggedy Rose*, Mabel Normand is carrying the ball alone. There's no Chaplin, no Fatty, no Keystone Kops, and she is clearly taking herself more seriously as an artist. In a frail story about a little ragamuffin who works for a junk dealer, she's partly reminiscent of Chaplin's Little Tramp and partly a satire on the waifs with fluttering hands played by Lillian Gish. (In some scenes, she looks a bit like Giulietta Masina.) Her comedy playing is, as always, perfectly timed, sharp, and precisely delineated. When Mabel is given the typical Keystone comedy routine to do, she's superb. Having heard that a friend of hers who got run over by a car was given a thousand dollars and put in a hospital where she could "eat anything" she wanted, Mabel sets out to get the same treatment. Standing in front of a speeding open-air automobile, she is firmly resigned. The car, a rattletrap, slams on its brakes and falls totally to pieces, and the driver gets out and bops Mabel with one of the fenders. She starts a pillow fight with a rival and her mother, jumps in and out of bed, and does a splendid routine in which she finds a dime in the pocket of one of the old coats she is gathering in her rag-picking work. And there is a glamorous moment in which she dreams of herself dressed beautifully in one of the dresses she's collected, an elaborate costume with ruffles. In her mind, she dances with her dream prince, wearing the dress and a beautiful hat.

During these years, Mabel's private life continued to spiral downward. On September 17, 1926, she suddenly and inexplicably married the actor

Lew Cody, a heavy-drinking disaster of a man who allegedly proposed to her in a drunken state and was accepted in the same condition. Descriptions of their wedding party, in which they zoom to a justice of the peace with a motorcycle escort and their dinner guests falling out of their overcrowded car, sound suspiciously like a Mack Sennett comedy chase scene. The elopement of two well-known drinkers was met with nothing but cynicism on the part of their friends, the press, the film business, and even the bride and groom themselves. (On the morning of September 18, Cody showed up at a Breakfast Club broadcast in the Hollywood Bowl. He was late, a mess, and dressed in his dinner clothes from the night before. "Fellas," he admitted, "I went to a party last night . . . I married Mabel Normand.")

After her marriage to Cody, Mabel's career slowly dried up. Her last movie was *One Hour Married,* released in February of 1927. In 1928 she made no movies at all. By 1929, sound had taken over the industry, and Mabel had other problems anyway: She had been diagnosed early in the year with a serious tubercular infection. About the same time, Cody collapsed with a heart attack and was himself hospitalized. In August, Mabel was taken to Pottenger's Sanitorium in Altadena, California, and on February 23, 1930, she died. In one of her diaries, dated February 1927, Mabel had written her own best obituary: "WHO CARES?" It was both a plea and a cynical shrug.

The early death of the beautiful and talented Mabel Normand is one of the greatest of all the silent film star tragedies. Wasted and ill, her career more or less in ruins, Mabel died at the age of thirty-seven. The diagnosis was pulmonary tuberculosis. Mack Sennett, on the other hand, lived to a ripe old age, dying at eighty on November 4, 1960. Whereas Mabel hardly had time to put anything in perspective, Sennett lived to write his autobiography, an "as told to" series of inaccurate memories published in 1954. He began his book—and thus the story of his life, with all its events, successes and failures, and parade of celebrities—by saying, "I am an old storyteller, long in the tooth and willing. Once upon a time I was bewitched by an actress who ate ice cream for breakfast." In other words, when he added it all up, it was Mabel Normand who was on his mind. He called her the "most important thing in my life." For film fans and scholars, the question is always, Why, finally, did Mack and Mabel never wed? The mystery of their romance and why it failed them is one of Hollywood's saddest ironies. In their personal relationship, their timing—always so impeccable on film—was obviously way, way off.

Of their famous romance, Mabel Normand said little other than "I made a tremendous fortune for that Irishman." Sennett was more revealing, saying, "The worst predicament of all is to fall in love with an actress with whom you are in business." Whatever their relationship off-screen, in the business, it was a power struggle between two artists, each of whom felt entitled to control and to a superior status. Sennett was the driving force behind Mabel's success, but it was Mabel who was adored by the public. She wanted the kind of growth a big star needs to remain popular. That meant feature films, possibly even dramatic parts, and the same status as others like Mary Pickford and Norma Talmadge, two of her chums when she first entered the business. Sennett was a businessman, and he wanted to keep things low-cost. And he was a down-to-earth maker of comedies who was determined to give the public what it clamored for. It was the age-old Hollywood argument. From Sennett's point of view, why should he pay Mabel a fortune or let her make decisions? It was also his style not to put stars under contract or let them demand exorbitant salaries. (Over the years, a wealth of talent moved through the Sennett studios, going on to better salaries and star status, if not always better material.) Mabel's attitude was based on what she knew to be her worth.

Sennett's book reveals his appreciation of how special Mabel really was. "When Mabel Normand went anywhere at all, or did anything at all, it was with all flags flying. When she bought hats, she bought thirty, wore one, and gave the others away. When she had those French people make her gowns and evening dresses, she ordered by the dozen—and wore only one. Mabel was like—she was like so many things. She was like a French-Irish girl, as gay as a wisp, and she was also Spanish-like and brooding. Mostly she was like a child who walks to the corner on a spring morning and meets Tom Sawyer with a scheme in his pocket . . . Mabel was all about emotion." Obviously he loved her. When asked why he never married her, he said, "I can't explain it, even to myself." In the very last interview of his life—June of 1960—he said, "I've always regretted not marrying her."

There is an explanation of sorts. Mabel wasn't just a girl who ate ice cream for breakfast. She was also a girl who partied all night, came to work late, and disappeared for days on end. She was involved in the scandals of William Desmond Taylor's murder, of her chauffeur's shooting of her boyfriend, of the rumors of drugs and the curse of bad health; she was tubercular, and clearly burned the candle anyplace she could get it lit. For whatever reasons, the perfect comedy marriage never took place, and Mack Sennett died a bachelor. Their story is a kind of warped *Citizen Kane* of comedy, only Mabel really has talent, unlike Susan Alexander, and they never marry. But Kane/Sennett ends up old and alone, remembering, and whispering his last fond memory. And it's . . . "Mabel," his Rosebud. It's hard to fashion a comedy out of the private lives of Mack and Mabel, but everything else about all of them—Mack and Mabel and the Kops—is as wonderfully funny today as it ever was. They are the geniuses of American movie chaos.

The quintessential Mabel in full crisis

DOUGLAS FAIRBANKS

ONCE UPON A TIME, and that time was not so very long ago, when little boys dreamed of grand heroes who dared and dueled, who fought and won, who leaped and flew through the air, and who always, but always, carried the day, their dreams came true in the form of Douglas Fairbanks. As Frank Nugent's obituary tribute in the *New York Times* of December 17, 1939, said:

> Doug Fairbanks was make-believe at its best, a game we young-sters never tired of playing, a game—we are convinced—that our fathers secretly shared . . . There wasn't a small boy in the neigh-borhood who did not, in a Fairbanks picture, see himself tri-umphant over the local bully, winning the soft-eyed adoration of whatever ten-year-old blonde he had been courting, and wreaking vengeance on the teacher who made him stand in the corner that afternoon.

Douglas Fairbanks was a macho dream come true—the hero who was brave and honorable, clean and gallant, full of optimism and conviction. Although he had many imitators in a later age, there was never anyone quite like him.

Fairbanks is not forgotten, and he isn't unappreciated—but he is remembered as much less than he really was. His career, one of the greatest in film history, has separate halves. Up until 1920, he made energetic comedies in which he played young men who personified the optimism of America in the teens—always on the move, always pursuing a goal, and always the win-ner of the brass ring through determination and perseverance. After 1920, he stepped out of that pseudorealistic world of the all-American man-boy and began making highly romanticized adventure movies. Today, he is remem-bered for the latter, and few realize he began as a comedy star, and that it is his comic timing and energy that make his adventure movies great.

It is ironic that Douglas Fairbanks's career took him forward into a never-never land. Instead of aging into King Lear, he aged into Robin Hood. Instead of beginning to play the fathers of the leading ladies he once courted, he grew ever younger, casting aside all pretense of modern life and carrying the viewer into a land of visual enchantment. For a star with less to offer, such a career move would have meant disaster, but it makes Fairbanks unique. Inside his original movie persona—a young man running down the streets of old Los Angeles, leaping over rooftops, clambering aboard moving trains—was contained a spirit wanting to be free. And free it gets. He steps out of business suits and drawing-room sets into Sherwood Forest . . . or onto a magic carpet . . . or a pirate ship . . . or the streets of old Paris. Boys will be boys, Fairbanks seemed to say . . . and so will men.

On-screen, Douglas Fairbanks appears as very vital, very virile. He wasn't a large man, though he wasn't tiny like some of Hollywood's male stars. His height is variously listed as between five feet seven inches and five feet ten, and his weight between 145 and 155 pounds. He had dark brown hair and piercing gray-blue eyes. He was somewhat of a health nut, and certainly an early advocate of physical fitness (although off-screen he was a heavy smoker). He kept himself deeply tanned year-round, which not only made him look healthier both on- and off-screen, but seemed to turn him into a magic person from another world where the sun was always shining. (Cary Grant was said to have patterned his own year-round tan on that of Douglas Fairbanks, the man whose style and look he most admired.) He has the kind of physical radiance that is usually associated with female performers, although he is quintessentially masculine. He has *it*. Sometimes he reminds me of the equally exuberant Al Jolson of *The Jazz Singer*, *Mammy*, and *The Singing Fool*. Like Jolson, he jumps around gracefully, swinging his arms, making broad gestures. He seems about to erupt in song but, unlike Jolson, he erupts by leaping up onto something. One of Fairbanks's most distinctive physical movements is his upward jump, sometimes facilitated by a trampoline or a springboard, sometimes enhanced by a fence or wall designed to look much higher than it actually is. Everything he did to "act" was physical—the word most commonly used to describe his performances at the time was "exuber-ant"—and this acting style was perfect for silent films because it was all about using the whole body to express character, attitude, and emotion.

Fairbanks is a joy to watch. He has a light, unpretentious touch. The reviewers of his day always refer to his gusto, his energy, and to his combination of robust and romantic traditions. He appeals "to the young," they said, and also "to the young in heart." Inside that cliché lies one of the secrets of the Fairbanks stardom—his ability to connect with grown men as well as with little boys. He understood the male desire for escape, and his movies are a kind of "man's movie" not unlike the old women's pictures that gave women a form of pseudoliberation and lots of terrific clothes and furniture to ogle. He welcomed the grown-up masculine viewer into a world of games and exploits, but without asking him to surrender his dignity. It's highly unlikely that any star could reach the heights that Fairbanks reached and stay at the top as long as he did without having some sense of himself, some sense of the business, and some sense of the medium itself. Fairbanks had all three but was particularly smart about how to reach the adults in his audience. Male stars who have lasted for decades at the box office all had a sense of humor about their image, and have put a touch of irony into their macho heroes.

The three top male box office stars of the sound era, John Wayne, Clint Eastwood, and Bing Crosby, all offered the audience a private wink at their images. Wayne's swagger and raised eyebrows, Eastwood's squint and laconic dialogue, and Crosby's casual ad-libs were the equivalent of Douglas Fairbanks's mocking laughter. With his head thrown back and his fists on his hips, he is not only embodying the male hero but also laughing joyously at the very ridiculousness of it all. Fairbanks is not cynical the way Eastwood is, but he radiates self-humor. He communicates directly with the audience, suggesting that we're all in it together, to take things seriously but only as serious escape. Serious fun.

Fairbanks was also a good businessman and a shrewd judge of his own abilities. Griffith, Pickford, and Chaplin, he said, were geniuses, but "I am not a genius." He knew he pleased crowds, but he also knew his range was narrow. To compensate—and because it was good business—he learned everything he could about making movies, and he surrounded himself with the best of everything. He became a consummate craftsman, with a thorough knowledge of the filmmaking process. Joseph Schenck, the producer, said of him, "This fellow knows more about moviemaking than all the rest of us put together." Fairbanks hired excellent character actors, none of whom threatened him and all of whom enhanced him. He spent money, especially on his later films, building gigantic sets so that the pageantry of his stories was supported visually. He made furniture and sets and costumes to delight the eyes of his audience, and he was clever enough to realize that such money spent brought double value—these things looked impressive in themselves but they also served as props for his adventure stunts. He always hired the best—the top-ranked directors, writers, designers—and he knew how to get good value out of them for his money, treating them to saunas and sleeping quarters at his mansion (Pickfair), and having his chauffeur drive them to work.

When you went to a Fairbanks picture, you often got more than one Doug Fairbanks. He was constantly donning disguises, assuming different walks and attitudes, undertaking masquerades. He liked to play two versions of the same character—old and young, effete and strong—and besides giving a marvelous performance, he did exciting stunts and acrobatics, anything physical he could think of to do. When all his character variations were supplemented by excellent supporting actors, beautiful leading ladies, superbly designed sets and costumes, lavish production values, solid writing and directing, he had a full house. And there were also imaginative and innovative tricks of cinematic technique to wow the audience even more.

Fairbanks put his knowledge of cinema to good use, coming up with a bag of sly visual tricks. He shortened the legs of a table he was going to jump over so that he would appear to soar. He could easily and swiftly *whoosh* down a hanging tapestry, because a slide had been built and concealed inside the fabric. He found just the right number of frames to use per minute in a sequence to give added pace and acceleration. Although he spent significant sums of money on clothes and props and sets, he tried never to hire a double. "Don't cheat the audience of yourself" was one of his rules. (Cheat them the respectable way—through top-notch special effects.)

Above all, Fairbanks became a master of scale. When he leapt from the floor up onto a table, or from a window onto a tree trunk, he knew how to make the leap look more impressive than it actually was. By building huge sets, he made all his feats look bigger and grander than they were . . . although they were, in fact, pretty big and grand. His ideas were inherently cinematic and he used the medium in bold ways. For instance, in *The Mollycoddle* (1920), his character is put belowdecks on a ship to stoke the furnaces. Not used to such labor, he collapses from exhaustion. Suddenly, the audience is shown the other stoker as Fairbanks's character would see him (in an imaginative point-of-view shot): the stoker with his shovel, the flaming furnace, the pile of coal—all revolve around in a circle, as if encased inside a drum.

If Doug Fairbanks had possessed only his athlete's agility, a little humor about himself, and a strong business sense, he might never have become popular. But he had something else that every star must have: magnetism. When Fairbanks is on the screen, you don't feel like looking at anyone else. He glows with good health and that oft-remarked-on energy. He commands attention. He is—quite simply—a likable fellow who's very hard to resist.

The critics of his time, who were almost universally male, definitely could *not* resist him. They appreciated and loved Fairbanks. (Their affection is in stark contrast to their hatred of Rudolph Valentino.) The first significant criticism started to appear only in 1930, when the scholar Paul Rotha's assessment of Fairbanks's persona hinted at the limitations that were built into his work: "Fairbanks, one feels, realizes only too well that he is neither an artist nor an actor in the accepted understanding of the terms. He is on the contrary (and of this he is fully aware) a pure product of the medium of the cinema in which he seeks self expression . . . his rhythm, his graceful motion and perpetual movement . . . Fairbanks is essentially filmic . . . No other talent than his rhythm and his ever present sense of pantomime, except perhaps his superior idea of showmanship and overwhelming personality."

One of the few to discuss his limitations seriously was Gavin Lambert, who, writing a full decade after Fairbanks's death, said that "Fairbanks had the exuberance of the virtuoso, but there is no poetry in his movements, agility and vigor rather than grace. *The Thief of Bagdad* showed his feeling for the exotic to be ludicrously undeveloped." (Fairbanks's sense of "the exotic" was never sexual or decadent; it was fanciful and playful. On that basis, perhaps it is not exotic at all, but it certainly was well developed.) In fact, the primary appeal of Fairbanks lay in his quintessentially American, and therefore unthreatening, presence. He was closer to imaginary male heroes like Jack Armstrong, the All-American Boy, the lads of Horatio Alger, or even the Lone Ranger, than he was to someone like Valentino, who was erotic, foreign, and sexually ambivalent. Fairbanks was a man's man, and he stood for fair play, decent behavior, and rapidly evolving upward mobility.

FAIRBANKS WAS BORN Douglas Elton Thomas Ulman to Hezekiah Charles Ulman, a New York lawyer who was the son of a wealthy Pennsylvania family, and Ella Adelaide Marsh of New Orleans. Ulman had met his wife when he helped her settle her affairs after the sudden death of her first husband, John Fairbanks. (He then helped her obtain a divorce following a disastrous second marriage.) The couple settled in Denver, where the restless Ulman practiced law but also unsuccessfully tried his hand at gold mining. Two children were born, Robert in 1882, and Douglas in 1883. Five years later, Ulman disappeared and never came back, becoming yet another of the disappearing fathers who mark the lives of so many silent film stars. The bitter wife changed her name back to that of her first husband, Fairbanks, and Douglas never saw Ulman again except once when he showed up to cadge drink money after Douglas had become a successful stage star.

Fairbanks showed an interest in performing at an early age. A November 19, 1898, program for "Living Pictures," a children's matinee sponsored by the woman's club and art leagues of Denver, names a "Master Douglas Fairbanks," a pupil of the Tabor School of Acting, as presenting a "selected recitation." In 1899, when he was just sixteen, Fairbanks went on tour with Frederic Warde's famous Shakespeare company, and a year later, he was on Broadway. During the next fourteen years he established himself solidly as a leading man. In 1906, with his appearance in *Man of the Hour*, he officially became a star. By 1919, a theatrical journal referred to him as "generally regarded as the leading exponent of light boys and young men of today . . . He has an ingratiating personality, charged with health, directness, breeziness, and a certain patrician quality which contributes an attraction to any part he plays."

In 1907, Fairbanks married Beth Sully, a stagestruck heiress, and he gave up theatre for a one-year period to work for her father's soap company. (On December 9, 1909, the couple had a son, Douglas Fairbanks, Jr., who would himself become a successful film and stage star.) Fairbanks did not like business, and returned to the stage, eventually being lured west to make movies by Harry Aitken of the Triangle Film Corporation, who also had under contract the Gish sisters, the Talmadge sisters, Bessie Love, and others, including the prize catch, the renowned stage actor Sir Herbert Beerbohm-Tree. Fairbanks made his film debut in Triangle's *The Lamb* in 1915.

In this first feature—playing a starring role—he was directed by Christy Cabanne and costarred with Seena Owen in a story written by "Granville Warwick" (a pseudonym for D. W. Griffith). The question naturally arises—when *The Lamb* is shown today, does it look as if a star is being born? Definitely. Like Clara Bow and Valentino, who would come along later, Fairbanks stands out in the frame, causing those around him to pale by comparison. Unlike Bow and Valentino, however, Fairbanks had more than just his fabulous looks and the kind of vitality the camera responds to: he had stage presence, physical skills, and a solid comic ability. He plays a "son of the idle rich" who is "the lamb" of the title. The first sight of the soon-to-be star finds him looking perhaps a bit stocky but very fit and well dressed, giving a fully developed performance as a silly and somewhat fuddled young man. Flashing his million-dollar smile, Fairbanks seems totally at home within the frame, easily deploying his acrobatic skill to portray a physical bumbler who, though he can jump with ease over a hedge, has to take boxing lessons (with a "white hopeless") and jujitsu instruction to become "manly." Peppered with current slang and snappy one-liners (he's going to get married and become a "lamb led to the halter"), *The Lamb* tells a rollicking tale of Fairbanks in one dilemma after another. On his way to Arizona, he gets rooked by Indian traders, left behind by his train, taken out into the desert to be robbed and dumped by crooks, and finally embroiled in a fight between Yaqui braves and Mexican bandits. Naturally, all ends well, as he rescues Owen and proves his mettle.

The Lamb set the pattern for Douglas Fairbanks's early years as a star— he's a resolutely cheerful go-getter, a kind of all-American guy who always comes out on top no matter what the odds. He's almost a straightforward version of Harold Lloyd, but he plays his early comedies to emphasize excitement over laughs, whereas Lloyd stressed laughs over excitement. Both were masters of presenting young men who were faced with physical and social obstacles to overcome, and both represented the essential optimism of their era. Doug's character in *The Lamb* starts out as a jerk, but he finds out, under duress, that he has good stuff in him and that, in fact, he secretly harbors the heart and soul of a hero. This idea—that ordinary people were really special if only life would give them a chance—was an idea that America was ready to embrace. His was the *Zeitgeist* of the optimistic post–World War I era, and no other star represents it as well as he does, both on- and off-screen.

Between 1915 and 1920 (when he released his first big costume film, *The Mark of Zorro*), Fairbanks appeared in twenty-nine movies. Except for *The Half Breed* (1916), which was purely a love story, all were about comedy, romance, and adventure. Sometimes it was romantic adventure, and sometimes it was romantic comedy, and sometimes it was comedy adventure. For instance, *Arizona* (1918) was a romantic drama set in the West, *When the Clouds Roll By* (1919) was an action romance, culminating in a huge flood sequence, and *The Good Bad Man* (1916) was a romance about a Robin Hood of the Old West. *A Modern Musketeer* (1918) was a fantasy-comedy, and *The Man from Painted Post* (1917) was a romantic comedy melodrama . . . the mix was slightly different from movie to movie, but the basic ingredient was always Doug Fairbanks doing his thing. At some point, he would scale a wall, climb a tree, jump off a building, sock the villain, and rescue the girl and save the day. It was an excellent formula which he executed to perfection, and with great joy and panache.

All these early comedies are peppy exercises in how Doug Fairbanks Can Solve His Problem. He charges through the plots, always seeming to be genuinely enjoying himself. Watching Fairbanks in these movies, it isn't hard to see why he became so popular. He is the very definition of what makes a great film star: he and his screen character seem totally unified. It's impossible not to believe that we aren't watching Doug Fairbanks be himself. There is no distance between a film viewer and this character. Fairbanks, however, was not really playing himself, but a character he devised for himself. People could come to the movies and watch a good-looking young man having a great time up on the screen chasing and catching crooks, becoming rich and successful, winning the girl. How reassuring and how satisfying. And what fun!

Fairbanks himself described his second film, *Double Trouble* (1915), by saying, "In my second picture I ran a car off a cliff, had six rounds with a pro pugilist, jumped off an Atlantic liner, fought six gunmen at once and leapt off a speeding train." Both *The Lamb* and *Double Trouble* were supervised by D. W. Griffith, but the artistry of Griffith and the exuberance of Fairbanks were not really compatible. Fairbanks said, "D. W. didn't like my athletic tendencies. Or my spontaneous habit of jumping a fence or scaling a church at unexpected moments which were not in the script. Griffith told me to go to Keystone comedies." (Both movies were Triangle features. Triangle's creative force was Griffith, Thomas Ince, and Mack Sennett, the three producers who had each signed a contract to release a three-hour program every week.) At Triangle, the writing-directing team of John Emerson and Anita Loos was also unpopular with Griffith, who considered Loos's titles altogether too snappy, so Loos and Emerson began working with Fairbanks. They were a highly effec-

Fairbanks and
D. W. Griffith

tive trio, and they started right out with a hit, Fairbanks's third movie, *His Picture in the Papers* (1916).

The Douglas Fairbanks movies of 1915–20 all have certain things in common: Doug, of course, looking handsome, suave, and bursting with energy; a very pretty girl who has relatively little to do; and a full-scale action sequence in which Doug performs acrobatics, stunts, and various forms of derring-do. Usually these films have more than a little comedy, and some are out-and-out spoofs or farces. The plots follow a pattern, basically, adding up to snappy entertainment with little depth. Seen today, they are endearing for their innocence and zest, for their boundless enthusiasm for the possibilities of life. The great thing about Douglas Fairbanks on film was that he not only conquered his world but also made it seem as if anyone could do the same.

In 1916 alone, he made eleven films, five of which involved either Emerson or Loos in some capacity. In *His Picture in the Papers,* he is the son of a health-food magnate, but he hates health food. He conceals the fixings for his cocktail shaker inside a box of Prindle's Toasted Tootsies, and after a family vegetarian dinner, he dashes to the nearest restaurant for a bloody steak. The film's opening title warns that "Publicity at any price has become the passion of the American people," and Fairbanks is put to the test when he falls in love with a vegetarian's daughter. (She, too, sneaks out for a little red meat now and then.) The girl's father tells him that he cannot marry her unless he claims his rightful inheritance—half his father's business. When he goes to his father, he's told he can have the money only if he can publicize "Prindle's 27 Vegetarian Varieties" by getting his picture in the papers. Thus a typical Fairbanks comedy dilemma is set up—he sets out to get publicity of any kind and can't even get arrested. Nothing works. In the end, after much dashing about, he rescues a train and makes the grade. The little moral about the emergence of celebrity, and how ludicrous the concept of celebrity really is, gets lost in the rush, and everyone has a good time. (*Variety* liked what it saw in *His Picture in the Papers,* writing, "Douglas Fairbanks again forcibly brings to mind that he is destined to be one of the greatest favorites with the film-seeing public.") In this early movie, the power of the Fairbanks personality is stunning. It's also evident that he was playing in a somewhat superficial mode. This shows up again in *Reggie Mixes In,* also from 1916. Although he has real charm, he is clearly letting his good looks, strong body, and athletic ability carry his performance and stand for his character.

The timing and flow of the chase sequences that Fairbanks participates in for all these early movies are perfect, and it's startling to realize how common such first-rate comedy action was in those years. *Variety,* for instance, stated flatly about *Flirting With Fate* (1916): "There is nothing unusual about the feature." Today a sequence like the one that Fairbanks executes so easily would require stunt doubles (unless it involved Jackie Chan) and would be tarted up with explosions, fake camera angles, and computer assists. Fairbanks just steps out and does it. This chase is a particularly good one, and is the central action of the movie, which uses three reels to set up a plot and two reels to do nothing but run and chase. Fairbanks plays an unsuccessful artist who, dejected at the way his life is going, hires an assassin to sneak up on him and kill him. Suddenly, his luck changes. He sells a painting, gets the girl, and inherits a fortune! Now he's got to evade his killer, but he has no idea what the guy is going to look like, since he has ordered the assassin to wear a disguise. (This plot is similar to Warren Beatty's 1998 *Bulworth.*) Obviously, Fairbanks spends the rest of the movie running . . . from everyone. (I am highly partial to the assassin, who turns out to have a conscience and a dying mother. "Even assassins have mothers," he weeps to the Salvation Army workers who reform him.) In the freewheeling chase, Fairbanks jumps up from the sidewalk onto a store balcony, jumps into the back of a fast-moving automobile, jumps from a moving car onto the back of a second one that drives up alongside, scampers over rooftops, and leaps up things and over things in a lumberyard. Despite *Variety*'s quibble about the chase being old hat (which it isn't), the review praised him: "Mr. Fairbanks is a comedian first, last, and always."

All the early Fairbanks chase scenes take place across actual landscapes and city streets—they're inventive, well shot, and played out in the most natural yet sophisticated way possible. Two of the finest are in the 1916 releases *Manhattan Madness* and *The Matrimaniac* (one of the best of his titles). In *Manhattan Madness,* he assaults a mansion to rescue his girl. On location in an actual three-story house, Fairbanks climbs in and out of win-

dows, clambers up to the rooftop, struggles with a villain, jumps off the roof
into a tree and shimmies down it. The house has a wide eave at every floor, so
that he and his adversaries can go in and out of windows, run around, and leap
down from one eave to another in an amazing burst of action which the viewer
can see is honestly dangerous. Fairbanks even climbs up this house from the
ground floor . . . and the reward is all his. In the end, he sets his beautiful
prize on a horse, and the two lovers gallop away to happiness.

Matrimaniac presents an elopement. Constance Talmadge and Fairbanks run away to be married, only to confront a series of disasters that separate them. He spends the entire remaining running time of the movie trying to
get to the girl in time to marry her before her father catches up with them.
With a justice of the peace in tow, he chases madly by train, car, reluctant
mule, and on foot—all with both the police and Daddy in pursuit. It is a buoyant, joyous romp across logic and through time and space. Doug has to leap
across buildings, climb trees, walk a tightrope, and tiptoe (literally) along a
telephone wire.

Less fun, though successful, was *The Americano* (1916), a romantic
adventure story set in "the little Republic of Paragonia" which is "hidden in a
bend in the Caribbean." Fairbanks plays a young mining engineer who falls in
love with the president's daughter (the languid Alma Rubens, looking as if
she's in a tragedy). He ends up rescuing her from an unwanted marriage and
her father from death in prison at the hands of revolutionaries.

The eleven 1916 movies that made Fairbanks a household name had
one bizarre entry among the titles. John Emerson directed Fairbanks in *The
Mystery of the Leaping Fish*, taken from a story by Tod Browning. When modern audiences come across it, they're usually astonished at its joking references to drugs, as Fairbanks plays "the world's greatest scientific detective,
Coke Ennyday." Obviously intended as a satire on Sherlock Holmes and his 7
percent solution, the movie opens with Fairbanks sitting beside a large con-
tainer clearly marked COCAINE, and he is repeatedly seen injecting himself.
This may have seemed appropriate material for comedy in 1916, but it's a bit
unsettling today. The story itself is rather fevered, involving counterfeiters,
Japanese opium dealers, and "the little fish blower of Short Beach," the leading lady "Inane," played by Bessie Love. Fairbanks ends up as a sort of
human submarine, but there's a visually imaginative use of large inflated fish,
which swimmers use to ride the waves at the beach and the smugglers use to
hide their drugs in.

Fairbanks's string of hit movies continued with five releases in 1917,
seven in 1918, and three in 1919. All these followed the established pattern.
Four typical examples of the work in this period are *Wild and Woolly* and
Reaching for the Moon (both in 1917), and *His Majesty, the American* and

In Again, Out Again
(1917), with
Arline Pretty

When the Clouds Roll By in 1919. *Wild and Woolly* is one of the favorite Fairbanks comedies with fans today. With a script by Anita Loos and direction by John Emerson, it is a completely wonderful spoof of westerns. (It is interesting to note that western movie conventions were firmly in place by 1917, probably based on dime-novel awareness, so that the traditional action could be spoofed with audience understanding and participation.) Once again Fairbanks plays the wealthy son of a tycoon (this time, a railroad baron), and once again he will be tested in a great finale of action, comedy, and excitement. He is first seen sitting beside a campfire outside a teepee, cooking his stew in an iron pot, wearing a large cowboy hat. As the camera slowly pulls back, it is revealed that he is in his own bedroom, which is decorated with guns, western gear, and drawings and paintings of the Old West. He is a romantic—dreaming of the glory of the Old West and firmly believing that his vision is exactly what it's still like out there. When his father is offered the opportunity to build a railroad spur to a mining camp in Bitter Creek, Arizona, he sends his son to look into the situation. Meeting the camp representatives in New York, Fairbanks mistakenly thinks they've dressed up like "easterners" for their trip; and they understand that his vision of their modernized western town is a fantasy. In order to win the father's support, the entire town decides to stage a real "western" for Fairbanks when he arrives. They dress in costumes, don guns, erect new signs, redecorate everything to make their town look like a western

He Comes Up Smiling: the perfect modern hero of 1918

movie set. When Fairbanks arrives, they even start talking western talk: "Wish you'd a come last Thursday. Thar wasn't a killin' all day." When their fake holdup goes awry because of some real crooks, Fairbanks, who has been practicing his western tricks by roping the butler back home, rises to the occasion. In a grand finale—with a bunch of Indians running across country on foot intercut with a gaggle of mothers with crying babies rushing around town—he executes a splendid crescendo of activity. The film has a witty ending. As Fairbanks leaves town, waving good-bye gamely to the little gal he fell for, a title says, "But wait a minute, this will never do! We can't end a western romance without a wedding. Yet—after they're married, where will they, shall they live? For Nell likes the east—and Jeff likes the west—so where are the twain to meet?" In a comic finale, Jeff and Nell come downstairs in their mansion, with two footmen standing by. They are dressed in classic English riding style, but when their front doors are opened, outside is a typical western street.

Reaching for the Moon demonstrates the classic silent-film-era format of "two for the price of one"—Fairbanks starts out as a button-factory worker and grows into the king of Vulgaria. Such transformations obviously appeal to the audience, who saw themselves similarly elevated, transported, or liberated, but they are also an extension of one of Fairbanks's primary trademarks: movement. His ascents to glory were symbolized by his performing a stunt that looked unperformable for an ordinary person—a jumping up, as it were, out of poverty to wealth or from ineptness to agility—visualized as a leap from ground to tree branch.

Reaching for the Moon's button maker is "a young man of boundless enthusiasm." In other words, he is Doug Fairbanks. He yearns for wealth and royalty, but when he turns out to be the heir to a throne and is placed in a series of comic situations in which the forces of evil in Vulgaria try to murder him, he just keeps on surviving. ("Long live the king!" his subjects are always shouting, just as he once again narrowly escapes a would-be assassin.) Of course, his royalty in the end turns out to be that solid plot device of American movies and television—nothing but a dream. When he wakes up, he learns the movie's moral—"Keep your feet on the ground and stop reaching for the moon"—and settles down in a little cottage in New Jersey: talk about keeping your feet on the ground! (This movie should not be confused with the sound film of the same title that Fairbanks made in 1931.)

The polish and confidence of the Fairbanks comedies reached its peak with the release *His Majesty, the American*. It's a perfect title for the Fairbanks franchise: the elevation of an ordinary American go-get-'em guy to royal status. Audiences were treated with a special opening: Doug breaking through the titles to proclaim *His Majesty, the American* to be the very first picture to be brought to them by the newly formed United Artists. The movie presents Doug as yet another enterprising American loaded with energy and optimism. This time, he's the millionaire version of his persona, a "Fire-eating, Speed-loving, Space-annihilating, Excitement-hunting Thrill Hound." He spends his free time—which his wealth gives him plenty of—participating as a member of the police (capturing a criminal) and the fire department (he rescues helpless victims from a blazing tenement fire). Those colorful events, however, are only appetizers—later, he takes a trip to Mexico and gets involved with Pancho Villa. But the heart of the plot takes place in "Alaine," an imaginary European kingdom, where "agitating demagogues have changed a peace-loving people into a rioting succession of mobs." In order to straighten out Alaine—and find his secret destiny—Fairbanks runs up the sides of buildings, jumps around all over the place, and shows himself to be the most self-confident of performers, a star who knows what he has to offer the public and how to give it to them.

By the end of 1919, everyone loved the well-established Fairbanks comedy persona. The August 30, 1919, issue of *Picture and Picturegoer* defined it: "Doug is, perhaps, the type par excellence of the modern American—restless, dissatisfied, a little careless and fond of getting-there-quick, but cheerful, persevering, resourceful and clean."

*The Man from
Painted Post*

  Mollycoddle (1920) and *The Nut* (1921) are like parentheses around *The Mark of Zorro* (1920), one released immediately before and one immediately after. They are his final comedies, the last hurrah of his original modern movie persona. *Mollycoddle,* as reviewed by *Variety,* is indeed "one peach of a picture." Directed by Victor Fleming, the movie presents Fairbanks as the son of a succession of brave Americans, from a Revolutionary War hero to a pioneer to a cowboy, etc. However, the family has become rich, and this new generation's representative has been raised abroad and is something of a "mollycoddle." Doug's given a perfect plot for undergoing one of his character changes. In the early scenes, in which he is the Europeanized American, he uses his excellent physical control to create a new walk, in which he bends slightly forward, sticks a cane under his arm, tightens up and tenses his body as if he were a bit of a stiff, a man out of shape and not entirely comfortable with his body. When confronted with the movie's plot problems, in the shape of Wallace Beery as the seemingly grand "Van Halker," who is really a diamond smuggler, Fairbanks rises to the challenge, and becomes loose, free and easy, full of fight. Beery mistakes Fairbanks for a Secret Service agent (who is actually the leading lady, played by Ruth Renick) and smuggles him aboard his yacht to America. Fairbanks performs the usual list of exciting acts, including being put overboard to drown, disguising himself as an Indian, falling off a mountain, and going over a waterfall. *Mollycoddle* is typical of the boisterous comedy years, a kind of summing up. It's fun, fast-paced, and provides an opportunity for Doug to do his acrobatic stunts and act out a kind of Charles Atlas ad come to life.

The Nut was his final modern comedy, and it is a magnum opus, a fitting finale for the first phase of his work. He pulls out all the stops, and his comic play is a cross between Charlie Chaplin in *Modern Times* (several years before that film was made, of course) and Buster Keaton's gadget-obsessed two-reelers. The opening sequence is one of his most original and best-sustained sight gags; his timing, excellent pantomiming, and mastery of physical shtick are beautifully combined. Fairbanks plays an inventor. ("He invented ways of pleasing his girl and then he invents ways of getting out of the trouble caused by his inventions.") The first scene carries a title card that charmingly sets the tone of the movie: "Chapter I. In which we introduce our hero—" The audience is presented with a straightforward view of a set—there is a floor, a rug, two arched windows, a vase of flowers on a sill, a standing birdcage, with bird, and a bed. Lying facedown on the bed is a man who is sound asleep. Suddenly, a close-up of the bird shows a cartoonlike caption in which the bird is singing out, "Ten o'clock!" The man's eyes fly open. Immediately, covers are raised off his body by a set of automatic strings that hoist them to some imaginary space above. The mattress section of his bed slides forward and is revealed to be on wheels. The sleeper is rapidly rolled forward to a sunken bathtub, with the bed conveniently upending itself at tub's edge in order to slide him, pajamas and all, into the waiting water. In his bath, he removes his pajamas (revealing a heavily muscled back), and an automatic arm with three giant sponges attached begins to whirl and wash him. As he finishes his bath, he moves to the end of the tub and begins to get out of it. As his presumably naked body rises up out of the water, a large roll of towel on a spindle rises up in the foreground, neatly covering him. The roll, like the sponges, whirls around, drying him from head to toe, while he turns back and forth. Dry, he steps out from behind the protection of the spindle, but before we can see him, a title card cleverly interjects some information: "He isn't lazy. He's just different and eccentric—but then—so were Christopher Columbus—Sir Isaac Newton—Lydia Pinkham—and Ponzi." When the card disappears, Fairbanks has miraculously progressed to a semidressed state. He is combing his hair and wearing an undershirt, shorts, black shoes, and socks and garters. He presses a switch, and a conveyor belt carries him toward a long closet marked by a series of panels that open automatically by sliding upward and then back down. The first panel opens and hands out a clean white shirt . . . the second a pair of pants. Another cleverly placed title card ("Maybe necessity is the mother of invention—but the father of these is a nut") masks the progress of the dressing man. The next time we see him, he is tying his tie, then donning his jacket, and completing the effect with a pocket handkerchief. However, the first hanky that comes out he rejects—a neat little touch. It goes back in and a second choice emerges. In this excellent opening, Fairbanks and his team have understood that they are working a one-joke gag, and while it is inventive as it proceeds from bed to bath to closet, they must shorten the time presentation to keep the pace moving and the comedy fresh. By working with the audience's desire to see Fairbanks emerge naked from his bath, they hold interest, but jump forward over a cut—a little joke on the audience. This is an example of Fairbanks's brand of physical comedy. Granted, he's not as skilled at moving the narrative smoothly forward or as inventive in his action as Keaton, nor is he as talented a pantomimist as Chaplin, but he's good. And he's a legitimate romantic leading man in a way neither Chaplin nor Keaton could ever be.

In *The Nut,* Fairbanks fully indulges his interest in movie special effects. In an extended sequence, the hero and the leading lady (Marguerite De La Motte) are shown climbing through the heating pipes of a house via trick photography. The audience is allowed to look through the walls, as it were, to see them climbing up and down inside the pipes and the furnace. There's also an excellent scene in a wax museum in which he pretends to be a dummy; a routine with a wax "cop" he loses in the street; and a marvelous visual joke in which he performs for guests by impersonating Lincoln, Napoleon, and others, including Charlie Chaplin. Each time he goes behind a screen to transform himself into a historical person, another actor comes out who is short, or tall, or whatever the impersonation requires, with the grand climax being Chaplin himself in his surprise cameo. (It was probably no accident that Fairbanks's character's name in *The Nut* is "Charlie." The two men were very close friends.) It was almost as if Fairbanks had stored up a bank of comedy routines and decided to use them all in *The Nut.*

The reviews that Fairbanks received for his comedies from 1915 to 1920 trace his rise and help define his popularity. As early as *Reggie Mixes In,* a *Variety* review pointed out that "D'Artagnan and other swashbuckling heroes were mere children alongside the physical prowess of Douglas Fairbanks in his latest Fine Arts Feature . . . Some scrapper that Doug Fairbanks. Jess Willard has nothin' on him." *Matrimaniac* was dubbed "a great picture for the Fairbanks fans . . . The picture will get the money." The *New York Times* referred to *The Americano* as "a typical Douglas Fairbanks film, with the star as his irresistible, athletic self." By the time of *The Mollycoddle* in 1920, reviews pay tribute to Fairbanks as the be-all and end-all of his movies, and to his contributions to the entire production: "One reason why the Douglas Fairbanks pictures hold their popularity is that Mr. Fairbanks does not depend entirely upon himself, nor upon a hackneyed story, to keep the public interested. In nearly all of his productions there are extraordinary scenes that

could be shown in no way except by motion pictures and are conspicuously within the scope of the motion picture cameras."

THE THIRTY COMEDY MOVIES are the films that made Fairbanks a star. When he expanded his movie universe into the swashbuckling films he is more readily identified with today, he was smart enough not to abandon his original successful persona: he simply took his comedy self and moved it to another part of town. With *The Mark of Zorro,* Fairbanks lifted his daring young man out of the ordinary and into history. It was not that the mythical kingdoms of some of his comedies (such as "Paragonia" and "Alaine") were realistic, or that he was presenting a documentary approach to the West, or to daily life in the teens. His millionaires and playboys and enterprising button clerks were hardly the stuff of realism. But his comedies were connected directly to the daily life of people in the audience, and they had modern settings, however fanciful or decorated or embellished. With *Zorro,* Fairbanks went where he was always destined to go: into the realm of adventure fantasy, that particular place little boys long to inhabit. He took the well-cut suit of clothes off his hero and dressed him up in a hat with a feather, or an earring, or a set of Arabian Nights pantaloons, but he didn't let go of the comedy. As Gavin Lambert put it, writing in *Sequence* in 1949, "He will be remembered as the only figure of his time to attempt a revival of the heroic spirit in popular terms. What was overlooked, perhaps, in the excitement of the moment, was that Fairbanks had to create an old fashioned world to contain his antics." His great gift was understanding that these hammy macho men would be totally irritating if they weren't ingratiatingly amusing. He knew that the swashbuckler *must* be fun—a kind of comedy character in costume—and that the audience must feel that, underneath, he is totally wise to himself.

All eight Fairbanks silent swashbucklers have in common excellent production values, exciting action, large doses of good-natured comedy, a dash of satire, and at the center, Douglas Fairbanks, who had already created his persona and was now about to create a genre. Before he became a movie star, Fairbanks spent more than fourteen years as a stage actor, and his theatrical instincts were strong. He knew how to make an entrance in the dramatic traditions of the stage. *The Mark of Zorro,* the first of the swashbucklers, opens inside a busy tavern on a rainy night. The patrons are discussing the dreaded Zorro, who has carved his trademark *Z* on the cheek of one of the hapless drinkers. Suddenly, the door swings open, revealing the darkness and the pounding rain outside. Out of the inky blackness, stepping slowly inside, comes a pair of boots protected from above by a gigantic black umbrella, slick with rain and shiny from the lights reflecting off it. All action stops. The audience watches intently: an umbrella and a pair of boots. When the umbrella is

The disguised fop . . .

slowly, slowly lowered, we do not see the dashing Zorro, with his cape and sword, but instead his alter ego, the foppish Don Diego. It is very effective filmmaking, delivering the unexpected, but it also could have taken place on the proscenium-arch stage.

Zorro took the audience by storm. Everyone loved it, and critics raved. "Here is romance and into the bargain a commercial film," said Variety, adding that "Douglas Fairbanks is once more the Doug that crowds love." The New York Times added, "There's no fault to find." (However, in true critical tradition, the reviewer did find fault, pointing out that whereas the comedy films were lean and mean, Zorro's action was slower to incorporate the more complex plot, the romance, and the beautiful scenery. It was also pointed out that the action was "tamer" because there were no mountain slides or floods.) The Mark of Zorro presented an extravagant Fairbanks, a larger-than-life figure, in keeping with the status he now occupied as a superstar. There were races, pursuits, entrances and exits, disappearances and reappearances, splendid quick changes, marvelous dueling scenes, and a fully developed romantic love story, pairing him once more with the beautiful Marguerite De La Motte. If The Mark of Zorro seemed tailor-made for Fairbanks, it was. Not only was it a United Artists/Douglas Fairbanks production, with him in total control of all aspects of production, but he wrote the script under his pseudonym, Elton Thomas. (Fairbanks had written scripts throughout his career, and

. . . and the masked
hero of *The Mark of
Zorro,* with
Marguerite De La
Motte and Robert
McKim

all his adventure films, except *Don Q,* would be written by him. Elton Thomas
was part of his real name, as he had been born Douglas Elton Thomas Ulman.)

Off-screen, 1920 was the year Fairbanks married one of the few stars
whose fame was even greater than his own—Mary Pickford. They were wed
quietly on March 28, 1920, and it was probably the last moment of quiet they
ever had except when they could hide out together in Pickfair. Fairbanks and
Pickford were American royalty. By 1919, he had become the nation's number
one male box office attraction, and she was even bigger—the absolute number
one of all stars, male or female. Their wedding—the marriage of two superstars—remains unprecedented in film history. (Tony Curtis and Janet Leigh
were stars, but not nearly the equivalent of Fairbanks and Pickford, and that
is also true of Bruce Willis and Demi Moore. Elizabeth Taylor was a superstar,
but Burton wasn't one when they wed, and never became one.) It is hard to
imagine today what such a wedding meant to the media of 1920. Stardom was
new to the world, celebrity was still an emerging concept. (When William S.
Hart visited a camp of German prisoners of war and they called out his name,
he was astonished . . . and more than a little upset.) Alistair Cooke assessed
their union by saying, "Douglas Fairbanks and Mary Pickford came to mean
more than a couple of married film stars. They were a living proof of America's
chronic belief in happy endings." At the time of their marriage, both were at
the very top of their popularity and success, and the wealth they accumulated

The fans' couple, "Little Mary" and "Swashbuckling Hero,"
and the couple in real life, suave Doug and chic Mary

in the decade of the 1920s lifted them to the heights. They were the richest,
the most famous, the most talented and successful, and the most physically
beautiful and beloved of their era. Nothing like them had been seen before or
really ever would be again. Their celebrity mattered; it wasn't the fifteen-
minute kind.

After *The Mark of Zorro,* all of the Fairbanks silent movies were swashbucklers. His next was *The Three Musketeers,* and he, of course, played
D'Artagnan. (In 1918, he had succeeded in a comedy called *A Modern Musketeer,* in which he played a young man who dreams of being D'Artagnan. It was
a role that many had thought would be perfect for him.) In September 1921,
the *Variety* review describes how a huge crowd had lined the sidewalks on
both sides of the street outside the theatre for more than an hour in advance,
because both Doug and Mary were to make a personal appearance at the
opening. Unexpectedly, Charlie Chaplin and Jack Dempsey also appeared,
and the mob went wild. The movie tickets, which cost an astonishing two dollars, were being scalped for as high as five, as people pushed and shoved to

The Three Musketeers

get inside. Fairbanks spoke before the film, during the intermission, and at the end—all at the insistence of the audience, who clamored to see him. The review was positive, saying that "Fairbanks and D'Artagnan are a happy combination, the character providing the star with what will probably go down in film lore as his best effort, for Fairbanks is just a modern bust of the mold of the Dumas hero."

It was clear from the success of *Musketeers* and *Zorro* that Douglas Fairbanks had found his perfect niche in portraying the romantic heroes of legend and literature. His next choice for a role was inevitable—the bandit of Sherwood Forest. With *Robin Hood*, in 1922, he moved toward a spectacle on the grandest scale . . . so much so that he almost outsmarted himself. Wilfred Buckland, the art director who created the huge castle set, reported that when Fairbanks first saw it, he was momentarily dismayed: "I can't compete with that!" he cried. But, of course, he could—and did. The sets, the pageantry, the costuming added up to supreme movie grandeur, and the film had an enormous impact. But although everyone agrees that *Robin Hood* is spectacular, it may be the least appreciated of the eight adventure movies. Sometimes Fairbanks looks like a midget, hopping around on the huge sets, and there is a slight odor of Peter Pan. Critics of the day complained of a "slow first part" and declared it "a great production but not a great picture." One critic nailed down the pageantry: "Where once he danced on air, Doug now stands on ceremony." However, *Robin Hood* has a splendid cast and excellent direction (by Allan Dwan), and when the action starts moving in the second half, it takes off. The massive sets—the drawbridge, the castle, the convent, the banquet room—are all stunning, and the costumes, by Mitchell Leisen, are outstanding.

It was Leisen who made the enormous drapery that Fairbanks slid down in his most spectacular stunt in the movie. The drape was seventy feet long, and according to film historian David Chierichetti's book *Mitchell Leisen: Hollywood Director,* "It hung from the top of the set and had to be carefully arranged to conceal the slide in back of it which was really how Doug got down. There was nowhere to buy any cloth that large. Mitch made it out of burlap and painted it himself to look like tapestry." Leisen remarked that "Fairbanks was really . . . fascinated by the period and was very knowledgeable about everything in it. Once he got wound up in a project he couldn't stop."

A way of understanding Fairbanks's appeal is to compare his Robin Hood to Errol Flynn's. In the Fairbanks version, the star is introduced at the beginning of the film at a jousting tournament. He enters the frame dramatically, in the Fairbanks tradition, as a romantic medieval knight. A title card announces "The other contender for the championship—the favorite of King Richard—The Earl of Huntington, Douglas Fairbanks." He moves into the frame wearing the armor of knighthood. His full-face helmet is lowered over his countenance, and over his head a huge white plume is flying. He pauses in the frame for a moment, obviously giving the audience a chance to observe him and think: "It's Fairbanks!" Seen from his waist upward, his gloved hands on his hips, he surveys the scene through his helmet's eyeholes. Suddenly his head begins to twitch, but he cannot reach inside the helmet with his large gauntlets. He pulls the elaborate headdress off, revealing the handsome, mustached face of Douglas Fairbanks; he then looks at his own reflection in the shiny armor of the cuffed gloves he wears, rubs his mustache, and laughs. It is a perfect blend of stagy drama, romantic costuming, and low-level physical humor. A storybook knight with an itch!

The Fairbanks *Robin Hood* stresses spectacle. The story line contains a fully developed Crusades sequence, and the first appearance of Fairbanks as the traditional Robin Hood appears well into the film. It, too, is a dramatic entrance, almost of a second character. In this sequence, his entrance is not announced by a title card but by a swiftly flying arrow that whizzes through the window of Prince John's castle and pins a writ of capture for Robin Hood to the desk on which it is being scribed. At an open high window, Fairbanks is seen leaping onto the ledge, turning, and jumping down out of sight. When everyone in King John's large hall turns to look, he is gone. Outside, a hand is shown, shaking a large vine to test its strength. Suddenly Robin Hood swings across the frame, and up onto the window ledge again. "Robin Hood!" cries out a servant, and he is seen laughing, dressed in the traditional garb associated with the character, carrying his bow and arrow and casually eating an apple. A marvelous action sequence follows in which Robin Hood romps through the king's castle, leaping up and down, running up and down, and descending from a high parapet to the floor below via that famous and unbelievably long drapery. It is a passage of humor, robust athleticism, and dangerous action, and it gathers speed as it goes.

Errol Flynn's *The Adventures of Robin Hood* (1938) is enhanced by glorious color, natural settings, and one of movie history's best musical scores, by Erich Wolfgang Korngold. Flynn's entrance is somewhat simpler. He is seen riding with Will Scarlet, moving into frame for the typical star close-up of the time. In the sequence that follows, he rides to the rescue of an ordinary Saxon who is being persecuted for having killed one of the king's deer to feed his family. Flynn is already dressed as the genre's typical Robin Hood, and this film contains no pageantry of knighthood or Crusades scenes. It's as if everyone had watched the Fairbanks version and said, "Bag the knights. Keep the forest." However, the action is all in the tradition of the Fairbanks mode: Flynn jumps up on tables, climbs up vines outside the castle, swings across the frame and poses atop a tree trunk. He does acrobatics and employs props in the same imaginative way Fairbanks does. He's called "impudent" and "a bold rascal"—typical Fairbanks phrases. He puts his hands on his hips, smiles broadly, and brings humor and his own robust athleticism to the part. Flynn's Robin is certainly as handsome as Fairbanks's, and he wears a similar wig and an identical mustache.

Just as the Fairbanks influence on the costuming and makeup of the character is clearly felt, the Fairbanks influence on the acting style is there, too. Errol Flynn is himself a master of this type of role, and he is a big star in his own right. In no way does the shadow of Douglas Fairbanks diminish him; rather, he pays homage to it, showing how much Fairbanks has influenced the concept. The latter-day Robin Hood has shed the more old-fashioned, stilted aspect of the earlier film, and concentrated on the cheeky aspects of the character. The addition of sound allows for dialogue that modernizes the character, defusing anything out-of-date with snappy repartee. Furthermore, the addition to the story of a strong social conscience—much emphasis on the starving peasants—moves the story into the 1930s.

One of the most important aspects of the silent cinema is spectacle, and no film of Fairbanks's presented a greater spectacle than *The Thief of Bagdad*, his magnum opus of 1924. Having dazzled audiences with his enormous sets

Fairbanks's mastery of spectacle: the huge castle set of *Robin Hood* (OPPO-SITE) and the flying carpet of *The Thief of Bagdad* (with Julanne Johnston)

for *Robin Hood,* he chose to outdo himself for his Arabian Nights movie. Working with William Cameron Menzies, Fairbanks oversaw the construction of a city with domes and minarets, a palace of enormous size, and tiny streets with archways, bridges, stairways, and passageways to nowhere that seem to rise up, up, and away into the very heavens themselves. It was a dream city out of a fairy tale, and was specifically designed to give the impression that it was floating over its own streets, a weightless universe of the imagination. The final touch was the Adventures of the Seven Moons sequence, in which trick photography and animation were put to ingenious use.

"Our hero," Fairbanks was quoted as saying, "must be every young man of this age and any age who believes that happiness is a quantity that can be stolen, who is selfish, at odds with the world and rebellious toward conventions on which comfortable human relations are based." And so Aladdin, the hero, becomes the kind of happy-go-lucky rogue that Fairbanks was so adept at embodying, a handsome young man who dares to dream and to fight for the hand of the fair caliph's daughter even though he is not much more than a common thief. After he wins his fair maiden, they disappear into the heavens and the stars spell out a beautiful title that reads, "Happiness Must be Earned." The movie—superbly directed by Raoul Walsh, and costarring Fairbanks with the lovely Julanne Johnston as the princess, Anna May Wong as the princess's slave, and Snitz Edwards as his faithful companion—is a masterpiece of romantic fantasy, possibly the greatest Arabian Nights movie ever made (although the 1940 Technicolor remake, also called *The Thief of Bagdad,* and directed by Michael Powell, is a great movie as well).

On the one hand, *The Thief of Bagdad* is a movie you want to have seen as a kid, when its wonderful special effects can work their best magic. On the other hand, its magnificent design, its sophisticated sense of Arabian Nights fantasies, and its tongue-in-cheek star may best be appreciated by adults. In other words, it's a film for all ages and for all decades. It's a feast for the eyes, a humor-filled adventure story, and a great star vehicle.

The Thief of Bagdad opens on an extended action sequence featuring Fairbanks. Bare-chested, wearing gold hoop earrings and decorative pantaloons and sporting a handsome silver crescent-and-star design on his arm, Fairbanks looks tanned, muscular, and fit as a fiddle. He begins as if he's asleep in the Bagdad city square, using the ruse to deftly pick the pockets of unwary citizens who stop to drink from the fountain he rests above. As they bend down to drink, he lightly lifts their money purses, then starts to move about, pantomiming in a broad and exaggerated style that is not just about silent film but about fantasy. Fairbanks is a beautiful man with a beautiful body, and he also exudes an amazing life force. Everything he does is fluid and graceful, and as he discovers a magic rope that can be thrown up into the air and climbed, he easily pilfers it, moving on to such activities as rolling under a wealthy woman's carriage and hanging there until her hand, adorned with rings, droops down out of the vehicle. He then cleverly removes one of her rings and easily rolls off and away again. There's always a new, somewhat comical piece of dashing action. He twirls about, flashes his grin, and lifts his arms joyously—it's a magnificent dance of pantomimed action, almost a musical number or a brief ballet. At this point in his career he is forty-one years old, yet he looks youthful and performs energetically. There is no need for the audience to suspend disbelief as they watch an "older" star pretending to be young. Doug *is* young, boisterously so.

The scale of the objects gives the movie an impressive look—gigantic drums, huge oil jars, tall stairways, and high windows. Everything is enormous, with walls that dwarf Fairbanks, though he can still leap over them or climb them with the aid of his magic rope. Everything in the film is visually sumptuous yet modern in its stark settings, which emphasize interiors of great luxury set inside beautiful white spaces. The parade of thrilling effects is endless—from the wonderful processions of merchants and princes bearing gifts to the grand moment when Fairbanks becomes "invisible" inside a small triangle of movement. It's all fresh and funny and stunningly beautiful.

Science and Invention magazine of May 1924 carried a two-page layout on "The Mechanical Marvels of 'The Thief of Bagdad,'" pointing out how effective Fairbanks is in creating an illusion that takes away from the audience the easy explanation of the effect. For instance, the film presents "the magic rope" that miraculously rises into the air where it hangs suspended so Doug can climb up it. There is no support visible to the naked eye. The viewer immediately decides there's a wire at the top of the rope that can't be seen. Knowing this, Doug has his character hang on the rope and bend the top of it over, effectively demonstrating that there's no wire attached. Of course, there really *is* a wire, and a property man to pull up the rope, and a clever use of photography to conceal what is manipulating the rope from above.

Thief of Bagdad also contains a "flying carpet"—on a wooden frame supported by steel piano wires—which was photographed against a black background so the film could be reexposed to show clouds painted on a rolling canvas fly by. To complete the effect, a large fan blew the fringe on the carpet edge to give a sense of motion. There is also "the cloak of invisibility," "the flying horse," a "magic chest," and a highly effective monster. All these superb effects make the story magical, and they rely on the most innovative techniques, such as the use of black backgrounds, stop-motion photography, glass paintings, treadmills, wind machines, and double exposures. When you went to a Fairbanks film, you got your money's worth. And as the years went by, he increased the ante, never settling for what he had done before but always pushing to create a greater illusion and a more entertaining film.

In *Don Q, Son of Zorro* (1925), Fairbanks dares to do the Valentino tango. It's interesting to compare the two superstars and their versions of the Argentine dance, which is seldom seen anywhere outside a movie theatre. As Don Q, Fairbanks goes out on the town in Old Spain with some pals, visiting a dive, where they encounter a lovely woman dancing alone. Fairbanks joins her, and they tango wildly, energetically, and his tango is very, very good. He is extremely graceful, and has his entire body totally under masterful physical control, one of the primary requisites for the tango. But where Valentino's dance is sexy and clearly focused on seducing the woman, Fairbanks's is really not sexy at all. If it *is* sex, it's that of two sixth graders whose idea of it is knocking each other around, each one more focused on self than on the other. Fairbanks's interest in the woman barely exists. Where Valentino drew his woman closer and closer, bending her backward, looking deep into her eyes, pressing his body into hers, Fairbanks eventually ditches *his* woman to jump up on the table several times to do a solo set of masculine kicks and spins and jumps. The woman is a prop, not an object for seduction. Valentino's dance is clearly only a prelude to a later, more satisfying physical action. In fact, both tangos are a prelude to a later physical action, but with Valentino, the postlude is never shown, only implied, as the point is to let the women in the audience (and/or the men) imagine it for themselves, later when they are at home, with themselves playing the partner. For Fairbanks, the dance is an introduction to an extended and highly imaginative action scene which becomes the on-screen release or postlude. He has to fight his way out of the bodega after the villain locks him in. The ingenious way he escapes—swinging on chandeliers, leaping through windows, tumbling out doorways, and dueling his head off—is a perfect release.

Son of Zorro is one of the best of the Fairbanks swashbucklers. It's funny, lively, and exciting—full of satisfying title cards that say things like "For two pins, I would twist your nose!" The love interest is the exquisitely beautiful young Mary Astor, and two excellent character actors provide support: Jean Hersholt as a secondary villain, and Donald Crisp (who also directed) as the primary villain, Don Sebastian. Fairbanks's sister-in-law, Lottie Pickford Forrest, plays Don Q's servant girl, Lola, and Warner Oland plays the archduke. "It is Fairbanks as the public wants Fairbanks" and "designed for the Fairbanks fan," said *Variety*.

Fairbanks handles the whip, Don Q's main prop and weapon, with great aplomb, even flicking it into a burning fireplace to pluck a tiny spark with which to light his cigar. The action scenes, especially those involving the escape from the bodega and the capture of a mad bull, are extremely well presented. When Fairbanks is accused of murdering the archduke at the queen's ball, he leaps up onto the sill of an open window, shouts, "My father always said, 'When life plays you a trick, make it a trick for a trick,' " and pretends to stab himself to death, falling backward out of the large window, which is located high, high above a dangerously rushing river. (Of course, he lives.)

Fairbanks as Don Q has his hideout in the ruins of an old castle, complete with trapdoor, and all the settings are carefully designed and beautifully photographed. One of the high points of the movie is a scene that returns the audience to Old California so they can see the original Zorro, now an old man. He remembers how he threw his sword up into the ceiling "until he would need it again." The movie then flashes back to a scene from the original movie, *The Mark of Zorro*, to show this happening. Upon returning to the present, the movie shows the old man pulling down the sword and going to help his son. As the two Zorros—and the two Fairbankses—fight side by side, with the father carving a *Z* on the cheek of the villain, it's a great moment of a kind that comes along all too seldom: one in which the romance of an old movie is evoked to enhance another movie in which the same actor is still alive and kicking and on top of his form. (In 1926, Valentino would do a similar turn in *The Son of the Sheik,* playing both the title character and his father—the original from *The Sheik*—with a scene from the earlier movie included.)

By the time of *The Black Pirate* in 1926, the world was eagerly awaiting the next Fairbanks adventure. The ads screamed out the news, "Only Douglas Fairbanks could make such a picture . . . in glorious natural colors (Technicolor Photography)." Illustrated with beautiful photographs and drawings, the copy referred to "the rollicking zest of Doug himself!" and added, "Here is a film that will fill your lungs with the adventurous air of Pirate Days." And, in fact, *The Black Pirate* went all out, and it is a particular favorite of many of Fairbanks's loyal fans. Perhaps the most common image people have of Douglas Fairbanks today is his character from *The Black Pirate.* It is an especially dashing Fairbanks, with a head of thick, black, curly hair, an earring, short pants, a torn shirt, and seven-league boots turned over at the top into cuffs— all, of course, in darkest black. He is first seen standing on a ship's rail, fists on hips and throwing back his head to give a hearty laugh that allows him to flash his beautiful teeth.

The Black Pirate is greatly enhanced by its beautiful Technicolor photography (which *Variety* complained about, saying it's good the running time is short "so that the eye strain doesn't become too trying"). It has what reviews called "a corking underwater effect," in which pirates sneak up on a ship. The underwater photography sequences were spectacular in their day, and are still highly effective. Fairbanks looks terrific in *The Black Pirate,* but he is beginning to pose more than perform, and a highly romantic, exaggerated style of acting is beginning to dominate his work. Where once he was natural and his hands-on-hips, big-grin routine looked fun and cocky, it all begins to seem like posturing. Yet he is still his old amazing self, especially when he executes a grand stunt in which he slides down a ship's sail. He mounts to the cross- arms of the ship, pierces the white sail with his sharp sword, grabs the hilt, and plummets to the deck, the force of the descent tempered by the sword's ripping of the canvas as he moves downward. (It's not unlike his slide down the curtain in *Robin Hood* but is even more spectacular.) This effect is so good it's repeated, and when the smiling and dashing image of the handsome Fair- banks performs it, it becomes not just spectacular but utterly memorable.

The Black Pirate was a huge hit, receiving both critical raves and box office patronage. *Variety* asked a good question, after complaining that the story was little more than an excuse for the action, as to why, if he wanted to make a pirate story, he didn't use *Captain Blood,* the famous novel by Rafael Sabatini? That pirate story, said *Variety,* "was a Fairbanks set up if there ever was one." (The young Errol Flynn would make his first big hit as the hero of *Captain Blood* in 1935.)

The Black Pirate,
with Billie Dove

The Gaucho (1927) is the film that fans like least of the Fairbanks swashbucklers. This is no doubt due to a maudlin religious motif that crowds in on the action, and from time to time the action is stretched to a point that's almost self-satirizing, as when an actual house is moved forward off its base by a string of a hundred horses—an elaborate plot setup that is barely worth it. *The Gaucho* opens with "a miracle" involving a small girl falling into a canyon. Her life is saved by the Virgin Mary, who appears in a vision and brings her back to life.* After this sequence, as *Variety* reported, "Doug Fairbanks is at it again." He is indeed "at it again" with the usual acrobatics and spectacular scenes, including one in which cattle are stampeded, a real pip. Doug does his usual hop-skip-and-a-jump stuff, looking tanned and fit and very self-confident about what he is up to. The word "dashing" was invented for Fairbanks. In *The Gaucho* he dashes here, he dashes there, and he manages to turn the entire world of the movie into a kind of gymnasium for his stunts. What is different about *The Gaucho* is the leading lady. No longer a pure virgin, a damsel in distress who needs rescuing (there is one of those, but she's not the Fairbanks love interest), this "mountain girl" is played by the fiery Lupe Velez. Her character is a definite departure for a female role in a

---

*In a cameo, Mary Pickford, backed up by a penny sparkler to provide a suitable halo, plays the Virgin Mary.

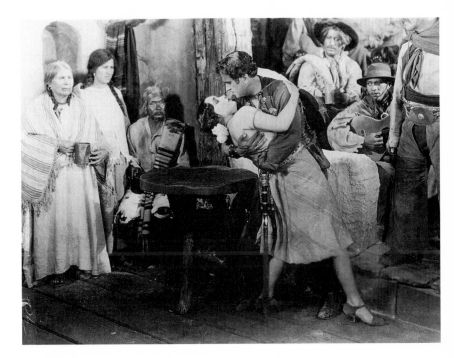

The Gaucho, with
Lupe Velez

Fairbanks movie—she plays a true hero. After betraying Fairbanks because
she thinks he is leaving her for another woman (the grown-up "miracle" girl,
who is actually busily helping him cure himself of leprosy by teaching him to
pray—you can see why this movie is no one's favorite), she rides to save him by
alerting his band of men. She then beats up on his chief enemy, jumping him
from a rock above, punching him repeatedly, pounding him into the ground,
and winning the fight. Velez acts with her elbows, the apparent source of all
her emotional response, but she looks fabulous—radiant with sexual tension
and lush in her appeal. She acts out a female role that is a feminine version of
Douglas Fairbanks, as she leaps around, matching him dido for dido. They
also play out a sort of Petruchio/Kate match at a banquet, arguing, shoving,
and bonking each other like a madcap variation on the Liz Taylor/Dick Burton
version of *The Taming of the Shrew.* (Velez earned excellent reviews, such as
"This baby goes over . . . She scores 100% plus . . . a beauty . . . a great sense
of comedy value to go with her athletic prowess.")

The last Fairbanks epic adventure was *The Iron Mask* (1929), directed
by Allan Dwan, who was quoted years later as saying, "Doug seemed to be
under some sort of compulsion to make this picture one of his best productions. He has always meticulously supervised every detail of his pictures, but
in this one I think he eclipsed himself. It was as if he knew this was his swan
song." There were two reasons why Fairbanks might, indeed, have known *The*

Fairbanks's silent farewell, *The Iron Mask*

Iron Mask would be his silent-film-hero swan song: first of all, he was forty-six years old when he made it, and secondly, sound had taken over the industry. Whatever he may have felt, Fairbanks gave *The Iron Mask* everything he had. Once again, he wrote the story under his pseudonym, Elton Thomas, creating the screenplay out of two of Dumas's novels, *The Three Musketeers* and *The Man in the Iron Mask*. And he assembled a wonderful cast, with Belle Bennett as the queen mother, the lovely Marguerite De La Motte as Constance, Rolfe Sedan as Louis XIII, and himself, of course, as D'Artagnan.

Fairbanks very much treated the movie as a sequel to the 1921 *Three Musketeers*. Critics loved it, saying, "photography and titling top grade," "enjoyable screen material," "a lilt and verve to his D'Artagnan," and "a role which fits [him] like a glove." The movie was advertised with the announcement that the star would TALK, although it didn't say how much. Fairbanks's voice was heard only in a minute and a half of prologues for the first and second halves of the picture. There was no dialogue at all in direct action, but the movie had a great many sound effects and a suitable score especially composed by Dr. Hugo Riesenfeld.

The Iron Mask has a great deal to recommend it. In particular, the early love scene between Constance and D'Artagnan is excellent. Constance is leaving to go to the palace, and D'Artagnan tries to find a private place in which to kiss her. He leaps gracefully upon a wall, swinging her effortlessly up by one arm, continuing the action over the wall as he leaps down with her to the other side. They then run here, run there, but everywhere they go they are spotted. Finally, in a hidden garden, they believe themselves to be alone at last, only to look up and see a washerwoman grinning down at them from the wall above. However, she turns out to be a helpful ally, dropping her wicker wash basket to cover their heads so they may kiss inside it. The audience can see only De La Motte's little hand moving to embrace Fairbanks . . . until they finally stagger back out from under with De La Motte wiping her brow. It's a charming scene, well handled by both players, who strike the right note of playful fun, innocence, and sex to make it interesting.

Perhaps the most famous example of Fairbanks's theatrical flair is *The Iron Mask*'s finale. Seen today, it feels like an epitaph for his career. Fairbanks, playing a now-aged D'Artagnan, has returned to save the good king from his iron mask by mortally wounding the bad king. As everyone celebrates, he walks outside alone, reaching upward toward the open sky. The image of his three dead musketeer companions is superimposed above him, beckoning him to come up and join them. As he once again leaps "up," the four of them are seen again as young, vigorous, and happy. It's one of the last hurrahs of silent action and certainly the last great hurrah of Douglas Fairbanks. "Only think! And we live again!" they cry out to viewers. It can't help but tug at a movie-lover's heart.

THERE IS SOMETHING grand, something majestic, in these Fairbanks romantic costume films. They are beyond. They go to exotic locales, dress people in fantastical costumes, make everything bigger. Where a grand stairway leading from the city plaza up into the cathedral might logically be two flights of stairs, it becomes four. Where a tall ceiling might be twelve feet, it is built at twenty-four feet. Where a hero running up the trunk of a palm tree would be impressive at twenty feet, Fairbanks runs forty feet. Bigger. Grander. Beyond. And the acting styles have to match or the actors would be dwarfed. A Fairbanks picture is partly about size, which is partly about abundance, which is partly about excess, which is partly about America.

The tragedy, if there is one in a career that is such a huge success, is that time ran out. Not only did sound render the Fairbanks type of romantic adventure temporarily old-fashioned, but he himself aged past the point at which such roles felt right for him. The wonderful illusions he presented, and the escapist world of pirates and thieves and swashbucklers, passed over into the world of tough-talking gangsters, a new kind of western hero, and a more disillusioned audience.

After *The Iron Mask*, things came unglued. It was not that Fairbanks lost his money or his reputation or even his status as a beloved star. But things

Fairbanks and
Pickford in their
only screen pairing,
*The Taming of the
Shrew*

came to an end. (His storybook marriage to Mary Pickford was over in 1936, his career dead two years earlier.) His sound debut was swiftly made in 1929, following *The Iron Mask,* and it was an appearance costarring with Pickford in *The Taming of the Shrew.* His years as a stage actor prepared him for sound, and he had a good voice and could handle dialogue. But somehow the new medium wasn't right for him, and he made only four more movies. In 1931 there was *Reaching for the Moon* (a modern romantic comedy with music) and *Around the World in 80 Minutes,* a comedy travelogue. In 1932 he made only *Mr. Robinson Crusoe,* a romantic comedy melodrama, and in 1934 he made his final screen appearance in the kind of feature his audiences loved, *The Private Life of Don Juan,* a costume drama about a man who falls in love with his own wife. Unfortunately, the title was a bit too prophetic—rumors of dalliances emerged and after he and Pickford divorced, he married Lady Sylvia Ashley, whom he had met while filming his final movie in London.

Fairbanks's career ended in 1934, but not his influence on other actors. His is the dominant image of the masculine fantasy adventure hero, and actors like Errol Flynn, Burt Lancaster, and Gene Kelly—not to mention his own son, Douglas Fairbanks, Jr., in movies like *Sinbad the Sailor*—all borrowed from the Fairbanks image. Each of them had his own particular persona, yet each of them was young during Doug's heyday, and each at some time in an interview acknowledged his affection for the films of Douglas Fairbanks.

More than twenty years after *The Black Pirate,* Kelly impersonated a notorious pirate named Mack the Black in *The Pirate* (1948). In a fantasy ballet sequence (imagined by Judy Garland), he dances a number dressed in earring, head scarf, and short, torn pants, whirling and leaping and jumping like Fairbanks, after entering the action by sliding down a long rope. Kelly could easily appropriate the image of Fairbanks, since he was committing his impersonation (or homage) in a musical dance number, which didn't require narrative credibility or modernity.

Lancaster, four years after Kelly, presented *his* pirate, satirically called "crimson" rather than "black." The film opens with a precredit sequence in which a bare-chested Lancaster swings dramatically across a ship's deck from sail top to sail top. He addresses the viewer directly, "Gather round, lads and lassies, gather round . . . You've been shanghaied aboard for the last cruise of

Fairbanks adrift in 1930s art deco: *Reaching for the Moon,* with Bebe Daniels

The Fairbanks influence: Errol Flynn in 1938's *The Adventures of Robin Hood*
and Burt Lancaster in 1952's *The Crimson Pirate*

the Crimson Pirate . . . Ask no questions. Believe only what you see." After
flashing a big-toothed grin, he swings back to the first sail top (actually a
reverse of the first shot). "No," he grins. "Believe HALF of what you see." The
film that follows, a joyous romp in the Fairbanks tradition, clearly borrows
both plot and character devices from *The Black Pirate*. Lancaster decks himself out in a thick head of hair (although blonde and his own), an earring, and
costumes that display his muscled chest. There can be no doubt about what
inspired *The Crimson Pirate*.

Nearly sixty years after his death, Fairbanks is still the perfect model for
boyish male action in which the hero takes a somewhat tongue-in-cheek
approach to himself and the story. He is not old-fashioned, because his comedy skills draw the seriousness out of the material, telling a modern audience
that it's okay to be amused. With Fairbanks, it was always the action that mat-

tered, not the killing. He fought by a code, and only for the joy of it, and only when forced into it by bad guys. His was a clean, larking sort of action.

Fairbanks was not given to serious public self-examination, yet there is every indication that he understood clearly who and what he was on-screen. In his book about Fairbanks (*His Picture in the Papers*), Richard Schickel evaluated him perfectly: "There is absolutely no evidence that as an actor—or, to risk a pretentious term, an artist—Douglas Fairbanks conceived of himself as anything more than a fabulist and fantasist. And the idea that he might have held a mirror up to life probably would have appalled him. What he did was hold a mirror up to himself—to endlessly boyish Doug—and invite his audience to join him in pleased contemplation of the image he found there, an image that very accurately reflected the shallow, callow charming man who lived by the simplest of American codes, and eventually died by it."

When Fairbanks died, on December 12, 1939, he was only fifty-six years old. The silent film era, of whose royal family he was indisputably a member, had been gone little more than a decade. It might as well have been gone a hundred years. In 1938, Errol Flynn starred in *The Adventures of Robin Hood*, and few reviews mentioned the Fairbanks version. Clark Gable was the king where women were concerned, and most of Fairbanks's contemporaries were either retired or dead. When notified of his passing, Mary Pickford rose to the occasion and gave a statement to the press. "He passed from our mortal life quickly and spontaneously as he did everything in life, but it is impossible to believe that vibrant and gay spirit could ever perish." She spoke in words appropriate to a silent film title card, and even more significantly, she spoke of his image rather than of his person. It was Pickford who had always understood their stardom and what defined it: business. She closed his door with dignity, but with an appropriate commercial understanding. In this sense she was his true widow, both of the man and of his image.

All through his career, Fairbanks excited commentators to an almost purple evaluation of his assets. Booth Tarkington, for instance, went all out in describing him, but underneath the gush there was a solid understanding of Fairbanks's appeal: "I don't know his age. I think he hasn't any. Certainly he will never be older—unless quicksilver can get old." Thanks to what we fondly like to call "the magic of the motion picture," Douglas Fairbanks never *will* be any older, and no other star ever earned the right to remain magically young as truly as he did.

SISTERS
The Talmadges,
Norma and Constance

SISTERS WHO BECAME STARS were a phenomenon of the silent era.* Granted, we have Joely and Natasha Richardson or Michelle and Dedee Pfeiffer today, and there were Catherine Deneuve and Françoise Dorleac in the 1970s and those two famous feuding siblings, Olivia de Havilland and Joan Fontaine, of the 1940s and 1950s, Constance and Joan Bennett in the 1930s and 1940s, the Lanes, the Blondells, the Wilde twins, Marisa Pavan and Pier Angeli, the Redgraves, and Juliet and Hayley Mills, all topped by the Gabors, Eva, Zsa Zsa, Magda, and their unstoppable mother, Jolie. Still, there has never been an era for sister acts like the 1920s. Mary Pickford's Lottie had a minor career (as did their brother, Jack), and sisters Shirley Mason and Viola Dana were both solid successes. The spectacularly beautiful Young daughters—Gretchen (who became Loretta), Sally (Blane), and Polly Ann—began in silents, and, of course, the remarkable Lillian and Dorothy Gish as well as Jane and Eva Novak, Mae and Marguerite Marsh, Katherine MacDonald and Mary MacLaren, Mary Miles Minter and Margaret Shelby, Marceline and Alice Day, Priscilla and Marjorie Bonner, Sally O'Neil and Molly O'Day, Dolores and Helene Costello, and Constance and Faire Binney. But of all the sister acts of those years, none was bigger or better known—and none fell faster with the coming of sound—than the celebrated Talmadges, Norma and Constance.

In many ways, the story of the Talmadge sisters is the definitive silent film show business story: deserted by their father, driven by their mother, supported by a strategic marriage, raised to immense success in a new medium that made them household names, and then wiped out by sound. Their story illustrates an aspect of stardom that people tend to forget: in the early years, it

*It was also an era of famous brothers: Dustin and William Farnum; Owen, Tom, and Matt Moore; George and Raoul Walsh; and, of course, the famous Barrymores, Lionel and John.

was a way out of poverty for women who had been abandoned by men, a way to make a living, because it was a new business with no gender bias. Most of the young girls who became stars—Pickford, Swanson, Negri—had a voracity for success that never really left them, but the Talmadges were different. They worked hard and did what was expected of them, but in the end, when fame abandoned them, they seemed to walk away with a "who cares?" attitude. Of course, they walked away wearing silk and fur, and that *did* make a difference. Norma and Constance Talmadge are forgotten today, as hardly anyone understands how very important they were. Except for *Intolerance,* in which Constance appears, their films are almost never revived. Yet in their day they were both hugely popular; Norma, in particular, was one of the top three or four most famous actresses of the silent era, the epitome of stardom. (A 1924 *Photoplay* contest elected her America's most popular female star.) As Richard Koszarski points out in *An Evening's Entertainment,* "Of all the silent stars whose reputations collapsed with the coming of sound, Norma Talmadge was certainly the most important one." The almost total unavailability of her films (as well as the loss of many to the ravages of nitrate disintegration) renders her more than obscure today. She is practically invisible. To put this in perspective, it is roughly equivalent to eradicating the name of Bette Davis from film history.

In the beginning, there were four Talmadge women: Norma, Constance, their hapless sister, Natalie, and their formidable mother, Peg. Theirs is a tale of how women survived in an unliberated era, and the plot is simple: four women, no man, no money. What to do? The story would naturally open up with the mother, Peg, the gigantic figure who stood behind her girls every step of the way. The very tough and manipulative Margaret Talmadge was the Mother of all Stage Mothers. Where her daughters were slim and beautiful, Mama was a lump of overabundant flesh. The large and luminously expressive eyes of the actress daughters were not matched by Peg's small and, some said, mean little slits. The sisters were always fashionably gowned and impeccably turned out, but Mama was an off-the-rack specialist who couldn't have cared less. The glamour coiffures of the beautiful sisters so copied by women of the audience had no influence on Mama, whose hair looked like a "neglected bird's nest." About her appearance, Mama just didn't seem to give a damn, and the famous beauty of her daughters was, by default, attributed to their father, who had disappeared long before the family arrived in Hollywood. (Peg always referred to him as "that skunk.") She was unsentimental, and having had to take in laundry, rent out rooms, and pinch every penny, she had a right to be bitter and angry. Instead, she kept her humor, and tough and domineering though she was, she held her family together. She had brains and drive and one simple goal: survival. She wanted bread on the table. Life had been tough for her, and it was potentially tough for her girls, but Mama knew they

Constance
and her
mother, the
unsinkable
Peg

had beauty—and they could buy class. (Anita Loos once called the Talmadges "class trash.")

Mama came up with a plan. What she was interested in was financial
security, so she took stock of her assets and found two very beautiful daughters and a not-so-bad-looking one. If worse came to worst, she could marry
them off, but she decided it might be safer to bypass men and put her daughters to work. And what Mama wanted her daughters to do, they did. (As she
herself put it, "I've spent years driving those wild horses to a trough, and I'll
be damned if I don't make the bastards drink!") She knew the family could
survive if they stuck together and used their heads—and their faces.

Norma and Constance, the two beauties of the family, found work in
movies early on and, under Mama's determined tutelage, soon were providing
for the family. Once the girls had a foothold in movies, they started pushing for
Natalie to have small parts, but Natalie had to be written off in the movie star
category; she just didn't have it. Mama Peg realized she would have to pursue
her fallback career tactic for her third daughter—marriage to wealth and success (a ploy she also used as a safety measure for both Norma and Constance,
just in case stardom let them down). The melancholy Buster Keaton was
selected as the bridegroom, or depending on how one sees it, the victim.
Natalie Talmadge became Mrs. Buster Keaton in 1921, and that became her
chief claim to fame, although she did actually star opposite him effectively in
Our Hospitality (1923). After her daughters hit the top, Mama didn't spend all
their money, marry a gigolo, or get drunk every afternoon. She just relaxed,
enjoyed her wealth and leisure, and kept a sharp eye on her brood, their husbands, and their careers, stepping in as she felt it was necessary to keep
everything—and everyone—shaped up. Margaret "Peg" Talmadge is the kind

of woman who is frequently criticized and ridiculed, when in fact she probably should be respected if not admired. However questionable her plan to
exploit her daughters might have been, at least it was a plan. And it worked.
The family *did* stick together. They *did* become rich, with plenty of bread on a
very expensive table. And with the possible exception of the dour Natalie, no
one seemed to suffer from it.

The films of Norma and Constance Talmadge should be required viewing in women's studies courses. Taken together, they present the sum total of
the woman's filmed universe. Norma appeared mostly in stories that touched
on the typical tragedies of the woman's life—bad men, bad luck, and bad marriage—while Constance usually played in movies that provided escape and
the promise of a better deal: good men, good luck, and good marriage. In many
ways, they were filmic opposites: Norma suffered, Constance sparkled. On a
simple level, Constance was a blonde and a comedienne, and Norma was a
brunette and a dramatic actress, although both of them could and did play in
all kinds of movies. And although Norma's fame was bigger than Constance's,
Constance was not a poor second, like Dorothy Gish to Lillian.* Both played
real women, not little girls, not exotic divas, not sex symbols. Sometimes these
women were pretty fantastic—Arab dancing girls, Chinese maidens, aristocratic playgirls—but they were recognizable women. And something else they
had in common was glamour. In tragedy or comedy, both wore superb costumes, plenty of fur, and very good jewels. Their films are guidelines to the
moviegoing tastes of the teens and twenties—to the clothes, to the manners
and mores, and to the changing attitudes toward what a woman's life was supposed to be or to what women secretly wanted it to be. Each is a symbol of the
fantasized woman the movies sold to the public . . . and each, especially
Norma, helped shape the concept of the woman's film. Except for *Intolerance,*
and possibly Norma's Frank Borzage movies, neither sister ever appeared in a
truly outstanding motion picture, and the fact that neither of them can be considered part of the "art" of the motion picture makes them all the more important to an understanding of the culture, the audience, and the social values of
their time.

Today, it is difficult to understand why Norma was the bigger star,
because Constance plays a type of character that points ahead to the 1930s,
whereas Norma usually plays the kind of woman associated with the silent era.
Constance prefigures Carole Lombard—blonde, sophisticated, well dressed, a
pretty comedienne with a slightly screwball touch. Norma's type of character
was a dead end, because the thirties made her brave heroines who rose from

---

*The Talmadges were more like de Havilland and Fontaine. De Havilland's career outlasted
her sister's, and she won two Oscars instead of one, but Fontaine was definitely a star of the first
rank herself, and both women were respected actresses as well as movie stars.

rags to riches look too sentimental, too satisfied with just achieving wealth as a goal. (The Depression movie tended to suggest that being poor was really to be rich.) Norma and Constance Talmadge are like two bookends facing in opposite directions, but they were never rivals. They never feuded like de Havilland and Fontaine, and they were always supportive of each other, remaining best friends until they died. They were sisters who happily divided up territory—"you take drama, I'll take comedy"—living out a movie plot in real life in which the older, more beautiful sister looks after her madcap younger sibling partly by marrying a man who could take care of both their careers.

NORMA'S CAREER

Norma Talmadge is the proof of the basic fact about stardom: clearly in her case, you had to be there. That, however, is the main point: the immediacy of the appeal of great stars, the connection they make to the viewing audience of the day, is what defines their success. Since you can't reconstruct the audience of the time, and since you can't reconstitute yourself into a 1920s person, you can only view the work and speculate. What is clear is that Norma's image and performance style seem dated. She looks neither embarrassing nor ridiculous today, but she seems rather passive and quite dull. She's very attractive, but not strikingly beautiful like Greta Garbo or Dolores Costello. She isn't touchingly appealing like Lillian Gish, or timelessly modern like Louise Brooks, or knockabout funny like Mabel Normand, or weirdly representative of the styles of her era like Gloria Swanson. She isn't a subtle actress of both comedy and drama like Mary Pickford, although she performs both with competence. Her type of physical beauty is of its era—slightly plumpish, round-faced, and with a nose untouched by surgery. (A nose like that wouldn't last past eighth grade in a would-be actress today.) Her eyes are her best feature, large and lovely. She is able to depict emotions in the traditional silent film acting mode, and she wears clothes beautifully. How, then, does she differ from hundreds of other young girls who had good looks, good figures, and solid if not spectacular acting ability? The answer has to do with determination— Norma was her mother's daughter. She was tough herself, and very hardworking. Furthermore, she married one of the most powerful men in the film business, Joseph Schenck, and he guided her career wisely. It was the combination of Norma's natural gifts and willingness, Mama's manipulations, and Schenck's powerful business sense that lifted Norma to the top of the heap.

As a result, Norma Talmadge cannot be denied, but the fact that she was *so much* of her time made her quickly lose popularity. Paul Rotha, writing in *The Film Till Now*, which was originally published in 1930, was already com-

Norma Talmadge's range: from Suffering Woman to Exotic Creature

plaining about her: "All through her career Norma Talmadge achieved success by looking slightly perplexed and fuzzy about her eyes . . . but audiences worshiped her." The latter is key: they *did* worship her. She didn't surpass Mary Pickford in popularity, but she probably came as close as anyone, and she is still remembered fondly by those old enough to have seen her at the time.

Norma Talmadge never developed a single persona, a "role" that audiences thought was actually *her* in private life. Instead, she was considered to be a Great Actress who took on all kinds of roles—a kind of a Meryl Streep of her day. There are two main categories in her "Great Actress" definition: traditional contemporary woman's films in which she is half modern and half old-fashioned, and exotic films in which she impersonates non-Waspy females, such as Arab dancing girls, Asian maidens, Native American princesses, and tropical beauties. (Presumably the former category appealed mostly to women in the audience, and the latter to men.) She often was presented as a transitional figure—a woman forced out on her own who could and did cope but who really wanted and needed love. In other words, on the one hand she was a "new" woman who worked at a real job or was independent in the big, wide world, and on the other hand, she succumbed to the traditional romantic expectations of love and marriage. She had one foot in the 1890s and the other in the 1920s. (Sadly, she never got either one into the 1930s. By the time she retired, she had appeared in more than 250 movies, most of which, after her early years, were what would today be called "weepies." The great stars of a particular era who are associated with "weepies"—Greer Garson in the 1940s, for instance—are rarely appreciated by latter-day moviegoers.)

Norma Talmadge began appearing in movies in about 1910 (when she was barely fourteen years old) as a member of the New York–based Vitagraph Studios. She came to attention in the 1911 version of Dickens's *A Tale of Two Cities,* starring Maurice Costello. (She was "The Girl in the Tumbrel," her dark-eyed beauty and luscious form helping her to stand out in the crowd.) Later in the same year, she was featured in *An Old Man's Love Story,* in which she is very, very pretty, with a thick head of dark hair, a full bosom and slender waist, and a lovely smile. (Perhaps that was all it took in 1911, before stardom was fully defined.) Whereas later in her career she began to look a little like the Pillsbury Dough Girl, here she is slim and attractive and can depict emotion with a direct simplicity. In 1913, she stars in *Father's Hat Band,* a complicated plot involving lovers sending each other notes via a disapproving father's hat band. Norma is charming enough, but the role could have been played by anyone. In 1914, she began to stand out more in *The Helpful Standard,* about the evils of a snobbish sorority. Norma, a poor girl, craves acceptance so desperately that she turns to shoplifting to afford the kind of clothes the girls require for entry into their sacred circle. She shows a little spunk here, and wears smart-looking outfits that suit her well. Later that same year, in *Sawdust and Salome,* she plays a circus performer who marries a man whose family spurns her. ("You have married a woman who has worn tights!" they cry out.) In *John Rance, Gentleman* (1914), *His Official Appointment* (1914), and *The Devil's Needle* (1916), she is just a cog in the overall plot construction. None of these movies is built around her, and none is outstanding. However, she was appearing in a great number of films a year, in stories that appealed to the general audience. She always looked lovely, and always gave a credible performance. Two of her best films from this period that are available for viewing today are *The Social Secretary* and *Fifty-Fifty,* both from 1916. *The Social Secretary* is particularly interesting because it showcases her comedic skills, which would not often be deployed later on. In it, she keeps losing her job as a secretary because she won't sleep with her boss or because some hot Italian count or an old widower from the Purity League (a place she thought she would be safe) makes a pass at her. Finally, in desperation, she answers an ad for a secretary who is "unattractive to men." A society matron is fed up with training girls and then losing them when they decide to marry. Norma disguises herself in the tried-and-true woman's film manner: she puts on glasses and a frumpy dress. After endless plot complications, she foils an evil reporter from the tabloid press (played by Erich von Stroheim), saves the rich family's honor, wins the full respect of the society matron, and captures the son in marriage after being caught with her glasses off. *Variety* described the movie as "a comedy/drama in which Miss Talmadge has a role she can play to perfection, and the feature is one that will hold any audience from start to finish." As always, Norma is highly skilled and competent, but there is no particular sparkle or charm to her presence. What one misses is the presence of blazing charisma.

In *Fifty-Fifty* Norma plays "the Nut," whose profession is china painter and whose nature is hopelessly hoyden. She is given a scene in which she is allowed to imitate a "Popular Dance Artiste" and she dances wildly around, looking much more animated and lively than usual. Soon enough, however, she is married, a mother, and losing her husband to another woman who is "a riddle the highbrows can't solve." (This movie has titles that act as warnings for the women in the audience: "When a man comes home from the brainstorm of work, he wants more than half-hearted caresses" and "When a man catches a streetcar, he stops running.") Norma is half playful and half pathetic in this film. Again, there is no indication of the kind of powerful presence associated with stardom, although her pale, white hands are very expressive, and her gestures, while melodramatic, hold one's attention. In *Going Straight*, also from 1916, there is still no sense of a special quality that could be labeled "Norma Talmadge." Norma looks pretty but undistinctive, and she is once again put to the service of the plot—this one about a couple who used to be criminals but have become refined and now have a family, only to be confronted by their past. The story is the thing, not the star.

In 1916, however, Norma's personal life—and her career—were permanently changed by her marriage to the dynamic Joseph M. Schenck, one of film's authentic pioneers. Schenck fell in love with the velvet-eyed young girl, and his love, her beauty, and her mama's ambition made a fabulous union. Schenck and his brother, Nicholas, had risen up through the ranks to part ownership of a chain of movie houses. (They were Russian immigrants who found their way into the film business via amusement parks.) Determined to become more than just an exhibitor, Schenck wanted to break into the world of actual movie production. In Norma, he saw not only beauty but dollar signs. For her part, Norma probably saw power, strength, a father figure (Schenck was nineteen years older than she was, and she always called him "Daddy"),

Norma in *Ghosts of Yesterday*

career support, and her own dollar signs. Mama Talmadge no doubt saw all of these and even more.

When Norma Talmadge married Joseph Schenck in 1916, he immediately took charge of her career. In 1917 he established a producing company of her own for her (at Mama's suggestion), after her current contract had fortuitously expired. The arrangement for Norma (and later also for Constance) was to release her films through Lewis J. Selznick's successful company, Select Pictures. From that moment onward, starting with *Panthea* in 1917, the first Select release, and the debut of the Norma Talmadge Film Company, Norma's career moved to another level.

Panthea had the distinction of being one of the first movies ever to open simultaneously in two Manhattan theatres: the Rialto and the New York, which were within walking distance of each other. Both houses played to overflow crowds, and Norma's reputation as a box office draw and a fine actress was solidified. Set in Russia, *Panthea* was the story of a woman who sacrifices herself to help her husband get his opera produced, with a dubious happy ending in which the couple are seated by a campfire en route to Siberia, with the husband cheerfully promising his wife that he's sure her release will soon be forthcoming. (He's just going along for the trip; she is the one being exiled.)

Panthea illustrates what Schenck did for Norma Talmadge. In addition to the releasing advantage he secured with the Selznick organization, and the stunning two-theatre opening, he surrounded her with excellent, experienced talent in all departments. She was directed by Allan Dwan, and the settings, costumes, and production details were first-rate. *Variety* said, "If future Talmadge special releases are of equal caliber . . . Miss Talmadge is certain to remain in the front rank of sensational drawing cards." From *Panthea* onward, Norma's releases were treated with importance, and she began moving up to the top ranks, always showcased in woman's stories that also had something for the men (in *Panthea* it was a shipwreck). *Panthea* was Norma's most successful film of 1917, and it is clearly the film that made her a true star.

For the rest of her career, her films would be prestigious in every way, although her next, *The Law of Compensation*, was a routine tearjerker. But the one that followed, *Poppy* (1917), which exists in fragmented form at the Library of Congress, casts her as Eve Destiny, a woman who, in classic woman's film tradition, finds "success—fame—fortune—everything but happiness." She suffers a lot, triumphs a little, and shows off a closetful of wonderful clothes and hats, with several different hairdos and lots of spectacular jewelry along the way. *Poppy* was followed by *The Moth* and *The Secret of the Storm Country*, her last 1917 release.

By the end of 1917, Norma Talmadge, under the shrewd management of her husband, had climbed to the absolute top of motion pictures. Throughout the next three years, she appeared in film after film, in an ongoing run of success. A look at the titles of these films indicates what they were like: *Ghosts of Yesterday, The Forbidden City, By Right of Purchase, Deluxe Annie, The Safety Curtain, Her Only Way*, and *Heart of Wetona* in 1918; *The Probation Wife, Way of a Woman, New Moon*, and *Isle of Conquest* in 1919; and *She Loves and Lies, The Woman Gives, Daughter of Two Worlds, Yes or No?*, and *Branded Woman* in 1920. All were successful with her fans, but not all were successful with critics. Although reviewers always mentioned the extravagant production values, Norma's beauty, and definitely her outfits, they did not always buy into the frequently silly plots and somewhat bizarre casting of Norma in some of them. (For instance, in *Heart of Wetona* she plays a Native American half-caste, who, when told by her proud father that she is to play the virgin at the annual Corn Fest, begins to look pretty concerned, since she knows she no longer has the primary qualification for the part.)

One of her best films in this period is *The Forbidden City*, directed by Sidney Franklin and giving her dual roles in an old-fashioned melodrama. A Madame Butterfly story, introduced by the Kipling quote "East is east . . . ," it is set in China. Norma, a Brooklyn girl, plays San San, "the motherless flower of Wong Li's house." (The titles that represent San San's conversation are especially horrifying: "San San die if love-man go away," and "Oh, Budda, please send love-man here to give me million sweet kisses.") *The Forbidden City* is a lavish production, very beautiful to look at, and Norma gives a fine performance, low-key and understated even though it's hard to respond

The Forbidden City

directly to her work. (In comparison, consider Lillian Gish's performance in
The Wind or *Way Down East* or *Broken Blossoms*. The decades simply fall
away and viewers of all ages start to weep.)

Even so, the film contains a moment of great visual power, in which Talmadge rises to the occasion and shows what she is capable of. San San
secretly marries her American lover, but her father is hoping to restore himself to favor with the emperor by delivering his beautiful daughter to him.
(This means that when her lover returns, he cannot find her, and he goes back
to America without her.) When Norma is summoned to the emperor's throne
room, its large, heavily carved doors open to reveal her standing alone, small
and delicate, protectively wrapped in heavy, embroidered Chinese robes. She
moves forward—tentatively, humbly. Norma moves with grace, and she has
never looked more beautiful. Upon reaching the now-delighted emperor, she
bows low in front of him, her soft and lovely eyes downcast. Slowly she opens
her beautiful robes . . . to reveal the child she has concealed within them. It's
a terrific moment, exquisitely done. She pleads eloquently for the emperor's

mercy, and, smiling, he falsely promises her sanctuary. After having her murdered—a shocking treachery—he allows her child to be raised in the palace,
although a virtual outcast due to her ancestry. ("I American. I need no ances-
tors," is her evaluation of the situation.) After an exciting escape, the grown
daughter (also played by Norma) is reunited with her father and finds her own
American lover to wed. *Variety* says, "Miss Talmadge plays both roles with a
skill and artistry that will enhance her already big reputation as a screen
favorite."

What one sees in a Norma Talmadge performance is professionalism.
She did her job. Although she could shine in something like *The Forbidden
City* as the Asian maiden, her best parts were generally those in which she
played what might be called "the woman's role." In *Way of a Woman,* she is
the daughter of one of the first families of Virginia, but rich and well bred
though she is, she has the usual problem: men. Her family doesn't let her
marry the man she loves—he isn't good enough—so she settles for one with
money because her family needs cash. He then *really* turns out not to be good
enough. At the time, no doubt, Schenck, Norma, and family all believed in
this kind of work, but a review of the plots of those films unavailable for
screening and a look at those that are is a fairly dismal experience. One
reviewer comments that Norma always brings "her pleasing person" into
"such stuff as is provided for her." (That about sums it up.) In *New Moon* she's
a Russian, and in *Isle of Conquest* she gets shipwrecked on a desert island
with only one man for company. He hates women and she hates men, since
both have been involved in bad marriages. (The film is noteworthy only for
being the screen debut of sister Natalie, about whom the *New York Times* cruelly stated that she "does not show what, if any, unusual talents she has.") In
The Woman Gives, it is Norma's job to go into an opium den and drag a friend's
husband out. For this she receives no thanks, one marriage proposal, and the
loss of her own true love, who misunderstands. (Later, things are reconciled,
but one review complained about accuracy, saying that a thug uses the Shakespearean " 'tis" and that a man who has been smoking opium for days "rises
from his couch and beats a Chinaman up . . . a physical impossibility.")

Yes or No?, which I wasn't able to see, is a story constructed out of flashbacks. Norma plays two roles—a rich wife and a poor wife, both of whom feel
they are neglected, and are tempted by other men who promise a better deal.
The rich wife gives in to temptation and gets jilted, while the poor wife soldiers on until her husband invents a washing machine and she gets "everything," setting an example for us all. *Branded Woman* was a blackmail story,
with Norma, the child of a cheap (and naughty) chorus girl and a wealthy man,
having to pay for her mother's sins. In *Daughter of Two Worlds,* she is a poor
girl who goes to school among the rich and suffers wardrobe inadequacy
accordingly, shortly before again winning everything for herself.

Between 1921 and 1926, however, Norma Talmadge made some of her best films, and these were her most fruitful years. Her first release in 1921 was *Passion Flower*, a story of hate between a man and his stepdaughter, which turns out in the end to be an almost insane love. It received outstanding reviews, being called "probably the strongest piece Norma Talmadge has ever appeared in—an artistic achievement . . . atmospheric, romantic, and well directed." In another 1921 film, *The Sign on the Door*, she plays a stenographer who is subjected to unwanted advances by her boss's son, and who has to save her stepdaughter from the same man. In that year, she also undertook one of her few comedies, *The Wonderful Thing*, in which she played—talk about variety—the wealthy daughter of an American hog raiser who marries a titled Englishman, only to learn that it was her money that motivated him.

Nineteen twenty-two would be a banner year. She released three highly successful features, one of which is among the best she ever made. First up was the rather ordinary *Love's Redemption*, in which she played a "waif of Jamaica . . . who mothers all the spiritual cripples that drift her way," but next came a movie that was so popular it was remade twice, in 1932 (with Norma Shearer) and 1941 (with Jeanette MacDonald), always with the same title so fans could recognize it: *Smilin' Through*. Norma, though beautiful, was never ethereal, being too solid and too real-looking for that. But dressed and made up and superbly lit as she is in *Smilin' Through*, she makes a highly romantic image, standing out in the moonlight, tiny blossoms in her hair, bare shoulders reflecting light as she stands quietly wearing a long, shimmering gown. Her dual role is that of Moonyean, a doomed young woman who will be killed at her wedding ceremony, and her counterpart in a later generation, Kathleen, a "cousin" who just happens to look a heck of a lot like her. *Smilin' Through* has proved itself almost foolproof material over the years, and it was an excellent vehicle for Norma, whose fans loved her in it. Some consider it the most popular film of her entire career. *The Eternal Flame* (her final film of 1922) is based on the Balzac novel *The Duchesse de Langeais,* and it costars Norma with Conway Tearle and Adolphe Menjou. Reviews were solid, referring to Norma's "special type of beauty, her eloquent face," but striking an ominous note by conspicuously focusing on her outfits. "Miss Talmadge, as always, exhibits a ravishing assortment of frocks, an important production feature where this star is concerned." (One minute she is decked out in the most opulent Louis XVIII–style gowns, and the next she's suffering away in a convent in elegantly simple all-white nun garb, posed beautifully at the organ.) *The Eternal Flame* is an expensive production, but with very little emotional or dramatic power.

What followed was more of the same: *The Voice from the Minaret, Within the Law, Ashes of Vengeance,* all typical and undistinguished by today's standards, but good box office and popular in their day. A particularly dreadful

In *Secrets*, Norma depicts the woman's life: Pampered Girl . . . Brave Pioneer Wife . . .

movie is *Song of Love* (a late December 1923 release reviewed in 1924)—also known as *Dust of Desire,* but terrible under either title. It is interesting today only because it was codirected by screenwriter Frances Marion. Norma is cast as "Noorma-hal," an Arab dancing girl—of all things—who works in the "gambling den of Chandra Lal." The plot involves the efforts of the locals to sweep the French out of North Africa, and toward this goal Norma is given the job of spying on one of the enemy. ("I will skillfully beguile him.") Instead, she falls in love with him, even though he is Joseph Schildkraut in a striped desert robe and what appear to be white anklets and flats. (He makes a very poor Valentino stand-in.) Norma is all empty posturing and totally external.

However, one of her other 1924 releases, *Secrets,* directed by Frank Borzage, is perhaps her best performance. (Her other Borzage movie, *The Lady,* made in 1925, was also outstanding.) Reviews immediately responded, with *Variety* claiming that the movie showcased Norma in "the greatest role she has ever been seen in on screen." It is one of those stories that actresses of

. . . Stalwart Mother . . . Old Woman

the time would kill for—the chance to be seen in various episodes that allow
her to age from a young girl into a seventy-year-old woman. We see her in
1865, as a young girl eloping with her sweetheart against her family's wishes;
in 1870, as a young wife on the frontier, helping her husband withstand a bandit attack and losing her newborn child; in 1888, as a wealthy matron living in
a robber-baron palace, whose husband has fallen in love with a younger
woman; and in 1923, as an elderly grandmother bravely facing the death of
her devoted husband, who has long since seen the error of his ways. *Variety*
praised Borzage's handling of Norma, saying that "he has taken Miss Talmadge and handled her in a manner that makes her reveal artistry such as she
never displayed heretofore . . . [*Secrets* is going] to be one of the biggest box
office knockouts of the year."

   The print of *Secrets* that I watched had untranslated flash titles, and it
was not complete, yet Borzage's mastery of cinematic technique and Norma's
expressive performance made it completely comprehensible. The audience
first sees her character at the end of her life, and then is returned to her youth.
The transition of the "old" Norma, sitting in a chair with white hair, wrinkles,
and a little lace cap, into a vibrant, beautiful, and happily excited girl is marvelous. For once, an old woman played by a young woman in makeup really
looks like an old woman, so the change is impressive. Norma varies each of
her "lives" of the woman she is playing in small, perfect ways. Her young girl

is really girlish, full of hope and optimism and shy modesty. She plays the scene with an appropriate touch of comedy, as she and her lover climb down the balcony and ride off on a unicycle in the moonlight. (There is one pure Norma episode, in which an extended period of time is spent dressing her for a ball. First her hoop skirts are put in place, then layers of elegant petticoats, then her elaborate overdress, her little nosegay, her handkerchief, her little satin slippers, her hair decoration . . . fans expected to see Norma in all her finery, and they certainly do here. The plot stops dead for this event.)

In the western sequence, Norma is a totally different person, yet not unconnected to the young girl we've seen. She is now brave, stalwart, and resourceful—the logical outgrowth of the girl who dared to defy her family and elope with the man she loves. In the scene in which she discovers her baby is dead by holding a mirror under its nose—and the resulting close-up suffering—Norma is lyrical, and her grief is both moving and believable. In her next sequence, as the matron who now has four children—an ironic note, as the prior sequence closed on the memory of the baby's death haunting her—she is appropriately dignified, well mannered, and knowing. Her parents—now reconciled to her marriage, as her wealth has no doubt brought them around—come to help celebrate her birthday, but she is forced to put on a brave front because she knows that her husband is having an affair. She suffers quietly, almost politely, her expressive eyes filling slowly with tears. Finally, again as the "old" woman, she shows strength and courage once more as she visits her dying husband's sickroom. Watching *Secrets,* we can finally grasp what made Norma Talmadge a star. She is skilled and subtle in this movie, and there are lots of close-ups to show her at her best. Her warm and expressive eyes do much of the acting for her. There was probably not a dry eye in the house for this one.

In *The Lady* (1925), Norma is again given the opportunity to portray a woman in various stages of age and success in life.* First she's a cheap dance hall girl named Polly Pearl who is married above her class to a young man who turns out to be no good. A few years later, he is unfaithful with one of his own kind, and Norma responds in a way suitable to her background—she beats the stuffing out of her rival. He is horrified and says, "You common little trollop! My father was right. I was a fool to marry a little guttersnipe like you." Left on her own, she wanders into Marseilles and collapses outside the establishment of the tough old bird Madame Blanche, where she eventually gives birth to the baby she is carrying. (One of the best scenes in the movie is the

---

The Lady was made with sound in the 1930s under the title *The Secret of Madame Blanche,* starring Irene Dunne in the Talmadge role, and *Secrets* was redone in 1933 with Mary Pickford. (Talmadge also appeared in *The Only Woman* in 1924 and *Graustark* in 1925.)

baptism of the baby in what is obviously a whorehouse.) The plot is pure melo-drama—the husband dies, the old father wants to claim his grandchild—but Norma and Borzage give it credibility. Norma makes a noble sacrifice, hand-ing her son over to good people who will take him away "somewhere and never tell me" so that the evil old grandfather can't "ruin him like he did Leonard." The final touching gift she has for her child is to instruct the new parents: "Don't let him know that his mother wasn't a lady." When she meets her grown son years later—naturally, he doesn't know she's his mother—she bravely states, "Thank God my boy is a gentleman." The inevitable wise reply comes, for a perfect final film line: "And do you know why your boy is a gen-tleman . . . Because his mother happens to be—A LADY."

The Lady is of its time, and times have changed, but it is intelligent work, presenting its sentimental tale with dignity and simplicity. It is defi-nitely one of Norma's finer performances, low-key and touching, as she changes from showgirl to society wife to cabaret singer to aged flower woman to bar proprietress, and she holds the audience's eye every minute.

In *Kiki* (1926), Norma takes on one of the few comedy roles she played in the later stages of her career, well directed by Clarence Brown and well supported by Ronald Colman (who was also an effective leading man for her sister). As Kiki, she receives one of the most crucial pieces of advice one could get in a woman's movie. Wondering how to rise out of the gutter, she is told, "All you need is some nifty clothes." At this stage of her career, Norma Talmadge shows a great deal of self-confidence, and she is a much more dis-tinctive personality than in her earlier work, where she just seemed to be inserted into a role to flesh it out. Here she *is* the role, and she knows it. She has fun in this movie, demonstrating that Constance wasn't the only one in the family who could do physical comedy. She perfectly executes an extended sequence in which she pretends to be unconscious and stiff as a board. Her timing, as a doctor lifts her leg up and down and her arm flies up, is worthy of Mack Sennett.

As Norma's career moved forward through good material and bad, reviews constantly paid tribute to the quality of her productions, the first-rate casts, the excellent production values, the beautiful clothes and settings. Over and over again, the critics say things like "There has been no money saved on this production or cast . . . ," "production is high class in every respect—the technical details, direction lighting and uniformly excellent acting . . . ," "the usual lavish production values of a Talmadge film and eye filling sets." Not unnaturally, Norma begins to be seen in part as an actress who is present in the story only to wear clothes. Her costumes and appearance begin to get reviewed as much as her performance. "Her gowns are all creations and eye-smashing" and "She has never looked so beautiful" and "She's a miracle of

Kiki: a rare comedy role

youthful slenderness" and "She looks tired" or "has circles under her eyes."
Her acting is almost always discussed with the same words: She is given credit
over and over again for her "expressive eyes," her "tenderness of expression,"
and her "naturalness." Sometimes she is called "dignified" or is said to have
"a high degree of sincerity." In fact, the kiss-of-death word most often used is
"sincere"; it means nothing, and is a way of avoiding the fact that she has no
unique characteristic or quality to take hold of. A definitive statement sums
up her acting: "Miss Talmadge's reputation rests on her naturalness, the simple, straight-forward wistful appeal she gets onto the screen." She is given
credit for treating her audiences as if they were intelligent, and for bringing
the quality of intelligence to her characterizations. "There's no talking down
to the audience," says more than one review. When Norma is criticized, it's for
becoming "so much the actress" that she's not as natural as usual.

Norma Talmadge's bad reviews were usually for her material, not for her.
She was too professional simply to walk through even her worst roles, yet
despite all the different eras and settings in her movies, it becomes apparent
that her work is about genre. She has beauty and skill, but she is basically
serving the plots of her films, dressing them up with her presence. Her movies
are star vehicles, but their significance today lies outside *her.* She was the
genre she inhabited—the woman's picture. This is not in and of itself a bad
thing, but it denies her the significant place in film history that her popularity
would ordinarily have earned her. She cannot stand the test of time.

Joseph Schenck obviously wanted to feature his wife in material that
had a certain high-level tone to it. It was his plan not only to make money with

her and for her (and off her), but to turn her into a Queen of the Motion Pictures (an interesting foreshadowing of what a latter-day mogul, Irving Thalberg, was to do for his wife, another Norma). He went after what he considered "quality" material—Broadway plays, novels, and historical documents—and the fact that much of it was turned into expensive trash didn't matter to him. The movies made money, her fans loved her, and she was a star. What was wrong with any of that, and what, in fact, could possibly go wrong with it?

The answer was about to hit Norma right where it would hurt most—in popularity. After *Kiki*, Norma Talmadge had only three movies left in her silent career. But who could have dreamed of such a thing at the time? It was unthinkable to imagine that someone of her star ranking—and with her powerful husband behind her—could just disappear from the silver screen, yet that is exactly what happened. Norma made *Camille* in 1927, then *The Dove* and *The Woman Disputed* in 1928. These movies were virtually the end of her. She was off the screen during 1929, and came back in 1930 to try sound in *New York Nights* and *Du Barry, Woman of Passion*, both failures. Then she was officially gone, and never made another film.

Her final movies are uneven. *Camille* paired her with the very handsome Gilbert Roland, whose career would last well into his old age. He made an elegant Armand, and with the fine actor Maurice Costello as Monsieur Duval and the elegant Lilyan Tashman as Olympe, Norma had her usual excellent cast. And, as *Variety* remarked, "Norma Talmadge has never looked better in her life and the picture is an excellent example of photography and production." The movie itself, says the reviewer, as directed by Fred Niblo, "lacks punch." Or, as another reviewer said, "In these times when hotsy-totsy film fare is splashed across the screen in unmistakable gestures . . . [*Camille*] is apt to leave an audience cold." Norma received positive reviews, both for her beauty and for her "sterling performance," but there wasn't much enthusiasm. Perhaps indeed she lacked the "hotsy-totsy" needed for the viewers of 1927. Norma had become famous as a perfect identification figure for the years between the Victorian woman and the flapper. On-screen, she suffered and loved, and rose from rags to riches. Off-screen, she was frequently publicized as a businesswoman and a shrewd investor in real estate. She was half old-fashioned and half modern, part Norma Talmadge, star, and part Mrs. Joseph Schenck. From silence to sound wasn't the only transition taking place in her world. There was also the transition from the subservient stay-at-home female over to the working girl with more freedom and independence. Norma's time had passed. Ahead lay a world of women with exotic sexuality (Garbo) and tough assertiveness (Crawford).

The Dove, Norma's first release of 1928, was set in an imaginary "Costa Roja, somewhere on the Mediterranean coast," with Norma reverting to one of

Norma as an elegant courtesan in *Camille* (with Maurice Costello)
and as a woman of the streets in *The Woman Disputed*

her roles as a woman of another culture. Here she is an exotic "guitar girl," who constantly repeats the line "You betcha my life!" The *New York Times* was succinct: "The story—caramba!" *Variety* was cruel, opening with "The Dove ain't what she used to be." Although later the reviewer admits that Norma's still "fair of form and face," it remarks that she doesn't appear to be trying. Her drawing power was still intact, but both she and the reviewers were getting discouraged. Her final silent movie, *The Woman Disputed*, was released later that year. Allegedly inspired by Maupassant's "Boule de suif," it was neither reviewed nor received with joy.

By 1929, sound had arrived, and Schenck was out of her life, although they were not yet officially divorced. Norma did not appear on the screen at all during that year; instead, she spent the entire time taking voice instruction. Her two final movies, in which she "talked," as it were, were not successful. Talking pictures had been around long enough so that the reviews were not only about how Norma's voice sounded. *Variety* cut right to the issue: "If

Talking Pictures:
Norma in *New York
Nights*

Norma Talmadge has retained her drawing power of other days, [*New York
Nights*] will need it." Although it paired her again with Gilbert Roland, and
was directed by Lewis Milestone and written by Jules Furthman, it was tired
material, "another underworld and backstage film." Norma's personal review
in *Variety* was a good one: "Miss Talmadge looks as well as she acts and
talks . . . A better picture will give her an even break. Recording favorable."
In general, reviews of her speaking voice were not bad, although they weren't
raves. Norma speaks extremely carefully as she veers from swallowing her
vowels to enunciating every word with a kind of pseudo-high-class diction, à
la "thee-ah-tuh." About her voice in *Du Barry, Woman of Passion, Variety*
says, "Miss Talmadge speaks, but her voice has no flexibility." The film itself
seemed halfway between comedy and drama, so that the reviewer ends up by
evaluating it as "coo coo for the box office . . . Often when trying to be serious,
it is just travesty." One critic wrote of her, "She speaks the Belascoan
rodomontades with a Vitagraph accent." This time, the beautiful sets, costumes, photography, and strong support—William Farnum, Conrad Nagel,
and Hobart Bosworth—didn't help. Norma Talmadge's career was over.

    Sensible advice came to her from her beloved sister and fellow star.
Constance saw Norma's sound movies and, according to Anita Loos, wired her
sister: "Quit pressing your luck, baby. The critics can't knock those trust
funds Mama set up for us."

Constance's Career

Constance Talmadge was in many ways the opposite of her sister Norma, and their careers are also opposites, and not just because Constance mostly made comedies. The key difference is that Constance developed a persona and Norma did not. It is a subtle, almost ironic, distinction, in that both women were identified with a recurring type of movie. For Constance, this became a plus, as she pinned down a role that became *her,* both on and off the screen—the hoydenish, devil-may-care, flirtatious sophisticate. Norma won the larger fame as a Great Actress in prestige productions, but this later became her kiss of death; she remained merely representational, not individual, and by standing in for every woman in dozens of geographies and settings, she never found the one character that could be her. Constance, who was pretty, though not as beautiful as her sister, was peppy, sparkly, and famous for her wit and charm both on and off the screen. Her movies fell into the pattern of sophisticated comedy, forerunners of the screwball tradition of the 1930s, but she shaped the type into "the Constance Talmadge comedy." Her screen self was a limited one, but it was specific. She was "Connie," and she had adventures, with titles like *A Virtuous Vamp, A Pair of Silk Stockings, Her Night of Romance, Venus of Venice,* etc.

Seen today, Constance is everything Norma is not: vibrant and saucy with plenty of the old hotsy-totsy. Her style was detached and rather cool, and thus more modern, more aware of itself. She doesn't always seem to be fully committed to the roles she's playing, although, like Norma, she is clearly a serious professional who fulfills her obligations. However, there's a slightly breezy quality to her work that isn't *all* in the script and character. To understand the differences between the two sisters, one has to compare Norma's comedies, like *Kiki,* with Constance's more serious roles, like *The Dangerous Maid.* Norma can effectively manipulate all the silent film acting traditions and emotional techniques to reveal her character's feelings, but Constance seems to stand back from such histrionics. Thus when Norma takes on comedy, she overdoes it, and when Constance takes on drama, she doesn't move an audience.

Constance was born in Brooklyn in 1899, although her birth date is sometimes listed as 1900.* From early childhood, she was always called by

---

*Constance was not the middle sister of the Talmadge trio, but the youngest, being three years younger than Norma. For many years, everyone believed Natalie to be the youngest, but she was actually the middle sister, taking the traditional role of the overlooked middle child. (Natalie was only one year older than Constance.)

her nickname, "Dutch," given to her because she had very fair hair in a family of brunettes. According to her mother's dubious book, *The Talmadge Sisters,* written in 1924, Constance always had "shock proof courage," and was never as moody or emotional as Norma. "Constance was saved, I think, from a great deal of emotionalism by the fact that she released so much energy in her tomboy outdoor playing. For a prolonged period she cared for the company of boys, not merely because they were boys, but because . . . she could equal them in their daring stunts. She rarely played with girls other than her sisters." (Maybe Constance would become famous for light roles and Norma for dramatic because these were the roles in life their mother had assigned to them.)

When Norma became a Vitagraph player in New York in 1910, Constance was full of curiosity, and soon was hired as an extra. (Norma was never an extra. From the beginning, she assumed specific roles, with suitable billing.) Constance liked to clown around, and she loved being among the actors at Vitagraph. Her high spirits and great charm soon attracted attention, and she began to be cast in comedies as "the Vitagraph tomboy." She also played in two dramas opposite Maurice Costello. Throughout 1914 and 1915, Constance made movies, with her official debut in a credited role often said to be *Buddy's First Call* in 1914. The approximately twenty-nine films she made in those two years had such titles as *In Bridal Attire, Forcing Dad's Consent, Billy's Wager, Spades Are Trumps,* and *The Boarding House Feud.* The first film the sisters made after going out to Hollywood in 1915 was *Captivating Mary Carstairs.* Constance played a bit part and Norma starred. Later that year D. W. Griffith placed both Talmadges under contract, and Constance appeared in a Griffith scenario (written under his pseudonym, Granville Warwick) which was filmed as *The Missing Links.* It starred Norma, and Constance played the daughter of a village merchant.

The earliest of these films I was able to see was *Billy the Bear Tamer* (1915). Billy Quirk plays Constance's father, who spirits her away to his hunting lodge when he finds her smooching with a young man. While Quirk spends his days hunting, Constance resourcefully sends her pet carrier pigeon (which she has conveniently brought along) with a message to her lover. This enterprising young man turns up, disguises himself in a fairly moth-eaten bear suit, and he and Constance hatch a scheme whereby the "bear" captures her and he rescues her, thereby earning her hand in marriage from her grateful father. The young and inexperienced Constance is as cute as can be, tricked out in a striped scarf, a long skirt and bulky sweater, and a big tam that allows her little curls to peep out around her face. Her performance style is utterly casual, as nonchalant as if she had just dropped by the set and decided to jump in and help out the rest of the cast. She's fresh and natural, and the film is unpretentious fun, with good pacing. All the assets that would make Constance Talmadge a popular star are here—the looks, the sense of fun, the ease—but in an unpolished form. This makes it all the more delightful to see her; there's a strong sense that one is definitely looking at the real Constance Talmadge, a girl for whom life would be fun, a lark, a romp—not to be taken too seriously.

In 1916, Constance made Griffith's *Intolerance*, her first important film, and the one that ensures her place in film history. She was cast in the tailor-made role of the Mountain Girl in the Babylonian sequence, and also as the flirtatious Marguerite de Valois in the medieval story. The latter role is very small in many of the prints seen today, and it is the former that made her a star.* As the Mountain Girl, she's completely delightful. Because her character is the only comic relief in the film, she is one of the main sources of audience pleasure (together with the scantily clad "maidens from Ishtar's temple of love and laughter," of course). Many people feel she's the best thing in *Intolerance*. The first glimpse of her is a haunting close-up, showing her young and unlined face. She is sitting, pensive, surrounded by male figures, one of whom starts to tease her. Instantly she changes into a hellion, throwing a rock at him. Constance has lovely soft eyes, much like Norma's, and a mass of thick hair (which looks quite dark, although family lore said she was always a blonde). She wears a sort of hat made out of leaves and twigs, and an animal skin around her waist. She plays a classic tomboy, fighting, kicking, socking would-be lovers, and swaggering around like a pseudo little man. In fact, Constance as the Mountain Girl might be said to be—not a child-woman like Pickford or Gish—but a cute little boy–woman.

This boyish female full of high spirits and the desire to be free becomes her film persona. Even though some of her characters would be married women, and she would grow more and more sophisticated as she aged, she was always the slightly boyish, gee-whiz gal who wheeled out into the world with a will of her own. The Mountain Girl, sent to the marriage market, eats onions to ward off suitors and warns, "But touch my skirt and I'll scratch your eyes out." Constance is fresh and funny, and she plays her commitment to the Babylonian leader like a teenage crush, vowing eternal allegiance to him with an innocent kind of passion that is both charming and believable. She later emerges as the central hero of the Babylonian story, riding out in a swift char-

---

Intolerance circulates today in copies with various running times. DeWitt Bodeen (in an article on Constance in the December 1967 issue of *Films in Review*) says that Griffith, realizing that her role as the Mountain Girl would make her a star, originally changed her billing as Marguerite to "Georgia Pearce," so as not to dilute her impact as the Mountain Girl. This billing was later dropped, and when the film was reissued in 1919—according to Bodeen—Griffith shot new footage of Constance so the film would have a happy ending for her character. As Marguerite, she is briefly seen today riding in a carriage, wearing a little pearl cap and smiling flirtatiously behind a lacy fan.

Constance as the Mountain Girl in Griffith's *Intolerance*

iot to warn her compatriots that the enemy is coming, and dying bravely during the final enormous battle after she has put on an armored vest and taken up weapons to fight among men.

The public's love of Constance Talmadge was born with *Intolerance*. She was young enough (barely seventeen) to seem authentic as a little girl playing soldier and yet grown up enough to be beautiful and appealing. She is utterly natural, completely at ease, with no artifice or guile. Griffith always liked Constance, both on- and off-screen, partly because she wasn't afraid of him. In her book, Peg Talmadge wrote, "Part of Constance's value to Mr. Griffith lay in the fact that she amused him . . . She made him laugh largely because of her absolute disregard of his importance, in contrast to the awe and respect and head-bowing accorded him by all the others." Bodeen wrote that Griffith told him personally that his two favorite actresses were the obscure Clarine Seymour (who died young in 1920) and Constance Talmadge. (Griffith said he respected Lillian Gish, but declared that for all her fragility, she had a masculine mind and thought like a man.)

The success of *Intolerance* lifted Constance into stardom, but of the next four films she made for Triangle, only one showcased her effectively. The four movies were *The Microscope Mystery* and *The Matrimaniac* in 1916, and *A Girl of the Timber Claims* and *Betsy's Burglar* in 1917. The most interesting of these is *The Matrimaniac*, partly because Anita Loos wrote it, and partly because it paired Constance with Douglas Fairbanks. *Matrimaniac* is a romantic comedy, a sort of early screwball effort, in which Fairbanks and Constance are trying to marry despite her father's opposition. The bulk of the film is taken up with Fairbanks's efforts to corral a minister, elope with Constance, and get the ceremony performed. Her role is relatively small, but she makes the most of it.

In 1916, she was a young colt of a girl. She is playing opposite a man who is not only a great star, but quite a lot older than she is (Fairbanks was thirty-three in 1916.) She is *very* pretty as first seen waiting to elope, stylishly dressed in a tricorn hat and modish suit, with a fur ruff around the collar. Her hands are primly folded in her lap, and she is the perfect picture of a sweet young lady, yet alert and anxious, cocking an ear to every sound, every nerve awake to what is happening. Constance is focused, playing tension very believably without waving the emotion at the audience. Her entire performance in the movie is unaffected and under control, and she makes a great foil for Fairbanks. This was their only pairing in motion pictures, which is a shame because they were perfect for each other, particularly in the modern comedies that make up the early part of the Fairbanks career. Constance is not just pretty, a beautiful prop to provide a love interest; she can hold her own when chaos crashes in on the characters, herself contributing to the comedy. *Matrimaniac* was a great showcase. It's fast, funny, inventive, and astonishing—with the marriage finally taking place with Doug atop a telephone pole, the minister performing the ceremony in jail over the telephone, and Constance in her hotel, also on the phone.

After her Triangle contract expired in 1917, Constance joined her family to return east largely because her new brother-in-law, Joseph Schenck, was setting up his production company there for Norma. It was the shrewd Mama Talmadge's fondest hope that he would do the same for Constance and, in fact, he did, putting his sister-in-law under contract in June of 1917. This was not mere familial generosity on his part. Constance was a worthwhile project in her own right, and the closeness of the sisters made his working with the two of them easy. After her own company was established, Constance embarked on the career for which she is best known, creating her image as a sparkling and glamorous comedienne, as opposed to the slapstick queen like Mabel Normand that she might have become.

Her first film under her own banner was *The Lesson*, in which she played a role that was not quite what Schenck had in mind for her, that of a woman whose unhappy marriage inspires her to undertake a career. It was a low-key comedy, rather grim, and her natural brilliance was not put to good use. For this reason, *The Lesson* was not immediately released. (It finally came out as her sixth feature for Select.) The other Select movies released ahead of it were *Scandal, The Honeymoon*, and *The Studio Girl* from 1917, *and* 1918's *The*

Shuttle and *Up the Road with Sallie,* and each of them presents the persona that would be associated with her throughout her career. She is rich, beautiful, spoiled, and full of high spirits. She wants her own way and gets it, but then she meets a man . . . and he tames her. (DeWitt Bodeen has pointed out that "all sixteen of the feature-length comedies Constance filmed for Select owe more than a minimum of their plot to *The Taming of the Shrew.*")

Throughout 1918 and 1919, Constance's movies were all hits, and their titles are an indication of what mood and style they represented: *Goodnight, Paul; A Pair of Silk Stockings; Mrs. Leffingwell's Books; Sauce for the Goose; A Lady's Name; Who Cares?; Romance and Arabella; Experimental Marriage; The Veiled Adventure;* and *Happiness à la Mode. A Pair of Silk Stockings* is a prototypical Constance Talmadge film of the period, an imitation French farce in which she plays with grace and elegance while perfectly turned out in an ermine-and-sable-trimmed coat. Her role is the kind that best suited her—an attractive young matron whose natural sophistication and polish see her through a series of compromising situations. Bedroom doors open and close, thieves hide under beds, divorced husbands climb in and out of windows— and a pair of silk stockings finally explains everything satisfactorily. The audience of the day was treated to the sight of a wealthy mansion, lots of gowns, some excellent farce, and the sight of Constance, pretty and well dressed, playing her role with a beautifully light touch. Constance Talmadge made a name for herself by being very good at deftly handling material that was never meant to be anything but fun.

Peg Talmadge, ever vigilant, began to worry about the sameness of Constance's roles. (Norma, of course, was playing everything from an Indian maiden to a Russian countess to an Asian unwed mother during this time frame.) When Schenck moved Norma's company from Selznick's Select to Associated First National, Peg started working on him to do the same for Constance. Ever the dutiful son-in-law, he complied. Schenck then hired Anita Loos to write for Constance, as he had liked the role Loos had created in *Matrimaniac.* Loos and her husband, John Emerson, wrote Constance's next six pictures, actually contributing to the "sameness" Peg was worried about: *A Temperamental Wife* and *A Virtuous Vamp* in 1919; *Two Weeks, In Search of a Sinner, The Love Expert,* and *The Perfect Woman* in 1920. Loos understood what Constance's strengths were. She wrote her as a fun-loving, witty woman in a contemporary setting, with a good wardrobe and a handsome costar, and then she let her romp through a plot that contained a little bit of farcical misunderstanding, a solid battle of the sexes, and a good deal of romance. This recipe becomes—with suitable variation—the Constance Talmadge film. In these Loos/Emerson scripts—comedies of manners of their time—Constance played in her usual rather narrow range. She was a chorus girl chased by a bounder who hides in the house of three bachelors; a widow whose husband

Constance as an
ingenue in two 1918
films, *The
Shuttle . . .*

bores her, so she sets out to find a sinner to have some fun with; a young
woman trying to marry a man shackled by two maiden aunts (she finds husbands for them, neatly freeing him from the problem); a secretary who vamps
her boss; a flighty young girl who marries a sober, older senator; and a well-
bred vamp who learns that flirting and a successful business career won't mix.
All these characters were somehow the same person—Constance Talmadge.
Her final release for the year 1920, not a Loos/Emerson project, was *Good
References,* in which she becomes a secretary and marries her boss.

     After *Good References* was completed, Mrs. Talmadge and her daughters
took time off to sail to Europe on an extended vacation. When they returned,
Constance married her first husband, John Pialoglou, a handsome Greek
tobacco importer whose chief asset seemed to be the one that the newspapers
seized upon: "exceptional ballroom dancer." He was Constance's first husband, but not her first fling. Dorothy Gish once said, "Yes, Constance was
always getting engaged—but never to less than two men at the same time."
Her many boyfriends included Irving Berlin, Richard Barthelmess, Jack
Pickford, Buster Collier, Michael Arlen, and a really serious one, Irving Thalberg, the boy wonder of MGM. The Thalberg/Talmadge love affair was legend
in Hollywood. Then as now, men of power, no matter how short, sickly, and
mother-ridden they might be, attracted the most beautiful and desirable
women. Constance was beautiful and desirable, and Thalberg was very short,
quite sickly, and had a formidable mother who could equal Peg, but without

... and *Sauce for the Goose*

the self-humor. Henrietta Thalberg was horrified at the thought of her boy marrying Constance Talmadge, the woman F. Scott Fitzgerald called "the deft princess of lingerie and love . . . the flapper de luxe." Constance was a flirt, and a well-known girl about town. She liked to stay up late, dance all night, and play cards with a set of cronies notorious for their intemperate habits. She was capricious, leading Thalberg a merry chase and endlessly frustrating him, but she was just too full of life, too much fun, and too adorable for him to ignore. He fell madly in love with her, but every time he tried to pin her down, she would waltz off to New York or Paris and leave him behind. Unlike her sister Norma, Constance felt no pressure to marry someone who could guide her career, possibly because Norma had done it for her, and she finally told Thalberg she was fond of him but could never consider marriage. This crushed Thalberg, who everyone said sparkled and came alive when he was with Constance in ways he never had with any other woman. (Henrietta was relieved, and a marriage with the more pliant Norma Shearer soon took place.)

Constance's marriage to Pialoglou was brief, and after a few months she went back to work, appearing in five more movies written by Loos and Emerson in the next three years: *Dangerous Business*, *Mama's Affair*, and *Woman's Place* in 1921, *Polly of the Follies* (1922), and *Dulcy* (1923). (The final one, *Learning to Love*, didn't appear until 1925.) From 1921 to 1924, she also starred in seven other movies: *Lessons in Love* (1921), *Wedding Bells* (1921), *The Primitive Lover* (1922, written by Frances Marion, based on Edgar Selwyn's *The Divorce*), *East Is West* (1922, also by Marion), *The Dangerous Maid* (1923), *The Goldfish* (1924), and *Her Night of Romance* (1924). Thus, in these few years she was the leading lady in twelve successful films. (She and Norma also made cameo appearances in a 1924 movie called *In Hollywood with Potash and Perlmutter.*) Her films, like her sister's, were all definitely vehicles especially designed for her. They are formulaic, in that they all emphasize fashion and glamour, and they have their roots in typical bedroom farce. Audiences loved them, and critics almost uniformly gave Constance excellent notices.

Three typical examples of the Constance Talmadge early 1920s comedy are *The Primitive Lover, The Goldfish*, and *Her Night of Romance.* Each one has complicated twists and turns to its story, and each is light, silly, escapist fare. *The Primitive Lover* opens on a raft in the middle of the ocean—no sense wasting any time. Four people have been shipwrecked—a woman, her husband, a virile young man, and a third man who apparently is on board so he can go nuts and be wrestled bravely overboard by the virile hero. The husband, weak and delirious, needs more than his share of the precious water supply, so the young man, announcing that all he cares about is that the woman be happy, volunteers to jump overboard, only requesting that before he goes he may be allowed to kiss the wife good-bye. He then jumps, leaving the lawfully wedded couple to whatever their fate may be, but at least to the privacy of their legally entitled comforts.

This beginning—appropriate to some old-fashioned, hyped-up melodrama—is ahead of the audience all the way, and turns out to be the sentimental ending of a romantic book the heroine (Constance) is reading, and is only her own hilarious visualization of its events. The book, *The Primitive Lover,* inspires Constance's idea of what a real man should be like. (The audience has, in fact, been given some hints that the opening might not be legitimate. For instance, the life raft is carrying, among other supplies, a large box labeled CAKE.) The film rushes into a mad whirl of plot development: The book's author, thought to be lost in the African jungle, turns up (his disappearance was only a publicity stunt), and Constance wants him instead of her tame husband, an inventor. She craves "the caveman style" of lover, and goes to Reno for a divorce. Her husband chases her, enlisting an Indian chief to help him fake a holdup and kidnapping, etc., etc. In the end, the husband turns out to be more of a caveman than the author. In such material, Constance played with aplomb, carrying her load as if it were light as a feather. No matter how bizarre the plot twist, she could handle it.

In *The Goldfish,* which exists only in fragmented form at the Library of Congress, she plays a very rich, very Long Island heroine. She and her newlywed husband agree that if either one ever tires of the other, they won't belabor the issue with endless arguments and discussions; instead, there will be an

The Goldfish, with ZaSu Pitts

act of great dignity—the simple presentation by one to the other of a goldfish in a bowl. (This film contains one of my favorite title cards: "Take me away from here. Take me to Detroit and teach me to make shoes.") The couple decide to use the prop at the same time, setting Constance off on a journey in which she tries to become a lady, marries two more husbands, and finally returns to her original love, played by Jack Mulhall.

In *Her Night of Romance,* she was directed by Sidney Franklin and paired with the very handsome Ronald Colman and the solid Jean Hersholt. The movie is greatly helped by a nice script by Hans Kraly, who often worked with Ernst Lubitsch. In yet another comedy-farce with mistaken identities, entrances, and exits, and complications that the audience must tolerate until they are sorted out, Constance plays an American heiress whose father is "the brush king." When she and Colman meet cute, the plot takes off—he pretends to be a doctor, diagnosing her as being threatened with a nervous breakdown. Her father buys Colman's country manor house without Colman knowing the buyer is her father or the father knowing Colman is the owner. The material cries out for a Lubitsch to turn it into something imaginative and cinematic, but that never happens. Talmadge and Colman play with panache, however, and it's easy to see that Colman is headed for big stardom.

When Constance strayed from her established character and what audiences expected from her, she didn't have much luck. Perhaps in imitation of her sister's ability to play women of all lands and cultures, Constance undertook—or was assigned—the leading role of the Chinese Ming Toy in *East Is*

West, in 1922. Fay Bainter had played the role on the stage, and most critics felt that Constance was badly miscast. "She is an actress of undeniable charm in light comedies and school-girl stuff, [but] seems strangely out of place as Ming Toy . . . She doesn't rise to the comedy heights that Miss Bainter did . . . [She] hasn't come up to expectations." This was also true when she tried a more serious costume picture, à la Norma, with *Dangerous Maid* in 1923. Set in 1685 England, the movie cast her as a young woman trying to save her cousin, a fugitive rebel, from the king's officers. It isn't heavy drama, and Constance gets to pretend to be a boy for some of the time, but although reviews called her "sweet and sympathetic," it was clear that everyone liked her best when she played the role she had become identified with early in her career. She returned to form in *Dulcy* (1923), one of her biggest hits. Dulcy is a nitwit blonde, but as the *New York Times* pointed out, in Constance the audience found, instead of a beautiful nitwit, "a delightful and charming actress" who brought "the full perfection of her talents to a most ungrateful part." She was praised by everyone as the well-meaning young wife who nearly ruins her husband's career—in notices that called her "adorable," "plausible," "sweet," "amusing," "fetching," "nifty," and "head and shoulders above anything she has ever revealed before in her electric person and her delightful talents." *Variety* went all out, praising Dulcy as "the highest accomplishment an ingenue can achieve in farce in any form." Constance had taken a potentially annoying character and turned her into a charming and lovable person.

After the last film written for her by Loos and Emerson, *Learning to Love* (in which she plays yet another heiress who is a flirt), Constance was at the peak of her popularity, and part of her success may have had to do with her very intelligent ability to assess herself and her talents. In a December 1920 issue of *Moving Picture World,* she said, "I enjoy making people laugh, because this type of work comes easiest and most naturally to me. I am not a highly emotional type. My sister could cry real tears over two cushions stuffed into a long dress and with a white lace cape made to look like a dead baby, and she would do it so convincingly 900 people out front would weep with her . . . My kind of talent would lead to bouncing that padded baby up and down on my knee with absurd grimaces that would make the same 900 people roar with laughter. In my way I take my work quite as seriously as my sister does hers—I would be just as earnest about making it seem real. That, I think, is the secret of being funny . . . one has to be serious in one's levity."

By 1925, Constance had it all. She was rich, famous, and adored, and she loved her life, kicking up her heels off-screen whenever she felt like it. She was only twenty-six years old, and seemed to have an unlimited future ahead of her. Actually, she would make only five more movies, but these final films are among her best, a grand swan song for a lighthearted career. *Her Sister from Paris* (1925) reunited her with the *Her Night of Romance* team: Hans

Kraly wrote the story, Sidney Franklin directed, and Ronald Colman costarred. Constance plays twins, one a sweet little wife to a highly successful Viennese writer, the other a sophisticated glamour girl from Paris. (This plot is not unfamiliar. It was made in 1934 as *Moulin Rouge* with Constance Bennett and in 1941 as *Two-Faced Woman,* the film that drove Greta Garbo into her apartment for the rest of her life.)

My favorite Constance Talmadge films are her next three. *The Duchess of Buffalo* (1926) paired her again with Kraly as writer and Franklin as director, but this time her costar was the inexplicable Tullio Carminati. ("Who's Tullio Carminati?" asked *Variety,* and nailed the movie, saying, "Not much reason in the plot to start the story and not much more to keep it going.") This is true enough, but Constance gives it a touch of pizzazz. She plays an American dancer (presumably from Buffalo) who falls in love with a young lieutenant of the dragoons at the same time that an elderly Russian grand duke falls in love with her. She looks her best, and she is splendidly dressed in well-designed gowns that suit her perfectly, and with furs that must have cost a fortune.

In *Venus of Venice,* Constance's creative team changes to Wallace Smith

The Duchess of Buffalo

as writer and Marshall (Mickey) Neilan as director. It was 1927, and since she had, after all, been playing in the same kind of roles for half a dozen years, reviewers were starting to complain. *Variety* laid it out: "Nonsensical, dumb and dull." Although they were willing to say that Constance "looks good," they felt that the "story isn't there and Marshall Neilan has done nothing with it." For today's viewer, not sated with a dozen similar appearances, *Venus of Venice* is an amusing, elegant production in which she excels. She plays the assistant to a crook who disguises himself as a blind peddler; whenever she's chased by the police, she escapes by diving into the canal. During one escape, she takes refuge in the gondola of a handsome young man played by Antonio Moreno. The movie has splendid sets, and an eye-popping masked ball at which a pearl necklace is stolen. Constance is suitably reformed before the fadeout, but not before she has to jump in the canal once again and demonstrate her expert Australian crawl. The movie is fun—exciting, light, and charming, again with fabulous clothes.

Breakfast at Sunrise (1927) was directed by a master of sophisticated comedy, Mal St. Clair, whose *The Grand Duchess and the Waiter* is one of silent film's least known and best examples of the type. By this point, Constance is becoming rather grand. Her clothes are beyond luxurious, and the settings are stunning—gigantic bathrooms and bedrooms. She has become completely and utterly the star, and her movies must present her as such, since she is no longer a boyish little girl. Constance plays a wealthy young woman who loves a marquis (Bryant Washburn) who is wooing a little tart named Loulou (Alice White) who is loved in turn by a handsome, but naturally, very poor young man (Don Alvarado). It all takes place at a newly opened luxury hotel. The owner, wanting the hotel to appear full, has stocked the place with nonpaying guests who are mingling with the paying variety. (These deadbeats, however, have been given their instructions in regard to the menu: "Nonpaying guests will not be served with wine and caviar.") When all four lovers are in the dining room at the same time, Constance comes up with the brilliant scheme that she and Alvarado should pretend to be lovers to make White and Washburn jealous. In the end, they go so far as to marry to accomplish this goal . . . and end up falling in love. It's a deliciously contrived, well-plotted little comedy, light and pleasing—a trifle, but a good one.

In between *Venus of Venice* and *Breakfast at Sunrise*, Constance had married her second husband, Captain Alastair MacIntosh. The two went to London to live, but soon Constance, saying she was "bored to death," returned to Hollywood where the ever faithful, ever resourceful Schenck ended the sisters' contracts with First National (which had been known briefly as Associated First National when they first signed) and moved them over to release at United Artists. After *Breakfast* appeared in 1927, Constance made her final movie, *Venus*, the only film of hers actually handled by United Artists.

Constance in her
final film, *Venus*

Venus, which was made in France and had the plus of location shooting, broke no new ground for her. Why should it? She had found fame and fortune by playing in romantic comedies with complicated and farcical plot lines, so why change? This time, she is a princess who is president of a steamship corporation. While out cruising on her yacht (the "Venus" of the title), she decides to impersonate the goddess in a moonlight swim, and is unfortunately observed by a passing shipload of gawkers. She rides a surfboard at high speed, clad only in a shimmering evening gown and a long string of pearls. When the gown gets in her way, she decides to doff it. Scandal follows, until finally she finds true love with a sea captain. The movie is more of a romance than a comedy, and it was slight, very slight. The *New York Times*, ever the sober lady, referred to her as having become "unduly gay" and referred to the movie as having "glum moments and unconscious humor." The audience hadn't tired of the charming Constance, but they had tired of her plots, and sound films were already changing their tastes. Constance never appeared in another movie, not even in a cameo role. She married twice more (the fourth marriage apparently a happy one) and lived out her life in wealth, burying her beloved sister Norma in 1957. (The hitherto indestructible Peg had died of cancer only a few years earlier.) Once when in Hollywood on business, she was asked if she intended a comeback. After a noticeably extended silence, she replied, "Why on earth would I ever do a thing like that?" She had worked hard for her living all her young life, and despite the glamour of fame, was glad enough to get out of pictures and finally quit the work her mother had directed her toward. She had enjoyed her career, but she had never taken herself very seriously. She had never tried to exaggerate her own skills, or stretch herself much beyond the qualities she possessed in life. She was deft but she wasn't deep, and she was never interested in becoming the world's greatest actress. Constance Talmadge always left a lot to the audience, trusting them to like her, assuming they would know she was just "acting natural." She was comfortable on film, comfortable with the light roles assigned to her, and her comfort showed.

IN ORDER TO UNDERSTAND fully just how popular the Talmadges—especially Norma—really were, one has to look into the sacred relics of the mystery of stardom, the fan magazines of the day. The sisters were regularly featured in *Photoplay* in beautiful full-page portraits in which their two lovely heads were bent close together. The Talmadges had cachet. They were successful. They were beautiful. They were fashionable. And they were sisters. The public couldn't get enough of them, so the fan magazines promoted them heavily, selling each one according to her adopted screen image or latest role. Norma was always put forth more seriously than Constance. She was consulted as a fashion oracle, or for her nuggets of wisdom on marriage, motherhood, and life in general. Constance was usually written about as if she were a heroine of one of her own zany plots—she was out shopping, having madcap adventures, and spilling tea on her best new bombazine. It was common to find both of them in the same issue, such as the September 1920 *Photoplay*. Norma is the alleged author of an article on fashion, in which she suggests that "it's the little things that count." "The little things," according to Norma Talmadge, include "a sash, a headdress of pastel buds, and new double-strapped sandals," which she assures her readers will "help a costume along." In a cheerful piece called "A Date With Connie," Constance is swanning about the city, shopping and planning her evening, with her entire family nearby "at the Savoy." The author assures everyone that "Connie" is "the very spirit of sunny American girlhood." Norma, never hurting for space, turns up in a second layout in the same magazine, modeling a series of weird hats, one with a fluted edge, one trimmed in raw ostrich feathers and monkey fur, one hung about with wooden beads, and one made out of taffeta "embroidered in gold."

Eventually, Norma began writing a regular monthly fashion advice column for *Photoplay*. Ever her mother's practical daughter, she asks her readers, "How many of you girls actually know how much it costs to dress yourself for a year? Not many I am afraid. It seems to me that there would be many earlier marriages if girls would only be satisfied to make the best of little things, and get out of the way of thinking that expensive gloves, silk underwear and imported hats are essential to their happiness." This sage advice appears in the very same issue in which she models all the crazy hats! The fact that she herself was so often photographed in silk and satin and undoubtedly had no clue what it cost to dress her didn't slow her down; she was more than ready to lecture her audience severely on their tendencies to fashion nonsense. "Can you cook and sew?" she asks. "Well, you simply must." And as far as she's concerned, that question—"Can you cook and sew?"—should be added to the list one fills out for obtaining a marriage license. Ultimately, Norma became "fashion editor" for *Photoplay*, billed as "the screen's acknowledged leader of fashion."

Norma's rise through the ranks of stardom can easily be tracked through these magazines. In an early issue of *Motion Picture*, in 1918, she is listed among those who are beginning to get large numbers of votes for star popularity. By October of that year, she is given the full star treatment in an article entitled "The Tantalizing Talmadge." In full movie-business propaganda, the magazine tells readers that "no sooner do you think you have her personality chained to your imagination via the typewriter route than you see a different phase, a more alluring characteristic peeping out at you, and it seems as if a little imp laughs mockingly, 'As if you could ever catch me on paper!' " The article claims La Talmadge will always be "elusive."

By May of the next year, the magazine acknowledges her rise, saying that "Miss Talmadge continues to advance in popularity. No star has made the strides of Norma Talmadge in the last two years." By 1921, *Motion Picture* presents one of its longest and most elaborate articles on her, celebrating her amazing success and her now lofty status as a top star. In a piece entitled "Floating Island on Olympus," by Adele Whitely Fletcher, all of Norma's trappings as a glamorous screen queen are described in breathless detail. She has a huge car, a chauffeur, and an adored Pomeranian ("Dinkie"—whom someone naturally has to take for a daily walk). Her arrival at the studio is treated as if it were the arrival of a visiting queen, which in a sense it was, even though the queen was arriving to work. The doorman runs out to welcome her and help her out of her car while her chauffeur holds the door open. A specially hired minion then runs ahead of her, booming out, "Miss Norma's working on the set," to alert everyone that A STAR has arrived and is advancing toward them and they had better darn well believe it. With typical irony, this same article does a sudden switcheroo, so as not to alienate the fans. Readers are quickly assured that Miss Talmadge, despite all these servants and trappings of position, is just a swell gal. In fact, the main question on the glamour queen's mind that day is "How long does it take to make stew?" It seems she's planning to whip up a batch that very evening! She'll prepare dinner with her very own hands in the kitchen adjoining her dressing room, "and there will be floating island for dessert." Norma confides that she always does her own cooking, although all she can make is stew, lemon meringue pie, chocolate cornstarch fudge, and floating island. (A menu for a star—a touch of democracy in the stew, and a dash of glamour in the floating island.)

Norma is presented in this article as "a star at whose shrine thousands worship." Pressed for details about just exactly how this feels, she is claimed to have said, "I'm not exactly unhappy because I haven't had time to reign supreme in a tiny kitchen . . . [in] a tiny flat. Whenever I read about someone with stacks of money wishing for an apron and a kitchen stove, I wonder why they don't sell one Rolls-Royce or one gown and get them." The interview ends with the usual female call to arms, the statement that no matter what, love is everything: "We love our careers, our successes, and sometimes what others call our failures, but more than these we love our Loves—our families and our romance." It was time to remind everyone just what stardom was really all about: just being one of the little people, although naturally with more money.

While the fan magazine presentations of Norma became grander and grander, more and more directed at her stardom and luxurious lifestyle, Constance's became more and more down-to-earth, with every effort made to present her as *real*, honest, and natural. A typical article about her appeared in *Motion Picture* of September 1920. Called "Name It!," and written by Gladys Hall, it was supposed to be an interview with Constance. The author, however, cleverly sets it up by saying that it isn't really an interview like those you read in other magazines which are phony, because Constance "has agreed with me that the one and only thing to do is tell the truth and nothing but the truth . . . She does not . . . believe in deluding the unsuspecting public." However honest she might have been, Constance was nevertheless "two hours late" to the session because she had "been attacked by the shopping fever." She was wearing one of her new "frocks" to show Ms. Hall: a navy blue dress embroidered in rose-colored beads, tied carelessly with a rose-colored rope about the waist; she also had bought a new hat, a perky black thing that looks as if a saucer had landed on her head. When asked by the interviewer if she was always in such high spirits, she replied (no doubt with complete honesty), "No, really I'm not, but you know, I've just got to appear to be. I've started the pose now and I have to live up to it . . . If I ever draw a serious breath, there's an avalanche of questions . . . I have a lot of jinx

The Fashionable
Talmadges:
Constance (OPPO-
SITE), showing a fan
magazine writer her
latest purchase;
Natalie, Constance,
and Norma in full
flower (RIGHT)

hours, but I have them behind closed doors . . . Some day they'll all wake up
to what a joke I am." In this article, the ever present other Talmadge sisters
were hovering on the fringes. Norma was taking a nap, so sister Natalie was
pressed into service to take Connie and her interviewer out in her new roadster and then deposit them at the Vanderbilt for lunch. (This type of job was
usually given to Natalie, in addition to her main assignment of being Mrs.
Buster Keaton.)

By the beginning of 1931, Norma and Constance Talmadge were gone
from both the fan mags and the movies. Norma settled into her off-screen life,
finally divorcing Schenck in 1934 and marrying Georgie Jessel the same year.
(She later divorced him, too, in 1939, and married Carvel James in 1946.)
Although Norma had tried to have a sound career, Constance never did; she
quit movies cold in 1929, and her last movie, *Venus,* was silent. She married a
very wealthy man in May of that year, and vowed she would stay with him forever and never make another film. She kept her word about the movies, but
soon enough ditched the husband. Norma officially retired in 1930, and an

anecdote surrounding her retirement years has often been repeated. Apocryphal though it may be, it's a grand exit line for one of the greatest of all the female movie stars of the silent era. Norma, it is said, dealt with an eager fan who was pressing her for an autograph as she left an expensive restaurant by drawing her furs around her, standing up tall, and carefully intoning in a loud voice, "Get away, dear. I don't need you anymore."

It is remarkable that two such successful movie stars as Norma and Constance Talmadge could walk away from it all and never look back, but when the end came, they actually did do just that. It says a lot about old Peg and her sensible, hard-nosed values. Apparently, the sisters had absorbed her idea that film acting was a means to an end, and the end was security. They took their fame for its cash value, and their lives—and their money—went right on. (In their time, the kind of celebrity that movie stars have today was not yet an end unto itself.) Norma and Constance Talmadge turned out to be good daughters, dutiful children. A little naughty, perhaps, and not always quite so obedient as they should be, and with not much better taste in men than their mother, but they did what was expected of them, and Peg and her girls got their independence. Whatever skunks they took up with or married, they didn't have to worry about any walkouts or desertions. And because they were Peg's daughters, they mostly took up with rich skunks, believing that marriage, like stardom, was basically a kind of career move.

In 1978, the never very reliable Anita Loos wrote a book about the Talmadge sisters in which she claimed to have witnessed the retired, older Norma and Constance—slightly drunk, slightly sad, and slightly lost—reeling down a city street together in a semistupor. I suppose there's no reason to doubt her, although I have my suspicions that her attitude might have been the final revenge of a behind-the-scenes writer who never got to be a star herself, even though she had plenty of personality and pizzazz of her own. Perhaps what she wrote was true, and Norma and Constance were pathetic old ladies. But I doubt it. There was nothing about the Talmadge women that ever suggested pity, and I like to see Loos's scenario differently. In my version, Constance, ever the comedy queen, whispers to Norma, "Here comes that mean little Anita Loos. Let's fool her," and they link arms and perform their last great sister act together. In my mind, Norma and Constance—with their unfortunate third sister, their "skunk" father, and their Dickensian mother—could easily be the subject of a great comic novel. Better yet, how about a hilarious epic movie about Hollywood's history? One thing is certain. They should not be forgotten. They were the top of the top in their day, and they more than earned the bread on their table.

Sisters and Stars: Constance and Norma Talmadge

Very Sincerely Yours.

William S. Hart

COWBOYS
William S. Hart
and Tom Mix

AMERICA IS FAMOUS for its magnificent westerns, and rightly so. From the very beginning, a moviemaking staple was a story shot on location involving cowboys and Indians, train robbers and bandits, stagecoaches and horses, sheepherders and ranchers. Over time, Hollywood has given us an excellent lineup of masculine types to grace these stories, and in the silent era there are two perfect prototypes to represent polar opposites of the western hero: William S. Hart, stark and realistic, and Tom Mix, flamboyant and flashy. Both are distinctive, colorful, and iconic, and their movies are great entertainment.

Each man clearly defined his visual world and his type. Where Hart gave audiences the hardships of the West, its violence and cruelty, Mix emphasized its optimism, its openness, and its limitless opportunities. Hart was about suffering and doubt, sometimes with religious overtones, and he portrayed his world as harshly and authentically as he could in an entertainment medium. Mix was about dash and flash, and he played for the fun of it, rushing through his slam-bang adventures as if his pants were on fire. Hart's heroes were not pure, and they didn't always avoid bad women, but the Mix hero didn't drink, smoke, swear, or fall prey to saloon girls, and he never killed his enemies unless it was absolutely, unequivocally necessary. Hart went for grit and reality, Mix chose showmanship and brilliant stuntwork. In real life, Hart could prove that he had worked the land and could ride and rope and do basic stunts, but Mix was an authentic rodeo champion and a superb cowboy. Hart performed his action sequences as realistically as possible, but Mix liked to wow an audience. Instead of just getting on his horse and riding well, he would show off—standing up in the saddle or jumping on his mount while the horse was at full gallop.

Hart anticipates the modern cowboy—intense, with deep strains of violence—while Mix leads to the comedy cowboy character. (He is often described as the inspiration for the singing cowboy, though without the music, of course, because his fancy clothes and modern settings foreshadow the Gene Autry and Roy Rogers movies of the late thirties and early forties.) Both Hart and Mix valued the filmmaking process, and their films presented excellent production values and location shooting that make the most of America's dramatic natural scenery. Hart's are prized for their somber portraits of a dusty Old West, and Mix's for their outstanding outdoor photography by Daniel Clark, an artist in his own right.

Although Mix started working in movies earlier, it was Hart who became a big star first. But later Mix took over the genre, breathing life and fun into the stark landscapes of Hart's westerns, replacing Hart's simple clothes and plain look with his all-white outfits set off by black boots and peaked sombreros.

Today, both Hart and Mix are shadowy figures, although Hart's name is frequently listed among the greats of the silent era, and he is often called, in an oversimplified and inaccurate historical summary, "the first western hero." However, he hardly qualifies as one of the names and faces from the silent era that are still somewhat familiar to the general public—Chaplin, Keaton, Fairbanks, Pickford, Gish, and Valentino. A photograph of his stern visage, with its tight lips and slightly squinty eyes, may be recognizable to people as the archetypal cowboy of the silent West, but asking them to come up with his name is more of a challenge. Is he Broncho Billy? Is he Hoot Gibson? Is he Yakima Canutt? In a sense, Hart is none of them and all of them, as well as so many others who came after, including Gary Cooper, Randolph Scott, John Wayne, and Clint Eastwood. William S. Hart *is* the grandfather of all cowboy heroes, and although there were some before him and many after him, his particular brand of taciturn hero who lived a tough life, spoke little, and did what he had to do—but always by a particular code of honor—is still our most familiar definition of a movie western hero. Although he stressed authenticity of location, weaponry, and action in his movies, he was also responsible for helping to shape the western genre into a romantic story with heightened drama. He fused the truth of the West from his own life with the imagination of the theatre, and put it into a new form, the motion picture. When the legend became fact, he printed the legend, and became the first real mythic definition of the western hero in the movies.

Hart's personal story is an interesting one. Born in 1865 (some sources say 1870) in Newburgh, New York, he nevertheless spent years homesteading and traveling the unsettled West before the turn of the century. A skilled horseman and hardscrabble dirt farmer, he was paradoxically also a successful Shakespearean actor of the Broadway stage. In the nomadic years of his youth, Hart's family had settled in the Dakota Territory near a Sioux reservation, and he claimed to understand the language and customs of Native Amer-

Hart as Shakespearean actor and as definitive western hero

icans. For certain, he knew what it was to be poor, and to scratch a living out of an unforgiving and uncooperative western landscape. (The illness of Hart's mother later forced the family to return to the East, where Hart, desperate to make a living, went on the stage after first working as a postal clerk.) For twenty years, Hart was a successful theatre actor, touring in both America and Europe, with his first great acclaim coming for portraying Messala in the original stage company of *Ben-Hur.* When he saw his first western film, he vowed someday to make one of his own, and to make it realistic in its portrait of the life he had lived as a boy. While touring California, he was reunited with an old friend who had been his roommate when they were both struggling actors. This was Thomas Ince, who had become the head director for the New York Motion Picture Company, which boasted such names as Charles Ray, Frank Borzage, Enid Markey, Sessue Hayakawa, and Louise Glaum. Ince hired Hart for his first movies, *His Hour of Manhood* and *Jim Cameron's Wife,* two-reelers in which Hart played the villain.

Hart was already at least forty-four years old when he made these movies for Ince in 1914. By 1920, he was one of the top three male stars in the

The Unexpected Hart: Indian chief (*The Dawnmaker*), tuxedoed man-about-town (*Branding Broadway*) . . .

business, and he remained on top through 1921 and 1922, but by the mid-twenties he had begun to seem old-fashioned. In 1925, he released his final film, one of his best: *Tumbleweeds,* a story of the land rush in the Cherokee Strip in 1889. Although it was successful, it was not a smash hit, and Hart retired from the screen.

That Hart began his movie career by playing villains is not without significance; he would later come to be known as "the good bad man." It is the unrelenting sense of an austere nature, perhaps a cruel one, that gives Hart his strength as a filmed image. His characters contain that touch of the outlaw that is a basic aspect of so many of the greatest western heroes. His image is stark and uncompromising, a classic look that was on full display as early as 1916 in *The Return of Draw Egan,* one of his most successful movies. Hart stands tall in the frame, arms folded in a stance that is calm and assured, even slightly menacing. He is head to toe a man of the West: cowboy hat, boots, neckerchief, vest, chaps, and guns. He doesn't smile. He doesn't lift an eyebrow. He doesn't deliver a clever titled line such as "Smile when you say that, pardner." His eyes contain no warmth, no little twinkle to signal to the audience that he actually has a heart of gold; in fact, his eyes are mean—small and hard. He gives off no sign of emotion or attitude, no hint of what he may do next. He just stands there, like a rock in Monument Valley, and it's up to us to figure him out. He doesn't even seem to be an actor. Rather, his presence seems to say, "This is what a western hero looks like"—his behavior, his look, his truth. Whatever action Hart takes will explain what the American West

. . . sermonizer (*The Disciple*), creative chef (*Singer Jim McKee*)

was all about. Naturally, he takes dramatic and violent action, appropriate to a story of guns and outlaws. In establishing stardom in movies, presence is everything, and Hart certainly has it. It's not good looks or sex appeal or elegance that made him—it's authority. He has a commanding presence.

The movies that William S. Hart made from 1914 to 1925 were sometimes written by him, and even produced and directed by him. Since he didn't come to films as a young and inexperienced actor, he was able to assert himself in the filmmaking process. (After he attained his footing in the film business, he formed his own production company.) It was Hart's determination to make his films a cinematic equivalent of Remington paintings and the drawings of Charles Russell, and he really did know what the West looked like. Authenticity became everything to him. "The truth of the western meant more to me than a job, and always will," he wrote in his autobiography, *My Life East and West*. The films he created with his collaborators paid close attention to detail, striving for the presentation of an atmospheric West that contained real dust, real dirt, and a strong sense of the power of nature. He also prided himself on being able to do his own stunts, and he always tried to do his own riding, mounting, and dismounting, and his own fight scenes. Certain historians believe that Hart *did* use doubles. Probably he used doubles for the more dangerous falls or trick rides, as most actors of the day—and today, of course—always did. Some of his films had really exciting stunts. In *Singer Jim McKee* (1924), Hart and his horse—or his double and a horse, although Hart claimed to have done the action himself—took a spectacular fall over a dirt cliff. The action required them to drop some twenty-five feet, ending with a spectacular roll on the ground. Audiences were thrilled.

The Hart westerns mix elements of religion, comedy, passion, rage—all primal concepts to go with his primal presence. The stories he tells are as stark as the landscape and his presence in it. He is definitely a minimalist artist. His looks, which have an almost evangelical intensity, often led him to be cast as a preacher, or "sky pilot," as in *The Disciple* (1915), in which he plays Jim Houston, "the shootin'-iron parson of the frontier, strong of jaw and good at prayin'." In *Travelin' On* (1922), he managed to have it both ways, playing a preacher who holds up stagecoaches to get money to build a church. Most of Hart's stories were obvious, but very strong. They tended to be somewhat similar, and they were almost always westerns, although he did make other kinds of movies. For example, there was *The Rough Neck* (1915), with Hart looking strange in a business suit, playing a miner who has come east; *The Whistle* (1921), in which he played a factory worker; and *Cradle of Courage* (1920), in which he was a city cop.

Perhaps his most representative film, and the one, along with *Tumbleweeds* and *The Toll Gate* (1920), that is most often revived today, is *Hell's Hinges* (1916). It is a clearly developed narrative featuring a list of characters we now think of as typical for westerns: the weak brother, the beautiful, virtuous sister, the saloon hall gal, and the slick villain, all inhabiting a rootin'-tootin' western town that's so wide open it's called "Hell's Hinges." The most complex of these archetypes is Hart's own character, Blaze Tracy, who is original in that he is frankly presented as an "evil" man, but one who, stunned by the virtue of the leading lady, reforms, finds religion, and saves the day. A title card describes Blaze as "the embodiment of the best and worst of the early West. A man-killer whose philosophy of life is summed up by the creed, 'Shoot first and do your disputin' afterwards.' " The first sight of Hart is a medium close-up in which he's sitting on his horse, laughing somewhat contemptuously while looking down at the decent townspeople. He's dressed unusually for a cowboy in that he is wearing a patterned shirt with a differently patterned vest. He also has on the traditional neckerchief, but what catches attention is his hat—it looks more like a World War I cavalry officer's hat than a typical cowboy Stetson. Recruited to scare off the new parson (the weak brother), Hart enters the town saloon with a laughing sneer on his face. A title tells us there's neither law nor religion in "Hell's Hinges," in case we hadn't figured that out. Hearing that the stagecoach bringing a new parson and his sister—and institutionalized religion—into his world is about to arrive, Hart sets out to meet it. Telling a pal that he'll probably only have to scare them a little bit, he walks down the street, rolling somewhat in a cowboy gait, smoking a cigarette, his guns on his hips. And then the stage pulls in—

and he sees her (Clara Williams). ("One who is evil, looking for the first time upon that which is good," says the title card.) His face indicates little at first, but slowly, slowly he registers change. And then, after taking all the time he needs, William S. Hart doffs his hat, acknowledging the purity of the heroine, and also the emotional power she has exerted over him through her beauty. It's a thrilling moment—and a wonderful presentation of ritualistic behavior. Hart's taking his time before performing the simple action gives it all the meaning and character and event anyone could need. This is a prime example of the stark acting that lifted Hart to stardom.

In *Hell's Hinges,* Hart created some great action for himself. When the heroine's brother is tempted by the dance hall queen and becomes depraved (in about two minutes), he goes so bad that he helps the villains burn down his own church. Hart steps in, six-guns blazing, and frenzied by his passion and determined to clean up his town to please the woman he loves, he is willing to destroy it totally. He directs a splendid action sequence, with townspeople running everywhere, guns shooting from all directions, dust flying in huge clouds, and a wow of a fiery finale in which the church burns down and so does everything else. The sequence is well cut, and the energetic rushing around of extras who look undirected and thus give a strong sense of real chaos taking place is excellent. The camera provides a distanced view of the town burning, and the sensible placement of it during the action sequence keeps the audience totally clear as to what is going on. This is an excellent, focused piece of entertainment. When Hart gently, but firmly, takes the romantic leading lady away from her brother's corpse, the title card gives us the simple words of a western hero, "We'll be goin' now."

The Toll Gate showcases the Hart good/bad outlaw figure in its purest form. He plays Black Deering, the leader of a band of raiders. Dressed entirely in black, he is tough and menacing, but true to his personal code of honor. He tries to tell his men that they have pushed their luck and shouldn't attempt any more holdups. Led by his closest lieutenant (who later betrays them), they out-vote him and he accompanies them in a train holdup that goes wrong. Captured and tied up in a railroad car, he looks like a trapped animal, but the soldiers guarding him recognize him as the man who once rode eighty miles to warn the fort that the Apaches were coming. Since he had saved their wives and children, they allow him to escape. In the strong and simple drama that follows, he resumes his outlaw ways until he encounters an abandoned wife, played by Anna Q. Nilsson, and her small son. Because he saves the child from drowning, and because he honestly tells her he's an outlaw, she takes him in. The man who betrayed him turns out to be the husband who had deserted her, and as Hart prepares to avenge himself through Nilsson, he sees the words "By their fruits ye shall know them" in her Bible, and miraculously sees the error of his ways. After killing the villain and again being spared by the grateful posse, he kisses Nilsson—but gently rejects her offer to stay with him. Telling her it will be best if she and her son go to live with her family, he literally rides into the sunset—a classic example of the noble westerner who must, no matter what, live by his code, do what a man's gotta do, and go his way alone.

Hart's westerns have a recognizable format. What action they have moves fast, but they usually stress character over action, and they develop tension over time in a somewhat melodramatic story construction. At their worst, they're old-fashioned and marked by a sentimentality that is difficult for modern audiences. In *Pinto Ben* (1924), a short film based on a poem that Hart wrote, a cowboy recites a poem around the campfire about his dead horse ("So long, you son of a gun"). And, indeed, Hart was deeply attached to his own horse, Fritz.

Writers and reviewers of the time always paid tribute to Hart's sincerity, and to the character of a man who kept himself apart from the sometimes wild social life of Hollywood in the 1920s. Reviewing *Wild Bill Hickock* (1923), *Variety* wrote, "Bill Hart is a regular guy, on and off. He never has been a faker, on the stage or on the screen. He holds a national wide regard and respect among all the theatrical folks because he is an actor, was an actor when on the stage, one of the best, playing red-blooded roles . . . He went into pictures and made a name second to none in all of picturedom for the work he specialized in, and Bill Hart did it so well he has been fruitlessly copied by others." The movie itself is said to "bring in a great western character . . . the sort of story that Young America wants, that Young America should watch. It sets them tingling. It lets them know that there were great men of the west in the days when the west had to have great men, and it is brought out by a great actor . . . William S. Hart."

In an era of razzle-dazzle style and plenty of off-screen shenanigans and movie hype, Hart seemed to have the respect of everyone—the machinery that sold the movies and the public that bought them. In the April 1921 issue of *Motion Picture,* he acknowledged this by writing, "Knowing and loving the west as I did, I believed that I could make pictures that would be a truthful mirror of all its fascinating and colorful charm . . . I am always grateful to the American public who understand what I am endeavoring to present."

Hart's feelings for the West were deep, poetic. In a movie like *Three Word Brand* (1921), this feeling is directly conveyed by the on-location wide open spaces. There is a magnificent look to the landscape—clean and spare like Hart's face and the story lines he chose to tell. (He seems to physically represent the entire American western landscape.) As James Agee described it, "There was William S. Hart, with both guns blazing and his long, horse face and his long, hard lip, and the great country rode away behind him as wide as the world." Hart commanded his space, elevating it to something elemental.

One tough gun handler in *The Silent Man*, and twins in *Three Word Brand*

Richard Schickel has written, "If the West seemed like a lost Eden, Hart seemed to be the last Adam." Hart doesn't act, really, which is not to say that he can't. Acting just isn't the point with him. He's *epic*, representational. Because of this, his films get their points across very directly. "Boys," he says, playing a preacher who knows how to get the congregation of tough guys to do what he wants in *The Disciple* (1915), "this is Sunday and we're going to have services." As they balk—he's come into the saloon to round them up—he draws his guns and adds, "Are you going to force me to preach to cripples?" This was the kind of title card Hart liked. He kept dialogue simple and frequently violent. (An exception would be *Three Word Brand*, whose three words turn out to be a terse "I love you" delivered to his leading lady. Hart makes up for this uncharacteristic love talk by designing a story that gets off to a super-dramatic start. He plays three roles in the movie: a father and the twin sons whom he saves from massacre out on a lonely trail. He distracts the Indians by blowing himself up, creating a diversion so the boys can escape.)

The movie magazines of the day contributed to the idea of Hart as an authentic western hero. In one layout, he is shown in a series of photographs teaching readers simple examples of Indian sign language, about which he is said to be "an expert." These magazines present him as if he's one of the characters from his films—an austere man but one who loves horses and dogs and playing poker, all highly suitable for a western hero. Legend has it that Hart—a romantic—always proposed to his leading ladies, and he finally married one of them, Winifred Westover, his costar in *John Petticoats* (1919).

(The couple had a son, William S. Hart, Jr.) Westover was twenty years younger than Hart, and the marriage ended in divorce after six years, on the grounds of desertion.

Of all the cowboy stars of the silent era, it is William S. Hart—his face and attitude—that most influenced the sound era. It's an inscrutable face, reflecting a loner's innate secretiveness. And it's a direct line from the hardness of Hart's eyes in *The Return of Draw Egan* to that in the eyes of Clint Eastwood's Billy Munny in *Unforgiven*. In fact, to understand William S. Hart and his enormous influence, one has only to look at the cowboy heroes who followed him in our own time. Whereas the 1930s were influenced more heavily by Tom Mix, the postwar complex, even psychologically driven, western hero was definitely cast in the William S. Hart mold. Randolph Scott, Gary Cooper, and Clint Eastwood are the Hart type of laconic, taciturn men of the West, tall in the saddle and riding lone across the prairies. All these latter-day western stars, including Henry Fonda, Joel McCrea, and Jimmy Stewart, portray characters not unlike Hart's in some of their films. (John Wayne, the greatest icon of the sound western, who had no real rival until the emergence of Clint Eastwood, interestingly straddles the Hart and Mix prototypes. He played both a "singing cowboy" in low-budget westerns in the 1930s and a more complex modern hero in the postwar period.)

Perhaps the actor in sound westerns who is closest to Hart is Randolph Scott. It isn't much of a stretch to see Hart's face and Scott's as one and the same. Scott was the star of a series of movies brilliantly directed by Budd Boetticher in the 1950s: *The Tall T, Ride Lonesome, Seven Men from Now, Comanche Station,* and *Buchanan Rides Alone.* An excellent horseman, Scott began his career in musicals and screwball comedies, but matured into playing westerners who employed a minimum of dialogue. His silent, strong masculinity was highly appealing to audiences. (It's easy to forget that Randolph Scott was one of the top ten box office draws in 1950, 1951, 1952, and 1953, a four-year reign as a western hero.) Hart, Scott, and Clint Eastwood have in common an inscrutable face, a tall, lean body, and considerable physical skills in riding, roping, and doing stunt work. With their large physical stature, they seem somehow to be detached from ordinary life, above it, or at least beyond its pettiness. Each man is best showcased in stories that offer little explanation of who or what his character is really feeling. Resolution of his conflict comes with action, and the audience is allowed the privilege of providing its own explanations of the hero's interior self. All three stars hold the frame in a rugged landscape, with close-ups displaying their remarkable faces—Hart, planed and plain; Scott, noble and angular; and Eastwood, beautiful yet strong—and defining the ideal western hero in a visual medium.

.   .   .

IN THE 1920s things began to jazz up in America, and just as the Victorian suffering heroine and little girls with curls morphed into flappers with cigarettes and whiskey flasks, the cowboy hero also began to change. Hart was nudged out of his popularity by a new kind of western leading man, one who jumped off speeding trains and was a larger-than-life action hero. Hart's brand of severity and his insistence on realism began to seem dull by comparison. The man who finally took over Hart's title of King of the Cowboys was the glamorous Tom Mix.

Mix is considered by many film historians to be the greatest cowboy star of them all. His popularity in his day was enormous, but his influence has been less on the modern concept of the western hero than on the concept of the Hollywood (or rhinestone) cowboy, as his is essentially the image being presented whenever a loud, overdressed western hero with a big "seegar" shows up in a movie. Today, people who recognize the stereotype of the "drugstore cowboy" in the ten-gallon hat, who drives a low-slung car with Texas longhorns mounted on the front fenders, and who has his monogram embroidered in rhinestones on his all-white suit, may not know the name of the man who inspired the joke: Tom Mix, King of the Cowboys and the highest paid western hero of the 1920s. There is much more than this to the real Tom Mix, who is truly delightful, and much more fun than that grouchy old William S. Hart! He's the Jackie Chan of cowboys, with his breakneck pace, his action just for the sake of action, and his amazing stunt work. Riding forward at full tilt on his faithful horse, Tony, Tom Mix can't help stirring the blood. No wonder everyone loved him—he was enjoyable rather than admirable.

Tom Mix was born in Du Bois, Pennsylvania, which doesn't suggest a western background. However, Du Bois was rural, and Mix learned to ride everything while growing up there, including workhorses and mules. He spent his spare time practicing mounts and dismounts, bareback riding, and standing up on a galloping horse, and became an excellent horseman in early childhood. He saw knife-throwers performing in itinerant circuses, and he practiced their skills on his little sister, Esther. He learned to shoot straight, with both rifle and pistol. He may not have been born in the West, but he had authentic western skills.

After two enlistments in the army, during the second of which he went AWOL, he ended up around 1906 working for the famous 100,000-acre "Miller Brothers 101 Real Wild West Ranch," near Bliss, Oklahoma. The custom had emerged of letting the cowboys who worked the ranch entertain and amuse themselves at the end of a cattle drive by staging contests and sports events, and these events came to be staples of Wild West shows, rodeos, and Frontier Day celebrations. The "101 Wild West Shows" developed out of these events, and soon Mix joined the shows, while also finding work as a deputy sheriff and night marshal in the area. In 1909, he won the "101 Ranch Champion All-Round Cowboy" award, which entitled him to be called the "King of the Cowboys." Hired as a cattle wrangler for the movies in 1910, his good looks and riding ability soon won him supporting roles.

Mix was no overnight success, but he worked steadily, appearing in over a hundred one- and two-reelers between the years 1911 and 1917, and when he was signed by William F. Fox at the end of that period, he began starring in a series of westerns. By 1922, Mix, age forty-two, was one of the ten biggest box office draws of the year. He officially became the "King of the Cowboys" on film, too, and his popularity and fame were red hot, earning him $17,000 a week on a fifty-two-week basis.

Mix's westerns were the polar opposite of William S. Hart's. They featured dangerous stunts, all performed by Mix himself, and they were the sort of slam-bang, fast-paced, exciting action-packed westerns that appealed to young boys. (Mix's stunts, although performed by him, sometimes cheated the viewer through editing and manipulating camera angles. They were frequently undoable as seen on film.) Mix wore fancy duds, high-heeled boots, embroidered shirts, and hats that looked more twenty-gallon than ten-gallon in size. His movies changed westerns from the sober, rather dark and realistic stories favored by Hart into glamorous and unrealistic presentations. Like Hart, however, Mix paid attention to detail, and his films were extremely well made and well directed.

Tom Mix's life story, though interesting, isn't a patch on the one invented for him by Fox publicists. He is a classic example of the Hollywood tendency to take what was more or less true and embroider it, as if it were one of his own cowboy shirts. A 1925 issue of *Photoplay* carries an article entitled "My Life Story," by Tom Mix. Comparing it to the real story provides a textbook example of Hollywood hype. Tom is reborn—this time just north of El Paso, Texas, obviously a much more suitable birthplace for a western star than Pennsylvania. As a child, he "watches bravely" while his mother shoots two angry mountain lions as they leap through the family's log cabin window. (Naturally, he was born in that log cabin.) As a young man, he enlists in the army, and instead of spending his years in lackluster activities and ultimately going AWOL, he "sees plenty of action." He's with the Rough Riders at the Battle of Christabel. He becomes a scout and courier to General Chaffee because of his extensive knowledge of the Spanish language. ("It was pretty much hand-to-hand fighting," he is quoted as saying.) He's wounded, but comes back just in time to go to China for the Boxer Rebellion, where he was in charge of a rapid-firing gun during the siege of Peking. Next he's in the Boer War, switching sides from the British to the underdog Boers, and is taken prisoner . . . etc.,

etc. The publicists at Fox convinced Mix that it was in his best interests just to go along with the nonsense, because it was all business, and the business was that of selling images and stories to the public. He was told he could tell anyone the truth in private if he wished to, but publicly he was to endorse the legend. Mix more than endorsed it, he embraced it, and to this day it's difficult to sort out fact from fiction. Mix *was* a U.S. marshal at one time, and he *was* a champion rodeo rider, and he *did* do his own stunts.

The plot of a Mix film was straightforward, linear, and full of energy. Mix described himself as a character who was always "getting into trouble when doing the right thing for somebody else." While Hart went for poetry and portrayed a bleak world, Mix went for showmanship that helped audiences escape into something that moved so fast they wouldn't have time to remember their troubles until the lights came up. Because they were breezy and cheerful, with a lot of comedy mixed in, his movies appealed greatly to children, especially young boys. In some ways, these movies are like the early westerns of Douglas Fairbanks, which also were energetic romps across the landscape. But Mix's movies have an even lighter touch, and the role of the romantic leading woman is completely unimportant. Mix's characters seldom form any serious romantic liaisons, which was another reason they appealed to young boys. (His huge following among young boys shouldn't be taken to mean that he wasn't popular with the wider audience. As *Variety* pointed out in its review of his *Riders of the Purple Sage* (1926), "every boy wants to be a Tom Mix. Every girl wants her boy to be a Tom Mix. And not only to the youth does the heroic figure of Tom Mix appeal as the daring, riding, shooting, handsome westerner, but it hits the grit and sympathy of the grownups—those who in their youth also wanted to be or have a Tom Mix." In other words, everyone responded to the joy of a Tom Mix movie.)

Mix's movies were filled with action, as was reflected in their energetic titles, such as *Mile-a-Minute Romeo* (1924), and they place Mix front and center at all times. Because they were so successful at the box office, money was spent on making them. Spectacular and breathtaking stunt work is always featured, and Mix is often supported by excellent casts, including such names as Alan Hale, Bull Montana, and, of course, his famous horse, Tony, a beautiful black stallion that became the most famous horse star of the twenties.

The Great K and A Train Robbery (1926) is the definitive Tom Mix western. It runs a quick fifty-five minutes, and as the *Variety* reviewer of the day said, "The impression you have is that it has not run over 30 minutes," adding that it was "probably the fastest picture in action ever filmed," as it "starts in action and never stops." Others said it could safely be billed as the fastest moving picture ever put on the screen, and even today this applies. The most striking thing about *The Great K and A* is indeed the speed at which the story moves, coupled with the stunts that Mix performs. Mix enters the frame hang-

Tom Mix with his beloved horse, Tony . . .

ing over Colorado's Royal Gorge in a basket suspended on a long rope that runs from the top of the gorge down to the saddle of his old reliable, Tony. When he spots the train, the Old K and A, coming through the gorge, he slides down the rope into his saddle and gallops off. From that moment on, except for a few minutes spent winning the heart of the leading lady, he's off and running, climbing, swimming, riding, fighting, and rescuing everyone.

Like most of Mix's films, *The Great K and A* is shot on location, and in the American tradition it presents speed, thrills, danger, some comedy—even a little love. The villain works for the railroad president but is secretly in cahoots with the bad men. He is described in his introductory title as a "college man," but the college "must have been Vassar." (Some of the humor is definitely politically incorrect; the black porter is described as "one of the few dark clouds without a silver lining.") When Mix encounters a former comrade-in-arms from the Signal Corps at Verdun—now a hobo—he is reminded of the time when he "rescued" his pal. This comedy sidekick reminisces about how he had met a beautiful French girl, and borrowed fifty dollars from a friend to take her out, "But you borrowed that fifty dollars from me," he tells Mix, "and bravely took her out yourself." Mix westerns tended to be set in more modern times, whereas Hart's were clearly in a re-created Old West. Here, Mix plays a World War I veteran, and the clothes and props are up-to-date. (This became typical of many of the 1930s B westerns.)

. . . and on the set
for *Mile-a-Minute
Romeo*

Dick Turpin (1925) is interesting because it isn't a western. In it, Mix plays a highwayman in Old England, and is dressed in lacy period costumes. Yet despite these outfits and the untypical British setting, Mix is still moving right along, riding his horse, rescuing the leading lady, and escaping his enemies. *Variety* called the movie "absolutely sterling, pure entertainment," and pointed out that it was "the best Mix film to date," adding that first-run houses, which had largely ignored him, would now have to play his films. He had "crept along" from starring in ordinary westerns to the point where his box office pull in state after state was greater than that of most other stars, many of them more widely advertised. (Mix had just secured a $2,000,000 contract for three years with Fox, and *Dick Turpin* had an unusually high budget for a Mix movie, $400,000.) *Variety* summed up Mix's appeal: "As an actor, he is on a par with thousands of others . . . but as a rider, fighter, and general all around stunt man, he makes others in the same business look foolish."

Mix had fun with his stardom, and once having accepted the hoo-ha of press agents and publicists who turned him into a war hero and a former Texas Ranger, he seemed to just go with the flow. And the flow was cash. Mix took up a lifestyle as colorful as anything he ever put on the screen. He married five times and did not lack for female companionship in between engagements. He created a brand for himself that consisted of his initials, TM, and a single bar, and put this "TM bar" brand on everything in sight, including the outer doors

Mix as modern cowboy in *Ladies to Board* (ABOVE), and as old-fashioned highwayman in *Dick Turpin*

to his magnificent home, his fireplace mantel, his saddles and cowboy gear—anything he could find that it would go on. Outside his $250,000 Hollywood Hills mansion were electrically operated gates with his initials on them—decades before Elvis's musical-note motif. It was said that he had special tires made for his Rolls-Royce with TM embossed on them, so that when he drove around the dirt roads of California, his monogram would be left behind. And in case anyone didn't know where the fabulous Mix mansion was located, these initials were blazing outside in hot neon every single night, highly visible to anyone and everyone. (There was also a fountain spraying water with lights that rotated from red to white to blue.) Built to his specifications in 1922, Mix's house had four bedrooms and three baths, encompassing 4,000 square feet of living space. Behind it was a guest house with two bedrooms and its own kitchen and bath. The main house featured stained-glass windows, beamed ceilings, a seven-car garage, and a handmade rock fireplace that stretched all the way from the floor to the ceiling. His wife at the time, Virginia Forde (a former leading lady), decorated her space with Louis XVI furniture and Aubusson carpets, while Mix decked his out with Navajo rugs, animal heads, and western mementos. (He also had acquired his dream ranch out in Arizona, for when he wanted to escape the Hollywood tinsel.)

Mix dressed beyond the nines—he went for the high teens. He had a purple tuxedo and six hundred pairs of boots and shoes—all with his initials on them, of course. He wore a diamond-studded belt buckle and diamond-studded spurs. He had ten-gallon Stetsons in different colors, mostly white, and suits embroidered with TM, sprinkled with stars, and covered with beautiful beadwork. He amassed a huge gun collection (now displayed in the Tom Mix Museum in Dewey, Oklahoma), including a matched set of Colt Police Specials, a Browning semiautomatic, a custom German Mauser bolt-action rifle, and a custom 1890 Winchester rifle. Once Tom Mix accepted stardom, publicity, and fame, he went all the way.

HART AND MIX were not the only great cowboy stars of the silent era, of course. There were also Broncho Billy Anderson, Hoot Gibson, Fred Thomson, and many others, including Dustin and William Farnum, Bull Montana, Harry Carey, Ken Maynard, Tim McCoy, Jack Hoxie, Art Acord, and the charming Buck Jones. Each of these men had his own particular slant on the western genre, and his own unique persona. Anderson, whose name was officially G. M. Anderson, established his screen character Broncho Billy around 1910, a few years after participating in movie history by appearing in *The Great Train Robbery* as a bit player. (If anyone deserves the title of "first western star," it's probably he.) Ironically, he had no real connection with the West, and couldn't even ride a horse when he started out. However, he was a big man, solid and masculine, perfect for silent films and even more perfect for outdoor dramas. Anderson was a shrewd man who realized that in the new medium of motion pictures no one really knew what he was doing. On that basis, he figured he could create a central character for his audiences to like, play that character himself, and make a series of movies in which he could both star and direct. Pioneering the concept of western hero on film, he supposedly made over four hundred Broncho Billy one- and two-reelers between 1910 and 1920. These movies had titles like *Broncho Billy and the Outlaw's Motion* (1913), *Broncho Billy's First Arrest* (1913), *Broncho Billy's Christmas Deed* (1913), *Broncho Billy and the Settler's Daughter* (1914), and *Broncho Billy's Cowardly Brother* (1915). They were simple and direct, strongly presented in the western pulp-fiction tradition. Sometimes Billy was a bad guy, sometimes a good guy. Sometimes he even died in the end. By 1920 Broncho Billy—his deeds, his redemption, and his cowardly brother—were all off the screen. (Sometime in the mid-1950s, a fan asked him what he had been doing with himself since he left the movies. His reply was a line worthy of any western: "Just driftin' along with the breeze.")

Hoot Gibson, unlike Broncho Billy, was an authentic cowboy, with a diamond-studded belt inscribed "World's Champion Cowboy, 1912" to prove it. He was born on a ranch in Nebraska, and he had spent his youth as an itinerant cowboy on the ranges of the West. His natural athleticism led to his being hired by a traveling Wild West show, and he entered westerns in 1910 in D. W. Griffith's *The Two Brothers*, eventually becoming a stuntman and double to the actor Harry Carey in early John Ford westerns. (It was on the 1917 Ford film *Straight Shooting*, which starred Harry Carey as a reformed outlaw, that Gibson was promoted to feature player.) After serving in the Tank Corps in World War I, Gibson began starring in his own series of two-reel westerns. His persona in the genre was very different from most of the others of the time. He wasn't stern and stoic like Hart, or flamboyant like Mix. Instead, he created a kind of Destry-like character who was clumsy, very human and flawed, and seldom wore a gun. Any villain could knock him down with little effort; in fact, Hoot fell on his butt more than once. His movies were light-hearted and good-natured, and he himself was an unpretentious man off-screen, so confident as an athlete and as a cowboy that he dared to be less than heroic. He emphasized comedy, and his gosh-darn, fumbling hero appealed to the entire family.* He seemed real, even ordinary, and his ability to do deadpan comedy made him very popular, particularly with small-town audiences. He kept on making movies after sound came in, with irregular success, although he did costar with Ken Maynard in a 1940s series called *Trail*

---

*One of Gibson's movies, *Galloping Fury* (1927), is the story of a ranch that contains a peculiar mud that will cure adolescent pimples. It may well be the only western in history that involves the beauty clay market!

Blazers. Hoot Gibson died in 1962, broke, but with a secure place in western movie history.

Fred Thomson was somewhat like Tom Mix, in that he stressed action over character, and his depiction of the Old West was glamorized. Although he liked to dude himself up and his movies were flashy and even superficial, he was an excellent athlete who performed most of his very tricky stunts himself. Thomson is probably best remembered today only for being the husband of the famous screenwriter Frances Marion, but during his era, he and his big white horse, Silver King, were enormously popular—he was definitely one of the top three western stars along with Hart and Mix. His off-screen image was that of the squeaky clean hero, since he came from a highly religious background and had even trained for the ministry.

Big, handsome, and appealing, looking like the Rock of Gibraltar if ever a movie star did, Fred Thomson died suddenly and unexpectedly from pneumonia at the height of his fame in 1928. In his own era he was at the top, and who knows what additional heights he might have attained in western movie history had he lived. As it is, he simply was gone in mid-career and quickly forgotten, dying early in an unglamorous way that didn't give him legendary stature like a Valentino or James Dean. His rivals, Hart and Mix, however, both exited public life in a style appropriate to the image they had created.

There is perhaps nothing more satisfying in film history than the star who manages to find an appropriate way to say good-bye to his or her audience—John Wayne's courageous walk down the big Academy staircase to present the Best Picture Oscar in 1979, for instance. Wayne, who would be dead of cancer within two months, stood, stoic and calm, while the audience gave him a prolonged standing ovation. But not even he could top the exit of William S. Hart.

In 1939, Hart rereleased his silent feature *Tumbleweeds* with a musical track and a spoken introduction. In an eight-minute appearance, Hart describes the film the audience is about to see, and then bids farewell forever to his fans. First, an old-fashioned title card tells us, "From Horseshoe Ranch at Newhall, California, the Foremost of Western Stars Tells Us the Story of His Greatest Picture." Hart is seen walking down a small hill. In the background are pine trees, sagebrush, and a clear and open sky. He is dressed in a cowboy hat with Indian beadwork on the crown and a small feather tucked in it. He wears tall boots, a vest, and a large, full neckerchief knotted on his shoulder. Around his waist is a colorful, striped sash edged in fringe, and at his side is a hunting dog. Birds are heard chirping in the background, and a gentle western breeze moves the branches of the trees. In medium close-up, Hart stares directly into the camera, giving the impression that he is looking the audience straight in the eye. He is, as always, tight-lipped. After a lengthy, colorful description of the story behind *Tumbleweeds*, Hart suddenly removes his hat.

The breeze comes up stronger, ruffling his thinning white hair as he holds the hat awkwardly, momentarily looking down at it. Then, straight as an arrow again, he pauses, looks into the camera, and suddenly changes tack, saying:

> My friends, I love the art of making motion pictures. It is as the breath of life to me. But through those hazardous feats of horsemanship that I loved so well to do for you, I received many major injuries that, coupled with the added years of life, preclude my again doing those things that I so gloried in doing. The rush of the wind that cuts your face. The pounding hoofs [*sic*] of the pursuing posse. Out there in front, a fallen tree trunk that spans a yawning chasm. The old animal under you that takes it in the same low grounding gallop. The harmless shots of the battled ones that remain behind. And then the clouds of dust through which comes the faint voice of the director: "Okay, Bill, okay. Glad you made it. Great stuff, Bill, great stuff. And say, Bill, give old Fritz a pat on the nose for me, will ya?" Oh! The thrill of it all! You do give old Fritz a pat on the nose, and when your arm encircles his neck, the cloud of dust is no longer a cloud of dust, but a beautiful golden haze through which appears a long phantom herd of trailing cattle. At their head: a pinto pony. A pinto pony with an empty saddle! And then a low, loved whinny, the whinny of a horse so fine that nothing seems to live between it and silence, saying, "Say, boss, what you ridin' back there with the drag fer? Why don't you come on here and ride point with me? Can't you see, Boss, can't you see the saddle is empty? Up ahead the boys are calling. They're waiting for you and me to help drive this last great round-up into eternity." Adios, amigos. God bless you all, each and every one.

After delivering this astonishing speech, in which he allows himself to choke and almost sob, Hart looks down at the ground, turns, and walks back up the hill.

In this unprecedented "farewell to the screen"—and it was a farewell, because although he lived until 1946, he never appeared again, spending his retirement writing his autobiography and coauthoring a series of children's books with his sister—Hart is both magnificent and foolish. To watch this old-fashioned man deliver his sentimental speech is almost heartbreaking, but, as he always did, Hart triumphs. He is too tough to seem pathetic, and a viewer feels like saying "hats off" to the old bird. (Or, as one of my students yelled out at a screening, his nose ring flashing in the light reflected off the screen, "I can't help but like this old fart!") Hart seems to come down the hill from another time, another place. His voice is the voice of a stage-trained actor from another century. He speaks from his diaphragm in a clear, ringing voice that has clearly had elocution lessons. His clothes are a bit hokey, and so are his words, but his face, that fabulous face, is authentic. It is the face of the Old West as we have known it. Hart has conviction. His is the first and truest face of the Old American West on film.

Hart had spent his final years in comfortable retirement, but Mix had gone on working. His career didn't die out completely, although age had become his enemy, since he was so well known for doing his own stunts. He had also lost money in the stock market crash, and his days of top stardom were more or less finished by the coming of sound, although he appeared in a 1935 serial, *The Miracle Rider,* for Mascot, and toured the country in the Tom Mix Circus. He became a kind of pioneer "media cowboy" in vaudeville, circuses, and comic books. His radio program, *Tom Mix and His Ralston Straight Shooters,* was a huge hit, although he himself never played Tom Mix in it. Generations of boys and girls learned to recite the Straight Shooter Pledge from the Ralston Purina box: "I promise to shoot straight with Tom Mix by regularly eating good old Hot Ralston, the official Straight Shooter's cereal, because I know that Hot Ralston is just the kind of cereal that will help build a stronger America." When it came to advertising, it might be said that Tom Mix, old rodeo rider that he was, always came first out of the chute.

The end came suddenly. He had always loved fast cars, and had bought himself a customized 1937 supercharged Cord, Model 812. Some say it was pure white, like the suits he loved to wear. Some say it was a dramatic black. Still others claim it was green or even yellow, and some argue that he had *two* fancy Cords, a 1934 model as well as the 1937. A master mechanic who later claimed to have bought and restored the car stated definitively that it was the color of "cigarette cream," and that the top was made of genuine black mohair with red piping around the front and rear edges. There is one agreed-upon, hideous final fact: on October 12, 1940, Tom Mix, said to have been driving at eighty miles per hour, crashed through a workmen's barricade at about 2:15 p.m. just eighteen miles outside Florence, Arizona, and roared down a dry wash. The Cord overturned, pinning him beneath the wreckage, and a metal suitcase that had been sitting in the back seat flew forward and hit him from behind, breaking his neck. He was killed instantly.

Mix had been alone, driving to Florence to visit a former son-in-law. The highway workers he had whizzed past ran to the wreckage, overturned the Cord, and found the body of their cowboy hero, Tom Mix. He was wearing a pair of his famous boots, his diamond-studded belt buckle, and a white ten-gallon Stetson. In his pockets there was $6,000 in cash and $1,500 in traveler's checks, and some say there was a bag of jewels in the car. None of that wealth had helped him, however.

Although Mix's accident robbed him of any potential filmed farewell, in a sense this was the exit his films might have prepared us for—it was active, it was unsentimental, and it was at high speed. It was *modern*. It also motivated a last scene that had all the showmanship and style that Mix loved. On December 5, 1947, cowboy star Gene Autry—one of the 1930s movie cowboys Mix had inspired—traveled to Florence, Arizona, to appear before a crowd of about three hundred people to help dedicate a seven-foot statue marking the spot where the fatal accident occurred. The statue depicted a riderless pony, and the inscription read: "Jan. 16, 1880–Oct. 12, 1940. In memory of Tom Mix, whose spirit left his body on this spot, and whose characterizations and portrayals in life served to better fix memories of the Old West in the minds of living men." Autry sang "Empty Saddles in the Old Corral," and most people cried. All things considered, it was a final show as appropriate for Mix as Hart's had been for him. It had flamboyance (the song), glamour (the presence of Autry), great audience response (the tears), and an authentic western zing (a riderless pony to look over the endless Arizona landscape). And it was fast.

Hart and Mix. Mix and Hart. Two monosyllabic names, two actors who played heroes of the imaginary American West. Each was a very big star. Although both claimed to be from the West—Hart from Dakota Territory and Mix from Texas—they had both been born in the East. Each was influential in movie history, doing his part to define the concept of the western hero. Hart gave us the complex, taciturn concept that is the modern movie cowboy, and Mix defined the B-western hero and the fancy dude cowboys of the 1930s and 1940s. Taken together, they make a perfect composite of the main appeals that silent film had for an audience: the ability to re-create a world visually with seeming honesty, and the ability to lift viewers out of their seats with escapist action. In Hart and Mix—and the other early cowboy stars—one sees the concept of the movie star legend in its original form. These men had lived at least a part of the life that they depicted on-screen, and they believed the public would want them to be at least a little bit real. Since they were going to be photographed in action and on location, they assumed that this meant they would need to be able to do the things their characters were supposed to do. They would need to *be* cowboys both on- and off-screen. In this honesty lies the appeal of both William Hart and Tom Mix. Each in his own way really *was* a cowboy. In the end, the difference between them is that Hart aspired to be a western hero and Mix was content to be a cowboy star. My Stetson is off to both of them, and I wouldn't want to have to choose one over the other.

Two styles of
American cowboy:
the realistic William
S. Hart (LEFT) and
the flamboyant
Tom Mix

WOMEN OF THE WORLD
Gloria Swanson and
Pola Negri

ONCE UPON A TIME in the movies, women walked in beauty like the night, trailing behind them—well, whatever. Usually a lot of yardage trimmed in fur. During the silent film era, the concept of woman as an object of great beauty, great mystery, and great outfits was commonplace. Once the motion picture was invented, it gave men and women a place to sit in the dark and have secret thoughts and secret experiences. Movies freed the mind if not the self, presenting their audiences with new opportunities for turning both men and women into sex objects. Sometimes both sexes were wholesome and lovable, and sometimes they were pure and virginal, and sometimes they were "ordinary" and "believable"—and then, sometimes, they were wildly peculiar, living in strange places and walking around in clothes never seen anywhere on the globe in any possible situation. They were exotic. This explains how we watch Gloria Swanson, a lively and cute young girl, turn into an actress who stands about with a long cigarette holder, wearing what appears to be a lampshade on her head. She had become exotic. "Exotic" didn't mean that a heroine wouldn't fall in love, or suffer, or dance the waltz. It didn't mean she couldn't live in the United States of America, either. It didn't mean she couldn't get married and settle down, be a mother, or preside at a dinner table. It meant that she wasn't commonplace. She was the Other. She wasn't going to be washing dishes, and she wasn't going to be *explained*. She was desirable, even dangerous (the vamp was an exotic), but above all, she was about physical things. Her looks. Her figure. Her hairdo. Her wardrobe. It was a type that cried out for one of its later representatives, Hedy Lamarr, the perfect exotic. Too beautiful to be imagined, with thick black hair, alabaster white skin, full luscious lips, wide sparkling eyes, and a slender figure, Lamarr had an authentic foreign accent to lend credibility to her status. She was born to stand around, and she wore a turban better than anyone in the history of the cinema.

The silent era defined the type, and from the very beginning there were many exotics, the most famous early one being the highly original Theda Bara. Born Theodosia Goodman in Cincinnati, she found stardom in 1915 playing in the accurately named *A Fool There Was*. The name Theda Bara was said to be an anagram for "Arab death," and since her role in the film was based on Kipling's "The Vampire," the jazzed-up label of "vamp" soon stuck to her.

Some of the most beautiful of these women were Barbara LaMarr (called "too beautiful to live" and not to be confused with Hedy), Valeska Suratt, Louise Glaum, and Alma Rubens—all names barely known today, and for a good reason: an exotic beauty was good to look at, but after a while, she wasn't all that interesting. The careers of Bara, Glaum, LaMarr, and the others didn't last long, because men got tired of looking at them and women felt no connection to them. Around 1915, however, two women got their movie careers going who really knew what to do about that last problem—Gloria Swanson and Pola Negri. Swanson and Negri knew how to be exotic in ways that made it last: first, they connected their strangeness to the ordinary woman in the audience by translating it into a form of pseudoliberation; and second, they started playing the role off-screen as well as on. They were exotics who became divas, and, more importantly, they came to represent "the modern woman." They played good women and bad, in contemporary settings and historical ones, in comedy and drama, but they played their roles to the hilt and took them home with them at night.

Swanson and Negri were on their own very early in their lives, and when they came into the new art form of motion pictures, they seemed to understand instinctively that, despite the glamour and the fame, the movies were nothing more than a business. So they became businesswomen whose business was performance. On-screen, Swanson played a modern woman who was independent and/or who questioned the traditional value system that victimized women, while Negri challenged the old sexual double standard. Off-screen, Swanson played it straight. She was outspoken and shockingly frank, knocking everyone over with her liberated ideas. Negri went for the European version: "I-am-a-passionate-artiste-and-thus-might-just-go-mad-and-do-anything." They combined their movie roles with colorful off-screen antics. They married royalty, demanded extravagant salaries, conducted a famous feud with each other, had affairs with such men as Joseph Kennedy (Swanson) and Rudolph Valentino (Negri), and gave outrageous quotes to the fan magazines. Ambitious, talented, and smart, they became a form of surrogate escape for American women, who followed their every move and checked out their every hat. They were so very convincing that today people confuse their crazy publicity with who they really were, which is unfortunate because who they really were matters. They were modern women, career pioneers who lived liberated lives. They were women of the world.

GLORIA SWANSON

Gloria Swanson is yet another of those dinky little women who became great silent film stars. Only four feet eleven inches tall, she managed to strut across the screen in outfits that would have overwhelmed many a larger leading lady. I'll say this for her: she may have been short, but she acted tall. (And she knew the difference, once saying to a fan who had gushed about "finally meeting" her, "And I bet you were surprised at what a sawed-off little shrimp I really am.") Like all silent film stars, Swanson knew how to use her entire body. Mary Astor, in her autobiography, described Swanson as having "expressive shoulders," an astute observation from a rival actress. Swanson always made the most of everything she had, and this drive and determination turned her into one of the very biggest stars of the silent era.

She was born Gloria Josephine May Swanson on March 27, 1898 (she said 1899), in Chicago, an only child whose father, a military man, moved his family around frequently. She made her debut in movies in 1915 at Essenay in Chicago and very soon came out to Hollywood and signed with Mack Sennett to play in two-reelers at Keystone. Since she posed for publicity stills at Sennett wearing one of the typical bathing girl costumes of the day, Swanson was often said to have been one of Sennett's Bathing Beauties. This she denied vehemently all her life, in almost every interview she gave as well as in her excellent autobiography, *Swanson on Swanson* (published in 1980). Since she had been a featured player with Sennett, she felt demeaned by the idea that she had been just another pretty face among a troop of bathing beauties. She had acting experience before ever arriving at Sennett. Her Essenay roles in 1915 had included *The Fable of Elvira and Farina and the Meal Ticket* (said to be her debut), in which she plays a young girl with social aspirations; *Sweedie Goes to College* (opposite her future husband Wallace Beery—he plays a big Swedish maid and she plays a deb in a girls' dormitory); *The Romance of an American Duchess* (she has the title role, perhaps her first moment on-screen in the kind of glamorous roles she would later make famous); and *The Broken Pledge* (as one of a trio of young girls who vow to become old maids until a camping trip—and three good-looking guys—change their minds).

Swanson's first Sennett-Keystone movie was *A Dash of Courage* (1916), and after that she was in a series of comedy two-reelers with names like *Hearts and Sparks*, *Love on Skates*, and *Haystacks and Steeples*, all in 1916. Her best-known comedy from this period is the likable *Teddy at the Throttle*

Gloria Swanson, under contract for Sennett, posing at the beach. The actress pulling the boat ashore is sometimes identified as Phyllis Haver, sometimes as Marie Prevost.

(1917), in which she costars with Bobby Vernon, Beery, and Teddy, the famous dog star of the Sennett menagerie. (Swanson had married Beery in 1916, but the marriage lasted only a month, although they didn't officially divorce until three years later.) *Teddy at the Throttle* is a terrific comedy in the Sennett tradition, with a slam-bang story of skulduggery in which Beery ties Swanson to the railroad tracks and Teddy has to save the day by jumping up and taking over the throttle, stopping the train just in time to rescue Gloria. Swanson is lively and animated in this film, a respectable rival to Sennett's great star comedienne, Mabel Normand, and appears totally unrelated to the staid clotheshorse she would become in just two years.

A lesser-known film from the same year, *The Pullman Bride,* paired her with the comedy greats Chester Conklin and Mack Swain in a romp that takes place largely on a speeding train. Swanson is exceptionally pretty, and her little well-dressed body seems almost detached from the chaos of the action. She looks surprisingly modern, in a smartly cut suit and flower-bedecked hat. As the action unfolds (the film is wild, charmingly vulgar, and really funny), Swanson is like a calmer, less physical version of Normand, maintaining perfect comic consistency in her part as the unhappy, slightly reluctant bride.

She takes her falls—most notably an amazing backward drop that she does without hesitation, falling flat, her body like a stiff board—but she holds down her role, which is that of the comedy ingenue lead. Swanson already has that charisma that great stars all exhibit in their earliest work. You can't help looking at her, and not just because you know she's Gloria Swanson. Even in her earliest years, and with less of the comedy action belonging to her, Swanson makes her mark.

In later interviews, Swanson said, "I hated comedy, because I thought it was ruining my chance for dramatic parts. I didn't realize that comedy is the highest expression of the theatrical art and the best training in the world for other roles . . . The mark of an accomplished actor is timing, and it can be acquired only in comedy . . . Comedy makes you think faster, and after Keystone I was a human lightning conductor." At the time, however, she wanted to be more like the emerging Norma Talmadge, so she left Sennett and moved to Triangle Studios, making her first film there in 1918, *Society for Sale*, directed by Frank Borzage and costarring her with William Desmond. She went on to make a group of movies with typical titles of the time: *Her Decision, You Can't Believe Everything, Every Woman's Husband, Station Content, Secret Code,* and *Wife or Country*—all in 1918. Her other Triangle release of the year was *Shifting Sands*, which represents her work of this period very well. It has a twisted plot stuffed with events that swamp the poor heroine. First she's a slum girl trying to earn a living painting (though she has no talent). Then she's attacked by the rent collector when she can't pay, and refuses to give him her "favors" in exchange. After dropping his wallet as they struggle, he comes back to arrest her for the theft. She goes to prison, and comes out with a baby! (Who knew?) After she gives this child up to the Salvation Army, they hire her, and the next thing you know she's married a very rich young man because, as we all know, very rich young men frequent Salvation Army headquarters. (Actually, he invites her to his estate, telling her to bring the poor kiddies she takes care of for a picnic.) As a rich wife, she looks lovely in white organdy with a satin bow, but good clothes do not put an end to her troubles. Counterfeiters turn up to blackmail her (some accounts say German spies but they were counterfeiters in the version I saw). All mercifully ends well, but a modern audience might question Swanson's judgment, wanting to play in junk like this instead of the delightful Sennett comedies.

Her performance style in these 1918 films is restrained and subtle, sensibly underplayed. She can't summon up the radiant suffering of a Lillian Gish or the passionate histrionics of a Negri, but she's very appealing. She seems to have a kind of real American honesty—plain and simple, straightforward and direct. *Variety* paid her tribute, saying, "Miss Swanson gets all she can out of the part." Precisely. Swanson elevated herself out of the slapstick world of Mack Sennett by participating in these less-than-stellar movies.

Swanson in her
Keystone years:
*Teddy at the
Throttle . . .*

Her next goal was to take another step up the ladder of success by finding
some *good* serious material, and it didn't take her long; the next rung was
waiting. In 1919, she left Triangle to make her first movie with Cecil B.
DeMille at Artcraft (which released its movies through Paramount). DeMille
was already a big name, and coming under his aegis was a giant step for a
young actress like Swanson, who had only four years of moviemaking experience behind her. Yet she didn't come to DeMille empty-handed; from her
slapstick years, she had learned timing and professionalism. At Triangle, she
had found two kinds of roles for herself—the poor working girl who rises and
the bored society woman who has to learn a moral lesson. Swanson was ready
for her DeMille close-up. Furthermore, she had driving ambition and a willingness to work herself to death. And she had something that DeMille certainly noticed—she was a very beautiful young woman.

Today it's often said that DeMille discovered Swanson and developed
her into a star. The truth is more complicated, in that Swanson had already
played leading roles. She hadn't, however, become a name, and she had no
real persona of her own. It was DeMille who found the Swanson definition. In
their six films together from 1919 to 1921, he turned her into a symbol of a
particularly new kind of American woman: sophisticated, soignée, and definitely not a virgin. Although young, this woman was married, so she already
knew about the birds and the bees. She was rich, magnificently and luxuriously dressed, with jewelry to knock 'em dead in Peoria. She was not to be

... and a typical
1917 release

found sitting home by the fireside; she was out in the world, ready for something to happen, riding in fast cars, shopping, dancing, smoking, doing pretty
much whatever she felt like. One thing was certain—she was meeting lots of
men. There was no implication that she was wicked, or promiscuous, but she
was out there, and thus possibly available. There was a sense that anything
could happen to her—and in the DeMille plots, it did. There was also the
sense that the Gloria Swanson woman might even think for herself, no doubt a
thrilling idea for her female fans.

With DeMille, Swanson's career took off. DeMille appreciated her style,
and he knew she had that extra something that stars must have. He said that
one of the first things he noticed about her was "the way she leaned against a
door . . . She showed complete poise, repose and grace." Their first film
together, in 1919, was *Don't Change Your Husband* (advice she herself
ignored). In this cautionary tale, Swanson plays a dutiful wife who has to ask
permission from her husband to buy a new dress. Granted, the dress is a haute
couture frock made of pure silk and dusted with precious beading, but
still . . . why should a woman have to suffer like that? In all the DeMille films,
Swanson is awash in the world of fashion but also trapped in a world dominated by husbands, most of whom don't have a clue. The main events in the
lives of the Swanson women are Fashion and Husbands, Husbands and Fashion, but of the two it's Fashion that's the more potent force. A dress is everything. In *For Better, For Worse* (1919), she plays a rich young girl who calls

Swanson's first DeMille film, *Don't Change Your Husband*, with Lew Cody. A proper little wife . . .

her lover a coward when he chooses to stay out of World War I and care for crippled children, only to learn his true worth much later on. Her nobility is primarily expressed by her superb taste in clothes.

One of her greatest hits under DeMille was *Male and Female* (1919), based on James M. Barrie's *The Admirable Crichton*, and featuring her in a famous prolonged scene in which nothing happens except her bath. In a presentation that might be thought of as extended foreplay, the audience is first prepared for the delicious thrill it's about to have by a card that says, "Humanity is assuredly growing *cleaner*—but is it growing more artistic? Women bathe more often, but not as beautifully as did their ancient Sisters. Why shouldn't the Bath Room express as much Art and Beauty as the Drawing Room?" Why, indeed? Especially when the viewer is going to be allowed to peep in and watch the beauty disrobe and enter her tub. First, two attendants prepare Swanson's bath—dropping in bath salts, adjusting the water temperature, and putting rose water into the shower she will take afterward. The narrative flow stops dead while Swanson enters and prepares to step into the sunken tub. Carrying loofahs and huge towels, the two attendants step regally forward to assist her in dropping her dressing gown to reveal the very white skin of her lovely back. As they raise a huge towel to cover her, she lowers herself majestically into the water with all the aplomb that a four-foot-eleven-inch woman in a Hollywood bathtub scene can possibly summon.

Gloria Swanson is not being presented as a mere sex object; she's being

. . . and a glamorous figure
of fashion and power

presented as the representative luxury bather for the entire audience, male
and female. (Everything about the movie—a kind of *Upstairs, Downstairs*
story about the mingling of the classes on a desert island—stresses wealth
and consumer goods.) She's first seen following an introductory title card that
presents her character name, Lady Mary, against the background image of a
peacock with a fully spread tail. Her undergarments are shown in close-ups,
spread out on a chair for the camera to linger over lovingly: lace underwear,
silk stockings, frilly garters. The audience is given a look at her fancy silk
shoes with enormous buckles being delivered outside her door by a houseboy,
and our first sight of her presents her sleeping in a magnificent bed of silk and
satin.

After her bath, further details of her ritzy life are depicted in an
extended scene in which she does nothing except eat her breakfast. A butler,
three maids, and a footman arrive to serve. One carries the tray, and another
carries the little silver box that keeps her toast warm. The butler has to over-
see everything, and one of the maids has to lift Swanson's elbow and place a
tiny pillow embroidered with little roses under it. There's silver and crystal
aplenty, and while Swanson lounges, the camera makes sure to show us her
little feet in their beautiful stockings and white shoes. Everyone scurries
around, indicating that this outrageous pampering is a daily routine.

It's no wonder Gloria Swanson finally wanted out of these DeMille epics.
Although later in the film she has more to do, and there's exciting action

involving a shipwreck and survival on the island, she was primarily being used as a clotheshorse, a female fantasy figure. Even on the deserted island, she's decked out in a couple of fetching numbers made of leaves and twigs and skins, both of which have matching hats. She might also have wanted to leave DeMille while she could escape with her life. *Male and Female* is the movie with the famous scene in which Swanson lies down and lets a real lion put his paw on her back. In a "flashback" to Babylonian times, Swanson, a captive in chains and an excellent leopard skin, refuses the lust of the Babylonian king by biting him viciously on his hand. As a result, the "sacred lions of Ishtar" have to be trundled out so that Gloria, in yet another dramatic getup, can be carried in on an elaborate litter and tossed to them. ("I'll tame her," threatens the king . . .)*

During 1919, Gloria Swanson began to be a favorite with fan magazines, especially in fashion layouts. *Motion Picture* of August 1919 carried an article entitled "HATS! HATS! HATS!" in which she models a series of really bizarre chapeaus. "Gloria Swanson," gushes the article, "is a svelte, stylish little person." Gloria poses in beautiful close-ups in a "shopping hat" (which looks like a cereal bowl turned upside down, with a fern growing out of its bottom), an "afternoon hat," a "boudoir cap," a "bathing cap," a "sport hat," and a fish-scale turban that flaunts "gorah [*sic*] feathers." (The turban has no specific function, except possibly to frighten people.) In the final portrait, "Gloria is not wearing a hat, but a unique hair arrangement which resembles her favorite turbans." She looks dwarfed under a tower of hair, and highly uncomfortable.

Fan magazines featured her as a major spokesperson for their female audiences. In the December 1919 issue of *Motion Picture,* there is an article entitled "Gloria Swanson Talks On Divorce." Gloria, aged twenty at the time, holds forth: "I not only believe in divorce, but I sometimes think that I don't believe in marriage at all . . . After all, marriage is just a game. The more elastic the rules, the less temptation there is for cheating. I think that divorce should be made more easy, instead of more difficult. Yes, I believe in divorce as an institution!" (Swanson took the advice she gave her readership and used the institution of divorce herself a solid five times.) After all this, the magazine reminded readers that Cecil B. DeMille had personally chosen Gloria Swanson to represent the typical society woman in his "exquisite satires—satires that are doing their share towards forming a literature of the screen."

As the calendar turned over from the teens to the twenties, ushering in

---

*After Gloria had gamely let the lion put its paw on her, she marched into DeMille's office and informed him that she was shaking with hysteria and probably wouldn't be able to work the next day. Apparently DeMille then presented her with an open box of jewelry for her to select something that might soothe her nerves. "I picked out a gold mesh evening bag with an emerald clasp and immediately felt much better," she said.

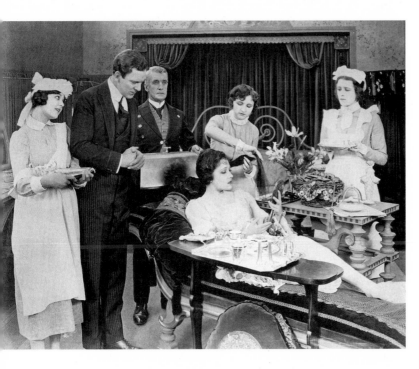

Male and Female: first waited on hand and foot, fulfilling the audience's dreams of luxury (LEFT), but later paying her dues, shipwrecked, reduced to rags, and doing the waiting herself

the Jazz Age, Gloria Swanson was front and center as the representative of the modern American woman with style. Audiences loved her, and off-screen, Miss Gloria Swanson was strutting her stuff. Showing an amazing disregard for what others might think, she had begun to live a life similar to that of the glamorous women she played on-screen, women who pretty much did what they pleased. Having been married at so young an age to Beery, she now took on husband number two, Herbert K. Sonborn (in 1919), and made no attempt to hide the fact that she gave birth to his daughter, Gloria, even though motherhood was thought to diminish a star's appeal in those years. In her autobiography, Swanson refers to the escalating troubles in this marriage ("I finally snapped over a remark he made about the number of internal baths I took") and says she moved out on Sonborn in May 1920. ("In May *The Great Moment* was a huge success and I broke up my marriage with Herbert.") She had barely passed her teenage years, and had already married twice and become a mother. Even more shocking, on her own during this time period she adopted a baby boy she named Joseph. For years, the rumor mill implied that this son was actually Swanson's illegitimate child by Joseph Kennedy, father of the future president. In her autobiography, Swanson is very vague about the dates of her marriages, births of her children, and of this adoption, but most sources indicate that she hadn't yet met Joseph Kennedy when she brought Joseph home, and that he was named for her own father.

In 1920, her fourth film with DeMille, *Why Change Your Wife?*, was released to great success. Swanson played a rich man's unglamorous wife, who learns a great fashion lesson when her husband is stolen from her by a well-dressed rival. The implication is very clear: if she had worn better clothes, this calamity would not have taken place. To get her husband back, the wife has to subject herself to ostrich feathers and furs and long ropes of pearls.

Her last DeMille in 1920 was *Something to Think About,* in which she's a poor blacksmith's daughter. It's an interesting film to watch because its plot is what many people believe all silent films to be—a melodramatic, old-fashioned story with religious overtones. Yet, recounting the events of the movie in no way gives a sense of how effective Swanson makes the material. Cast as the smith's daughter, Ruth ("the flower of the forge"), she is at first only a schoolgirl. Her transformation from this happy creature (who jumps around hugging everyone) into a lovely young woman—and ultimately into an elegant matron—has the influence of Mary Pickford all over it. DeMille uses one of his favorite leading men, the popular Elliott Dexter, as a crippled philosopher (conveniently wealthy) who pays for Swanson to go away to school and proposes marriage to her when she returns home.

Swanson and Dexter plan to wed, but trouble arrives in the form of "strong young manhood" from a "straight and faultless mould." Played by

Swanson with
Wallace Reid in
DeMille's *The
Affairs of Anatol*

Monte Blue, Jim cannot stop himself from loving Ruth—and the two run away
to the city on the eve of her marriage. Her father (famous character actor
Theodore Roberts) is humiliated, and as he pounds out a horseshoe, he cries
out, "I pray God I may never see her ungrateful face again." Sparks fly up, and
he is instantly blinded, or as a tart title card reminds the audience, "If we ask
a curse—we got a curse!" Swanson's husband, a sandhog, dies a hero's death
saving his comrades from the collapse of an underwater tunnel, while at home
Swanson makes a pie. Left pregnant and alone, she returns home. Her father
throws her out, but as she considers hanging herself in the barn, Dexter rescues her by generously offering a marriage "in name only." Years pass, and
Swanson grows to love her husband, but he gives her only coldness. (Meanwhile, her dad is blind in the poorhouse.) Suddenly, things are neatly wrapped
up. Dexter's faithful servant (Claire McDowell) has been lurking around,
reminding everyone to have faith. She collects Swanson and the two do some
serious praying, with excellent results. Dexter finds he can walk without
crutches, and Grandpa, fishing blindly down at the stream, is united with
Swanson's little son. Sunshine floods the world.

No recital of a story like this can possibly do justice to the competence
of the filmmakers, the visual imagination that is employed in the storytelling
process, and particularly to Swanson's graceful ability to make her character

attractive and believable. She wears only a few beautiful outfits in this movie, and is called on to prove she can act. She more than meets the challenge, and *Something to Think About* fueled her desire to do more, and to be taken seriously as something other than a clotheshorse.

Her last DeMille, *The Affairs of Anatol* (1921), loosely based on Arthur Schnitzler's play, took her back to the more typical DeMille formula. She suffers the affairs of a philandering husband, always nobly taking him back, until he finally learns his lesson. In all such soap operas, Swanson never plays the other woman; she is always the focal point of sympathy for the audience—the wronged wife or the dutiful daughter—so that women in the audience could sympathize with her, while considering her the absolutely last word in chic. Swanson worked very hard for DeMille, cooperating fully with anything he asked her to do. At the time, she said, "I have gone through a long apprenticeship. I have gone through enough of being nobody. I have decided that when I am a star, I will be every inch and every moment the star! Everybody from the studio gateman to the highest executive will know it." And she kept her word. "She is a sullen, opaque creature, an unknowable, but as enkindled as a young lioness," said Adela Rogers St. Johns.

The DeMille/Swanson films are considered highly significant for providing modern audiences an insight into the manners and morals of their time. But they're really about only three things: sex, women, and clothes. They reflect a flirtation with a new morality, and in particular, they begin to show a subtle questioning of the double standard, so they're definitely about sex, but always in good taste—so good that sometimes the issue gets lost. In all of them, Gloria Swanson wears incredible outfits: fur-trimmed lounging robes; long necklaces with crystals, onyx, and jet; turbans with feathers and plumes; evening gowns with long trains covered in beads and bands of ermine. She wears her hair piled high on her head, skyscraperish (partly because this gave her height), with these elaborate structures decorated with silk bands, golden stars, and tiny white pearls. Many of her costumes have an oriental flavor, and others are art deco with angular cuts and matching headdresses of jeweled material. She sleeps in beds of satin and ruffles, and when she sits down, she sits on brocaded chairs. But best of all, when she takes one of her baths—and these bathroom scenes became a Swanson/DeMille trademark—she enters a chamber as big as a football field, luxuriously decorated with chinchilla rugs and black marble fixtures. The public loved her, but it also loved the clothes, the beds, the chairs, and especially the bathrooms. "The public, not I, made Gloria Swanson a star," said DeMille, but he and his bathrooms played a major role in her success. He always showcased her, calling her his "young fellow" and praising her professionalism.

Alexander Walker described the Swanson role in DeMille films as that of "the playmate wife," and historians cite her character as *the* modern female of the post–World War I years in America, the one most admired by American women. Swanson's success in representing this creature was due both to her midwestern solidity and comic timing, which made her seem down-to-earth and basically good, and to her ability to dress up in exotic clothes, wield a cigarette holder, and look and act incredibly worldly-wise and sophisticated. (DeMille had been right—she knew how to lean against a door.) She effectively straddled the fence between realistic and fantastic, which was what the DeMille films made a fortune doing. (His method was shrewd. Show an orgy, and then put the idolators to death. Tempt the good wife and take her right to the edge, but let her come to her senses at the last moment. Have it both ways for the audience, the hallmark of the Hollywood film.) The DeMille/Swanson films are key to an understanding of the evolution of the female role in movies.

By the end of 1920, Gloria Swanson had become a household name and a top box office draw. Her movies with DeMille had all been first-class: well directed, brilliantly produced, and written with clarity and imagination. They had costarred her with such solid silent film names as Elliott Dexter, Lew Cody, Thomas Meighan, Theodore Roberts, Monte Blue, and Wallace Reid and contrasted her favorably with the other women in the cast—Julia Faye, Wanda Hawley, Bebe Daniels, Lila Lee. Swanson, however, wanted more, and when she got more, she wanted even more than that. She began to feel that DeMille was limiting her growth. (Certainly he stifled her considerable comic gifts, which were being put to no use.) Swanson had also learned about money, as Sonborn had shown her how to read a contract, shrewdly pointing out that DeMille might be her mentor, but he was not paying her the top salary that other stars were getting, or even always giving her star billing.

She left DeMille and began making movies exclusively for Artcraft's parent company, Famous Players–Lasky/Paramount, where she would remain until 1926. Her first starring vehicle, in which her name appeared above the title, was *The Great Moment* in 1920.* It was an original Elinor Glyn story— the mark of 1920s class—and paired her with handsome Milton Sills, a matinee idol of his time. She plays a noble young English girl who falls in love with an American engineer. The high point, a tribute to Glyn's idea of romance, occurs when a rattlesnake bites Swanson on the breast and the hero has to suck the poison out to save her life. Just how that pesky rattler got up there without her noticing is a bit of a puzzle, but it was hot stuff for an audience under the Glyn influence. Swanson appeared in two films in 1921, *Under the Lash* and *Don't Tell Everything*. In 1922, she made *Her Husband's Trademark, Beyond the Rocks* (which paired her with the up-and-coming Rudolph Valentino), *Her Gilded Cage*, and *The Impossible Mrs. Bellew*. At this point,

---

The Great Moment was released one month prior to *The Affairs of Anatol*, and Swanson had actually gone to Artcraft to make it prior to her final DeMille.

she began to take full charge of her own career, and assert her independence. She made herself constantly available for publicity, and throughout 1922 countless articles about her life, her clothes, and her films appeared everywhere. The April issue of *Motion Picture* presented a large layout of photographs from *My American Wife*, which was planned for a 1923 release and would costar her with popular Antonio Moreno. The full story of the film is reprinted, from start to finish—Swanson was to play a young daughter of a Kentucky gentleman, a character who was "for all of her lack of years, a woman of the world." She loves horses and horse racing and has captured blue ribbons around the world, racing as "N. H. Chester," a name everyone knew but that "comparatively few people knew . . . was a woman." Going to Argentina, she meets and falls in love with Moreno, whose mother cries out, "Never! Never while I live shall a LaTassa marry a woman of the race tracks!" (The photo caption above a shot of lovely Swanson dressed to the nines and holding a bunch of flowers answers back, "Gloria tosses her flowers in gay abandon.") After it's all settled, they get married and Moreno becomes ambassador to the United States, promising to "glorify the Argentine Republic with the aid and inspiration of my American wife." So much for Mama LaTassa! All these photographs feature Gloria carefully posing to show off all the details of each outré outfit.

The 1922 fan magazines reveal two things about Swanson's image. One is that she had a strong group of detractors, and the other is that everyone in the business was aware of her driving ambition (which she herself never tried to keep secret). In *Picture-Play* of September 1922, a writer named Ethel Sands comments on Swanson, "Either you are fascinated by her . . . or you don't like her at all. People . . . argue about her . . . pro-Gloria and anti-Gloria. She's called weird and freakish by many." Some even thought she wasn't very attractive. Adela Rogers St. Johns, who first met her at Triangle in 1917, later described her this way: "She was awful. Short and inclined to be dumpy. A strange face dominated by sullen grey eyes, with a long nose tilted upward, and a defiant mouth, whose upper lip seemed too short to cover her big strong white teeth."

Motion Picture of June 1922 comments on Swanson's ambition and her hard business sense with a thinly veiled critique: "Much as she loves her baby and her husband and her home, they could never mean *everything* to Gloria. Her career, her work in the studio is as vital to her as the oxygen she breathes . . . She is beautiful, as flawlessly beautiful as a diamond—and as cold." To find such overt criticism of a star in a movie magazine of the 1920s is rare, although sly attacks were fairly common. About Swanson they came right out in the open. This article nails her, saying, "Gloria loves clothes, loves luxuries, *loves fame.* [She is] possessed of a will to get and keep the lux-

Bluebeard's Eighth Wife: glamour post-DeMille

uries of this life . . . She is a dominating little woman . . . maneuvering her course with a careful rudder."

The lady herself seemed unfazed by any of this. She never apologized for her ambition, later saying, "I've always been my own business manager and agent. Mary Pickford had her mother, Chaplin had his brother, Lloyd had his uncle, the Talmadges had Schenck, the Gishes, Griffith. I was always alone." (Those who might want to point out that Swanson had plenty of business support from the powerful Joe Kennedy would do well to remember that he made a series of ruinous investments for her from which she almost didn't recover financially.)

In 1923 and 1924, she went on making the kind of romances that audiences liked her in, but she also made a successful return to comedy, and found a director, Allan Dwan, whom she liked and felt understood her abilities. By 1923, she had worked out a new contract, which raised her salary to an astronomical $6,500 per week, and that allowed her to move to New York City and make her movies there. Swanson's 1923 releases included the aforementioned *My American Wife*, plus *Prodigal Daughters* and *Bluebeard's Eighth Wife*, and along with *Zaza* and *Manhandled*, she released *The Humming Bird, A Society Scandal, Her Love Story,* and *Wages of Virtue* in 1924.*

One of the most successful of these movies was a Dwan film and the first of her New York–made movies: *Zaza*. The story of an actress, *Zaza* shows how intelligent Swanson was about her own image. She selected a story that contains humor and lively action—at one point she takes on another woman in a fight scene—but doesn't forget the clothes and glamour that had lifted her to stardom with DeMille. After her six DeMille features, she understood how important clothes were to a visual characterization, and she knew what her fans expected. Zaza starts out as a rather low-class cabaret star, dressed in gaudy emblems of her success. She wears a diamond bracelet set with two big *Z*'s and has huge monogrammed *Z*'s on her gloves. She also wears a flashy necklace with a chain holding another big *Z* and her hair holds little crystals with tiny triangles at the base of them. These hang out of her puffy curls, catching the light so that Swanson is literally sparkling. She looks fabulous. Seven years later in the plot, her clothes have become very simple and elegant, signaling to viewers that Zaza has changed. She's now a sophisticated lady, with a finer understanding of life because, after all, clothes make the woman.

During these years of success, fan magazines continued to point out that Swanson incited negative as well as positive feelings in moviegoers. The February 1924 issue of *Picture-Play* ran an article called "WHAT DO YOU THINK OF GLORIA?" by Norbert Lusk. The answer was ambivalent: "Either you rave about Gloria Swanson or you rage against her." Referring to the many letters the magazine received regarding her stardom, Lusk said fans wrote either that "Gloria is a great actress or a terrible one," that "she is endearing or repellant, beautiful or otherwise, and so on." (As for himself, he comments that he found Gloria's eyes "cryptic" because when he "looked into them, they told me nothing.") Swanson was masterful at publicity, but she cut no slack for anyone, not even when she knew she was deliberately under scrutiny. Lusk interviewed Swanson in person, and he points out that although her day had begun at 6 a.m., it was nearly midnight by the time she could see him. He asks her boldly why some people hate her, and she replies with wonderful evasion: "Oh, it's because it's a matter of vibrations." Not to be sidetracked, he presses on, "How much of your real self do we see on the screen?" To this, Gloria fires off, "Oh, do you mean am I a clotheshorse or just pretending to be one because it's the most I can do? I love clothes—beauty—luxury—extreme styles. The urge for these is a part of me. It is what you might call my real self, I suppose, though there are other things in life. Don't think I walk around in

---

*In addition to the titles discussed, she made *Coast of Folly* in 1925 and *Untamed Lady* and *Fine Manners* in 1926.

Zaza

twelve-foot trains at home." In conclusion, she reminds her interviewer that her pictures sell. For himself, he is willing to admit that Gloria Swanson is "polite," but he adds that like "all these actresses," she is definitely "different" from an ordinary person. (Wasn't that the point?)

Picture-Play claimed that such movies as her earlier *Don't Change Your Husband* were popular only with women, not men. In assessing Swanson, the magazine once again refers to her "hard-driving career," but adds that she "represents sophistication combined with freedom and extravagance and success with men." In a perceptive discussion of her acting, the author, hostile to Swanson personally, pinpoints her ability by saying that her acting skills are "spontaneity, fire, mood, feeling, unselfconsciousness." He concludes, however, by describing her as "grimly ambitious . . . just as determined now to be a great actress as she was once to get out of slapstick comedies. [Hers is] not a yielding nature, and she wants to hold on to what is hers." Reading an article like this, one feels that all this is exactly why women and girls adored Gloria Swanson. Somehow she didn't care what anyone thought of her. It wasn't that she was insensitive, but she knew that for a woman to be successful she was going to have to forgo the idea that everyone in the whole world would love her and approve of her.

Gloria Swanson
Apt 124

OPPOSITE: Gloria Swanson, Queen of Bizarre Fashion. RIGHT: The costume that got away— Bebe Daniels in *The Affairs of Anatol*

Swanson lived lavishly and didn't care who knew it. Once described as "the second woman in Hollywood to make a million [Pickford would have been the first], and the first to spend it," she liked to give parties and have fun. "Oh, the parties we used to have!" she said. "It was not uncommon to have 75 or 100 people for a formal, sit-down dinner. But they weren't stuffy. We all knew each other, and we had fun. In those days they wanted us to live like kings and queens . . . so we did. And why not? We were in love with life. We were making more money than we ever dreamed existed, and there was no reason to believe that it would ever stop." In 1924, *Photoplay* reported on the ways Swanson spent her money one year: purses, $5,000; furs, $25,000; lingerie, $10,000; silk stockings, $9,600; perfume, $6,000; and gowns, $50,000. As for jewelry, she rented it at 10 percent of its total cost, running up a bill for $500,000 in one year alone. (Swanson also made some significant purchases. Her legendary one-inch-thick bangle bracelets made of rock crystal disks with circular and baguette-cut diamonds and crystal beads threaded on elastic were displayed alone in a specially designed case at the Metropolitan Museum of Art's Cartier show in the spring of 1998.)

The two best Dwan/Swanson comedies are *Manhandled* in 1924 and *Stage Struck* in 1925. In both, Swanson manages to utilize her considerable comedic skills, send up her DeMille image with grace (but without malice),

and deliver a heroine who wins the man of her dreams. *Manhandled* begins
with a title that lays its morality out clearly: "The world lets a girl think that its
pleasure and luxuries may be hers without cost—that's chivalry. But if she
claims them on this basis, it sends her a bill in full, with no discount—that's
reality." Gloria plays "Tessie McGuire, one of the mob," a low-level sales-
clerk in the basement of Thorndyke's department store. This movie connects
her directly to her female fans in the audience—the ordinary young girls who
admired her for her glamour and grit—through the device of having her play
one of them. The opening sequence, one of her best comedy scenes, has
Tessie, tired at the end of her day, struggling with her journey home on a
crowded subway. Swanson skillfully plays out the role of the little person, buf-
feted and wedged in by bigger riders. First, she has trouble just getting
through the turnstile, as others keep shoving her aside. Once she's on the
train, she keeps up her spirits as best she can, energetically chewing her gum
and trying to hang on. Her hat keeps getting knocked down over her eyes, and
her feet are constantly stepped on. Finally, she drops her purse. All the con-
tents spill out and as she bends down to retrieve things, two men also bend to

help her, so that her arms become entangled with their elbows. When they stand up to grab the subway straps they had been hanging on to, Swanson is lifted off her feet into the air, a prisoner. Later she is squashed on all sides, bumped back and forth as the car roars onward; her hat is knocked off and stepped on and the grapes it had been so ridiculously adorned with are ripped off. Then comes the final indignity—a guy winks at her. She pulls herself up into a pose worthy of one of her baroness roles and cold-shoulders him. At her station, she can't get through the door because she's so small. Every time she pushes toward the exit, she's carried backward by the incoming rush of humanity. Finally, she makes it, flopping down over the turnstile as she exits.

By beginning *Manhandled* this way, Gloria Swanson, the great and glamorous star, shows what a swell fella she really is. Having objected to slap-stick in her Sennett days, she now was a big enough star to feel she could get away with it. She had already proved her dramatic ability and sealed her image as a glamour queen. There's also a sly subtext, a private conversation between Gloria and the shopgirls in the audience. "This is what men do to me, even though I'm Gloria Swanson. I just have to pick myself up and keep on going."

As the story proceeds, she gets bored because her true love, Jimmy the garage mechanic (Tom Moore), is so caught up in work he never takes her out. She goes to a party with "Pinkie, who believes heaven will protect the working girl and send some bracelets, enough to keep her wrists warm." At the party, Swanson is shown eyeballing the "ladies," who are beautifully dressed and very sophisticated. Swanson admiring Swanson-ites! She ogles the "name" guests, such as Ann Pennington, a star from the Follies, who plays herself in a cameo role. Pennington, who is even smaller than Swanson, does her famous dance, and Swanson later gives a brief imitation, but her underpants fall down. Eventually, she moves up out of Thorndyke's. First she becomes an artist's model, striking a pose that presents her in elaborate oriental garb. She looks like the DeMille Gloria, serene and mysterious in an outlandish head-dress and gold-embroidered costume, but after holding this pose for a while she's told she can rest, and then she swiftly turns into an entirely different person with a comic stretching of her limbs and a funny little shake.

In the end, of course, she learns that the rich life is not for her, just as her Jimmy returns from Detroit, where he's sold an invention that makes him a millionaire. (He enters the apartment house and instructs the landlady: "Step aside, madam! I'm a millionaire!") Later, seeing Swanson dressed up like a Gloria Swanson glamour figure, he suddenly spurns her, saying: "You're like the goods you hated to sell in Thorndyke's basement—rumpled—soiled—pawed over—MANHANDLED!" Everything gets sorted out, needless to say, and the two end up in each other's arms. *Manhandled* is one of Swanson's most

Swanson as a waitress who dreams in *Stage Struck*, with Lawrence Gray . . . and
what she dreams of—beads, bracelets, and victim

representative films because it shows us all possible Swansons: the elegantly
dressed clotheshorse, the exotic mannequin, the lovely leading lady, and the
deliciously comic little girl.

In *Stage Struck*, Swanson is wonderful. Working as a waitress in a pancake house, she is seen flipping a pancake onto her own head, juggling trays,
getting kicked in the seat of the pants, and, amazingly, donning a mask and
boxer's outfit to enter the fight ring as "Kid Sockem" so she can knock the
block off Gertrude Astor in a boxing match. It's pure slapstick comedy. (Those
who think Gloria Swanson is nothing but Norma Desmond have to see this
movie.) The shrewdness about her image is again on display. The movie opens
with magnificent color sequences (color by Technicolor) in which she is seen
in a series of fabulous costumes, supposedly portraying a famous actress who
is re-creating the great roles of theatre and history, such as Salome. This turns
out to be a dream sequence, and the little pancake waitress is then introduced
in plain clothes, hilariously practicing her acting lessons in front of a distort-
ing mirror. Everything Swanson does is very precise, very small, very on the
mark—she's a controlled pantomimist and a good mimic. She's a natural
clown, a kind of female Charlie Chaplin due to her small stature (which is why
she could imitate Chaplin so well in *Sunset Boulevard*).

In 1925 Gloria made off-screen history by being officially the first big star to marry European aristocracy. On February 5, she wed Henri, the Marquis de la Falaise de la Coudraye, husband number three, and on her way back to Hollywood from Europe, sent Adolph Zukor a famous cablegram: "Am arriving with the Marquis tomorrow. Please arrange ovation." The arrival was indeed something. She was met by a brass band, and she and her prize-catch husband (and Louella Parsons) drove in an open car through the streets from the station to the studio. Gloria stood up in the backseat holding huge bouquets of flowers and blew kisses to her loyal fans who lined the streets and cheered their heads off. (This marriage ended in divorce in 1930, after which the Marquis went on to marry another glamorous movie star, Constance Bennett.) Of her many failures in marriage Swanson would say, "The mess I made of marriage was all my own fault. I can smell the character of a woman the instant she enters a room, but I have the world's worst judgment of men. Maybe the odds were against me. When I was young, no man my age made enough money to support me in the style expected of me. There's no sense kidding myself—I loved all the pomp and luxury of that style. When I die my epitaph should read: She Paid The Bills. That's the story of my private life."

Swanson had met her marquis on the set of one of her movies. She had always wanted to play the role of Madame Sans-Gêne from the successful play by Victorien Sardou and had managed to persuade Adolph Zukor, her boss, that she would not only be perfect in the role but that it would be a financial blockbuster. He had acceded, and in November 1924 she traveled to Europe for the authentic French locations. The marquis was hired to be her interpreter, since the movie's director, Leonce Perret, spoke very poor English. *Madame Sans-Gêne* was the most ambitious screen role Swanson had undertaken.

The plot sounds like a perfect Swanson story.* According to reviews, she begins at the bottom, as a little laundress who does the young Napoleon's washing. She's all sympathy and support when he can't pay his laundry bills, stealing stockings from other customers for him and mending his shirts and darning his hose. Reviews indicate that Swanson's gift for comedy is well used, and that she's lively and clever—an altogether appealing laundress. Later, she emerges into her other Swanson self: the well-dressed duchess of Dantzig, very beautiful and elegant but not without her comedy touches. The duchess loses her petticoat when she climbs into her carriage (no other star ever had as much trouble with undergarments as Gloria Swanson), and happily sheds her elegant shoes when they pinch her feet.

Variety, like the *Times*, spent more time reviewing the audience than the film itself, which they dismissed with a coldhearted "If it were not Gloria Swanson appearing in the title role . . . Famous Players would have nothing to brag

---

Madame Sans-Gêne is a famous "lost film," unavailable for screening.

The famous lost film,
Madame Sans-Gêne

about as far as motion picture entertainment is concerned. Gloria . . . does make it possible for one to sit through the feature." According to *Variety*, the publicity and exploitation campaign behind the movie were unprecedented.

> Never has Broadway seen a splash such as was given to this star. Her name in the largest electric letters ever given to an individual on Broadway decorates the facade of the Rivoli; the house is shrouded in the tri-color of France and the Stars and Stripes, and all the other buildings on both sides of Broadway from 49th to 50th streets are similarly decorated with the result that one can hardly get standing room in the theatre . . . Outside the theatre the police reserves from the West 30th and West 47th street police stations were trying to hold back the frantic mob of the sightseers who were trying to glimpse the star . . . So intent on rubbering were they that they did not notice the dips working in the crowd, and many a one went home lighter in pocket because of the light-fingered gentry present.

(There was a similar crush when the film opened in Los Angeles shortly afterward.) How did Swanson feel about the adulation? Ever the realist, she wrote in her autobiography that she had been thinking, "I'm just twenty-six. Where do I go from here? . . . I was thinking that every victory is also a defeat. Nobody gets anything for nothing."

In 1926, Gloria Swanson did something that few actresses had dared to do—she left the security of Paramount and went out on her own to produce her own features, forming Gloria Swanson, Inc., with her movies to be released by United Artists. In order to make the break from Paramount, she had turned down an impressive million-dollar offer from Zukor, so she felt she should make the most of her freedom and resolved to try artistically bold movies.

Unfortunately, her reputation as nothing but a clotheshorse is partly substantiated by the first of these, *The Loves of Sunya* (1927), a story about a woman who has no fun being a dutiful wife but who also has no fun being a career woman. (The life of a woman, it seems, just isn't much fun.) Sunya's compensation, however, is that she *can* wear very good clothes and particularly dramatic jewelry, all of it made of diamond-designed triangles, circles, and squares, very art deco in style. Swanson again gets to present her screen character in several different modes. At first, she's a sweet young girl learning from a traveling soothsayer what her future might be, according to the choices she makes regarding her life. What she sees inside his crystal gives her a chance to be pure, then sophisticated, then remorseful, and finally downtrodden. In particular, she plays a terrific drunk scene as a soused opera star who has to go on to sing *Tosca*. "Once we have made our choice," the movie tells women, "we must be honest. If it were not for that . . . what?" Swanson lives out the various female choices in great style on behalf of her audience—and she knew what her audience wanted from her. Heavy publicity combined with her glamour to draw big audiences; her company netted a hefty $630,370. Gloria Swanson, Inc., was off to a strong start.

Two of her best movies, both made in 1928 for her own company, are available today in incomplete forms, *Sadie Thompson* and *Queen Kelly*. Many feel that her *Sadie Thompson* is not only the best version of the Somerset Maugham story ever filmed, but also her best performance. The last scenes are missing from the only existing print, but Dennis Doros of Milestone Films has restored and released the film using stills, remaining footage, and the original script to guide him. This affords today's audience a chance to see the mature Gloria Swanson at the peak of her career and her beauty, performing confidently in a role that uses all her potential. Swanson was at this point totally unafraid to look and dress cheap; after all, she had more than proved herself as a fashion plate. Her eloquent and expressive face is used equally well for scenes of flirtatious behavior, comic playfulness, desperate fear, and passionate anger. Swanson exudes a healthy sexuality, a wholesome sense of herself as a woman. She doesn't simper or vamp in her scenes as the sexy Sadie; rather, she just moves forward in the frame as if she were an attractive woman who knows she's attractive, and who knows, understands, and likes men. When she and Captain Tim O'Hara, played by a roguish Raoul Walsh, who also directed, grow attracted to each other, their desire takes a playful form.

As Sadie Thompson: happy before conversion . . . and miserable afterward,
with Lionel Barrymore as Reverend Davidson

(Walsh is excellent as the simple hero who, as someone remarks, "is a beautiful bird, but he flies straight.") Swanson hides his hat behind her back, and he
pushes her forward across the room in mock battle, the two of them sparring
and playing and flirting in high spirits and with obvious pleasure. Theirs is not
steamy sex, as depicted in the 1953 *Miss Sadie Thompson* starring Rita Hayworth, and it's not low-down and cash-on-the-barrelhead sex as in the 1932
Joan Crawford version, *Rain.* When Sadie repents, Swanson plays it in a
highly original way—she just lets all the life go out of the character. She
deflates Sadie, makes her into what is almost a collapsed bag of a woman.
She's still beautiful enough to tempt Reverend Davidson, but it's as if the
essence of who and what she was had been killed. Lionel Barrymore, in the
role of the twisted reverend who temporarily crushes Sadie's spirit, is austere,
with an almost evil cunning about him. Barrymore isn't yet debilitated by his
arthritic condition, so he stands ramrod tall, rigid, unbending.

Swanson's notorious lost epic, *Queen Kelly*, was begun in 1928, as sound
hovered over Hollywood. If the film had been finished, it would have run for
thirty reels, or approximately five hours. The movie was a "Gloria Swanson
Pictures Corporation" production, with Swanson in partnership with her lover,

Joseph Kennedy. Direction was under the leadership of the great Erich von Stroheim, creator of such masterpieces as *Greed, The Merry Widow,* and *Blind Husbands.* Had it been completed, it would have been von Stroheim's eighth movie; as it turned out, it was his final silent film. Infuriated by what she considered his excesses, Swanson closed down production after approximately one-third of the script had been shot, and based on what is available for viewing today, the stoppage was a major loss to film history. Eventually, *Queen Kelly* was handsomely restored to a ninety-seven-minute version, using remaining footage, stills, and the original full orchestral score that was discovered during restoration. (In 1985, Dennis Doros, who had also directed the restoration of *Sadie,* made available to audiences the most complete version of *Queen Kelly* ever assembled.)

Queen Kelly showcases Gloria Swanson at her best. In a sense, it's an overview of her career, an epic that allows her to go from being a playful, amusing convent girl (her Sennett days) to a beautifully turned-out young woman (her DeMille spectacles) and on into an actress of maturity and subtlety, a sophisticated woman of the world (the kind of roles she hoped her own production company would provide her). She is ravishingly beautiful in the footage, which includes the famous images of her in close-up, kneeling to pray amidst a screenful of lit candles. This scene was later used in *Sunset Boulevard* to show what Norma Desmond had been like as a young actress. "We had faces!" is a line inspired by Gloria Swanson in *Queen Kelly.*

Swanson as Patricia Kelly, or "Queen Kelly," as her lover dubs her, has everything it takes to portray a character full of curiosity, life, and desire, but who is still innocent of love, though eager to be initiated. She is like a pure jewel inside the very, very oddball setting provided by the perverse talents of von Stroheim. His stunning images include the naked, wild-haired Queen Regina the Fifth (Seena Owen), drunk in her bed, cuddling her fluffy white cat (decked out in ribbons) to her naked body . . . Swanson, a virginal convent girl in white, with her bloomers down around her ankles, laughed at by the handsome prince and his troops because her elastic gave way . . . the kinky byplay in which Swanson boldly picks up these same undies and flings them in the face of the prince (Walter Byron), only to have him respond with delight, sniffing them delicately and claiming them as a token . . . the mad queen whipping Swanson, driving her out into the darkness in her white nightie . . . and Swanson's arrival at her aunt's brothel in Dar es Salaam (where she will end up as owner, a power figure dressed totally in black).

Von Stroheim's gift was for detail, and *Queen Kelly*'s visual world of decadence and sophistication is unparalleled. The underpants scene is a perfect example of his talent for suggesting ripe sex mixed with a level of innocence and purity without which his particular brand of kinkiness doesn't

work. Swanson's convent girl knows her undies should never be seen, particularly by a troop of soldiers, and she knows that above all else, she should never let a man handle any clothing that had touched her private parts. Yet her considerable fire and anger motivate her to toss the garments in the prince's face. She wants to be rid of her innocence, and shows her penchant for passion, her fiery nature. Swanson plays her role perfectly, capturing all its anger, humor, sexual heat, and innocence. She was perfect material for von Stroheim to mold. In a sense, her career ended just as she hit her peak, and her gifts for comedy, tragedy, bizarre sexuality, and passion would not find a movie outlet again until she was fifty years old, in the hands of another German, Billy Wilder, in *Sunset Boulevard*.

The disappearance of *Queen Kelly* and *Sadie Thompson* for many years, so that modern viewers didn't get to see them even in the rare instances when silent classics were revived, diminished Swanson's reputation as an actress. ("I was a star at twenty-one," said Swanson, "and a has-been at thirty-three.") Although she is known as one of the four "fabulous faces" of American movies—along with Garbo, Crawford, and Dietrich—hers is often thought to be the least beautiful, least interesting face of the group. Seeing her animated, alive, and moving, and watching her magnificently expressive face at work reveals quite a different story. A touch of meanness settles around her mouth and eyes in still photos, but this disappears when she is involved in movement

In the film that was never finished, *Queen Kelly:* from convent girl (OPPOSITE, with Seena Owen) to brothel madame (RIGHT)

and action. (Arthur Bell, the poisonous but funny writer for the *Village Voice,* once wrote of Swanson, "I'm sick of seeing her mean little face all over town.")

Despite her best efforts, Swanson's career floundered in the 1930s. It wasn't because of sound, because she had a lovely speaking voice and could sing reasonably well. In her first sound movie, *The Trespasser* in 1929, she not only introduced the song "Love, Your Magic Spell Is Everywhere" (written especially for her), but she received her second Oscar nomination as Best Actress of the year. (Her first was for *Sadie Thompson,* and *Sunset Boulevard* was her third, but she would never win.) Her reviews were excellent, and she seemed to have glided smoothly from silence to sound, making possibly the easiest transition of any of the great 1920s names. She was only thirty-one years old, a tremendous star, and a two-time Oscar nominee. For reasons that are not entirely clear, however, nothing seemed to click for her ever again, except for *Sunset Boulevard.* She made *What a Widow!* in 1930, *Indiscreet* and *Tonight or Never* in 1931, *A Perfect Understanding* in 1933, and *Music in the Air* in 1934. None of these films was particularly successful, and none did anything to revitalize her career. She told David Chierichetti in 1975 that "the picture thing was very difficult for me at that time. It's a long, tiresome story. They didn't want stars to be producers." Her strong will, her independence, and her very 1920s "modern woman" image may all have worked against her as the new decade took hold. Swanson also had other interests, and from 1934 on, she was off the screen for seven years, until *Father Takes a Wife* in 1941. After that, she didn't appear again in movies (except in a compilation of clips from Sennett comedies called *Down Memory Lane* that was released in 1949) until *Sunset Boulevard*. (And for that matter, the latter didn't do much for her, either. After her huge success in it, she made only *Three for Bedroom C*, a lackluster comedy in 1952, and *Nero's Mistress*, a European mishmash in 1962. There was also a second compilation film, *When Comedy Was King*, in 1960.)

Sunset Boulevard, directed by Billy Wilder and written by him with Charles Brackett and D. M. Marshman, Jr., costarred Swanson with the young, handsome, and talented William Holden. Her old director, Erich von Stroheim, played a supporting role as Max, her former director now turned lifetime butler and confidant. The movie was an enormous success for everyone involved, and for Swanson it meant that she was back in the limelight again. Although she lost out in the Oscar race to Judy Holliday (who won for *Born Yesterday*), Swanson had come back after a long dry spell, and she came back at the very top.

Sunset Boulevard is about a silent film star who wasn't just an ordinary silent film star but was unique, beautiful, talented, and legendary. ("Madame is the greatest star of them all," intones Max.) There has always been much speculation as to just whom Norma Desmond was modeled on, but it was probably no one actress. She's most likely a combination of the ego of Negri (who always knew what she was doing) and the genuinely crazy Mae Murray (who apparently *never* knew what she was doing). Having Swanson play the part verifies the character, and, in fact, gives the entire story a credibility it might not otherwise have. She's magnificent. Who could know better than she did how to play an exotic diva from the era? Everything about her, from her leopard trim, her cigarette holders, her bangle bracelets, to her bed shaped like a golden swan and her outré open-air automobile seems completely authentic—because it is. And when Norma goes on the lot, to Swanson's old studio Paramount Pictures, and meets her old director Cecil B. DeMille playing himself, everything rings true. For many people in the audience, it was an extraordinary blurring of fact and fiction, since for them it had been less than twenty-five years since it had all been real. Swanson herself was just past fifty years old, yet she and the world of the movie seemed to come from a time and place so remote that few could remember it. When Norma's bridge group meets, and the other players include Anna Q. Nilsson, Buster Keaton, and H. B. Warner, older people in the audience gasped. (I know. I was there, ushering, watching it numerous times.) And, of course, being able to use clips from the never-released *Queen Kelly* not only gave viewers Norma as she authentically was as a younger woman, but also convinced them that it could have been Norma, not Swanson, in the part, because they themselves had

Swanson in her last great role, Norma Desmond in *Sunset Boulevard*

never seen it as a Swanson film. This was heady stuff, and when you add in Swanson's imitation of Charlie Chaplin, the superb writing and directing, the other members of the fine cast, the art direction and music, the moody cinematography—you have a masterpiece. Few actresses ever find a role like Norma Desmond. In truth, only one did, and she more than met the challenge. When Swanson rises up in the flickering light coming down from the screen, and with genuine passion—and considerable nuttiness—cries out, "We didn't need dialogue! We had faces!"—her profile stops any arguments.

After *Sunset Boulevard*, Swanson's name came alive to a new generation who did not know her and was born again for those who did. Yet the role of Norma Desmond was so powerful, and depicted such an obsessed character, that perhaps it doomed her. People began to think that Gloria Swanson *was* Norma Desmond. She never quite shook off Norma's shadow. Even though she made comedy appearances on television, starred on Broadway in a revival of *Twentieth Century* (with Jose Ferrer), and took over another leading role on Broadway in *Butterflies Are Free,* her career was once again associated with tragedy and confused by the mingling of her personal life with her performance life. Gloria the Great finished her remarkable career on film in a way that was totally appropriate for her: her final role, in *Airport 1975* (1974), is a cameo as herself—what could be more perfect than that? Hearing that the plane is going down, Swanson elects to forget her jewel case and save her autobiography—a shrewd business move by the character/movie star who had always known how to run her own business better than anyone else, and who was always a good judge of value for her money. And she looked youthful, slim, and still beautiful.

Gloria Swanson was a true film phenomenon. She endured past the end of her movie career in ways that few of her silent contemporaries could match. Always a capable businesswoman, she found an outlet for her energy and intelligence in many ventures. There were her fashion designs ("Gowns by Gloria") and her health food lectures. Swanson was famous for having become a health nut very early, a nutritionist before it was fashionable. Sometime in the 1920s she stopped eating salt, red meat, and dairy products, existing on a diet of seaweed, bread, herb tea, and organically grown vegetables cooked in her own pressure cooker, which she hauled everywhere with her. (Scoffers should consider that she lived to the healthy old age of eighty-four or eighty-five, dying in 1983 at home in New York, still looking slim, energetic, and smooth-skinned.) She also married three more times, and gave birth to another daughter, Michael, and remained devoted to her children.*

In fact, one of the most interesting aspects of Swanson's career is her motherhood. More than any other actress of her time, she was charged with having a raging ambition that bordered on ruthless; like Mary Pickford, she had tried to direct her own career, shape it, and control it. Yet despite this, plus all the foolishness of her personal life with its luxury, publicity, rumors, and marriages and divorces, she raised two daughters and a son and never made any attempt to hide them away or deny her motherhood. And then she openly celebrated becoming a grandmother to seven grandchildren. Swanson, the woman who had had it all, claimed that the most exciting moment in her life was the first time she held "my child in my arms. I wanted children more than anything else," she said. "Oh, I could say it was coming back from Paris with a new husband, the marquis, and taking a private train across the country, or I could mention the film festival in Belgium, where every theatre was playing a Swanson picture. But when you come right down to it, and you get old and they put you out to pasture, who's around? Your family and your dear ones, that's who." (Yes, it was the family, but she threw in Paris, the private train, and the film festival.)

---

*Gloria got around. Husband number four in 1931 was Irish sportsman Michael Farmer, number five was investment broker William N. Davey in 1945, and number six was William Dufty (1976), a writer who helped her with her autobiography. She also had her share of glamorous affairs, with, among others, writer Gene Markey and actors Joel McCrea and Herbert Marshall. Her romance with Marshall was described by fan magazines as something "beautiful and brave with dialogue by Noel Coward."

Swanson's movie career, as Richard Koszarski points out in *An Evening's Entertainment,* is not one that displays a "conventional arc of achievement," but rather a "series of plateaus." She isn't easily categorized, and she doesn't have a single dominant persona . . . other than that of Gloria Swanson, Movie Star, her off-screen self (or possibly the erroneous "Norma Desmond" label). Over the years, she received many accolades, among them a tribute at Eastman House in Rochester, New York, where at her retrospective in 1966 she proved herself still a colorful quote machine, saying, after the films were shown, "I must say I got fed up looking at this face of mine. First it was a pudding, then it was an old dumpling. Talk about the face that launched a thousand ships—this was a thousand faces that launched I don't know what—a career, I guess." She also showed her serious side by saying, "Failure is never easy to deal with. Success is impossible unless you've had the experience. I like making movies better than anything else."

Although she was probably associated with the silliness of movie stardom as much as anyone in the business, there was always something profoundly sensible about Swanson. ("I guess I'm an old ironsides," she once said.) No matter what, she always kept her head straight and her feet on the ground. Instead of relying on men to make her deals, she became her own agent and learned how to handle her own business. She was as colorful and quotable and demanding of her rights as any star, but she was always practical and cut her losses. She kept advancing her product, improving it, updating it—the product being herself, Gloria Swanson. "I saved my own career," she said.

To the end of her life, Gloria Swanson knew how to play her part. No Norma Desmond, she was nevertheless always ready for her close-up. When she was eighty, she was still walking around grandly, carrying a single red rose and demanding that her theme song, "Love, Your Magic Spell Is Everywhere," be played. ("Her greed for fame is amazing," wrote James Robert Parish.) And yet she never became one of those aging movie stars for whom there is no life, no laughter, no honest human contact. Somewhere deep inside her there still seemed to live that little clown from her Keystone years. No matter how grand she acted, or how expensive her clothes were, no one could possibly believe that she was really from the upper echelons of society. Like Joan Crawford, who took her place as the representative shopgirl aspiring to wealth and society, Swanson was common clay. The audience knew it, but they loved her lifelong performance as the crazy movie star. Furthermore, they forgave her for it in the end, and let her escape from it.

That would not be as true for Pola Negri.

POLA NEGRI

Pola Negri may have been the most colorful star ever to appear in silent films. Her over-the-top antics off-screen seem to have totally obscured her actual career, and certainly her talent. She was an excellent actress, capable of playing with real passion and fire, but her shenanigans turned her into the fundamental caricature of a silent movie star, almost a real-life Norma Desmond. (It's rumored that Billy Wilder first offered the role of Desmond to Pola, who is said to have thrown him out. She took her career seriously, and to lampoon herself was unthinkable to her.) Although her remaining fans are still loyal, even fanatical about her, Pola Negri today is almost entirely forgotten.

One contemporary critic called Pola "all slink and mink," and another wrote, "You had the feeling that the back of her neck was dirty," by which he was making a clumsy attempt to say that Pola Negri seemed earthy, like an early Anna Magnani. Whatever she was, she knew how to sell it. She had a real talent for front-page publicity, and she represented, as well, that inevitable lure for Americans—the European sensibility. She was foreign, and that meant unencumbered by puritan ideals.

The story of Pola Negri, like its leading lady herself, is a colorful one. Her birth date, as with so many birth dates of female movie stars, is subject to negotiation. Some say she was born in 1894, others in 1899, but the general idea is that she was born during those last years of the nineteenth century. There are many versions of her story, and which of them (including her own) is true is hard to decide. Here's one of them: She was born with the impossible name of Barbara Apollonia Chalupiec in Janowa, Poland. She studied at the Imperial Ballet School in St. Petersburg and at the Philharmonia Drama School in Warsaw, and made her debut in Poland as an ingenue at the Rozmaitoczi Theatre. She received excellent notices, particularly for her performances as Hedvig in Ibsen's *Wild Duck* and the title role in Gerhardt Hauptmann's *Hannele*. These successful appearances led her to be invited to make films in Poland, and her movie debut is assumed to have been in 1914, in *Niewolnica Zmyslow* (no American title). She became a top star quickly, and during this period she also appeared in Max Reinhardt's celebrated stage pantomime *Sumurun*, first in Poland and later in Berlin. Arriving in Berlin in 1917, she made a series of films there, some of them wonderfully comic shorts. For five years, she was at the very top of the German film industry, and also became a favorite stage actress. The most important thing that happened to her, however, was meeting the great actor/director Ernst Lubitsch. Together,

Negri and Lubitsch made a series of films in Berlin that included *The Eyes of the Mummy* and *Carmen* in 1918; *Madame Du Barry* in 1919; the filmed version of *Sumurun* in 1921 (with both Negri and Lubitsch repeating their stage roles); *The Wild Cat* (also 1921); and finally *Die Flamme* (called *Montmartre* in the United States) in 1922.

Negri and Lubitsch found popularity with American audiences when three of these films were released in the United States: *Carmen* in 1921, retitled *Gypsy Blood; Madame Du Barry* in 1920, retitled *Passion;* and *Sumurun* in 1921, retitled *One Arabian Night.* When these imports arrived on American screens, audiences were bowled over by Negri's strong sexuality, her fearless portrayals of passion, and her animal magnetism. She was promoted as a descendant of Polish Gypsies, the implication being "and that means she's not bound by our rules." Pola Negri brought Americans her own kind of "new modern woman"—an openly sexual and sensuous creature who made absolutely no apology for it.

Negri's German films by Lubitsch represent her early years very successfully. Her talents are easily observable in *Passion.* She holds a viewer's attention, and she plays a fully developed character. In the silent era, glamour girls were usually one thing or another—good or bad. Stars were divided into those who scampered and those who simpered, the virgin or the whore, the girlishly attractive or the womanly seductive. Negri in *Passion* is everything. She is scintillating and extremely attractive, with the implication that men are drawn to her not for her decadence or erotic posturing but for her impulsive, hearty sexuality, which they long to experience. She's unafraid of sex, and makes it clear she wants it, too. (Negri will not be jumping off any balconies to avoid a "fate worse than death.") The men in her movies can't resist her. They drop like flies. Imagine the impact it must have had on audiences in 1921 when they saw Pola Negri, as Madame Du Barry, and Emil Jannings, as King Louis XV, enact the real thing in *Passion.* While Negri leans back sensuously on her luxurious bed, King Louis is seen slipping her little shoes on and off her feet. (She won't get up until she's properly shod, and properly shod means a king must do the job.) Louis kisses her feet and calves, licking one toe. Then he clips her fingernails for her . . . and you didn't see that every day of the week (and still don't). When Dan Duryea paints Joan Bennett's toenails in *Scarlet Street* (1945), directed by another German, Fritz Lang, the scene is chillingly decadent, sinister in its implications. In *Passion,* Jannings playing with Negri's feet and nails may seem slightly besotted, or possibly hilarious, but it also seems like real love.

In the scene in which Negri first meets the king, bringing him a petition from her penniless lover, Louis presents his hand to her to be kissed in the traditional formal greeting. Negri takes one of his fingers, kneels down, then impulsively jumps up and kisses his cheek instead. He's so startled, he plops

Negri in the three German films that were reissued to great acclaim in America: LEFT, *Carmen* (*Gypsy Blood* in U.S.); BELOW, *Sumurun* (*One Arabian Night*) . . .

. . . Madame Du Barry (Passion), before (RIGHT) and after the revolution

backward into his chair. Before he can get up again, she falls into his lap as naturally as anything, her bosom right beneath his nose. She has cleverly put the petition there, so he has to reach in to draw it out. He reads it carefully, signs it, and then, pretty clever himself, insists on returning it to its "envelope." As he slowly, very slowly, inserts the thinly rolled parchment down the front of her dress, she begins to giggle, twist and turn, and dimple at him. They kiss, the king with one hand on her breast and one on the petition, which is now once again snugly down her front. She seems to enjoy all this so much, as if it were the most natural thing in the world: All kings should have their hands down the front of her dress. It's such fun! It feels so good! It's so healthy for both of them! Let's all try it at home for similar results!

Passion is a well-directed movie, a model of what an epic film should be. It combines historical sweep with intimate portraiture, and there is no overestimating what having a good director can do for the later reevaluation of an actress's career. Lubitsch doesn't use reaction shots in *Passion,* nor does he use many close-ups other than at medium range. When he wants to emphasize Pola Negri—as when she appears in male garb to overhear her ex-lover plotting her death—he first shows her walking between her lover and the other patriots he's plotting with. Then he irises down onto her, shutting everyone else out of the frame. This gives Negri an almost superhuman quality, and makes her supremely important in the image. (The advertisements for *Passion* said, "POLA NEGRI AND A CAST OF 5000 PEOPLE IN *Passion,* A Mighty Epic of the Screen. This is the story of a wonder woman—the world's most daring adventuress.") Ads also referred to *Passion* as "the acme of dramatic art." Today, it is known, if at all, as the chief film that made Negri an American star, and it is respected for its action scenes, its richly detailed sets and costumes, and its very sophisticated visual presentation.

In *One Arabian Night,* Negri plays "the dancer," and Lubitsch, who both acts and directs, plays "the hunchback." The movie is a comic farce, with characters running in and out of rooms, jumping in and out of trunks, and delivering such lines as "the market place is choked with the gaping rabble." It's a glorious tale about a hag, a hunchback, a juggler, and a dancer who are "wanderers out of the desert wilderness." Pola more or less plays it straight, allowing the comedy to swirl around her. It shows, however, what a range she had, as her most imaginative work was always done with Lubitsch, who saw more possibilities in her than most of her other directors did. (That would be true for other actresses who worked with Lubitsch; who ever got more out of Merle Oberon, Kay Francis, and Miriam Hopkins than he did?)

Gypsy Blood, the third of these German films, opened in the United States in spring of 1921. (The *New York Times* explained to the reader that "as in the cases of [the other] importations, its name has been changed to suit a supposed demand for a peppy title. Originally it was called 'Carmen' and it is a motion picture version of the story by Prosper Mérimée.") Both Lubitsch and Negri are highly praised in the *Times* review: "Once more Mr. Lubitsch has made a motion picture that can hold the interest and excite the discriminating admiration of intelligent people and once more Pola Negri has endowed a character with the attributes of reality." The role of Carmen gave Pola Negri everything she was best at—primarily the chance to be fiery, tempestuous, and passionate and to break through the boundaries of a woman's ordinary life. She plays with enormous energy—a radiant and compelling figure on-screen. *Variety* stated it simply: "This Negri is amazing."

After these films were released so successfully, Lubitsch and Negri were inevitably invited to come to America. Negri was canny and took her time deciding just which company she would sign with, thereby upping her financial offers. She finally chose Paramount, and was said to have met Mabel Normand on the boat coming over. The two became fast friends, which might seem strange until one remembers that Negri, like Mabel, had once appeared in knockabout comedies. (Everywhere she went, Negri seemed to make friends. People liked her, although she was frequently described as a loner.)

When Negri finally arrived in Hollywood, she knocked 'em dead. She bought herself a white Rolls-Royce upholstered in white velvet and equipped with ivory door handles and dashboard. When she went for a ride, she placed an enormous white fur rug across her lap, and took along her two white Russian wolfhounds, one sitting on each side of her. Her chauffeur was dressed in an all-white uniform—unless it was raining, and then he wore black. She wrapped herself in ermine and chinchilla and mink and draped herself with diamonds and rubies and emeralds and sat up straight in the back, staring stonily ahead, drawing all eyes. (She also kept a pet tiger on a leash, and frequently paraded down Sunset Boulevard with him.) She had her dressing room decorated exclusively with Chinese furnishings, and insisted the floor be strewn daily with fresh orchid petals. Her wardrobe was dramatic, either black silk, black velvet, or sable, or the opposite—white silk, white chiffon, and ermine. She started the fad for toenails painted fire-engine red. Furthermore, she had the guts to chase a man, and once she caught him, she knew how to conduct a torrid love affair twenties-style, worthy of the plots of her movies. Both Charlie Chaplin and Rudolph Valentino became her lovers. Chaplin couldn't take the heat and begged out as soon as he could, but Valentino could match her style, having had considerable training with other women who knew how to get attention. (For years, everyone assumed that the famous "woman in black" who showed up annually at Valentino's grave was Pola Negri. Who else, they figured, would think up a dramatic scenario like that, and who else would have the nerve to pull it off, year after year? However, it wasn't really her.) Among Negri's other lovers was rumored to be Adolf Hitler, but this idea was put to rest by Negri's wardrobe mistress, who scoffed,

"Miss Negri is herself a dictator. She would never take orders from Hitler." (It made sense.) And when it came to marriage she was no slouch, either. She married and divorced three times—two counts and one prince. Pola Negri never went second-class.

Negri's American film debut was in *Bella Donna* in 1923, directed by George Fitzmaurice, costarring her with three male actors, Conway Tearle, Conrad Nagel, and Adolphe Menjou. Her flair for publicity was already gaining wide attention, as *Variety* commented in its review that "Pola Negri seems to have some peculiar draw over here . . . lately gained through publicity." The review also points out that the novel the film is based on, by Robert Hitchens, "was to book readers what 'The Sheik' was to the flappers." For the debut of the great European star, Pola Negri, Famous Players pulled out all the stops, giving her a very grand set of clothes to wear and placing her at the absolute center of the film. The story concerns a woman who leaves her British husband for an Egyptian tycoon, who cruelly spurns her after he has flirted with her like mad. Negri has to jump in a rowboat, row over to the desert, and stagger around in the sand, threatened by tigers and jackals. (As *Variety* snottily pointed out, "What a tiger or jackal or [Negri] was doing in that part of the desert just then is picture stuff, but the animal must have gotten [Negri] out there in her semievening clothes . . . There must have been three or four barrels of sand used for the storm. Also one camel. And Pola knows how to get off a camel even if the picture doesn't show her getting on." The review also complains that Negri's scheme for anguish seems to be a drop of glycerine under the left eye. "One-eyed criers are new over here.") From the very beginning, Negri's off-screen antics affected how reviewers saw her. They just couldn't take her seriously, even though this negative review is forced to admit that although the story was "applesauce," Negri would no doubt become a "star vamp" because the picture would give her "a big start."

Pola's next American film was a remake of the Cecil B. DeMille success *The Cheat*, also directed by George Fitzmaurice. This time the cad who brands the straying society woman is a Hindu instead of a Japanese, but the plot is more or less the same. According to *Variety*, the audience at the Rivoli "laughed at it." Tribute was paid to the sets and clothes, which would "make the women talk," but Negri was said to "throw upon the screen a distinctly hard personality." She fared better with her final 1923 release, *The Spanish Dancer*, in which she was said to be "fiery and flashing" and could hold interest in "a straightforward tale." Negri was directed in *Spanish Dancer* by Herbert Brenon, and at the same time that her film was released, her friend and frequent coworker Lubitsch was releasing his first American film starring Mary Pickford, *Rosita*. Ironically this movie, long considered a flop and hated by Pickford, is compared favorably to *Spanish Dancer* in a *Variety* review.

In *The Spanish Dancer*, Negri plays opposite Antonio Moreno, with Wallace Beery as King Philip IV of Spain. It's the kind of movie in which the characters don't drink from a glass, they use a flagon. They don't gather twigs in the woods, they gather faggots. It tells a complicated but quite entertaining story about—a Spanish dancer. Or, as the opening title puts it, "This is the story of a great love—a tale of passion swift and romantic, that caught and held, through danger and high adventure, the hearts of a Gypsy lass and a grandee of Spain." The first sight of Pola shows her as the head of "a lawless, carefree band . . . for her skill in dancing and her gifts as a teller of fortunes, Maritana, the Gypsy, was known the length and breadth of Spain." She is seen in medium close-up, laughing, her head thrown back, and wearing the traditional movie-Gypsy garb of peasant blouse, scarf

The Spanish Dancer

around the head, big bangle earrings and strand of beads. Her first action consists of a merry shrug that allows her to lift her arm and show off an armful of bracelets.

It is easy to see that Negri had been a dancer, as she moves with grace and a specific physical eloquence. She is very beautiful in this movie, and her large eyes and expressive white face register a wide range of various feelings easily. The plot, which has enough complications for three movies, concerns the king of Spain, his French queen, the Infante, court intrigue, a downtrodden apprentice boy, and a "reckless, carefree noble" (Antonio Moreno) who spends all his money and falls in love with Pola. For authenticity, perhaps, they threw in Velázquez.

The Spanish Dancer is beautifully shot by the famous James Wong Howe (still being billed as James Howe) and is well directed, with rapid pacing, by Brenon. All in all, it was a first-class production, with large sets, hordes of extras, and wonderful crowd scenes, in particular one in which masses of people surround a duel that takes place with tons of confetti falling down over the crowd. It was not an accident that Pola Negri's early films found welcome. They were extremely well produced, and she was superb in them.

Negri's 1924 movies included *Shadows of Paris, Men, Lily of the Dust,* and *Forbidden Paradise.* In *Shadows of Paris,* she does the woman's film thing, rising from the underworld as a girl in an apache den in Paris to the heights of wealth as mistress of a mansion. Typically, she's first seen wearing a checked skirt, tight top, and a cheap hat covered in feathers. Later, she appears in the latest Parisian couture, with jewels at her throat and all over her arms and fingers. After her sweetheart is killed, Negri, as Queen of the Crooks, pretends to be a Polish countess who is a war widow, and she meets and marries a wealthy and powerful man. In the traditional language of women's films, it is her clothes that always indicate who she is. When she revisits the apache den, she dresses like an apache. As a rich wife at home, she's in silks and furs. When her lover returns (he was presumed dead, but like countless World War I movie casualties, he was alive all the time), she meets him dressed as the wealthy woman, jeweled to the teeth, to let him know immediately who she has become. Like the thief *he* is, he robs her, and she realizes he never really loved her.

In *Men,* which *Variety* called "Box office sure fire," she was reunited with Dmitri Buchowetzki, one of her directors from her years in Polish films. Obviously comfortable with her countryman, Negri played well and earned excellent notices. She first appears in the movie as a little country waitress, who, betrayed by one of her father's friends, naturally becomes the queen of Parisian nightlife, dressed in the most splendid costumes. Later, of course, she finds true love, but again Negri is playing first a poor girl, then a woman of clothes and jewels, with a touch of sex and wickedness thrown in. In *Lily of the Dust,* based on Hermann Sudermann's *The Song of Songs,* Negri was again directed by Buchowetzki, who, apart from Lubitsch, was her best director. Reviewers were now becoming more respectful, as she really *could* act. The *New York Times* commented on how quickly she could show emotions such as "anxiety, affection, nervousness, interest, pleasure and despair . . . Her eyes are soft, and as usual, wonderfully expressive."

Negri's best work of 1924 is in *Forbidden Paradise,* which reunited her with Lubitsch. In this, she was on home territory, back in the safe arms of her first great director and in material that was European and sophisticated. She played the royal Catherine, a perfect role for her, and was supported by an excellent cast that included the handsome Rod La Roque as her lover Alexei, Adolphe Menjou as a suave chancellor, and Pauline Starke as the ingenue who loves Alexei. The material is a superb combination of comedy, romance, and intrigue, and Negri rose to the occasion, earning some of her best reviews. *Variety* said, "If ever a star did good work, Pola Negri does it here." Lubitsch earned raves: "If ever a director used his head and artistic sense, Lubitsch

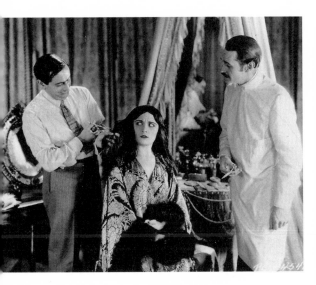

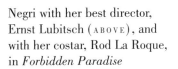

Negri with her best director, Ernst Lubitsch (ABOVE), and with her costar, Rod La Roque, in *Forbidden Paradise*

did." And, significantly, the production company got a rave, too, because "If ever a film company threw in the hot love scenes, Famous has."

The movie was expensively produced, with huge palace interiors and expensive gowns for Negri. She was very good at playing both "hot love scenes" and light comedy, and here she has a chance to do both. She's both flirtatious and autocratic, making it completely plausible that these two qualities might coexist in an empress. She looks lovely, and brings a clever, sly quality to the role of a woman who frankly likes men. She's earthy without becoming smarmy, and she makes everyone in the audience enjoy the fun without feeling the need to judge the morality being presented. One of her best scenes comes early in the action. She sits in her magnificent boudoir, dressed all in billowing white, and the moment is treated as high drama. Two ladies-in-waiting begin to weep. Is it the end of her reign, the death of a loved one? No. In a typical Lubitsch touch, it's revealed that the queen has decided to cut her hair! She solemnly inspects a series of young women, each one wearing a different style of haircut, and finally chooses the one she wants. The barber comes forward like an executioner, and as he cuts one hank of hair after another, he carefully hands each one to a lady-in-waiting, who, sobbing openly, places it gently into a special basket. The scene is presented almost religiously, as if showing a life-or-death operation. Negri knows exactly how to play it: she always responded to the Lubitsch touch.

Rod La Roque, her leading man, was a good foil for Negri. He was tall and handsome, and she has to stand on a little stool in order to give him the royal kiss. She is clearly indifferent when he first begins to explain to her that her troops have rebelled, but suddenly she gets a good look at him! After that, each item of information he presents earns him a promotion, and he heads for her ultimate accolade: a special decoration. (Everyone knows what it takes to earn that particular award.)

Forbidden Paradise earned Negri excellent reviews. Seeing her in it, and seeing how effective she is, gives credence to the theories expressed by film historians like DeWitt Bodeen, who felt that Hollywood actually destroyed Negri because it didn't give her enough material like this—sophisticated and intelligent—to showcase her range of abilities. When she had stepped away from such sophisticated characterizations in her earlier German films, she had found rejection from American reviewers. "Pola Negri does not shine in the 'sweet simplicity' roles," said *Variety* about her 1922 *The Devil's Pawn.* "Her work makes you think of Theda Bara playing Juliet." Regarding her performance in *The Last Payment* (also a 1922 German import), *Variety* went into detail:

> When one takes into account her work in all the pictures in which she has been shown in America, the conclusion must be reached that Miss Negri shines in roles depicting her as a woman of no morals—an unmoral rather more than an immoral screen female. Hers is not the doll type of beauty we worship in this country, and her acting is of the kind that demands strong roles visualizing women of the people. This limits her characterizations and debars her from enacting modern society women, and as everyone knows, the pictures that draw the most money in America are those portraying our heroines residing in mansions.

What the review did not understand was that Pola Negri was creating her own special kind of modern woman, a heroine harder to pigeonhole, but who appealed in her own way to audiences. Never timid, Negri was totally unafraid to go all out with her emotions on-screen, but she was never unintelligent about it. She's grandiloquent, but she's in control. She *dares,* so she was right for an era in which the idea of women starting to let go, to have feelings and act them out, was a social triumph and an act of bravery.

In *Sappho,* one of her German films that had been released in America in 1921, she challenged conventional thinking. "But why this fear of love?" she asks a man who tells her that her brother is in an insane asylum because he is being rejected by a woman. She's very matter-of-fact . . . love can make you crazy, so why not accept it? Later she gives an impassioned speech about what it has been like for her where men are concerned: "SOLD AND SOLD AGAIN! I WANT TO BE FREE!" She makes it clear that the idea that women have no choice but to give themselves to men in order to survive, and to go from one to another if necessary, is a kind of slavery. "I WANT TO BE FREE!" Her fearlessness, her defiance, was *her* link to the women in her audiences. These qualities also helped her command the screen. She can hold the silent moment and she is prepared to appear evil and defiant. Swanson was willing to be unloved off-screen by the movie magazines, but Negri is one of those rare female movie stars (like Bette Davis) who are unafraid of having their characters go unloved by the audience.

The fan magazines jumped on Pola's bandwagon early, because she was ready-made for them. In *Motion Picture* of June 1923, a long article by Henry Carr, entitled "Behind the Scenes With Pola Negri," calls her "a wild wind . . . who doesn't calculate . . . couldn't tell you how she does it because she just does it." The article says that Negri "walked into Hollywood with the hauteur of an empress" and that she has what few Hollywood American actresses have—"power." *Photoplay*'s sober article on "character nose readings" said Pola Negri's nose spoke of a "strong, domineering" person who was "vital and wild, with executive ability and a keen sensitivity to art," and "bold and resolute." (Gloria Swanson's was said to reveal "strength of character, luxury loving, and a quick mind and ready wit." She was "shy and suspicious.") Another article called Pola "an exotic sorceress" who lived "a crepe-georgette existence."

Negri was also hyped by studio ads in a highly dramatic way. She was called "the magnificent wildcat" and "a tiger woman with a strange slow smile and world-old lure in her heavy lidded eyes—mysterious, fascinating, an enigma." Much of this advertising material was directed at women, stressing how beautiful Negri's costumes were, how romantic her love scenes were, but adding an important extra twist: her daring and independence. She was described as "all fire and passion that speaks of the perfumed Orient of smoldering passions and hidden storms." The studio also released constant bulletins describing her temperamental outbursts, her tears, her hysterics. How many good girls and wives in her audiences were secretly thinking, "Go on, Pola!," identifying happily with the fact she felt no pressure at all to behave well. If she didn't get her way—well, look out, world. For the men, she was billed as "the most fascinating love actress in the world."

Magazine articles on Negri carried such titles as "The Loves of Pola Negri" and "How Pola Was Tamed," or stressing how exotic and enigmatic she was—"Who Is Pola Negri?" and "The Real Pola Negri." She was no slouch in the quote department. For instance: "I do not believe in marriage. It is not for me. I am selfish, no, not selfish, for I have sacrificed everything for love. I am

The Faces of Pola Negri (CLOCKWISE FROM TOP
LEFT): *Shadows of Paris, Woman of the World,
The Cheat, Men*

independent. Freedom comes before anything. I am a Gypsy, like my father."
Hedda Hopper repeated one of her good ones, and threw in the requisite Polish accent: "I am slave. We slaves loff to suffer. When I played a sad part on
the screen, I leeved eet, and when I didn't have anything to feel bad about, I
invented something so I could soffer." One of her very best quotes was her
statement on her romance with Rudolph Valentino and how she would remember him: "He loved to make spaghetti and meat balls. He had his own special
recipe. I never tired of it, and I will never share with anyone else the secret of
his . . . meat sauce." Now *that's* a quote for the history books. (And the idea
of Pola Negri and Rudolph Valentino sitting around the house sharing a bowl
of homemade spaghetti is a real showstopper, too.)

Much space in the magazines and newspapers was given over to Pola's
romances, in particular the celebrated affairs with Chaplin and Valentino. In
her autobiography, Negri writes,

> A great deal has been written about my relationship with Charlie
> Chaplin. Unfortunately, much of it was written by Mr. Chap-
> lin . . . Charlie shares something with a great many comedians—a
> total lack of a sense of humor about his private life. It was all so
> many years ago . . . It impresses me as phenomenal that his vanity
> is still so wounded, that he cannot see some of the comic aspects of
> what happened between us.

Negri then assures the reader that her version of what happened will be *the
absolute truth.*

One of the most amusing aspects of the Negri hype was the celebrated
feud between her and Gloria Swanson. When Negri first arrived in Hollywood
in 1923, both she and Swanson were under contract to Paramount. Naturally,
the publicity department saw a ripe opportunity to create a feud. According to
movie lore, it was natural to expect that two such women of the world would be
enemies. Both were big stars and expected to be number one at Paramount.
Both made women's pictures, with glamorous clothes and jewelry. Both had
affairs off-screen, and were famous for their independence. And both were
exotic types, outspoken and colorful. The first news on the feud front was the
mysterious "case of the studio cats." Swanson disliked cats, and this fact had
been well documented by the rapacious fan magazines that mined everything
for copy. Negri, on the other hand, was promoted as a lover of animals (don't
forget that tiger on a leash). This was instantly translated into good feud material by the Famous Players–Lasky publicity department. Pola was claimed to
have unleashed a pack of felines of all colors, shapes, and sizes onto Gloria's
set, driving Gloria home, ill and terrified. Swanson wasn't having any of that.
"Me afraid of cats?" she snorted. "Didn't I let the King of Beasts rest a paw on
my back in *Male and Female*? Really, they'll have to do better than that."

They kept on trying, but neither Negri nor Swanson was dumb enough to get drawn into the fray personally. Although they never became friends, they were never really enemies, either. Friends always reported that they avoided comment on each other, and they were known to be very polite whenever they met. If asked, both women denied there had ever been a feud, and Negri repeated that fact more than once in her memoirs.

Years later, Swanson pointed out how silly most of this hype really was by saying, "I'm not a stupid woman and I hope I have common sense. Someone wrote . . . that Pola and I always tried to see who could make a later entrance to a party. What did I do, sit outside in an automobile until she went in first? Or be in cahoots with the butler who would call me up and say, 'She's arrived, now you can come over'? I never heard such nonsense in my life." At the time, however, they seemed like perfect foes and it made great copy.

In 1925, Negri appeared in *East of Suez, The Charmer, Flower of Night,* and *Woman of the World,* and in 1926 *Crown of Lies* and *Good and Naughty.* Many of these movies were weak and silly stories that didn't allow her to use her very real dramatic talent. An exception was *Woman of the World,* directed in the elegant European style of Mal St. Clair. Based on Carl Van Vechten's novel *The Tattooed Countess,* the movie presents Pola as the ultimate example of such a woman—a countess with a skull and butterfly tattooed above her wrist, who walks around dragging a ten-foot chinchilla train behind her spangled gown. This was good enough for me, but there's more. Confronted with a faithless lover who more or less feels she should just accept his treachery, Pola announces, "I'm a woman of the world, but not the world's woman. I'm going far away, to the other side of the world." The other side of the world turns out to be a small midwestern town, Maple Valley, and the audience is treated to the sight of her, loaded down with pearls and diamonds, making her way amongst the porch swings and the church bazaars.

When Pola gets off the train in Maple Hill, she stands underneath a sign that says "127 miles to Des Moines, 210 miles to Davenport." Her clothes, demeanor, and black onyx cigarette holder with two diamond circles on it indicate that it's probably about six thousand miles back to her home base. The charming story that ensues might have been called "POLA COMES TO AMERICA." Every scene is a culture clash, as she lolls in a hammock, having her satin shoe put back on by a handsome young bumpkin who is overwhelmed by her glamour . . . or as she reacts with horror to realizing that she is the main event at the fund-raising Water Works Bazaar ("Talk to a real countess for 25 cents"). Pola copes, telling the young man, "Remember me as half lover and half mother," which seems to successfully deter him, and cooperating with the townspeople despite her humiliation. The big crisis comes when she falls in love with the local reformer, and he with her. True to his rigid morality, he tries to drive her out of town, but the female relative she is staying with tells her how to handle him, handing her a long black whip! Pola interrupts one of his meetings and whomps the daylights out of him, leaving a bloody mark on his brow. Naturally, they immediately get married. *Woman of the World* is a perfect example of what Pola Negri had to offer: glamour, acting ability, and genuine charm and sophistication. It's marked by an attitude of tolerance and sympathy for all parties concerned, and the alliance of two women from different backgrounds over their outrage at male behavior is very modern.

In 1927, Pola Negri made two of her best films, and she is excellent in both: *Hotel Imperial* and *Barbed Wire*. (Her third film of 1927 was *The Woman on Trial*.) *Hotel Imperial* is directed by Mauritz Stiller (Garbo's Svengali), and is a beautiful film. Unfortunately, it doesn't tell a particularly interesting story. (Nevertheless, it was remade in 1939, formed the basis of *Hotel Berlin*, and was not dissimilar to the plot of *Five Graves to Cairo*.) It is no longer fresh or particularly involving, with its tale of a servant girl who makes a noble sacrifice for an aristocratic soldier. The best thing in it is Negri. She looks very beautiful, although physical beauty alone was never what she was about. (She *was* stunning, with large, dark gray eyes, a full figure, and the prerequisite white, white skin of 1920s movie women, and a magnificent head of thick, black hair.) She doesn't have the glorious face of a Barbara LaMarr, or the exotic looks of a Gloria Swanson, or the sweetness of the very pretty Mary Pickford, or the ethereal beauty of Lillian Gish. What she has is a face full of character, an expressive face that seems human and real. When she smiles, her face lights up, and her eyes are always full of a very specific response to her situation and her character.

To me, the face of Pola Negri is one of the great faces of the silent screen. In one of her luminous close-ups in *Hotel Imperial,* she is radiant, her eyes wide, her lips slightly parted, but what makes her fascinating is not the beauty but the ability to convey with enormous subtlety a flickering range of emotions from fear to love to uncertainty. When the Russian general who has tried to seduce her hears her alibi for the Austrian soldier she loves—he was in her room all the time—he threatens to tear the clothes he purchased for her off her body. She stops him dramatically—she'll do it herself! She goes into a frenzy, ripping, tearing, breaking her beads and rolling her eyes. This was Negri's specialty: unbridled passion. (This was thought to be great acting.) But it's her small, subtle emotions that make us believe her today. A comparison of her bodice-ripping scene to a later one in which, after the war is won, her soldier returns proves the point. She has helped the hero escape and has told her friend she will never see him again because "he is an aristocrat, and I am a servant." As he rides past her in the parade, triumphant, she is shyly proud, slightly overcome with tears, but too happy to see him alive to break down.

Two of Negri's final (and finest) silent films: *Hotel Imperial* . . .

She runs along the street without him seeing her, full of joy and yet sadness. (Her soldier spots her, and in receiving his medals, brings her forward as a true hero of the war, honoring her and embracing her for a happy ending.)

Barbed Wire is well directed by Rowland V. Lee. Set in World War I, it's a story of a French girl who is ostracized by her village when she marries a German prisoner of war. (The very British Clive Brook plays the German soldier.) The movie sets out to depict what happens to ordinary people's lives and emotions when war breaks out. Before the war, the French farm peasants are happy—perhaps too happy—but when war overtakes their lives, they are slowly changed into people of grief and hatred. Their shock over one of their own consenting to marry an enemy prisoner is palpable, and Negri is at her finest, particularly in a scene when she walks slowly homeward after defending her husband at a French court martial. Her neighbors have gathered to revile her, but as she walks by the barbed-wire fences of the prison camp, the German soldiers line up to tip their hats to her.

Barbed Wire has the usual inexplicable plot complications of the World War I film. For instance, yet again a soldier thought to be dead—Negri's brother—turns up alive after all, and of course he is blind. After the war, this character, convincingly played by Einar Hanson, gives an impassioned plea for everyone to realize that old hatreds must be abandoned. Negri shows a range of emotions—happy, energetic, and positive as a farmworker . . . sad, listless, and discouraged as war comes and her brother is apparently lost . . .

... and *Barbed Wire*

touchingly passionate and tenderly in love as the German enters her life . . . and finally, disbelieving and numb as her neighbors turn against her.

Barbed Wire is one of the strongest stories about World War I to be produced during the 1920s, and its antiwar message is effectively presented. Negri's personal notices in it were not all positive, however. Perhaps offended by the somewhat pro-German sentiment of the movie, *Variety* panned her by saying, "The star does not convince in appearance or performance as the French peasant woman." *Variety* also mentions one of the commonest criticisms leveled against Negri, and one that often appears in writing about her today, which is that not only is she "camera conscious" but "except under the guidance of certain directors, she is lost." The idea was that Pola Negri, temperamental European diva, was out of control, an egomaniac, and a liability on the set unless someone dominant, like Lubitsch, had her in check. Her film performances, seen today, do not necessarily verify this point of view. Certainly she did some of her best work with Lubitsch, but then, who didn't?

By 1928, the shadow of sound began to fall over the kings and queens of silent film. Negri, however, released four films: *The Secret Hour, Three Sinners, Loves of an Actress,* and *The Woman from Moscow.* These movies were more of the kind she had been making, and she then allegedly retired from the screen, making one "part talkie" in England, titled *The Woman He Scorned* in America and released in 1930, which was easily dismissed by critics. She was off the screen until 1932, when she returned to Hollywood to make her official

talking debut in a movie called *A Woman Commands*. It was heavily publicized and promoted, and Negri appeared in New York City on the arm of
Mayor Jimmy Walker for the premiere. She was spectacular, dressed all in
stark white, with a fabulous tiara sitting atop her dark hair, but nothing could
disguise the fact that the film was poor. One review called it an awkward combination of "a musicalized 'Zenda' and a weak stab at continental elegance
and a flavoring of both 'Peck's Bad Boy' and 'Nellie the Beautiful Cloak
Model.' " The bottom line was that the film was "confusing." It presented a
mishmash of torch songs, czarist revolution, hot romance, Ruritanian court
intrigue, and low comedy.

Needless to say, Negri's entrance into the world of sound showed that
she spoke with a thick foreign accent, but so did Garbo, and Negri sang a
snatch of a torch song well, revealing that she had an agreeable alto voice.
Her voice was not the problem, but there was nowhere for her to go in sound in
America. She was not young, and as with John Gilbert, her trademark type of
passionate movie behavior was going out of style. Her lush image, her furs and
jewels and silk shoes, her Gypsies and czarinas and apache crime queens,
just didn't work in the hardscrabble world of the 1930s. Compared to the
tough working girls and gun molls of the period, Pola's tantrums no longer
seemed like much of a defiance, and certainly not a liberation. For all practical purposes, the American movie career of Pola Negri was finished. However,
the hype surrounding *A Woman Commands* ensured that she would go out
with her usual flourish of publicity and glamour, keeping her forever associated with such nonsense. It's too bad that Pola Negri paid so high a price for
her publicity. Over the years, it has tended to overshadow her genuine talent,
as most books and articles write about her off-screen antics rather than her
performances. Negri always gave all she had to her film roles, and she is
unfailingly absorbing and entertaining even in the wildest junk.

After *A Woman Commands*, Negri received no offers, so she returned to
Europe, making a film in France and going back to UFA in Germany in 1935.
There she was starred in a series of solid movies, and she also found some
success as a cabaret singer. When World War II threatened, she returned to
the United States and remained there until her death in 1987. She made only
two more films, a piece of nonsense called *Hi Diddle Diddle* in 1943 and Walt
Disney's *The Moon-Spinners* in 1964.

The Moon-Spinners was a vehicle for the very popular young star Hayley
Mills, and Pola was persuaded to come out of her retirement (in Houston,
Texas, a place no one would expect to find a Pola Negri—Havana, maybe,
Helsinki even, but Houston, no). She played a small but showy role as
Madame Habib, a jewel thief who lives on a luxury-laden yacht called "The
Minotaur." Pola's footage is brief, but she makes every moment of it count.
She's seen only inside her salon, which is cavernous—not unlike an old silent

Pola Negri, Queen of Pearls and Furs

film set. There are Egyptian and Asian artifacts all about, and a leopard sleeps on a large stool with a cushion on it. Pola is given a grand star entrance—sitting in an ornate chair with its back to the viewer, with only her hand visible. At first glimpse, she is busily cleaning her jewelry, dipping a large diamond necklace into a glass of champagne and then scrubbing it with a little brush. She wears gold brocade and a mink stole. Her thick black hair is arranged in a simple pageboy, with an elaborate braided chignon on top. At this point, Negri is at least sixty-five years old, possibly even seventy, but she looks literally twenty years younger. Her face is unlined but without that frightening look that face-lifts can give (the smooth, unearthly skin punctu-ated by two hot little holes for a pair of seemingly unrelated eyeballs). She is slender, and moves with the ease of a much younger woman.

Negri fully understands her purpose in *Moon-Spinners*—to be colorful and amusing for those who have never heard of her, and to touch base as her old self with those who do. She delivers her lines in a strong but not unintelli-gible accent, and she is expert with dialogue. Her large and expressive eyes are very much alive and alert, and she can still blaze fire out of them. She plays straight, rising above camp but putting a twist on the part that is cleverly comic without losing the dignity she obviously feels she is entitled to. Her

Pola Negri in her farewell to the screen, *The Moon-Spinners,* with Hayley Mills

performance was greeted warmly, but she felt she would not like to do any more film work. It was enough for her, seemingly too exhausting after years of retirement that involved no pressure.

Pola's final film gave her a very fine curtain speech, just before she and her leopard retire for a nap. After she has sold out the villain she was formerly in cahoots with, she calmly tells him, "Everyone lies when it suits their purpose . . . even the stars." She then wraps up all the chaos of the story by saying: "I lived through two wars, four revolutions, and five marriages." It was a perfect self-referential salute to Pola's own life, her former roles, and her own unique personage.

POLA NEGRI AND GLORIA SWANSON, who played overdressed, oversexed, suffering clotheshorses, were on their own in private life. Neither was protected by a powerful man, and neither had her career managed for her by someone else. Yes, Swanson temporarily had Joe Kennedy, a somewhat dubious support system, and yes, Negri did become a kind of semi-partner with Lubitsch for a portion of her career. But neither of them was dependent on a man for success, and neither of them was dependent on men in life. Despite their different backgrounds—Pola with her European upbringing, and Gloria with her very American one—they had a lot in common, not the least of which was their beginning in comedy. The crucial thing about them was their refusal to be ordinary—to be dutiful girls who behaved properly. They had nerve—real nerve—at a time when few women in film could make that claim.

Both women wrote their autobiographies. Swanson's cover presented a René Bouché sketch in which she looks youthful and modern. Although she appears very glamorous, with long gloves, earrings, and her trademark mole, she also appears relaxed and natural, very down-to-earth. Negri, on the other hand, whose book came out a decade earlier, took the high ground. Calling her story *Memoirs of a Star*, in case we had forgotten, she had no photograph on the cover, but introduced the reader to herself inside the covers with the reproduction of a portrait painted of her in her prime by Tade Styka. This frontispiece presents Pola (apparently naked except for a string of pearls hanging down her back), wearing a large globular ring on her finger, an exotic silk headband, and, of course, a wide swath of expensive fur that she has wrapped around herself. She is looking over her shoulder toward the reader with a slight smile on her face. In the foreword, she modestly tells us she will present herself as "the private individual I always was beneath the extraordinary facade of glamour and exoticism." Publicity conscious to the end, she has the inside covers of the book reproduce a series of old headlines: POLA NEGRI JILTS CHAPLIN; RUDY'S LAST WORDS OF POLA; THE WOMAN WHO WAS ONCE THE GLINT IN EVERY MAN'S EYE; HAIL POLA AS THE VENUS OF 1922; ARTISTIC POLISH COUNTESS GREATEST OF ACTRESSES; RAREST OF SCREEN TYPES; THE REAL POLA NEGRI— CREATURE OF FIRE; and "O-O-O-oh", CRIES POLA AS SHE GLIMPSES NEW YORK. It is pure Belle Poitrine. Never mind that the spotlight had departed long ago. Never mind that she had helped manufacture all the nonsense the public believed about her. Never mind any of it . . . it was time for a final bow. Swanson's book undercut her stardom, saying that writing her own story was an "agonizing experience, a bit like drilling teeth." She made every effort toward honesty and toward revealing her behind-the-scenes pain, although always with humor and common sense. (Her book, in fact, is one of the best star autobiographies ever written.) Negri, as might be expected, went in the other direction, beginning her book with "I was a young swan gliding along the rich green darkness of a place I could not quite make out." Each woman's book was true to her lifestyle, her image, and her awareness of what her public would expect. They remained masters of performance to the very end, and neither ever lost her clever perspective on the humbuggery of motion picture stardom.

Until the day she died, Swanson knew how to make an entrance, and how to maintain the illusion of glamour and mystery; in short, how to capture press ink. She was no fool, and her autobiography reveals her to be a shrewd analyzer of the behind-the-scenes hijinks of the film business, but she was willing to do what she had to do to get attention. Attention, she had learned, is what keeps stars on top. (Cecil B. DeMille had dubbed her "the movie star of all movie stars.") Pola also knew how to claim her share of the limelight, although once she retired, she was more willing to be left alone. (She may

Gloria, the all-American girl, gardens . . .

have been the true Garbo, in that she really *did* want to be left alone.) She captured publicity because she was a sophisticated European woman who knew that outré behavior appealed to people with dull lives. Pola was self-confident and outrageous in a way that Swanson wasn't, but there's no evidence to indicate that either of these women was really fooled by her own publicity.

Exotics they were, flamboyant they were, good publicity machines they were, but each one knew who and what she was and how to sell it. Pola Negri and Gloria Swanson were women of the world. They were liberated ahead of their time, and the significant thing about them was this: from the minute they first began to act in movies, they knew that being a movie star was a twenty-four-hours-a-day job. They accepted the business contract. In the end, Gloria Swanson said of herself, "I never regret. I have excitement every waking minute . . . I never look back. I always look ahead." Negri, childless and more alone, admitted in her final years that she had asked herself, "What to do with time? What to do with my life?" But she also made a simple, yet telling statement: "The past was wonderful; it was youth and exhilaration. I would not have missed it for worlds. The present is tranquil; it is age and a little wisdom. I am grateful to have survived long enough to have experienced it."

. . . Pola, the European exotic, sculpts, reads, and plays her harp in satin.

Gloria and Pola,
the rivals: They
drive expensive
cars . . .

. . . They pose with their portraits in front of the fireplace.

RUDOLPH VALENTINO

POOR RUDOLPH VALENTINO! Or, better yet, poor Rodolfo Alfonzo Raffaele Pierre Filibert Guglielmi di Valentino d'Antonguolla, because in some fundamental way he never quite shook off his background. He was an Italian immigrant boy who lived the ultimate 1920s "New World" dream to the max. He didn't merely become rich and famous, he became rich and famous and desired and envied and imitated and adored and even worshipped. He rose to the heights of movie stardom during the years when the term really meant something, when it was all new and fresh and joyous, when the curse it brought wasn't yet fully understood. Valentino got the glory, but he had to pay the heavy price that as later decades more clearly would understand, came with the territory. He pioneered the pain and the contempt, as well as the triumph. Even at the peak of his career as the most popular male star of his day, he was in danger of sliding past the status of household word into the ignominy of fraternity joke, and he was shrewd enough to know it. He chafed at bad reviews and grew enraged at the critics who labeled him a "pink powder puff" or "a no-account, no-talent nothing in tight pants." His secret fear that his detractors were right, that he was a ridiculous figure, saddened his eyes and drove the curves of his mouth downward—and the curves of his box office returns up. The more he looked slightly unhappy, the better his adoring audience of women loved him; no doubt each of them felt that she (and only she) could lead him out of his secret sadness. He was a one-name wonder— Valentino!—but he grew hurt and bewildered by the dark side of the fame he had at first seized with relish, and he lost his way in his off-screen life.

His female audience didn't give a damn what the critics (mostly male) had to say about him. They thought he was wonderful, and they made him a star, never losing their passion for him, and lifting him to a fame that outlasted his time: although his films are rarely revived, people know his name and they know his game—Latin Lover Extraordinaire. Yet Valentino's role in defining that concept, and the real flamboyance and style he brought to it, have been neglected, leaving him both misunderstood and unappreciated. Valentino has become an image frozen in time, a still photograph emblematic of the world of the 1920s, that crazy outmoded world of sheiks and flappers. He poses grandly, in his burnoose and high boots, his hair slicked down and his eyes narrowed, representing something that might once have been the perfect object of repressed desires but that today is merely a curiosity, a shorthand definition of another time, another place.

And so it's "poor Rudolph Valentino." Once a great star and a true original, he has become a joke, held up as proof that modern audiences are more clever and more sophisticated than those of the past. People who have never seen him on film dismiss him as silly or, worse yet, "effeminate," presumably the greatest insult that can be tossed at a man in our culture. The best that is said about him is that, untalented and hilarious as he was, he has the right to his photo in the history books—a good-looking guy in an outfit.

What a fate for a man who moved with a panther's ease, whose tiny flick of a cigarette was an inimitable come-hither gesture. Immobilized, Valentino is robbed of his essence: a dancer's grace. Valentino has to be moving to be appreciated; a photo robs him of his amazing ability to draw the eye and hold it. Almost any good-looking man can put on a sheik's costume and become a Valentino, but not once the camera is turned on. What is missing in a still portrait is Valentino's energy, his sass, his slightly mocking self-humor. When Valentino walks into a movie, he isn't just handsome, he's hot. There's no denying that his films express attitudes toward male sex symbols, women's role in society, and love and romance that are far from our own, but Valentino himself can still deliver the goods. He swaggers in with his little ironic smile, his mysterious androgyny, and his strong cinematic presence—and it all begins to work. He carries a modern viewer past the dated nonsense of his movies, and deserves credit for making so much out of the trash he was given. No major star ever had less to work with than Valentino, and he not only got through it but also defined a type that is still with us today. We still have our Valentinos, but they aren't as original, or as effective.

In the 1920s, Valentino provided a sharp contrast to the hearty, honorable American movie heroes who would never, but never, do wrong by a gal. Valentino *would* do it, and would enjoy doing it, even though, except for early in his career, he wasn't playing the villain. He was a new type of exotic hero with a different set of morals, a man who offered women outlaw romance, a total escape on a swift stallion making a desert dash in the moonlight to a remote place where the rules no longer mattered. Polite society wasn't home out there on a desert oasis. With Valentino, a woman was going to be able to ditch the shackles of the double standard, and best of all, because he was an abductor, whatever happened wasn't going to be her fault. After all, she hadn't asked to be captured, had she? The Valentino abduction, first presented in *The Sheik* in 1921, became the perfect liberation fantasy of an audience of women who knew they weren't going to get to go any other way.

The Valentino style of seduction in *The Sheik* and *The Son of the Sheik* was new and raw, and he played it boldly, with confidence, and with no lack of clarity about what was really happening. When he brings his captured lady into his tent, his gestures are eloquent and highly specific. Firmly directing the woman toward his bed (a mass of satin pillows), he begins to disrobe, removing his flowing outer garments and his heavy weapons. He moves around on his light little cat feet, creating a minor ballet. Seen repeatedly in close-up, he broods, he sighs, he smokes, he smiles. Then, suddenly, he swoops the lady up into an intense kiss: passionate, seemingly abandoned, and yet, oh so carefully posed for the camera. Valentino knew exactly how to pull off this type of maneuver, and as his career progressed, he just got better and better at it, becoming the master of the simple, focused physical action in which he paraded around showing his stuff and then—pounced! It became his trademark, with audiences awaiting breathlessly the moment in which he would strike, grabbing a woman up like stolen goods, sweeping her off to some guilt-free paradise—a tent, a hotel, an atrium. Any place would do.

It is assumed today that Valentino's appeal lay in his looks, or perhaps in the fantastic roles he played—the sheiks, the counts, the foreigners, the romantic outlaws. But his appeal actually lay in his sensuous physicality, his graceful movements and precise gestures. Furthermore, he was one of Hollywood's first really brilliantly packaged stars. To his looks and physical grace the movie business added glamorous costumes and settings, romantic and sexy stories, hyped-up publicity and fan mag junk designed to lift him way up out of the ordinary. And as the machinery ground on, Valentino turned out to be even more exotic than expected. He bought expensive cars and moved into a house he called "Falcon's Lair." He carried on torrid romances with other famous stars. He married badly. He quarreled with his studio. And, in the ultimate payoff, he died young and tragically.

Behind the scenes, Valentino was an ordinary Italian boy from an ordinary background, but when he came to Hollywood and stepped in front of the camera, he took on an air of mystery that fascinated everyone, even those who despised him. Valentino's mysterious quality hinted at several different things; throughout his career, people speculated on whether he was superficial or deep, kind or cruel, stupid or smart, male or female. He might be anything, anything at all. That was his gift and what made him a star.

What he wasn't, certainly, was a great actor. Valentino is at his worst when he tries to "act." When he goes over the top, nostrils flaring and eyes popping, he becomes the caricature people think he always was. These acting disasters are emphasized by bad camera angles that exaggerate his nose, make his mouth look mean, and point up his small stature. He can shrivel up fast, or look oily and snakish, but when he's relaxed, laughing, and moving with his natural ease, Valentino still looks terrific and immensely appealing.

Who was Rudolph Valentino, really? For many years, people accepted as fact the biography written by Herb Howe in the April–May issues of *Photo-play* in 1923. This bio, however, was the usual fanciful hype created by the joint imaginations of Howe and the star himself. In it, Valentino was presented as a fairly well born Italian, a gentleman, whose life of ease and glamour included wonderful escapades in Monte Carlo and Paris. In truth, Valentino *was* born in Italy, but he wasn't a gentleman, and he had barely average schooling before escaping his life of relative poverty. Immigrating to America, he landed in New York on December 23, 1913. His life in Manhattan was, at best, hand to mouth, and possibly shady. He made his living as a café dancer and was rumored also to have been a gardener, a petty thief with a police record, even to have been for hire sexually. After filling in for Clifton Webb on a dance tour, Valentino ended up in Hollywood, where he started dancing in cafés, hoping his handsome sexiness would be noticed. Inevitably, he drifted into the movies, although in the beginning his very Latin looks were not considered appropriate for leading roles. From approximately 1918 to 1921, Valentino played in about sixteen movies, films with titles like *Alimony, The Married Virgin, A Society Sensation,* and *A Rogue's Romance.* Since his roles were usually small and many of the films are no longer available, it's difficult to trace his work. However, we know that sometimes he was an extra and sometimes he had a more significant part—an Italian count, an Irishman, an apache dancer. Occasionally he was the villain, and at least once, in *All Night* (1918), starring Carmel Myers, he was a lead. Two of these movies starred the popular Mae Murray (*The Delicious Little Devil* and *The Big Little Person,* both in 1919), and *Out of Luck* (also 1919) was a Dorothy Gish picture.

All Night, one of his earliest films, is revealing. First of all, he isn't cast as a Latin type, but as Richard Thorpe, an obviously wealthy young man who is in love with a Kentucky colonel's daughter (Myers). Secondly, he's playing comedy, and doing it well. The movie is a sort of early screwball story, in which Valentino and Myers must pretend to be a married couple, trapped in a compromising overnight situation and constantly spied on by an overbearing millionaire. Valentino is the romantic lead, with his handsome profile on full display, and he is superbly dressed in cutaway suits, coats with fur collars, and silk pajamas, so he's not that far from the Valentino we know. However, he's cast as a shy young lover who can't work up the courage to propose to Myers. What's clear is that Valentino has remarkable self-assurance and easily holds the viewer's attention. He has focus and intensity, and he never looks awkward or uncomfortable. He has everything it might take for stardom: exceptional looks, grace, ability to wear clothes well, and the talent to play comedy. Had the 1920s not been a decade that called for a romantic sheik, he could easily have become a star of light romantic comedies.

There is one other existing movie from Valentino's non-star years that presents him perfectly: *Eyes of Youth* (1919), starring Clara Kimball Young. It

Early Valentino:
A Rogue's Romance,
with then star Earle
Williams

was probably his first really showy "Valentino" role, even though it's a relatively small part. Young was a star with status, so she was surrounded by an
excellent cast of experienced actors whose names are not well known today
but who were well respected in 1919: Gareth Hughes, Pauline Starke, Sam
Sothern, Edmund Lowe, Milton Sills, and Ralph Lewis. Valentino was in distinguished company in *Eyes of Youth*, and he plays a man hired to trap Young
into a compromising position so that her husband can divorce her on the
grounds of adultery.

   Eyes of Youth is standard fare. Its trite story grinds along, with its cast of
troupers doing yeoman service, very polite, very well dressed, and moving
about very carefully. Suddenly, Rudolph Valentino enters the frame. Almost
instantly, everything lights up. Handsomely attired in a well-cut coat with a
fur collar, Valentino looks modern, sleek, and cool, totally at home in his role
of gigolo. His presence makes the movie's other leading men look like pasty-
faced wimps, but that's the least of it. He also makes them appear totally sexless. Valentino oozes sex appeal, and it's frank and open, unafraid. Even in his
clichéd role, with very little screen time, Valentino generates the kind of
screen importance that is associated with movie stars. Watching *Eyes of Youth*
today, and watching Clara Kimball Young learn that "Duty, Ambition and
Wealth" are lousy choices for a woman to make in life (only true love will do),
makes it obvious why Valentino became a star. He's a breath of air in a stifling
drama.

Valentino apparently appeared in six movies in 1920—*An Adventuress,
The Cheater, Passion's Playground, Once to Every Woman, Stolen Moments,*
and *The Wonderful Change.* Still being cast as heavies, or Italians, or in
insignificant parts, he kept up his looks, dressing as well as he could on limited funds, and stayed in circulation by doing what most good-looking actors
in Hollywood did at that time: he turned up at the Alexandria Hotel bar every
afternoon around five o'clock, to cadge drinks, eat the free sandwiches, and
parade around hoping to be noticed. As a result of showing himself off this
way, he was hired by D. W. Griffith to dance with Carol Dempster onstage in a
prologue for Griffith's *The Greatest Thing in Life.* The audience was so enthusiastic that the run of the show was extended by three weeks. After that, his
name was a little better known, and he kept working, both dancing onstage
and in clubs and playing his smallish film roles. In his daily and nightly
prowls about town he bumped into the beautiful Dagmar Godowsky. She was
under contract at Metro, and she invited him to a dinner party being held to
celebrate the great Alla Nazimova's latest movie, *Stronger Than Death.* At
that party, he met, allegedly for the first time, a woman named Jean Acker, a
young Metro actress who, like Valentino, was looking for better parts and more
recognition. They were drawn together by their mutual interests, and almost
immediately, and without much of a courtship, they married. This mysterious
union has been the subject of much gossip, as by all reports the new Mrs. V.
slammed the door in her groom's face on their wedding night, saying it had all
been a horrible mistake. It was the beginning of what might be called
Valentino's legendary bad luck with women. For all the magic he created for
women on-screen, he had the opposite effect on the women he chose to love
and marry. Confused and unhappy over his marital failure, Valentino went on
working and trying to be noticed. His personal situation was dismal, and his
professional situation was not much brighter. And then he met a woman
named June Mathis.

Mathis, a shrewd and intelligent screenwriter at Metro, was not especially beautiful or glamorous, but she was very good at her job. She had been
hired to write a film adaptation of Vicente Blasco Ibáñez's famous novel *The
Four Horsemen of the Apocalypse,* and when asked who she thought should
play the role of the romantic and dashing young hero, Julio, she surprised
everyone by recommending Rudolph Valentino. A great deal of legend sur-
rounds Valentino's casting as Julio and Mathis's attitude toward him. Fan
magazines later claimed that Mathis had fallen in love with him when she saw
him on the screen, and demanded he be cast. Others claimed that he had read
the novel and written to Blasco Ibáñez, begging to play the role he was sure he
had been born for. There was speculation that Mathis had threatened to with-
draw her script unless Valentino played Julio, having expressly negotiated the
purchase of the novel so that Valentino could bring the role to life. The reality

is that June Mathis was a talented and intelligent professional who was also highly perceptive about stardom and a good judge of what audiences would like. She had seen Valentino in *Eyes of Youth*, and had noticed his obvious raw sexual power. She knew what she wanted for Julio—and Valentino had it. However the deal was worked behind the scenes, the relatively unknown Rudolph Valentino was given the role, and as a result, the immigrant youth with the shady background was automatically elevated to the top of the Holly-wood heap. He was to be directed by the respected Rex Ingram in an expen-sively mounted production written especially for him. It was the stuff dreams are made of—and it worked.

Once rehearsals began, Ingram and Mathis agreed that Valentino's role should be expanded. Originally, the character of Julio was one of several important figures in an ensemble story. With Valentino in the part, the script was rewritten so that Julio became its center. The balance of events was shifted to him, with new scenes tailored especially to his strengths.

The Four Horsemen of the Apocalypse is a sweeping epic covering the events of World War I as they affect the lives of a Spanish family living in Argentina. Over the generations, the family has intermarried with both the French and the Germans, so that the war in Europe divides their loyalties. As the story opens, Julio is living the life of a dissolute young scamp in Argentina, and after the death of his beloved grandfather he goes to Paris to live in Montmartre and become an artist. There he falls in love with a beauti-ful married woman (Alice Terry), and they are caught in the act by her hus-band just as the war breaks out. Ultimately, they accept responsibility for what they have done. She returns to her heroic husband, now blinded by the war, and Julio, deciding to fight for France (his father's country), dies nobly in combat.

Metro Pictures went all out for *Four Horsemen*. Even though war films were not particularly popular in 1921, they decided to spend something between $600,000 and $800,000—a huge sum for those days—in bringing the story to the screen. It was a great financial risk, and to fuel audience inter-est, a big publicity push took place. The fan magazines of the day were agog with the well-documented extravagance that audiences were going to be treated to in *Four Horsemen:* fourteen assistants were hired for director Ingram, and each had his own cameraman . . . 125,000 tons of masonry were used to build an entire village and a huge castle . . . more than twelve thou-sand people were hired to work on the movie in all its aspects . . . thirty-two principal roles were written, many of which were cast with fresh faces for the public to discover . . . $75,000 worth of insurance was carried on the art works, furniture, and decorations used . . . more than a dozen fully appointed interior sets were built . . . and an amazing array of beautiful clothes and cos-tumes were all specially designed for the stars. *Four Horsemen* was in every

way a massive undertaking and no expense was spared, which makes it all the more remarkable that the further risk was taken of starring an unknown in the central role.

As filming got under way, it immediately became apparent that Valentino was going to justify the faith Mathis and Ingram had in him. In his own mind, Valentino was Julio, and everyone else began to agree. There was an ease to his performance at this stage of his career, a kind of abandon, that was not always evident later. He seemed to be one of those natural actors, so much so that D. W. Griffith, watching him, said, "Is this fellow really acting, or is he so perfectly the type that he does not need to act?" It was an astute question from a wise old judge of both star talent and acting ability, and it was going to be the central question of Valentino's acting career.

So what was it about Valentino in *Four Horsemen*? The answer is simple: as Julio, he has raw star power, though not much else. His triumph is that he seems utterly at ease, completely unrehearsed. When he's first introduced on-screen in medium close-up, he is uncommonly striking in his good looks. Furthermore, like Lauren Bacall or Audrey Hepburn or Robert Mitchum, he doesn't resemble anyone else, and he stands out for his unique physical qual-

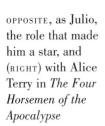

OPPOSITE, as Julio, the role that made him a star, and (RIGHT) with Alice Terry in *The Four Horsemen of the Apocalypse*

ities. In this movie, Valentino's looks are more modern than in some of his later roles. Although his hair is dark and rather slick, and he wears elaborate sideburns, it isn't heavily pomaded down to his skull, nor does he appear to be powdered, lipsticked, or mascaraed. He seems like a real man, and he appears to be enjoying life, especially in the famous scene in which he dances the tango.

Despite its opulent sets and its epic tale of war, the highlight of *Four Horsemen of the Apocalypse* is definitely Valentino's sassy tango, the dance that made him famous. It's a straightforward scene. The spoiled young Julio is sitting around an Argentine dive, looking terrific in the traditional black, flat-rimmed gaucho hat, a loose blouse with vest, and wide floppy pants tucked into shiny boots. He flashes a beautiful smile, and then drags deep on his cigarette. Spotting a young woman doing the tango, he moves to cut in on her partner. After a scuffle with this badly outclassed bit player, Valentino sweeps the woman into his arms and tangos off into film history.

Valentino takes the floor to dance with all the masculine self-confidence in the world. (After all, this is how he had once made his living.) His dance is both good enough and imperfect enough to suggest a real man in a real situation, which adds to his appeal. Our sense that the tango is, in fact, his dance, the only one he really knows and the only one he cares to execute, works perfectly, since it is the dance of seduction, of male mastery over the female. Valentino is going to dance his partner down—literally. He pauses and dips, smiles and sneers, twirls and stops, with just the right timing and precision. But—always—Valentino makes the dance about his attitude toward the woman.

Is Valentino really a great dancer? Who can say? The tango number, for all its fame, is constantly intercut with reaction shots of the cast of motley customers who are watching. They certainly all try to indicate by their responses that he's the greatest dancer who ever lived. The few glimpses available of the tango itself look good enough. The important thing is that the tango is a sexy dance, giving Valentino the opportunity to pull a woman low between his legs, to insert his leg between hers, to bend her over and press against her, to put his face next to hers and transfix her with a sexy wink. He spins, he twirls, he dips and bends. And he looks fantastic. If he's not Fred Astaire—or even Gene Nelson—who cares? At least he can *do* the dance. Valentino's tango isn't about dancing, anyway, it's about sex, and the women in the audience clearly got the message. With most star careers, you can't pinpoint the exact moment that stardom struck, but with Valentino you definitely can: this tango on an Argentine dance floor is it. As the old movie dialogue has it, he went out there a nobody but he came back a star.

The success of Valentino's appearance in *Four Horsemen* is that, as Griffith noted, he really doesn't appear to be acting. It's as if he doesn't fully understand what is expected of him other than to look good and have a good time. When he laughs, it's very real. When he looks at a woman and winks, it's as if he's really flirting. And when he drags down hard on his cigarette, or holds it gracefully in his hand, he makes the cigarette into a kind of secret, an intimate communication with the audience. (Rudolph Valentino has only one rival in film history when it comes to smoking a cigarette with great style and confident sexuality, and that's Marlene Dietrich. What a shame they were never paired—two androgynous figures in tuxedos with their cigarettes aglow . . . what a loss to film history.)

Throughout *Four Horsemen,* Valentino is presented front and center in the very best clothes in the very best sets and under the very best lighting, and he never puts a foot wrong. He wears his tuxedo with ease, as if he had been born in it, and the specially designed, well-cut suits and beautiful cashmere coats with fur collars set him off splendidly. Even when he appears as a mere doughboy in nothing but combat boots, a uniform, and a bedroll on his back, he looks fantastic. And, of course, he's particularly effective in his love scenes. Clearly, Valentino could handle making love to women. Even when he's sitting in his foxhole, bombs bursting about him, and he slowly, sensuously kisses a photograph of his beloved which he carries in a locket, he's a wow. You have to give him the credit he deserves. *Variety* did. In its review, the official bible of show business acknowledged what had happened: "Rudolph Valentino . . . proves his right to stardom in motion pictures."

The casting of the young Valentino in *Four Horsemen* paid off. The movie drew rave reviews and earned an astonishing $4 million worldwide. Valentino's career was made, and he was immediately put to work in his next movie.* It, too, would be a prestige production directed by Rex Ingram. *The Conquering Power* (1921) was adapted from Balzac's *Eugénie Grandet,* and once more June Mathis wrote the script, paying special attention to Valentino's role. To say that liberties were taken with Balzac's story would be an understatement, since the movie ends with Eugénie in the arms of the man who, in the novel, squanders her savings on riotous living. (Needless to say, it is Valentino who plays that man.) The movie has also been updated because, as an opening title card points out, "commercialism tells us that you, Great Public, do not like the costume play. Life is life, so we make our story of today, that you may recognize each character as it comes your way."

It is obvious that the script has been designed with Valentino's new stardom in mind. His role is flashy, cut to order for his strengths and skills. He plays a pampered twenty-seven-year-old playboy who, at the start of the film, is celebrating his birthday with a somewhat risqué party. The camera lingers on him in this opening sequence, allowing the audience to appreciate his looks and his tuxedo. Later, when his character arrives at the little French village of the Grandet family, the entire sequence is about him rather than the pure girl he will meet and fall in love with (Alice Terry, again). Valentino arrives in an expensive automobile, which is driven boldly by a chauffeur right into the midst of a group of local village peasants. Valentino opens the door and stands on the car's running board, elevated among them like a prince. He casually knocks the ashes from his onyx cigarette holder into the ear trumpet of one of the oldest among the villagers—we're close to von Stroheim territory. When he goes to the humble cottage of the Grandets, he's allowed yet a third dramatic entrance. As the family sits inside in their peasant clothes, their door swings suddenly open, and there stands Rudolph Valentino in all his glory. He is wearing yet another well-cut suit and a suave bowler hat, and he carries a magnificent cane. He looks relaxed, again smoking a sexy cigarette, and holding a barbered little poodle on a leash. A star has been born, the movie seems to say; let the audience gaze on the star.

It is clear that everyone connected with *The Conquering Power* knows perfectly well what is happening with Rudolph Valentino, including Valentino himself. He is showcased as a sensuous man, equally effective at hugging his old father or his beautiful leading lady. Time is provided so that the audience can stare at him head to toe and appreciate his clothes and his stance. He cuts a grand and confident figure, though he doesn't have much to do—the official leading role is played by the character actor Ralph Lewis as the old Grandet

*Four Horsemen was released in early March of 1921, and *Uncharted Seas* came out in late April. Valentino plays the "other man" in this movie, which received bad reviews, most of which didn't mention him. *Uncharted Seas* was unavailable for viewing, and it is unclear whether it was made before *Four Horsemen* or when *Four Horsemen* had finished shooting but wasn't yet released. *The Conquering Power* was his first post-recognition project.

Valentino with Dorothy Dalton and cast in *Moran of the Lady Letty*

who goes mad with desire for gold. But Valentino is the effective center of the movie and the most interesting thing in it.

By the fall of 1921, Valentino was solidly established in the movies, and he was a name. He began working steadily, and his next film to be released* signaled the prestige he was rapidly acquiring. He had been cast opposite Nazimova herself in her production of *Camille*, a movie that she designed and created in conjunction with her friend Natacha Rambova, née Winifred Hudnut, and June Mathis. The decision was made in February of 1921, shortly before the New York premiere of *Four Horsemen*, when Valentino was not yet a star. He was signed to play the role for $350 per week, the same salary he had been paid for *Four Horsemen*.

Playing Duval to Nazimova's modern-dress Camille was no easy assignment. Nazimova, a powerful creative force, was what might be called "something else." With her pumpkin head and gunboat feet, she cut a very strange figure indeed. Valentino, by comparison, looks modern, sleek, and strangely calm in her presence. Against her somewhat cold but forceful performance, he seems low-key and subtle, and he blows her off the screen. She knew, and cut him completely out of her death scene. It is in *Camille* that the real sense of what Valentino is going to be in movie history emerges. *Four Horsemen*

The Conquering Power was released and reviewed in *Variety* two months before *Camille*, even though it had been shot later, after Valentino's stardom was secured.

The Conquering Power, with Alice Terry

could have been a fluke, *The Conquering Power* capitalized on *Four Horsemen*, but *Camille* reveals the truth.

Valentino's role is that of a weak and callow young man, and he's required to spend a lot of time standing around while Nazimova preens. He sits quietly and observes her, waiting for his big acting moment, which will consist of dropping to his knees and begging her to allow him to be her "servant, her dog." It must have been a shock to Nazimova, an actress of great experience and talent, to look at the dailies and see this upstart Italian boy absolutely commanding attention and drawing every viewing eye away from her, despite her art deco getups and bizarre settings. Valentino steals the show; he seems to have a sly instinct about how to survive in a role designed *not* to showcase him, just as he knew how to rise to one that did. (Suggestions that Valentino was not very bright or that he was completely dominated and directed by the women in his life may or may not be accurate, but one thing is obvious: he had an animal cunning when it came to movie acting. In *Camille*, he was expected to carry the can for Nazimova, yet he managed to establish himself much more strongly in the film than she did.)

Camille was not a financial success, but Valentino was not harmed by it. He and Nazimova make a curious pair and a sharp contrast in film acting styles. Valentino is what we now know to be the definition of a movie star as opposed to an actor. He can hold the camera doing nothing, while inspiring an audience to supply his character, his essence, and his thinking process. He

Traditional Valentino: the aggressive lover who makes Nazimova swoon in *Camille*

succeeds on film because audiences think they know what is going on inside him; it may be nothing, but they think it's something, and furthermore they think they know what it is. Nazimova is more theatre-oriented. She is all surface, and her inexplicable presence deflects an audience's understanding. That is her brilliance, and it carries its own weight. *Camille* was designed with magnificent sets and costumes that could have overpowered two lesser personalities, and Nazimova and Valentino deserve credit for what they accomplish in it.

Off-screen, Valentino's life was something of a mess. All through the filming of *Camille*, he had two major problems to juggle. He met and fell in love with the exotic Rambova, beginning an affair with her, and he had to cope with Jean Acker, his reluctant bride. She had filed a legal case for separate maintenance, and her lawsuit claimed that Valentino had, in fact, deserted her. But while Valentino was grappling with love and the law off-screen, he was moving toward the most important role of his career. Already important before he made it, Valentino found superstardom in *The Sheik*, which gave him his signature role, the kind of part every legendary movie star must have.

One has to respect him—it's tough to have to make a living in movies like *The Sheik*. Even in its day it was thought to be foolish. (On November 11, 1921, *Variety* wrote, "Bad as this Lasky production now at the Rivoli and the Rialto is, the public has nothing but the public to blame for it.") Calling the material it's based on "preposterous and ridiculous," the reviewer goes on to point out that it's a hit because "it dealt with every caged woman's desire to be caught up in a love clasp by some he-man who would take the responsibility and dispose of the consequences." (Precisely.) As to Valentino, the review says that "the acting could not be worse than the story, but it is bad enough. Valentino is revealed as a player without resource. He depicts the fundamental emotions of the Arabian sheik chiefly by showing his teeth and rolling his eyes." So much for the male perspective, and so much for the reviewer's lack of audience awareness. The point about *The Sheik* is its very silliness, which provides protective cover for something that is deeper, slightly sinister, and definitely on the audience's mind. They weren't in their seats for realism, common sense, or good acting, they were there to get sexed up, and that was something Valentino understood and could deliver.

The Sheik was sold boldly and dynamically, with advertising copy that screamed: "SEE—the auction of beautiful girls to the lord of Algerian harems! SEE—the barbaric gambling fete in the glittering casinos of Biskra! SEE—the heroine, disguised, invade the Bedouin's secret slave rites!" And, of course, most important of all: "SEE—Sheik Ahmed raid her caravan and carry her off to his tent!" Probably no one who worked on *The Sheik* had any illusions about its artistic worth or its fundamental qualities, but everyone knew what it was that would bring in the audiences and keep them coming back for more. It was Rudolph Valentino.

The Sheik is an anomalous occurrence in movie history—a really bad movie that was so popular with the public that its star achieved legendary status from it. Based on a novel by Edith M. Hull, it starts out with a title card that sets the tone: "Mohammed's land—where saint and sinner chant as one." Valentino is introduced almost immediately, presiding over a marriage market at which Arab men are purchasing new wives. "The Sheik," reads his introductory card, "Ahmed Ben Hassan, upon whose shoulders has fallen the heritage of leadership." Valentino is sitting cross-legged, dressed in flowing robes and high leather boots. He once again languidly smokes a cigarette, posed against a background of striped desert tents. His eyes are sharp and shrewd, and he casually holds a rope of beads in his hand. A medium close-up shows him smiling sympathetically at a young man who doesn't want the woman he loves to be sold at this market. "When love is more desired than riches, let another be chosen," Valentino decrees.

The movie's leading lady, played by Agnes Ayres, is "Lady Diana Mayo, the orphan daughter of an English poet." Diana is supposed to be a 1920s

Valentino all
togged out

THIS PAGE:
LEFT: *The Four
Horsemen of the
Apocalypse*
RIGHT: *Blood
and Sand*
BELOW: *Son of
the Sheik*
OPPOSITE PAGE:
TOP LEFT: *The
Young Rajah*
TOP RIGHT: *The
Eagle*
BOTTOM LEFT:
Beyond the Rocks
BOTTOM RIGHT:
*Moran of the
Lady Letty*

modern woman, who declares "marriage is the end of independence . . . I am content with my life as it is." Diana and Ahmed Ben Hassan first lock orbs as he prepares to enter a casino restricted to Arabs only. He sees her, and the impact is registered by both players, but Valentino's response is given maximum screen time in an intense close-up. His eyes dilate slightly, and a little smile turns up the corners of his mouth. As he frankly appraises Ayres, his eyes take on a look that can only be defined as SEX. He exudes appreciation of her beauty, and a strong, sensual quality. Sex is fun for everyone, he seems to imply, so let's all have some fun here tonight.

Throughout the rest of the film, the only interesting thing is Valentino's performance. Sometimes he is given ridiculous action, like standing under Ayres's window to sing "Beautiful Dreamer" (without sound). Sometimes he looks slightly homely and even runtish. And sometimes his acting is out of control, false and hammy. But when he smiles, he lights up the screen. Unafraid to swagger and twirl whenever he moves about, he has amazing style. Laughing, smoking, swanning around in his burnoose, he's pretty wonderful even though he's playing a ridiculous character—an Arab educated in Paris who turns out not really to be an Arab after all, because not being one suits the ethnic attitudes of the time better.

The plot of *The Sheik* is total nonsense. The high point occurs when Valentino gallops up to Ayres out in the desert and rescues her from a bandit attack by carrying her off to his tent. That's when the movie gets right down to business. "Why have you brought me here?" asks Ayres, in a card title. "Are you not woman enough to know?" sneers Valentino. While she struggles in his muscular arms, he barks out (through another title card) *The Sheik*'s most famous line: "Lie still, you little fool." Not only is he unimpressed by her virtue, he is amused by it. He wants what he wants, and is impatient to get it. (Adolphe Menjou, showing up as a French writer who drops by for a visit, explains it for the audience: "When an Arab sees a woman that he wants, he takes her.") Of course, the story is ridiculous, and of course it doesn't work on a level of art or realism. But was it ever meant to do so? I doubt it. It's supposed to work as escapist fare, but more importantly as a metaphor for sex in a repressed era. And it's not all that metaphorical, it's pretty overt. It's not hard to grasp why it stunned audiences of its day. Even now, it's naughty fun, and Valentino is glamorous, humorous, and full of life. Unfortunately, he also shows signs of beginning to "act." His ease, his natural grace, and his sense of joy in himself as an actor are occasionally intercut with a florid, overwrought style that was probably how he was being directed at the time. It's interesting to speculate how he appeared to audiences then: Was it the posturing that made him popular and his more modern ease that caused critics to call him a bad actor? Or was it the cool modern style that audiences loved and the traditional acting they forgave? Either way, the point is that Valentino, like all the really great lover/sex-symbol/adventure stars—like Errol Flynn, Burt Lancaster, and Clint Eastwood—carries within himself and his performance his own critique, his own self-mockery. This can only come from intelligence, and it makes one wonder why everyone assumed Valentino didn't have at least a little sense of humor.

Following his enormous success with *The Sheik* in late 1921, Valentino went on to make four movies in 1922. Stardom had to be earned in those days, and although everyone understood that Valentino was a star as far as the audience was concerned, he still was listed as a featured player in two movies. His first release was *Moran of the Lady Letty,* in which Dorothy Dalton starred and Valentino was her leading man. *Variety,* however, pointed out the truth in its review of February 10, that "the real star of the picture" was Valentino. Playing a rich young idler who gets shanghaied, Valentino earned excellent notices. "As a rough-and-tumble fighting hero, Valentino is a revelation," said *Variety.* "Physically he looks the part, but it comes as something of a shock, probably because he has so long been identified with roles of a daintier kind." He hadn't been around long enough to be identified with much of anything, but we can see that even at the beginning of his career, Valentino was being typed as a "woman's" actor, suitable only for boudoir roles. Yet, as the reviewer perceives, Valentino had much more to him. Given a chance to portray an active hero or throw in a touch of comedy, he more than met the challenge. But the review also marks the beginning of what would increasingly become Valentino's problem: he would be locked into his Latin Lover fame, and the very basis of his success was going to restrict and frustrate him within another year.

In *Moran of the Lady Letty,* he is actually playing against this type. Although he begins the film as a dandy, after he is shanghaied he is forced to become physically strong and active; this is a seafaring adventure movie, with Valentino running, fighting, climbing ship riggings, and showing off his muscles in sleeveless shirts. The movie features Dalton in the title role, that of a motherless young woman raised to be an "able seaman" by her father. Valentino comes to appreciate her, saying, "I never knew a girl like you— never knew a girl could be like you. You swear like a man and you dress like a man and you're strong. I know you are as strong as I am. You have no idea how different you are from the kind of girls I've known." Dalton tells him she isn't interested in men—or women either—and that he should forget about it. Later, however, she realizes she loves him. The movie presents an interesting take on sexuality, although that may or may not have been its intention. Dalton wears men's clothes, and proves she is as good a sailor as anyone. Valentino, the well-dressed lover, is easily knocked down by the sailors when he's first hauled aboard a smuggler's ship. He has to learn to be a man; she has to learn to be a woman. The casting, which pairs Valentino's extreme good looks with Dalton's strong, almost masculine face, questions traditional sexuality despite his vigorous action scenes and her beautiful close-ups.

Beyond the Rocks, his next movie, paired him with Gloria Swanson, who in every way was a top-drawer star. Again Valentino was listed as a featured player, but considering that *Beyond the Rocks* was a tale of nonsense penned by Elinor Glyn and that he once again played an ardent lover, there was good reason to believe that it was Valentino, not Swanson, who was going to put the customers in their seats. Reviewers labeled *Beyond the Rocks* a "program feature," by which they meant a slight project built to capitalize on star power. Valentino's next movie, however, was a major effort of which he himself was unquestionably the star. *Blood and Sand,* released in August of 1922, became one of his most famous roles.

Blood and Sand costarred Valentino with two leading ladies, Nita Naldi and Lila Lee. His popularity was in full flower, and the movie perfectly illustrates the image that most people today associate with him—that of the nocturnal seducer with flaring nostrils. His persona was clearly in place, so that *Blood and Sand* offers a chance to glimpse a young and buoyant Valentino in his earliest, happiest days as a star. (Since he plays a bullfighter and the movie is set in Spain, it also epitomizes his "Latin Lover" image, and it gives viewers another look at the famous Valentino tango.) He is confident and in great form, accepting the challenge of a senorita with a rose in her teeth, twirling his cape, strutting about in tight pants, and scowling darkly before and after such card titles as "I hate all women . . . but one."

Blood and Sand is glamorous corn, and much of it looks very foolish today. It's mainly a matter of posed images, with less cinematic flow than Valentino's best films. The movie's high point is the magnificent pantomime in the Valentino/Naldi seduction scene, which contains a quintessential image of Rudolph Valentino in his prime. His skill lay in his ability to turn a seduction into a dance. First, he accepts a rose from Naldi, his would-be seducer, then angrily pushes her away. Suddenly, however, he relaxes his body and succumbs to her determined sexual power. As he himself becomes the master, he grabs her into a fierce embrace, his decision made, his choreography complete. Naldi, all twenties flamboyance, rises to his level. (She was a competent silent screen vamp, who, alas, looks to a modern viewer a shade too much like Margaret Dumont for her own good. The madness that is Valentino can cover any such distraction, however.) Naldi glories in his brutality as he hits her with a telling insult ("You serpent from hell"). Naldi responds, "I want to feel your strong hands on me," and her body posture and his look suggest very clearly that there is something going on between them other than standard love and kisses. Valentino can convey more than desire, he can convey a passion that is slightly kinky, with a touch of rape and sadism, and Naldi was his perfect foil. They enact a battle of the sexes worthy of the term as they dance around each other, hissing and vamping. He slowly, confidently, turns Naldi around and around in his arms, delaying her pleasure, increasing the audience's anticipation . . . and not incidentally maneuvering to get his own full-face on camera. And why not? He was at the top of his form, handsome, intense, and absolutely a star, and not the least confused about whom he was really making love to. Valentino could always focus past those feathered-serpent ladies in his movie arms and out onto the ones who really counted: the women in the audience, the ones who truly loved him.

Blood and Sand was a huge hit, but again an ominous note was struck in the *Variety* review of August 11, 1922, describing the movie's opening night. The theatre had been decorated lavishly with Spanish and American flags, and the theatre's working personnel all flaunted specially designed bull-ring costumes in various gay colors. The house was sold out from midafternoon through the final show. The crowd's behavior, however, was reported negatively in *Variety:* "Along toward the middle of the screening, [they] showed a disposition to scoff at the play. Some of the serious scenes, particularly those 'vamping' episodes involving Juan the bullfighter and Doña Sol, the vampire widow, touched their sense of humor. Joshing a matinee idol like Valentino is fatal. It's only a short step from public worship to public ridicule . . . His bullfighter was just a movie hero." The reviewer had firmly established the attitude that would haunt the remainder of Valentino's career, and defined a problem that was built into the plot of *Blood and Sand.* Valentino's hero has to become weak in order to be seduced by Doña Sol, and his adulterous behavior leads him finally to be humiliated before his noble wife and to lose his strength in the bull ring. (This problem exists also in the Tyrone Power remake, in which the fabulous Rita Hayworth plays the temptress and Linda Darnell the virtuous wife.) Valentino and Power are both best, most exciting, in the early scenes in which they're playful and physical. Both are good in their scenes of passion, but the story gets too religious and moralistic, and has to undercut the handsome hero to make its point. Valentino does his best, harnessing his natural power by hanging back and waiting to be seduced, to have his lust released by a woman. However, the role weakens his energy and robs him of his trademark: he's at his best when he plays the aggressor.

Valentino finished out 1922 with *The Young Rajah,* which was poorly received by reviewers, and which today is unavailable for viewing. *Variety* reported that his role "was not an especially fortunate part for Valentino. His successes have been made in roles that called for hectic romance with a dash of paprika in their flavoring. This one is a milkshake." Although the review grudgingly admits that "the star has a pull," because the theatre was packed even on a rainy night, *The Young Rajah* seemed to make no one happy. The stills from it show a grumpy-looking Valentino, ludicrously dressed as an Indian rajah, tricked out in gold thread and wearing a fancy headdress. By now, the male critics who loathed him were loud in their criticisms, and *The Young Rajah* is frequently cited as an example of what went wrong with his career. Natacha Rambova, who had become his wife on May 13, 1922, is considered key in the "feminizing" of Valentino. She designed his *Rajah* costumes, and encouraged him toward the exotic and away from the humorous. The resulting unsatisfactory material and bad reviews were beginning to make Rudolph Valentino very unhappy about his screen career.

Off-screen, Valentino behaved like a movie god. His life was turned into fan magazine fodder, and everything he did was scrutinized and publicized. His troubled love life—the mysterious marriage to Acker, the torrid love affair and marriage to Rambova—was fuel for publicity, but was also apparently leaving him sad and confused. Who Valentino really was off-screen is still a mystery. He is alternately described by those who knew him as "never the lady killer type; the ladies killed *him* . . . He was a weak man, a bit on the stupid side as well" (Colleen Moore) or "perfectly delightful with a great sense of humor" (actress Lois Wilson). Carmel Myers, who appeared with him in one of his earliest movies, *A Society's Sensation* in 1918, described him in those years as "charming . . . gracious . . . with a great, great sense of the dramatic. When he'd drive down Hollywood Boulevard, everyone would say, 'Here comes Valentino.' And at the beach, when we would be sitting there on Sundays, telling lies to each other, he would come by in a white bathing suit with two white Russian wolfhounds on a leash, and they'd say, 'There goes Valentino.' He was the most, most attractive man." Research on him turns up two opposing views. In one, he is stupid, dominated by women, vain, and effeminate. In the other he is modest, shy, rather sweet, and inherently sexy. The first Valentino likes to shop and buy fancy cars, and the second likes to sit home at night and make his famous spaghetti sauce. Who can know the truth about Valentino after all these years? But whatever else was going on with him, he was apparently enjoying his money. Having been born a poor boy, he spent wildly, and silent film stars earned big money before there was an income tax to eat it all up. He bought the expensive home he romantically christened "Falcon's Lair." He purchased more than one fancy automobile. He stuffed his closets full of elegant, hand-tailored clothes.

Throughout 1922, all the popular movie magazines were filled with Valentino stories. His rapid rise to fame is clearly chronicled in their pages. In July 1922, *Motion Picture* calls him "a new face, scarcely known even after years of effort in the very midst of the film world." Valentino hadn't really put in "years of effort," but the star-selling machinery was grinding into action and it sounded good. *Motion Picture* says that in addition to being a new face, Valentino suggested "background" (no mention that he was an Italian immigrant from a poor family), "a provoking wisdom" (no suggestion that he was weakly educated and that many people found him dull and unintelligent).

The article states clearly that just because he had "rocketed into fame overnight" in *Four Horsemen*, he isn't threatening the solid stardom of Wally Reid, who is still "Sheik Supreme of Feminine Hearts." Valentino is only one of several young male stars written up in this article, which is covering "all new faces" in Hollywood that summer. In fact, it warns him that climbing up behind him is one Ramon Samanyagos, a Rudy look-alike. Samanyagos, says *Motion Picture*, "was born to be mispronounced and to be famous." (Fifty percent right, anyway.)

By February 1923, the fan passion for Valentino had rocketed out of control, as is illustrated in an article called "The Vogue for Valentino" in *Motion Picture*. Purporting to explain the "underlying sex psychology" regarding Valentino's huge popularity, the magazine had commissioned a piece by "one of America's most eminent psychologists, who, for obvious reasons, does not wish his name to appear." (Indeed.) Readers are further lured in by a tag line that says the article will contain a tremendous indictment of the American businessman (whose fault it all will turn out to be) and a warning that no man or woman should fail to heed. How could anyone pass it up? The article, full of the usual 1920s fan mag–invented nonsense, does contain an interesting take on Valentino's persona. Saying he has "inflamed the feminine imagination of an entire country" with an overnight leap to stardom that is "almost unprecedented in motion picture history," it analyzes the source of the craze that motivated his popularity. First, it announces that Valentino

> epitomizes the lure of romantic passion. He represents the stolen kiss . . . He is the "fancy man" deluxe—the male Helen of Troy . . . He stands for . . . perpetual romance. He is the Romeo of all the ages, the deathless troubadour at every lady's casement window . . . He is every woman's husband by proxy . . . the Phantom Rival . . . the standard by which every wife measures her legal mate. And he is also the young lover's rival . . . the third party on every honeymoon . . . the absent correspondent in every divorce proceeding.

After this—and no wonder men hated him—the article gets down to the somewhat more objective business of coolly appraising Valentino's real assets. The list is to the point: an almost perfect physique, good grooming, excellent knowledge of how to dress, poise and dignity, and a Latin look that implies depth and a wealth of hidden resources.

As foolish as this article is, it does touch on another aspect of Valentino, one that is particularly apparent today. Without hinting at bisexuality or androgyny, and with no indication of Valentino's ambivalence about his life or his stardom, the article tries to define his "mystery" by saying he is both Apollo and Dionysus, both sophisticated and primitive, both graceful and

Valentino as
hot lover:
with Agnes Ayres
in *The Sheik* . . .

. . . Nita Naldi in
Blood and Sand . . .

... Vilma Banky in
The Eagle ...

... Vilma Banky in
The Son of the Sheik

aggressively masculine. He is said to have both beauty and strength. Undoubtedly, both male and female viewers responded to these ambiguities. (Although Valentino is always said to have appealed only to women, no star rises to the very top without having some popularity with both sexes.)

There is often a hint of cruelty in Valentino's look. He has a slightly sullen demeanor that masks his passion, and he often enacted a cold indifference that suddenly ignited. He *is* both beautiful and strong, and watching him you can't help wondering just what was really going on inside him. This, of course, is what made him a star: everyone wanted to know. His ambivalent quality is still apparent on the screen today. He looks very sexy, but his sexual nature isn't always specific. There's a touch of weakness about his mouth, and his famous hooded eyes reveal—what? As Mae West might have put it, Valentino looks as if he could be had, but exactly what having him was going to mean was unclear. After struggling with all this for several pages, the "eminent psychologist" of *Motion Picture* draws his conclusion: "George Washington may be the father of this country, and Mary Pickford may be its sweetheart. But Valentino is its lover." Who was going to argue with that in 1923?

Valentino was the victim of a great deal of such movie magazine hokum, but he himself contributed to it. He published a book of rotten poems under the title *Day Dreams,* in which he claimed that the real author was a power working through him to help him pen such immortal lines as "Your kiss, a flame of Passion's fire." There was also the recording—allegedly the only record of the sound of his voice—in which he sang "Pale Hands I Loved Beside the Shalimar." Sometime during 1922, he began giving out tragic quotes such as "I am beginning to look more and more like my miserable imitators" and "A man should control his life. Mine is controlling me." (Writing five years later in *Photoplay* of April 1927, H. L. Mencken said of him, "He was precisely as happy as a small boy being kissed by two hundred fat aunts.") Trying to assert himself, or being pushed by Rambova, Valentino quarreled with Famous Players/Lasky, the organization that controlled his contract. As a result, he abruptly left the screen and did not make a movie for nearly two years, from *The Young Rajah* late in 1922, until *Monsieur Beaucaire* in mid-1924. Instead, he embarked on a national personal appearance tour with Rambova, in which the two lovebirds danced the tango for enthusiastic audiences in the hinterlands. This tour, a trial for Valentino, who was mobbed by female fans everywhere, was sponsored by a mineral water called Mineralava, and was dubbed the Mineralava Tour.

After Valentino returned to the screen in 1924, he would make only five more movies before his death. Anyone who doubts what an extraordinarily big star he was should review the facts of his remarkable rise to fame: arrival in Hollywood in 1918, a virtual nobody in 1919, a star in 1921, off-screen from 1922 to 1924, dead in 1926. Despite his layoff in an era in which stars ground out four or five movies per year, Valentino remained a household name, and never lost his red-hot box office appeal. When he returned to moviemaking, his loyal audiences were waiting for him, as passionately committed to him as ever. The ludicrous Mineralava Tour, ridiculed by the press, did nothing to diminish his popularity with moviegoers.

Recognizing this, the fan magazines immediately set to work again, carrying a great deal of coverage of *Monsieur Beaucaire.* The October 1924 issue of *Picture-Play* had a breathless article "by an extra girl" who was "On the Set with Valentino" for the movie. In addition to her girlish descriptions of seeing Valentino emerging from his bungalow "eating a red apple" and making a three-act drama out of "Rudy having trouble keeping his lavender silk stockings up," she contributes a vivid portrait of the ballroom scene in which she was an extra. Eagerly she describes "the magnificent Rudolph in gleaming lavender satin embroidered in purple, stitches on back of his chamois gloves embroidered in heavy, scintillating gold thread studded with small jewels." He wears only one of the gloves, she tells readers, "over which there are huge cabochon rings" and, in case we were wondering, "he carries the other glove" alongside his satin coat.

In August 1924, *Motion Picture* carried a major article containing sketches of the costumes to be worn in *Monsieur Beaucaire.* Valentino's "walking costume . . . is pale grey velvet with chenille braid. It is brilliantly lined with purple and red shot taffeta. The waistcoat is pink velvet, embroidered with silver. And the breeches and boots are grey suede." The only photograph accompanying the story is a large one of Valentino, posed in the exaggerated garb he wears in a sequence in which his character appears in an amateur theatrical. "Here he wears a suit of pale blue taffeta, rose shot, with a cape of silver cloth. This cape is beautiful with its lining of rose colored velvet and its silver lace collar and rosettes." The article points out that "five years ago" no producer would have made such a fuss over a man's costumes, and certainly this kind of publicity contributed to the scorn with which many viewed Valentino. What other male star ever appeared in fashion layouts? Many actors pranced around in lace and taffeta in a costume picture, but they weren't celebrated in this way for their efforts.

Some of Valentino's costumes are amazingly elaborate, and if one sees only the photographs of him in these getups and not the film itself, an idea of him as a fop emerges. In the movie itself, Valentino actually arrives at a big ball disguised as a woman, carrying a red rose, wearing a long, full cloak with a hood, and flirtatiously holding a fan over the lower half of his face so that only his very distinctive hooded eyes can be seen. When he casts off the cloak, his "masculine" costume underneath is even more bizarre. He wears a satin and brocaded jacket, flared out stiffly at the bottom like a heavily pleated tutu. He has a large jewel at his throat, a lace handkerchief, and high heels. He

Valentino as dancer: rehearsing on the set of *Four Horsemen*,
and executing the deed in costume . . .

parades into the room with a model's grace, carefully placing one foot in front
of the other. Much of the criticism of Valentino's appearance in this movie was
generated by photos of him in these outfits. He never loses his sense of comedy
about himself in this scene, however, and it's only a small part of the overall
action. There is an extended dueling episode later that strongly presents him
as an action hero. By now Valentino was juggling his image, his somewhat limited acting ability, his female fans and his male fans, with a great deal of skill.
The movie, directed by Sydney Olcott, and based on a famous Booth Tarkington story, gives us an interesting look at a man somewhat weighed down by his
reputation but managing to play with it and give good entertainment value.

When Valentino returned to the screen in this expensive production,
there was no longer any pretense that anything in the movie mattered except
him. He had traveled the sex symbol road from lively discovery to product.
Monsieur Beaucaire clearly has only one thing to sell: Valentino. *Variety*
reported on "the wholesale relegating of practically the entire cast to the
background, so that this feature amounts to nothing less than 100 minutes of
Valentino." This, concludes the reviewer, means that "women will 'go' for this
one by the thousands." *Monsieur Beaucaire* is a vehicle, but Valentino rises to
the challenge; he more than lives up to the stratagem. In one scene, he is
shown bare-chested, and plenty of screen time is given to allow the audience
to ogle his muscles and shapely back. Yet there's affectionate fun made of

. . . in *A Sainted Devil* with Helen D'Algy and in *Monsieur Beaucaire*
with Doris Kenyon

him, too. When the leading lady shows no interest in him, a title refers to her
having given him "the shock of his life—a woman not looking at him."

In speculating on what happened to Valentino's career, writers often cite
this movie as an example of how feminized he became, or how his movies grew
static, overcostumed. Actually, there is much lively action and humor in *Monsieur Beaucaire,* and some of the fancy costuming is presented as a problem
for the young hero who would like to lead a more vigorous life, and who loves
fighting. This way, of course, the movie gets to have things both ways. The first
scene that presents Valentino has him playing a role onstage to amuse King
Louis XV, a play-within-the-movie conceit that has a foppish Valentino strum-
ming a mandolin, posing in full profile, wearing not one but two beauty marks,
a powdered wig, and lipstick, and sporting painted eyebrows. He is weighed
down by ruffles and satin and brocade . . . but this is for fun, to amuse the
king. Valentino postures, shows off his profile, and his legs in tights, but he
cuts any such nonsense with an attractive smile. He has a tongue-in-cheek
quality that deliberately refers to his own image and stardom. (After he begins
his masquerade as an ordinary barber, he says, "I was never so happy. Nobody
knows me. Nobody expects me to make love to them.")

Valentino's other 1924 release was *A Sainted Devil.* (*Monsieur Beaucaire*
was reported to be something of a flop outside the big cities, although it did
well enough in urban areas.) *A Sainted Devil* was received by reviewers with

less than enthusiasm, and the kind of sardonic attitude that Valentino inspired more and more as his career advanced. *Variety* snorted that the movie "may be what women want," because it's "more of a personal Valentino vehicle than a regulation picture." Somewhat cruelly, the review makes sport of "soft close-ups on Rudy, lots of them, close-ups which give full face, profile, ear, eye, nose and throat views . . . Maybe it'll satisfy the Valentino rooter," and adds, "Most of them are women, and this is a woman's film." This was meant to be the killing put-down to a story that actually is an undistinguished tale of a young South American and his rocky road to love.

After *A Sainted Devil*, Valentino's career headed rapidly to its abrupt ending. In 1925, the year before his death, he released only two films: *The Cobra* and *The Eagle*. Both were star vehicles, but *The Cobra* had only Valentino to recommend it, whereas *The Eagle* is a well-made movie.

The Cobra is an example of what happens to a movie star who becomes locked into an image and a specific kind of film. It knows that Valentino is its main asset, once again setting up events so that everything is on standby while he is afforded the star entrance. The movie opens up on a title card that announces: "In scrapes or out of them, there was always something magnificent about the young Count Torriani." The first visual presents him dressed in black, smoking a cigarette at an outdoor European café, and eyeing a beautiful young woman at a nearby table. Clearly, this is the Valentino audiences expect, and a small, viewer-pleasing tableau is worked out as the opening action. The young woman smiles, flirting openly with him. He responds with an ever-so-slight play of a smile around his lips. Then, he slowly, carefully, lifts his small glass of wine to his lips while looking pointedly at her. He's giving the woman an open invitation with simple, practical, highly physical movements. This is Valentino playing to the women in his audience. His smile and his lips are for them—it's a trademark hot Latin Lover moment. This first scene is wisely followed by a sequence played for comedy, in which he is chased by an irate father.

The Cobra perfectly reflects the Valentino legend and demonstrates the truth about what made him popular. The opening flirtation is grounded in the audience's knowledge of his persona. They see him enacting the role of a great lover who just can't stop himself where women are concerned. ("Women fascinate me," his character will say later, "just like that cobra fascinates its victims.") He is the languorous, legendary Valentino, beautifully posed in a well-cut suit, showing his profile in close-ups. However, almost immediately afterward, in the extended comedy-action sequence, he is running and hiding, amused by his own legend, sending it up with great skill. One scene sums it all up: Valentino, dressed in a beautiful tuxedo, carefully removes an elegant ring in order to sock an adversary on the jaw and knock him flat. (The action is in response to a character who calls him an "indoor sheik," a direct reference to Valentino's effeminate image.) There were always the two sides to the

Valentino presence: the Latin Lover and the active send-up. When a film presented both with equal skill—and in balance—Valentino had a hit.

The Cobra pairs him once again with Nita Naldi, his costar from *Blood and Sand*. And once again, it presents him in a detailed seduction scene with her, another indication of how much the filmmakers understood what the audience wanted from him. Again, Naldi is the aggressor, Valentino the seduced. (Naldi is the "cobra" of the title role, although people today often erroneously believe it to be Valentino, because of his hooded eyes.) Naldi advances on her costar, and she is dressed up to the challenge, wearing a velvet coat massively trimmed in chinchilla. As she moves forward, she drops the coat to the floor, revealing a slinky black dress. When Valentino, looking her over, chokes out, "Aren't you forgetting your husband is my best friend?," Naldi sensibly replies, "I've made him happy. Aren't I entitled to a little happiness, too?" The logic of it apparently makes sense to Valentino, because soon enough he is kissing her in a hot embrace that goes on and on and on in the 1920s style of romance. (Naldi gets punished for her sins, of course. After Valentino comes to his senses and flees the hotel room, she calls in another man and immediately gets her comeuppance: the hotel burns down, killing both of them.) *Cobra* finishes with Valentino taking on the female role in a woman's film: he sacrifices himself for the one good woman in his life (Gertrude Olmstead), returning to Europe alone so that his friend (who seems to get all the women whether the women want him or not) can marry her and give her the stable life she deserves. Valentino ends the film, still elegant, still well dressed, still smoking his lonely cigarette, all by himself on a ship carrying him away. It's a weak and old-fashioned movie, but Valentino rises to it, looking good and making the nonsense relatively believable.

His two final films—*The Eagle* and *The Son of the Sheik*—are probably his two best other than *The Four Horsemen of the Apocalypse*. In *The Eagle*, for one thing, he isn't left to carry weak material all by himself. He has an excellent supporting cast, including the exquisitely beautiful Vilma Banky as his leading lady, and the great character actress Louise Dresser as Catherine the Great. The film is a handsomely mounted production, with impressive set designs by William Cameron Menzies, costumes by Adrian, and an excellent screenplay by the witty Hans Kraly. The story—somewhat of a *Mark of Zorro* rip-off—is directed with pace and humor and cinematic flourish by Clarence Brown. Not many of Valentino's films have any kind of visual style other than that which comes from costumes and set designs, and *The Eagle* actually has a distinctive look. For one thing, it contains one of the most famous tracking shots in film history, as the camera moves backward down a gigantic banquet table loaded with food. (Brown mounted the camera on a wooden beam, which was itself mounted on wheels by the sides of the table. The wheels rolled on tracks that ran close alongside the table. As the camera tracked backward, props that were too tall were pushed into place at the last moment, so that the audience sees expensive dishes and foodstuffs revealed item by item, but up close on the table.) Also, in *The Eagle*, Valentino is humorous, light, and very active. Instead of always standing around in careful poses, he's an action hero in every sense of the term. He plays a young cossack in Catherine's court, and he is beautifully paired with Banky: she is blonde and delicate, an excellent visual contrast to his swarthy complexion and shoe-polish black hair. Where he seems earthy and highly physical, she is delicate and ethereal. Together they make a perfect pair of silent film lovers, all image and looks and visual contrast.

Valentino's opening sequence in *The Eagle* is totally different from the careful poses of *The Cobra*. Instead of sitting there in good clothes letting everyone eyeball him, he is introduced in a superb action sequence in which the young cossack jumps on Catherine's horse in order to chase down a runaway carriage—and rescue the leading lady, who is riding in it unprotected. (Banky gets her own excellent introductory moment—she is swathed in velvet and lace, hiding in fear behind a large fur muff, her wide eyes seen just above the fur line.) The opening sets the tone. *The Eagle* is adventurous, and Valentino will not just be a handsome and desirable man, he will also be an exciting figure leaping from one adventure to another. In fact, he gets to be an extravagant, sexy version of the more boyish and uncomplicated heroes that Douglas Fairbanks was famous for; Valentino's version naturally has more love and romance than the typical Fairbanks, but the similarity is there.

Perhaps feeling more comfortable in such a role, Valentino is at his best, relaxed and appealing, and free of false posturing. He still cuts a very fine figure in his well-designed all-black ensemble—tall, shiny boots, little mask, tall Russian hat, loose blouse and pants, all tricked out with leather straps, sash, whips, pistols, and swords—but for once he doesn't seem to be on-screen solely to be admired. His character is given moments of comedy, as he tries to pry off a ring that's stuck on his finger, or when he puts too much pepper in his soup (because he's gawking at the gorgeous Banky), but, of course, there are the obligatory Valentino love scenes. He strokes Banky's neck with his impeccably manicured hands, sensuously moving her head back and forth, and he sweeps her into his arms as he is expected to do, covering her with kisses. (The Valentino swoop is referred to in a somewhat joking manner when he leaves a note for his nemesis which says, "I hover over your lands—ready to swoop down on you.")

Despite its obvious assets, *The Eagle*, which received very good reviews, was only a modest financial success. For the modern audience, it puts on full display many of those characteristics of Valentino's that are seldom associated with him; it's a textbook display of how he has been misunderstood and underappreciated. He has solid timing, a dashing demeanor, and if not a great acting style, at least a serviceable one. In fact, *The Eagle* is nearly a comedy, full of pratfalls and jokes capably directed by Brown. Valentino makes an excellent swashbuckler, and he isn't the only source of the action—nor the only source of entertainment, as was true in so many of his poorer films. There is more here to enjoy. And he gets to poke fun at himself, playing a czarist version of Zorro who disguises himself as a foppish French tutor. And for once, his wonderful costumes aren't just there to stand out in the decor; this time, they're a part of him, like a natural skin. One of the most glorious moments on film occurs when, after blowing a kiss to his leading lady, he leaps from a tall window into the moonlight, disappearing into the shadows as he's about to be captured.

Tragically, Valentino had only one more film to make, *The Son of the Sheik*. Like *The Eagle*, it was directed by a strong man with a personal style, George Fitzmaurice. It also had a good supporting cast, and excellent production values. And, like *The Eagle*, it gave Valentino more to do than just look exotic in costumes and lipstick. *The Son of the Sheik* is, in fact, the movie that people imagine the much weaker *The Sheik* to be. It's a rip-roaring story of rape and action in the Arabian desert, and the physical overpowering of the leading lady by Valentino is even more explicit. What's more, Valentino plays not one but two Arab sheiks! He re-creates his old role of Ahmed Ben Hassan from the original film and creates a new part, that of the Sheik's son, now a grown man. The leading lady from *The Sheik*, Agnes Ayres, as Diana, "graciously consented to re-create her original role as a favor to Mr. Valentino and his producers." Thus, the movie cleverly brings back the original characters—even including a small "memory" that once again shows the original Sheik carrying Ayres off on his horse and warning her to "Lie still, you little fool." At the same time, it offers an entirely new plot, a tougher, sexier, more physical young hero (Valentino as the son), and a far more beautiful and talented leading lady, Vilma Banky. And there are lovely costumes and an exciting sandstorm that covers the whirling action sequence of the finale.

This time, the romantic leading woman is not British but an "Arab dancing girl, Yasmin," which the blonde Banky somehow manages to make credible. Banky and Valentino are already lovers when the film begins, but only in the most youthful and romantic sense of that term. Right away, the audience is treated to several scenes of them in medium close-up, kissing, nibbling, nuzzling, and murmuring to each other. The lovers are introduced with an extreme close-up of Banky's fabulous face, which dissolves into another extreme close-up of Valentino.

Valentino is even more self-confident in this film than in the original *Sheik*, in which he was not exactly timid. But here he knows he is a star and, more important, he knows why he is a star. He knows what is expected of him, and he gives it full force. He has also upgraded his outfit. Instead of standard

movie-Arab garb, he is now in costumes that were clearly created with his figure and persona in mind. Where he once was merely handsome, he is now
astonishing. He has gold braid on his burnoose, and more than one ring on his
finger. He has tasteful necklaces and bracelets, and fine silks and handwoven
linen. He's got beads all over! (This bejeweled look is part of what has made
Valentino a subject of scorn for so many years. Ironically, it makes him highly
fashionable today.) In addition, the film features much more lovemaking
between the leads. There are lingering shots of the two gorgeous stars in profile, leaning toward each other for a kiss that is delayed, delayed, and then
delivered. And the close-ups of Valentino (which are everywhere) include one
in which he kisses his way down Banky's arm, with particular attention to the
inside of her elbow. Hot stuff!

The defining of Valentino and his image that has taken place—by his
agent, his studios, the strong women in his life, and, to whatever degree, himself—has by now made it clear that both sexes find Valentino attractive, and
that his appeal is not exactly Sunday school. Valentino is captured and hung
up by his arms. As he dangles there in an attractively ripped and torn silk
shirt, his chest bare and his eyes dilating, he is menaced, whipped, and
pinched. Those who think of Valentino as a "pink powder puff" should see
The Son of the Sheik. His arms are heavily muscled in an age in which body-
building was not the norm. He looks strong, and his biceps bulge. Yes, he
appears to be wearing just a touch of eye shadow and lip rouge, and he does
have those beads, but he successfully presents the image of a macho desert
chieftain.

The Son of the Sheik is packed with action. In addition to stirring chases
and nocturnal rides across the moonlit desert, there are fights with swords,
guns, knives, and fists. There are doors to break down and walls to climb—
Valentino is alive and moving, and therefore becomes not only more interesting, more masculine, but more of a real character. *The Son of the Sheik* is less
a woman's fantasy or cheap romantic fiction than *The Sheik.* It's an action-
adventure film—with romance. In fact, *The Son of the Sheik* had it all as far as
Valentino's admirers were concerned. While the movie was being made, he
was in his prime, successfully restored to a career that now seemed secure.
His personal life was in its usual chaos, but no one associated with the movie,
including its star, could have possibly thought of *The Son of the Sheik* as his
swan song. Yet it is a true last hurrah, not only in being his final film but also
in terms of its giving audiences everything it possibly could that was associated with his fame—and when it decides to take the time to deliver the
Valentino trademark, his Latin Lover self, it slows down and really goes all
out. The big seduction scene is a pip, as Valentino roughly drags Banky, who
he believes has betrayed him to his captors, into his tent. In action that is sexier than that of *The Sheik,* he is seen framed by flickering phallic candles

Valentino's dual role: as the hero of *The Son of the Sheik*,
and as his father, the original hero of *The Sheik*, now an older man

while he snorts and sneers just before engaging with her. He tosses her
around, displays his anger, and finally is seen herding her ruthlessly toward
his bed as he slowly raises his arms up to both push her down and embrace
her. (Rape as romance!) Valentino gives a solid performance in both his roles,
doing the best acting of his career. He makes subtle delineations between his
young self and the old sheik, for whom he wears a beard and mustache and
grayed-down eyebrows. His facial expressions alter, as well as his body movements and gestures. It isn't a profound performance by an accomplished actor
but a solid performance by a competent actor who understands his own appeal
and persona.

All in all, *The Son of the Sheik* was very good entertainment, with broad
audience appeal. It was premiered in Los Angeles four months before its general release, and reviewed in *Variety* on July 14, 1926. The reviewer paid it
reluctant tribute: the film is called "an outstanding success" and the conclud-
ing line states that "the new Valentino picture should go a long way to once
more endear 'the sheik' with picture fans." The premiere—at Grauman's Million Dollar Theatre—was one of Hollywood's most glamorous affairs.
Valentino arrived with his latest flame, Pola Negri, on his arm, and she rose to
the occasion by wearing a tight silver gown and a diamond tiara. Everything
indicated not only that Valentino was on top but that he had a long and fruitful
career ahead of him. He began a trip across the country that would see an
equally successful premiere in Chicago, marred only by a vicious article in
the *Chicago Tribune* that coined the "pink powder puff" epithet. Valentino
was furious, and he issued a public challenge to the unidentified writer.

The glamorous Rudy relaxing
at home, whipping up some
spaghetti (for Pola Negri, perhaps)

As the train carried him east, he read and rested and planned his next film. When he arrived in New York City on July 20, it was unbearably hot, but the film's July 26 opening was a smash hit. The *New York Times* review reported, "The sands of the desert weren't any hotter than the crowd which stood in the sun and stretched around the corners nearly to 8th Avenue, waiting to see if 'The Son of the Sheik' were as good as his old man . . . They stuck to it and crowded the Strand to storm its doors." Valentino's presence— he vanished through a side entrance under police escort—had required picket lines to control the mobs. The review says the film is full of "desert rough stuff and bully fights," and "wild riding and fighting which leaves no doubt" about Valentino's masculinity. (The review refers to the "pink powder puff" contretemps and Valentino's having challenged his detractor to a fight. If it happens, says the review, "the sheik has an arm that would do credit to a pugilist and a most careless way of hurling himself off balconies and on and off horses. One leap from a balcony to a swinging chandelier is as good as anything Douglas Fairbanks ever did.") Valentino was very pleased, as the movie opened to tremendous business.

Since Valentino's next film was not scheduled to go into production until October, he devoted his attention to promoting *The Son of the Sheik* and planning a trip to Europe. Things were going well for him, and he ordered a new set of luggage with matching wardrobe trunks, and two dozen new suits to be custom-made by a New York tailor. To make amends for the time he spent off-screen in his quarrel with Paramount, he arranged a meeting with Adolph Zukor to apologize, and Zukor, according to his autobiography, said, "It's water over the dam . . . You're young. Many good years are ahead of you."

Ten days later, on Monday, August 16, 1926, Valentino was in a hospital near death. It was that sudden. He had been in his suite at the Ambassador Hotel, in the company of his valet, when he abruptly doubled over, clutched his stomach, and fainted. He was taken to a hospital where two emergency operations were performed. His condition was announced as "fair." On August 23, he was dead, at the age of only thirty-four. By the time *The Son of the Sheik* went into general release late in the fall, Valentino had been gone nearly three months. Imagine the impact this entertaining movie—one of his best—must have had on viewers. Here is Rudolph Valentino at his sexiest, most energetic and alive, most self-confident. No wonder his legend soared. He had this final signature film, released wide to his adoring public weeks after his tragic and unexpected death. And it presented him in a pseudo–old age he would never attain, and renewed the audience's memory of *The Sheik*, the movie that had secured his legend. No better posthumous memento could exist. It was as if Hollywood had written Valentino's story . . . which in a sense, of course, it had.

Valentino's death, and the mob hysteria that followed, was one of the earliest instances of what movie fame was about: people went crazy. His death at such an early age and in conjunction with such a huge new hit took everyone totally by surprise. No one could believe it, and no one could absorb how it had happened or why it had happened. Confusion reigned, and even today his death is variously described as having been due to a burst appendix, with peritonitis resulting, or a perforated ulcer that would not stop bleeding. (There is, of course, the usual conspiracy theory. It was rumored he had died of a gunshot wound, delivered by an irate husband or a spurned woman, and, in the modern tradition, there were also rumors that he was still alive.) As news of his death hit the newsstands and radio reports, mobs of mourners appeared in the streets outside the hospital, and there was a near riot at his funeral. Newspapers, magazines, radio, and newsreels from all around the world put Valentino's death front and center for days. Women tore their clothes and clutched their bosoms. Poems were written. ("His feet had carried him so very swiftly, / into the lands of wonder and romance; / And yet, although they traveled far, / they never forgot how to dance," from *Photoplay*, October 1926.) Natacha Rambova started writing her memoirs of their marriage . . . Pola Negri claimed they had planned to be wed . . . and bagfuls of mail arrived anyplace fans felt might connect to him: the funeral home, his studio, the cemetery, the homes of other stars, the offices of the mayor of Los Angeles and the governor of California, and, sadly, addressed just vaguely to Valentino himself. And a grand new legend was born: The Lady in Black. This mysterious woman would appear every year at Valentino's grave, on the anniversary of his death, until she herself apparently died or gave up in 1955. Dressed all in black—hat, hose, shoes, dress, and veil—she always carried thirteen roses, twelve red and one white, which she placed lovingly on his grave.

And then there was the dramatic and tempestuous Pola Negri, who had been conducting a torrid affair with Valentino. After her announcement that she had been scheduled to be the third Mrs. Valentino, Negri stepped forward into the spotlight. She sent blood-red roses to the funeral, four thousand blooms assessed to be worth a cool $2,000, a six-foot-wide beautiful carpet of

Valentino's funeral:
the procession down
Broadway, with
police escort and
stunned crowds; the
grieving Pola Negri
in full mourning

flowers that stretched eleven feet in length, with POLA spelled out in the center in white blooms. (God forbid she wouldn't get her money's worth.) No slouch at publicity, Pola Negri claimed the playing field as Valentino's official "widow," and as she prepared to go east for the services, Adolph Zukor, her boss at Paramount, was supposed to have said, "Get her first-class accommodations, a doctor to travel with her—and, of course, a good publicity man." Negri made her definitive statement on Rudolph Valentino in her 1970 autobiography, cleverly understanding what his appeal really was: "It was not his physical perfection nor the blithe charm of his manner. It was in the way in which he moved! . . . In dancing with him, his true sexuality reached out and captured me."

And so it was that, after a brief career plagued by self-doubt, weird marital behavior, and many bad reviews, Valentino disappeared, wiped off the screen about a year before sound began to creep in and ruin the lives of many of his colleagues. He was so totally unique, and so much a creature of his era, that it is difficult to get his career fully in perspective. Assessment is aided, however, by remembering that he was not the only Latin Lover of his time—he was simply the best. It's tempting to laugh at the concept today, yet it was a type that did not disappear with Valentino, bringing us Gilbert Roland, Ricardo Montalban, Fernando Lamas, Antonio Banderas, Armand Assante, Anthony Quinn, Cesar Romero, and plenty of others. In his own day, Valentino had three major rivals: Antonio Moreno, Ricardo Cortez, and Ramon Novarro. Some might also include Rod La Roque, but he was a Chicago-born actor of French extraction whose work didn't really fit the description. Tall, handsome, and versatile in his roles, he made film history by marrying—and staying married to—the beautiful Vilma Banky (known as "The Hungarian Rhapsody"). It is only his name, really, that makes him seem "Latin." Many of his most famous roles, such as Dan McTavish in the modern portion of DeMille's *Ten Commandments,* were in no way associated with the concept, although his good looks and dashing appearance also cast him as romantic leads.

Moreno, Cortez, and Novarro all made movies during the period that Valentino dominated, and assessing their looks, talent, and careers sheds light on the Valentino phenomenon. Antonio Moreno, who never rose to the heights of a Valentino-like stardom, began his career in 1921, living on to work in such classics as John Ford's *The Searchers* in 1956, in which he plays a Spanish-American. In fact, Moreno *was* a Spaniard, having been born in Madrid. He was an exceedingly handsome man, with large, dark eyes, a strong profile, and a beautiful smile. His looks are more modern than Valentino's and less exotic. There is no hint of the sly, no sense of danger to him. He was a capable actor, able to play both comedy and drama, and he found success in many different genres, including epic westerns, women's pictures, romantic comedies, and serials. Moreno showed good judgment in the management of his career, and the work he left behind far surpasses Valentino's in quantity and quality. He appeared opposite Greta Garbo in *The Temptress* (1926), and starred in Rex Ingram's greatly respected opus *Mare Nostrum* (1926). His roles usually capitalized on his exotic looks, as when he supported Marion Davies in *Beverly of Graustark* (1926), playing a Graustarkian goatherd who turns out to be a count. His other leading ladies include Constance Talmadge, Dorothy Gish, and Clara Bow. (Clara Bow was the "It" girl, but Antonio Moreno was the "It" guy, playing opposite her in the famous film of that name. Elinor Glyn, that grand humbug, had decreed that only four Hollywood personalities really had "It": Bow, Moreno, the doorman at the Ambassador Hotel, and Rex, King of the Wild Horses.) Moreno's flame burned at a considerably lower wattage than Valentino's, but he lived a long, full life and worked on into the late 1950s, dying at the age of eighty.

Ricardo Cortez looked the most like Valentino, and he was invented, named, and groomed to become a direct rival. Ironically, he wasn't Latin at all, having been born as Jack Kranze in Vienna, and having immigrated with his family to America at an early age. He became starstruck growing up in Manhattan, began playing bit parts in New York–based films, and after moving to Hollywood, his appearance in a dance contest won him a Paramount contract. Cortez was a superb ballroom dancer, and he and a partner were taking part in a dance contest at the Coconut Grove in 1922. In the grand "a star is born" tradition, Jesse L. Lasky of Paramount was in the audience and noticed at once how much Cortez resembled Valentino. *And* he could dance! Valentino was at the height of his popularity, with both *The Sheik* and *Blood and Sand* behind him, and he was already giving the studio a difficult time, demanding much more money, more control of his career, and better roles. Lasky immediately offered Cortez a contract and began preparing him to take Valentino's place. (The first step, of course, was the invention of a suitable Latin name, with "Ricardo Cortez" supposed to have been thought up by Lasky's secretary. The name was so successful that Cortez's brother would also adopt it, becoming the cinematographer Stanley Cortez.)

Ricardo Cortez really did look like Valentino. His eyes had the same somewhat hooded quality, although to a lesser degree, and his nose and facial shape were very similar. And his hair was the same. What Cortez lacked was Valentino's physical grace, and his inner fire, even though he was a handsome man and a competent actor. During this period, he supported Garbo, Swanson, Bebe Daniels, the beautiful Florence Vidor, and the young Joan Crawford. After a tragic marriage to the morphine addict Alma Rubens, who died in 1931 at the age of thirty-four, Cortez moved easily into sound films and went on playing opposite big-name female stars, including Crawford, Barbara Stanwyck, Mary Astor, Claudette Colbert, Kay Francis, Irene Dunne, Bette Davis,

The rivals of Valentino: Ricardo Cortez, Ramon Novarro, Antonio Moreno

and Dolores Del Rio. And that is the difference between Cortez and Valentino: Cortez supported big-name women stars; Valentino was himself the star. Cortez eventually left movies, joined a brokerage firm, and made a great deal of money and a happy third marriage. He made one final film appearance, in John Ford's *The Last Hurrah* in 1958, and died at the age of seventy-seven, very rich and very comfortable, a Latin Lover who had lived down the term.

Ramon Novarro was the biggest star of the three Valentino rivals, and the one whose career most threatened Valentino. Many historians feel that he was the far finer actor and, in the long run, the more important personality, and that his fame was eclipsed by the brief, meteoric passion that Valentino inspired. Since Novarro went past the silent era into success in sound, Valentino detractors believe that it was his untimely death that elevated him above Novarro, and that it would not have happened otherwise. Certainly it is true that Novarro had the bad luck to come along after Valentino had already risen to the heights of stardom. This meant that he would inevitably be sold to the public as a Latin Lover, which made him automatically second fiddle to Valentino. But Novarro is really nothing like Valentino. His is not a frivolous sexual game, a flirtation with women in the audience. He plays a full character, with dimensions other than mere lover. The difference between the two men is one of substance as well as style. Novarro was more associated with serious acting than with making women swoon, although he definitely was in the Latin Lover category and was very popular with women moviegoers. Both men used humor in their "sex symbol" appearances. Valentino's was only a touch, but it was a touch that made the sex and danger all the more intriguing. Novarro's humor overtly suggested that he didn't take himself seriously as a lover of women. (This may have been a direct reflection of his private life. Novarro was brutally murdered in 1968 in what is supposed to have been a homosexual quarrel.)

Novarro, like Valentino, was small and perfectly proportioned. He was beautiful but not exotic. His photographs show eyes that are not sharp, and certainly not cruel, like those of Valentino and Cortez. He exudes a much more tender quality. What Novarro lacks, in comparison to Valentino, is raw sex appeal. What he gains is that he is actually a better actor than he is given credit for—more realistic, less of a poser, and with a wider range. Despite this range, however, the public seemed to like him best as a swashbuckling, romantic lead.

Born in Mexico in comfortable circumstances, Novarro became an avid movie fan at an early age. His family relocated to Los Angeles, and he turned to acting when the death of his father created financial difficulties. He was determined to succeed, and worked desperately hard at his craft. He did not have a glamorous and sudden rise to fame. He played small roles in important films until Rex Ingram chose him to play the leading role of Rupert of Hentzau in his 1922 *The Prisoner of Zenda*. The film made Novarro a success, and *Scaramouche*, which followed in 1923, made him a top-ranked star. As his career unfolded, his similarity to Valentino caused him to be presented in his own desert epic, *The Arab*, in 1924, a direct attack on Valentino's fame. In his private life, Novarro spent generously and lived like a star; furthermore, he was a clever businessman who knew how to hold out for the top dollar in contract disputes. One of his great interests was serious music, and he studied diligently, hoping to be able to sing in grand opera one day. As a result, his career continued well into the sound era, as he spent five years singing and dancing in a series of successful romantic movie operettas. He continued working in small roles for years, coming out of comfortable retirement in 1961 to play a minor part in his friend George Cukor's 1960 feature *Heller in Pink Tights*, starring Sophia Loren.

Unlike Cortez and Moreno, Novarro became a major star, undoubtedly because of his central role in *Ben-Hur*, the $5 million 1926 spectacle that is still successfully revived. Novarro played the hero of the title, and he is young, muscular, and vibrantly alive in the part. Unlike Valentino, Novarro would work often with great directors, including not only Ingram but Lubitsch, John Stahl, and Jacques Feyder. He made many movies that are considered "quality films" today, including *Ben-Hur, The Prisoner of Zenda, Scaramouche*, and *The Student Prince* opposite Norma Shearer.

Valentino's influence on others carried well into the sound era, to such actors as George Raft, whose clothes, slicked-down hair, and sensuous dancing style were clearly patterned on Valentino. Raft, although best remembered for his gangster roles, was a great master of the ooze-across-the-floor tango. He had the true sexual detachment required for the proper presentation of the dance, because he was a natural deadpan. Valentino's tango was never quite perfect, as Raft's was, but in terms of getting results, Valentino's was by far the stronger of the two. How many people today even remember Raft as a tango dancer?

IT'S HARD TO BE BRANDED a Latin Lover in any era. Any such actor has to have something else going for him. (Anthony Quinn, Ricardo Montalban, and Gilbert Roland all became serious actors. Fernando Lamas started directing. Cesar Romero developed a flair for musical comedy.) Nothing goes out of style faster than love scenes on film, as each generation has its own approach to romance. What we know today about Valentino's lovemaking on film is that, like Frank Sinatra, he made women swoon and annoyed men. Unlike Sinatra, who had a long career and plenty of time to live it all down, Valentino died young. He seemed to understand well enough what was required of him in the context of any movie he was in. What he seems not to have understood was what to do with the label in his off-screen life. Although many who knew him described him as a very nice fellow, gentle, athletic, and possessing a good sense of humor, others, particularly biographers, described him as a hen-pecked husband who married two lesbians without having a clue about it.

In reading about Valentino, it is striking how negatively his biographers have seen him. Surely no superstar was ever less appreciated. Significantly, his biographers have all been male, and practically nowhere except in a few articles and fan magazines does one find the female response to his work. The portrait painted of him is one of an uncertain, sexually ambivalent, weak man, dominated by the strong women in his life, particularly his second wife, Rambova. It is probably wise to remember that most of the opinions expressed about him after his death came either from critics who detested his films or from women who had been in his life—who gave their points of view, not his.

Who knows the truth about Valentino? In his own day, his background story was rewritten and designed by studio hype, and when he died so suddenly he was instantly elevated into legendary status, and—not unlike Elvis—became an object of both ridicule and adoration for the ages. Facts no longer mattered.

When Valentino's image is analyzed today, he is usually described as androgynous. However, he is not like a Marlene Dietrich, who clearly understood the term and definitely played with sexuality for a dual appeal. Valentino is from a less knowing, more innocent decade, and his films forthrightly present him as a Latin Lover for women. The fact that he is physically beautiful, wears magnificent clothes well, and twirls around in capes, was not a wink at men in the audience. (That he could still have a strong sexual appeal for men is another issue.) His filmed image was directed at women who wanted to escape the bounds of a constricting society that gave only men sexual freedom. He is not a hip, cutting-edge bisexual figure but a creature out of a romance novel. He is there to rip bodices.

This is borne out by the fact that male reviewers seemed to hate him so much. (Did female reviewers and females in the audience hate Marilyn Monroe like this?) These men clearly just resented Valentino, and wanted to discredit his sexuality. Or else they were frankly embarrassed by him. It's entirely possible that, in his image, which offered women sex directly and freedom indirectly, they smelled trouble, the winds of change that were going to unseat their authority. Even a rational film historian like DeWitt Bodeen, who loved and respected films and film stars, wrote with contempt of Valentino in 1968, referring to his "long-lashed myopic eyes, his child-bearing hips, his outrageous attire or bold partial nudity." Bodeen states that Valentino today looks more like Nita Naldi than like a male movie star.

Over the years, Valentino's image has captured the imagination of film-makers. Two movie biographies have been made about him: *Valentino,* starring the lackluster Anthony Dexter in 1951, and *Valentino* in 1977, directed by Ken Russell and starring Rudolf Nureyev in the title role. Neither film offers any real insight into the Valentino legend or life, and neither understands anything about silent film stardom. Both are crippled by weak performances by the leading men, and neither Dexter nor Nureyev seems to have a clue about what made Valentino great.

No one ever suggests that Valentino could have survived the sound era. Unlike other male sex symbols or action stars—Clint Eastwood, for example—Valentino died too young to have a chance to grow, develop, and triumph as producer-director-actor and award winner. It is assumed that he didn't have the intelligence or the range to do anything other than be a Latin Lover. The general consensus is that his career was some sort of aberration, and that at any moment he was about to be laughed off the screen. Watching him, however, I find myself wondering. Valentino might actually have been *better* in sound. Freed of the extravagant romanticism of the silent era, and detached from his attempts to "act" in its highly emotional style and very histrionic situations, he might have been liberated into his natural comic mode, and made an excellent "other man" in a screwball comedy. More interestingly, he could have been a fine Italian gangster in the many hard-boiled crime movies of the early 1930s. George Raft, after all, was little more than a Valentino carbon copy; Valentino would have been a better George Raft. And think of Valentino playing the lover in the pre-code era of early sound or in support of Garbo in one of her exotic romps. His sexuality could have been fully unleashed. Instead of hinting at being hot, he could have been overtly low-down and sexy, which was his natural talent. Valentino might have surprised everyone if he had lived and been allowed to play comedy, or play really tough and sexy, or even do a musical. And who knows how his voice would have recorded? Carmel Myers told an audience in 1980 that "if he had ever talked, in talking pictures, if he had lived that long, he would have been a much bigger star, because his voice was just beautiful." (When I played Valentino's recording of "Pale Hands I Loved Beside the Shalimar," I heard a strong baritone voice with a pleasant tone.)

Seventy years after his death, the Valentino legend is not yet exhausted. His name is still known, and he brought a new word into the vocabulary: *sheik*, meaning "a masterful man to whom women are irresistibly attracted." In his brief stardom, a nation of Emma Bovarys gorged themselves on his distinctly Latin style and went crazy when he died young and tragically, paying his dues not only for being sexy but also for being so successful. As with Harlow and Dean and Monroe after him, early death ensured his legend, because Valentino's story had no mundane finish like that of Moreno and Cortez, and no sordid one like that of Novarro. Valentino is still a magic name. How many women out there are secretly hoping some good-looking sheik will carry them off? His is the Latin beat that all other heartthrobs are measured against. He may have had nothing but the style of a gigolo—but what a gigolo!

A saucy Rudolph
Valentino

MARION DAVIES

FROM A HISTORICAL PERSPECTIVE, no one has it worse than Marion Davies. Over her successful career hangs the ghastly shadow of Susan Alexander, the no-talent wife of Charles Foster Kane. Marion Davies was a delicious comedienne whose films are unpretentious entertainments in which she is beautiful, peppy, funny, and highly appealing. She was a big success in silent movies, and popular with audiences . . . but nobody believes it. It is generally assumed today that William Randolph Hearst, newspaper tycoon, manufactured her career, that she had no talent, and that she survived in motion pictures only through the efforts of his publicity people. Hearst *did* manipulate Marion's career, he *did* produce her movies through his company, Cosmopolitan Pictures, and his newspapers *did* give her consistently good reviews. However, it was Marion Davies whose image appeared on the screen, and it was her considerable talent and great personal charm that audiences responded to. And she got good reviews on her own from less-than-sympathetic rival publications. Why does nobody believe it? It's the curse of *Citizen Kane*.

Citizen Kane, as perhaps everyone knows, tells the story of a newspaper tycoon, Charles Foster Kane, who makes an unsuccessful marriage for politi-cal reasons but later falls in love with a pretty young girl, Susan Alexander. After first making her his mistress and later marrying her, he tries to turn her into an opera star, even though all she has is a rather sweet little singing voice. Alexander, the movie makes clear, hasn't the brains or the talent or the incli-nation for stardom, and the result is a total disaster. Since Hearst allegedly was the model for Kane (which Orson Welles and others deny) and Davies was his mistress, it must follow that Marion Davies had no talent.

No one who has watched her films with an open mind really believes that Marion Davies couldn't have become a success on her own—she's too pretty, too talented, and too good a comedienne. If there's a problem with her career, the fault should probably be laid at the feet of the man who loved her, Hearst himself. He was the one who placed her in the scandalous position, and how-ever well intentioned his sponsorship was, he frequently made bad choices in material for her. He was old-fashioned, and loved to see her in costume dramas or sentimental romances. This tended to hold her back, since her real gifts were in comedy timing and an ability to do wonderfully wicked imitations of her fellow stars. (She also could sing and dance, which helped when sound came in.) However, everything about the Davies career always comes down to William Randolph Hearst. Reviews of her own day constantly gripe about the money being spent on her movies, about her privileged treatment in Hearst reviews, about how no one is allowed to see her on her own terms because of his publicity machine. Although critics often gave her excellent notices, they never forgave her for the sin of William Randolph Hearst. No doubt many sincerely resented the immorality that Marion represented in those more restrictive years; for many people in the press, as well as in the audience, Marion Davies was a "fallen woman." The fact that she not only wasn't suffering for it but apparently was having a heck of a good time—and becoming a big-time movie star while having it—must really have irritated them.

In his autobiography, *A Tree Is a Tree*, written in 1952, King Vidor, one of Marion's best directors, spoke warmly of her and her career, but also shed light on Hearst's participation in it. ("I directed Marion in three comedies and I considered her to be a most accomplished comedienne.") Vidor details how he wanted to make a picture about Hollywood, and, in particular, to satirize the career of a famous female film star. He and writer Laurence Stallings quickly agreed that the object of satire would be Gloria Swanson, who started out in Mack Sennett comedies but had graduated to Cecil B. DeMille dramas and beyond, marrying a marquis along the way, and that the material would make a perfect Marion Davies movie. When they motored up to San Simeon to enthusiastically present to W. R. Hearst and Marion their hilarious idea for the screenplay in which Marion would do comic imitations and get hit with a custard pie in the face, Marion said, "I like it," but Hearst was silent. He finally gave consent, but only if Marion did not get hit with the custard pie. She disagreed and later quietly suggested to Vidor that he wait until she could persuade Hearst to come around, but before shooting began, Vidor was summoned to a meeting with Louis B. Mayer* and Hearst in which, despite his best arguments, entreaties, and justifications, the final word was handed down by Hearst: "I'm not going to let Marion be hit in the face with a pie." The issue was settled.

---

*At that time, Hearst's production company, Cosmopolitan Pictures, which featured Marion Davies, was on the lot at MGM and released its product through MGM. Over the years, the company moved several times. Following *Adam and Eva* in 1923, Hearst moved Cosmopolitan from Paramount to Goldwyn. When Goldwyn merged with Metro Pictures and became MGM in 1924, Hearst, Marion, and Cosmopolitan were housed there until the completion of *Operator 13* in 1934. In 1935, Cosmopolitan was moved to Warner Brothers, where Marion made her final four movies.

Davies and the objectionable pie, in *Show People*

In this story lies the clue to Hearst's role in Marion Davies's career, and in her life. He loved her, and he wanted her to be treated with dignity and respect. When he had first fallen in love with her, she was a softly beautiful young girl, and that was how he wanted others to see her. That she was also a saucy, fun-loving little imp was not lost on him, but he must have been conscious that his relationship with her was denying her the full acceptance of society. In threatening her reputation, he threatened her dignity, so dignity ("always dignity") became one of his greatest ambitions for his Marion.

Whenever Davies had directors or writers who couldn't handle Hearst, her movies were not as good as they should have been. When she had a shrewd and talented director like King Vidor, they turned out well because Vidor simply found a way around the problem. In *Show People,* a riotous comedy, Marion Davies isn't hit in the face with a pie, but she *is* hit in the face with a forceful stream of water from a soda siphon bottle. (On the day the scene was shot, Marion cleverly had the publisher of the *Los Angeles Examiner* telephone Hearst and call him off the set to a conference, so Hearst knew nothing until it was too late.) The scene is one of the best in the picture, and Marion plays it to perfection. An audience seeing it seventy or more years later easily appreciates her talent, and she loses no dignity whatsoever.

The Hearst/Davies romance is a curious tale that defies all the odds. Despite its trappings of "old lecher picks up young chorus girl" or perhaps "young gold digger traps old lecher," theirs was a true romance, a great love story. Hearst and Davies, who undoubtedly would have married if his wife had

given him a divorce, stayed together until his death. She was at his side
through thick and thin. She gave her youth to him and never complained when
it was all over.

The legitimate question to ask about the career of Marion Davies is not
whether she had talent—she did—but what her career might have been without Hearst. With his guidance, she found popularity but never became a top
box office draw. There is a good deal of evidence to suggest that she could
have been an even bigger star than she was. One thing is certain, however:
even if Marion Davies could have had more success without Hearst, she
wouldn't have wanted it that way. Hearst was central to her life, and no one
ever questioned her devotion. She was 100 percent loyal. If Hearst wanted to
see her in a certain kind of film, she made that kind of film. If he wanted her to
be available in the summer months, she did not make any film at all. Her
"W. R." always came first.

Marion Davies's story is interesting because it is not like anyone else's.
(Yes, Norma Talmadge's career was managed and shaped by her lover, Joseph
Schenck, but after she married him.) Davies was forced to proceed without
portfolio in polite society. All the successful movie stars of the silent era
became stars partly because the public discovered them, embraced them, and
began to believe something about their screen presence, something easily
labeled. Chaplin was "the Little Tramp." Pickford was "America's Sweetheart." Valentino was "the Latin Lover." Colleen Moore was "the perfect flapper," Clara Bow was "the 'It' girl." Marion's film presence didn't suggest any
such simple identification. Stars also extended their fame and glory when
their off-screen lives reflected the public's image of them, or when dramatic
events elevated them to romantic heights. Pickford and Fairbanks got married, Valentino went on tour and really danced the tango, Swanson married a
marquis, Tom Mix was an authentic rodeo champion. Marion Davies could
compete in this area, but unfortunately the certain something in her private
life that made her glamorous and interesting—she was Hearst's mistress—
became the thing that destroyed her reputation (the curse of *Citizen Kane*).

Marion Davies on-screen was apparently just being herself. She comes
across as highly likable, a quality she had in abundance in real life. Considering that her career was shaped and protected by one of the most powerful
and hated men in America and that she had everything material that anyone
could possibly want, people might easily have hated her. But they didn't.
Everyone loved her. She didn't seem to inspire dislike or jealousy, even in a
business famous for unpleasant competition, because she didn't take herself
seriously. Her fabulous onyx-and-diamond cigarette case had a rubber band
around it to hold it together, and she loved a bargain. She was down-to-
earth, natural, and very funny. One of her costars, Antonio Moreno, praised
her as the "most fun" of all the women he had worked with, adding, "She

was the cutest thing on the screen. Always the same—gay, unassuming, and considerate."

Writing of her in *Films in Review*, Earl Anderson summed her up: "In her private life, she radiated a warm personality and a delightful sense of humor that gained her the largest army of sincere friends in Hollywood. Fun-loving, wildly sentimental, and extraordinarily generous, she was throughout her life one of filmdom's more genuine human beings." Her kindness to her former rival, the tragic Alma Rubens (who became a drug addict), was known to many. She arranged for Rubens's memoirs to be published in a Hearst newspaper when Rubens needed the money, and later paid for her funeral, rounding up friends for the service so that Rubens could be properly remembered. She did much charity work, particularly for children and veterans. And in what is perhaps the most telling Marion Davies story of all, she bailed out Hearst himself when he needed help. At a moment in the late 1930s when he was hard pressed for cash, she instantly turned over to him $1 million of her own money with no strings, no interest charged, and no hesitation. This is a very special kind of mistress, and a very special kind of woman.

MARION DAVIES WAS BORN Marion Douras in Brooklyn on January 3, 1897, the youngest of four daughters. She had a powerful brother-in-law, the theatrical producer George W. Lederer, and it was natural that, with her lovely looks, she would drift toward show business as her older sisters had done before her. Her biographer, Fred Lawrence Guiles, marks her Broadway debut as an appearance in the chorus of *Chin-Chin* in 1914, and she described this experience to an interviewer years later: "I was one of 500 chorus girls, more or less. We had to stick our heads through holes in the backdrop. We were supposed to be flowers. I was on the top tier. All went well until the framework I was standing on crashed down on the girl below. She had to go to the hospital. It left me chinning myself on the backdrop. I hung there until rescued, a most unhappy looking blossom."

There are many versions of how William Randolph Hearst first met Marion Davies. The one closest to those old backstage musical plots is the one in which he spots her hoofing in the chorus line, falls in love at first sight, and comes every night for eight weeks just to see her, reserving two seats, one for himself and one for his hat. Davies never acknowledged this romantic story, and after Hearst's death even claimed she didn't meet him until 1918, after she had already made her first film. Her matter-of-fact description of the big moment was as close as she ever came to explaining their first discovery of each other: "I bumped into Mr. Hearst . . . I called him 'Sir' then . . . and we became friends after that." Earl Anderson's article says he believed this story because "it's banal enough to be true, it's in character, and it's not self-serving."

William Randolph Hearst was already in the film business when he and Marion first met, sometime between 1915 and 1918. He not only ran the International Newsreel but had produced some early serials, such as *The Mysteries of Myra* and the very popular *Exploits of Elaine*. After Davies was signed by Hearst to work for his company in 1917, she never made a film for anyone else. Hearst's motives for putting her into his movies cannot have been sheer, blind love. She not only had a bubbling personality that came across on film, but she was also quite beautiful. (When Cecil Beaton came to Hollywood in 1930 to photograph "the six most beautiful women in the movies," he chose Marion, in addition to Lillian Gish, Dolores Del Rio, Norma Shearer, Alice White, and Greta Garbo, giving as his reasons the "delicacy and elfin qualities of her features, which remind one of a Greuze painting.")*

Marion Davies made her film debut in 1917 in *Runaway Romany*, which was shot in Florida and released by Pathé. She played a Gypsy girl who turns out to be the long-lost daughter of an important man. The film was not particularly successful, and Davies was in it only because it was directed by her brother-in-law, George Lederer. According to Davies herself, years later, Hearst saw the film and signed her for his film company for $500 per week.

For his first production starring Marion, Hearst stuck to what he had already done, creating a serial called *Beatrice Fairfax*, the chapters appearing in theatres throughout the calendar year of 1918. Marion played the title role, that of a wealthy young woman whose curiosity leads her into a series of adventures, but *Beatrice Fairfax* was a flop. According to Guiles, Hearst then went into high gear. Instead of trying to feed her to the public slowly and let them make her a star, he decided to present her as if she already *was* a star. Guiles states that "Marion's rise to star status with all its prerogatives was achieved in a matter of weeks through extraordinary publicity in the Hearst press, huge infusions of cash into her personal bank account, with unlimited charge accounts at all the best stores, and by moving her and her family into a white marble townhouse, remodeled along palatial lines . . ."

In 1918, Davies starred in two more Hearst movies, *Cecilia of the Pink Roses* and *Burden of Proof. Cecilia's* story sets a pattern that would be repeated many times throughout Davies's career, and was obviously the kind of thing that Hearst thought was right for her. It is the basic Cinderella plot, with Marion presented in two different guises. At first, she's a cheerful girl of the slums, the daughter of a bricklayer, who spends her days looking after dear old dad and all the household chores—a situation that shows off a boyish Marion Davies as an ordinary gal with a good heart and plenty of spunk. Then her father comes up with one of those miraculous inventions that turn up in so

---

*Whether Beaton's list reflected his real beliefs, or was something he was hired to produce, is open to question.

many 1920s movies, and they suddenly become extremely wealthy. Cecilia is sent off to a finishing school, where she has to learn how to dress, how to talk, how to eat, and how to behave in a suitable way. Naturally, she ends up teaching the snobs a few things, but not before she's beautifully finished and comes out looking ravishing, a stunning woman in gorgeous clothes.

Marion appeared in four movies in 1919: *Belle of New York, Getting Mary Married, The Dark Star,* and *The Cinema Murder.* They cast her in roles that didn't add up to any particular persona, and they were merely typical movies of their time. Hearst made every effort to surround her with the best talent, however. Anita Loos and John Emerson wrote *Getting Mary Married,* and Allan Dwan directed both that film and *The Dark Star.* For Marion's final 1919 movie, Hearst made an even greater effort. For the large fee of $2,000 a week, he hired the extremely successful screenwriter Frances Marion, who had written for Mary Pickford, to create seven special scenarios with Davies in mind. The first of these was *The Cinema Murder,* in which she plays a young girl who is trying to break into the movies, but who falls in love with a playwright accused of a murder he didn't commit.

By 1920, Marion had a solid three years in the business and seven films under her belt. She was doing well, but nothing distinctive had occurred. In this year, she made *April Folly* (another of those diamond robbery/masked ball stories in which she outwits the crooks) and *The Restless Sex* (a messy tale about an adopted daughter who falls in love with her "brother"). In 1921, there would be *Buried Treasure* and *Enchantment. Buried Treasure* was a silly story about reincarnation, which prompted the *New York Times* to predict that audiences were going to ask themselves, "Why do they do this, when they have so much money to spend on something good?" . . . one of the first reviewer complaints about Hearst's money. *Variety* was enthusiastic about Marion, however. Its reviewer says, "Before 500 feet of *Enchantment* have been unwound, it is apparent to the most casual spectator that high comedy is the forte of Marion Davies in pictures . . . Miss Davies has the role of a carefree, egotistical flapper, all wise, the pampered only child of doting parents of wealth who deny her nothing and whom she winds about her finger at will." (Davies is one of the first of the 1920s leading ladies to be cast in a role in which she is defined as a flapper. This movie predates Colleen Moore in *Flaming Youth* by almost two years. Davies herself might have become the fan idol most associated with the flapper concept had Hearst not wanted her to appear in more romantic roles.)

By the end of 1921, Marion was a pronounced success, and her career was growing. However, she still hadn't found a truly suitable métier. In 1922, something began to take shape, a concept that had surfaced successfully in *Cecilia.* Often in the 1920s, movies set up situations in which popular actresses could play two people: a boy and a girl; a homely sister and a beau-

tiful one; a mean one and a kind one; a poor girl and a rich one. This duality
allowed an actress an opportunity to stretch her talents, of course, but it also
afforded the possibility of her wearing tight pants, taking part in action
scenes, revealing hidden nuances about herself—and possibly appealing to
slightly offbeat tastes. Davies was a natural mimic and clown, but she was the
mistress of a man who liked her to look very feminine. The popular "duality"
ploy offered a way of resolving their conflict; Marion could be the woman
Hearst wanted her to be on film and still exercise her talents and have some
fun. She could sit swathed in furs and draped in diamonds—the equal of any
of the great divas of the silent screen—and also get a chance to screw up her
face, wiggle her nose, and make herself homely and hilarious.

In 1922, Marion Davies made four films: *Bride's Play, Beauty's Worth,
The Young Diana,* and *When Knighthood Was in Flower,* and all of them presented her in these "duality" roles. *Bride's Play* was a modern story with a
flashback to earlier times in the Cecil B. DeMille tradition, with Davies playing both an up-to-date 1920s girl and "Enid of Cashel," a well-costumed and
romantic heroine. *Beauty's Worth* presented her first as a drab little Quaker-
ess, and then transformed her into a drop-dead gorgeous leader of society.
(Never mind the logic of this.) In *The Young Diana,* she is first an unattractive
spinster with no clothes sense, but then she meets a scientist and submits to
his experiments, emerging as a radiant young beauty who will later be gor-
geously gowned. (He practiced the Science of Fashion, apparently.) In the
end, this experiment turns out to have been a dream, but two Marions for the
price of one seemed to please everyone. The format had been found.

During 1922, the reviews became overtly critical of how much money
was being spent on Marion Davies movies. This would become a common
theme. In its evaluation of *Beauty's Worth,* for instance, the *Times* says, "She
has had more in the way of rich settings, fine costumes and careful direction
thrust upon her than almost any other screen player has enjoyed." This leads
directly to complaints about how title cards keep saying that her beauty is
"pure gold" or that she is a "diamond among rhinestones." In fact, the *Times*
gives Marion a royal pan: "Unfortunately, she was not born with acting ability
and she has not been able to achieve it. They have taught her how to move
around the stage more freely than she used to, they have made her laugh and
scowl and pout, but they have not made her act. Her role . . . doesn't mean
anything, except that Marion Davies is in another movie." This type of negative review, obviously grounded in resentment about her sponsorship by
Hearst, was going to haunt Marion Davies one way or another all her life. In
fairness, the settings of *Beauty's Worth were* spectacular—Hearst had hired
Joseph Urban, a celebrated Viennese set designer who had come to America
in 1913 to do some of the *Ziegfeld Follies* sets as well as operas for the Metropolitan. (Urban took movies seriously, calling them "the art of the twentieth

How Hearst liked to see Davies: romantically dressed in period costumes, in *Janice Meredith* and *Yolanda*

century, and perhaps the greatest art of modern times.") If critics had complained about the money spent on *Beauty's Worth*, they needed to brace themselves for Marion's next, *When Knighthood Was in Flower*, her final 1922 release. Hearst put Urban under contract, and let him loose to design streets, villages, and a fully detailed Tudor court.

When Knighthood Was in Flower is the kind of movie historians would have us believe always evoked poor reviews—the historical costume film. Yet she gets an excellent review from *Variety:*

> Miss Davies as the sweet, impulsive and loving Mary, emoted when that was called for, coquetted as nicely with her sweetheart, and sent the fierceness of her wrath when aroused out of the screen and over the footlights, while at all times making a charming etching, perhaps never more so than in the view as she kneeled before the cross praying that Brandon should be saved . . . While this is a fine picture for all concerned, it is a finer one for Marion Davies for *When Knighthood Was in Flower* implants this handsome girl right among the leading players, those who can act—something mighty few beautiful women of the screen ever accomplish.

(*Variety* wasn't owned by William Randolph Hearst.)

Every possible dollar was spent to make *When Knighthood Was in Flower* into a first-rate production—and it cost an amazing sum for the times: a whopping $1.5 million. Davies is surrounded by a cast that, as reviewers noted, "reads like a composite of the leading drama and musical comedy of Broadway. It's a collection of names seldom met other than at a benefit." (Cast members included Pedro de Cordoba, William Powell, Gustav von Seyffertitz, and others.) *When Knighthood Was in Flower* (which is not about knights, even though it opens with a tournament) reeked of money in all production aspects—sets, costumes, cast, props. (The opulence of the silent film costume drama—its spectacle—is comparable to today's over-the-top special effects. It's all for the eyeball, and to lift a viewer out of reality.) When the movie opened in New York City at the Criterion, the evening was an invitation-only affair. Inside the theatre, a huge and glittering sign presented the beautiful Miss Davies as a star, and outside the theatre there was an even more telling one. At the point of the Times Square triangle, Broadway and Forty-seventh Street, on the downtown side of an old building could be read ZIEGFELD'S FOL-LIES GLORIFYING THE AMERICAN GIRL. Immediately underneath was the new ad for the Davies film. Passersby thus read, ZIEGFELD'S FOLLIES GLORIFYING THE AMERICAN GIRL MARION DAVIES IN WHEN KNIGHTHOOD WAS IN FLOWER.

When Knighthood Was in Flower is a romantic and sentimental story about "the right of youth to love." Davies appears as a pseudohistorical Mary Tudor, who at first refuses to marry King Louis XII of France. ("But he is King of France! What more could any woman want?") She marries him, though, in order to save the man she loves. It's an old-fashioned tale of great sacrifice, but it was well received in its time. Because it marked the beginning of Marion's true stardom, the one she earned for herself, it's curious that it has such a bad reputation. It's true that she spends a good share of her time standing around with her hands in a fur muff, immobilized by yard goods. However, the other Marion definitely exists, particularly when she dresses up as a boy in order to flee with her lover. She duels, she swaggers, she minces around as a pseudo-male, swinging her arms and plopping her big boots up on a table, cutting a very fine figure indeed. ("You're more a handsome girl than any man I ever saw," says one smitten taverngoer.) Throughout the film, Marion alternates between posing in an astonishing series of hats and making faces at the Spanish ambassador. Her character is presented as unafraid of authority ("I have been defiant, but I am not a wanton"), clever (she outsmarts Henry VIII), and up to any trouble that comes along (the film climaxes in a dramatic chase).

In 1923, Davies appeared in several movies to good notices. For *Adam and Eva,* she was praised for "her knack of carrying off breezy comedy parts with a certain jaunty chic." In a section of the movie I saw (the entire footage was not available), Marion seemed self-confident, easy and natural, as if she knew that this kind of lighthearted comedy was better suited to her talents than anything else. When she enters the frame, she whirls in with a radiant smile, full of life and energy, the way any actress who knows she's got it and deserves a star entrance might do. Ironically, the scene I saw shows her giving all her jewels to her bankrupt father. "Daddy, ruined? Never mind, I'll take care of you," she says, in an almost eerie forerunner of the scene she would later play in real life with her sugar daddy, W. R. Hearst.

Next was *Little Old New York,* one of her most celebrated movies. It has marvelously detailed sets, with "little old New York" in its early days being presented as a friendly, bucolic place. The costumes and decor are outstanding, especially in a long sequence in which Robert Fulton introduces his invention, the steamboat. In *Little Old New York,* Marion does the "double" again, playing a young girl whose brother dies en route to America to claim their inheritance. Since the female cannot inherit, Marion poses as her brother to save the family from ruin. She is feminine and pretty as the Irish "Patricia O'Day," a very lively and feisty little colleen, and equally cute as a boy, wearing boots, tight trousers, and a short haircut. She plays the boy with self-confidence and charm, and a somewhat cheerful wink at the audience, as if to say, "We all really know I'm not a boy." The *Times* pointed out that she was too feminine ever to be mistaken for one, but a clever scene plays with this. When "Pat" refuses to kiss the hand of a woman, the woman is heard to remark, "What an impossible little boy!" Very impossible, as it were. Davies has an opportunity to play several comedy scenes. In one, she is sent after dinner to the smoking room with the men and becomes ill after puffing on a pipe. In a somewhat bizarre sequence, she attends a bare-knuckle fistfight, breaks it up by ringing the fire bell, and is captured by the angry mob and tied to a post. As one of the fighters, the Hoboken Terror, prepares to horsewhip her, she breaks down and confesses that she's a girl.

The costly presentation of Marion's movies was matched by the advertising. In *Motion Picture* magazine of August 1920, a full-page ad proclaims, "COSMOPOLITAN PRODUCTIONS WITH MARION DAVIES." The text reads, "Marion Davies, starring in Cosmopolitan Productions, is shown at all leading photoplay theatres. THE CINEMA MURDER, APRIL FOLLY, and her latest production, THE RESTLESS SEX, were selected for the screen from the writings of the world's most famous authors, and have appeared in one or the other of the great chain of Hearst magazines and newspapers. Cosmopolitan Productions are distributed by Paramount-Artcraft Pictures." (Talk about synergy!) The ad features a huge photograph of Marion Davies in profile, wearing a luxurious fur collar and fresh roses in her hair.

Like all stars of the day, Davies was featured in fan magazines. (If she hadn't truly been popular with the public, there wouldn't have been so many articles about her.) In the June 1920 issue of *Motion Picture,* she gives a bit of

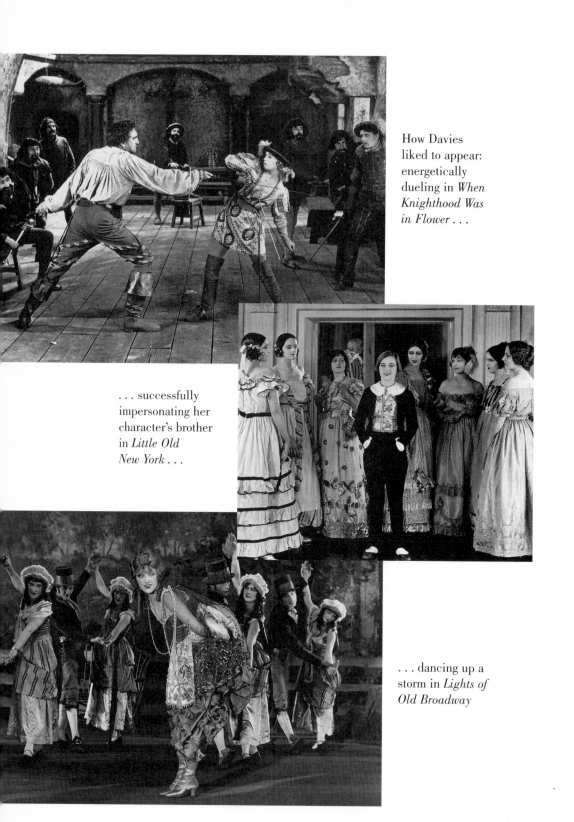

How Davies
liked to appear:
energetically
dueling in *When
Knighthood Was
in Flower* . . .

. . . successfully
impersonating her
character's brother
in *Little Old
New York* . . .

. . . dancing up a
storm in *Lights of
Old Broadway*

advice "anent June Brides and Trousseaux." Says Marion, who married once and very late in life, "Of course, you know I have had no experience in trousseau-shopping, but, like every other girl, I have ideas on the subject, very decided ideas, in fact . . . It would be a great pity to miss it all, wouldn't it? . . . If I were planning a wedding and my funds were limited, I'd manage a wedding gown and veil somehow." Marion Davies, of course, was not planning a wedding and her funds were not even remotely limited. (Later in the article, Marion confesses, "It is difficult for me to remember the slim purse.") The magazine observes, "There is an air of efficient practicality about her . . . and you inadvertently wonder how she had come to know of conservation, economy." The subtext is unavoidable.

In an article entitled "Rose and Old Lace," which appeared in the September 1920 issue of *Motion Picture*, Adele Whitely Fletcher wrote, "Among . . . people seemingly belonging to those days when romance suffused in her roseate hue, I would place Marion Davies . . . her quiet manner of refinement—it may be her utter soft femininity—rose and old lace seem to fit her somehow . . . lunch at Delmonico's." (There was, needless to say, no mention of William Randolph Hearst in this discussion of the feminine Marion.)

In fact, no direct mention of the relationship with Hearst was ever made in the fan magazines, but nothing was hidden from the public about Marion's wealthy lifestyle. About that, publicity abounded. In 1926, *Photoplay* breathlessly described a typical week for the "socially prominent" Marion Davies: "On one day she gave a small dinner party for Lady Ravensdale. The next day was Rudolph Valentino's funeral in Hollywood, with Marion escorting Pola Negri through the ordeal. Then the Goldwyn baby was born, and Marion and Mrs. Goldwyn are great friends. And the following day, the Boardman-Vidor wedding was celebrated at Marion's home."

During the 1920s, Marion Davies lived like a queen. Her Santa Monica beach house had seventy rooms, and it was three hundred feet wide and three stories high, with a gold-leafed ballroom, a huge dining room, a reception hall, a drawing room more than sixty feet long, an Italian marble swimming pool over one hundred feet long with a marble bridge across the center of it, an antique rathskeller removed from a 1560 Surrey inn and brought over to be installed, and an enclosed garden adjacent to the Pacific. Marion and Hearst also, of course, lived at their fabled San Simeon estate.

San Simeon, which is now a California State Park open to tourists, is one of America's greatest castles, with its refectory, indoor Roman pool, outdoor Greek pool, assembly hall, zoo, massive rooms and suites. In addition to her impressive beach house and San Simeon, Marion had a well-appointed bungalow on the studio lot, and the couple also entertained at Wyntoon, a spectacular country compound on the McCloud River in northern California. It was like a little village, containing the Cinderella House, the Bear House, the

Sleeping Beauty House, the River House, the Cottage House, the Honeymoon Cottage, the Swiss Chalet, and the Early American Bend House—nine houses in all, including the main house itself.

The parties Marion and W. R. gave at San Simeon are legendary—the photographs that survive are legendary in themselves. They reveal the most famous people of the 1920s and 1930s, all having a fabulous time, laughing, smiling, and dancing. Sometimes they're in tennis clothes or riding habits, and sometimes they're dressed in tuxedos and elegant evening gowns, but mostly they are gotten up in spectacular costumes for the masquerades and costume parties that Marion presented. W. R. loved these events; the photographs show him as President Madison, Norma Shearer as Marie Antoinette, Irving Thalberg as a Tyrolean in lederhosen, Clark Gable as a cub scout in knee socks, Claudette Colbert as an Indian princess, David Niven as a pickpocket, Sonja Henie and Tyrone Power as circus clowns, Cary Grant as a jockey, Joan Crawford as a little girl with a hair bow and a hoop, and actor Fred Stone as an onion. (There's even the omnipresent Elinor Glyn, suitably outfitted as Catherine the Great.) Marion was famous as a hostess, and could charm everyone and put the shyest at ease. Every noted person who came to Hollywood was wined and dined by her, a phenomenon that is beautifully summed up by a photograph in which Marion sits in style at a sumptuously laid table. On one side of her are Louis B. Mayer and Clark Gable, and on the other, George Bernard Shaw and Charlie Chaplin. No doubt about it, Marion Davies was the hostess with the mostest. Her skill in handling people was well known. At her luncheon for Charles Lindbergh, Mary Pickford, seated next to the notoriously shy aviator, sent a desperate note over to Marion, seated on his other side. "He won't talk!" Marion sent back her solution: "Talk about airplanes." When Shaw visited the lot at MGM, Marion showed him around a set, and he pronounced, "I don't think anybody knows what they're doing . . . They're all stupid." However, when he came up to San Simeon, he fell under Marion's spell, finally admitting to her, "Pretty shrewd you are, young lady." Hearst and Marion had fun together, although the many stories recounted from the San Simeon days indicate that much of the time he held back while Marion partied with her friends. Yet on certain occasions, she was able to get him to join in the fun, and it's easy to imagine that his devotion to her was based on the fact that she wasn't afraid of him, and that she took him out of himself with her parties and her jokes. In one telling photo, taken in front of a massive fireplace at San Simeon, Marion and Hearst are seen dressed in western costume, the theme of that particular party. They have assumed the mock stance and facial expressions of an old-fashioned photograph. Marion sits, wearing a silk "school marm" gown trimmed in ruffles and lace. On her head is a demure bonnet with a ring of little posies around her face. Her hands are folded carefully around the ribbon that lies in her lap, with one of the long strings from the bonnet (tied under her chin)

Typical San Simeon costume party fun: Davies with songwriter Harry Ruby and his wife, film star Eileen Percy; Hearst and Davies in western garb, one of the few photos of them together

twisted around her fingers. She is an actress, and the pose and the facial expression are perfect. Hearst, on the other hand, looks uncomfortable and phony, though game. He's wearing a bandanna around his neck, a plaid western shirt, and a patterned vest buttoned over his very ample front. His dark pants and shoes don't look very western, but he holds a ten-gallon hat in the crook of his elbow. His expression seems resigned, as if he's not sure whether this is fun or not, but he's willing to believe it might be. The one touch of honesty and relaxed effort on his part is in a simple gesture: his hand is resting lovingly, protectively, on Marion Davies's shoulder.

By the time Marion appeared in *Yolanda* in 1924, she was being billed as "The Queen of the Screen." (Allegedly, this was a title she had won in a recent voting contest.) Like all her films, *Yolanda* is well produced, and although she gets a rave from *Variety,* the reviewer points out, "Those who have watched the Marion Davies pictures continuously will miss the elf-like, cheery, charming cuteness and roguishness no one else on the screen can give to a light character."

The quality of the Davies productions, and the care with which they were released and advertised, meant that no one could ignore her. She was a major player, always appearing in prestige movies. Furthermore, she was good in them, and the public, while not making her a top box office draw, nevertheless liked her very much. Her next film, *Janice Meredith* (1924), propelled her even further forward toward the top ranks. As the *New York Times* had to admit, "No more brilliant achievement in ambitious motion pictures dealing with historical romances has ever been exhibited than Marion Davies's latest production, *Janice Meredith* . . . The audience was often thrilled, constantly interested, and frequently amused."

Janice Meredith took more than eight months to make, and it cost what the *Times* called "a fabulous sum." It's an epic movie depicting events of the Revolutionary War, including Paul Revere's ride, Washington crossing the Delaware, and other historic moments. The presentation of colonial homes, costumes, and parties was again a spectacle that audiences adored. Davies, in the title role, was given a chance to play a wide range of emotions—she's angry, she's petulant, she's happy, she's tearful, she's mischievous, she's imperious, she's brave. AND she has twenty costume changes! Furthermore, her character was firmly embedded in the action, providing her with a chance to be a proper heroine. She climbs out of a window and rides off to help rescue the troops by warning them in the nick of time. The sight of little Marion riding over hill and dale and finishing the last mile on foot (through the driven snow) is still pretty impressive.

When Knighthood Was in Flower, Little Old New York, and *Janice Meredith* were the three films that secured her stardom. As 1925 got under way, she had become a name that meant something at the box office: expensive production values, excellent costumes and clothes, suitable mixtures of comedy and romance, and perhaps a historical setting. She was "Marion Davies," which meant a lovely comedienne who was going to be very honest and down-to-earth in her characterizations. There was no particular shading to this. She was not a flapper, like Colleen Moore, or a sexpot like Clara Bow, or a sophisticated madcap like Constance Talmadge, or a suffering woman like Norma Talmadge. She was just Marion Davies. Since her image was a reflection of herself, it came with the off-screen baggage of Hearst, the money, and the special treatment regarding exhibition, publicity, and reviews.

When Davies wasn't well directed, she wasn't at her best. *Zander the Great,* directed by George Hill, suffers in this way. Released in 1925, it's a good program comedy and nothing more. It does showcase Davies fully, however, and as *Variety* commented, "Marion Davies once more, after spectacle, has found a happy medium in comedy." *Zander* starts out with Marion in Pickford territory, an orphanage. She is a freckle-faced little girl with braids, and although abused by the matron, shows plenty of spunk and a good heart. Davies is actually almost doing a Pickford imitation as she capers cheerfully about until a kindly trustee takes her to live with a woman who needs help with her son, Alexander, or Zander. In a plot that must have appealed to the many women in the audience who had been abandoned by their husbands, the woman (Hedda Hopper) waits for the man who went off to Mexico to return . . . or at least to write her a letter. Years go by, and Davies grows up into a very pretty young woman. As the mother lies on her deathbed, a letter finally comes—telling the wife to forget him, he is going to a town in Arizona and will never return, but to make Hopper happy as she dies, Davies pretends that the letter says he's coming home. And to prevent Zander from being taken to the same orphanage she herself suffered in, Davies runs off to Arizona with him in search of the father. This rather sentimental and predictable movie takes a turn for the athletic out west, suddenly involving rumrunners, wicked Mexicans, Black Bart, a huge windstorm, gunshots . . . and a romance for Davies and an explanation about the father. (After the shooting, one of the rumrunners observes, "Soon as a woman comes around, something like this is bound to happen.") Throughout all the shifts in tone and plot complications, Davies is true to herself—charming and unpretentious, willing to go along with the nonsense. And once again, there are two Marions—the comic little orphan and the grown-up beauty.

Her next movie, *Lights of Old Broadway* (1925), was directed by Monta Bell and her costar was the handsome Conrad Nagel. She was effectively cast in her by now trademark double role, this time as twins separated at birth. (Their mother dies on shipboard, an emigrant en route to America.) One twin is adopted by poor Irish, who name her Fely O'Tandy; the other goes to live with an exclusive Old Dutch New York family, and she becomes Anne De Rhondo. As Fely, Marion gets to dance around, and, of course, marry the wealthy Dirk De Rhondo (who is, in a crazy way, thus marrying his sister). The grand climax of the film is the moment when electric lights first blazed out on Broadway, simultaneously creating a lovely visual scene and solving a plot problem. *Variety* called it "a corking picture from almost every angle."

A perfect role was designed for Davies in *Beverly of Graustark* (1926), which was directed by Sidney Franklin and costarred her with the very handsome Antonio Moreno. This lighthearted and well-executed tale from the best-selling novel by George Barr McCutcheon has a fanciful plot in which Davies, as Beverly, sets out to help her cousin Oscar when he is offered the crown of Graustark. He's ill, and his ascendancy to the throne is contingent on his being there by a certain date. Beverly takes his place, once again giving us two lively Marions. First, she appears as a typical New York flapper, very perky and modern and good-humored. She's extremely attractive, and as usual, very well dressed and coiffed. When she first reappears as "Cousin Oscar," she looks equally fantastic, and perhaps even better to the modern eye. She's presented à la Julie Andrews in *Victor/Victoria*—short hair, flat

The male and female Marions, both in charge of Antonio Moreno
in *Beverly of Graustark*

chest, wearing extremely well tailored and decorated military uniforms and superbly cut men's suits. With this super-duper masculine look, she could step right out in 1990s America without changing a thing.

Marion Davies probably assumed the guise of a boy more often in her movies than any other female star, and she's better at it than either Katharine Hepburn or Julie Andrews because she never really is a "boy." (Her "Oscar" wears lipstick and eye makeup, and no one seems to notice.) Her triumph is in her ability to create accurately the physical sense of a male in her movements, gestures, and reactions. Like Marlene Dietrich, she becomes male casually, though without the sexuality. Her goal is comic androgyny, and she burlesques masculine behavior while maintaining physical credibility. There's a sense about her that she's too sophisticated to imagine that someone as feminine as she is could ever get away with *really* fooling anyone. Instead, she appears to be totally comfortable with the idea that she's a female man, or perhaps a masculine female—whichever. She's grown-up about the idea. Where Katharine Hepburn lowers her voice and slouches around in a mockery of a young man, or Julie Andrews takes on a camp identity designed to titillate, Davies just shows up, saying, "I am now Marion Davies dressed as a male." What's remarkable is the nonchalant manner with which she assumes the male disguise, seeming to suggest that any girl has this in her.

Beverly of Graustark gives Davies an excellent chance to show off her skills as a comedienne. She carries off an extended drinking scene with the aplomb of a Buster Keaton. Required by the plot to show that she's both terribly drunk and under great pressure to fake sobriety, she is hilarious. A scene in which a hired vamp sets out to seduce the future king—Marion—is played for a kind of fresh and innocent comedy, with the suggestion that all this is just going to be terribly awkward for both women. (When her advances are rejected, the vamp immediately knows that something is wrong, and starts telling everyone Davies must be a fake.)

Marion Davies has spirit. It's impossible to watch her and not feel that she's having a grand old time—the very quality that must have endeared her to Hearst. Marion brought life to his party and to everyone else's, both on and off the screen. This quality is well illustrated in *Beverly* when she appears on-screen carrying an enormous ostrich feather fan and wearing a jeweled lace cap—and she sticks her tongue out unexpectedly. She enters as Gloria Swanson, switches rapidly to Mabel Normand, and then goes back to her own funny self. She can move across the comedy/glamour boundary with as much ease as any other actress.

The Red Mill (1927) had been an enormous success on Broadway. It was a musical comedy by Victor Herbert and Henry Blossom, and it seemed an ideal movie adaptation for Davies—yet another Cinderella story. This time she plays a Dutch girl who works at the inn of the title. (No expense was spared in creating a small Dutch village, with the inn, a canal, and a large windmill.) Marion went all out in her comedy sequences, and she took the idea that she was playing an unglamorous drudge very seriously, wearing freckles and little makeup, and keeping her beautiful blonde hair tucked inside a mobcap. Reviews of the day praised the wonderful ice-skating scenes but panned the slapstick comedy, which included having Davies crash through the ice, fall down a well, get spanked by the inn's owner, spend about twenty minutes trying to set up an ironing board, find a mouse in her wooden shoe, throw flowerpots around, and end up locked in the old mill. The climax put her in a skating race, during which, when a dog chases a white mouse, she grabs hold of the dog and is pulled along at top speed. (This mouse has his career made. He also causes panic during church, breaks up a wedding, and hides inside the proprietor's pipe.) As is usual with silent film adaptations of musical hits, something is clearly missing. Without the songs, *The Red Mill* has to fall back on its story, which is less than scintillating. However, Marion once again was liked by audiences in a role in which she starts out without glamour and acquires plenty of it before the finale.

After *The Red Mill* (her first release in 1927), Davies made a string of six movies before the advent of sound and her talking debut in *The Hollywood Revue of 1929*. Five of these are her finest comedies: *Tillie the Toiler, The Fair Coed, Quality Street, The Patsy,* and *Show People,* of which the last two are by far the best. *Tillie the Toiler* (1927) isn't a great script, nor is it particularly well directed by Hobart Hanley, but Davies is able to elevate it out of the junk heap. The popularity of the comic strip on which it is based (and Marion's charm) was expected to overcome the weak material: Davies plays a typist in the office where her boyfriend is the bookkeeper. Tillie presents herself as a girl who wears two pairs of garters, "one pair to hold up her stockings and the other pair to hold up traffic." Reviewers of the day were not fooled: "Mildly amusing," said *Variety*, adding that there was "not much doing . . . little action, no sex stuff, and the romance is a little dizzy." The final straw was that there was "not even a big cabaret scene." Seen today, however, *Tillie the Toiler* has more charm than this review indicates. For one thing, it's possible now to see it as a perfect example of 1920s attitudes. It has the slang, the clothes, and the male/female mating patterns of its time—consider a title card that says, "He's the kind of man who got married in the back yard so the chickens could eat the rice." And Marion Davies is adorable. In the very opening sequence, she is seen strutting down the city streets, in a big hurry on her way to land a job. As she runs along, focused on her destination, she looks like a cartoon Tillie, teetering on high heels. Suddenly, a cigarette ash flies into her eye. As she goes hurrying along, she starts winking and blinking to remove it, not wanting to stop. Men on the street think she's winking at them, so she starts accumulating a parade of men from all walks of life, all ages, all occupations, following her as she trots along. This is an extended comedy sequence in which everything works to perfection: Marion's focus and wink, her boop-a-doop walk, the camera movement, and the variety of men, each with his own characterization. Unfortunately, nothing in the rest of the movie comes up to that level, but the film is a lot of fun and should be better known.

In *The Fair Coed*, also in 1927, Marion plays the unexpected: women's basketball champion. Her costar was the handsome young John Mack Brown, said to be her personal choice for the role. In this college comedy, full of smart talk and sassy slang, Marion plays a free-spirited tomboy who has a necklace made out of "popularity pearls," which reflects her motto "Don't let the boys string you. You string them." Most of the time, she's romping up and down the basketball floor in gym shorts and sneakers, throwing up a mean jump shot, and responding to the cheers of the crowd (led, of course, by boy cheerleaders). *Variety* called it a "snappy, jazzy comedy of college life from the modern female angle, done in a breezy way . . . Picture has special appeal from its spirit of youthful nonsense and provides the best light role Marion Davies has had in some time." The movie opens with a highly unusual sequence in which the student body is returning to campus. Having been told by the faculty that student motorists will now be forbidden, the young people arrive in every kind of comedy conveyance. There's a burlesque version of a Roman chariot drawn by two mules, a squad on bicycles, and a Gypsy wagon. The women play a mean game of full-court basketball, and the entire focus of the movie is on women's sports. It makes for a modern story, but, as *Variety* points out, not without presenting some old-fashioned attitudes toward women: "As the flirta-

Davies as basketball star,
checking out the competi-
tion (Jane Winton) and
her final goal, John Mack
Brown, in *The Fair Coed*

tious basketball star of Bingham College [Davies] had a conspicuous opportunity to spread-eagle on the gym floor in 'shorts' and the trimmest of trim jer-
sies, all duck soup for the one time 'Follies' girl."

Quality Street (1927), based on a famous James M. Barrie play, has the
excellent production values that are typical of all the Davies movies.
(Katharine Hepburn appeared in a remake in 1937.) It's a period story of a
young woman who fails to land a proposal from her beloved before he leaves
for war. When he returns, she has become old and drab, and he's no longer
interested in her. To punish him, she takes on an assumed identity, that of a
younger, sillier woman (her own niece) of the kind he imagines he wants—
until she shapes him up. It was yet another movie in which Marion played a
dual role. *Quality Street* was a good showcase for her, but its restrained and
genteel story was not ideally suited to her gifts.

By now, audiences understood and accepted the on-screen Marion
Davies. She was a Cinderella figure, a "duality" queen who could be both
slavey and fashion princess. In fact, over and over reviews of the day refer to
her plots as "Cinderella stories." The fact that her off-screen life was a per-
verted version of the fairy tale—Hearst was no Prince, and her shoe may have
fit but she never got the ring—must have been buried somewhere in everyone's subconscious. The "two Marions" format became a formula—any variation that allowed her to be both the Hearst Marion and the Marion Marion was

okay. Her duality was not designed to provide her with a great actress turn, as when Norma Talmadge played both a mother and a daughter, or when Norma Shearer played twins, or when Mary Pickford gave the public the "little Mary" they craved as well as her mature self. As a result, Marion's "duality" didn't add up to a real persona. She never became separate from her image—she was a Cinderella girl off-screen, and a Cinderella girl on-screen. Marion Davies may have come closer to playing herself on-screen than any other silent movie star.

In *The Patsy* (1928) she received superb reviews. It was a comedy directed by King Vidor, and Davies effectively mimics Pola Negri, Mae Murray, and Lillian Gish. *Variety* not only called it "an excellent laugh picture," but praised Davies, saying she "does some really great comedy work." The *New York Times* said that she "not only holds her own in the matter of vivacity and appearance, but she also elicits more fun than one would suppose could be generated from [the story]." *Variety* went so far as to boldly suggest that *The Patsy* was so outstanding that maybe it was "a good opportunity for the soft-pedaling of the customary Hearst hokum publicity to see if the picture and the star cannot stand up and get by without the bolstering." The reviewer pointed out that the audience that saw the movie when he did actually burst into applause after Marion did her terrific imitations of Gish. Marion plays the neglected sister in a superbly dysfunctional family that presents the marvelous Marie Dressler as the mother and the very beautiful Jane Winton, one of Flo Ziegfeld's "glorified American girls," as the other sister. Constantly pushed aside—like her hapless father—Davies, who is always seen doing the dishes, resents it and fights back. Naturally, she is going to blossom out of that kitchen into some excellent duds, and along the way she delivers such inexplicable lines as "A worm is nothing more than an upholstered caterpillar."

Her Cardboard Lover gave her a chance to do more of her clever imitations, this time of one of the other actresses in the movie, exotic Jetta Goudal. Goudal plays a glamorous and sophisticated Parisienne, and Davies gets herself up to look like her, pulling off a marvelous comic turn that earned her good reviews. She plays a schoolgirl visiting Monte Carlo, where she meets a handsome tennis champ (Nils Asther) and sets her cap for him. Her character is an autograph hound, and resorts to dressing up like a bellboy to pursue her quarry. As usual, Davies looked great as a boy, and was admired by the *Times* as looking "stunning in braided trousers and a coat of many buttons." To get her man, she ends up socking him on the jaw.

The appeal of Marion Davies is clearly identifiable in what is generally thought to be her best film, *Show People* (1928), brilliantly directed by King Vidor and costarring William Haines. It was a grand send-up of the Hollywood star system, and it was to be her last silent film. Shot on location around Los Angeles and, in particular, on the MGM studio lot, it contains cameo

The Davies balancing act: period lady in *Quality Street*, with Conrad Nagel;
modern flapper in *The Patsy*, with Marie Dressler

appearances by many of the greats of the day: Chaplin, John Gilbert, Lew
Cody, Douglas Fairbanks, William S. Hart, the ubiquitous Elinor Glyn, and—
Marion Davies, in a very funny scene in which Davies, playing newcomer
Peggy Pepper (who becomes Patricia Peppoire) bumps into Marion Davies on
the lot. Davies (as herself) jumps out of her roadster, dressed in pleated skirt
and sweater and low-heeled shoes. She's carrying a tennis racket, and has a
simple 1920s hairdo. Peggy Pepper, in period movie costume, has masses of
golden curls and a fussy ruffled silk dress. "Who's that?" asks Pepper of her
companion. "That's Marion Davies," he replies. Pepper studies Davies, first
registering shock that she could look so ordinary, then making a face as if to
say, "I never thought she was much." (When she encounters Chaplin, he asks
her for her autograph. "Who is that little guy?" she asks afterward.)

Throughout her life, Marion Davies was described as a "regular" person,
someone down-to-earth and completely without airs. These qualities are well
displayed in *Show People*, as she shows fully how much she understood the
nonsense of moviemaking and stardom. There are a series of scenes that
showcase her making fun of movie acting. In the first, she's an innocent girl
from Georgia who shows up at a Mack Sennett–like comedy factory, believing

In her best comedy
role, as plain
Peggy Pepper who
becomes movie star
Patricia Peppoire,
in *Show People*

she's to act a serious dramatic role. As she is sucked into the action and given
that healthy squirt of seltzer in the face, she plays out the resulting comedy
mixed with genuine outrage—in just the right proportions to show she could
have been yet another possible rival for Mabel Normand. When she and her
father, Colonel Pepper, arrive in Hollywood, she proves to the casting director
that she can act by demonstrating emotions while her father calls them out to
her. "Meditation, passion, anger," he barks, while Davies changes by holding
his bandanna over her face, and then lowering it to reveal each new attitude.
"Sorrow! Joy!" he barks, and every new face is a comic masterpiece, yet still
related to the fundamental concept of the emotion.

After Peggy leaves her comedy troupe and goes over to "High Art Studios," there's a hilarious send-up of silent film acting technique. Sitting alone
on a throne, she is commanded by her director in a series of exercises. He
tells her that the man she loves is off to screen right, and the man she hates
screen left. "I love you," and "I hate you," says Davies as she swivels from
right to left, left to right, over and over, rearranging her features each time
with swift skill. When told to suffer and cry, she screws up her face but can't
do it. Then she asks that the musicians on the set play "Hearts and Flowers,"
and when that doesn't work, she yells "Louder—and sadder!" (These musicians were an inside joke. Hired to follow Patricia Peppoire around the set,

they were, in fact, the actual musicians Hearst hired to follow Davies around her sets.) In an effort to feel something, Davies bangs her head on a post, stamps her feet, and pinches herself . . . finally, some peeled onions get her going.

The high point of the movie is Davies's extremely funny imitation of Gloria Swanson. Even Swanson fans can't help loving it, because it's not mean-spirited. Davies, now taking herself very seriously as Peppoire, is dressed in the kind of romantic nonsense that Swanson was famous for. Wearing a pseudo-Russian outfit of fur and beaded headdress, with tons of rings on her fingers, she is being interviewed. Her leading man, done up as a cossack, acts as her spokesman, informing the interviewer: "Being a lady of quality, she chose the cinema as a medium of self-expression." (Just the sort of stuff that stars were expected to be saying in interviews in those days.) "She has the temperament of Nazimova, the appeal of Garbo, the sweetness of Pickford, and the lure of Pola Negri." During all this, Davies is doing her Swanson. She purses up her mouth to look like Swanson's small lips, bares her two front teeth in the Swanson smile, and places her beringed hands under her chin in a perfect pose. She even manages to get the little pointy teeth of Swanson just right. From time to time the pose slips, and when she pulls it back into place, she's hilarious. Yet, as if Vidor and Marion wanted to compensate Hearst for the slapstick comedy she's going to be performing in the movie, the first sight of her in *Show People* is the sweet image of her that Hearst most adored. She's riding in the back of an open touring car, holding a ruffled parasol and wearing a big hat with a curved brim, tied under her chin with a big satin ribbon. She has on a ruffled dress and has long, golden curls and a little locket around her neck. She's thrilled and excited to be driving down the streets of Hollywood, and as she smiles and looks around her, she's a truly beautiful sight. No doubt Hearst forgave all the pratfalls after that entrance.

IN JULY OF 1928, Marion Davies and William Randolph Hearst left Hollywood for an extended journey through Europe, taking along with them about a dozen of Marion's girlfriends. By the time they returned in October, sound had taken over the movies. This was a potential disaster for Marion because all her life she had stammered. Fred Lawrence Guiles reports that Marion and a friend went together to see Al Jolson in his second talking film, *The Singing Fool*, and that when Jolson began to sing "Sonny Boy," she started sobbing, "I'm ruined. I'm ruined." Because of her speech problem, how was she going to talk in movies? And what was she going to do with herself all day if she didn't have a film career?

As it turned out, Marion Davies had a good voice, pleasingly low and with what Guiles called "a tinge of humor in it much of the time." Unlike stars who had foreign accents, voices too high to record well, and no singing ability,

Marion Davies actually was in a good position. After she made her sound test, it was determined that her voice was fine, and that her stammer could be worked around. She was amazed to be one of the stars of the silent era who ended up making the transition to sound without any real trouble.

Marion Davies made her sound debut in 1929 in *The Hollywood Revue of 1929,* along with a crowd of big stars of the silent era: John Gilbert, Norma Shearer, Joan Crawford, Buster Keaton, and others. Since she had started her career singing and dancing on the Broadway stage, and she had no fear of adding this dimension to her work, her debut was a musical one. She appeared supported by a chorus of male singers and dancers, all dressed as grenadier guards. When first seen, she's a tiny figure amidst the huge soldiers, but then her image is blown up to full size while she executes a "hard shoe" dance on a big drum and sings "Tommy Atkins." (*Variety* griped: "If it weren't for Miss Davies, this 9-minute number wouldn't be in.")

Marion went on to make fifteen more sound films. Although these movies did well, most do not have great reputations today. Some of them, however, are very good, in particular the delightful musical she made with Bing Crosby, *Going Hollywood;* her great screwball comedy with Clark Gable, *Cain and Mabel;* and *Hearts Divided,* an unusual story of Napoleon's younger brother in America, in which the brother is played by Dick Powell, Claude Rains is Napoleon, and Frank Borzage directed. Two of these, *Cain and Mabel* and *Hearts Divided,* both in 1936, were made for Warner Brothers, since Hearst's long-time releasing relationship with Metro-Goldwyn-Mayer had fallen apart after Marion finished *Operator 13,* a Civil War story made in 1934 in which she played a Northern spy who masquerades as an octaroon laundress. Hearst and Marion had taken another trip to Europe to rest, and after a visit to Versailles, Hearst had become convinced that Stefan Zweig's biography *Marie Antoinette* would make a perfect vehicle for Marion. MGM owned the property and Mayer was willing to let Hearst have it—if he would pay the full cost of production. However, there was another problem: Norma Shearer, whose husband, Irving Thalberg, wanted her to play the plum role. (This was not the first problem Hearst had encountered with Shearer and Thalberg. He had wanted Marion to play Juliet, and Marion had wanted to play Elizabeth Browning—but both roles had gone to Thalberg's wife.) Mayer and Hearst entered delicate negotiations, with Hearst finally deciding to move Marion away from MGM—and Norma Shearer. Marion herself said, "Marie Antoinette was the straw that broke the camel's back at MGM . . . The studio said no . . . I was frustrated . . . W. R. was much more mad than I was. He said, 'I don't want you to ever have anything more to do with the MGM studio.' We went down the road—but fast . . . I don't think Louis B. Mayer minded losing me so much. He did mind losing Mr. Hearst, if you know what I mean. Later he said to me, 'We have lost our queen.' What he meant was that he had lost

Two sound successes: *Not So Dumb* and *Polly of the Circus* (with Clark Gable)

the power of the chess game—the visitors—and the press." Within days after the decision was made, Marion's famous bungalow was moved—piece by piece—over to Burbank and the Warner Brothers studio, the deal having been settled down at Marion's beach house in five minutes of talk between Hearst and Jack Warner.

On the whole, Marion had a respectable sound career. She lasted longer than many of her silent contemporaries, including Pickford, the Talmadges, Moore, and Bow. Her final film, released in the spring of 1937, was *Ever Since Eve*. Once again she gave her audience two Marions, playing a good-looking secretary who, tired of running around desks, disguises herself as an ugly duckling (using the traditional pair of glasses and wardrobe of frumpy fashions). It was a fitting finale.

Although Marion occasionally considered other properties and did a few radio shows, for all practical purposes she had voluntarily retired from motion pictures. She said, "Although I was only making two pictures a year, I couldn't enjoy myself. Even though I could travel for about three months a year, when I knew I had to get back to the studio by a certain date and that I couldn't eat too much or get sunburned or freckled, I couldn't really have a good time." Since Marion liked to have a good time, and since Hearst liked having her with him as much as possible, they apparently enjoyed her retirement. However, on May 8, 1941, they had *Citizen Kane* to deal with. Guiles says that they probably saw the film together in a local movie house in San Francisco. Hearst's biographer John Tebbel believed that Hearst enjoyed the idea that the movie was about him. He was, of course, no stranger to criticism, and why should he object to being portrayed as a clever rascal by a handsome young actor like Orson Welles? In comparison to some of the attacks that had been made on his character and abilities over the years, *Citizen Kane* probably seemed mild indeed, and perhaps even a bit glamorous. The problem, of course, was that he loved Marion Davies, and the possibility that people could think Susan Alexander was an accurate portrait of her was a different matter. About that, he was furious.

Marion Davies reportedly was very hurt by *Citizen Kane,* but wise in her response. "Years ago," she said, "W. R. gave me some good advice. He said 'Never make anything out of an insult or a slap at you. Ignore it. Make as little of it as possible.' That's what I've done with *Citizen Kane* and apparently a lot of people agree with me." Then she added, "It never made any money." (The ultimate Hollywood put-down.) Davies could never imagine that a minor RKO film that didn't do well at the box office and which had been directed by a newcomer could really wipe out her twenty years of stardom. After all, she had just quit the movies four years earlier, and it was too soon for her to be forgotten. Nor was anyone going to believe she had no talent. But she reckoned without the long-range power of *Kane* and Welles, and without the strange turn of history that literally eradicated silent film from the screen for so many years. During the 1950s, Marion Davies became a forgotten name except as the role model for Susan Alexander. It's a tragic misunderstanding, and a major historical gaffe.

Hearst and Marion lived on together until the end. On April 29, 1951, he turned eighty-eight, but he was too weak to come downstairs for his birthday party. Marion carried out his wishes by inviting five close female friends for a small party in his room, and Marion presented her lifelong love with an oil painting of Phoebe Hearst, his mother, holding him as a baby in her arms. When Hearst saw it, he began to weep, and Marion, sitting at his feet, was reported to have embraced his legs, saying, "It's all right, W. R., it's all right." Now she was taking care of him as he had always taken care of her.

William Randolph Hearst died on August 14, 1951, while Marion, who had been tending him, was getting some much-needed sleep. By the time she woke up the next morning, his body was gone. His sons had come for him and taken him away to his wife, who had never granted him the divorce he wanted. Marion's sad statement was, "I asked where he was, and the nurse said he was dead. His body was gone, whoosh, like that. Old W. R. was gone. The boys were gone. I was alone. Do you realize what they did? They stole a possession of mine. He belonged to me. I loved him for thirty-two years and now he was gone. I couldn't even say good-bye."

Ten weeks after Hearst's death, Marion Davies got married for the first time, to Captain Horace Brown of the California State Guard, whose most distinctive characteristic was that he looked very much like a young William Randolph Hearst. On September 23, 1961, she died of cancer, and was buried in the Douras family crypt in Hollywood. Her famous jewelry collection was immediately inventoried, and it included, among many impressive items, a 29-carat pear-shaped diamond pendant, a platinum diamond watch, a platinum sapphire brooch, an emerald-and-diamond brooch, a platinum marquise solitaire ring (21 carats), a cabochon emerald ring with ten diamonds, a 17-carat emerald solitaire ring, a diamond choker with fifteen marquise diamonds and two pear-shaped diamonds, a marquise diamond bracelet with two square diamonds, and one gold toothpick worth ten dollars. She also left behind a group of tape recordings that were notes for a book on her life. Her memories were all happy ones, particularly about "W. R.," who was the hero of every anecdote. These memories are touching. "W. R. did a tap dance [for Lindbergh]. He was the best tap dancer you ever saw. And he accompanied himself. He didn't need any music, just one, two, three, bum-bum . . . Whenever he felt the urge, he often used to get up and do a little tap dance . . . He was the kindest, most innocent, naive person you'd ever want to meet . . . He wouldn't have harmed anybody, ever . . . W. R. would say, 'I'm in love with you. What am I going to do about it?' And I'd say, 'Well, let it ride. It's all right with me.' " She had let it ride for a lifetime.

A Marion Davies will never emerge in film history again. Although famous women might have their careers shaped, directed, or even managed by powerful men they also marry or become involved with—think of singers Celine Dion and Mariah Carey—the old-fashioned tradition of the mistress is dead. The name Marion Davies will stand as the most famous example of the phenomenon in Hollywood history, an actress who was always seen first as a mistress and second as a movie star—in her own mind as well as in the public's. Her powerful lover had been born in the 1800s. His idea of a mistress was a Victorian one, which meant that as a rich man of honor, he would take care of her financially and provide her with something to do with herself after she aged and was replaced by a younger woman. A gentleman would, for instance, set his woman up in business—perhaps with a little hat shop. William Randolph Hearst never replaced Marion Davies, but he did set her up with the most glamorous hat shop in the history of mistressing: he made her a movie star, and she lived up to her part of the bargain.

LON CHANEY

Perhaps it is inappropriate to include such a universally respected actor as Lon Chaney in a book about "forgotten, misunderstood, and underappreciated" silent film stars, but there is much more to Chaney than most people realize. Yes, Lon Chaney is not forgotten, and no, he is not unappreciated, but he's generally defined as much less than he is, treated as a kind of weirdo who loved pain and wore elaborate makeup, leaping around Notre Dame or lurching through underground caverns in a death mask. He's described far too glibly as a "horror" actor, a creator of monsters and nothing else.

In the early years of his career, Chaney played any kind of role that was available to him—drama critic, Italian count, German admiral, idle society playboy, whatever was needed. He was a stage actor who had developed a marvelous mastery of makeup skills, so that unlike many early movie stars he wasn't limited to roles that fit his physical identity. He could transform himself through makeup and costume, and since he desperately needed work, steady work, he began to do just that. Did someone need a western hero, a circus clown, a cripple, or the type that was then known as a "Chinaman"? Chaney was made up, dressed, ready to go, and highly credible. His famous nickname—"the Man of a Thousand Faces"—was more than just publicity hype. ("Don't step on that spider. It might be Lon Chaney" was a popular joke of the 1920s.) As his career advanced, he began to be associated more and more with creatures who were bizarre creations of the makeup box and his physical dexterity: a sham cripple, an armless man, a legless man, a one-eyed crook, a vampire, all kinds of brutal gangsters, and literary figures like Blind Pew and Fagin. Once he was a star he almost never looked the same way twice on the screen, and it's hard to picture him as he looked in everyday life. Instead, we visualize him in one of his famous guises—most likely the hunchback of Notre Dame or the phantom of the opera, his two best-known roles. Watching the Chaney movies available today, I was almost shocked when I encountered him as an ordinary human being—say, as a marine sergeant in *Tell It to the Marines*. Chaney as a normal man doesn't look normal! (In an era of men and women movie stars who were ethereally gorgeous, Chaney was somebody you might see out on the street. He had an excellent physique and an attractive face, but he wasn't a Gilbert or a Valentino, or even a Rod La Roque or an Antonio Moreno. In no way, though, did he resort to bizarre makeup to hide some real—or imagined—ugliness.)

As Chaney's career developed, he was drawn to playing two basic types of social outcast: the criminal and the cripple. He seemed to identify deeply with characters who were outsiders and loners. No matter how twisted mentally or physically these characters were—either human or monster—he played them as having recognizable emotions. He impersonated wicked people in the most human way possible, so the audience could understand their evil, realize where it came from, and even sympathize with it if they chose to. He brought understanding and tolerance to these outsiders, and a conviction that there was another side to their lives beneath the obviously ugly surface. Audiences responded to this conviction, and they still do.

As an actor, Lon Chaney was in the right place at the right time, when films were new and special, and melodrama and exaggeration were common. Twisting the body into strange forms and letting everything rip was not only accepted as an acting style, it was welcomed and rewarded. Like most of the successful stars of silent movies, Chaney could use his whole body as an expressive force, and eliminate the need for titles with a single gesture, an eloquent movement, or a cruel half-smile. He was enormously focused on-screen, and his intensity was palpable. These qualities—focus and intensity—came from his youth, his home life, and his background, and were so much a part of him that there was never a time they weren't there.

Lon Chaney's career was a slow climb from obscurity into stardom by a professional, a man who both paid his dues and learned his craft. As his fame grew, his movies became star vehicles, but they were always well made, and he is a much better actor than he is usually given credit for. He was born Leonidas Frank (not Alonso) Chaney on April 1, 1883 (or 1886), in Colorado Springs, Colorado, the second of five children whose parents were deaf—a fact that has been made much of in discussions of his outstanding ability to pantomime and signal meanings with his hands and body. His mother was born deaf, and his father, a barber, had gone deaf at the age of three. Their children, however, all could hear, which is not untypical. When Chaney was just nine years old, his mother was stricken with inflammatory rheumatism and became bedridden for the rest of her life. It was the boy's job to take care of her during the first three years of this illness, and it became his habit to act out for her whatever he had seen or done during his absences. The need to clarify silently and provide detail was thus born during Chaney's early years. "Acting out" was associated with love, with his mother, and with her returning love to him in gratitude for his efforts to entertain, amuse, and inform her. She and his father were Chaney's first audience.

When his older brother John went to work at the Colorado Springs Opera House, Chaney followed him there, first working as a prop boy, scene painter, and stage hand, and then acting in small roles or crowd scenes. By the time he was seventeen, he considered himself an actor and was on tour with a traveling group. Young and insecure, he often hid behind elaborate makeup, and soon he knew everything there was to know about creating any kind of character, age, or special effect. (In fact, he was the author of the *Encyclopaedia Britannica*'s section "Stage Makeup.") While he was touring, around 1905, he met a young actress named Cleva Creighton, and on February 10, 1906, she bore him a son, Creighton Chaney (who would later change his name to Lon Chaney, Jr., and enjoy a long career, with a fine list of credits and his own loyal fans; however, he lacked his father's consummate skills). Records indicate that Chaney and Cleva were probably not married until May 31 of that same year, and it was an unhappy and unsuccessful union. They divorced in 1914, and Chaney was given custody of Creighton. His second marriage, in 1915, was to a chorus girl named Hazel Hastings, a very happy pairing that lasted until his death.

Eventually, Chaney, the traveling professional, arrived in California. It's pleasantly romantic to picture Lon Chaney, a poor young actor with his makeup box under his arm, drifting slowly, inexorably toward Universal Studios in California, working as he went at whatever roles paid him enough to live on. The image is so appealing because it gives us a loner linked to the kind of characters he would eventually play. One thing is certain: Chaney was used to being alone and moving through the world in silence, communicating through gesture, pantomime, and specific physical action.

How did fate lead him to the world of silent film—the world, as it were, that he had been born to star in? Chaney, who usually spoke very little about himself or his life to anyone, and least of all to interviewers, once explained his entry into the movies by saying that in 1912 he was appearing in a musical that got stranded in Santa Ana and that he spent his last money on streetcar fare.* The streetcar took him into Los Angeles and out to Universal City, where a friend got him work as an extra in the movies. For a year, he worked steadily, playing bits and extras—whatever he could get to feed himself. Obviously, his ability to create believable character makeup made him a useful employee, but he could also write scenarios and direct. In the beginning he did anything that was needed. It seems that he received his first billing as an actor in 1913 in a comedy called *Poor Jake's Demise*.

It's impossible to trace all the films Chaney might have appeared in before that date, since cast lists weren't kept and credits didn't include actors'

*Michael Blake's excellent biography *Lon Chaney: The Man Behind the Thousand Faces* discusses all the various versions of Chaney's life story.

names. Treating *Poor Jake's Demise* as his "first" movie, it's possible to put together a long list of Chaney appearances before he finally got a part that brought him serious attention. In these films he played policemen, lawyers, villains, foreigners of all types, mob leaders, seducers, violin makers, dukes and royalty, and society husbands. These movies had such titles as *The Trap, Discord and Harmony, The End of the Feud, A Ranch Romance, Richelieu, The Measure of a Man, The Stool Pigeon, The Oyster Dredger, Hell Morgan's Girl, The Grip of Jealousy, Grasp of Greed, If My Country Should Call,* and *The Piper's Price,* to name only a few.

A film typical of the work he did during this busy period was *By the Sun's Rays,* in 1914 (the earliest Chaney work I have seen). In this western, Chaney plays a villain. He wears no special makeup and no physical disguise; he's just a capable actor holding down his corner of the standard hero-villain-girl triangle, but he stands out for his power and presence, and his face registers sharply in the movie medium. Around him are a group of pudding faces; he alone seems to believe totally in what is happening. A movie like this makes it clear why Universal used Chaney over and over again during this period. He could be counted on to give an above-average performance no matter how slight the material. In other words, he was a total professional.

Hell Morgan's Girl (1917), a movie that helped gain him real attention, was a melodramatic story of San Francisco's Barbary Coast in which Chaney played a tough politician (and gang leader) who dies in the 1906 earthquake. His work was dynamic enough to attract the attention of William S. Hart, who invited him to play the villain in his 1918 movie *Riddle Gawne.* Skeptics thought the pairing wouldn't work. Chaney was short, Hart was tall, which meant that, visually, the villain wasn't going to measure up. But as Hart later claimed he told the dismayed Chaney when they met—and the difference in their heights was strikingly apparent—"Inches never made an actor. You get the part."

To appear in *Riddle Gawne,* Chaney moved from Universal to Paramount/Artcraft, where Hart's films were made and released. His role was a significant one, and it earned him good "by name" mention in most of the reviews of the time. *Variety* referred to him as "the villain" and as one of several "prominent film artists" in the cast without evaluating his performance, but any mention in a William S. Hart film was to the good. *Riddle Gawne* was a strong story, in which Hart is pitted against Chaney in a central conflict that was very much equal-to-equal because it lasted for years over both their characters' lifetimes. According to reviews, Chaney was well cast to provide a strong balance to Hart's well-known image and star power.

After *Riddle Gawne* Chaney returned to Universal and made three more films in 1918 and seven more (plus *Daredevil Jack,* a fifteen-episode serial) the following year. The first of these was probably *The Wicked Darling,* the

The Miracle Man

first of ten movies that paired him with the great director Tod Browning. *False Faces,* his next, presented him as a German spy; *A Man's Country* was a western in which he was a villainous gambler; and in *Paid in Advance,* set in Alaska, he was again the villain. His other three releases in 1919 were *The Miracle Man, When Bearcat Went Dry,* and *Victory,* the last an adaptation of the Joseph Conrad novel, in which he played the villain. (*Bearcat* was a mountain romance in which he provided the plot problems.) His real achievement in 1919 was *The Miracle Man,* one of his most successful and respected movies, and unquestionably the film that brought him forward out of the pack.

Audiences for *The Miracle Man* were stunned at the scene in which, acting the complex role of a con artist who pretends to be physically disabled, Chaney undergoes a phony "miracle." To see a twisted Chaney, apparently in agony, crawl toward the miracle maker (who doesn't know the truth) and slowly, painfully untwist his body and rise to his feet, was astonishing—an acting tour de force. Inspired by this phony miracle, a crippled child suddenly walks. Chaney's big moment was then extended into a scene in which his shocked and frightened reaction to a real miracle happening before his eyes gave viewers a chance to appreciate his acting range. The hero of *The Miracle Man* was played by the very handsome and popular Thomas Meighan, and the leading lady was Betty Compson. Chaney's role was more or less a supporting one, but he stole the show. Even hard-hearted critics felt compelled to describe the scene of the false cure and the little boy. (*Variety* kept apologizing for liking it, saying it was "contrived" and "sentimental," but admitting,

"We cannot believe it and yet we are so anxious to believe it that we will pay well to be fooled.") The *New York Times* gave the movie a rave, calling Chaney's work "unusually good" and also describing in detail the scene with the little boy.

After *The Miracle Man,* Chaney was a name. Although he would still play supporting parts until the major stardom he achieved with *The Hunchback of Notre Dame* in 1923, many of his films from then on saw him in the central role. During 1920, Chaney played both Blind Pew and the pirate Merry in an adaptation of *Treasure Island,* directed by Maurice Tourneur. In *The Gift Supreme* he portrayed a drug addict. His other two films of that year were *Nomads of the North* and *The Penalty.*

Proof that Lon Chaney did not always impersonate a twisted criminal type lies in *Nomads of the North,* in which he plays an outdoorsman living in the Canadian wilds. Not only is he a normal man, he is, in fact, the romantic lead, married to the beautiful Betty Blythe, and father of a baby. The story is from one of the wilderness novels by James Oliver Curwood, popular generic tales of their time that provided the basis for more than one stirring outdoor drama in the teens and twenties. In this romantic tale, Chaney and the love of his life (Blythe) are forced to flee to the Far North when Chaney kills a man in self-defense. They live in an Eden-like world, with a pet bear and their faithful dog, until the villain of the piece—the evil city-bred Bucky, who sells whiskey to the Indians—comes across them by accident in their forest paradise. When a Mountie who once loved Blythe is assigned to bring Chaney in (this role is played by Lewis Stone, and you know you are in a silent movie universe when one of the romantic leads is Lewis Stone), they encounter a forest fire in which the young couple rescue Stone, who ultimately lets them go. The simple and beautiful way of life that Chaney and Blythe take up with their child, their bear, and their dog romanticizes the great outdoors, and in this regard Chaney is merely another element in the tale, with none of his unusual gifts required. He's highly competent, as always, but seems somewhat false and stagey alongside the more modern Lewis Stone.

The Penalty is the story of a master criminal who concocts a plot to take over the world. Blizzard, played by Chaney, had his legs amputated when he was a boy due to a young doctor's error. What's more, the accident that destroyed his legs also caused a "contusion" at the base of his skull, giving him not only an extremely high intelligence but also a deep penchant for evil. Blizzard is the mastermind of the "Frisco Barbary Coast," and his life is dedicated to a vendetta against the young doctor, who has gone on to fame and success. There is a disturbing quality to *The Penalty.* When Rose, a government spy, infiltrates Chaney's lair, he forces her to work the pedals of his piano while he plays beautiful music. ("You're a real find," he tells her.) She's so good at it that even when he discovers she's a spy, he decides not to murder

As a legless man in *The Penalty* (with Charles Clary), and as Fagin in *Oliver Twist* (with Jackie Coogan and Edouard Trebaol)

her because "you're the best pedaler I've ever had." Rose (Ethel Grey Terry) doesn't care, because by now she's fallen in love with him! In fact, glad to be found out, she kneels before him, exclaiming, "Master!" He embraces her, and they kiss, although later he shoves her roughly away. Chaney's big plan is to use disgruntled foreign workers as slave legionnaires and to ruin the doctor's life by amputating the legs of his daughter's boyfriend. (What a plan!) Instead, the doctor operates on *him,* fixing the "contusion," and Chaney is transformed into a good man. And then he's shot. *Variety* remarked, "It is not a great feature." (Chaney's second wife, Hazel, had been previously married to a man with no legs, and the idea for *The Penalty* was said to have come from that source.)

How many actors today could make a film like this work at any level? The idea of a legless man who builds a pristine operating room in an elaborate underground chamber, with foreign slaves working away in it, is simply nuts. But Chaney does make it work. He keeps his acting minimal in the central scenes; he just *exudes* inner rage. Nothing more is needed. He can convey danger or evil or just plain weirdness through his intense physical focus and inner power.

During the 1920s, Chaney's films were sold to the public partly on the idea that he was willingly undergoing great pain in order to produce his remarkable disguises. Most people today, however, feel that his mastery of his devices and makeup tricks was such that his discomfort was probably minimal. He was a professional, and in control of what he was doing. (In *The Penalty*, though, he was said to have worn his leg supports for only twenty minutes at a time, so as not to cut off his circulation.)

Chaney's next movie paired him again with Tod Browning, the Edgar Allan Poe of movies and his most compatible director. In *Outside the Law* (1921), he was given a showy opportunity to contribute to the overall emotional impact of the movie, even though he isn't the star. (The credits announce: "Priscilla Dean in *Outside the Law,* A Tod Browning Production.") The lovely Dean is the leading lady and central character, but Chaney is given not one but two flashy roles. The first is Ah Wing, a servant who is also a Confucian scholar, and the second is "Black Mike" Sylva, "a rat, a vulture, and a snake." There seems to be no logic to this double role; the two characters are in no way related—they're just two characters played by the same actor. The cast list lays it out: in the number four billing spot is "Ah Wing . . . Lon Chaney," and number five is "Black Mike Sylva . . . Lon Chaney." Chaney appears as his own physical self as Mike and as a heavily made-up "Oriental" in the other role. The point can only have been to show off his skill with makeup, because the two faces are distinctly different and he is almost totally unrecognizable as Ah Wing. (This also affords him a unique piece of screen action: with the benefit of trick photography, he gets to murder himself.)

In watching Chaney play two different parts at this early stage of his success, it becomes obvious that usual standards of acting don't really apply to his performances. He isn't attempting to, in modern method terms, *become* his characters as much as he's creating a visualized concept of the qualities his characters embody. As Mike, he is evil, so he looks mean. As Ah Wing, he is the mysterious wisdom of the East, so he looks inscrutable. The main story line has Dean, a former crook known as "Silky Moll," having to choose between a life of crime and a domestic existence with husband and child. Chaney lurks around the edges of the plot, representing a powerful physicalization of her two choices, while filling the frame and dominating the story. What Browning seemed to understand about Chaney's work was that he should be allowed to twist himself into the wildest contortions he could manage and erupt into over-the-top violence as needed. If he was going to play "a rat, a vulture, and a snake," let him. His roles were representative, even symbolic—beyond melodrama. Let him go all out, and the audience would respond. Chaney's performance style is *uber*-realistic—as totally realistic as possible in his professional use of makeup skills—yet completely allegorical, in that his characters represent concepts such as good, evil, and fear. At the climactic moment, Chaney, often restrained and low-key in his conveyance of power, would go into maniacal superdrive. Audiences began to wait for these moments when he unleashed his very considerable power and rage. In *Outside the Law,* Chaney is given a star turn in the final gang fight, which escalates marvelously inside a complex physical space played on two levels and involving hundreds of breakable props (dishes, vases, etc.) and several different groups of antagonists, all running in and out of doors, up and down levels, and fistfighting, bashing one another with props, and shooting at one another.

What *Outside the Law* did for Chaney's career was to demonstrate how effective he could be in moralistic stories, and it probably suggested to Browning and others that vehicles could be built around his ability to generate a larger-than-life force that could command center stage. Such movies—exhibiting Chaney's primal force—would work particularly well if they had exotic settings or unusual backgrounds. He would then be free to do anything, creating characters as bizarre as anyone's imagination could make them. Such movies would have two assets: their own story and drama, plus the ongoing cachet of Chaney, with the "What's he going to look like this time?" and "What evil will he do next?" suspense that he offered fans.

Outside the Law was heavily promoted, and its advance ad campaign ran for weeks in a kind of modern superhype. "IF YOU PLAY CARDS ON SUNDAY," screamed one of the teasers, "you are OUTSIDE THE LAW." The movie did excellent business, and Chaney's career continued to climb. He was working steadily, turning out one feature after another, most of them undistinguished vehicles, and not all of them available for viewing today. In 1921, following *Outside the Law,* he made *For Those We Love,* in which he played a sympathetic role; *Bits of Life,* a four-episode feature in which he appeared in the Chinese sequence playing an Asian villain who menaces the beautiful Anna May Wong; and *Ace of Hearts,* in which he plays a highly complex character who is both hero and villain. The story concerns a secret society that decides when someone is "too evil to live" (because he or she is letting society down). Members of the club draw lots to determine who will perform the assassination—the ritual selection is made by dealing out cards until someone draws the ace of hearts. Chaney is one of the group, but when the woman he loves (Leatrice Joy, also a member) marries a chosen assassin, he is driven crazy with jealousy. Yet when the happy couple are transformed by their wedding night and wish to disavow any future assassination, Chaney spares them the club's revenge by blowing himself and the entire group to smithereens.

In 1922, he made eight movies: *The Trap, Voices of the City, Flesh and Blood, The Light in the Dark, Shadows, Oliver Twist, Quincy Adams Sawyer,* and *A Blind Bargain.* These films set the pattern that was to define his career. He played a crooked hotel proprietor, a criminal, a man seeking revenge, an Asian—and dual roles, as in *A Blind Bargain,* where he is the mad scientist,

Dr. Lamb, and also his apelike hunchback assistant (a forerunner to Igor in the Frankenstein series and Chaney's own *Hunchback of Notre Dame*, which would follow).

Flesh and Blood (1922) is almost totally focused on Chaney's character, a man erroneously sent to prison. It begins with an escape scene in which he breaks out, aided by two mysterious Chinese men who pick him up and hide him in a wagonload of fruits and vegetables. The story is set in two of Chaney's favorite haunts, Chinatown and a slum mission. It's a tale of woe in which Chaney's wife dies before he can escape and get to her, and his beloved daughter—who believes her father dead—disappears. Aided by a tong boss who shields him from the police, he finally locates her and helps her marry the man she loves, who turns out to be the son of the man who ruined him in the first place. In the end, Chaney lets this enemy go free, tearing up the confession he has forced him to sign, as a gesture of love to the son and daughter. He then returns to prison voluntarily: "I went out a hunted and marked man. I come back—free!" The main point of *Flesh and Blood* is Chaney's opportunity to disguise himself as a crippled beggar, and the audience sees him more than once twist himself, draw up one leg, and heave himself onto crutches. He also reverses the process, slowly lowering the leg, tossing off the crutches, and standing tall. He employs no facial distortions, so here is an opportunity to observe how he really looked, and he plays the role with a great deal of emotion, using his natural face to convey his tortured inner self.

He seemed to have a genuine fascination with physical infirmities, and also with the criminal mind, and was proud that his movies were popular with convicts. "I have dozens of letters from convicts . . . and they all say the same thing: that they appreciate my characters because no matter how evil they are, there is always some redeeming spot of good in them." His criminals find redemption, as in his next film, *The Light in the Dark* (1922), directed by Clarence Brown, in which his thief finds the Holy Grail, and his cripples often get operations that allow them to walk again, as in 1923's *The Shock*. It's a tribute to the power of his personality and his mastery of makeup techniques that he stands out so beautifully today in such old-fashioned stories.

Shadows (which followed *The Light in the Dark*) was one of the typical "yellow peril" dramas of this period in which the Asian-American world was presented as menacing. Whereas blacks are seldom key characters in the movies of the silent era, Asian characters seem to be everywhere, and are almost universally presented as evil beings who smoke opium, run the white-slave trade, have mysterious hypnotic power, and inhabit rooms with secret doors. These Fu Manchu creatures sitting around in brothels with beaded curtains swaying are very unsettling to modern viewers. It's blatant racism, and Chaney played more than one of these characters, although his were not always villains. For instance, Yen Sin in *Shadows* is a superwise, caring man who suffers persecution at the hands of a small fishing village. Eventually, he gains acceptance after rescuing the young minister and his beautiful wife from a villain—just before he conveniently dies. The title cards of *Shadows* present Yen Sin speaking in pidgin English, and refer to him as "the Chink." Chaney's physical characterization is remarkable, including makeup that transforms his face, a stooped posture, and a scurrying walk. In creating Yen Sin, Chaney doesn't just squint up his eyes and grin. He invents his character from head to toe, using a bent-over walk and slight stoop to suggest the years of hard labor Yen Sin has undergone. His makeup is realistic—medium close-ups reveal no sense of anything artificial. He *looks* Chinese. His use of his hands, his little gestures, the careful way he takes a litchi nut out of a bag in order to break it open for a small child, all happen with a rhythm and attention to detail that totally transform him into Yen Sin.

In 1922, Chaney, although a big name, was still on occasion playing supporting roles, such as his Fagin in First National's presentation of Dickens's *Oliver Twist,* a Jackie Coogan vehicle directed by Frank Lloyd. Chaney is a first-rate Fagin: pinched, hunched over, rag-clad. He uses his hands as if his fingers were claws, and his shaky and nervous scuttling back and forth around his sordid quarters perfectly physicalizes what Fagin represents. (It has been pointed out justly that Chaney's Fagin doesn't resort to the racial stereotyping of the original text.) His brilliant pantomime is on display in a wonderful scene in which he teaches his young boys to pick his pocket with just the correct light touch. He mimes the action of an innocent man walking down the street, to be stopped by one urchin who will distract him while the other slyly lifts his money.

Four Chaney movies came out in 1923: *All the Brothers Were Valiant, While Paris Sleeps, The Shock,* and *The Hunchback of Notre Dame.* A very revealing photograph of him was taken on the set of *All the Brothers Were Valiant,* a melodrama of the sea. Chaney, a private and quiet man, is sitting completely apart from the filmmaking team. At his feet is a large sewing kit, and he is concentrating on stitching up the costume he has on, which is in obvious need of repairs. Because he's wearing torn pants and vest, his muscular body is in evidence, and his ability to shut out everything around him is fully observed. He simply has no idea that anyone is near him, much less taking his photograph.

Chaney once said, "Some people are especially born for characterization. You feel the call of it and you answer the call. It is your dramatic destiny." Chaney's dramatic destiny lay in such roles as that of the crippled criminal "Wilse Dilling, a dope-peddler, safe-cracker, gun-man" in *The Shock.* "Wilse Dilling was something of a mystery, even to Chinatown—he baffled the police, though he was listed on a page-long record at headquarters as 'dangerous.'" Wilse makes his headquarters in Chinatown's Mandarin

Chaney in one of his "normal" roles, *All the Brothers Were Valiant,* with Billie Dove and Malcolm MacGregor

Café, where people dare to eat with chopsticks and the man behind the checkout counter taps out secret codes with his long fingernails. (Wilse responds by banging his chopsticks on a rice bowl.) The Mandarin Café is "a whirlpool of vice and intrigue," a front for the evil Queen Ann (Christine Mayo), who dispatches one of her henchmen (Chaney) to a small town to await orders.

The Shock is an old-fashioned story of utter simplicity and sentiment. The plot with all its ramifications holds little interest for modern viewers; what is interesting is Chaney's ability to portray a cripple. He never slips. Hauling himself out of his wheelchair, crawling on his belly, humping along on his crutches, he makes every move perfectly. It's impossible not to believe he *is* crippled, or that he doesn't need those crutches. It's not just that he's physically adept at the twists and turns, but that he manages to make his characterization *total,* to give a sense of a man who lives with a twisted body and cannot make a move of any sort—physical, mental, emotional—without taking that factor into account. *The Shock,* a movie barely known today, provides good entertainment value despite its melodramatic tale of crime, fathers and daughters, stolen bonds, etc. (Just when you think it's about to fizzle out, the San Francisco earthquake occurs! The audience of the day loved the quake—and so did I.)

The Hunchback of Notre Dame, his next movie, gave him a classic role that has been repeated by other actors in later years, notably Charles Laughton in 1939, Anthony Quinn in 1957, and Anthony Hopkins in 1982. (The Walt Disney Studios created an animated version in 1996.) The story has lasting appeal, but no version is better than the silent one, and no Quasimodo is better than Lon Chaney's. It stands the test of time.

The first thing to be said about *The Hunchback of Notre Dame* is that it is marked by outstanding production values. It was a massive undertaking for 1923, requiring 750 crew members to build its huge re-creation of the medieval world, a set that covered nineteen acres of land on the Universal lot. Chaney himself created one of his most challenging makeup jobs, designing a look that had him carrying around forty pounds of rubber on his back and shoulders in order to produce a large hump that wasn't just a little designer bump on the back. He added another thirty pounds of weight with a breast-plate and leather harness, and blocked out most of the vision in his right eye with a specially made eyepiece that distorted his face. Since he had to jump around on the sets and leap across parapets, the extra weight and blurred vision made things extremely difficult for him. (Although he did some of his own stunt work, he was aided by the efforts of two famous stuntmen, Joe Bonomo and Harvey Perry.)

Chaney's Quasimodo is great because he allows himself to appear as completely grotesque. His teeth protrude, and his swollen, distorted cheek-bones stand out over a broken and twisted nose. His blind eye bulges out, prominent but totally useless, and his distorted and deformed body gives nei-ther him nor the viewer any relief. He is in every way Victor Hugo's "mon-strous joke of nature." Also, he is unafraid to act barbaric, to become an animal. He thumbs his nose. He swings on the gargoyles. He hunches around in apelike behavior. Yet his triumph in the role is that he manages to convey the sense of the hunchback's essential innocence—his almost childlike response to the world—within the grotesque. He portrays a "monster" who is also human, and audiences responded emotionally to his performance. Undoubtedly part of Chaney's appeal in those more repressed times was his ability to "let loose" with evil behavior and primitive emotions—and nowhere more so than with Quasimodo. Charles Laughton, himself a successful actor of unusual characters, said of him, "Chaney was not only a great actor; he was a magnificent dancer. The famous ballet stars, like Nijinsky, could express every emotion and every shade of meaning in the movements of their bodies. Chaney had that gift. When he realized that he had lost the girl (in *Hunch-back*), his body expressed it—it was as though a bolt of lightning had shat-tered his physical self. Extraordinary, really!"

Oddly enough, *Variety's* review was highly negative. Calling it "a huge mistake," and "a two-hour nightmare," it went on—in case exhibitors hadn't got the point—"it's murderous, hideous and repulsive." Admitting that Chaney's "performance as a performance entitles him to starring honors," the review still warned that "no children can stand its morbid scenes" and con-cluded "let the matter . . . be decided by personal observation." This review,

Chaney's two most
famous roles: *The
Hunchback of Notre
Dame* (ABOVE) and
*The Phantom of the
Opera*, with Mary
Philbin

by the trade paper designed to tip off exhibitors as to the potential box office appeal of any movie, indicates just how powerful *Hunchback* was in its day. The *New York Times* put things in better perspective: "Naturally there is much in this picture which is not pleasant any more than the works of Poe, some of Eugene O'Neill's strokes of genius, the stories of Thomas Burke . . . and many of the masters of the pen in olden days." But the review goes on to call it "a strong production" that will "appeal to all those who are interested in fine screen acting, artistic settings and a remarkable handling of crowds." Chaney's personal reviews were excellent, and the huge success of the movie around the world bagged him a lucrative long-term starring contract with MGM.

As the year 1924 opened, a minor Chaney film for Paramount was released, *The Next Corner,* in which he portrayed a Spaniard, and then he moved to Metro-Goldwyn-Mayer where, except for *The Phantom of the Opera,* he would spend the remainder of his career in star roles tailored exclusively for him. Almost every movie he made from then on was a success, and all but four are available for screening today. (Missing are 1927's *The Big City* and *London After Midnight,* in which he played the dual role of a Scotland Yard officer and a vampire. This latter feature, directed by Tod Browning, is one of the most sought-after of the famous "lost films" of the silent era. Also gone are 1925's *The Tower of Lies* and 1929's *Thunder.*)

His first MGM film, released in 1924, has a very distinguished reputation. *He Who Gets Slapped* is a collaboration of the talents of director Victor Seastrom, his coadapter Carey Wilson, and a cast that included not only John Gilbert but the very young Norma Shearer, who was on the brink of major stardom. Chaney again plays a role with built-in duality—first he is a respected scientist, and then he becomes the circus clown known as "He Who Gets Slapped." The plot tells of a greedy baron, who steals Chaney's scientific discoveries with the aid of his faithless wife. Chaney goes slightly mad, and when he tries to claim his work in front of "the academy," the baron slaps him—and the crowd of fellow scientists laughs! Stunned into total silence, Chaney later realizes, "They laughed as if I were a clown." When his wife, too, calls him "Fool! Clown!," he accepts the challenge—and becomes a successful circus clown, a perfect gesture of contempt.

Chaney's great scene comes when he locks the baron and Shearer's evil father in a room together. He has locked only one door, however, knowing that when they open the other one to escape, a circus lion will attack them. Grinning, laughing, even though he has been fatally stabbed, he awaits their inevitable death. Finally he staggers out into the clown arena one last time to philosophize: "The world must have its love, the world must have its tragedy, but always the clown comes out to make them laugh . . ." This wisdom is intercut with his getting his face slapped—so much for philosophy. The film

ends by asking the audience meaningful questions in three sober titles—
"What is death? What is life? What is love?"—so *He Who Gets Slapped* was
high art as far as movies were concerned.

In addition to its cinematic elegance, *He Who Gets Slapped* has three
major assets: Chaney, the handsome Gilbert, and the radiant young Shearer.
Chaney's role is relatively small, but when he is on-screen, he's powerful, concentrated, and focused. His rictal grin as he awaits the lion is awesome, and
he has once again become a totally different person, unrecognizable as Lon
Chaney or as one of his own earlier characterizations.

Chaney's 1925 movies were *The Monster, The Unholy Three, The Phantom of the Opera,* and the missing *The Tower of Lies,* in which he played a
Swedish peasant in a psychological story. The first three were huge successes,
and may be thought of as typical Lon Chaney movies. *The Monster,* directed
by Roland West, presented him as the classic mad scientist. The movie is a
somewhat bizarre mixture of comedy and horror, with a correspondence-
school detective trying to figure out what has happened at an asylum the
inmates have taken over. Chaney, the crazed Dr. Ziska, is running things and
implementing his scheme for capturing innocent travelers to be fodder for his
surgical experiments. The *New York Times* complained that the movie had too
much "light comedy," so that although it possessed "a degree of queer entertainment" it was "neither fish, fowl, nor good red herring." The reviewer
added, "One does not expect much fun in a film featuring Lon Chaney," an
infelicitous wording for what he was trying to say.

The very qualities that made the reviewers complain in 1925 tend to
make this film particularly entertaining today. The crazy house is full of oddball mechanisms like iron panels that crash down, hidden chutes, and walls
with sliding panels for Chaney to peep through. Mysterious arms reach out
from behind chairs, and the heroine disappears into a couch when two big
arms enclose her. It's all pretty peculiar, with torture scenes and comedy
shtick side by side. The *Times* suggested that "Mr. Chaney looks as if he could
have enjoyed a more serious portrayal of the theme."

The Unholy Three is one of my favorite Lon Chaney movies. (I'm also
partial to the sound remake of 1930, which most Chaney fans like less.) The
silent version, directed by Tod Browning, has Mae Busch as the heroine, Matt
Moore as the hero, and Victor McLaglen, Harry Earles, and Chaney as "the
unholy three." *Variety,* calling it "a wow of a story," said it had "everything—
hoke, romance, crook stuff, murder, suspense, trick stuff and above all it is as
cleverly titled as any production in many moons." As for Chaney, the review
says he "stands out like a million dollars . . . He's done that before, but always
with a more or less grotesque makeup . . . No makeup this time. He isn't all
hunched up, he isn't legless, he isn't this, that or the other thing in deformi-
ties. He's just Lon Chaney, and he's great." The *New York Times* found it

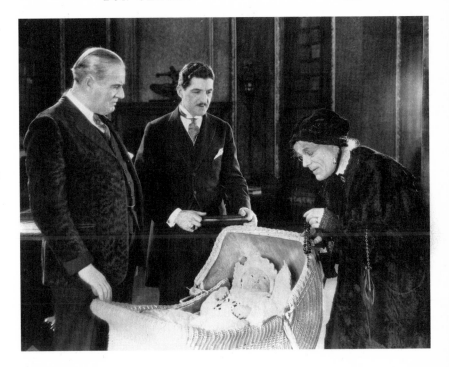

Chaney in drag, in
The Unholy Three

equally wonderful, saying that it was "stocked with original twists and situations . . . surprises . . . suspense." As for Chaney, he is said to "give a brilliant performance, restrained and earnest."

The story concerns a carny girl (Busch) and the unholy three—a ventriloquist (Chaney), a strongman (McLaglen), and a midget (Earles). The plot is a
wonderful opportunity for Chaney, whose ventriloquist impersonates a little
old lady who runs a parrot shop. This charming old girl sells talking parrots to
rich people—*only* to rich people—and the parrots talk amazingly well as long
as his ventriloquism is there to help them along. Once the rich folks get the
birds home, of course, they turn out to be slightly defective. The old lady then
makes a house call, once again inspiring the birds to blab, but also allowing
"her" to case the joint for burglary. So the parrots, the pet shop, and the old
lady are a cover that allows the three crooks to rob the wealthy. *The Unholy
Three* was a huge hit for everyone involved.

Chaney's next movie, *The Phantom of the Opera*, is his single greatest
success and his most famous role. As much as any story in movie history, the
tale of the phantom has captured moviegoers. The plot has been used for later
movie versions (1943, 1962, 1983, 1989) and also for television (1990) and,
of course, a successful Broadway musical adaptation. It's one of those stories
that have universal appeal—a man cursed by ugliness but with a heart full of
love, a great wardrobe, and spacious living quarters. And Chaney's *Phantom*
is an authentic classic. Originally released with Technicolor sequences, the

marvelous designs of the opera house with its subterranean channels are wonderfully photographed and made atmospheric by shadows, subtle lighting,
and a cavernous appearance so real that you can almost hear echoes reverber-
ating off the walls. In fact, the massive sets contribute a great deal to the terror
the Phantom evokes. The vast spaces seem inhuman and menacing, an equivalent of the Phantom's soul.

Although later versions explain the Phantom's story in different ways to
make him less evil, Chaney's Erik is an authentic villain. He was born during
a massacre and has "self-educated" himself in music and the black arts. An
escapee from Devil's Island, he apparently was born deformed, an endorsement of the idea that evil is as evil looks. (He tells the leading lady that her
love will remove the evil his face represents.) One of the most elegiac pas-
sages in the film is that in which the masked Chaney leads the beautiful young
Mary Philbin down, down into his underworld. There are five different layers
of imaginative settings to descend, including passageways through backstage
areas with discarded props and bizarre furnishings of all kinds, long, deep
stairways, and canals of black water—a labyrinth of space that leaves behind
all reason and civilization. As he poles Philbin along on the "black lake" in
his boat, a tiny lantern at the front, her white chiffon stole glides along on the
water behind the boat, mysteriously staying afloat. It's great stuff, and Chaney
at the center is a magnificent figure.

It is remarkable how briefly Chaney is actually seen on-screen in the
movies in which he is wearing one of his most famous disguises. He holds the
power of his appearance back from the viewer; he's almost stingy with himself,
a very clever move indeed. The Phantom remains a phantom for much of the
early part of the film, appearing only as a shadow or a half-seen figure. When
he finally emerges, masked, he's still scary . . . but when Philbin sneaks up on
him and pulls off his mask, even though he has especially warned her not to—
true horror! He looks bad, really bad. His revealed self is no disappointment
for modern viewers. "Feast your eyes, glut your soul on my accursed ugliness!" he cries out pathetically, and the sight of his death's-head skull with its
hot-coal eyes is as unsettling today as it ever was. It is one of Chaney's greatest makeup jobs. *Phantom of the Opera* provides a masked ball, some comedy
relief, a dramatic entrapment in which the hero and a secret service man are
both nearly drowned, an exciting chase through the underground and out onto
the streets of Paris, and a fabulous moment when the Phantom hovers above
the lovers, who think they are alone atop the Opera House overlooking Paris.
As Philbin betrays the Phantom to her love, Chaney eavesdrops and feels the
pain, his huge cloak billowing in the wind, the giant feather on his hat quiver-
ing like a wounded animal.

Phantom of the Opera was reputed to have cost over a million dollars to
film, with retakes alone costing $50,000, a large sum for 1925. Critics paid

tribute to its expensive sets and ambitious production values, and Chaney earned solid reviews. Considering how much audiences loved the movie and how famous it has become, *Variety* was not very enthusiastic about it, questioning whether or not a "majority of picture goers . . . [will] prefer this revolting sort of tale." Its technical expertise was called "mechanical" by the *Times,* and there was a feeling that perhaps this film had gone too far in the horror vein, and wasn't going to be all that appealing. Once again, the critics were dead wrong. The film was a huge hit and is still one of the very few silent films to be revived on a regular basis.

By the end of 1925, Chaney was in every way a star, one of the greatest names in the film business. He seemed to have an unlimited future, yet he would have only five more years to live, and although he would make fourteen more features, which sounds like a lot today when stars may make only one movie every two years, he was in the final stage of his remarkable career.

Blackbird (1926) is a solid vehicle for him, the kind of movie that shows what his stardom was all about. It's one thing to create *Phantom of the Opera* and *Hunchback of Notre Dame,* but *Blackbird* is the bread and butter of the working actor in silent films. It efficiently displays the persona he has developed—the Man of a Thousand Faces—and it has been totally constructed around him. Without Chaney, there would be no movie.

It's a simple story, well told. Chaney plays two brothers—but not really. They're both the same person: a crook who disguises himself as a crippled bishop who supervises a Limehouse mission. It's the perfect masquerade for a criminal. It also provides Chaney an opportunity to undergo another of his famous "twisting" transformations right in front of the audience, as he screws his leg and arm into the strained positions required for the role of the bishop. Like John Barrymore's Dr. Jekyll and Mr. Hyde, Chaney's "brothers" and the differences between them are presented as an actual acting process, in which the actor's body control accounts for the change from good to evil (Barrymore becoming Mr. Hyde), and from evil to "good" (Chaney's disguising himself as a bishop). Barrymore's work is based on the craft of the stage and is partly psychological in its presentation. Chaney's work is more purely physical. Like Sonja Henie's ice skating and Esther Williams's swimming, Chaney's power to transform himself is a unique physical gift. No other film actor has matched him in it.

In *Blackbird,* Chaney again was directed by the excellent Tod Browning, who played such an important role in his career. It's evident that Browning totally trusts his star performer. Browning guides the audience cleverly, without their fully realizing it. For example, when the leading lady, Renée Adorée (playing a dance hall puppeteer named Mademoiselle Fifi Lorraine), joins Chaney at his table after her act is finished, she looks around at the rich people who are "slumming" in Limehouse, wearing all their finery. She sees an expensive diamond-and-pearl choker necklace on the throat of one of the women, and the audience is allowed to see how she eyes it, how Chaney sees her eyeing it, how he eyes it, and how he eyes her afterward with a knowing smile. We follow her desire to have the necklace, as well as his observation of that desire and his acknowledgment that he will be able to use the desire against her. This type of directing skill, which involved the audience in the scripting process, was fundamental to the silent film tradition, but it was also key to building up the viewer's involvement with the unsavory villains played by Chaney.

In 1926, there was also *The Road to Mandalay*, in which Chaney played a one-eyed criminal called Singapore Joe. (Despite the title, the movie has nothing to do with Rudyard Kipling.) It's one of those movies in which a dive in the slums of Singapore is clearly meant to be taken as a bordello. (One of the proofs of its being a very low-down joint is that all the classes and races mingle there.) Essentially, *Mandalay* is an old-fashioned melodrama in which Chaney's convent-bred daughter (who, of course, doesn't know Singapore Joe is her father) must be saved from the traditional fate worse than death. Chaney's big scene is a spectacular twenty-foot fall from a balcony down onto his various motley customers, who are apparently so tough they're no worse for wear afterward. His chief makeup disguise is his "bad eye," a white orb that stares coldly out at the viewer. At first, it just seems foolish, even hokey, but as the movie proceeds, that eyeball takes on an increasingly sinister quality, and its very simplicity ends up being a strong definition of a relentlessly single-minded man.

In 1927 Chaney continued his string of successes with *Tell It to the Marines* (as a sergeant, in one of his most normal characterizations), *Mr. Wu* (yet another dual role, first as the vengeful villain, Wu, and then as His Honorable Father), *Mockery* (one of those late-1920s Russian Revolution movies, with Chaney as a serf who pretends to be the husband of a countess), the two famous lost films (*London After Midnight* and *The Big City*), and the splendid *The Unknown*, one of his very best. In *The Unknown*, Chaney is paired with the young and radiantly beautiful Joan Crawford. The movie tells a completely bizarre story about an armless man (Chaney, of course) working in Crawford's father's carnival. Chaney loves Crawford, but she thinks of him only as a dear friend. When the carnival strongman tries to make love to her, she rejects him as well because she fears men's hands and hates them pawing her. Secretly, Chaney actually does have arms, but he hides them, keeping them strapped to his back in order to disguise his criminal past. In one of the most distressing plot developments I've come upon in films, Chaney blackmails a doctor into performing surgery on him: he has his arms amputated for real, because he fears that if Crawford ever embraced him, she might feel them . . . and she hates men's hands, remember? This is about as grim as it gets in films. Craw-

Chaney's amazing dexterity (*The Unknown*)

ford is a tremendous plus in the movie because somehow she seems worth it all. At this point in her career she's totally unaffected, very natural in her acting, and inherently sexy. Yet she has a sweet shyness to her and she makes a good foil for Chaney because her image is so strong. (In later years she commented, "Lon Chaney was my introduction to acting . . . Watching him gave me the desire to be a real actress.")

In 1928, Chaney made *Laugh, Clown, Laugh* and *While the City Sleeps,* and in 1929, *West of Zanzibar, Where East Is East,* and *Thunder.** These films in no way broke with what had gone before in his career, although in *While the City Sleeps* he is a plainclothes detective, not a typical role, and in *Thunder* he is a railroad engineer, also a departure.

On July 6, 1930, Chaney's career was in its final year, and he was close to death when he released his sound debut movie, a remake of *The Unholy Three. Variety* treated his sound debut with indifference, feeling that Chaney's portrayal of the old woman was more convincing in the silent version, but the overall comment wasn't a criticism of his speaking ability. The *Times* felt the remake was not as gripping as the original, but it paid tribute to Chaney's use of five different voices. In a clever marketing ploy, Chaney produced an affidavit that guaranteed audiences that only *his* voice was used for his roles in *The Unholy Three,* since he was talking for his basic character, the ventriloquist's dummy, various parrots, the old lady he pretends to be, etc. This document was signed by Chaney and notarized and used for publicity. The ads then dubbed him "the man of a thousand voices."

Lon Chaney's one and only sound film was directed by Jack Conway. It starred Chaney with the stunningly beautiful Lila Lee in Mae Busch's role, Ivan Linow replacing Victor McLaglen as the strongman and Harry Earles repeating his part as Tweedledee, the midget. The romantic leading man originally played by the handsome Matt Moore is now the callow Elliott Nugent. Watching Chaney in a sound movie is at first very disconcerting. Sound changes everything, and the experience helps to explain what happened to John Gilbert when his public first heard him talk. In the beginning, Chaney's voice just seems so much less than it ought to be. He's somehow diminished, rendered less frightening, less weird. Since this is the only Chaney talking feature, it's the only time his audience experienced what must have been happening again and again for audiences in the late twenties when they went out to the movies and suddenly discovered that their formerly silent gods and goddesses sounded like ordinary mortals. (James Card once described it in a lec-

---

**Thunder,* for which no known prints exist, was actually his final silent film, and was released with sound effects and a musical score in July of 1929. Production on *Thunder* had been halted due to his being ill, but the movie was eventually completed. The illness, a cold which developed into walking pneumonia, was the beginning of the end for Chaney.

Chaney in *West of Zanzibar*, with Mary Nolan, Warner Baxter, and Lionel Barrymore

ture to an American Film Institute audience as being "as if a beautiful woman opened her mouth to speak, and something ugly and stupid fell out.") Chaney's persona—that of the twisted, unique creature—is naturally undermined by having to render dialogue such as "How'd ya like a sock in the nose?" As the movie unfolds, however, Chaney takes hold . . . or the viewer adjusts . . . and Chaney seems as natural and effective as he always did.

With sound added, *The Unholy Three* takes on a new quality that can only be described as screwball. With one slight shove in the right direction, it could have been the funniest comedy ever seen. As it is, it's comic enough. The unholy three are still the ventriloquist, the midget, and the strongman. They still run a pet shop and make their living by selling talking parrots, etc., etc. Chaney is fine when he's playing the criminal ventriloquist, but he becomes magnificent dressed up in a long dress, ruffles, beads, earrings, and a white wig as the old grandma, Mrs. O'Grady. A later sight of him in this getup, but with the wig off and an apron on, his earrings bobbing while he makes breakfast and lectures the midget, is astounding. He's talking to "the baby," who wears a little bonnet and christening-style dress (but who is really the foul little midget, smoking a cigar and mouthing off), while the strongman sits playing with an elephant toy. This is a domestic breakfast scene to remember: granny in drag, the "baby" midget with a cigar, and the big guy playing with a kid's toy. Granny crabs away at everyone while she cooks, and the three of them, unholy indeed, argue over the murder they have just committed as if they were talking about who should take out the garbage.

Naturally, the three thieves begin to quarrel. ("You're the one who should have been the old woman," the midget says slyly to the strongman, in an attempt to flatter him over to his side.) They end up trapped in a hideout together, and the sound continues to add a bizarre note. While Chaney cooks, cleans, and swats at their cranky circus ape (don't ask), Lila Lee sits crying and sobbing, the strongman cleans his rifle, and the midget, with the ventriloquist's dummy on his knee, sings, "Oh, I wish I had someone to love me . . ." Sound throws these characters even further off balance than they were in the silent version. They are more than standard villains, more than standard oddball characters. Sound renders them inexplicable, unlike anything you've ever seen—or heard. When the midget, pretending to be the baby, sees a policeman pick up the toy elephant in which they've hidden a stolen ruby pendant necklace, he sets up a diversionary tactic. "My dog, my dog," he wails, clutching his fat little hands open and shut, reaching out to take the elephant back. "He calls it his little dog," explains Chaney grimly, knitting away at about a hundred miles a minute in the granny's rocking chair. When the policeman shakes the elephant and, hearing it rattle, starts to investigate what's inside, the strongman grabs it away, yelling, "I don't like people to play with his toys." The evil little "baby" immediately opens the elephant and pops the big fat ruby into his mouth, crying out, "My candy, my candy!" The sound of Chaney's fake female voice, the click of the knitting needles, the rattle of the elephant, the yell of the strongman, and the insane little pseudo-baby voice come together to render the scene tense, frightening, and yet somehow hysterically funny.

At the movie's end, when all is resolved, Chaney, near his death in real life, looks handsome and virile on-screen. After he has helped the young lovers get together, he flashes a big smile, looking both normal and attractive, just an ordinary man in a bowler. There can be no doubt that this movie introduced him successfully into sound, and that he would have gone on to an even bigger career. Ahead in the 1930s lay some of Hollywood's greatest horror films—*The Mummy, Frankenstein, Dracula*—and in 1941 would come *The Wolf Man:* roles tailor-made for Chaney's talents. In fact, he was scheduled to portray Dracula when he was diagnosed as having bronchial cancer. *Dracula,* of course, made the career of Bela Lugosi, Boris Karloff became a name playing Frankenstein's monster and the mummy, and Chaney's own son, Lon Chaney, Jr., portrayed the wolf man. None of these actors might have had the careers they did if Lon Chaney, Sr., had lived a normal life span.

Lon Chaney, with his bizarre plots and grotesque characters, carved out his own territory in film stardom. There was no "Lon Chaney type" except for Lon Chaney; in his category, he was it. Modern attempts to classify him simply

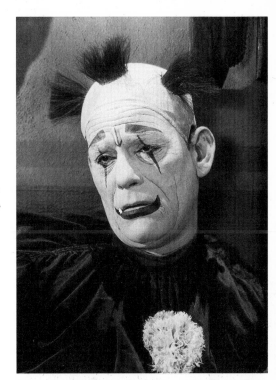

Three faces of Chaney:
He Who Gets Slapped (RIGHT),
While the City Sleeps (BELOW),
Mr. Wu (BELOW RIGHT)

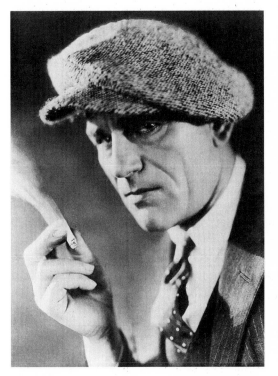

as "a heavy" are mistaken in their oversimplification of his career. There was, of course, a classic silent film "heavy," and there were significant actors to play these roles. The very Prussianesque Erich von Stroheim played both Huns (skewering babies on his bayonets) and seducers (leading beautiful wives astray in sophisticated sex stories). The Japanese star Sessue Hayakawa received raves for playing the villain opposite Fannie Ward in Cecil B. DeMille's 1915 version of *The Cheat*. (*The Cheat* was the shocker of its day. When Hayakawa pulled Ward's dress off her shoulders and branded her exposed flesh with a hot iron, he inadvertently became a pre-Valentino sex symbol, the glamorous "other" kind of man, from a different culture.) Von Stroheim and Hayakawa were "heavies," men from foreign lands with different morals and different social customs, and such types were very useful in the visualized melodramas of the silent era. Classically American types like Wallace Beery and Ernest Torrence alternated between movies that exploited their comedy skills, turning them into buffoons or bumpkins, and movies that used their large size, grim faces, and menacing manner to advantage as "heavies." (Beery ended up in sound films carving a niche as a lovable old scalawag who was no better than he should be, but who would be reformed before the movie ended.)

An all-out heavy was Louis Wolheim, who was, by his own description, "the ugliest son of a bitch in the world." His broken nose had left him with a face that looked twisted and menacing, and he played sadists, gangsters, killers, soldiers, and prizefighters, with only an occasional loyal sidekick, stalwart pal, or comedy relief character. His characters were often quiet, with a strong sense of brutishness underneath. (Wolheim found fame as the lead in Eugene O'Neill's play *The Hairy Ape*. His stage ability might have led him to a solid career in sound films, but he died in 1931 of stomach cancer.)

None of these typical "heavies" ever became a major star, except possibly Beery in the sound era, and no other actor made a great career playing monsters, criminals, and oddballs the way Chaney did. His characters had shadings and dimensions of morality that lifted them out of the usual silent era "bad guy" category. There is something about him on-screen that not only transcends the standard villain type but that remains mysterious and compelling over time. Perhaps it is only because he refused to allow his personal life to become the property of his fans, his studio, and the magazines of the day. His famous comment "My personal life is nobody's business" sums up the situation, and, unlike most stars, he really meant it. Surrounded by publicists and salesmen and other actors who loved the limelight, Chaney just stood his ground. Nowhere is this more evident than in a Metro-Goldwyn-Mayer promotional film of about 1925. The newsreel camera roves slowly down a well-dressed and well-posed lineup of Metro's top stars, all of whom are grinning and vamping for the photographer. (John Gilbert and Norma

Shearer look particularly aware of the camera's presence.) Chaney, standing near the very end of the line, turns his back on the camera as it moves by. He alone does not present himself for exploitation. "I care nothing whatever about fame," he told *Motion Picture* magazine in 1922. "The less I have of it the better for me personally. I work for money and I work because I am interested in the things I do. If I were not, I wouldn't do them."

Why should he pander to the public as a private man when he gave so much to them professionally? This sense of privacy has given rise to rumors that Chaney was unhappy and tormented, antisocial and reclusive. However, his hobby was moviemaking, and since he loved the filming process, he often made home movies, a few of which still exist. They give the lie to the idea that he was a twisted character from one of his own films. The Chaney-made movies show him clowning around with his wife, kissing her at their cabin retreat, and talking happily with a roomful of dinner guests. The idea that he didn't lead a normal life seems utterly erroneous when one watches these home movies. It's far more likely that he simply shunned Hollywood's idea of "society" and that because of the roles he played on film, he developed an exaggerated reputation as a peculiar man.

Chaney had been unwell during the shooting of *The Unholy Three,* and after it was finished, he went to New York to consult throat specialists and was diagnosed as having bronchial cancer, although it has been said that he wasn't told he had only a short time to live. While resting in his cabin in the Sierras, his throat began hemorrhaging, and he was brought to a Los Angeles hospital where he underwent a series of blood transfusions. Some sources claim he lost his voice and spent his last days pantomiming to his friends and family. Chaney died on August 26, 1930, of a final hemorrhage of the throat. He was only forty-seven years old. Two minutes of silence were observed on all of Hollywood's sets. A squad of marines lowered the flag at MGM and blew taps, and nearly everyone in the studio commissary ordered the "Lon Chaney sandwich" (bacon, cheese, and tomato). His death was a great shock to everyone in the industry, and to his legions of fans, who could never get over the loss, since no one could take his place.

In 1957, Universal made *Man of a Thousand Faces,* a biographical picture about Chaney starring James Cagney. Cagney, who respected Chaney, gave a terrific performance and the film made Chaney's name live again for a new generation. Cagney portrayed Chaney as moody, somewhat tormented, but hardworking, loyal to friends, and dedicated to giving the best performance he possibly could. Despite this biopic, several books, and numerous articles on his work, Chaney still seems mysterious, and probably always will.

He took his acting seriously but he treated it like a job. He was twenty-nine years old before he ever made a movie, and it took him seven years of performing in bit parts and secondary roles to earn his star billing. He crafted his stardom out of hard work and a set of skills he had spent his youth mastering. His craft meant everything to him. He once told a costar that real crying on-camera wasn't necessary, glycerine tears were just as good. "The point isn't that you cry," he said, "but that you make the audience cry." His was a style of acting that grew from understanding how to use the tools of the trade, but he also understood that a good actor used the tools for a serious goal. "If I played the role of an old man, I tried to crawl into the old man's mind," he said. "Rather than merely build up a putty nose, and don white whiskers, I tried to inject into it some distinctive mannerisms—a limp perhaps—or broken arm, or maybe just a slight nervous twitch of the face. I want my makeup to simply add to the picture, to show at a glance the sort of character I am portraying, but I want my role to go deeper than that. I want to dig down into the mind and heart of the role."

What, after all, *was* Chaney's appeal? The answer is simple: he was unique. There hasn't been, and no doubt never will be, anyone like him on the screen. He stands alone in film history. He brought the audience to himself on his own terms. He was not a woman's romantic hero, a lover to dream of, nor was he a delightful, swashbuckling role model for male fantasies. He didn't play slapstick comedy, and he didn't present the lives of noble heroes for young people to emulate. Although in his long career he was versatile and essayed many kinds of roles, he came to be associated with flawed characters, and therein lay his magic. On behalf of the lonely and worried and frightened and ugly in the audience, he was willing to be an outsider, to be unloved, to be less than beautiful, and to be unrewarded by the joys of life. As it turned out, there were many less-than-perfect people out there to appreciate him.

Lon Chaney and
the tools of his
trade—mirror
and makeup kit

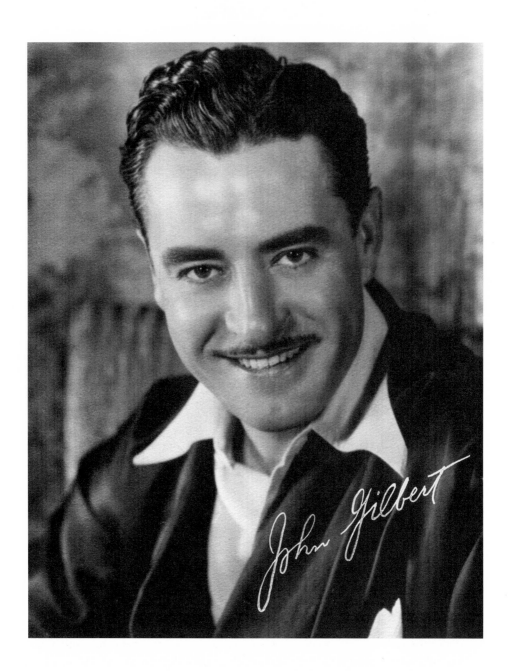

John Gilbert

JOHN GILBERT

JOHN GILBERT IS triple-cursed: forgotten, misunderstood, and underappreciated. Once one of the most popular stars of the 1920s, he carries the burden of the "matinee idol" label, as well as the dubious distinction of being the official poster boy for the "ruined by sound" movie star. This combination has relegated him to a name without a persona, even though—ironically—some of his movies are among the most revived of the silent era. In his own time, to be a matinee idol was a respectable goal, and Gilbert embraced the term. It meant that he was not only a handsome guy, but the guy all women wanted to be their very own. It didn't imply "ham actor," as it does now, or merely "pretty boy," although there *was* a touch of scorn attached, since men were always supposed to be manly. (The November 1918 *Motion Picture* defined the term as "an actor with eyelashes," and Frank Capra's 1928 comedy *Matinee Idol* casually threw out a comment on what it meant to be one: "You're getting over 500 letters a day—all from women.") Over the years, the term has increasingly become pejorative. Today it suggests a male clotheshorse standing around holding a cocktail and smoking a cigarette in an ivory holder, looking bored and coming alive just long enough to deliver a witty putdown with casual ease. A sexless second lead. Or the type usually played by Adolphe Menjou, the Parisian man of the world.

This modern misunderstanding has very little to do with John Gilbert. He was a serious actor, part of a tradition: a long line of respected stage actors admired by female theatregoers (a line that still exists today in its modern version, sexy hunks who draw at the box office). He was the male equivalent of the female sex symbol, and was valued because he inspired romantic dreams in the opposite sex. (This doesn't mean his own sex couldn't dream about him too—those were just different times.) Gilbert gave the matinee idol heat. The movie camera brought his audience in close, so they could look into his eyes—and feel the sex on his mind. He faced the lens without fear, and he knew how to smolder. He projected the image of a handsome, passionate, somewhat brooding man, but at the same time he seemed real, tangible. He was not exotic and remote, a dream man you were never going to meet in your ordinary life, like Valentino. Meeting John Gilbert might be a stretch, but it seemed possible. Koszarski calls Gilbert "the first successful link between the romantic traditions of Valentino and Wallace Reid." In other words, Gilbert had the outrageous good looks and sensuality of the former, combined with the boyish charm of the latter. He bridged the gap between fantasy and reality.

Gilbert has been written about disparagingly in the modern era by critics who find him too weak as an actor or too excessive in his emoting. There's no doubt that he acts in the silent film tradition, but one has to consider him in the context of his times, and to compare him with other leading men of the era. Only then is it clear why he was so popular: he cuts a far better figure than most of them, and he has personality, real personality. And his voice *was* adequate for sound. No matter how many historians try to explain that Gilbert made eleven reasonably successful sound movies, or that it wasn't his voice that killed him as much as it was the changing times, which rendered his brand of heated romance outdated, no one wants to believe it. It's a better story the other way. So Gilbert winds up as the matinee idol with the lousy voice, little more than a footnote in the transition to sound, proof that it turned the world of movie stardom upside down. It's a neat and easy way to dismiss a top box office draw of the 1920s.

John Gilbert deserves much more. He *was* a matinee idol, but one whose career transcended the term both then and now.

GILBERT HAD NO DISTINGUISHED professional family background. He was born in 1897 in a cheap rooming house in Logan, Utah, where his mother, an unknown actress, had dropped out of a low-level touring company to give birth to a child it was clear she didn't want. Gilbert underwent a fairly long apprenticeship, working in films for over a decade, sometimes writing and even directing movies as well as acting in them. He first appeared as an extra, possibly in William S. Hart's *Hell's Hinges* in 1916 (sources differ), and he slowly worked his way up, appearing in films at Triangle, Paramount, Metro, and Fox.

Handsome and likable, Gilbert inevitably began to be noticed. Several film historians believe that *The Great Redeemer* (released in October of 1920, starring House Peters and Marjorie Daw) is the film that determined that he would, in fact, become an actor rather than a behind-the-scenes contributor, but reviews of the day don't mention him as an actor in *The Great Redeemer* and do refer to his having adapted (with Jules Furthman) the story on which it is based. On the other hand, two 1919 releases feature him: *The Busher,* with Charles Ray and Colleen Moore, and *The Heart o' the Hills,* a Mary Pickford vehicle. In the first, he has a small role as a well-dressed banker's son who believes that he is "the social overlord of his native town." He has obviously been cast for his good looks and for his ability to wear clothes well and look wealthy; he has very little to do. But in *The Heart o' the Hills,* he is featured in a showy part, and anyone who was in a 1919 Mary Pickford film received attention. Pickford's popularity and the quality of her movies ensured Gilbert a chance at an acting career if he did a creditable job, and he did more than that. He is excellent in the second romantic lead of "Gray Pendleton, a blue grass aristocrat." (It's as if almost from the beginning everyone understood that Gilbert must play someone with clothes and manners.) The first glimpse of him in *The Heart o' the Hills* is a disappointment: he doesn't look at all like himself—he's very young, and he has no mustache—and I started to wonder if it was really he. Suddenly, however, his character is given something to do. He smiles, laughs, and reacts to Pickford, who is playing a barefooted little mountain girl. In other words, he comes alive, looking relaxed and natural. He *is* John Gilbert, after all.

Gilbert has two wonderful scenes in the movie. In the first, he's a young boy, filled with joyful energy as he claps enthusiastically along the sidelines at a wild mountain hoedown (or, as it is described, "a jollification"). Caught up in the foot-stomping abandon of the dancing, he takes to the floor solo and throws himself into the dance with arms, elbows, and torso all gyrating, his feet thumping the boards a mile a minute. He blows everyone around him—except, of course, for Pickford, who couldn't be upstaged by anyone—off the screen. In his second big scene, he's grown into an elegantly turned-out young man in love with Pickford. He kneels by her chair to propose, and despite a bad camera angle which makes his nose too big and bestows a mysterious bump on his forehead, he takes his time with the lovemaking, kissing her hand gently and with a modest passion appropriate to Pickford, who is, after all, not Garbo. When she gently turns him down and walks out of the frame, Gilbert stands there alone holding the moment for an extraordinarily long time. He is slim, handsome, and charismatic. As the young girl who loves him enters to take his hand, and he goes on looking after Pickford, it is a perfectly presented tableau in which Gilbert already seems to have all the experience he will ever need to become a star. Watching John Gilbert in *The Heart o' the Hills* explains everything, and it is fascinating to see him before he became a matinee idol, when he was so young and energetic.

Whatever the film was that made everyone take notice (and I would vote for *The Heart o' the Hills*), it was a 1923 John Ford* movie, *Cameo Kirby,* that brought him to real prominence and gave him the chance at stardom. Besides being uncommonly handsome, he is given a showy role as a riverboat gambler whose trademark is his cameo jewelry. Commanding the screen with a cameo

---

Cameo Kirby is today known to film scholars as the movie on which Ford officially changed his directorial credit from the informal "Jack Ford" to the more serious "John Ford."

Gilbert on the brink
of stardom, in John
Ford's *Cameo Kirby*

at his throat, several cameo rings on his fingers, and a wide bracelet of matched cameos on his wrist, Gilbert makes a dramatic picture. Dressed in a white ruffled shirt, pale tight-fitting trousers, high boots, black hat and jacket, he is beautiful to look at. Furthermore, he's mastered the final detail of his dramatic outfit—a full black cape that he twirls with great skill and panache. Although there isn't much for him to do but pose, he poses well and manages to project considerable presence. The story is standard melodramatic stuff, but well directed by Ford, and Gilbert makes it work. He is calm, cool, and collected in front of the camera, seemingly born for roles in which he can wear costumes, suffer, strut, and seduce.

Although Ford's *Cameo Kirby* focused attention on him, it was King Vidor who elevated Gilbert into real stardom, and it was Gilbert's 1924 move to the brand-new MGM studios that boosted his career to top-level fame. Two of the movies he made at MGM in 1924—one directed by Vidor (*His Hour*) and one by Victor Seastrom (*He Who Gets Slapped*)—solidified his reputation.

His Hour gives Gilbert the kind of role in which he was to be fervently embraced by audiences. He cuts a great figure as a Russian prince who stands around on elaborate sets, awaiting an opportunity to make love to his leading lady, Aileen Pringle, who plays a straitlaced British girl. Gilbert has dark hair, a full mustache (said to have been grown to balance his somewhat-too-large nose), a good smile with even teeth, and beautiful dark eyes that literally

Gilbert with
Norma Shearer,
in *He Who Gets
Slapped*

sparkle.* He's very, very pretty! And like Valentino, who was his major rival
with women, Gilbert moves with grace and plays with style, exhibiting self-
confidence as an actor and presenting his silly character without apology or
embarrassment. *His Hour* was one of the many ridiculous plots dreamed up by
Elinor Glyn, the high priestess of twenties romance, whose strong suit was in
writing stories in which pale and correctly raised young women met up with
pseudo-savage men of wealth and/or royalty. (These men were usually European, the idea being that nice American boys would never behave that way.)
His Hour is a typical Glyn piece of nonsense, but it doesn't seem particularly
committed to its decadence. Gilbert, on the other hand, does seem committed,
and very willing. When he first encounters Pringle, she pretends to be asleep,
and he boldly kisses her neck and slowly runs his tongue along her hand. This
was hot stuff! After Gilbert sweeps her up and off to his snowbound country
lair, she asserts herself by pointing one of his guns at her head and crying out,
"Touch me again and I'll shoot!"

   He Who Gets Slapped is entirely different material. Gilbert plays a rela-

---

*Gilbert's mustache undoubtedly played a large role in his success, because without it his face
loses its symmetry. Suddenly, his nose is too big, his mouth too small, and his cheeks too flat;
his head looks too big for his body, and nothing works. But put his mustache on him, dress him
up in a slouch hat and a good suit—or a tuxedo, or a Russian cossack uniform with plenty of fur
trim—and he becomes a handsome, exotic figure. Cinematographers also learned how to
bounce light off the bridge of his nose, reducing its size.

tively small role in what was designed as a starring vehicle for Lon Chaney, already at the peak of his popularity. Presenting the lovely young Norma Shearer in one of her best silent films, the movie has Gilbert in the romantic lead, playing Bezano, a circus daredevil rider who falls in love with Shearer. His footage consists of a few scattered moments, with one extended sequence in which he and Shearer go on a picnic together. Shot in glorious sunlight, which gives everything a romantic glow, both young stars look innocent and radiant. While ants devour their food, Gilbert weaves a garland of flowers for Shearer's hair. They romp about, falling in the grass, kissing and laughing. Gilbert's job has been reduced to the essence of what will become the central element of his persona: the man in love. He performs the role with great skill, and those who think he was good at appearing to be in love in *Flesh and the Devil* only because he *was* in love (with Garbo) should see him here with Shearer. Being featured in a prestigious Chaney movie elevated Gilbert's status, but the key to his career was that he had appeared in two movies back-to-back that presented him as the ultimate lover. Female fans responded accordingly, he was labeled a matinee idol, and his career took off.

Gilbert finished out 1924 with two other movies, *The Snob* and *Wife of the Centaur,* and the following year appeared in two of Hollywood's most celebrated films: *The Merry Widow,* directed by Erich von Stroheim, and *The Big Parade,* by King Vidor. Many movie stars go through an entire career without participating in even one film of such quality, and Gilbert, a relative newcomer as a leading man, had two in that one year. It was the making of his reputation, and from that time on, he was a star of the first rank, with an avid following.

In the first of these two films, *The Merry Widow,* Gilbert was not the primary focus. The film was designed to belong to Mae Murray in the title role, and if not to her, then certainly to its colorful director, the legendary von Stroheim. Murray, an actress famous for her "bee-stung" lips, brought her own hairdresser and makeup man. She looks gorgeous, the quintessential little 1920s leading lady draped in beads. She has no apparent acting talent, but she's very good at standing there, hand on hip, showing off her extremely expensive wardrobe. In this sense, Murray knew her job, and she is well supported by Gilbert as the romantic lead, and also by Roy D'Arcy, the consummate villain for silent costume films, and Tully Marshall in one of his best crackpot roles, this time as a foot fetishist. They are all superb, and outclassed in raw talent though she may be, Murray is appealing as the widow. Everything about the movie was given first-class treatment, including the ticket charges: $1 for matinees, and evening performances at the sensationally steep prices of $1.50 and $2.

Gilbert is subtle and honest in his role as the handsome Danilo, and his low-key work in this film doesn't seem dated today. This is partly because the film as a whole is a masterpiece. The wonderful directorial touches von Stro-

Gilbert and Mae Murray alone in a crowd,
and facing the villain, Roy D'Arcy, in *The Merry Widow*

heim provides include a royal funeral, suggested through a corps of drummers slowly descending a long flight of stairs, dissolving in and out and repeating their movements; the brilliant silhouetting of gems adorning Mae Murray to the exclusion of her face and figure when she is gazed upon by the mercenary prince; the beautiful way freezing rain on a window is used to indicate the passage of time; and a marvelous sequence that establishes subjectively how each of her three different male admirers actually sees Murray: Gilbert, the romantic, sees only her face; D'Arcy, the sensualist seducer, sees her body; and Tully Marshall, the fetishist extraordinaire, sees her tiny feet in their little shoes.

Gilbert's performance is in significant contrast to D'Arcy's. D'Arcy has been skillfully directed to give his character an insane comic touch. He's totally in control of the role, and plays it to the hilt with deliberate exaggeration. Nevertheless, the performance—meant to be satiric—doesn't go over well with modern audiences who don't appreciate the tradition. By contrast, Gilbert seems far more modern, and thus more appealing. He is outstandingly handsome, relaxed, wearing a 1990s haircut, and very trim in his smart white uniforms. And again, he is the intense lover, the man who, when he sees the woman he wants for the first time, stops everything to appreciate her and to make love to her with fire and passion. He shows up well in a movie that has a great deal else to take attention away from him.

As good as it was, *The Merry Widow* presented Gilbert as part of an ensemble under the guidance of a unique director. His next movie singled him out and put him front and center. Every great movie star career needs a definitive role in a blockbuster that catches on with the public, and for Gilbert that blockbuster was *The Big Parade*. Directed by King Vidor from a story by Laurence Stallings, *The Big Parade* was a war movie made with "the cooperation of the Second Division, United States Army and Air Services Units, Kelly Field." It is unquestionably a great film, one that stands today as an undisputed classic and that plays with almost the same power it generated on the day it opened, only half a dozen years after the war it depicts had ended.

King Vidor had wanted to make a film about World War I for a long time, but he wanted it to be a realistic and honest film. When Gilbert was suggested to him for the leading role, he balked. He had already directed Gilbert in two romantic pictures, and what he had in mind for the lead was anything but a "matinee idol." He didn't dislike Gilbert but felt that a Romeo deluxe was not appropriate for the movie he wanted to make. Gilbert, for his part, was also not enthusiastic—he would have to have dirty fingernails and go without benefit of makeup, so that he could look like a real soldier in the trenches. The two men were reluctantly persuaded, and the result was one of those happy accidents of the kind that kept Ronald Reagan and Ann Sheridan out of *Casablanca*. As soon as filming got under way, everyone knew the outcome was going to be good. The movie looked so impressive in rough cut that it was expanded, with new money invested. The final film cost about $250,000, a lot for the time, but it earned an enormous $15 million at the box office. It was the most popular film of 1925, playing a record ninety-six consecutive weeks at the Astor Theatre in New York City.

Just as Lon Chaney had Tod Browning for ten movies and Gloria Swanson had Cecil B. DeMille for six, John Gilbert was lucky to work with King Vidor in five silent films. There were two to launch him (*His Hour* and *Wife of the Centaur*), one to make him a star (*The Big Parade*), and two to prove the status was permanent (*La Bohème* and *Bardelys the Magnificent*). (In a sixth Vidor silent, *Show People*, he appeared as himself in a cameo.) John Gilbert was in the right place at the right time to become the leading man in King Vidor's *The Big Parade*, one of the greatest war films ever made, and the film that adds a dimension to his career that takes him beyond the terms "matinee idol" or "sex symbol."

It's true, however, that he *was* a sex symbol of his time. And like female sex symbols such as Marilyn Monroe and Rita Hayworth—both of whom had considerable acting talent that often went unused—Gilbert was often denied the respect he deserved as an actor. His range is somewhat narrow, but he is superb at what he does, and *The Big Parade* showcases him at his best. It's an epic story of the infantryman's life in World War I, mixing comedy and tragedy in its account of an ordinary young American who goes over, falls in love, fights a war, loses a leg, and returns home a changed man. In his early scenes, Gilbert is youthful, filled with energy and life. At the end of the war, back in America, when he's being driven home from the station by his father, he looks gaunt, haunted, years older. This is not just makeup at work; it is Gilbert's ability to internalize an emotional state and reflect it in his face. He has gone from a lively young boy to a broken man, nervously smoking a cigarette, distracted, looking away from his father, not even listening to him as they drive.

As the young hero from well-to-do circumstances who joins the army for a lark, Gilbert is first-rate. He's standing on the sidewalk, idly watching a parade, listening to a stirring military march, when his pals ride by in an open-air automobile and cry out to him, "Come on! The whole gang's going over!" He laughs and, taking another glance at the uniformed band smartly stepping down the street, goes to join them, and in just that casual way his life is changed forever.

It is a significant comment on Gilbert's underrated acting ability that the film that made him a great star doesn't present him only as a lover. The scenes in which he woos and wins his costar Renée Adorée (as the French girl, Melisande) are utterly charming, but they are hardly the entire film. Gilbert is called upon to act a character who will experience young love but will also become a disillusioned soldier in battle. The love scenes, which come relatively early in the story, are sweet and funny, and the success with which Gilbert and Adorée enact them makes what follows—the horror of war—even more effective. They're playful with each other. He teaches her how to chew gum, and she, not understanding, swallows it. He kisses her and wins her heart with his shy yet purposeful manner. The fact that they are not supposed to understand each other fully because of their different languages lends an innocent quality to their wooing, making them seem inarticulate and thus inexperienced.

One of the most famous moments in movie history—and justly so—is the farewell scene in which Gilbert's unit is called up to battle and Adorée tries to find him to say good-bye. The couple have parted sadly because Gilbert is engaged to marry a girl back home, but when he is called up, they both realize their true feelings and in the chaos of departure try to find each other. Adorée searches hopelessly in the crowded streets of her village while men and machinery swirl past her in a blur. She's pushed along, pulled at by others, as she frantically calls his name and looks around everywhere, her head swiveling in a frenzy of fear that she won't find him. Meanwhile, he is up ahead, looking back, calling out her name. The tension builds through cutting until he finally spots her, jumps down off the truck he's climbed into, and runs back to her. They embrace, and he cries out, "I'm coming back—remember, I'm coming back!" Adorée won't let go of him, clinging to his leg as he climbs back up into the troop transport, hanging on to the truck as it begins to drive away, looking up at him, her face a mixture of love, fear, and pain. Finally, she can't keep up any longer and falls down in the dusty road, clutching the dog tags he's thrown to her and one of his old worn boots. (It's the boot that makes it perfect.) The scene ends with Adorée sunk to her knees in the dirty street, no one left but her. Audiences ate it up.

Despite these powerful moments of romance, Gilbert's finest acting is the scene in which, having gone out to rescue his buddy, only to find him dead, he pursues the German soldier who killed his friend. As they both crawl into the enemy trench, Gilbert draws a knife to kill, looking full into the face of the wounded and helpless enemy who is, in fact, also a young boy. As Gilbert hesitates and the two lock eyes, the boy makes the sign for a cigarette and Gilbert gives him one, lighting it for him. Half laughing at himself, still filled with rage at the death of his friend and obviously stunned by the madness of war, Gilbert plays the scene to perfection. (The German dies anyway.) After *The Big Parade*, Gilbert was given a four-year, million-dollar contract by MGM, proving his box office power.

In his next release, *La Bohème* (1926), the Gilbert "great-lover" acting style is on full display, and he is given star treatment. He is Rodolphe, the romantic hero, playing opposite the exquisite Lillian Gish as Mimi. Gilbert's presence is in the tradition of the 1920s matinee idol, but at the highest level of what that implies. He takes a wide-footed stance, hands on hips. He throws back his head, laughing gaily, his white teeth flashing. Playful and full of vitality, he is dressed in full-sleeved white blouses, big hats with feathers, and tall boots. In short, he sets a pose designed to capture female hearts. If this sounds dated and silly, it needs to be evaluated on its own terms, not today's. The issue is—can John Gilbert pull it off? He can. To watch him tackle the role of Rodolphe is to watch someone who understands and accepts fully the concept of romantic idol, and who plays it not only with pizzazz and dignity but with true and tangible conviction. For instance, in a playful picnic reminiscent of the one between him and Shearer in *He Who Gets Slapped*, Gilbert and Gish romp about on a happy outing in the country, Gish in gossamer white sleeves and little flowered cap and Gilbert in white blouse and artist's jabot. The two of them skip, dance, and play hide-and-seek in their pastoral paradise, and only their talent and complete acceptance of the action keeps it from being ridiculous. The sequence is beautifully, ethereally photographed in natural light to suggest innocence, happiness, and great purity. It is a romantic dream, shamelessly presented to viewers to touch their hearts as well as their libidos.

Renée Adorée
clings to Gilbert
in *The Big Parade*,
while outside the
Astor Theatre in
New York, mobs
line up to see
them (1925).

Gilbert and the exquisite Lillian Gish, and
the essential romantic Gilbert image, from *La Bohème*

In *La Bohème* can be seen what will become John Gilbert's complete
acting range in silent films. It is not so much a function of what he could do
but what he was asked to do, which in turn indicates what audiences wanted
him to do. First, he is young and athletic and devil-may-care, hanging out
with his male friends and living a boisterous life. Then, he meets The Woman
and goes into his second phase, in which his greatest natural ability is on display. He becomes a man suddenly inflamed by true love, changing from
capering boy into passionate man. He becomes John Gilbert, great
lover . . . and he is amazing. He takes his time with the feelings, looking long-
ingly at the woman, his eyes smoldering, lashes slightly fluttering. In *La
Bohème*, where the object is the somewhat sexless Gish, it takes everything
he's got. He draws her into his arms at a snail's pace, so everyone in the audience can fully savor what is coming. Then he starts murmuring words that the
audience naturally cannot hear but which they can surely imagine. Then he
starts to kiss her all over her arms and hands, then just her face, and then full
on her lips. This kind of slow, detailed lovemaking, seen in medium close-up
and lingered over, belongs totally to its time. Even now, however, it can be

appreciated for its sensuousness. Thinking about what it might have meant to audiences of its own day, it's easy to grasp Gilbert's impact. Women in the audience—and men—had never witnessed such behavior outside a movie theatre and had very likely never experienced anything quite like it either. It took people's breath away. After his "I'm in love" scenes, Gilbert usually was asked to go into the third phase of his three-step formula, which, alas, might be called "acting." He becomes angry, experiences grief, or goes berserk. In some of these scenes, he is over the top and somewhat hammy, though as his career progresses, he becomes better and better at handling them. What one sees in Gilbert's persona, which is fully in place with *La Bohème,* is the kind of man who is feminine in the sense that he totally embraces the concept of passion and emotion, yet who is totally masculine in his appreciation of a woman's allure and physical self.

By the middle of 1926, Gilbert was a top star whose only rival with women was the great Valentino. When Valentino died suddenly and tragically in August, Gilbert was left with the playing field all to himself, the undisputed king of the matinee idols. He became a major subject for the fan magazines, gossiped about, adored, and photographed everywhere he went. He received mountains of fan mail, most of it from women. Everyone knew John Gilbert. If he had never made another film, and never had anything sensational happen in his personal life, he would still be one of the primary names of 1920s film.

After *La Bohème,* Gilbert released one other highly successful movie, *Bardelys the Magnificent,* in 1926. Directed by King Vidor and based on a Rafael Sabatini novel, *Bardelys* is a celebrated "lost" film. A small clip of it exists in Vidor's Hollywood satire, *Show People,* with Gilbert looking handsome in his swashbuckling role. One review says, "John Gilbert shows that he has IT . . . he scores a 100% average in this work." And then Gilbert, the star, was paired with a young woman who was on her way up, and who would, of course, become one of the greatest stars in Hollywood's history, the one and only Greta Garbo. Pairing Gilbert and Garbo on-screen would have been exciting enough for fans, but there was an added dimension: off-screen, they fell in love, and Garbo would become the greatest love of Gilbert's private life. (Or so say some. Others believe it was Dietrich, or Ina Claire, or his beloved wife and the mother of his daughter, Leatrice Joy. Perhaps it was that Garbo became his greatest obsession.)

Clarence Brown, director of the movie in which they were first paired, *Flesh and the Devil* (reviewed in January 1927), described their love affair by saying, "They were in that blissful state of love which is so like a rosy cloud that they imagined themselves hidden behind it, as well as lost in it." The two stars were like teenagers. She called him "Yacky" and he called her "Flicka," the Swedish word for girl. Their romance was so hot that MGM rushed to pair them again immediately in a movie to be called *Love* (what else?). (Nobody

Gilbert with Eleanor Boardman in the lost King Vidor film, *Bardelys the Magnificent*

ever said the film business didn't know how to market its product.) By that time, Garbo was finished with Gilbert, but first there was *Flesh and the Devil*.

This film was the high point of Gilbert's romantic career. Its credits blazed "JOHN GILBERT in FLESH AND THE DEVIL with Greta Garbo" across the screen, which illustrates his star power: it was his movie, not hers. He exudes self-confidence in his performance, and he is physically at his peak—flat-stomached, handsome, and radiantly healthy. Everything in *Flesh and the Devil* is about love and passion, a love and passion that simply crowds everything else out of a man's life.

Garbo and Gilbert play long, detailed scenes of love. Gilbert's character, the young Leo, stops dead in his tracks when he first spots Garbo at a train station. He stands transfixed, jaw dropping, a perfect portrait of a romantic young man succumbing to love at first sight. He follows her to her car, picking up the bouquet she drops, boldly plucking one of the roses from it. When they meet again that evening at a ball, he is wearing his superbly tailored military uniform, and carrying the rose. Spotting Garbo through the crowd of dancers, he goes directly to her. There is nothing else in his world except her. He gathers her up into a majestic waltz, and as she enters his arms to become his partner, she almost lets her lips touch his. Off they go, round and round, again and again, and—like Elizabeth Taylor and Montgomery Clift dancing in *A Place in the Sun*—they make it clear to us how there is no one in the room but them. We feel their attraction. It becomes palpable, and real—which, of course, it was, as Garbo and Gilbert gave in to their true passion off-screen. Out they sweep into the moonlit night and into one of the most seductive love scenes ever shot on film. Moving forward through magnificent lighting by William Daniels, Garbo and Gilbert are two sensational-looking people who are shown to us in intense, half-lit close-ups. Deep in the garden, they speak. "Who are you?" Gilbert asks. "Does it matter?" she replies. "You are . . . very beautiful," he says, and she replies, "You are . . . very young."

If one had to choose a single scene to perfectly illustrate the no-holds-barred erotic romanticism of silent films, this would be the one. She places a cigarette between her lips, which are wet and open. Then she puts it in his mouth instead. He starts to light it and the light from the match illuminates their beautiful faces. She slowly blows it out, then remarks that blowing out a match is an "invitation to kiss." They come together in a lip-lock, up close and tactile. In today's world, where people disrobe and do everything right in front of us, it may be hard to imagine the impact of a scene like this on an audience. It was a time when couples still did not kiss in public, and to sit in the dark and be so close to such passionate intimacy must have been almost overwhelming.

A title card tells us, "The tragic, unquestioning . . . amusing love of youth. No one had ever loved before . . . Leo was sure of it." Following this, the audience was later treated to yet another hot love scene, the notorious one in Garbo's boudoir that most of the famous stills from the movie illustrate. Garbo is lying on her back against a brace of pillows, wearing a brocaded, sleeveless silk blouse. Gilbert sits on the floor, his head against her, the tunic of his uniform loosened, partially unbuttoned. He smokes, and the smoke curls upward about them, enveloping them in a kind of postcoital fog. Garbo plays with his hair. Suddenly, he takes her hand and places it over his mouth, not just kissing it but running her little finger back and forth, rubbing it sensuously over his lips, taking his time, focused on giving her pleasure. This kind of male character on film is the absolute embodiment of the female fan's fantasy of its time: a man who has a woman's appreciation of love and romance and its importance in the scheme of things—a man to shut out everything in his life except his love for one of her sex. Taking this kind of action is what a matinee idol was all about, and nobody did it better than John Gilbert.

The scene is interrupted soon enough. The lovers go on kissing, exchanging rings and sentiments, when suddenly a character we have been kept in the dark about enters the room. "This is Count Rhaden . . . my husband," says Garbo. Because silent films took so much time with the love scenes, played them out so slowly, in so much physical detail, the shock of the husband's arrival is all the greater, even though we have seen this unidentified character drive up outside and enter the building. Gilbert beautifully plays his surprise and shame, as he offers the husband satisfaction. The resulting duel ends in the husband's death and Gilbert's five-year banishment to Africa.

Gilbert and Garbo
make film history
in *Flesh and the
Devil* . . .

Meanwhile, we are given a glimpse into what kind of woman Garbo really is—
in case we were overlooking her carelessness in failing to mention that she
was married. She is seen trying on black hats with veils, admiring herself in
her widow's weeds. (She looks magnificent. An earlier title has explained to
viewers that "when the devil can't reach us through the spirit, he creates a
woman beautiful enough to reach us through the flesh." This is one of the better descriptions of Garbo's otherworldly beauty.)

    After the plot plays itself out, with Garbo marrying Gilbert's best friend
during his exile, there is yet one more great love scene. Wearing a magnificent
fur coat, Garbo has come to visit Gilbert while her new husband is in Munich.
Gilbert, a decent man who had been tricked by true love, is distressed. They
go outside to talk things over. A soft snow is falling. In his anguish, he walks
rapidly ahead of her. "I can't go on," she tells him. "You shall go on," he tells
her, and moves forward, while she scurries along behind. She's stumbling in
her thin, elegant, high-heeled silk shoes. He stalks grimly on. Her chiffon
scarf blows out of her fur pocket in the snowy wind. Gilbert, wrapped up in his
own 1920s fur coat, finally comes to a halt. She sees a fire in a conveniently
situated cottage, and in she goes, with him reluctantly following. Soon she's on
the floor in the firelight, and they're off again, two beautiful faces cheek to
cheek in the soft glow, with the snow flaking down outside.

    Garbo, playing a vain and shallow woman, finally gets her comeup-

. . . until the unexpected arrival of her husband (Marc MacDermott)

pance. While dashing across a frozen lake to stop the duel in which she expects her husband to kill Gilbert, she breaks through the ice and drowns, still in her magnificent coat, the greatest fur coat ever seen on screen. (The first time I saw this film, in about 1955, as Garbo fell through the ice a woman in the audience called out, "Quick! Save that fur!") Nothing is left of the selfish Garbo except her exquisite chiffon scarf, floating on top of the cold water, amidst the broken ice. Gilbert and his friend (Lars Hanson) reconcile. "Leo," says Hanson, "everything is suddenly clear to me." (This presumably ties up all the action and answers every question.)

Garbo became a star as a result of this film, and it's easy to see why. When she's preparing to run away with Gilbert and her husband unexpectedly presents her with a gorgeous diamond bracelet, she demonstrates the very best silent film acting technique. Having eased her husband out of her bedroom, she studies the bracelet, fingering it, trying it on, her face subtly revealing that she is only now realizing just what she will be giving up if she succumbs to her passion for Gilbert. When he arrives, she suggests that they abandon their flight and have an affair under her husband's nose instead. Somehow, Garbo makes this, if not acceptable to the viewer, at least understandable.

Flesh and the Devil was a huge hit, and Gilbert went on to make *The Show, Twelve Miles Out,* and *Man, Woman and Sin* in 1927, all three movies pairing him with significant costars in top productions. *The Show,* directed by

Tod Browning, reunited him with his *Big Parade* love interest, Renée Adorée, in a role for which he received good notices, but which, *Variety* thought, "will hurt his general popularity with the women, for while he is a great lover there is nothing romantic in the character." They were wrong, because the carnival barker he plays is a real Don Juan and the audience loved it. *Twelve Miles Out* put Gilbert "at his best," said critics, and paired him with the up-and-coming Joan Crawford, who earned rave reviews, with *Variety*, saying, "Two more pictures like this . . . and she's set." The movie was a lively story of modern pirates, giving Gilbert a chance at some comedy, some action, and also some typical love scenes. Viewed today, it is a startling movie, because of the intense close-ups of both Crawford (angular, strong) and Gilbert (soft, romantic) in one sequence aboard Gilbert's boat. They played well together, even though their face-offs are a bit like two different decades staring one another down.

Man, Woman and Sin paired him with the great stage star Jeanne Eagels. Eagels, a drug addict, was frankly reviewed as "looking haggard" and "contradicting the description in the subtitles." Perhaps because of her age and her diminishing looks, the movie cleverly reverses Gilbert's role. Openly representing itself as not much more than a woman's picture, the movie has Gilbert portraying a shy and virginal young man who is seduced by Eagels. Once smitten, however, he turns into the passionate Gilbert persona and the focus of attention shifts to him and away from her.

Gilbert's biggest movie of 1927, which opened almost simultaneously with *Man, Woman and Sin* in December of that year, was *Love*. *Variety* got right to the point in its review of December 7: "*Love* plus Gilbert, plus Garbo, is a clarion call to shoppers. Shoppers mean women, and women mean matinees. Big ones. Try and keep the femmes away from this one . . . The girls are going to pay off this production cost, and some more besides. And how often do the exhibs get a real 'matinee' picture?" The review also points out that crowds were standing two deep behind the last row in the 596-seat theatre the movie opened in, with SRO notices posted outside for several days in advance.

Here was perfect box office strategy. At the high point of the public's awareness of their love affair—and just as it was beginning to fizzle out on Garbo's part—MGM paired Garbo and Gilbert in this silent version of *Anna Karenina*. Directed by Edmund Goulding and written for the screen by Frances Marion, *Love* is the sort of literary adaptation that has given Hollywood a bad name in English classes. Although in the versions of the movie released in Europe, Anna does indeed throw herself under the train, the American version presented an upbeat ending in which Karenin is dead, Anna's little boy is happy as a clam at military school, Vronsky is back in the fold with his regiment, and Anna herself, decked out in an excellent outfit, arrives to be swept up in her lover's arms forever and ever. *Love*, nevertheless,

may be said to understand its job in adaptation: Wipe out all subplots. Eliminate all politics. Cut down on the moralizing. Reduce the pain level, and give
Garbo and Gilbert lots of lingering close-ups, faces backlit, and dressed in
great clothes. This is what the audience wanted to see—a story about LOVE
with two stars in LOVE on-screen and in LOVE off-screen. To hell with Tolstoy.

   Love fully illustrates why Gilbert was a big star. To find a partner for the
exquisite Garbo, someone equally beautiful and romantic, was not easy, and it
was especially difficult in the silent era, when the audience could stare at her
astonishing face in quiet privacy. What Gilbert had was the male equivalent
of Garbo's beauty and grace, and her ability to embody the concept of
romance, romance, romance. And he had another important plus: he seemed,
somehow, to believe in all of it. He never showed the slightest sense of discomfort in his stiff military uniforms, nor was there ever a touch of irony or
self-mockery. He never tips a wink at the audience, the way Valentino and
John Barrymore do—he just gives himself totally to the romantic excess, and
given the fact that the audience knew he was really in love with Garbo, the
movie worked beyond all logical expectations.

   In *Love*, everyone seems to know what to do. The action begins in a
beautiful, whirling Russian snowstorm, with sleighs dashing through the cold,
the occupants swathed in furs and robes. To ward off the stinging snowflakes,
Garbo's face is wrapped in a chiffon veil so that when she and Gilbert,
stranded, meet and are forced to take shelter at an inn together, he cannot see
her. The buildup comes: they enter, register, have their things taken to their
rooms. As they move toward the huge fireplace to get warm, he chatters away,
starting to light a candle. Then he turns, and she has removed her veil. Great
balls of fire—she's Garbo! And she never looked more stunningly beautiful.
Garbo's face is a showstopper in any scene, but here she is simply ravishing.
Yet Gilbert can match her. As he stares at her, his eyes widening, softening,
the match he is holding burns his finger. He shakes it off with a shudder that
indicates what else is passing through his body—a totally emotional response
to her face. His own face, also seen in radiantly beautiful close-up, softly, subtly registers the emotions of a man who is falling hopelessly, helplessly in
thrall to a magnificent woman he is seeing for the first time. It is a conspiracy
of actress, actor, writer, director, producer, cameraman, designers to present
to the audience a moment of the most intense emotional meaning.

   This scene will not be the only time Garbo and Gilbert and crew rise to
the occasion (slight as the occasion may be) in *Love*. There are many close-ups
of the two stars at the peak of their physical attractiveness and at the peak of
their physical awareness of each other. Gilbert looks Garbo up and down in
one scene, smiling at her, his eyes first devilish, then smoldering, then dumb
with love. He later takes her in his arms to whirl her around the dance floor.
Their two profiles are in full display, with Gilbert in the stiff collar of his

Gilbert as passionate
lover in *The Show,*
with Renée Adorée,
and (OPPOSITE) as
action hero in *Twelve
Miles Out,* with Joan
Crawford and Ernest
Torrence

impeccable white dress uniform, Garbo's enhanced by a dress with a high,
stiff standaway lace collar. *Love* is an exploitation film—using Tolstoy as a
footstool on which to rest the beauty and sexuality and love of Greta Garbo
and John Gilbert. Without Gilbert, however, it couldn't possibly work, which
is not to diminish the work of anyone else, and certainly not the remarkable
Greta Garbo. The point is that Garbo is Garbo—she's in a class by herself.
And her perfect partner in silent film was John Gilbert, whose contributions
have consistently been underrated.

    Garbo and Gilbert were declared the perfect movie love team, but by the
time MGM put them together yet again, in late 1928, their romance was at last
completely over.* Released in early 1929, the movie was *A Woman of Affairs,*
based on Michael Arlen's best-selling novel *The Green Hat.* It boasts the usual
quality production from MGM, with gowns by Adrian, sets by Cedric Gibbons,

---

*Gilbert's other 1928 releases were *The Cossacks,* with Renée Adorée, *Four Walls,* with Joan
Crawford, and *Masks of the Devil,* with Alma Rubens. About *The Cossacks, Variety* pointed out
that "the flaps who want to see John Gilbert mauling some dame in hot love scenes may not
fancy this" because he played a Russian villager thought to be a physical coward until trouble
comes and he surprises everyone, even kicking around his own father. A plus was supposed to
be "real Russian" horsemen who did the riding stunts. In *Four Walls,* he was a gangster, with
Crawford playing what one reviewer called "a round-heeled frail." *Masks of the Devil* was a
more fully romantic role, in which he was a libertine whose innocent face masked an ugly soul,
a variation on the *Picture of Dorian Gray* theme.

and photography by William Daniels. Gilbert and Garbo stand opposite each other in cavernous rooms done in art deco, and they wear fantastic hats, sleek coats, and superb formal dress. Gilbert looks particularly good in a 1920s tuxedo . . . but the two of them have precious little to do. The film is more Garbo's than Gilbert's, and his role gives him only odd moments in which to shine. One of these, however, demanded considerable subtlety. Having abandoned Garbo to please his father, he is preparing, seven years later, to marry the wholesome Dorothy Sebastian. When Garbo turns up to claim the help of her old friend, a doctor played by Lewis Stone, Gilbert, Sebastian, and the nosy-Parker father are at Stone's house. After Stone rushes off to Garbo's aid, the father seizes the moment to speak cruelly of her morals. Up until then Gilbert has been an all-cool dinner guest, impeccably dressed, charming and controlled, attentive to his intended bride. And he has appeared more or less indifferent to the news that Garbo has been in the house. But when his father speaks ill of her, his eyes take on a smoldering anger, very low-key. His mouth twists in a small smile of rage and resentment, and he speaks up for her in an offhand, yet revealing way. His performance here is in no sense of the term old-fashioned, and it is specific, clear, and precise in what it conveys to a viewer. Most of the time, however, Gilbert is either embracing Garbo or walking around in very good white flannels. Perhaps he is a bit bored, but that isn't inappropriate to many of his character's scenes.

Gilbert as the passionate lover: (ABOVE) with Greta Garbo in *A Woman of Affairs*,
and Joan Crawford in *Four Walls*; (BELOW) again with Garbo, in *Love*,
and with Renée Adorée in *The Cossacks*

By the time *Woman of Affairs* was finished, the public had become aware that the romance between John Gilbert and Greta Garbo was finished, too. (Many feel it was an even briefer affair than this, and sources differ on almost all the circumstances involving their liaison.) Rumors say that Gilbert got Garbo further than any other man—to the doorway of a justice of the peace— only to have her turn around and bolt at the last minute. Clearly he wanted to marry her and had no qualms about marrying so famous an actress. (In fact, all of Gilbert's wives were prominent actresses: Leatrice Joy, Ina Claire, and Virginia Bruce.) Garbo seems to have gotten under his skin. After their breakup, he soldiered on bravely amidst the luxury of Hollywood, becoming famous for his extravagant lifestyle, his generous hosting, and his madcap party-going. Sadly, he also gained notoriety for his heavy drinking, becoming an alcoholic, the fate of another matinee idol, John Barrymore.

In early May of 1929, reviewers addressed the quality of John Gilbert's final silent film, *Desert Nights*. "No Dialogue," screamed a headline beneath the film's title, and the opening words of the review state clearly, "Without benefit of dialogue, *Desert Nights* leans heavily upon its star and cast." Technology had already rendered a death blow to Gilbert's career, and the movie was not accepted on its own terms. It is actually quite an entertaining story, involving a clever band of diamond thieves who take mine-manager Gilbert hostage to secure their escape. Obsessed with the new dimension of sound, the review went on to explain that the exhibition theatre had "made a synchronized score . . . and this may be helpful on the sound angle." Sound had taken over motion pictures.

Gilbert's first appearance before his adoring public as an actor who could talk was in *Hollywood Revue of 1929,* in which silent stars more or less debuted anew, each singing, dancing, speaking, declaiming, or playing some role that seemed suited to his or her persona. Trial balloons were being sent up. Gilbert appeared, romantically dressed and coiffed, opposite Norma Shearer in the balcony scene from *Romeo and Juliet.* Considering that he had no formal stage training of any kind, he handles the lines well, and he speaks clearly in a somewhat "light" voice, but certainly not a "high and squeaky" one. Reviewers commented that this sequence, done in early two-strip Technicolor and directed by Lionel Barrymore, was "excellent" and "is played seriously"—which, if people had been laughing at Gilbert, would not have been said. Neither the *New York Times* nor *Variety* suggested that Gilbert's voice was inappropriate for the new medium.

The successful delivery of sound dialogue needs a certain nonchalance, an ease with words. Since the medium takes viewers in close to the actor, there is no need for declaiming or hitting a point so the back row won't miss it. The medium calls for naturalism, behavior that people in the audience somehow take for the essence of the actor. Gilbert does not lack an ease with words, but his strength lay elsewhere. He was best at conveying emotion directly through physical behavior and action—through his face and eyes, through taking Garbo's hand and rubbing her finger over his lips. Sound was a different world, and accordingly it called for changes in movie acting. Silent film actors and actresses needed visual eloquence to be great, but on the other hand, they could get away with a very narrow range if they had superb looks. Much of what the general audience required from its silent stars was outstanding beauty and sex appeal, at least until they grew sated with merely looking at pretty faces.

Gilbert's sound debut seemed to go well enough, if not brilliantly, and after all, he *was* hugely popular. Then he made his first full-length talking appearance, in *His Glorious Night* in 1929, followed by *Redemption* (1930), *Way for a Sailor* (1930), *Gentleman's Fate* (1931), *Cheri Bibi,* also known as *The Phantom of Paris* (1931), *West of Broadway* (1931), *Downstairs* (1932), *Fast Workers* (1933), *Queen Christina* (1933), and his last film, *The Captain Hates the Sea* (1934). This means that he made, not counting *Hollywood Revue,* ten movies in about five years. His career was hardly dead. The problem may have been that, just as sound unleashed the tough-talking gangster movie and the wisecracking musical, Gilbert's first two features were dated in content. *His Glorious Night* was given a royal pan: "A few more talker productions like this and John Gilbert will be able to change places with Harry Langdon. His prowess at lovemaking, which has held the stenos breathless, takes on a comedy aspect . . . that gets the gum chewers tittering at first, then laughing outright at the very false ring of the couple of dozen 'I love you' phrases." Gilbert's voice is seen as "passable" but his dialogue is called rotten. "The love lines, about pulsating blood, hearts and dandelions, read far better than they sound from under the dainty Gilbertian moustache." (The movie is a story about a princess and a captain who is an imposter.)

In *Redemption,* his next film, Gilbert plays a man who arranges to have his wife and friends believe he is dead. Based on Tolstoy's drama *The Living Corpse* (a prophetic title in Gilbert's life), it too received poor reviews. The *New York Times* said that Gilbert's "cheerfulness is not natural and his habit of smiling and laughing strikes one as though he did so to conceal his own nervousness." The final blow was sneering that when Gilbert's character finally commits suicide, "few persons who see this picture" will regret it.

It is clear that he was being given the kind of material he handled so well in the silent years, but that the times—and new technology—had made it seem old-fashioned. The public, as if ashamed of themselves for having liked such stuff, quickly abandoned it and embraced the new. They had outgrown Gilbert. He was their teenage crush, the man they had loved in the innocent days in which movies had no voice, and by the time he started playing more suitable sound roles, the damage had been done. His next picture, *Way for a Sailor,* found him supported by Wallace Beery, Jim Tully, Polly Moran, Leila

Hyams, and Doris Lloyd, all strong sound players with lively personae. Reviews say Gilbert "gives a better performance than he did in his previous audible production," and the story line—a kind of mixture of low comedy and light romance—places him on a freighter with a lot of rowdy shipmates. There's a big shipwreck, scenes of men working on the freighter, and lively action. By then, alas, it was too late.

One of Gilbert's typical sound films was *Downstairs,* based on a story he wrote himself. In it, he plays a cad, a conniving chauffeur who preys on women. (Gilbert still has billing over the title, so how far had he really fallen?) His costars are Paul Lukas and the beautiful Virginia Bruce, who would become his last wife. Gilbert still looks debonair and well dressed. His voice is not a heavy masculine voice, but it sounds just fine, and not inappropriate for the character he is playing. What is lacking is the fire and intensity he exhibited in silent films, his sense of totally believing in what he was doing. Yet he has an easy, nonchalant manner, and seems modern enough. (He was actually more dated in his performance in *Queen Christina,* something of a return to the type of role he had played in silent film.) He looks a bit tired, and occasionally has dark circles under his eyes, and sometimes he is a little wooden, or even a little dull. What is missing is the dash and flash of his silent lovers, the old swagger, the old self-confidence. Gilbert is fine, but he's just another leading man.

What really happened to Gilbert's career is still unclear. Various reasons for his precipitous drop from the very top in 1927 to a frustrated death in 1936 have been put forth over the years. There is the "victim of sound" theory, by which his voice at best "does not suit his image" or "did not record well with the initial crude equipment." There is his bad luck at having his first release be the Graustarkian and old-fashioned *His Glorious Night,* when the more believable movie he had actually shot first, *Redemption,* might have fared better at the box office. There is also his unpleasant relationship with the powerful head of MGM, Louis B. Mayer, who is alleged to have sabotaged him, preventing him from obtaining suitable sound roles and assigning him to several unworthy, low-budget projects. Finally, there is Gilbert's own personality. He was often rumored to be temperamental and difficult to work with (although his friends adored him), and he was said to be insecure, uneducated, and addicted to alcohol.

Each of these arguments can be refuted: his voice is not bad; he did have some good roles in sound, and Garbo insisted on his starring opposite her in *Queen Christina* in 1933; *Redemption* isn't really much better than *His Glorious Night;* and other stars lived down awkward sound debuts and personal problems. As to Mayer's contentious relationship with him, he was not the only star to have that problem, and in *An Evening's Entertainment,* Richard Koszarski points out that Mayer had a 10 percent share in the profits

Gilbert with Garbo
in one of his few
sound successes,
Queen Christina

from Gilbert's films, and Irving Thalberg had 5 percent. Koszarski's good
sense and solid historical research lead him to conclude:

> Conspiracy buffs attribute too much wisdom and foresight to
> Mayer. The fact is, most silent stars were very badly presented in
> their early talkies, even those producing their own films. Pickford,
> Gish, Swanson, Talmadge, Lloyd, Keaton and Gilbert were only
> some of those whose talking picture debuts were far below their
> usual standard . . . John Gilbert was a victim of the inability of
> Hollywood's best minds to predict a method of pushing silent stars
> to the edge of talkies.

No doubt it is the sum of all these possible explanations that did Gilbert
in: his voice, his alcoholism, the changing times, Mayer, and disappointed
audience expectations—all these combined are why his great career collapsed so suddenly. And yet studying Gilbert's silent films and his sound work
leads me to think that, despite everything, the original idea may be the correct
one. It *was* sound that killed Gilbert. Not because he had a bad voice or a high
voice and not because his sound roles were silly, since some of them (*Captain
Hates the Sea, Downstairs*) are quite entertaining and modern, and he's good
in them. It was sound that killed him because sound diminished John Gilbert.
Two other big matinee idols of the day were *not* diminished by it—Ronald
Colman and John Barrymore. Their extensive stage training and experience,
their beautiful voices, and their filmed images could carry forward. Barrymore

more or less ceased being a matinee idol when sound came in, but he became a great character actor *and* a romantic leading man. Colman developed a fine gift for comedy, as well as going on with his romantic leads. Barrymore's looks were adaptable to villains, rogues, and comedy characters as well as to leading men, and Colman's excellent timing and line delivery gave him the ability to play in a wide range, from Raffles to François Villon. Gilbert could be a cad, but he wasn't suitable for villainy, and he had only a minor comedy gift. His true forte was as the fulsome romantic idol. Sound added nothing to his ability to convey a man in love, to present a sensuous, impassioned romantic. On the contrary, sound subtracted heavily from it.

Whatever it was that happened, Gilbert's career slowly died. He languished at home, drinking heavily. On March 20, 1934, he took out an ad on the back page of the *Hollywood Reporter* that said, "Metro-Goldwyn-Mayer will neither offer me work nor release me from my contract. Signed, Jack Gilbert." After Garbo had helped him get the romantic lead opposite her in *Queen Christina*, he saw the billing: "Greta Garbo in *Queen Christina* with John Gilbert" where once it had been "John Gilbert in *Flesh and the Devil* with Greta Garbo." "Oh, what the hell," said Gilbert. "They liked me once. A man is an ass to squawk about life. Especially me."

Various accounts have been given of Gilbert's final years of misery. His daughter, Leatrice Joy Gilbert Fountain, wrote of his bleeding ulcers and chronic insomnia, and others of his severe alcoholism. In a November 1992 article entitled "Remembering Marlene," Fountain quoted director William Dieterle's conversation with her, forty years after the fact, recounting how he had told Dietrich of Gilbert's plight. "I told Marlene . . . 'There Gilbert sits in his palazzo on top of the mountain. He still looks wonderful, he's only thirty-five years old, all the talent still there, the wit, the intellect. But it's like a spell has been cast, those last bad years at MGM destroyed something in the center of him. We all used to drink. My God, how we drank, but Jack couldn't stop. He drank till he threw up blood, till he was totally unconscious. You'd look at this handsome guy with all the parts still together, it was unbelievable what happened to him.' " According to Fountain, Dietrich immediately tried to rehabilitate Gilbert, and they had a short, satisfying affair during which time he began to thrive again. She tried to help his career, and it says a great deal for Gilbert that powerful stars like Dietrich and Garbo went out of their way to help him.

Gilbert reputedly studied with sound coaches and vocal experts, but somehow nothing worked for him after the silent era. He had always had a mercurial temperament, which was part of what gave him his spark on-screen, and losing his first-rank status so rapidly unnerved him. Observers remarked how he changed from the happy-go-lucky guy who drove onto the MGM lot with his car top down, waving to fans and fellow employees, into an angry loner who wore his hat pulled down low over his eyes as he avoided contact with anyone. (Ironically, Gilbert and John Barrymore were neighbors, and in these last sad years of Gilbert's life, the two idols were said to be drinking buddies.) Then, on January 6, 1936, John Gilbert died at home, very suddenly, from a heart attack. Some say he died of a broken heart, a man who never understood what had happened to him. He was certainly not destitute, but the things he needed most—attention and fame—had abandoned him. He had been replaced by different kinds of leading men: Clark Gable, James Cagney, Fred Astaire, Dick Powell, Wallace Beery, Joe E. Brown, and Will Rogers, all on the list of top-ten box office draws of 1935. Adela Rogers St. Johns said of him, "He grew up with motion pictures and loved them and belonged to them. He wasn't any New York stage actor who came into Hollywood for money. He didn't look down on Hollywood. He looked up to it. He believed in movies as a great new art that belonged to the people and was closer to them, and gave them more real happiness than the other arts."

On that basis, Gilbert may yet have the last laugh. *The Big Parade, The Merry Widow,* and *Flesh and the Devil* are among the most revived and best known of all silent films (together with the great comedies, some of Chaney's work, and the major Griffith efforts). He had the good fortune to work with excellent directors, writers, and designers at MGM, and he costarred with the most beautiful and successful women of the day. His films were directed by King Vidor, Clarence Brown, John Ford, Tod Browning, Edmund Goulding, Victor Seastrom, Erich von Stroheim, Monta Bell, Maurice Tourneur, Jack Conway, and in the sound era, Rouben Mamoulian and Lewis Milestone. His costars included Norma Shearer, Joan Crawford, Lillian Gish, Jeanne Eagels, Renée Adorée, and, of course, Garbo. The revivals of his movies can put the lie to much that has been said about him, because in them he remains splendid: vibrant and romantic, handsome and untouched by time.

JOHN GILBERT wasn't the only matinee idol of the silent era, of course. There were plenty of good-looking men for the matinee crowd to enjoy—such as John Barrymore, Conrad Nagel, Richard Dix, and others. Two of the handsomest were Milton Sills and Thomas Meighan. Sills was the "strong, silent type" and he was a very popular star in his day. Six feet tall and stalwart-looking, he played opposite Clara Kimball Young in *Eyes of Youth* and Colleen Moore in *Flaming Youth.* He was definitely a major star until his untimely death at the age of forty-eight in 1930. Meighan had curly hair, masculine good looks of the Irish type, and an easy-going, natural style on film. He appeared in movies from 1914 to 1935, and his filmography—a large one—includes such well-known titles as *Miracle Man, Male and Female, Why Change Your Wife?,* and *Manslaughter.* He wanted to quit films when talkies came in, but his stage background made him a natural for sound. As he grew older, he shifted to character roles and simply kept going, becoming a wealthy man. He was stricken with pneumonia in 1935, and lingered on until his death in July of 1936 at the age of fifty-seven.

Three other male stars who were labeled matinee idols by the fan magazines of the day were Francis X. Bushman (one of the first of the type), Wallace Reid (the most tragic), and Ronald Colman (the one who managed to carry over into a major sound career).

Bushman was the greatest matinee idol of the early years, coming to films with experience both as a stage actor and as a sculptor's model. He was a big, good-looking man, a perfect sex object, so movies cast him almost exclusively in romantic roles. Looking good in tights and capes, he appeared in costume dramas and in Ruritanian romantic adventures. Bushman was one of the first fan magazine heroes, and his marriage to his leading lady, Beverly Bayne, was kept secret, as early press agents feared that if the women in his adoring public found out he was married, he would lose his appeal for them. Bushman, like Barrymore after him, was famous for his sharply delineated "classic" profile, but he would go unrecognized today except for his role as the villainous Messala in *Ben-Hur* (1926). (It's odd that he's best remembered as Messala, since he seldom played villains.)

Wallace Reid, called "the screen's most perfect lover" by *Motion Picture* in 1919, played a type of lead that was indigenous to the late teens and early twenties. Richard Koszarski defines him as "the final heir to the 'Arrow Collar' tradition of motion-picture stardom," by which was meant

> strong-jawed, all-American figures [that] exuded stability, friendliness, optimism, and reliability. He was at home in overalls or evening clothes and did very nicely in a uniform when the occasion arose. Their imitators were legion and, to modern eyes, indistinguishable. Few silent-film historians spend much time on these men or their films, but occasional lip service is paid to the last and greatest of them, Wallace Reid.

Reid, an unpretentious and likable actor, came from a show business family, and brought an ease to the business of performing that stood out among less comfortable, flashier actors. Although he came to epitomize the "all-American," he was also a matinee idol. The fan magazines described him glowingly as beloved by his mother—an expert swimmer, boxer, and dancer—an artist who was adept in oils—a daredevil who could drive a fast motorcar (*and* repair it). In an early *Photoplay,* Laurence Quirk said that the camera "caught a lovable quality in the man and reflected it on the screen." Reid married Dorothy Davenport, a young woman who also came from a prominent acting family, and the Reids were a glamorous couple about town. Reid became so popular during the period from 1915 to 1922 that he appeared in an amazing number of features—six in 1916, ten in 1917; he has been identi-fied as having appeared in over one hundred films prior to his role of Jeff the blacksmith in *The Birth of a Nation*.

Most historians feel that Reid might not be remembered, however, if he had not become the protagonist of one of Hollywood's earliest and most dra-matic tragedies. In 1919, he was injured when a special train carrying a com-pany to a location shooting was wrecked. In order to enable him to keep working until the movie was finished, a studio doctor prescribed morphine, and continued the dosage long past the safety point. Reid became an addict, and then started drinking to hide the addiction. He kept on working, making nine features in 1922, but finally collapsed during production, and the truth leaked out. Run-down and ill, Reid contracted the flu, went into a coma, and died on January 18, 1923, at the age of thirty and at the top of his fame. Later, his widow made his story known in order to educate others, and she kept his name and reputation alive for later generations. Reid, in fact, left behind a large and respectable filmography, including *Carmen, Joan the Woman, Affairs of Anatol,* and *The Birth of a Nation,* but when he is remembered at all today, it is largely for the scandal surrounding his secret addiction.

The very handsome Ronald Colman was a strong leading man during the last years of the silent era. Like all true matinee idols of those days, he was an exceedingly handsome man who wore clothes well and whose stance was grace-ful, poised, and soigné. He is solid in silent films, but his career was made by sound, when his distinctive voice, coupled with his highly nuanced and subtle delivery of lines, made him a top-level star and ultimate Oscar winner.

OF ALL THE MALE STARS labeled "matinee idols" or treated as sex symbols for women, the one who escaped both the limitations and history's scorn is John Barrymore, partly because he came from such a distinguished acting family. Although ultimately he got stuck with his own label—bad-boy brother of noble Ethel and sober Lionel—John Barrymore's name still has cachet. He is thought of as a glamorous figure, colorful and witty (though alcoholic). Bar-rymore's legend has endured. He is a "great actor" and Gilbert is only a "great movie star." These are two different things, not incompatible, and despite what some people think, not unequal either. In their day, Barrymore was not as big a movie star as Gilbert, but he was even then considered to be *the* name at Warner Brothers, his studio during the 1920s. He became Warners' most prestigious property, and they billed him as "The World's Greatest Actor." The Barrymore trio were the Royal Family of Broadway, and everyone in the movie business was suitably impressed. (These highfalutin credentials were sometimes said to have kept audiences outside the big cities away from Barry-more's movies, however, and this is one of the reasons why he never gained the box office status that Gilbert achieved.) Barrymore's acting ability was never

questioned in Hollywood, and he was always treated with the respect that his
theatrical lineage and his theatrical triumphs brought to the relatively new
medium.

Barrymore and Gilbert are two different types of matinee idols. Gilbert
was the man whose basic business is love; Barrymore was the man whose
basic business was giving a good performance. If love came into it, he played
it honestly and passionately, giving the ladies their lover—but if he could be
Mr. Hyde as well as Dr. Jekyll, he put his maximum energy into Mr. Hyde.
Gilbert is the movie version of the matinee idol par excellence, one of the earliest stars to give the term power. Barrymore is closer to the original theatrical
concept—a performer who is handsome, but who is first and foremost an actor
and secondarily a romantic object. Today we think of him primarily as a stage
actor, born into the profession; we've more or less forgotten that he was also a
matinee idol, known as "The Great Profile." Although Barrymore entered
movies in a period in which a man who was handsome—and thus a sex symbol—could still be taken seriously as an actor, his extraordinary good looks
meant inevitably that he would become a matinee idol. (In his autobiography,
Adolph Zukor called Barrymore "the handsomest man in the world, but a per-
fectionist, and a temperamental one at that.")

Barrymore lived with the label, and certainly enjoyed wowing the ladies
in his private life, but on-screen he seemed to take perverse joy in wrecking
his own looks, in twisting himself into old men, crazy men, mercenary men,
ugly men. He's the Lon Chaney of the tuxedo set. Dramatically handsome, and
making the most of his "Great Profile" identity, he played romance willingly,
and he could enter a drawing room and occupy the space as well as anyone
ever did. But he never relied on his looks alone to create a role, and he always
seems to have more fun with the parts that gnarl and twist him.

Barrymore appears in very few silent films—only twenty-two—and in a
remarkable number of them, he creates a dual personality, an opposite self,
or a masquerade of some sort so he can be both an idol *and* an actor. When
he was given a standard romantic role with no room to maneuver, he sometimes mocked himself, although without ever losing the larger meaning of his
role. It is clear from his silent career that in some way he wanted to deny the
audience his handsome profile—or at least make them wait for it. Yet despite
this tendency to fight his own looks, and despite his reputation as a serious
performer, the fan magazines always categorized him as a matinee idol. (The
August 1923 *Motion Picture* admitted that he was "greater than a matinee
idol" because "he is one of our greatest living artists," but six months later
the magazine reverted to form with a full-page glamorous portrait of him in
full profile and a caption that read "John Barrymore, the matinee idol.")

Looking at Barrymore as the gentleman thief, Raffles, in 1917, makes an
interesting comparison with Gilbert. He is a handsome figure with a dramatic

and sensational profile which is amply on display. He is adept at holding the moment: he remains still, concentrated, conveying an animal intensity underneath the most polished manner. His forte is intensity under control, and his appeal as a matinee idol no doubt partly stemmed from this, because women in the audience could sense the passion inside society's very best, most tailored clothes. (Inside that tuxedo beat the heart of a tiger!) This calmness is a large part of Barrymore's skill, and he had learned it from years of theatre work, of walking on and taking command, of knowing what to do, how to wait, how to control an audience. While everyone else in the movie hovers about, fluttering and fussing, Barrymore stands still, holding all attention to himself. When he does burst out—which he does—the result is stunning. Unfortunately, it can seem like too much, as, working in the tradition of the stage of an earlier time, he sometimes appears to overact wildly, with broad stage gestures and exaggerated facial expressions designed to be seen in the back row. But he always commands attention and seems to be utterly relaxed about it, casual even, almost cruelly uninterested in his audience. He looks fabulous in his tuxedo, and he can stand calmly smoking a cigarette with all the self-confidence in the world. "I can smoke better than most people can act," he seems to be implying.

Unlike Gilbert, Barrymore does not have the typical kind of charisma we associate with movie stardom—the understated, low-key, naturalistic behavior that binds us to star personalities and makes us feel that they are talking directly to us. He remains, instead, the consummate master of stage acting, which he shrewdly adapts to the movie format (and, of course, ultimately exploits at the end of his career when he begins to play "ham actors"). Barrymore doesn't have star radiance, he has stage presence; he stands out by some inborn grace and elegance, some inherent sense of his own royalty, the royalty of the theatre. In a flamboyant era, he could be extremely dramatic, but he could also take the tiniest gesture—the raising of one of his highly mobile eyebrows—and make it huge.

One of Barrymore's greatest hits was his 1920 version of Robert Louis Stevenson's *Dr. Jekyll and Mr. Hyde,* which received rave reviews. The *New York Times* gushingly refers to the "excellence of the photoplay," to Barrymore's "flawless performance," and to its being "something special and extraordinary." *Dr. Jekyll and Mr. Hyde,* depending on your feelings about a certain style of performing, is either one of John Barrymore's best films or one of his worst. Taking it on its own terms and placing it within the proper context, the former is a more appropriate assessment than the latter. As the celebrated scientist who searches for a way to separate the good and the evil in a man, Barrymore has the opportunity to present his two selves to the public. One is the young and handsome Barrymore, the one with The Great Profile, the matinee idol who plays the romantic lead. The other is the Barrymore who enjoys hiding behind false noses, domed heads, warts, and a misshapen body. It's a perfect vehicle for his talents, and illustrates how, although he played his love scenes well and there is a romantic aspect to the story, he himself emphasized the evil character.

As *Dr. Jekyll and Mr. Hyde* opens, a title warns us, "What we want to be, we *are*." The handsome and charitable young Dr. Jekyll is at work in his lab, where a fellow doctor is giving him the usual horror film warnings: "Damn it, I don't like it. You're tampering with the supernatural . . . Stick to the positive sciences, Jekyll!" Convinced by a worldly friend that "the only way to get rid of a temptation is to yield to it," Jekyll begins his experiments and soon enough wakens "his baser emotions." His goal—"to yield to every evil impulse—yet leave the soul untouched"—leads him to opium dens, prostitutes, and the company of Gina, an "Italian dancing girl who faced her world alone" (Nita Naldi).

To turn into Mr. Hyde, Barrymore undergoes a famous on-screen transformation, done without makeup alterations until the moment when a cut provides the viewer with a medium close-up in which he has added warts, new hair, and a false nose. What the audience sees when Jekyll turns into Hyde is a perfect tour de force of silent era/twenties stage acting. Having prepared a vial of his formula, Barrymore backs away from it, stares at it, and then strides purposefully toward it as it rests on his laboratory table. He hesitates dramatically, then lifts it, tilts his head back, and drains it. An immediate physical jolt hits his entire body. The handsome young man in the dressing gown begins to fall backward, head down, his hand at his throat. He then twists forward, his hands flailing, his hair flying loose. He clutches his head, writhing, his body going into spasms. His hair falls forward. He covers his face with his hands, as the twitching continues. Brushing back the hair, he slowly begins to rise. The young, pure-faced man with the noble mien has been replaced by an older person with a demonic stare—an entirely different creature. His eyes now look crazy. His mouth is fixed into an evil grin, and his hands are like claws. Then a cut takes the viewer close, and hideous makeup has been added to completely alter his appearance. To watch Barrymore enact this transformation without sound effects, color filters, superimpositions, or camera tricks is an awesome experience. Small and perfectly formed, with great physical control, he uses his entire body as a single unit of expression.

Barrymore's great strength as a silent film actor lay in this uncanny ability to change himself physically right before the audience's eyes. He was the master of transformation, but unlike Chaney's, his mastery is psychological more than physical. Barrymore is a man who must have thought of acting as more than a job in which you pretend to be someone else. For him, it was a job in which you *became* somebody else. Before method, he *was* method, although he surely would have denied it.

John Barrymore as
villain (LEFT) and
romantic idol
(BELOW), in *Dr.
Jekyll and Mr. Hyde*

Barrymore's last silent film, *Eternal Love* (1929), was directed by the great Ernst Lubitsch. It is not distinguished material, and only the combined talents of star and director keep it from being extremely dull. Even in its own time, reviewers complained about the "sentimentality" of its ending, in which a pair of doomed lovers pray to God for rescue from an angry mob and receive God's answer—an avalanche—by kissing, embracing, and walking joyously to their death. Both Barrymore and Lubitsch are pros who know what they are doing. Lubitsch's direction is tasteful and inherently cinematic, and Barrymore could play a role in which he conveyed passionate love—and an outsider's high spirits—in his sleep by this point. Watching *Eternal Love*, however, it's easy to conclude that it's time for Barrymore to move beyond the "matinee idol" label. He's too professional to turn in a lackluster performance, but one senses his awareness that this type of material is soon to be outdated. He seems to enjoy some drunk scenes, no doubt playing from an accurate grasp of the condition. In other moments, although handsome and quite virile, he flails about, swinging his arms wildly, and overworking his eyebrows. Clearly he's become bored with his "matinee idol" status.

Sound arrived in the nick of time to revive Barrymore's interest in his movie career. Both he and Gilbert started their sound careers in showcase films by reciting Shakespeare, and both made debut sound features that were period costume dramas. But whereas Gilbert was not accepted, Barrymore was embraced. He thrived in sound. His beautiful voice was one of his greatest assets, and his ability to deliver dialogue was a talent he had been born with. He played a wide range of roles in the early years of sound, enjoying success as the demonic hypnotist in *Svengali* (1931); the wonderful crook in *Arsène Lupin* (1932), in which his brother, Lionel, played his nemesis; the baron forced to become a thief (opposite Garbo) in *Grand Hotel* (1932); the wealthy criminal lawyer in *State's Attorney* (1932); and the troubled father of Katharine Hepburn in her debut film, *A Bill of Divorcement* (1932). Barrymore was never the victim of sound—only of his own excesses. He knew how to channel his flamboyance into a vocal advantage, simply turning his characters into theatrical types who were verbally overbearing but appealing. He shrewdly incorporated the label "matinee idol" into his bag of tricks. It became one of the characters he played, and thus he was the label's master, not its victim. Every role he played was one in which the character spoke well-written lines with style and distinction. An audience immediately knew to *listen* when Barrymore spoke on-screen, because he brought to sound the power of his family's acting tradition—and the foundation of years of experience on stage. In this he was very different from John Gilbert, who had learned his acting mainly in the movies themselves. When sound came in, Gilbert had to relearn and to adjust his silent film persona, but the public didn't give him the time in which to do it. Barrymore didn't need the time. He

Barrymore with up-and-coming star Colleen Moore, in *The Lotus Eaters*,
and with the beautiful young Mary Astor, in *Don Juan*

knew what to do. If he had been forced to speak aloud such dialogue as
"Snivel, you lying wretch!" or "My soul has been asleep—you have awakened
it!," he could have handled it. He never met a line he couldn't conquer, and
no amount of silly dialogue could have ruined his career. However, although
he survived the transition-to-sound era, and had a triumphant career well into
the 1930s, John Barrymore did not go out in a blaze of glory, with honorary
Oscars and the world at his feet. In his final years, he sank deeply into alcoholism and scandal. Frequently drunk and unable to remember his lines, he
became a joke, a satirical version of his earlier self. Some of his stage appearances were said to have been travesties, but, except for the very final works,
he remained more or less on top of his films. He stumbled on, famous for his
rowdy friends and sharp-tongued remarks, and died on May 29, 1942, at the
age of sixty. He himself had suggested that his best epitaph would be his
favorite line from Shakespeare: "Oh, what a rogue and peasant slave am I!"
He also played a magnificent deathbed scene, and he played it to a writer, his
friend Gene Fowler, who in his notoriously inaccurate biography, *Good Night,
Sweet Prince*—a huge best-seller—recorded how Barrymore, near the end,
suddenly rallied, opened his eyes, raised an eyebrow, and instructed Fowler
to lean down for a final question. It was a solemn moment of farewell between
two close friends. Fowler bent low for the golden moment. "Tell me," Barrymore asked him, "is it true that you are the illegitimate son of Buffalo Bill?"

He played a grand exit—good dialogue, perfect timing, twist of surprise, center of attention. And he chose to go out in a comedy role.

JOHN GILBERT WAS, of course, a type, but leading male actors of the silent era all tended to be types. In addition to romantic lovers or matinee idols, there were other categories of female favorites: cowboys, foreign sophisticates, country innocents, and—most popular of all—Latin Lovers. Many women seemed to be especially partial to the boyish heroes of those years, such as Robert Harron, Richard Barthelmess, and Charles Farrell. Harron was developed by Griffith as the perfect young man of innocence and decency. He rose to fame as "The Boy" in *Intolerance,* although he had begun playing leads as early as 1911 and in later films like *Judith of Bethulia* (1914). He was handsome and healthy, but his was not a muscled, tall physique. He was well cast as an ordinary young male, a homespun hero with typical, not remarkable qualities. His role really *was* that of "boy"—the innocent hero for an innocent time in innocent stories. Harron died tragically from a mysterious gunshot wound when he was only about twenty-four years old.

Barthelmess was a solid leading man who played with total conviction in any kind of role he was given. He was darkly handsome but not exotic, so his casting could stretch beyond the role of "lover" or "mysterious hero" into the kinds of stories that were American in setting and innocent in presentation. Barthelmess has been labeled "the hero of the last days of American innocence." At the same time, he could also play "the other," as in his excellent role as an ostracized Asian in Griffith's *Broken Blossoms.* Barthelmess had the good fortune to be developed by Griffith as a leading man for a series of films that have ensured his reputation today—including *The Idol Dancer, Way Down East* (both 1920), *Broken Blossoms* (1919), and *Tol'able David* (1921)—and also had non-Griffith hits like *The Patent Leather Kid* (1927). He had an excellent voice, which helped him make the transition to sound, appearing in tough little Depression movies like *Heroes for Sale, The Last Flight, Massacre,* and *A Modern Hero.* Although he left his days as a female favorite behind, his very respectable career lasted for two decades. He was nominated for the very first Oscar for Best Actor for his work in *The Noose* and *Patent Leather Kid,* but lost to Emil Jannings, who won for *The Last Command* and *The Way of All Flesh.* His reputation was made, however, in the earlier era, when he played simple heroes of decency and good values.

Farrell, over six feet tall and handsome almost to the point of being pretty, found fame playing opposite Janet Gaynor in a series of superb movies directed by Frank Borzage—*Seventh Heaven, Street Angel, Lucky Star.* He did not rise to stardom until the very end of the silent era, in approximately 1926, and he did not make an easy transition to sound. His voice initially seemed too thin for his size and robust appearance, but he took lessons to lower it and held on for a time. In the 1950s he became a television star, playing opposite Gale Storm in *My Little Margie,* and living to a ripe old age.

Most of these idols were family men, or men who were not womanizers, but John Gilbert lived up to his reputation as a "great lover" off the movie screen as well as on. He was the celebrated lover of both Greta Garbo and Marlene Dietrich, among others. Garbo nearly married him, and Dietrich is said to have sentimentally bid top dollar to purchase his satin bed sheets after he died. These are serious credentials!

JOHN GILBERT WAS GIVEN a perfect epitaph when Ben Hecht said, "In the time of Hollywood's most glittering days, he glittered the most," and went on to characterize him as "prince, butterfly, Japanese lantern, and the spirit of romance," adding, "There were no enemies in his life . . . He was as unsnobbish as a happy child . . . He needed no greatness around him to make him feel distinguished . . . He drank with carpenters, danced with waitresses and made love to whores and movie queens alike . . . He swaggered and posed, but it was never to impress anyone."

It is sad to think of such a beautiful and talented man, dead too young, living his last days riddled by alcohol and undoubtedly feeling both despair and disappointment. No one ever feels sympathy for the men who fuel female fantasies, but surely they suffer as much from the burden and limitation as female stars do. The life and career of John Gilbert suggest that it's no picnic being a "matinee idol," trying to live up to the label of "great lover."

Three great profiles of the matinee idol era: John Barrymore (ABOVE);
Francis X. Bushman and Ramon Novarro, in *Ben-Hur* (BELOW)

Sincerely
Colleen Moore

FLAPPERS
Colleen Moore and
Clara Bow

"FLAP, FLAP, FLAP," says the June 1922 issue of *Motion Picture* magazine. "A new vogue has swept across the country! Bobbed hair, low heels, pheasant quills, tweed suits and coats, rainbow hats and drop earrings are in order—There is a new language, too—flapper slang. It possesses menagerial tendencies. For instance, the dog's nightshirt and the cat's pajamas. Verily, it is the day of the flapper." Surrounding this pronouncement are the photographs of five actresses the magazine predicts "will become flappers": May McAvoy, Shirley Mason, Lila Lee, Marie Compson, and Gladys Walton, not one of whom is associated with the term today. In fact, if anyone thinks about flappers at all—the concept is itself a candidate for forgotten, misunderstood, and underappreciated—the actress who comes most readily to mind is Joan Crawford. She was definitely a famous flapper, but she entered the arena late, long after the term had been defined and developed by two actresses who are far less known today: Colleen Moore and Clara Bow.

The term "flapper" is said to have come from the flapping sound the galoshes young women wore in bad weather made if the flaps weren't closed up. This fad, somewhat like young men not lacing up their sneakers today, seems to represent defiance, or, more provocatively, looseness. A safe form of going half-dressed. ("See this? I dare go around with my galoshes unfastened. What's next?") The word "flapper" turns up in movie reviews as early as 1921, but not associated with either Clara Bow (who hadn't yet entered films) or Colleen Moore (who was still in her early years as a young leading lady support for top male stars). In a review of Constance Talmadge's *Woman's Place*, the October 28, 1921, issue of *Variety* says, "In this we have the woman's club offering the prettiest flapper in Fairfax the nomination for mayor." In September of 1922, a movie was released called *A Country Flapper* starring Dorothy Gish, whose character was defined as "a village flapper." Gish never became associated with the term, but Talmadge certainly did. However, she forged her own brand of madcap heiress role, and her characters were too sophisticated and often too mature for true flapperdom. The movie flapper really came into focus in 1923, when Colleen Moore appeared in *Flaming Youth*, and she more than anyone became the prototype. The popularity of her flaming youth character inspired another movie almost immediately, *The Perfect Flapper* (1924), and Moore went on to become a huge star. She is the person to whom the title belongs, as she was indeed "the perfect flapper." However, Clara Bow, who started in films after Moore, and who owns her own title (the "It" girl), was also labeled as a flapper over and over again in reviews of the day. Because only about fifteen of her movies exist to be screened, Moore is almost completely unknown today. Bow is better known, if only as a kind of catchall hotcha 1920s jazz baby. But both actresses were once household names, and they deserve to be better known.

It's unclear whether the movies invented the flapper or the flapper was just a fashion accident, but one thing is clear: it was the movies that made her into an icon. The movies told Americans who the flapper was, what she wore, how she behaved, and why she was different from other female movie types. The flapper wasn't a siren or a vamp or a femme fatale. She wasn't innocent, and she wasn't maternal. She was a naughty grown-up girl who wanted to play with boys, to cause trouble, to be mischievous. In fact, the movie flapper was a logical extension of the movie tomboy, that cute little girl who dug for worms and stole cookies in the earliest silent films. It was completely logical for the rule-breaking tomboy-girl of the teens to grow up to be a flapper, because breaking the rules was what a flapper was all about. The first steps of liberation for females on-screen were inevitably safe enough for the audience to watch comfortably, and the flapper fit the bill. She rode at high speed, but she was still just a nice kid who got her white dress dirty making mud pies.

The movie flapper was an escapist creation. The real thing may never even have existed. Her role was to embody the evolution of the old-fashioned girl into the modern woman. Picture the typical lovely young heroine of 1914 being transformed: her skirt goes up, and her neckline comes down. Her long, thick hair is cut short and bobbed. Her layers of petticoats and corsets are stripped off and replaced with a simple loose dress. Her legs, formerly hidden, are now not only on display all the way up to the knees, but the knees are rouged and the stockings rolled down under them. Gone was the demure American girl, all covered up; here is a girl who could jump into the shower, throw on a dress, and hop out the door. In her closet she had all kinds of new outfits—skimpier bathing suits, shorter tennis dresses, looser riding habits—all of which allowed her to move about freely. Freedom. It all spelled freedom, and with fashion freedom came other, more daring freedoms—staying out late at night, driving fast in cars, drinking from whiskey flasks, and of course the big one, the freedom to have sex.

For the movies, this was perfect. First of all, it meant roles for young, slender female stars who could be at the center of the story. It meant a whole new fashion concept, so that women in the audience would just have to buy tickets to understand what they were supposed to wear and how they were supposed to cut their hair. Girls who in the teens had dressed in hair bows and organdy and carried little nosegays began in the twenties to wear thin silk shifts and diamond earrings and carry long cigarette holders. Finally, it meant a different kind of woman's story in which these slim girls in those sliplike dresses and thin silk slippers and little capelets could go out into the world and have madcap, even sexy, adventures. They could do just about anything they wanted to do on-screen, with one caveat: in the end, they had to return home and regret it. Thus, the flapper acted out the change that was taking place for women in fashion, sex, social awareness, and politics. She represented women in transition from the old to the new, and not much had to be said about it because everyone could *see* it.

Colleen Moore's on-screen characters visually illustrate this transition. In her earliest films, she was usually cast as a demure (though perky) Irish colleen . . . or a small-town girl trying to make it in the big city . . . or a western tomboy. Tracing the career of Colleen Moore is tracing the arrival of the flapper, and she even enacts the change within the plot of *Flaming Youth*. By the time Clara Bow got started, in 1922, the flapper was already on the screen, but Bow was born to play her kind of freedom and daring. She never played sweet or proper young girls because from the very beginning she looked too hot to handle. There was no sense trying to make her into the innocent little angel next door. She might *be* next door, and she might even be kind of sweet (as in *Wings*), but Clara Bow was hot and the audience knew it.

Clara Bow and Colleen Moore offered audiences two different types of flapper: one that was sexy (Bow) and one that was wholesome (Moore). You only have to look at photographs of them to understand. Colleen Moore has an art deco look. She's trim, slim, and sleek, with the boyish figure of the 1920s silhouette. Even her hair is geometric, worn straight, short, and with no sense of softness. Her clothes are simple and elegant, with straight lines that reveal no curves. Bow has a mass of tangled, sleepy-time hair, thick and lush, and her breasts are not only generous but frequently spilling out of her blouse. Her line is the curve, and when she walks, she wiggles. (Moore never wiggles. In some of her comedy roles, she adopts an almost robotlike movement.) Moore and Bow are the straight line versus the curve. Both played images that were ultimately safe, because neither was ever presented as evil or seriously depraved; their flapper movies weren't tragic tales of unwed motherhood and abandonment. They were both typical examples of the same phenomenon, but there was a difference, and the difference was sex.

The two stars were contemporaries. They entered movies very young, and they were both very ambitious. Although each one finally found a man she could stay married to, neither of them really had an easy time of it with men. They were two attractive females who found freedom and financial security in the movies. The fact that they came to represent typical American girls on-screen was the usual ironic joke: neither was typical, in that no average American girl had the grit and the ruthlessness that movie stardom required. Their personal stories are especially interesting because they're the opposites of each other in terms of background, love, and security, and because they can be woven together to represent the 1920s, its fads, its movie stardom, and its attitudes toward the woman's role in society.

When Bow and Moore were starting out, things were very different from the way they are today, when everyone goes to college, people can buy on credit, and women are liberated by the pill and a morality that allows them to explore sex in ways only men could in the old days. Both girls had to face the limits imposed on their gender, and in Bow's case, poverty as well. But they shared a love of movies, and their escapist dreams were fueled by the tales of love, romance, and wealth they absorbed at the local theatre. By the time they entered their teenage years, they could see that other young women—Mary Pickford, Norma Talmadge—were becoming stars in the new medium. Escape was possible. They began not only to dream of this escape but to actively plan for it. Where Pickford had never thought of becoming a movie queen—she invented the term and pioneered the concept—Bow and Moore went to the movies and dreamed of becoming Mary Pickford.

Moore and Bow represent the kind of stardom that is partly an accident of casting and partly a force of personality but that certainly has to be earned the hard way. They aren't timeless stars like Garbo or Dietrich, but stars who represent their own time. To be that kind of movie star is the hardest job of all, because these are the actors whose films are about nothing much but themselves and their cool, cool (or hot, hot) images. The business attitude toward such actresses is always one of exploitation: make as much off them as quickly as you can before it all goes away. Sensational popularity—white hot and all consuming—doesn't last. As a result, Bow and Moore were inevitably pushed into movie after movie after movie. They were tougher than most, and managed to stay stars a full decade.

Colleen Moore was born Kathleen Morrison in Port Huron, Michigan, in 1900,* but she lived most of her childhood in the South, first in Atlanta and then in Tampa. By her own admission, she was ambitious; and from the very

*She frequently gave the date as 1902, but the correct date is 1900.

beginning she wanted to be a star. She had a strong sense of herself as someone special—hadn't she been born with one blue eye and one brown eye?
Didn't this mean a unique life? Didn't it make her a unique person? Moore
came from a solid Irish family, a relatively happy brood that included her parents, her brother, and her grandmother. They weren't rich, but they weren't
poor either, and as she wrote in her autobiography, *Silent Star,* "We did know,
my brother and I, what it meant to be loved." Furthermore, they knew what it
meant to have connections. Moore's Aunt Lib was married to Walter Howey,
the editor of the *Chicago Examiner* and allegedly the model for the editor in
Hecht and MacArthur's *The Front Page.* Moore begged her Aunt Lib and
Uncle Walter to help her get into the movies, and sometime around 1915 or
1916 Uncle Walter finally used his influence. In return for a favor, D. W. Griffith agreed to give young Kathleen a six-month Hollywood contract, and
Moore was on her way. (Her parents were always supportive of her career.)

Clara Bow's life was totally different. There was no Uncle Walter to help
her out. There was no one to help Clara Bow but Clara Bow. She was born on
July 29, 1905 (perhaps 1907), into poverty and sordid circumstances to a couple who clearly hadn't wanted her, or at least led her to believe they hadn't
wanted her. ("Nobody wanted me to be born in the first place," Bow was
quoted as having said.) Clara Bow was her real name. Her biographer David
Stenn says she "developed into a lonely, hypersensitive child, acutely self-
conscious of a slight speech impediment." He added that "Clara rarely spoke
of her early years, unwilling to exploit them for publicity . . . but when [she]
did discuss her youth, her tone was terse: 'I have known hunger, believe
me . . . We just lived, and that's about all.' " Bow was the Marilyn Monroe of
her day. She had the same voluptuous body, the same off-screen scandals, the
same touch of madness in her family tree, and the same background as an
unwanted child. Like Monroe, she was not taken seriously as an actress
although she was taken *very* seriously as a woman and as a personality. Like
Colleen Moore, Bow developed a passion for the movies and a driving desire
to be a movie star in her very earliest years. The way she got herself to Hollywood is the stuff legends are made of. Her ticket to stardom came through the
kind of luck and pluck she had to show to survive throughout her life: she won
a "Fame and Fortune" contest sponsored by *Motion Picture, Motion Picture
Classic,* and *Shadowland* magazines in 1921. First prize was her train ticket.
Thus, Bow's personal story is a 1920s movie plot about winning contests,
acquiring easy money, and reaching sudden stardom. Moore's personal story
is more conventional but is itself a form of 1920s movie plot: the one in which
a good girl with spirit goes to the big city and, despite various temptations,
keeps her values and her head screwed on right. (The two types of flappers
these stars were eventually to play reflected their own personal stories.)

Moore, a few years older than Bow, entered films about five years ahead of

The young Colleen Moore in *Bad Boy,* and in *The Sky Pilot*

her. By 1917, Kathleen Morrison (now rechristened Colleen Moore)* was making movies in Hollywood, turning out four feature films in her first year. Her first release, *Bad Boy,* was reviewed in *Variety* on March 9, 1917. It was a five-reeler from Fine Arts–Triangle, which starred Robert Harron as a typical small-town bad boy who grows up to be a criminal. Moore plays Ruth, a new girl who moves to town and temporarily takes him away from his steadfast childhood sweetheart, the reliable Mary (Mildred Harris). Moore was only seventeen years old. Of her debut, she wrote in her autobiography, "I made it through my first film, *Bad Boy,* simply by doing what the director told me to do."

Moore's other three movies in 1917 were *An Old Fashioned Young Man,* also with Robert Harron; *Hands Up* (not to be confused with the 1926 film of the same name); and *The Savage,* in which she played a half-breed girl named Lizette. (Some sources say she was in Pickford's 1917 release *The Little American,* but she isn't listed in the credits that were reprinted in *Variety.*)

Moore made only two films in 1918, *A Hoosier Romance* and *Little Orphant Annie,* but her career was solidly established. Her reviews for *Annie* were excellent, with *Variety* saying that she played "with such artistry that

---

*Even before she had left for Hollywood, her Uncle Walter had changed her name, on the theory that Kathleen Morrison was too long to fit on a movie marquee. Twelve letters, he said, was the limit, so they chopped Morrison down to Moore, which sounded very Irish, and he thought that creating an Irish type was a good idea. Kathleen was a good Irish name, of course, but there was already the famous Kathlyn Williams, so the even more Irish Colleen was selected. By her own consent, Kathleen Morrison became Colleen Moore before she ever entered films.

one's sympathies immediately go out to her in her misfortune . . . She has all the wistfulness of a homeless waif." It was a film that captured attention for her, both in the business and with fans, but the print I saw was such a poor one it was difficult to follow all the plot details. It opens by presenting the "late author James Whitcomb Riley" posing grandly with his little dog, and identified as the author of the story of "little orphant Annie." The visualized event presents a very young and pretty Moore, whose bright, wide smile is obviously a huge asset. The movie is enhanced by superimposed images of witches, goblins, scarecrows, and imps, as Moore's character herself becomes a storyteller to children ("and the gobble-uns'll git ye ef ye don't watch out"). For a movie that is obviously pitched at children, it ends sadly, with the grown-up Annie's beloved killed in World War I and her confined to her bed. What stands out about Colleen Moore in this early effort is that she can be both charmingly winsome and pathetic; hers will be the gift to play both comedy and drama when she matures.

Moore's beauty and intelligence made her easy to cast, and from the very beginning she was placed in quality films opposite name stars. Two of the best were *The Busher* and *Egg Crate Wallop* in 1919. In both she appeared in support of Charles Ray, whose particular niche was that of country bumpkin. (He was hugely popular with female moviegoers, who found his bumbling attempts to express himself both charming and lovable.) Since Ray was at the peak of his stardom, her roles as his love interest increased her visibility. In *The Busher*, she plays the ingenue, a typical small-town beauty, and in *Egg Crate Wallop*, she is the daughter of the manager of the express company where Ray works. Her character tends soda fountain at the local drugstore and since she looked sweet, innocent, and very Irish, she made a good costar for the "country boy" Ray. He is tall and she is short, and both are very young. Moore is what would be called "as pretty as a picture," but she isn't just another pretty face; she's distinctive-looking, and registers clearly on film. Her manner is very low-key, and she seems genuinely shy, genuinely innocent, and genuinely small-town. Together, she and Ray seem authentic, and audiences believed in them. They were particularly charming in *The Busher*, a solid film about a small-town baseball player who gets his head turned by success but who finally turns up back home, a wiser man. (Her other releases in 1919 were *The Wilderness Trail, The Man in the Moonlight,* and *Common Property.*)

By the end of 1919, Moore's career was rapidly escalating. In 1920, she made four more features, *When Dawn Came, The Devil's Claim, The Cyclone,* and *Dinty,* which was especially popular. She also made two short films for the Christie brothers, whose two-reel comedies rivaled Mack Sennett's: *Her Bridal Nightmare* and *A Roman Scandal.* Although many of Moore's films don't exist in any form today, both these shorts are available, providing a valuable look into what made her stand out from other pretty girls. In *Her Bridal Nightmare,*

"A Special Christie Comedy," Moore is fresh and pretty, and there is something utterly natural about her looks—she seems to be a real person, not a perfect little doll figure of the silent era. She projects a very specific quality of intelligence, and in its brief running time, the movie provides a look at everything she will give audiences in the future. She's beautiful, as innocently romantic as a bride. She's sophisticated and elegant in a party scene. She's hoydenish and clever dressed as a man in a baggy suit. And best of all, she's hilarious when she announces in a title card, "I'm going to commit suicide or die in the attempt." She marches out into the street and begins a comic dance of death as she stands in front of a series of oncoming cars that swerve, back up, turn around, and manage to avoid her, no matter what she tries. We see what will distinguish her: beauty, ability to wear clothes, perfect leading-lady looks, but also a remarkable comic timing and willingness to throw herself about as needed. In *A Roman Scandal* she plays a small-town would-be actress who goes on to play "the Christian maiden" in a howler called *The Fall of Rome*, put on by a traveling troupe of less-than-perfect thespians. Again, her physical comedy skills combined with her looks showcase her as a leading lady who will handle romantic lead and comic foil with equal aplomb. By 1921, Moore was established solidly enough to be directed by a top name like King Vidor (in *The Sky Pilot*) and starred opposite the legendary John Barrymore (in *The Lotus Eaters*). (Of Barrymore, Moore wrote, "He was almost unbearably handsome. In my first love scene with him . . . I was so overwhelmed, I froze.")

In *The Sky Pilot,** she isn't yet a flapper, and her famous "Dutch boy" haircut is not in evidence. She is, however, an extremely pretty young girl whose acting is better than average, who suggests a flair for comedy, and who might just turn into a serious rival for Mary Pickford. Although she's still several films away from her true stardom, she is both the leading romantic interest and a kind of child star, "Gwen, the one thing [her father] loved." *The Sky Pilot* is well directed by Vidor with his usual sensitive feeling for nature and out-of-doors sequences. There's also an effective touch of humor within the drama, and plenty of dramatic visual action, including an impressive cattle stampede and a final sequence in which a church burns to the ground.

Moore enters the action dressed in cowboy gear—chaps, neckerchief, western hat—and she's driving a team of fast horses at high speed. She's laughing—an unforgettable sight as she stands up in the back of a wagon. (This is a real star entrance!) Her character suggests one Pickford might play. She has long, curly hair, and she's one half coy young woman and the other half feisty tomboy, bouncing from one to the other of these two selves in a somewhat confusing manner. One moment she's wearing a gingham dress, a huge hair bow, and long black stockings, jumping around like a child and

---

*"Sky pilot" was a common slang term for a minister or military chaplain.

ineffectually threatening the big bad men. In the next, she's racing to the rescue of the hero by throwing him a rope and pulling him out of a rushing
stream, or surviving the stampede with courage and daring. Watching *Sky
Pilot,* it's easy to become confused as to exactly what her character is supposed to represent. She does play the grown-up love interest, but one of her
Christmas gifts is a great big doll!

Yet, Pickford imitation or not, Moore stands out immediately. Not
because she has curls, like Mary, or can emote while temporarily crippled,
like Lillian Gish, or because she plays her action as well as any serial queen,
but because she is bold in the story and bold on film. She makes an impression because she's not just another passive beauty of the silent era. In retrospect, she looks like a girl crying out to be modernized, to be swept forward
into the next decade and cut loose from earlier attitudes toward women. It's
easy to see in *The Sky Pilot* how the times were about to be very right for this
distinctive, pretty, lively young actress. (Her other 1921 release was *His Nibs,*
starring Chic Sale.)

Among her six 1922 releases, there was one, *The Wall Flower* (unavailable for viewing), that according to reviews gave Moore a chance to try out her
comedy skills. Cast opposite Richard Dix, a heartthrob of his day, Moore got
to show off her pantomiming with great success. *Variety* took note, saying,
"The work that Colleen Moore does . . . places her right in line to assume the
screen comedy honors that once so well fitted Mabel Normand. She has a role
as . . . an eccentric comedienne and makes the most of it." But in another
release, *Broken Chains,* she was back in the Pickford mold, sporting long
curls and suffering abuse at the hands of her improbably named husband,
"Boykan Boone" (played by an out-of-control Ernest Torrence). Her character
is actually more Gish than Pickford, as she is a child-wife who gets chained to
the floor in a log cabin for her efforts to do right by her awful husband. One of
the most fascinating aspects of this movie is a little bridge everyone has to
cross in order to reach the Boone cabin. So that no one will discover his wife
chained up, Boykan has cleverly rigged it so that stepping on a certain board
will plunge both the structure and anyone on it into a rushing mountain
stream far below. Boykan himself always remembers to step over that particular board as he comes and goes, and I spent the whole movie waiting . . . waiting . . . Moore's other 1922 releases were *Forsaking All Others, Come On Over,
Affinities,* and *The Ninety and Nine.*

She found better and better roles as she went along. In 1923's *Nth Com-
mandment,* she was directed by Frank Borzage in a Fannie Hurst story
adapted by Frances Marion. She plays a young wife whose husband becomes
ill shortly after their baby is born, plunging them into poverty. To escape, she
goes out to a party, where one of her former suitors, a rich young cad, dares her
to go out on the restaurant floor and dance alone. If she will, he'll give her

$100. Desperate for money, she does it . . . only to have him up the ante and tell her that if she'll jump into the fountain, he'll give her a further $200. With this preflapperish behavior, Moore earns $300, and after telling her husband an effective fib, packs him and the baby up for a new life in California. In general, 1923 was another year of good solid work and straightforward career advancement. She made films called *Look Your Best, Slippy McGee, April Showers,* and *The Huntress.* None of these are available for viewing today, but reading about them indicates that none are apparently what we have come to think of as "Colleen Moore" roles. In *April Showers,* an Irish love story, she played a girl from "the old country," and in *The Huntress,* reviews of which note that she has been promoted to stardom and deserves it, she plays a girl raised by Indians who finds out she isn't really one of them, so she heads for New York to find herself a proper husband. In *Slippy McGee* she's "a young miss" who helps reform a crook.

Broken Hearts of Broadway uses her youth to advantage, as she plays a little country girl who comes to New York to try for stardom on Broadway. When she arrives in the big city, she shares a room with a flashy young woman named "Bubbles" Revere (Alice Lake). (Colleen Moore's persona is rooming with Clara Bow's!) The plot is predictable: the heroine finds true love but can't find work. Broke and discouraged, at first she's tempted by the hotcha life, but she learns her lesson after nearly going to prison, and in the end, she becomes a big Broadway star. In this minor film and in a thoroughly unoriginal role, Colleen Moore shows herself to be a highly capable actress, able to project emotions very effectively. Her clothes are always simple and rather elegant, so that she looks extremely modern. This straight-lined, unadorned look suited her, keeping the emphasis on her soft face and beautiful eyes.

Moore had been promoted to stardom, but she hadn't yet found her screen persona. Her natural ability and wholesome good looks had carried her (there's an "Irish lass" quality to her—she looks rather like today's television star Dana Delaney), but there had been no single role that made her jump off the screen. She wasn't yet one of the definitive creations of silent film. However, her final film of 1923, released in November, was *Flaming Youth.* In it, Colleen Moore was going to play a flapper—and the persona issue would be permanently resolved. Indeed, *Flaming Youth* turned her into one of the biggest stars of the 1920s and made the term "flapper" a household word. "I was the spark that lit up flaming youth," wrote the Jazz Age chronicler, F. Scott Fitzgerald, "and Colleen Moore was the torch." Just as Fitzgerald became a glamour figure of American letters with his stories of a new type of carefree, reckless youth, *Flaming Youth* came along to further popularize the concept by visualizing just what a young woman who flamed and flapped really looked like. What she looked like was Colleen Moore: flat-chested and angular, big-eyed and lively, with her hair cut short, very short, straight across

Moore showing off her expressive face, which adapted to both comedy and drama well and expanded her career options

the bottom, and topped off with bangs. (This cut, called "the Dutch Boy bob," was popularized by Moore, not Louise Brooks.)

The *New York Times* review of *Flaming Youth* said:

> The beguiling and resourceful tactics of a flapper, from her plebe days to her graduation as a bachelor of hearts, are engrossingly portrayed in *Flaming Youth*, the new picture which is adorning the Strand screen this week . . . Colleen Moore gives a vivid performance of the jazz-devoted novice . . . She lives the part of the pert young thing whose hair is cut with a bang on the forehead, whose eyes are full of mischief and whose arms are long and slender.

The story isn't much. It's a cautionary tale about how life in the fast lane is dangerous for females, but before the big finale that proves the point, it takes time to revel in the fun to be had along the way. Reviews of the day almost all dwelt on the swimming pool sequence, in which party guests are shown shedding their clothes in semi-silhouette. In fact, this kind of titillation is exactly what the flapper film was all about—the audience doesn't see much of anything except a little underwear; everything is in silhouette, a kind of indirection that left everything to the imagination. The entire story of *Flaming Youth* fits this pattern, since the lesson is driven home that the wild life has no long-range rewards. Its heroine might be liberated in clothes, haircut, and social behavior, but the world still had its old-fashioned values to be reaffirmed. Colleen Moore's "Pat" became the emblem of what a flapper really was. She was cute and lively, but she wasn't sensual, like Clara Bow. There was no real suggestion that she might ever do anything truly stupid or immoral. Her galoshes might be flapping, but she was pretty zipped-up otherwise.

With *Flaming Youth* Colleen Moore had found her movie destiny. In the extant reels that I watched at the Library of Congress, she's a sight to see, and it's this image that really embodies the essential female spirit of the 1920s (a companion to Valentino's sheik). When first seen, she's sitting in front of her mirror, making faces, trying different perfumes and makeups on with great glee. She creates the popular "bee-stung lips" of the day for herself, and poses in various positions, checking herself out each time. A viewer watching her vamping around has the impression of a sweet young girl transforming herself into a flapper with all the store-bought props of the nation. It's a defining moment, in which a social transformation is enacted right on the screen by a charming actress with considerable comedy skills.

Moore's little flapper getting herself all dolled up still shows a lot of uncertainty, but it's clear she wants to take the social plunge. When she goes downstairs to a large party, her dress is too big, and so are her ideas, but she jumps right in. The film takes off from there, providing a willing audience with lots of images of the wild life, including the one mentioned above in which a bunch of half-drunk 1920s socialites take off their clothes and jump into a swimming pool. It was the old DeMille strategy—plenty of sin followed by plenty of reform—this time applied to the younger set instead of the married couples of the DeMillian universe.

Moore had begged for the role of Pat. She had read the best-selling book it was based on (by Warner Fabian) and felt that here at last was her chance at major stardom. As she put it in her autobiography, "Sweet young thing I was not. Pat, the heroine of *Flaming Youth,* I was." Moore writes of how when she was turned down because she wasn't "the type," her mother suggested, "Why don't we cut your hair and then make [them] give you a test?" The famous short haircut emerged, and Colleen Moore got the part and her stardom. "Never had I been so happy in a movie role," she wrote. "After six years of treacle, it was heaven to be given a little spice."

While Moore was climbing to fame, Clara Bow won her movie magazine contest and arrived in Hollywood. In 1922, with Moore solidly established and making six features, Bow appeared in her first films, *Beyond the Rainbow* (considered her debut) and *Down to the Sea in Ships.* Listed next to last in the cast (as "Virginia Gardener") in *Beyond the Rainbow,* she caught *Variety*'s eye: "The feminine characters form a galaxy of beauty. Lillian (Billie) Dove [the star] has a wealth of brunette loveliness and makes an attractive contrast to the other two beauties, Virginia Lee and Clara Bow, both blondes and both beauty contest winners." (Bow, of course, was a flaming redhead.)

Down to the Sea in Ships was a production made by the Whaling Film Corporation of New Bedford, Massachusetts—it's an attempt to accurately depict life on the whaling ships of Old New England. Backed by a group of ship owners, bankers, mill owners, and businessmen from New Bedford, *Down to the Sea in Ships* shows the actual harpooning of a sperm whale, the whale's attack on the small boat sent out to capture it, and the capsizing of the boat in shark-infested waters. The time given to an almost documentary detailing of how a captured whale is cut up and sliced for blubber definitely causes the narrative flow to stop. (*Variety* mused, "It will be interesting to see how New York takes it.") Clara Bow plays a life-loving, energetic young girl who shows no respect for the rules. Set down in the middle of this staid and unprofessional vehicle, she is like a breath of fresh air—vivid, alive, modern. She seems to have real passion rather than just imitating it. She's the very definition of the term "screen presence," particularly seen among the careful and stilted performances of the other actors. Cast as a young tomboy, she romps, she fights, she kicks and screams, and she seems utterly unselfconscious.

Clara Bow was very young when she began her career, barely more than sixteen, and since she caught viewer attention very early, she began to be cast in an amazing number of films every year, although usually in supporting roles. After her first two films in 1922 and a few undistinguished roles in 1923,* she made eight features in 1924. A typical example of Bow's 1924 work is in the successful melodrama *Black Oxen.*

Black Oxen—based on a notorious best-seller by Gertrude Atherton—is a big Hollywood movie, starring one of the popular beauties of the day, Corinne Griffith. It's a bizarre story about a woman who is kept young by a series of glandular injections, but despite its astonishing plot and its beautiful star, Clara Bow steals the film. She plays a wild little creature who's bursting with sex, dying to lose her virtue. (Almost from the beginning there seemed to be no way to contain Clara Bow, and it was certain that no one was ever going to cast her as a nun.) She's beautifully dressed and made up in this tightly produced melodrama, but somehow she manages to break free from the restraints of the good taste the film imposes. (*Black Oxen* seems to be wearing corsets. Clara Bow is the one free and natural thing in it.) Bow is deliberately used as contrast to the Griffith character who, although beautiful and dignified, isn't young anymore. A mature woman, she has depth and value, whereas Bow represents what youth is really all about: sex and silliness. She's terrific, and she's playing off the type that had been popularized in *Flaming Youth.* With the devil-may-care flapper officially on the movie rolls, Clara Bow's career was off and running. She was born to play a flapper, and possibly nothing else.

Her other 1924 releases gave her a variety of roles, one of which—

*Her 1923 movies included *Enemies of Women, Maytime,* and *The Daring Years,* and the other 1924 titles were *Grit, Poisoned Paradise, Daughters of Pleasure, Wine, Empty Hearts, This Woman,* and *Black Lightning.*

The young Clara
Bow in *Black Oxen*

Wine—had her as a proper socialite who cuts loose as a flapper after she finds out that her bankrupt father has gone into business with bootleggers. Most of these movies were not in any way exceptional (although she did play opposite the dog star Thunder in *Black Lightning*), but she was making a name for herself. At the end of 1924, she was chosen as one of the famous WAMPAS Baby Stars, an accolade from movie advertisers who singled out young women who had a chance to become stars. (WAMPAS was the acronym of the Western Associated Motion Picture Advertisers.) Bow was visible, and recognized as having the big chance, but she wasn't yet a star. Moore, on the other hand, had definitely arrived. Stardom was here.

While Clara Bow worked hard to move forward throughout 1924, in January of that year two new Colleen Moore releases were reviewed by *Variety: Through the Dark* and *Painted People*. *Through the Dark* was called "a wow of a crook thriller" that would "pull real business at the box office." Moore played a young finishing-school student who had no idea that her mother ran a refuge for bad boys and that her father had died in a state prison. *Variety* wrote: "It's a picture that will pull 'em, interest 'em and send 'em out boosting." *Painted People* was a comedy in which Moore played a washerwoman's tomboy daughter who becomes a successful stage actress. By the time this movie was ready for release, she was being billed as "THE FLAMING YOUTH GIRL!"

Next came a movie with a title designed to capitalize even further on her new fame. *The Perfect Flapper*—obviously the perfect title—asks the question, "The girl of today—herself a problem—has her own problem to face: 'What kind of a girl must I be to be the kind of girl the boys want me to be?' " Moore plays the girl who is going to answer the question on behalf of the audience. Her character is called "Tommy Lou" (sometimes spelled "Tommie Lou"), an appropriately tomboyish and modern name. At first, Tommie Lou is unfashionable, awkward, and lacking the required flapper social skills of drinking, smoking, and jazz dancing. She has to be made over: new clothes, new hair, and a whole new attitude. In the reels available for screening at the Library of Congress, she's made drunk by a friend, playing a perfect scene in which her entire body language changes from tense and nervous to loose and free. Such a scene, played by a young woman, must have been shocking in its day. A young girl drunk! And just for the fun of it! And with the suggestion that if she doesn't get with it in these matters, she's going to be left out of things. Naturally, Moore will eventually sober up and find herself, but once again audiences could track the emergence of the new movie heroine out of the old. In the end, her character lets loose with a passionate complaint against men on behalf of women in general. Thus Moore had given her flapper two qualities all her own: genuine comedy and a strong feminist attitude.

Her final two films of 1924 deserted the flapper role. In the first, *Flirting with Love*, she played a leading lady of the stage, a more sophisticated part. *So Big* (released on December 28) was based on Edna Ferber's famous novel. It afforded Moore the chance to play a serious role for which she received excellent notices—she aged decades during the course of the film. Barbara Stanwyck and Jane Wyman would do remakes in sound, in 1932 and 1953, respectively. Reviewers, however, referred to Moore as "a delineator of flappers" and wondered if she would return to her "flapperish parts."

In 1925, Moore was back on track in her more popular manner, playing the leading lady in three light movies: *Sally*, the film version of the Marilyn Miller stage success; *Desert Flower;* and *We Moderns*. In all three she essentially played the Colleen Moore persona—a sort of feminist hoyden with comic touches. (By now, she was completely associated with the term "flapper" and fan magazines identified photos of her as "the Irish flapper" or "the flapper Colleen of *Flaming Youth*.") She became a darling of the critics. *Variety* wrote about *Sally*, "Miss Moore reaches the high peak of her young career, an actress of versatility, charm, talent that knocks at the door of genius . . . With her face smeared with tomato as a foundling brat or covered with royal jewels and regal gowns . . . she gives the verity of life itself to the famous native Cinderella." The review remarks on her ability to bring truth to what she does, that rarest of talents, and once again goes so far as to say that she threatens Mabel Normand as a comedienne, because she is "funny with her eyes, her feet, her every gesture and glance" and that "as an emotional

Moore in *Flirting with Love* (LEFT) and *We Moderns,* with Jack Mulhall (ABOVE)

actress she is easily the grade of Mary Pickford's finest." Clearly, the reviewer had fallen in love with Colleen Moore. (He wasn't the first . . . and he wouldn't be the last—Moore was top box office in 1926, 1927, and 1928.)

Her fame hit its peak in 1926, and two of her films from that year—*Irene* and *Ella Cinders*—not only perfectly define her character but illustrate how far she had come from her early days playing ingenues with no distinctive traits. In both these movies, she's given plenty of time to clown around, and she appears in almost every scene. Both movies rely on title cards to provide some of the jokes (the hero of *Irene* is referred to as "a wild oats boy in a Quaker oats town"). Both are at the cutting edge of smart-talking attitudes: a gift card in *Irene* reads "From Sugar Daddy to Flaming Baby." Moore herself understood the source of her appeal. "No longer did a girl have to be beautiful to be sought after," she wrote in her autobiography, "Any plain Jane could become a flapper. No wonder women grabbed me to their hearts and made me their movie idol."

By this time, she had developed into a comedienne of the first rank. (In fact, all her 1926 releases are comedies,* although the last of them, *Twinkletoes,* contains other elements. *Irene,* based on a successful stage musical, seems to exist on film only because of Colleen Moore. It should have been called *Colleen.*) It's truly a star vehicle, presenting her front and center in every scene. She plays an Irish charmer, a down-to-earth girl who works in a department store window, holding up advertising signs to attract passersby. ("It's a pleasure to be sick in our bed.") The camera stays pinned to Moore while she makes faces, pantomimes, does imitations, and takes a series of comedy pratfalls. In a movie about the fashion business, stocked with clothes and glamour, she plays the role of female comic in the Sennett tradition. She even puts a lampshade on her head. By now, she is utterly distinctive, looking like no one else—the mark of a star. Her haircut makes a perfect dark frame for her face. Her large eyes sparkle mischievously, and are full of expression. She's apparently unworried about anything, as she dares to do many scenes another actress might not have wanted to undertake. She's a star, knows it, and she trusts the audience to love her.

In one of her best scenes, she stands on a dais while "Madame Lucy," a male dress designer, drapes fabrics on her to create some of his bizarre clothes. It's easy to overlook how modern and funny a scene this would have been in its day. For years, clotheshorse stars like Gloria Swanson had been treated like beautiful objects on which to hang garments and dazzle American female moviegoers. In *Irene,* Moore sends up the concept. As she stands on the dais, it turns around in a continuing circle, so Madame Lucy can easily drape

---

*In *It Must Be Love* she plays the daughter of a delicatessen owner, and *Variety* commented that she was "proving herself a comedienne of rare qualities."

the fabrics. Suddenly, the rotating machine goes berserk and starts whirling her around at high speed. As she tries to maintain her Swanson-like composure, Madame Lucy is still draping her with an exotic eastern fabric of the kind Swanson would wear. Moore plays the physical comedy easily, making fun of fashion, other movies, other stars, and the ludicrous use of women as objects to be draped. (And then later, in the ambivalent tradition of Hollywood women's movies, there is a huge fashion show finale in color in which Moore appears, beautifully gowned and romantically dressed, playing it straight.)

Irene reveals a great deal about the Colleen Moore flapper and the Colleen Moore persona. She has almost completely subsumed any external definition of "flapper." Her "Irene" flapper is not only independent and spunky, she's downright boyish. She wears plain, masculine clothes that set her apart from everyone else in the movie. In the movie's world of ruffled and curled women, she's practically an alien being. Her presence makes a clear visual statement about the female role. She looks somewhat androgynous, although in a unique way: she isn't both masculine and feminine, she's neither. She has become genderless as well as sexless, although she's still appealing. *Irene* demonstrates how important Colleen Moore really is as an image of women in film history. She has updated the "little woman" of the teens, turning her into a self-propelled doll* of a very different type, one that dares imply that sex needn't define a woman, that a woman may be considered attractive for reasons other than sex alone. Moore's characters were very popular with women audiences, since she represented what women were hoping to accomplish: the discarding of the traditional burdens of femininity, the usual restricted female roles of mother, sexual partner, and romantic object. However, Moore didn't appeal only to women; she was equally popular with men, and to this day has male fans who appreciate her originality and style.

Ella Cinders is a sweet comedy that reworks the old Cinderella story. Moore plays Ella Cinders, the put-upon stepdaughter who is victimized by her vile stepmother and two hideous stepsisters (The Pills). The plot has Ella entering a contest that will earn her a ticket to Hollywood and a movie contract. (Shades of Clara Bow!) Supported by her boyfriend, the iceman (whose name is "Waite Lifter"), she has photographs taken without realizing the pictures are awful. One of them shows her with a fly on her nose and with her eyes severely crossed as she tries to locate it. Ella wins, but when she gets to Hollywood she finds out that the two sharpies running the contest have gone bankrupt, and she's forced to look for work. An extended comedy sequence in

---

*Like other small actresses of the early years of film, Moore is quite tiny. She is very much like a living doll. It's interesting that one of her chief claims to fame is that she constructed a magnificent doll house, which now resides in the Chicago Museum of Science and Industry.

Moore as comedienne: *Irene* (with George K. Arthur) and *Ella Cinders*

which she tries to break into the well-guarded studio and grab herself a job is a forerunner of many such sequences that appear in sound films like *Star Spangled Rhythm* and *Anchors Aweigh*. When she finally gets inside after playing various tricks on the guard, she encounters two staples of silent film comedy: Harry Langdon (in a cameo) and a lion. Reminiscent of Mabel Normand's encounter with a studio lion in *The Extra Girl* and Charlie Chaplin's in *The Circus*, Moore's sequence gives her a chance to do some effective double takes and comedy pratfalls. After she runs into a "burning" set and starts screaming, she seems so real that she gets hired. In the end, *Ella Cinders*, in the tradition of Hollywood movies that promise women fame and riches but actually deliver them marriage in the last reel, comes up with the surprise that Waite Lifter wasn't really an iceman at all, he was a true prince—the football hero son of wealthy parents. He was just pretending to be an iceman!

Moore's last film at the end of the year was *Twinkletoes*, in which she plays Twinks, a dancer whose dad is secretly a crook. The story is old-fashioned and very sentimental, but she makes the best of it. She's given a star entrance—a shot of tiny feet running down a London cobblestone street toward a street fight. When she arrives, the camera tilts up to her cute Irish

Personae solidified: Moore sporting her trademark haircut in *Orchids and Ermine*, with Gwen Lee; Clara Bow, the hotcha flapper, just sporting, in *Mantrap*

face. She then jumps into the fight and stops it, distracting everyone by dancing for them. This would have been a typical Mary Pickford role five to ten years earlier, but Moore turns it into her own by the use of her comedy skills. She has a great scene in which she plays an untrained dancer in a chorus line, she and the other dancers all jostling each other for a good position, trying to gain the best vantage point from which to be seen. The old-fashioned melodramatic quality of the story gives her a chance to play both comedy and drama, to dance, and to ponder over such questions (seen in a title card) as "Am I fallin' for this big blister?"

By the time she appears in *Orchids and Ermine* (1927), Colleen Moore is locked into her persona. Playing yet another poor girl who is craving orchids and ermine and "a rich he," she represents the latest in fashion and attitudes, and the movie titles are up-to-date with slang terms, such as calling a checkbook a "dough diary." (Much of her comedy depends on titles like "Every girl today loves feathers, but she just can't find the right bird.") Watching Moore strut around in satin and fur, wearing an enormous spray of exotic orchids, must have seemed like the very latest in zing in the 1920s. Moore's other 1927 films were pretty much the same kind of thing: *Naughty But Nice* and *Her Wild Oat,* a late December release.

IN THE MEANTIME, Bow's career was also progressing. She rose to the top in 1925 and 1926, during which time she made an amazing total of twenty-two features. There is no question but that she was exploited, and exploited outrageously. Bow was never paid the top dollars that went to other stars, like Swanson or Pickford. A notoriously poor businesswoman and an even worse manager of her money, she also had no one to look out for her interests and help her learn how to cope (no mother to help her cut her hair and become a flaming youth). Furthermore, she seemed not to care about practical things. She liked to have fun . . . and she liked men. This quality came across on-screen, as it did with later sexy women like Jean Harlow and Marilyn Monroe, and also like Harlow and Monroe, Bow was going to pay off-screen for it.

The movies she made in 1925 and 1926 are mostly forgettable—a sampling of their titles says it all: *The Adventurous Sex, My Lady's Lips, Parisian Love, Eve's Lover, Kiss Me Again, The Primrose Path, Free to Love, Two Can Play, The Runaway, Mantrap* . . . These titles are themselves an explanation of Clara Bow's persona and career.* Out of all these movies, a few nice roles stand out. Two additional movies, *The Plastic Age,* made in 1925, and *Dancing Mothers,* in 1926, are key to her persona.

Kiss Me Again is significant because it's one of the few times Bow was featured in what might be called a quality production. Directed by Ernst Lubitsch, written by Hans Kraly, *Kiss Me Again* casts her with Monte Blue and Marie Prevost, and she received excellent notices for playing the little secretary, Grizette. As *Variety* said, "Clara Bow absolutely triumphs in the role." *Kid Boots* was another film that gave her an opportunity to work with top talent, as she played opposite Eddie Cantor in his film debut. Here was a chance to play wild comedy, and she was a perfect foil for Cantor in a cross-mountain ride on horseback, with Cantor tied onto the overburdened horse. One review said Bow was "just a world of merriment" in the role. Mostly, however, she didn't get a chance to appear in this level of material. Why bother giving her first-rate movies when she could carry the trifles? As Bow rose to stardom, most of her movies were poor. She makes them what they are, which is often delightfully fresh and entertaining, but the quality is low. They're formulaic—nothing more than "Clara Bow vehicles." Inevitably, her character is

---

*Bow's complete list of films for 1925 and 1926 is as follows: in 1925, *Capital Punishment, Helen's Babies, The Adventurous Sex, My Lady's Lips, Parisian Love, Eve's Lover, Kiss Me Again, The Scarlet West, The Primrose Path, The Plastic Age, The Keeper of the Bees, Free to Love, The Best Bad Man, Lawful Cheaters.* In 1926, *Two Can Play, The Runaway, Mantrap, Kid Boots, The Ancient Mariner, My Lady of Whims, Dancing Mothers, The Shadow of the Law.*

referred to as "a flapper" (*Adventurous Sex*), or "flapper trouble maker" (*Eve's Lover*). Her reviews are almost always excellent, and she's never panned. Yet the reviews also indicate what her career was all about, since they inevitably discuss her looks and almost never her performances. Typical Clara Bow notices say she is "pretty and active," "bright eyed and attractive," "vivacious and charming," and "pretty and vivacious and a little more." (It was the "little more" that kept her at the top.)

Two of her 1926 releases that lifted her to real stardom were *Mantrap*, directed by Victor Fleming, with whom she had an affair, and *Dancing Mothers*, directed by Herbert Brenon. The *Variety* review for *Mantrap* began with unrestrained enthusiasm: "Clara Bow! And how! What a 'mantrap' she is! And how this picture is going to make her! It should do as much for this corking little ingenue as 'Flaming Youth' did for Colleen Moore. Miss Bow just walks away with the picture from the moment she steps into camera range." Even today, this seems a fair, if somewhat hyper, evaluation. *Mantrap* is a thin story about a manicurist from Minneapolis who marries a big hick woodsman (Ernest Torrence) and goes to live with him in his isolated village of "Mantrap." When a sophisticated divorce lawyer, fed up with women, comes to town on a camping trip, Bow starts hungering for the city life again. Her first entrance into the movie is set up as a star turn—director Fleming obviously understood her appeal. As Torrence stands on a city street, he is seen looking goggle-eyed at something. A point-of-view shot reveals him to be ogling the silk-clad legs of Clara Bow as she gets out of a chauffeur-driven town car. As she turns back to say good-bye to the old man sitting in the car ("So long, Sweet Man, thanks for the buggy ride"), the camera lingers on her rear end. She is then shown in close-up, giving a saucy wink and a big smile to the old boy, who seems very pleased with himself. Bow's considerable looks and star personality are clearly being used to fill out a weak story.

Mantrap presents Bow in a star vehicle, although she is just becoming a star in it. She's shown in close-up after close-up, and allowed to dance, wiggle, and jump into the laps of unsuspecting—but delighted—men. She's outrageously flirtatious and highly aware of what she's doing. ("Why I never flirted in my life," she says, "unless it was absolutely necessary.") Furthermore, she takes charge of the two men who are fighting over her at the end by telling them off, jumping into a boat, and leaving them stranded on an island. Later, when she returns to her husband for a happy ending, the film provides a delicious punch line. Over his shoulder she spots a very handsome young Mountie arriving in town, and she begins giving him the eye as only Clara Bow knows how. Bow is the center of the movie. She's the prize to be won, and the primary plot motivation. After *Mantrap*, she *is* a star.

In *My Lady of Whims*, she plays a rich girl who's interested in living the wild life down in Greenwich Village. Her family hires a detective to find her and bring her back, but she's much too clever to be caught. (Her dad always pays these detectives with crisp, new fifty-dollar bills, so whenever she sees one, she knows to watch out.) The story is silly but fun, bolstered by Clara's pep and pretty clothes, close-up after close-up of her eyes, and a huge costume ball scene. In *Free to Love,* a foolish and badly written movie, she plays a girl sent to reform school by an unsympathetic judge. She plans to kill him when she gets out, but instead so impresses him with her passion and obvious innocence that he takes her in as his ward.

What one sees is that Clara Bow is very, very pretty, and that she is distinctive. She's a personality, not an actress, but that in many ways is the very definition of star. She can separate herself from any garbage she finds herself in, and she can always find at least one bravura moment to take advantage of—an opportunity to "let go," either by dancing wildly, kicking someone, punching someone, or, as in *Free to Love,* descending a gigantic stairway with six young men in tuxedos on two large satin reins that she's holding. (The young men are her ponies, and she wears a tiara, carries a huge plumed fan, and shakes her heavily beaded gown as she comes down.)

A rave *Variety* review for Bow in *Mantrap* appeared on July 14, 1926. The very next week, on July 21, *The Plastic Age* was reviewed. It was called "a nifty picture," with Clara Bow a "home run hitter." *The Plastic Age* was actually a 1925 production, but it had been playing out of town for several months, and had just come into New York on the heels of *Mantrap.* The two films together, coupled with her excellent reviews, solidified Clara Bow's status.

During these years, Clara Bow was under contract to B. P. Schulberg of Preferred Pictures, who made most of his money by loaning out stars to others, a practice David O. Selznick was later to imitate. Bow's 1926 success focused Schulberg on her enormous potential, especially when he realized that she was so popular with moviegoers that by the end of the year fans were writing her thousands of letters every week. He started to give her real attention, and *The Plastic Age* was promoted exclusively through her—she was sold as "the hottest jazz baby in films." (When Schulberg disbanded Preferred and returned to Paramount Pictures in 1926, he took Bow with him. She signed a contract with Paramount, where she remained until the end of her career.) Clara Bow had become a big name, although the movie that carried her to the very top, *It,* still lay ahead. Throughout 1926, she worked steadily, often playing roles that were somewhat small, although important to the action. Officially, she was only the co-lead or secondary character in both *The Plastic Age* and *Dancing Mothers,* but she had run away with both films.

Plastic Age is the story of a young athlete (played by the handsome Donald Keith) who goes away to college to run track and play football, but who falls afoul of the madcap Clara, whose high living eventually threatens his

Bow in two of her big hits: *The Plastic Age* and *Dancing Mothers* (with Alice Joyce)

training regimen. In *Dancing Mothers,* Clara is the spoiled and selfish daughter of the noble Alice Joyce, who has to become a "dancing mother" to save her willful daughter from ruining her life. In both movies, the story emphasis lies outside Clara, but in both she's the motivating force in the plot, and by far the most interesting and exciting thing on the screen.

In *Plastic Age,* Clara Bow is Betty Boop in the flesh. With her short hair, big eyes, bouncing body, and boop-a-doop personality, she's as cute as a button. Every time she comes on the screen—each time in a new outfit—she lights up everything around her. *The Plastic Age* of the title is youth, and the film is "Dedicated to the Youth of the World—whether in cloistered college halls, or in the greater University of Life." It's a story about a bunch of college kids, with the obligatory football games, snappy retorts, and slangy captions, and a wonderful raid on a roadhouse. Clara plays "the real hotsy-totsy Cynthia Day," the type of character most associated with her, a playful sexual aggressor who's so full of life and energy and spirit that she's leaping all over the place. It's clearly hinted that this means she's hot where sex is concerned, although the surface presentation is wholesome enough and Clara makes a noble sacrifice so that the young man can get back in shape and win the big game for dear old Prescott College. (In the end, of course, they reunite, aided by the formerly jealous but now understanding Gilbert Roland.) *The Plastic Age* was a huge hit. *Variety* wrote, "In it are yaps, saps, flips and flaps. For the flappers and their sundae buyers, *The Plastic Age* is perfect." This type of "with it" slangy review was aimed at the audience the movie was made for: those flappers and their sundae buyers. Clara Bow was becoming their sweetheart.

In *Dancing Mothers,* her role is similar, although she's presented as slightly younger than in *Plastic Age.* Whereas in the college movie she was a young woman with her own life, living away from her parents and driving her own car, in *Dancing Mothers* she's more a willful child just starting out in the world. She takes up the fast life, staying out late, going to nightclubs, lying to her mother, and flinging herself at an older, experienced man (Conway Tearle). She's meant to represent a kind of idealized modern girl, a girl who is more independent, more self-reliant, more daring—but who isn't really bad, just full of the devil. To represent this concept physically on the screen, Clara Bow is seen constantly hugging things to her plumpish body—pillows, little dogs, cocktail shakers—anything and everything, including men of all ages. She acts *out.* To personify "abandon," she smokes, drinks, dances, and throws herself around, shaking her big head and wiggling her little bottom. She plays a living cautionary tale for the modern girl, and seeing this sexy babe let everything hang out must have been very exciting to both men and women.

Clara Bow is certainly not a great actress, but she has two fine scenes in *Dancing Mothers,* a drunk scene that she handles very well, and a moment of shock, confusion, and heartbreak when she discovers it's her own mother who's her rival for Tearle's affection. (*Dancing Mothers,* one of her biggest successes, is extremely modern in its plot resolution. The mother, realizing that her philandering husband and her spoiled daughter are never going to be anything but the selfish creatures they are, just up and leaves them. She drives off in a taxicab toward the ship to Europe, and they're left to cope on their own, looking deflated and confused.)

Clara Bow's biggest personal success and the film that made her the "It" girl was her first release of 1927. *Flaming Youth* had come out in 1923, a full four years earlier, so she hadn't defined the term "flapper" as much as developed it, but she had managed to put her personal stamp on the term. Her area was specifically related to "It," or sex appeal. "It" was a social phenomenon of its day, rather like the hula hoop but more fun. It was a term coined by Elinor Glyn, that hack writer of the Barbara Cartland school who penned escapist romantic novels like *Three Weeks,* a Ruritanian story of love and sex. "It" was Glyn's concept, and she managed to parlay it into big-time fame for herself, which included not only an appearance in the film *It* but also big-time money in marketing the term. (Someone once said, " 'It' is a great concept, only Elinor left off the 'sh'." An even more persuasive analysis of what "It" really was, as embodied by Clara Bow, was provided by Dorothy Parker. "It?" she laughed. "She had THOSE!") Glyn, a Margaret Dumont type, was one of the great humbugs of the 1920s. Her philosophy of art was apparently "whatever will bring in the most money is the purest example," but she deserves credit for her canny exploitation of the press and the complete understanding she had of the nonsense of her day. When she came up with "It," she naturally looked to Hollywood for the biggest profit to be had from the concept, and after "picking" Clara Bow to be its embodiment, she sold it to Paramount Pictures for the neat sum of $50,000. "It," defined in the movie's titles, held long enough for even the slowest reader, was "that quality possessed by some which draws all others with its magnetic force. With IT you win all men if you are a woman—and all women if you are a man. IT can be a quality of the mind as well as a physical attraction . . . IT is that peculiar quality which some persons possess, which attracts others of the opposite sex. The possession of IT must be absolutely un-self conscious and must have that magnetic 'sex appeal' which is irresistible . . . Mothers spoil boys with IT—women never refuse them favors!" When "Madame Elinor Glyn," as she is billed, makes her grand entrance down an impressive staircase on the arm of a tuxedoed older man, she graciously consents to add to this definition: "Self confidence and indifference as to whether you are pleasing or not—and something in you that gives you the impression that you are not all cold. That's IT!" Clara Bow had "It." She could draw viewers with her "magnetic force," and please plenty of the opposite sex. (Looking at Clara, one character in the movie says to the hero, Antonio Moreno, "She's positively top heavy with IT." Indeed.)

For those who want to experience Clara Bow's particular appeal, *It* is the best place to start. It's a simple story: department store salesgirl marries rich boss. The movie smoothly introduces "It" as a concept, shows off Elinor Glyn, and allows the audience to watch Bow in all her glory. She is first seen behind the sales counter, selling lingerie, and she's adorable. "Sweet Santa Claus, give me him," she says when she spots the boss for the first time. Standing there in a simple black dress with a lace collar, she seems completely real and totally believable. Later, she dons a cloche hat with fake grapes dropping off it, and the sweetness and simple beauty of her face stand out even more. She has wonderful skin, satin smooth and alabaster white, and she really sparkles. The movie misses no opportunity to show her off, letting her cut apart her cheap dress to make an eye-catching outfit to wear out to dinner at an expensive restaurant, and taking time to show her slowly dressing for that same date, standing around in her silk stockings and lace teddy.

It was the final making of Clara Bow. Her popularity hit its peak, and, particularly since Colleen Moore was attempting dramatic roles and had reshaped the flapper concept to her own comedy design, she now became the ultimate flapper. Her success kicked off a string of new flapper movies, since Hollywood, then as now, repeated whatever worked. Madge Bellamy, Sue Carol (who later became an agent, and then Alan Ladd's wife), and Joan Crawford all played flappers with great success, in particular Crawford, whose *Our Dancing Daughters* made her a star. Today many people think of Crawford as the perfect embodiment of the 1920s flapper. However, she didn't originate the type, and didn't play it often. Since she went on to have a long and highly

Bow in *It*, as a shopgirl with an eye on the future . . .
and *with* the future, Antonio Moreno

successful sound career, which neither Bow nor Moore did, Crawford works as
an easy historical touchstone for flapperdom. Her legend was added to by
Scott Fitzgerald's calling her "the best possible example of the flapper . . .
those young things with a talent for living." She also was somewhat of a flapper off-screen, winning dance contests and being famous for her high energy
and active social life.

The difference between Crawford's flapper and those of Bow and Moore
is a level of sophistication. *Our Dancing Daughters* gets right to it, opening up
with the flapper in full flap. After a brief sight of a statue of a nude young girl
dancing, the audience is shown a pair of satin high-heeled slippers with large
lacy bows. These shoes are quickly filled by the superimposed dancing legs of
Joan Crawford, who is doing an energetic Charleston while she dresses to go
out. She gyrates wildly, pausing only to step into a pair of lacy underpants.
She adds a fringed skirt, checks her appearance, and dashes over to her bed
to throw on a fur-trimmed wrap. With a merry shout to her mother, "I'm going
to the Yacht Club. See you at dawn," she races downstairs, where her father
and three tuxedoed beaux await her. Each of the gents has a drink in his hand
for her to take a sip from, Dad instructing her to make a toast. "To myself!" she
triumphantly cries.

Crawford is not soft and luscious-looking like Clara Bow, nor is she the
perfect boy-girl like Colleen Moore. She's strong-jawed and angular, and

Joan Crawford's modern flapper, in *Our Dancing Daughters*

although extremely photogenic and beautiful, she doesn't seem to be either pliant or accommodating. Instead she exudes strength. She's all cheekbones and hips, and when she takes the floor to demonstrate her out-of-control Charleston, she's a vision of female power unleashed. In real life, Crawford was famous for these uninhibited Charlestons, and to watch her dancing is to see the real thing, unchoreographed, in the pure 1920s style, which was a rough, arms-akimbo, shake-it-baby-shake-it kind of dance. (Crawford is a great transition figure. She was a highly successful silent film actress, just on the brink of major stardom. Sound lifted her over. Her beautiful voice helped, but she also had the more angular, harsher looks tailor-made for the cynical 1930s.)

Our Dancing Daughters came out in 1928, not 1920, and the flapper by now was part of the landscape. The social change Crawford represented has partially taken place, and the concept not only needs no explanation but also asks for no apology and needs no reassurances to the audience about how it's all a pose. Crawford is not a sweet little girl who decides halfway through the movie to throw caution to the wind, lower her neckline, and risk a trip to a

Bow, the pouty
flapper, in *Rough
House Rosie*

roadhouse. This is a more advanced flapper, still virginal (although one of her
friends is not) but showing plenty of sex appeal and not afraid of it. "I'm
known as Diana the Dangerous," she tells the nervous John Mack Brown, who
looks as if he believes her.

CLARA BOW AND Colleen Moore were both at the top of their careers in
1927. If Bow had taken over Moore's role as the definitive flapper, Moore had
lost nothing. She was still on top, and by now she was more than just a flapper;
she was Colleen Moore, top box office draw. Bow had advanced herself considerably, and after *It,* everyone took her stardom—if not the woman herself—
more seriously. Immediately, Bow was given a chance to try a dramatic role in
Children of Divorce. (The male lead was played by Gary Cooper at Clara's specific request, since she was having a mad love affair with him at the time.)
Although her notices weren't bad, she seemed wasted in the role of a selfish
girl who maneuvers a man into marrying her and later kills herself, freeing
him to wed the girl he really loves. Three other 1927 movies capitalized on her
typical screen character: *Rough House Rosie,* in which she played a poor girl
trying to crash society; *Hula,* in which she plays a half-breed named Hula,
who lives on an island "where volcanoes are often active, and maidens always
are"; and her final release of the year, *Get Your Man,* directed by Dorothy
Arzner. Bow is an American girl who falls for a young duke, played by Mary
Pickford's future husband, Charles "Buddy" Rogers. She made only one other
1927 movie, but it was a big one, *Wings,* the first film ever to win the Oscar.
     Wings is a highly entertaining movie, with superb aerial combat scenes

LEFT: Bow making
film history in *Wings;*
BELOW: with Buddy
Rogers, her costar

and excellent pacing of the sort associated with its director, William A. Well-man, himself a veteran of World War I's Lafayette Flying Corps. "Reverently dedicated to those young warriors of the sky whose wings are folded about them forever," *Wings* tells a ripsnorting tale of war, but manages to place Clara Bow right in the middle of it. (It's an epic war movie enclosing a small Clara Bow movie.) Bow plays the small-town flapper-next-door who helps the hero build his own racing car, which she dubs "the shooting star." Naturally he loves someone else, but when he goes to war she follows him by joining the Women's Motor Corps. As always, Bow is vivid and alive, particularly when contrasted with the two leading men, Charles "Buddy" Rogers and Richard Arlen. Both are very handsome but not particularly lively, although Rogers has a good deal of charm. Bow would have been better paired with Gary Cooper, who has a small, showcase role of a doomed flyer. Handsome in a naturalistic way (no slicked-down hair or lounge lizard look), Cooper delivers the film's greatest line: "Luck or no luck, when your time comes, you're going to get it." In his big scene, he's given a large close-up and star treatment.

It's proof of what a big star and box office draw Clara Bow was at this time that the combat in the movie stops dead for a lengthy episode in which she encounters Buddy Rogers in Paris. This gives her a chance to change from her military uniform into a glamorous Parisian dancer's outfit. (Actually, she looked great in her tight leggings, high boots, little hat, and men's shirt and tie, but a ladies' room attendant gives her couture fashion advice on how to get Rogers to notice her, and that naturally involves a change of outfit.) Right in the middle of a war movie, Clara Bow steps out in a low-cut, dazzling gown with spangles, earrings, high heels, and diamond bracelets. After all, a star is a star. The public wants to see Clara Bow dolled up and shaking her hips around a nightclub . . . so they get to.

Both Clara Bow and Colleen Moore entered 1928 as huge stars. Bow would make more of the usual "Clara Bow" films—*Red Hair, Ladies of the Mob, The Fleet's In,* and *Three Weekends,* and Moore would make two of her own kind of comedies, *Happiness Ahead* and *Oh, Kay!* However, Moore would also make one of her best-known films, *Lilac Time,* a film that was something of a departure for her because it was partially a sentimental drama.

Lilac Time was Moore's last prestigious movie. It was an enormous hit, and its theme song, "Jeannine, I Dream of Lilac Time," also became a great success. (My parents always loved the movie. In 1936, hard-pressed for a new name for yet another daughter, they heard the "oldie" on the radio and named me for it, altering the spelling.) Like *Wings,* it was a World War I movie, and Moore was being paired with the man who should have been Bow's romantic lead in *Wings,* Gary Cooper. "Colleen Moore in *Lilac Time* with Gary Cooper," read the film's title card, showing how Cooper on his way up was being linked with Moore in the same way that she herself had once been paired with the

Bow in one of her "formula" films, *The Fleet's In*

then famous Charles Ray or Robert Harron. Moore and Cooper are two very
appealing stars, and their love scenes are touching and effective. Cooper is
clearly on his way to top stardom—he's a gorgeous young man, tall and lean
and natural and easy. However, *Lilac Time* is almost exclusively about
Colleen Moore, and it's in every way her movie.

Cast as a French girl named Jeannine (referred to in the titles as Jean-
nie), Moore is featured in almost every scene except for the air battles. Even
though it's a war story, she is the primary element, and the action frequently
stops in its tracks to feature her pantomiming skills, as when she tries to cheer
up the seven British flyers who are billeted on the lilac farm where she works.
One of their comrades has just died, so she enters dressed as a mock soldier,
with a little mustache and a broom for a gun, marching around, making faces,
posing, trying to get them to laugh. When that doesn't work, she starts juggling champagne bottles. Later, she dresses up in oversized mechanics' over-
alls, gets grease all over her face, and hides in Cooper's airplane. When it
starts up and runs away with her in an extended comic sequence, she accidentally starts firing its guns on the hapless flyers who are trying to recapture
it and rescue her. In *Lilac Time*, every possible use is made of her popularity;
every opportunity for her to dimple and smile and make comic faces is used to
advantage. At the same time, however, she is also presented as a beautiful
woman. She dresses in a lace cap and buries her face in huge bunches of
lilacs. She prays, she begs, she weeps. She's photographed in lingering close-
ups in which she is meltingly lovely. *Lilac Time* is a full showcase of the Moore
talent—she's both comedienne and dramatic leading lady, both half child (or
half doll) and emotional lover who responds to passionate kisses. With Moore,

Moore's great hit, *Lilac Time:* with her leading man, Gary Cooper, and clowning
around for the brave World War I flying corps

audiences got everything in one. But there's a scene that illustrates why the
character she played wouldn't easily carry over into the 1930s. When she's
dressed up in her Sunday best and prancing around like a little pony, trying to
attract everyone's attention, Gary Cooper—who will become one of sound's
biggest stars—sits apart from the other adoring men who surround her. She's
signaling to the audience in a typical series of 1920s attitudes—and doing it
efficiently—while Cooper is sitting back at the table. Narrowing his eyes just
a bit, he coolly appraises Colleen Moore as a woman with his pure, 1930s
"let's-go-for-real-sex" attitude. For one brief moment, a modern viewer can
identify two totally different decades: Moore is the perfect 1920s doll woman
and Cooper the perfect 1930s natural actor. She was a skilled and likable performer, but she wasn't a great actress, only a good one . . . and she wasn't a
universal archetype. She was an icon locked into her own decade.

THEN, SUDDENLY, IT WAS 1929, a year of reckoning for the two young
women who had been the embodiment of the 1920s flapper. Although they
were still very young (Bow was twenty-four, and Moore was twenty-nine), they
were top stars. Moore's influence on American fashion was tremendous.
Young girls cut their hair to look like hers and adopted her boyish look: short
skirts, flat chest, and low-heeled shoes. Any woman could get a haircut like
Colleen Moore's no matter what type of hair she had. (As early as 1922,

The transformation of Moore from Pickfordish sweetheart
to sleek 1920s flapper

Picture-Play had recognized Moore's fashion influence, saying that outside
the studio "she is a little flapper, dressed ahead of the style.") Bow, for her
part, had her own large effect on women's fashions. Her hair was luxuriantly
thick, and it curled wildly around her head; to get your hair to look like Clara
Bow's—that was a challenge, because nature had to have played a hand in it.
Her bow lips were another matter. No matter what shape of mouth any female
of the era had, she could use her lipstick to trace a "Clara Bow" mouth on her
face. Bow's lips, plucked eyebrows, and dark lipstick became a fashion trend.
To look at the designated sex symbols of the silent era is almost an exercise in
comedy. Here's Theda Bara—eyes like coal pits, overweight, and silly—or
Mae Murray, bee-stung lips, giddy stance, and batting her eyelashes. Clara
Bow, on the other hand, translates easily into modern times. It's easy to see
why she was the leading sex symbol of her time—she's *still* sexy.

By the time sound arrived, Moore and Bow were no longer naive girls dreaming over movie magazines. They were themselves inside the magazine pages, and they had changed. Moore's progress can be followed by comparing a 1916 photograph of her with one from 1928. In the early, somewhat sentimental portrait she wears almost no makeup and her natural looks are on full display. She wears a gossamer gown, and has the usual ton of long, thick, carefully arranged hair that marks the teen years. She stares straightforwardly into the camera with no guile, no flirtation, and no pose, her chin resting on her little hand. Twelve years later, in one of the publicity stills for *Synthetic Sin,* she's completely changed. She wears high-heeled shoes, shiny silk stockings, and reveals her bare knees. She sports her famous "Colleen Moore" bob, her dark black hair hanging loose and free around her face, cut in its harsh lines. On her arms are multiple bracelets, and at her throat an elaborate necklace. Her dress is made of material that is transparent at the top. Her arms are naked. Most significantly of all, she is striking a pose that is not only defiant but sexy. She's grinning impishly and waving flirtatiously. (You've come a long way, baby.) The difference between these two photographs is the exact story of what happened to the American girl in the decade of the 1920s, and part of the reason it happened was due to the young woman in these pictures.

The change in Clara Bow was not so much one of looks as of behavior. She had been a child of poverty and neglect and had suddenly come into money, fame, and if not business or political power, at least an understanding of her own sexual power. She became known for her very colorful off-screen life, and was eventually brought low by scandal. She could be seen about town driving her fire-engine-red car at full speed, and her many love affairs, madcap adventures, and careless, sometimes drunken exploits were well known to everyone in the business. Bow came to personify what the *New York Times* would later call (in her obituary) "the giddier aspects of an unreal era, the Roaring Twenties." Besides her gambling, carousing, and rumored affairs, Bow was splashed across the newspapers in 1931 when her former secretary, friend, confidante, and sometime manicurist, Daisy De Voe, tried to blackmail her. Bow sued De Voe and in retaliation, De Voe used the trial to publicize details of Bow's private life: bouncing checks, bouncing bedsprings, and plenty of drinks for one and all. De Voe was convicted and sent to prison for eighteen months, later to issue a statement worthy of the hardbitten 1930s: "I was a pet of all the prison wardens," she boasted, " 'cause I did their nails."

Bow's talking debut was in the 1929 *Wild Party,* directed by Dorothy Arzner and pairing her with Fredric March. In it, she looks fabulous, and she's so young it's impossible to imagine that her career was nearly over. Her entrance into sound was made much of, but with a slightly snooty attitude, since no one ever took Bow's acting very seriously. The *New York Times* trumpeted, "From Nome to Key West and from John O'Groat's to Tahiti, be it known that the voice of Clara Bow has been recorded in a motion picture, which, provided the theatres are wired for sound, can be heard by all nations . . . Miss Bow's voice is better than the narrative . . . It is not overly melodious in its delivery, but it suits her personality." But she had always been a critics' favorite, and she was to be forgiven things that John Gilbert would not. Besides, she sounded the way she looked, and her hotcha honeys were often lower-class, so any failures of diction or pronunciation could be overlooked. Since Clara's charm resided in her physical self, which was definitely intact, it was easy to assume that she could sail through the transition to sound, particularly since her sexy characters were still viable in the hard-boiled early thirties.

After her talking debut, she made two more films in 1929, *Saturday Night Kid* and *Dangerous Curves*. In 1930, she would do *Paramount on Parade* (taking her turn in an all-star musical revue), *True to the Navy, Love Among the Millionaires,* and *Her Wild Night,* and in 1931, *No Limit* and *Kick In.* These movies did not break with what had made her famous. She played such roles as a department store girl, a circus bareback rider, a soda jerk, a hash house waitress, and a movie usherette. She was charming in all of them, and her notices were good. Her voice sounded fine, and she even showed she could sing quite well in a warm contralto. Clara's career wasn't on fire, but it was far from dead. She had survived the transition to sound, and her movies, which cost little to make, were still clearing a profit. However, something else was happening to her. Bow was the daughter of a mentally unstable mother, and she began to suffer nervous breakdowns. Over the years since her death, the tragic circumstances of her childhood and family life have gradually leaked out—particularly the truth about her abusive father. Hers was an early world that was grim, humorless, disease-ridden, and cruel, with an unrelenting poverty. The pressures of constant work and the scrutiny of fame took their toll, and she felt she could not go on—her career would end with two highly entertaining movies, *Call Her Savage* (1932) and *Hoopla* (1933). After asking to have her contract with Paramount terminated, she entered a sanatorium for rest and recovery. It was not sound that destroyed Clara Bow, but heredity and the horrors of her youth.

What stopped Colleen Moore's career was apparently Colleen Moore. Like many another famous silent star, Colleen Moore was at the peak of her success at the end of 1928. In 1929, she released three movies: *Why Be Good?, Smiling Irish Eyes,* and *Footlights and Fools.* Her talking debut was in the second of these, about which one critic commented, "Miss Moore seems to have a good voice." In *Footlights and Fools,* she even sang to good notices. Since there was nothing wrong with her voice, and since she was still quite

Moore's *The Power and the Glory*, with Spencer Tracy

young and a top box office star, what happened to Colleen Moore's career? She chose to stay off the screen after *Footlights and Fools* until *The Power and the Glory* in 1933.* She signed a contract with MGM in 1932, but was loaned to Fox for the latter, which costarred Spencer Tracy. An excellent film, *The Power and the Glory* is the prototype of *Citizen Kane,* featuring out-of-sequence, overlapping flashbacks (it was written by Preston Sturges). It tells the story of a man's rise to riches and the effect this has on his family, particularly the loyal wife he married while he was still poor (Moore). Moore later said she thought it was the best film she ever made, but she was beginning to wonder about the world outside of Hollywood. "It seemed to me there had to be more to life than just work . . . I wondered if the success I had had in my career had to be compensated for by not having much personal happiness." She made three more films, all released in 1934—*Success at Any Price, The Social Register,* and *The Scarlet Letter.* The last was a dismal failure at every level, and according to her, she made it only to obtain enough money to finish building her beloved doll house. After that, she left movies forever, remarking that the public didn't want her in serious roles. "They wanted me to go on being a wide-eyed, innocent little girl. I was too old for that—and too tired of it in any case. So I bowed out." It seems to be a completely candid assess-

*Among other things, she did a Broadway play. Her marriage to John McCormack had broken up in 1929. This marriage was a disaster for Moore. She had married the alcoholic McCormack, a movie publicity agent, at a young age and suffered greatly in the relationship until she finally found the courage to divorce him. Her second marriage, to Albert Parker Scott, who had a seat on the New York Stock Exchange, also ended in divorce.

ment. Moore was a woman of intelligence, and she wanted something different. She had already lived her dream of stardom and found it wanting, and she
had put more than fifteen years of hard work into the business. The career of
Colleen Moore was over in 1934.

Colleen Moore was perhaps a bigger star than Clara Bow, but she was
not as big a personality. Bow had to carry weak movies that were designed to
capitalize on her fame. Despite her off-screen didoes, audiences loved her,
because she always seemed to be giving it everything she had. Critics who
wrote about her all used the same words—"vibrant," "energetic," "sparkling"—and her image still elicits these same descriptions from everyone who
sees her today because they're accurate. She really *is* extraordinarily vibrant,
energetic, and sparkling. Clara Bow lit up the screen as much as—if not more
than—any other star in movie history. She's three-dimensional in her presence, and this quality, projected onto her down-to-earth, regular-guy flappers,
makes her seem terribly real and true to audiences. Both men and women fell
in love with her natural charm.

Sometimes watching Bow on film one can only wonder—did she have
the itch? Was she a victim of that mysterious disease we heard about as children, Saint Vitus' dance? She jumps around, leaps up and down, and throws
herself into her movies with manic enthusiasm. Critics often pointed out her
aggressive physicality. Richard Watts, Jr., a New York film critic, once
described her as a sort of "Northwest Mounted Policeman of sex, who gets her
man even if she has to bludgeon him," and a review of her work in *Mantrap*
commented that she could "flirt with a grizzly bear." An amusing—and true—
comment about her came from Richard Schickel, who said, "Among the
heavy-breathing, comically serious 'artists' of the silent era, she was like a
sudden chorus of JADA at a Wagnerian opera."

Although Moore took a while to find her perfect movie persona (the flapper), she has a much greater range than Bow, who can really do only one thing
and that is be Clara Bow. As she gained her top stardom, Moore became free
and easy inside the frame of her own style. She doesn't become loose and sexy,
like Bow, but she uses her body with her own particular skill, making it tense
and robotlike for the purposes of visual comedy. When she rolls her eyes and
executes a pratfall, she defines for the audience the great inside joke of flapperdom: it's not really about having sex but about avoiding it. It's about women
liberating themselves *from* it, rather than liberating themselves to embrace it.

Both Clara Bow and Colleen Moore were out of the limelight before the
mid-thirties. In 1937, Moore was married a third time, and this time happily,
to Homer Hargrave of Chicago. She became a caring stepmother to his children, moved away from Hollywood, and became famous for her magnificent
doll house, which she exhibited in a nationwide tour of department stores to
raise money for charity. She wrote a guide to making money in the stock mar-

ket (she advised friends, "You simply can't be comfortable without six million dollars"), and had a solid success with her autobiography in 1968, dying in 1988 a wealthy and fulfilled matron. Of her fame, she said, "I had made a total of sixty motion pictures—one as a bit player, fifteen as a leading lady, nineteen as a featured player, and twenty-five as a star. I had given up my girlhood in order to pursue my burning ambition. If I had had it to do over, I didn't doubt that I would have done exactly as I had before. But I wasn't a girl any longer. And I had learned a number of things along the way which were more important to me in the long run than how to make successful movies."

Clara Bow married cowboy actor Rex Bell in 1931 and went to live on his ranch. She had two sons, Rex in 1934 and George in 1938, but mental illness finally claimed her, and she spent the rest of her life in sanatoriums or in seclusion. She was occasionally remembered, as when she impersonated "Miss Hush" on Ralph Edwards's radio show *Truth or Consequences* in 1947, or when Rex Bell was elected lieutenant governor of Nevada in 1954 and reelected in 1958. When her husband died of a heart attack in 1962, she came out of seclusion to attend his funeral, but she was accompanied by a nurse. She herself died three years later. For someone who was not rumored to be particularly bright and who certainly had no education, Clara Bow could be remarkably sharp in her observations. When asked what the difference was between the stars of her era and the more publicity-wary celebrities of modern times, she said, "They're sensible, and end up with better health. But we had more fun." About her life in Hollywood, she said, "It wasn't ever like I thought it was going to be. It was always a disappointment to me." Years ahead of Marilyn Monroe, she remarked that "a sex symbol is always a heavy load to carry, especially when one is very hurt, tired, and bewildered." In an obituary tribute in the *New York Morning Telegraph*, Whitney Bolton, who had known her, wrote, "She had fright in her . . . She had defiance that was a flower of fright. She had a kind of jaunty air of telling you that she didn't care what happened, she could handle it." Obviously, she couldn't handle it, but just as obviously, she could put on a very brave face. To Clara Bow may go the last word on the flapper phenomenon or, indeed, on any other movie fad or stardom. When asked, "Miss Bow, when you add it all up, what is 'It'?," after thinking for a moment, she replied, "I ain't real sure."

RIN-TIN-TIN

FORGET YOUR LASSIES, your Benjis, and your Beethovens, because great as you may think they are, amused by their shenanigans as you may have been, unless you have compared them to Rin-Tin-Tin, you cannot seriously discuss canine thespians. Other dogs may be good, but Rin-Tin-Tin was a *Star.* Consider the facts. At the height of his fame, in the middle to late twenties, he received as many as 12,000 fan letters a week. He earned $6,000 a month, was insured for $100,000, and had his own valet, chef, limo, and driver. He had an orchestra for mood music while he worked, a diamond-studded collar, and eighteen doubles to cover for him when he was tired. He ate only the best T-bone steaks, except when the story called for him to jump through a windowpane made of the finest spun sugar, because then he was allowed to devour the sweet as a reward. He had a personal secretary to handle his crowded schedule and his lucrative endorsement contract with Ken-L Rations, who featured his photograph on every box they sold—and with his help, they sold plenty. He was asked to pose for photographs with numberless visiting dignitaries. He lived a star's life, and he died a star's death: Rinty, beloved dog actor and greatest animal star in film history, met his maker while cradled in the lap of the blonde bombshell Jean Harlow.

There were an extraordinary number of animal stars in the silent era—animals of all kinds, not only dogs. Mack Sennett had a veritable menagerie under contract. In addition to his own famous dog, Teddy—the Great Dane who drove a train and had his own stunt double—Sennett had Fatty Arbuckle's sidekick dog, Luke, and Props, a stray who just showed up one day and, no doubt sensing a good deal, promptly started licking the tears off a baby and was awarded with a solid contract. Sennett also had Anna May the elephant, who, unlike so many of her fellow thespians, went on to a successful sound career in Tarzan films. She had true star temperament and such an affinity for the camera that it was said that the minute it started rolling, you could see a change come over her. There were the lions, Numa and Duke, Susie the chicken, and Josephine the monkey, who played pool and golf and could drive a car, to say nothing of Pepper, the Lillian Gish of cats, who could lick cream off her paws on cue and who was reputed to be so smart that when her costar Teddy the Dog died and a look-alike substitute was run in on her, she spat and walked off the set. (When Pepper just disappeared one day, Mack Sennett issued a statement to the press: "She retired at the top.") Sennett's troupe of animals was well documented because it had its own publicity machine, but animals were acting in films all over Hollywood in those days. There were Rex the Wonder Horse, Tom Mix's Tony, and William S. Hart's beloved Fritz, not to mention a group of acting monkeys called the Dippity-Do-Dads, a parrot, an alligator, and even a turtle—all with more than one movie to their credit.

The moviegoing public loved these performers, and anything the public loved, the fan magazines covered. They featured elaborate layouts of photographs and drawings of the animals, and fans cut them out and put them in scrapbooks and pasted them on their kitchen walls much as people today buy calendars with full-color portraits of cats and dogs. The magazines invented a genre of pseudo-articles allegedly written by the animals themselves—elaborate "biographies" and "interviews" that recounted the typical star story: discovery, rise to fame, adjustment to riches, all the while remaining the same simple animals they had once been back in the barnyard. Pepper, the Sennett cat, was given a star "interview" in the May 1920 issue of *Picture-Play*, in which she "discusses" her three years of stardom for Sennett, highlighted by such popular hits as *Back to the Kitchen* and *Down on the Farm*. She praises "costars" like Louise Fazenda, Ford Sterling, and Teddy, the Great Dane. (According to Pepper, Teddy was her "supporting cast," but Teddy might have put it differently.) She confesses that she absolutely hates having to do stunts, especially when forced to work all day with a mouse—without eating him. Sitting outside her very own little cathouse, the "Villa Paprika," Pepper assures her fans that she is always on the lot, always ready for her next scene, and heavily insured against accidents. In another article, Josephine, the monkey, shows off her huge wardrobe and her superb table manners for the interviewer, while her "manager" proudly boasts that Josephine has an "I.Q. of 140."

Of all the animal stars, however, it was the dogs that really reached the top. There were an amazing number of them, with the alleged "first" being the beautiful collie Jean, who could untie knots, thereby setting free any hero stupid enough to get himself tied up. There were Sennett's Teddy and Luke, of course, and also Sandow, Brownie, Strongheart, Silverstreak, Ranger, Fangs, Thunder, Peter the Great, Dynamite, Lightning, Peter the Second, Fido, Napoleon Bonaparte—and more. There were so many, and so many movies starring them, that a weary critic finally admitted in print to "a sinking of the stomach when another police dog was flashed across the screen at the Tivoli," because, as he frankly stated, "a new mutt is just an additional strain."

Throughout the twenties, dog stars held the public's attention, and the seriousness with which their films was taken is reflected in the reviews. Every dog was given a hard-nosed critical evaluation. Silverstreak was "a great dog actor" who could "put over a new trick or two in almost every new release." Thunder was "a police dog [who] has a corking trick of winking at proper moments." Fangs was "a good natured pup," but he would never really become a star because he "lacked fire" and was "averse to fighting." Sandow (billed as "Sandow, the Dog," in case people didn't notice) was panned for his performance in *Avenging Fangs* (1927): "Sandow was too playful to agree with the subtitles, feeling pretty happy over things when the printed inserts would have him grim and merciless . . . Sandow won't be proud of this [film]." The worst reviews always went to poor Ranger, the Vera Hruba Ralston of dogs. The bottom line on Ranger was simple: "not a good actor." He was called "an impossible animal star" who, even worse, was surrounded by "a poor supporting cast." In a review of *Breed of Courage* (1927), he was humiliated with "Ranger is still not a good actor, inclusive [*sic*] of all the progress he has made since last seen. In the fight scene, he is one of the tamest in the business. The heavy practically drags the dog toward him instead of the animal attacking. In several cases the menace falls to the floor, pulling the dog down on top of him in semblance of a fight." (Later, the reviewer relents and praises Ranger reluctantly for effectively eating a dynamite fuse to prevent an explosion.)

Whenever a new canine star appeared, reviewers took notice. "Napoleon Bonaparte" starred for the first time in a 1927 movie called *The Silent Hero. Variety* wrote, "The new dog star . . . looks okay. He can act nasty when asked, and fights without that playful spirit noted in others." He, like many before the arrival of Rin-Tin-Tin, was compared to the beautiful Strongheart, who was Rinty's greatest rival. Strongheart was known as "a good looking, upstanding animal," well worthy of "his starring honors." There were so many dogs appearing in movies that sometimes they were left nameless, as in *The Fighting Three* (1927), which starred western favorite Jack Hoxie and "a horse and a dog," or in *His Dog* (1927), whose lead was listed merely as "A Collie." There was no way reviewers could ignore these performing dogs, because they made money at the box office and had legions of loyal fans.

No animal, however, no matter what its reviews or box office success, was a patch on the great Rin-Tin-Tin. Like Tallulah and Elvis and Madonna, he had an unusual name. Like Bogie and Kate, he had that name shortened into a beloved nickname: Rinty. And like so many great stars, he came from humble origins with a rags-to-riches tale: a climb out of the trenches of World War I up to the heights of Hollywood movie stardom. It began on the morning of September 15, 1918, when an American soldier, Corporal Lee Duncan, came across an abandoned German war dog station. Huddled inside was a

Rin-Tin-Tin, handsome dog, in *Clash of the Wolves*,
with supporting cast, June Marlowe and Charles Farrell

half-starved mother with five newborn puppies, all of which Duncan rescued, eventually bringing two of them home with him to the United States. (The other three found new homes in Europe.) Duncan named his two dogs, one female and one male, for Nanette and Rin-Tin-Tin, the good-luck dolls carried into war by French soldiers. To Duncan's disappointment Nanette died upon their arrival in New York, but Rin-Tin-Tin survived. (Later, a semiautobiographical movie starring Rinty was made of this dramatic story. Called *A Dog of the Regiment* [1927], it presented him intrepidly performing first aid chores for his mistress, a Red Cross nurse behind combat lines. This makes Rinty the Audie Murphy of dogs.)

Corporal Duncan turned out to be an imaginative entrepreneur who, having realized Rinty's amazing ability to learn, decided to train him for the movies. When he first presented his dog for hire, his extravagant claims for Rinty's talents caused Jack L. Warner to exclaim, "This I gotta see. A dog that can act!" As it turned out, not only could Rinty act, he had plenty more going for him, too. He was handsome and he was smart and, like Joan Crawford among so many others, he seemed to know by instinct that stardom was a viable way out of bone-crushing poverty. Like Joan, he learned fast and was willing to do whatever it took to succeed. Jack Warner cast Rinty in his first starring feature, *Where the North Begins*, in 1923, and he was at once labeled "a good actor" by critics and accepted by the public.

Rinty quickly surpassed the very popular Strongheart, and the fan magazines dutifully covered the shift of fan loyalty from one dog to another. In the

Rinty's main rival, Strongheart, in *North Star*

December 1921 issue of *Photoplay*, two years before Rinty entered films, "The Story of Strongheart" is presented as the feature article of the month, with Strongheart photographs spread over a lavish layout. "Strongheart," the article gushed, was a stage name; he had, in fact, been born "Etzel," a German name because he was a German dog. (Readers were reassured that Etzel had "served nobly" in the German Red Cross during World War I, thus eliminating any fears that he had actually been a German trooper.) Strongheart, readers are told, is taking his place on the dog star roster alongside such popular canines as Sennett's Teddy and Universal's very popular Brownie. But Teddy and Brownie, *Photoplay* carefully points out, are comedy dogs, whereas Strongheart "is a dramatic dog; an emotional actor," which makes him unique. In other words, Strongheart is like all the other foreign actors and actresses who came over from Europe to straighten Hollywood out about just what serious acting really was.

Strongheart reigns supreme in the fan mags through 1923, but by March 1924 the handwriting is on the wall. *Motion Picture* publishes an article ominously entitled "The Rival of Strongheart." This new star, "Rintintin [*sic*]," is said to be "now competing with Strongheart for the canine celluloid honors," *Where the North Begins* (1923) placing him "in the stellar ranks." *Motion Picture* did not doubt "Rintintin's" movie power, particularly, as the story points out, "now that he has a press agent and a specially constructed motor car." By 1925, articles about Strongheart were fading, while Rin-Tin-Tin was appearing in almost every other issue.

Ultimately, Rin-Tin-Tin not only surpassed Strongheart, he became the biggest dog star of the era and Warner Brothers' top box office draw—he was nicknamed "the mortgage lifter," because his movies bailed Warners out of financial difficulties and kept them solvent. The films he made between 1923 and 1930 also earned Lee Duncan over $5 million. In addition, Rinty helped to advance the career of Darryl F. Zanuck, who was at the time a young writer at Warners, and who understood early on that Rin-Tin-Tin was box office gold. Zanuck played a key role in building Rinty into a superstar and a fan favorite. Jack Warner, who had at first been so skeptical, ended up loving the dog, pointing out that "he didn't ask for a raise, or a new press agent, or an air-conditioned dressing room, or more close-ups." (Since Warner was famous for being cheap with his actors and resenting their demands for perks, no doubt Rin-Tin-Tin was his ideal movie star.)

Watching Rin-Tin-Tin's films today, it isn't difficult to appreciate their strengths. They're enormously fast-paced, with an effective no-nonsense approach to storytelling. The production values are superior, with excellent outdoor location shooting, competent human supporting casts, and solid writing and directing. They understand how to please a crowd by including a little something for everyone: a little comedy, a little romance, a little sentiment, and a lot of danger and action. And the hard-nosed businessmen who supervised the Rinty pictures knew how to turn them out for a minimum of money, so that they were not only entertaining but hugely profitable.

The world of Rin-Tin-Tin is obviously of another time and another place. It is for the most part a bucolic world, with simple values and straightforward definitions of good and evil. Central to the appeal of his movies, there is always some key task to be performed: a gold mine to be found, a dam to be built, a stagecoach to be saved from robbers, wild wolves to be outrun, homesteads to be staked, even wars to be fought. Time's a wastin', and the humans need help, being the poor befuddled fools they are. In fact, the basic plot always consists of Rinty having to save the day because he's surrounded by human beings who are either remarkably venal, remarkably innocent, or remarkably stupid—often all three types in one film. The number of times that poor Rinty tries to tell people something important and they just don't get it is amazing. As his career advances, he looks more and more annoyed about this, but he is never less than a trouper; he always dashes into the situation at full speed, takes a quick look around to size things up, decides on a plan of action, and carries it out with excellent results. (Many actors would benefit from these skills.)

Rin-Tin-Tin's action stunts were cleverly varied to allow him to do the same thing many times while making it appear to be different. For instance, Rinty was a strong swimmer. Thus, he would jump into the water to retrieve a crutch for a little crippled child, or he would jump into the water to save a baby. He would also jump into the water to drown a villain or save a heroine from going over the falls. All that was required was that the river be rushing rapidly, and that he jump in, retrieve the item (or, in the case of the villain, leave it there), and bring it safely back to shore.

In everything he did, Rinty was humanized as far as possible. He was even given a love interest, finding himself a girlfriend in more than one film, and on occasion actually marrying and settling down with a wife and pups. In *Tracked in the Snow Country* (1925), he mates with a widow wolf, and in *Hills of Kentucky* (1927), he is a married dog when the film opens, "having fought the pack to win" his soul mate, played by the classy female dog star Nanette (not to be confused with his late sibling). In *Tracked by the Police* (1927), he falls for the leading lady's pretty "blonde" dog, also played by Nanette. ("After all, gentlemen do prefer blondes," says a coy title.)

The plain fact is that Rinty's movies are peppy and uncomplicated. They know how to bring an audience into their simple dilemmas and then step up the excitement so that, even today, you start caring about what happens. A typical example is *Jaws of Steel* (1928). It opens on a car driving across the Mojave Desert, carrying a little puppy (Rinty) and his "people": Jason Robards (senior) as John Warren, Helen Ferguson as his wife, Mary, and little Mary Louise Miller as "Baby Warren." When Baby's doll drops out the back window, Rinty jumps out of the car to run back and fetch it, but no one notices. He can't catch up to the speeding car and has no choice—after he has suffered enough—but to grow up and become a wild dog. (Title cards tell us that at first "Rinty was frightened, lost and alone," but one year later "He had conquered his fear and mastered the desert. He was no longer a dog, but a beast among beasts—known through the valley as The Killer.")

The Warren family lives in a deserted old town that they have been conned into believing will be a wonderful place to live while they work the worthless gold mine they have trustingly purchased. When grown-up Killer Rinty noses into town and reunites emotionally with Baby, the grown-ups don't trust him. ("He eats little babies!") Daddy even shoots at Rinty, since only the kid recognizes the truth of who he really is. Rinty and Baby start having secret play meetings, in which Rinty uses his teeth to pull a rope tied to the bottom of her swing. When she wants to remove her heavy boots, Rinty pulls them off for her, and when grown-ups show their intolerant faces, he hides in the laundry basket. Meanwhile, there's hanky-panky, as the villain murders "Alkali Joe," Warren's kind old partner, and steals the map to the gold mine that has suddenly and remarkably panned out. The villain then plants clues to blame the murder on Killer Rinty, but Rinty has other things on his mind. Baby is very, very ill: she misses her dog friend so much she just can't go on. Rinty sneaks into the languishing child's room, and as she perks up, her mother hesitates, giving Rinty the opportunity to do some tricks. He sits up, rolls over, and the mother suddenly gets it: This is Rinty! She sends

Rinty on the job: TOP, he attacks
(*Tracked in the Snow Country*) and
he brings the plasma (*A Dog of the
Regiment*); ABOVE, he picks the lock
and serves up the canteen (*A Dog of
the Regiment*); LEFT, he rescues Fair
Maiden (*Tracked by the Police*)

him off to fetch her husband and the townsmen, who have formed a posse to search out the Killer Rinty and dispatch him. Mom wants the men to go for the doctor instead, as Baby is once again fading. Rinty sets out, and here is where it becomes clear that this dog has real brains. Since the posse is after him, he figures the best thing to do is show himself to them, so he can lure them back home to rescue Baby.

A great outdoor chase ensues, in which Rinty breaks his paw in a jump to freedom. This action calls for all his acting skill. He has to fall, roll down a hill, express pain, and then get up and limp across the landscape as fast as he can with the posse in hot pursuit. (Rinty never forgets his limp, and always remembers which paw is supposed to be broken.) Back home, after the doctor tells the parents that Baby's dying from that prevalent film disease, Dog-Loss Grief, the parents understand that they must reunite their child with her dog. Then Rinty unmasks the villain, and all is right with the world.

This plot may sound silly, but it works, because it never stops moving and the dog is really very charming, the leading lady is very pretty, and everyone in the piece knows his or her job and does it well. It's not hard to understand why movies like this made money. They're simple and fun, and furthermore they're short—about an hour in running time. Nobody has a chance to get bored.

In one of his best films, *Tracked by the Police* (1927), Rinty is faced with a complex moral dilemma. Not one but two leading ladies get into deep trouble. First, the human female star (Virginia Brown Faire) finds herself hanging from a crane over a sabotaged dam. Next, Rinty's own leading lady dog is put in chains and thrown into the rushing river. What to do, what to do? Duty or Love? Should Rinty remain man's best friend and save the woman, or should he follow his heart and save his own true love? (Rinty and "Princess Beth"— played by Nanette—have done a lot of necking and nuzzling each other; the leading man, Jason Robards, Sr., and Ms. Faire, on the other hand, haven't shown us much of anything.) Rinty, being the brainy dog he is, uses his head—and his paws. First, he cleverly operates the crane to rescue Ms. Faire, choosing Duty, because that's the kind of noble dog he is. Then he rushes in to manipulate the dam's operating mechanisms, turning back the flood, and, although at first he thinks "Princess Beth" is dead, manages to save both females. (*Variety*'s reviewer does muse on this a bit: "It is hard to tell just why a dog is gifted with human intelligence." The *New York Times* complains outright: "His exploits in determining the levers that close the locks seems like asking almost too much of any animal.")

The astonishing thing about watching Rin-Tin-Tin is that you begin to agree that this dog *could* act. He could do a lot more than roll over and play dead. He could listen at keyholes, hide under beds and inside grandfather clocks, tug open bolted doors, and track and sneak up on villains. He could operate simple machines, put on little shoes and take them off, and he could run and jump on cue. This is already more than some human stars could accomplish, but Rinty could also stir up emotions by looking happy or sad or worried or hurt. And Rin-Tin-Tin was one fine-looking animal. When he moved in on a costar, plopped his big head down in the lap, and googled up with his soft brown eyes, it was all over for the human performer. Rinty was a real scene stealer. So subtle were the nuances of his performance that one reviewer commented on how he managed to rehabilitate a hero who had fallen into slovenly habits by making him feel so ashamed of himself that he got up and gave the house a thorough cleaning. (How this was accomplished the reviewer did not make clear.) *Variety* wrote of his performance in *Tracked in the Snow Country* that he "shows himself to be as effective a canine actor as ever, shedding real tears when his master dies and portraying most effectively the mental torture of a poor animal pursued and hounded by those who had formerly loved him."

Rinty's evolution as a dog actor is traceable. In his earliest films, while still a novice, he performs a few clever tricks but often seems to be looking off-camera, obviously watching for instructions from his master. As his confidence and experience grow, he more and more appears to be on his own, motivated by the narrative and carrying out complex instructions regarding action as well as conveying specific emotions in his close-ups. (Observers on the set often pointed out that Rinty increasingly was able to play lengthy scenes and go through complicated routines without stopping and without direction.) For instance, in the 1924 The *Lighthouse by the Sea,* Rinty accomplishes some amazing feats. When his master is shackled and incapacitated by the villains, Rinty brings him matches and a big piece of cloth so he can clumsily set the fabric on fire. Rinty then gallops up to the top of the lighthouse and rekindles its light with this flame. However, although he is a "retired Red Cross veteran" and manages to best a bulldog rival ("The Yukon Killer") in a fair fight, Rinty has less to do than the humans in this early movie. Rinty is heroic, but so are the leading man (William Collier, Jr.) and even the leading lady (Louise Fazenda). By 1927, however, Rinty is on a roll and needs very little human support. He is always introduced first, as in *Hills of Kentucky,* in which he plays "The Grey Ghost," so called because of his "phantom-like raids and escapes." In this excellent feature Rinty is the main show, and he rises to the occasion, giving a real performance. When he's wounded and helped by a crippled child, he begins to feel domesticated and slowly indicates the change. When the child leads him toward his home, Rinty wants to come, but is shy, apprehensive, reluctant. He comes forward toward the boy, then draws back, then circles around, ducks and runs, then returns. He even has his own subjective point-of-view shots, and his thinking process is clearly established through cutting and narrative. He's actually amazing. ("Doggie, I love you," says the little boy, and no doubt the audience echoed the sentiment.)

Over the years of his stardom, his stunts grew more complicated and his screen time was stretched out. His introductory titles grew more and more flamboyant, as in *Tracked by the Police* (1927): "Loyal and true, with the heart of a lion and the soul of a child, that was Satan, Sentinel of the Desert." The films themselves were also increasingly polished, as this same movie presents a complex overhead shot from which Rinty views the villain menacing the leading lady. (Poor Rinty is wounded, as he frequently is, and hiding in the attic. Unfortunately, he drips blood down onto the hand of the villain below, alerting him to his presence.)

Rinty's most dramatic close-up takes place in *Night Cry* (1925), in which, with his ears drooping and sagging, he lets his eyes tear up with emotion for his big break-down-and-cry scene—an Oscar-worthy performance. *Night Cry* is Rinty's *Hamlet*. Playing a faithful sheepdog suspected of killing lambs, he is shot and wounded by ranchers on the prowl for him. He limps home to his master—who has been ordered to kill him on sight because it's "the law of the range"—and comes in expecting the little family of rancher, wife, and baby to help him. As he begs for their attention, they ignore him, trying to cope with their emotions, knowing he must be killed. Rinty goes all out, resting his chin on their supper table, moisture in his eyes, turning his head slowly from one to the other, pleading, looking deeply hurt, sad, and bewildered. (One can't help feeling terrible for him.) Later, he redeems himself when the real killer, a giant condor that apparently has come north for the summer, carries off the baby and Rinty has to save her.

My favorite example of Rinty's ingenuity is a scene in which, having tracked a band of villains across the desert, he shows up in an isolated town only to realize he's the only dog around and is bound to be recognized. With a little help from the hero, Rinty goes into a general store, locates a beard, dons it, and emerges—well disguised as a kind of goat or a very weird-looking other dog. Rinty in disguise! (There is a stunning moment when he contemplates himself in the mirror in this getup, fleetingly looking depressed, as if to say, "Is this any way for a dog to make a living?") A moment of high suspense comes when the beard accidentally drops off and he is recognized (a lynch mob takes out after him). In this same movie, he also puts on little boots, partly because he has a bum foot. This means that eventually he has to use his teeth to unlace them (in full close-up, so we can see he's really doing it), because they hinder his climb up a slippery roof. Rin-Tin-Tin also spends a lot of time trying to alert the silly heroine to the fact that there's a message for her written on a water canteen he has efficiently delivered to her. Instead, she drinks from it while holding it the wrong way so the villain can read the message intended for her. Rinty is clearly disgusted. (This film, by the way, is very definitely not a comedy. It's called *Clash of the Wolves*, 1925.)

After a certain point, reviewers began to get really cranky about having to review dogs. After all, how were they supposed to evaluate these performances? To them, a dog was apparently just a dog. A sour note begins to creep in, and the sound of muttering can be heard. Writing about *Tracked in the Snow Country*, the *New York Times* reviewer sniffs that, oh, yes, Rinty's feats are "no doubt very difficult" but "there are some who will wish they were impossible." Later he adds with a touch of irony, "Let us, however, not be too fussy. Art is a democratic institution and if a dog has genius, by what canon shall self-expression be denied him?" Reviewers began to grapple with this issue. For instance, *Variety*'s review of the same film comments: "The most successful pictures featuring Rin-Tin-Tin, Strongheart, and other dog actors have not played up the canine side too strongly, but have introduced it merely as interwoven with a plot of human beings that holds a good deal of interest in itself. *Tracked in the Snow Country* makes the mistake of focusing the spotlight on its animal actors and on its star in particular, to the almost total exclusion of the men and women in the cast. The result seems to be a certain amount of monotony." The public did not agree, loving the movie and wanting even more of Rinty. *Variety* made one excellent point: "Rin-Tin-Tin's suffering and adventures are almost analogous to those undergone in countless films by Bill Hart and others of the school of martyred, silent, western heroes."

By the end of 1927, reviews were suggesting that everyone might be getting a little tired of wonder mutts and longing instead for just an old-fashioned *DOG*. In praising Silverstreak, one reviewer pointed out that "the dog remains a dog, not a mind-reading, miracle-performing, semi-human quadruped. Toward the end [of the movie] the pup does seem to get a little clairvoyant, but not absurdly so as in some other woof-woof operas. At no time does Silverstreak indulge in those prolonged dog soliloquies."

One of the dogs that reviewers most complained about in this regard was the luckless Ranger. His movie *Outlaw Dog* (1927) illustrated the worst of what everyone was beginning to find unacceptable. In this film, Ranger seems to be able to read, as he stops to peruse a sign offering a $1,000 reward for his own capture. He also has a remarkable grasp of English, as he clearly understands what he is supposed to do when told, "Go flag the Limited, and bring assistance. It's up to you, Ranger!" (Ranger does indeed flag down the train, bring assistance, and save the payroll.) *Outlaw Dog* goes over the edge, whereas while Rin-Tin-Tin's films gave him the human ability to think and plan, it was always somehow kept within a credible context. For instance, in *Clash of the Wolves*, Rinty climbs up a tree to hide so that his searchers will pass under him while he watches. When he tries to warn his two human friends, who are lovers, that her father is coming, he thumps the floor with his

Rinty relaxes at home and takes baby for a stroll

tail. (They ignore his signal, with dire results.) He knocks on a window with his paw to get the heroine's attention, and knowing his master is dying of thirst out in the canyon, he galumphs into town and fills the canteen himself by using his teeth to open it and turn a spigot on. At the movie's end, tribute is paid to him as a fellow "guy." He and the hero double date—the hero and heroine, and Rinty and the lovely Nanette—out in a canoe on a romantic lake.

Watching Rin-Tin-Tin perform his wonderful stunts and find his delightful plot solutions, it's almost impossible not to start thinking of him as a person instead of a dog. This is what makes him stand out. Lassie was an animal who helped out her human owners, but Rin-Tin-Tin was a leading man, a semihuman character in charge of most of the thinking and all of the action. As one reviewer wrote about him in *Dog of the Regiment:* "It is impossible to really present naturalism in a picture featuring a dog of pretended human intelligence, but a good attempt has been made here. Rinty is supported by several skilled players . . . and his director and photographer did well." Without realizing it, the reviewer had demoted two human beings—the director and photographer—and relegated the human actors to a status less important than the dog's.

Eventually, of course, as with everything that is popular with the widest audience, the craze for dog stars waned. Even as early as 1925, the *New York Times* review for Rinty's *Behind the Lines* had somewhat hopefully asked the question: "Is the public tiring of dog stars?" Ominous notes were struck even earlier for Rinty's rival: "Unless they get better material for Strongheart [in

Rin-Tin-Tin prepares for his sound debut, with trainer Lee Duncan

The Love Master, 1924] the day of the dog star is going to be a short one in the future." The craze lasted well into the end of the silent era, but as the fad began to die down, the fan magazines naturally jumped off the bandwagon. They began dropping their expensive photo layouts featuring dogs: dogs in their homes, dogs with their masters, dogs with other dogs, dogs with their dog dishes, dogs with their dog toys.

Perhaps Rinty felt the pressure. Although Lee Duncan always claimed that Rinty came to work prepared, because "he knows he's a movie star and therefore must do his duty as such," others were not so generous. Many claimed that Rinty definitely began to display a star's temperament in his last years. He was apparently not above attacking costars and directors if they irritated him, and he had to be handled carefully. He demanded so much attention, it was said, that he was actually cited by Duncan's wife as the cause of her divorce. (Rinty as "other dog.")

Ultimately, Rinty, like all the great silent film stars, had to face the coming of sound, making his debut in the 1929 musical review *Show of Shows,* which Warners used to introduce their "talking" players to the public. Rinty was given the important job of introducing the entire movie, which he did with a series of excellent barks, loud and sharp, with nothing effeminate or high and squeaky about them. His fans were not disappointed: this, after all, was pretty much how they imagined he would sound—like a dog. His bark recorded well, and he made the transition to sound without difficulty.

Off-screen, Rinty's story turned out to be a happy one. He "married" his beautiful costar Nanette, and together they had four sons. After a long and successful career, Rinty, still active at age fourteen, suddenly collapsed and died on August 10, 1932. He had spent a happy afternoon playing with his lifelong friend, rescuer, and trainer, Lee Duncan. In one last playful leap into Duncan's arms, Rinty suddenly became a dead weight, knocking Duncan to his knees. Across the street, Rinty's glamorous neighbor, the platinum girl herself, Jean Harlow, saw what had happened and came running. Sobbing, she took Rinty into her arms, and as Jack Warner so colorfully described it in his autobiography, "She cradled the great furry head in her lap, and there he died." What an exit!

After he was gone, other Rin-Tin-Tins took his place, although none were as great as the original who gave them all his name. There would be Rin-Tin-Tin serials, comic books, and even a television series, but there was never a dog to rival the real Rin-Tin-Tin, the greatest canine star of all time. His biggest competitor for long-lived stardom, Lassie, is still going strong in reruns, but Lassie was more of a franchise than a star, and several dogs played her over the years. (All of them were males, even though Lassie is always referred to as a female character, using "she" and "her.") Lassie was always

Rinty, wife Nanette, and the pups, *en famille*

popular, and appeared in several charming movies as well as a long-running television series. However, she was never herself a top-ranked box office star the way Rin-Tin-Tin was, and her films, except for the original *Lassie Come Home,* mostly subordinated her overall role in the story to the stories of the humans themselves.

To this day, moviegoers like to see dogs in movies, as well as other kinds of animals, with monkeys, chimps, and whales practically guaranteeing a box office hit. But no matter what animal stars have surfaced over the years, none are really as appealing as the amazing dog stars of the 1920s, the ones who played the leads and carried their films. To be able to shoot a movie outdoors and direct a dog across a real landscape in highly specific action sequences seemed an amazing, even heroic, thing to audiences back then. It made for great storytelling, and a satisfying kind of wishful thinking. After all, everyone had a dog. Maybe, if trouble came, Fido would save the family, or maybe— even better—Fido could learn to sit up and roll over, unlock a door, and res- cue a drowning heroine. Then he could go out to Hollywood and become a big star, with his own fan mail, his own limousine—and his own fat paycheck.

Rin-Tin-Tin, Dog Star

CODA: GARBO TALKS

IT IS OFTEN ASSUMED that the great stars of the silent era who didn't make the transition to sound are somehow tragic. Perhaps not. Many of them had already enjoyed long and full careers, and some, like the Talmadges, who had worked most of their lives, were content to give up stardom. And Colleen Moore, who had once wanted fame more than anything, was clearly happy to abandon it. Whether by choice or not, however, almost all the greats of the silent era were left behind when sound came in. This was especially true for those whose careers had begun in the early to mid teens, and an important factor in their failure is seldom mentioned: at a time when thirty-five was considered middle-aged, Fairbanks, Pickford, Swanson, Negri, Barrymore, Hart, Mix, Chaney, and Normand were past their prime. Furthermore, audiences—ever fickle—had already enjoyed ten to fifteen (or nearly twenty) years of them. They turned eagerly toward new faces and new personalities. Looking back from today's vantage point, one can see logical reasons why most silent stars didn't continue at the same level of fame—or continue at all: Valentino, Normand, and Chaney were dead before sound was well launched; Pickford, Norma Talmadge, Negri, and Hart had images that belonged to the 1920s or earlier and didn't translate well into the harsher Depression era; personal demons created problems for Clara Bow and John Barrymore. The great silent clowns—Chaplin, Keaton, and Lloyd—didn't seem as funny with dialogue as they had without. Even when it seemed odd that the careers didn't continue (Gloria Swanson) or perhaps unexpected that they did (Marion Davies), the bottom line is harsh: by the end of 1927, it was essentially over for the majority of silent film stars.*

*Exceptions that prove the rule are Laurel and Hardy—those two underrated geniuses of chaos—and Lillian Gish. The remarkable Gish more or less dropped out of movies during the 1930s, but she returned as a character actress in the 1940s. She had made her debut in 1912 and her last movie was *The Whales of August* in 1987, an unprecedented seventy-five years in movies, the longest career on record. Laurel and Hardy are more famous for their shorts than for their features, so they are frequently forgotten on lists of movie greats, but they were enormously popular in both the silent and the sound eras.

Sound changed everything, and as the motion picture business was transformed, America also changed, falling into a severe economic depression. The two phenomena combined to produce an appetite for new kinds of movies: harsh, unromantic stories with hard-bitten dialogue; gangster tales with sassy slang and the rat-a-tat of machine guns; musicals with songs and tapping shoes; Broadway plays with complex lines to be memorized; and pre-code plots about men and women living on the edge, drinking booze, and having sex openly. These movies cried out for stars with movie personae that fit into a world of noises and voices. Yet every star, male or female, who reached the heights in the silent era had already established a personal image. For them to change meant breaking the deep connections they had forged with their audiences. And there were other challenges, too. They had to relearn the moviemaking experience. Their directors couldn't call out encouraging words to them as they worked, providing instruction and reassurance. They had to remember where the microphone was planted, and control their movements accordingly. There were diction coaches to be dealt with, different types of shooting schedules, and new studio personnel in every category. They had been at the top of the heap, but now they were back at the beginning, just like any newcomer. With all this to face, they first concentrated on what seemed to be the two most important issues: Would their voices record well? Could they deliver dialogue convincingly?

Soon enough, the real issue became obvious. It wasn't so much a problem of recording or acting as it was one of image related to voice. Pirandello had said, "Film is the language of images, and images don't speak." But silent film stars were images that would now *have* to speak. Would their fans accept it? If a strong, virile man had a high-pitched voice . . . if a tiny little beauty talked with bass tones . . . if an ethereal blonde had a heavy foreign accent . . . if an elegantly dressed lover said "dese-dem-dose" . . . this was going to be a bigger challenge than adjusting to microphones. New stars starting out in sound didn't have this problem. They could speak in strange accents or weird cadences or voices that didn't match their bodies because the audience first met them in that condition and accepted them on those terms. The stars of the earlier era were different—their voices had already been "heard" in the heads of the moviegoing public who had met *them* in the silence, with only a piano or orchestra to intrude. To hear their favorites suddenly speak was a shock for fans. To hear them speak without the voices that had been mentally supplied for them wasn't acceptable.

The transition to sound revealed that the peculiar quality of the stars of silent film—no voice—was really an asset that had lifted them up into a godlike status. Sound brought them down to earth. It was not that silent film stars didn't seem realistic or approachable in their own era; on the contrary, many projected that kind of intimacy. But the illusion that silent film presents is removed from the everyday—even when it's about everyday things—because audiences supply sound in a world without voices.

For most silent stars, it was a no-win situation. Except for Greta Garbo, no one who had attained really great stardom before the mid-twenties carried over well—or increased his or her status—in the sound era. Many went on making films, among them Clara Bow, Colleen Moore, Marion Davies, Richard Dix, Richard Barthelmess—but their careers soon fizzled out and the decade of the 1930s did not belong to them. Garbo, of course, not only endured, but thrived. She made her first movie in Europe in 1922, found success there in 1924 with *The Story of Gösta Berling* and *The Joyless Street,* and earned her American success in 1927's *The Torrent* and *The Temptress,* and especially *Flesh and the Devil* with John Gilbert. Her throaty murmur, with its exotic foreign accent, verified her "otherness," and the detachment she had from the ordinary worked well in both eras. Ironically, her accent was originally thought to be a problem, so her sound debut was delayed until 1930's *Anna Christie,* and then treated like a major event. "Garbo Talks!" screamed the ads, and curiosity brought large crowds into the theatres. As it turned out, she not only talked well, but talked with a voice that fit her persona. Richard Watts, Jr., wrote in the *New York Herald Tribune* that "her . . . deep, husky contralto [possesses] poetic glamor" and Norbert Lusk in *Picture-Play* rhapsodized, "The voice that shook the world!"

Three actors who had begun early also made the transition: John Barrymore, Ronald Colman, and William Powell. Barrymore gave some of his best performances in early sound movies such as *State's Attorney, A Bill of Divorcement,* and *Grand Hotel,* but he soon became more of a character actor than a leading man. Colman started his movie career in British silents in 1917, and made his first American film in 1921. He went on to be paired with Lillian Gish in *The White Sister* (1923) and *Romola* (1924), and had attained star status by the time he played opposite Constance Talmadge in *Her Night of Romance* (1924). However, he had never been one of the top names of silents, and his mellifluous voice and polished appearance made him a far bigger star in the sound era. In retrospect, it's clear that his silent success depended on his good looks, as he mostly supported leading ladies of the era. It was his voice that made him stand out, and sound lifted him out of the category of "love interest" and gave him the opportunity to play more challenging roles. Powell is an odd case. He was solidly established as early as 1922 in *When Knighthood Was in Flower,* but he played villains, not leading men. Never the star, he played a thieving Legionnaire who reveals the family secret in *Beau Geste* (1926), a vengeful revolutionary in *The Last Command,* and a con man in *Feel My Pulse* (both in 1928). Like Colman, he had a cultured, well-modulated voice that gave his presence depth and credibility. His talent at delivering a witty put-down or a playful romantic line transformed him from a villain into one of the most sophisticated leading men of the 1930s, playing opposite the great beauties of the decade in both comedy and drama, including Myrna Loy, Jean Harlow, Carole Lombard, Hedy Lamarr, and Kay Francis. He gracefully continued until the mid-1950s, playing fathers, rich older suitors, and wise doctors.

Barrymore, Colman, and Powell, however, are special cases.* For most of the male stars, it was an especially difficult time. The coming of sound revolutionized the entire concept of "male" in the movies. The silent hero had been solidly located in the melodramatic tradition. It had seemed right—even necessary—for him to display extravagant emotion. He could cry, he could suffer over lost love, and the women in the audience loved him for it. Screenwriters now found it difficult to write dialogue for a hero who was sniffing a single rose, kissing the hem of a woman's cloak, or staring dreamily out the window while clutching a picture of his beloved. Actors were used to being highly emotional, but sound made them seem old-fashioned, even silly. Out went the sensitive lovers, the passionate men who would die for a woman, and the stalwart heroes of a gentler, more innocent and romantic time. In came the gangsters, the snappy-talking wiseacres, the tough guys, and the low-down chiselers. (It's the difference between John Gilbert and James Cagney—imagine pushing a grapefruit in Garbo's face!) It was a revolution, and it called for new talent.

Barrymore, of course, could handle it. A skilled stage actor, he had matured in dialogue performances, and his ability to deliver any kind of line was secure. Chaney could have done it had he lived. Chaplin refused even to try, and former stars like Richard Dix and Richard Barthelmess rode it out, their stardom diminished, ultimately accepting supporting roles. Charles Farrell faltered at first—then did well—but retired by the end of the thirties. One other male made the transition: Gary Cooper. But he was a newcomer to silents, not yet a real star, who was playing leads in support of big names like Clara Bow and Colleen Moore. His voice recorded well. He spoke casually, slowly, like the westerner he was, and he seemed utterly natural and uniquely American. He came into his own and rose to full stardom in the sound era.

The silent stars who survived and carried forward had risen to fame at the very end of the silents (1926 or later), and most of these, like Cooper, were not fully associated with the era. And most of them were women: Joan Craw-

---

*Charactor actors like Wallace Beery, or comedians like W. C. Fields, are also different. Beery became a star in sound, but was a supporting player in silents; Fields became really big only after sound wedded his unique speaking voice and verbal wit to his physical abilities.

ford, Constance Bennett, Norma Shearer, Janet Gaynor, and new players like Myrna Loy, Loretta Young, Carole Lombard, and Jean Arthur, who had begun to find significant roles in the late twenties.*

Young, who is seldom associated with the silent era, nevertheless began her career there. However, she was probably the least experienced of the women who made the transition, being barely into her teens when she got her first big break opposite Lon Chaney in 1928's *Laugh, Clown, Laugh.* She later said she survived because she was "so innocent I didn't know I was supposed to be afraid." Constance Bennett, who came from a theatre family and who understood the vicissitudes of show business, was solidly established by the mid-twenties, but wasn't yet a big name. Her type was the soignée sophisticate, and she properly belonged in the 1930s, where she became one of the earliest stars of the transition. (A perfect example of why she was right for the 1930s occurs in her silent film *Married?* Standing in a thick forest attired in high heels, furs, and a cloche hat, she grandly calls out to the ranger-hero, "Get me a taxi!")

Writing in *Films in Review* in 1956, the film historian John Springer assessed the female silent stars who "twinkled the most in the early days of sound" as "Gaynor, Crawford, Shearer . . . and, of course, Garbo." [†] According to him, "The first girl to reach stardom in the talkies had a negligible stage background and was practically unknown in the silent era." She was Nancy Carroll, "the first girl to sing a song into a movie mike and the first to do a tap dance on a studio sound stage." Carroll, unpopular with the press and uncooperative with studio publicity staff, had a very brief stardom.

Crawford, Shearer, and Gaynor shared these important assets: they were already well established when sound took over; they were beautiful in distinctive ways; and they were still young, with their best years ahead of them. However, the biggest asset they shared was the one that really counted: each had a unique voice that matched her looks.

Crawford and Shearer became rivals at Metro-Goldwyn-Mayer, with Crawford eventually winning the endurance contest. She had done well in silent films, playing opposite such superstars as John Gilbert, Lon Chaney, and Ramon Novarro. She had found fame as a typical flapper, but she easily transformed her image into that of an equally typical 1930s heroine. In fact, Crawford's strength turned out to be that she could transform herself over and over again, managing to look modern all through the 1940s, 1950s, and into

---

*Two of these women, Crawford and Loy, ended up enjoying more than three decades of stardom. Three others whose names might be mentioned were Marie Dressler, not a typical romantic leading lady; Dolores Del Rio, who was never a really big star in sound; and Mary Astor, who became a star opposite Barrymore in *Beau Brummel* in 1924.

[†] Springer lists some of the early sound stars who came from the stage, not silents, as Ann Harding, Claudette Colbert, Ruth Chatterton, Jeanne Eagels, Ina Claire, and Marilyn Miller.

Ronald Colman and Janet Gaynor

the 1960s. She became the consummate movie star. Sound presented no problem for her because she had a strong, clear voice, with a low register that
matched her basic toughness. Shearer's sound career was aided by mogul Irving Thalberg, who became her husband in 1927 (in the nick of time). Like
Joseph Schenck before him, who guided Norma Talmadge, Thalberg found
properties that were literary or stage successes he felt afforded Shearer the
opportunity to become a great actress in respectable material. Shearer's voice
had a light, elegant quality to it, giving credibility to her ladylike roles. Its lilt-
ing tone contained a sense of underlying amusement, which also worked well
in Noel Coward–type comedies.

Janet Gaynor, petite and adorable, began her career in two-reelers for
Hal Roach, but moved forward rapidly, appearing in films directed by John
Ford (*Shamrock Handicap* and *The Blue Eagle* in 1926), F. W. Murnau (*Sunrise,* 1927, *Four Devils,* 1928), and Frank Borzage (*Seventh Heaven,* 1927,
Street Angel, 1928). In 1927–28, she won the first Academy Award for Best
Actress for her work in *Sunrise, Seventh Heaven,* and *Street Angel.* (Awards
then were for multiple performances.) Gaynor, often called the "child-
woman," combines the sweetness and simplicity of the silent era with a more
sophisticated sexuality of the 1930s. It has been said that she played a character everyone in the audience wanted the world to be good to, a kind of mod-

ern Cinderella. Her voice was unusual, somewhat high and girlish, but not twittery. Sweet-faced and virginal-looking, yet flirtatious and warmly loving, Gaynor also had a voice that matched her looks.

The stars who survived the end of silent film retained everything they had learned from it, particularly their ability to use their bodies expressively. To this they added their distinctive voices, and had the best of both worlds. Unencumbered by the past, they embraced sound and never looked back. The future was theirs. Most of the silent stars, however, either went out with a bang or slowly faded away. Forgotten, misunderstood, or underappreciated, they still await wide-ranging rediscovery. Those who have seen their work know that they own a glorious past, a world of beauty, talent, originality—and silence—waiting to be rediscovered, admired, and enjoyed.

BIBLIOGRAPHY

For year of release and reviews of films in their own time, I consulted two major sources: *Variety*, from 1907 onward, and the *New York Times*, from 1913 onward. These two sources provided reviews for most of the movies screened, and they represented an urban point of view (the *Times*) and the accepted industry attitude (*Variety*). *Variety* was particularly helpful, as its reviews assessed box office potential in small-town areas, and often defined a star's persona as perceived in his or her own time. I also used reviews and articles from other newspapers and magazines, especially my extensive collection of early movie magazines, including *Photoplay* and *Motion Picture*. These magazines contain not only movie reviews but also revealing articles on a star's "life," beautiful portraits, fan letters, and advertisements for films and product endorsements by the stars. In all cases, including reviews, movie magazine materials, and quotations, I have referred to the source in the text, so these items are not listed below.

Anderson, Earl. "Marion Davies." *Films in Review*, June–July 1972, vol. 23, no. 6, pp. 321–53.

Ankerich, Michael G. *Broken Silence: Conversations with 23 Silent Film Stars*. Jefferson, N.C.: McFarland, 1993.

Astor, Mary. *A Life on Film*. New York: Delacorte Press, 1971.

Bainbridge, John. *Garbo*. Garden City, N.Y.: Doubleday, 1955.

Barrymore, Elaine, and Sanford Dody. *All My Sins Remembered*. New York: Appleton-Century, 1964.

Barrymore, Ethel. *Memories*. London: Hulton Press, 1956.

Beauchamp, Cari. *Without Lying Down: Frances Marion and the Powerful Women of Early Hollywood*. New York: Scribner, 1997.

Berg, A. Scott. *Goldwyn: A Biography*. New York: Alfred A. Knopf, 1989.

Berger, Spencer. "The Film Career of John Barrymore." *Films in Review*, December 1952, no. 10, pp. 481–87.

Blake, Michael F. *Lon Chaney: The Man Behind the Thousand Faces*. Vestal, N.Y.: Vestal Press, 1993.

Bodeen, DeWitt. "Constance Talmadge." *Films in Review*, December 1967, vol. 18, no. 10, pp. 613–30.

———. "Douglas Fairbanks." *Focus on Film*, no. 5, Winter 1970, pp. 17–30.

———. "Gloria Swanson." *Films in Review*, April 1965, vol. 16, no. 4, pp. 193–216.

———. "John Barrymore and Dolores Costello." *Focus on Film*, no. 12, Winter 1972, pp. 17–37.

———. "Lon Chaney, Man of a Thousand Faces." *Focus on Film*, no. 3, May–August 1970, pp. 21–39.

———. *More from Hollywood! The Careers of Fifteen Great American Stars*. South Brunswick, N.J.: A. S. Barnes, 1977.

———. "Ramon Navarro." *Films in Review*, November 1967, vol. 18, no. 9, pp. 528–47.

———. "Rudolph Valentino." *Screen Facts*, no. 17, 1969.

———. "Screenwriter Frances Marion." Parts 1 and 2. *Films in Review*, February 1969, vol. 20, no. 2, pp. 71–91; March 1969, vol. 20, no. 3, pp. 129–52.

———. "Sessue Hayakawa." *Films in Review*, April 1976, vol. 27, no. 4, pp. 193–208.

————, and Gene Ringgold. "Pola Negri." *Screen Facts*, no. 15, 1967.

Brownlow, Kevin. *Hollywood: The Pioneers.* New York: Alfred A. Knopf, 1979.

————. *The Parade's Gone By.* New York: Alfred A. Knopf, 1969.

————. *The War, the West, and the Wilderness.* New York: Alfred A. Knopf, 1979.

Cahn, William. *The Laugh Makers: A Pictorial History of American Comedies.* New York: G. P. Putnam's Sons, 1957.

Carey, Gary. *Anita Loos: A Biography.* New York: Alfred A. Knopf, 1988.

————. *Doug and Mary: A Biography of Douglas Fairbanks and Mary Pickford.* New York: E. P. Dutton, 1977.

Carol, David. *The Matinee Idols.* New York: Arbor House, 1972.

Carr, Chauncey L. "Janet Gaynor." *Films in Review*, October 1959, vol. 10, no. 8, pp. 470–500.

Chaplin, Charles. *My Autobiography.* New York: Simon & Schuster, 1964.

Cherchi-Usai, Paolo, and Lorenzo Codelli, eds. *The DeMille Legacy.* Pordenone, Italy: Le Giornate del Cinema Muto, 1991.

Chierichetti, David. "Gloria Swanson Today." *Film Fan Monthly*, no. 164, February 1975, pp. 2–8.

Cooke, Alistair. *Douglas Fairbanks: The Making of a Screen Character.* New York: Museum of Modern Art, 1940.

Cooper, Miriam, with Bonnie Herdon. *Dark Lady of the Silents.* New York: Bobbs-Merrill, 1973.

Crowther, Bosley. *The Great Films: 50 Golden Years of Motion Pictures.* New York: G. P. Putnam, 1967.

Dalzell, Tom. *Flappers 2 Rappers: American Youth Slang.* Springfield, Mass.: Merriam-Webster, 1996.

Davies, Marion. *The Times We Had.* New York: Bobbs-Merrill, 1975.

Davis, Henry R., Jr. "A John Gilbert Index." *Films in Review*, October 1962, vol. 13, no. 8, pp. 477–80.

DeMille, Cecil B. *The Autobiography of Cecil B. DeMille.* Englewood Cliffs, N.J.: Prentice-Hall, 1959.

de Mille, William C. *Hollywood Saga.* New York: E. P. Dutton, 1939.

Devon, Louis. "Douglas Fairbanks." *Films in Review*, May 1976, vol. 27, no. 5, pp. 267–83.

Dressler, Marie. *My Own Story.* Boston: Little, Brown, 1934.

Drew, William M. *Speaking of Silents: First Ladies of the Screen.* Vestal, N.Y.: Vestal Press, 1989.

Durgnat, Raymond, and Scott Simmon. *King Vidor, American.* Berkeley: University of California Press, 1988.

Dwyer, Ruth Anne. *Malcolm St. Clair: His Films, 1915–1948.* Lanham, Md.: Scarecrow Press, 1996.

Eames, John Douglas. *The MGM Story.* New York: Crown, 1979.

Edmonds, I. G. *Big U.: Universal in the Silent Days.* South Brunswick, N.J.: A. S. Barnes, 1977.

————. *Stars of the Photoplay.* Chicago: Photoplay, 1924.

Edwards, Anne. *The DeMilles: An American Family.* New York: H. N. Abrams, 1988.

Everson, William K. *American Silent Film.* New York: Oxford University Press, 1978.

————, and George Mitchell. "Tom Mix." *Films in Review*, October 1957, vol. 8, no. 8, pp. 387–97.

Eyman, Scott. *Mary Pickford: America's Sweetheart.* New York: Donald I. Fine, 1989.

Fairbanks, Douglas, Jr. *The Salad Days.* New York: Doubleday, 1988.

Fenin, George N., and William K. Everson. *The Western: From Silents to Cinerama.* New York: Bonanza Books, 1962.

Flamini, Roland. *Thalberg: The Last Tycoon and the World of MGM.* New York: Crown, 1994.

Fountain, Leatrice Gilbert. *Dark Star.* New York: St. Martin's Press, 1985.

Fowler, Gene. *Good Night, Sweet Prince.* New York: Viking Press, 1944.

Fox, Donald Charles, and Milton L. Silver. *Who's Who on the Screen.* New York: Ross Publishing, 1920.

Franklin, Joe. *Classics of the Silent Screen.* New York: Cadillac Publishing, 1959.

Fussell, Betty Harper. *Mabel.* New Haven, Conn.: Ticknor and Fields, 1982.

Giroux, Robert. "Mack Sennett." Parts 1 and 2. *Films in Review*, December

1968, vol. 19, no. 10, pp. 593–612; January 1969, vol. 20, no. 1, pp. 1–28.

Gish, Lillian, with Ann Pinchot. *The Movies, Mr. Griffith, and Me.* Englewood Cliffs, N.J.: Prentice-Hall, 1969.

Goldwyn, Samuel. *Behind the Screen.* New York: George H. Doran, 1923.

Griffith, Richard. *The Movie Stars.* Garden City, N.Y.: Doubleday, 1970.

Guiles, Fred Lawrence. *Marion Davies.* New York: McGraw-Hill, 1972.

Hampton, Benjamin B. *A History of the Movies.* New York: Covici, Friede, 1931.

Hearst, William Randolph, Jr. *The Hearsts, Father and Son.* Niwot, Colo.: Roberts Rinehart, 1991.

Herndon, Booton. *Mary Pickford and Douglas Fairbanks.* New York: W. W. Norton, 1977.

Holland, Larry Lee. "Francis X. Bushman, 1885–1966." *Films in Review,* March 1978, vol. 29, no. 3, pp. 157–73.

Hudson, Richard M., and Raymond Lee. *Gloria Swanson.* South Brunswick, N.J.: A. S. Barnes, 1970.

Huff, Theodore. "The Career of Rudolph Valentino." *Films in Review,* April 1952, vol. 3, no. 4, pp. 145–50.

———. *Charlie Chaplin.* New York: Pyramid Books, 1972.

Jacobs, Jack. "Richard Barthelmess." *Films in Review,* January 1958, vol. 9, no. 1, pp. 12–21.

Korda, Michael. *Charmed Lives: A Family Romance.* New York: Random House, 1979.

Koszarski, Richard. *An Evening's Entertainment: The Age of the Silent Feature Picture, 1915–1928.* Vol. 3 of *History of the American Cinema.* New York: Charles Scribner's Sons, 1990.

Lahue, Kalton C. *Gentlemen to the Rescue.* South Brunswick, N.J.: A. S. Barnes, 1972.

———, and Terry Brewer. *Kops and Custards: The Legend of Keystone Films.* Norman: University of Oklahoma Press, 1968.

Lambert, Gavin. *Nazimova.* New York: Alfred A. Knopf, 1997.

———. *Norma Shearer: A Life.* New York: Alfred A. Knopf, 1990.

Lee, Raymond. *Not So Dumb: The Life and Times of Animal Actors.* New York: Castle Books, 1970.

Lewis, Oscar. *San Simeon.* San Francisco: California Historical Society, 1960.

Limbacher, James L. *Four Aspects of the Film.* New York: Brussel and Brussel, 1968.

Loos, Anita. *The Talmadge Girls: A Memoir.* New York: Viking, 1978.

MacGowan, Kenneth. *Behind the Screen: The History and Techniques of the Motion Picture.* New York: Delacorte Press, 1965.

Madsen, Axel. *Gloria and Joe: The Star-Crossed Love Affair of Gloria Swanson and Joe Kennedy.* New York: William Morrow, 1988.

Manners, J. Hartley. *Peg o' My Heart: A Comedy of Youth.* New York: Dodd, Mead, 1913.

Marion, Frances. *How to Write and Sell Film Stories.* New York: Covici, Friede, 1937.

Marx, Samuel. *Mayer and Thalberg: The Make-Believe Saints.* New York: Random House, 1975.

McDonald, Gerald D., Michael Conway, and Mark Ricci, eds. *The Films of Charlie Chaplin.* New York: Citadel Press, 1965.

Meyers, Jeffrey. *Gary Cooper: American Hero.* New York: William Morrow, 1998.

Miller, Patsy Ruth, and Philip J. Riley. *My Hollywood: When Both of Us Were Young.* Absecon, N.J.: Magicimage Filmbooks, 1989.

Milton, Joyce. *Tramp: The Life of Charlie Chaplin.* New York: HarperCollins, 1995.

Mitchell, George. "Lon Chaney." *Films in Review,* December 1953, vol. 4, no. 10, pp. 497–510.

———. "William S. Hart." *Films in Review,* April 1955, pp. 145–54.

Mix, Olive Stokes, with Eric Heath. *The Fabulous Tom Mix.* Englewood Cliffs, N.J.: Prentice-Hall, 1957.

Mix, Paul E. *Tom Mix.* Jefferson, N.C.: McFarland, 1995.

Moore, Colleen. *Silent Star.* Garden City, N.Y.: Doubleday, 1968.

Morris, Michael. *Madam Valentino: The Many Lives of Natacha Rambova.* New York: Abbeville Press, 1991.

Munden, Kenneth W., ed. *The American*

Film Institute Catalog of Motion Pictures Produced in the United States. New York: R. R. Bowker, 1971.

Negri, Pola. *Memoirs of a Star.* Garden City, N.Y.: Doubleday, 1970.

Normand, Stephen. "Mabel Normand." *Films in Review,* August–September 1974, vol. 25, no. 7, pp. 385–95.

Oberfirst, Robert. *Rudolph Valentino: The Man Behind the Myth.* New York: Citadel Press, 1962.

Paris, Barry. *Garbo: A Biography.* New York: Alfred A. Knopf, 1995.

Parish, James Robert. *Hollywood's Great Love Teams.* New Rochelle, N.Y.: Arlington House, 1974.

———. *The Paramount Pretties.* New Rochelle, N.Y.: Arlington House, 1972.

———, and Don E. Stanke. *The Swashbucklers.* New Rochelle, N.Y.: Arlington House, 1976.

Peters, Margot. *The House of Barrymore.* New York: Alfred A. Knopf, 1990.

Pickford, Mary. *Sunshine and Shadow.* Garden City, N.Y.: Doubleday, 1955.

Quirk, Laurence J. "John Gilbert." *Films in Review,* March 1956, vol. 7, no. 3, pp. 103–10.

———. *Norma: The Story of Norma Shearer.* New York: St. Martin's Press, 1988.

Ramsaye, Terry. *A Million and One Nights: A History of the Motion Picture.* New York: Simon and Schuster, 1964.

Robinson, David. *Chaplin: His Life and Art.* New York: McGraw-Hill, 1985.

———. *Hollywood in the Twenties.* South Brunswick, N.J.: A. S. Barnes, 1968.

Rosenberg, Bernard, and Harry Silverstein. *The Real Tinsel.* New York: Macmillan, 1970.

Rosten, Leo C. *Hollywood: The Movie Colony, the Movie Makers.* New York: Harcourt, Brace, 1941.

Rotha, Paul, and Richard Griffith. *The Film Till Now.* London: Spring Books, 1967.

St. Johns, Adela Rogers. *Love, Laughter, and Tears: My Hollywood Story.* Garden City, N.Y.: Doubleday, 1978.

Schatz, Thomas. *The Genius of the System.* New York: Pantheon, 1988.

Schickel, Richard. *His Picture in the Papers.* New York: Charterhouse, 1973.

———. *The Stars.* New York: Dial Press, 1962.

———, and Douglas Fairbanks, Jr. *The Fairbanks Album.* Boston: New York Graphic Society, 1975.

Scott, Evelyn E. *Hollywood When Silents Were Golden.* New York: McGraw-Hill, 1973.

Selznick, Irene Mayer. *A Private View.* New York: Alfred A. Knopf, 1983.

Sennett, Mack. *King of Comedy.* Garden City, N.Y.: Doubleday, 1954.

Sherk, Warren M. *The Films of Mack Sennett: Credit Documentation from the Mack Sennett Collection.* Lanham, Md.: Scarecrow Press, 1998.

Shulman, Irving. *Valentino.* New York: Trident Press, 1967.

Skal, David J., and Elias Savada. *Dark Carnival: The Secret World of Tod Browning.* New York: Anchor Books, 1995.

Skretvedt, Randy. *Laurel and Hardy: The Magic Behind the Movies.* Beverly Hills, Calif.: Moonstone, 1987.

Slide, Anthony. *The American Film Industry: A Historical Dictionary.* Westport, Conn.: Greenwood Press, 1986.

———. *Early Women Directors.* South Brunswick, N.J.: A. S. Barnes, 1977.

———. *The Idols of Silence.* South Brunswick, N.J.: A. S. Barnes, 1976.

———. *Lois Weber: The Director Who Lost Her Way in History.* Westport, Conn.: Greenwood Press, 1996.

Spears, Jack. "Mary Pickford's Directors." *Films in Review,* February 1966, vol. 17, no. 2, pp. 71–95.

———. "Norma Talmadge." *Films in Review,* January 1967, pp. 16–40.

Sperling, Cass Warner, and Cork Millner, with Jack Warner, Jr. *Hollywood Be Thy Name: The Warner Brothers Story.* Rocklin, Calif.: Prima Publishing, 1994.

Springer, John. "Nancy Carroll." *Films in Review,* April 1956, vol. 7, no. 4, pp. 157–63.

Stenn, David. *Bombshell: The Life and Death of Jean Harlow.* New York: Doubleday, 1993.

———. *Clara Bow: Runnin' Wild.* New York: Penguin Books, 1988.

Swanberg, W. A. *Citizen Hearst.* New York: Charles Scribner's Sons, 1961.

Swanson, Gloria. *Swanson on Swanson.* New York: Random House, 1980.

Swenson, Karen. *Greta Garbo: A Life Apart.* New York: Scribner, 1997.

Thomas, Bob. *Thalberg: Life and Legend.* New York: Doubleday, 1969.

Thompson, Frank, ed. *Henry King, Director.* Los Angeles: Directors Guild of America, 1995.

Thomson, David. *Showman: The Life of David O. Selznick.* New York: Alfred A. Knopf, 1992.

Vidor, King. *A Tree Is a Tree.* New York: Harcourt Brace, 1952.

Vinson, James, ed. *Actors and Actresses.* Vol. 3 of *The International Dictionary of Films and Filmmakers.* Chicago: St. James Press, 1986.

von Sternberg, Josef. *Fun in a Chinese Laundry.* New York: Macmillan, 1965.

Walker, Alexander. *Rudolph Valentino.* New York: Stein and Day, 1976.

———. *The Shattered Silents.* New York: William Morrow, 1979.

Walsh, Raoul. *Each Man in His Time.* New York: Farrar, Straus & Giroux, 1974.

Weinberg, Herman G. *The Lubitsch Touch.* New York: E. P. Dutton, 1968.

Whitfield, Eileen. *Pickford: The Woman Who Made Hollywood.* Lexington: University Press of Kentucky, 1997.

Wlaschin, Ken. *The Illustrated Encyclopedia of the World's Great Movie Stars and Their Films.* New York: Bonanza Books, 1980.

Wray, Fay. *On the Other Hand.* New York: St. Martin's Press, 1989.

Wyatt, Edgar M. *More Than a Cowboy: The Life and Films of Fred Thomson and Silver King.* Raleigh, N.C.: Wyatt Classics, 1988.

Yallop, David. *The Day the Laughter Stopped: The True Story of Fatty Arbuckle.* New York: St. Martin's Press, 1976.

Zukor, Adolph. *The Public Is Never Wrong.* New York: G. P. Putnam's Sons, 1953.

INDEX

Note: Page numbers in *italics* refer to illustrations.

PHOTOGRAPHIC CREDITS

A Note About the Author

Jeanine Basinger is Chair of the Film Studies Program and Corwin-Fuller Professor of Film Studies at Wesleyan University, and Curator of the Cinema Archives there. She is the author of *The "It's a Wonderful Life" Book, The World War II Combat Film: Anatomy of a Genre, Anthony Mann, American Cinema: 100 Years of Filmmaking*, and *A Woman's View: How Hollywood Spoke to Women, 1930–1960.* She lives with her husband in Middletown, Connecticut. Their daughter, Savannah, and her husband and newborn daughter live in Wisconsin.

A Note on the Type

This book was set in a digitized version of Bodoni Book, a typeface named after Giambattista Bodoni (1740–1813), a celebrated printer and type designer of Rome and Parma. Bodoni Book is not a copy of any one of Bodoni's fonts, but a composite, modern version of the Bodoni manner. Bodoni's innovations in type style included a greater degree of contrast in the thick and thin elements of the letters and a sharper and more angular finish of details.

Composed by North Market Street Graphics,
Lancaster, Pennsylvania

Printed and bound by Quebecor Printing,
Fairfield, Pennsylvania

Designed by Iris Weinstein